Growth and Development

GROWTH and DEVELOPMENT

Karl C. Garrison

PROFESSOR OF EDUCATION
UNIVERSITY OF GEORGIA

with a chapter by
Florene M. Young

PROFESSOR OF PSYCHOLOGY
UNIVERSITY OF GEORGIA

and a chapter by
Florence Heisler

ASSISTANT PROFESSOR OF EDUCATION
BROOKLYN COLLEGE

LONGMANS, GREEN AND CO.

NEW YORK   LONDON   TORONTO   1952

LONGMANS, GREEN AND CO., INC.
55 FIFTH AVENUE, NEW YORK 3

LONGMANS, GREEN AND CO. LTD.
6 & 7 CLIFFORD STREET, LONDON W I

LONGMANS, GREEN AND CO.
215 VICTORIA STREET, TORONTO I

GROWTH AND DEVELOPMENT

PUBLISHED SIMULTANEOUSLY IN THE DOMINION OF CANADA BY
LONGMANS, GREEN AND CO., TORONTO

FIRST EDITION

LIBRARY OF CONGRESS CATALOG CARD NUMBER 52-5645

Printed in the United States of America

VAN REES PRESS • NEW YORK

To
the boys and girls
of today and tomorrow.

Preface

Although the child study movement had its beginning in the nineteenth century, the twentieth century has been correctly referred to as "the century of the child." The best measure of the value of child studies lies in its contribution directly or indirectly to the improvement of the lives of growing boys and girls. This purpose has constantly received the attention of the writer in the preparation and organization of materials relative to growth and development.

The vast amount of research now available has provided much stimulation to those concerned with analyzing the findings bearing on growth and development. These studies, however, present difficulties in selecting from the available data reliable and useful materials bearing on various problems of growth and development. Two ways of studying child development have been followed: (1) the cross-sectional approach, which makes use of data gathered on a large group of children during a brief period; and (2) the longitudinal approach, which deals with certain aspects of growth over a considerable period of time. Results from both of these approaches have contributed to our understanding of the nature and amount of child growth and development over varying periods of time. The results from both of these approaches have been used throughout this volume. The materials thus gathered tend to complement each other and thus provide a reliable and rather complete account of growth and development from infancy throughout the childhood years.

This book should be useful to parents and to young men and young women who will be the parents of tomorrow's children. A better understanding of the nature of development and of the importance of the interplay of parent-child relationships should provide a useful background for the guidance of children. Aside from the parents, and in many cases equal to the parents, the teacher is the most omnipresent individual in her relations with the growing boys and girls. An understanding of the nature of growth and development and the interplay of different forces on the child's development should contribute to favorable teacher-child relationships, and thus benefit the lives of growing boys and girls. Social workers meet children from varying hereditary and environmental backgrounds. An understanding of the interplay of different cultural forces on children is essential to them. The needs of all those who directly influence the lives of boys and girls were constantly in the mind of the writer in the selection and organization of the materials for this volume.

Many individuals have contributed either directly or indirectly to the preparation of the book. Students of child development, whose studies are referred to, as well as the publishers, were most co-operative in giving permission to use certain materials from their studies. These contributions were essential in the production of a complete account of child growth and development. The help provided by my wife, Linnea Malmborg Garrison, in collecting materials from the wide variety of sources available, was valuable in the development of this book. Professional associates and friends have offered useful suggestions relative to the selection and organization of certain materials. This volume, then, represents a wide range of experiences of teaching and research in the area of growth and development. If it provides for the enrichment of the lives of growing boys and girls, it will have fulfilled its major purpose.

KARL C. GARRISON

Contents

Part II. ASPECTS OF GROWTH

I

Introduction

1

Studying Child Growth and Development

Understanding the child

Importance of understanding the child. "He who would command nature must first obey her." This paradoxical maxim of Bacon's is most applicable to problems relative to the nature and development of children. The teacher, the parent, and the social worker, and many others working with children and youth need a clear understanding of the growth processes and the influences of the various factors and conditions upon development. The recognition of this need has brought about the widespread use of the scientific method in studying child growth and development. Out of the many studies that are being conducted, along with the information that has been collected for the past several decades, have emerged newer concepts of growth and more accurate notions of child nature. Results and generalizations from these studies will be presented throughout the subsequent chapters.

This age has been referred to as the "Age of the Child." Books, journals, magazines, the radio, and the movies have shown a great interest in the problems involved in child growth and development. As a result of the information thus made available, there is developing a changed concept of the child on the part of parents and teachers. There is, furthermore, evidence that the attitude of parents and teachers toward problems connected with child behavior and development is very important in affecting the future course of the child's growth and development. A recent study by Shoben bears this out.[1] In this study, fifty mothers of problem children were matched

[1] E. J. Shoben, Jr., The assessment of parental attitudes in relation to child adjustment, *Genetic Psychology Monographs*, 1949, Vol. 39, pp. 101-148.

for age, education, and socioeconomic status with fifty mothers of nonproblem children. These parents were given the *University of Southern California Parent Attitude Scale*. The items were then analyzed in order to determine which ones discriminated significantly, and these were retained to make up the tentative scale. The items were further classified as dominant, possessive, ignoring, and unclassified. These are illustrated in Table 1. Shoben concludes from his study that "parent attitudes are meaningfully associated with child adjustment." Just what knowledge and what attitudes are desirable for the development of well-adjusted personalities are problems which should receive further attention and study.

TABLE 1   Illustrative items from the U.S.C. Parent Attitude Scale

	Strongly agree	Mildly agree	Mildly disagree	Strongly disagree
1. A child should be seen and not heard.				
2. Parents should sacrifice everything for their children.				
3. Children need some of the natural meanness taken out of them.				
4. Children should not annoy their parents with their unimportant problems.				
5. A child should never keep a secret from his parents.				
6. Children should have as much freedom as parents allow themselves.				
7. Children should have lots of parental supervision.				
8. Children should not be allowed to play with youngsters from the "wrong side of the tracks."				
9. Children should be allowed to make only minor decisions for themselves.				

An understanding of child development is not a simple problem. All too often there are suggestions made that the child can be easily understood in terms of some simple formula. This was clearly set forth a number of years ago in connection with height-weight charts. Then, there are those who would ascribe all conduct and growth to some one element or a special combination of two or more elements.

By reducing these to a formula and applying it to the child's development, one is then able to predict and understand his growth needs and problems. The early views of child nature, which are presented later in this chapter, included, most of all, the fault of oversimplifying the child's growth needs.

A first essential in the understanding of the child is to regard him as a *dynamic living creature*. To understand him is to recognize that he must use, rather than hoard, his energy. This seems to have been a major point of difference between the attitudes of the fifty mothers of problem children and the fifty mothers of nonproblem children. Failure to provide guidance in the directing of this energy may eventually produce an individual whose abilities are developed in an undesirable manner and whose energy is directed into useless or undesirable channels. Another essential for the understanding of the growing child is the need to recognize each child as a *unique personality*. Parents and teachers who insist upon the child's following their particular pattern in development fail to realize that each child is unique, with his own needs, potentialities for growth, aspirations, and goals. Parents may cling to the child, hold him close by their side, and vow to make him into some special type of person. Such a treatment, however, must always operate within the framework of the dynamics and characteristics inherent within each living organism. Thirdly, it is very important to realize that the child *grows and develops toward maturity in accordance with certain fundamental principles*. Growth and development do not follow a haphazard course. Neither do they adhere to some simple formula that enables one to predict with certainty the nature and course of the child's future development. Teachers and parents should, however, be able to understand and direct growth more effectively as a result of their understanding the major principles involved.

Older concepts of child nature and development

Many of the generally held concepts of child development have been handed down during the course of the past generations and accepted as unverified but generally valid assumptions. History and literature are filled with examples of such unverified assumptions, and if one examines the attitudes and feelings of a large percentage of people, he will find that these have had their influence. Thus, many intelligent people are confused by conditions of fact and fantasy. This confusion has often been enhanced by various forms of indoctrinations introduced early in life and the integration of many of these faulty notions with such beliefs.

The doctrine of innate depravity. The notion that child nature is essentially evil has to some extent survived the teachings of the Middle Ages and is to be found in some circles today. The old adage, "Spare the rod and spoil the child," became a guide for parents and teacher alike. Schoolmasters were chosen partially because of their ability to impose order in the classroom. The whipping post was commonly used and the punishment inflicted in many schools was worse than that found in the great majority of prisons today. The poem by the English poet Crabbe cited by Cubberly reveals the attitudes existing toward child nature at the beginning of the nineteenth century.

> Students like horses on the road,
> Must be well lashed before they take the load;
> They may be willing for a time to run,
> But you must whip them ere the work be done;
> To tell a boy, that if he will improve,
> His friends will praise him, and his parents love,
> Is doing nothing—he has not a doubt
> But they will him, nay, applaud without;
> Let no fond sire a boy's ambition trust,
> To make him study, let him learn he must.[2]

The influence of Rousseau. In the teachings of Rousseau, a direct and effective attack was made on the doctrine of innate depravity. Rousseau was extremely disturbed by the political, social, and ecclesiastical conditions of his time, and tried to correct some of these conditions through writings of a critical nature about them. It was his belief that the best approach was to reject everything in existence and take the opposite view, since the prevailing conditions were so corrupt. His philosophy of education is presented in the book *Émile,* in which he describes the education of the boy Émile and his wife Sophie. His concept of the disastrous effects of the influence of men are set forth in the first sentence of his book.

All is good as it comes from the hand of the Creator; all degenerates under the hands of man. He forces one country to produce the fruits of another. He confounds climates, elements, and seasons; he mutilates his dog, his horses, his slave: turns everything topsy-turvy, disfigures him-

---

[2] Quoted from E. P. Cubberly, *History of Education* (Boston: Houghton Mifflin Company, 1920), p. 456.

self. He will have nothing as nature made it, not even man himself; he must be trained like a managed horse, trimmed like a tree in the garden.

This book did not set forth a philosophy of education in outline form, but it did present in an interesting literary style many of the educational paradoxes of the time. The emphasis throughout the book was upon the natural development of the child. According to the ideas presented, the best form of education for the child during the first twelve years was that in which the child was permitted to grow up without the interference of human guidance and direction. Thus, in literary style, Rousseau produced a boy who at the age of eighteen was unspoiled by the doctrines of the church and the ways of society.

Amid the interesting phases of life's growth, Rousseau was able to present a condition for growth that was free of the severity, restraints, and intolerable conditions of his time. His views of child nature soon had important effects on educational practices in Germany and were later felt in the United States as well as in other parts of the world. In *Émile* a new ideal for education is presented. Coming at a time in history when many of the political and religious practices of the time were in a state of flux, this ideal was enthusiastically received by many of the thinkers of Rousseau's day. Thus, we note that a doctrine of innate goodness came to be substituted by some for that of innate depravity. The fact that Rousseau made a valuable contribution to education and to an understanding of the needs of the child can hardly be denied. However, his concept of the child was destined to be studied and modified as a result of the use of the scientific procedure for studying children.

The child as a miniature adult. A theory widely held during the past century conceived of the child as a miniature adult. According to this view of the child, knowledge of right and wrong as well as various moral qualities were innate, and only maturity was needed to bring them into full development and utilization. Such a view could very well harmonize with the philosophy of the natural goodness of the child presented by Rousseau. The growing child, according to this viewpoint, was held responsible for his acts, just as the adult was, except for the fact that in some respects the moral sense was not as completely developed.

The materials presented in the subsequent chapters will show that the child is not a miniature adult physically, mentally, or emotionally. However, the miniature-adult concept of the child has had an important influence on the educational practices of the twentieth century. The widespread emphasis on education as a preparation for adult life, the attempts to teach children in terms of adult interests and aspirations, and the method of requiring children to adopt adult manners and ways of doing are evidences of this influence.

The mechanistic concept of the child. The theories of child nature and development just presented evolved as a result of man's efforts to better understand through critical thinking the nature of the universe and man's place in it. It was but natural, then, that the child would have been regarded at one time as a sinful and depraved creature. Also, the concept of man's innate goodness in a world of corruption found expression in the work of Rousseau. The development of psychology as a separate field of study paved the way for studying children in a more careful manner and under better controlled conditions. In an attempt to get away from philosophical and subjective procedures, many psychologists busied themselves with the development of techniques for studying individuals by the laboratory method. This movement opened up new fields for psychology, but when carried to an extreme tended to close others. The extremists of this school of thought, referred to as *behaviorists,* would dispense with all reference to consciousness and confine their considerations to studying observable reactions, i.e., the behavior of the individual in response to a stimulus. And, while this procedure led to worthwhile discoveries concerning the development of children, it failed to provide a complete picture of the child's growth.

Methods of child study

The widespread use of the scientific technique led to a general dissatisfaction among students of child development with the older subjective and philosophical methods of study. Thus, we note that by the dawn of the twentieth century students were becoming concerned with the application of the scientific method to the study of the growth and development of children. These studies have led to a more accurate and harmonious concept of the child as a dynamic growing personality. Two features in particular characterize the scientific method. In the first place, the scientist depends upon *careful observations.* If possible, these are made under laboratory or controlled conditions—oftentimes making use of instruments in order to secure more accurate and precise observations. Secondly, the scientist does not rely upon his memory but *records his observations.* These observations are recorded in a rather complete form in the order of their occurrence so as to eliminate errors resulting from forgetting, retrospections (confused associations), and bias. The methods commonly used in studying child growth and development make use of these procedures as far as possible. When direct observations cannot be made, ratings from the individual or others, interviews, tests, and other techniques of a like nature are used. Not all of these are wholly objective. However, when these are tested for their reliability and validity, and used by individuals who understand their limitations and possibilities, they have been found to be most valuable.

Direct observations. Recognizing the inaccuracies of ordinary observations made by parents and teachers, attempts have been made to improve these methods of collecting data. Also, strides have been made in recording observations in a more objective manner. Thus, personal biases, so prevalent in subjective judgments and estimates, have been largely eliminated or controlled through the use of systematic observations. Sometimes special conditions are established, designed to produce certain general types of behavior. The individual's behavior in such a situation is then observed and recorded. This technique has been used in particular in studying emotional and social development of children, and has furnished much material that will be referred to in later chapters dealing with these phases of the child's development.

Oftentimes, periodic samplings of a child's behavior are secured under different conditions. In this way the child's emotional characteristics manifested at home may be compared with those manifested at school or in some other situation. This method of child study has an advantage over the controlled experimental method in that many forms of behavior cannot be studied under definite laboratory conditions. Also, in the use of this method, attempts are made to secure the natural responses of the child.

The studies conducted at Yale University under the general direction of Gesell have made use of this method under somewhat controlled conditions. A dome-shaped compartment, equipped with cameras that make it possible to secure motion pictures of the child from several directions at the same time, is used. The child, who is inside the compartment, is free from distractions from observers, since the walls are constructed with one-way glass which enables those observing the child's reactions to make their observations without being detected by the child. Play materials, other children, special problems, and the like are introduced to the child, and his reactions are observed and photographed. Both still and motion pictures have been secured and analyzed for developmental stages. From these observations, some very worth-while facts and principles of child development have evolved, which will be referred to in a later chapter.

Genetic method. The use of the biographical or child-development method has brought considerable insight into the developmental characteristics of children. Studies have been made of the daily activities of a child before birth, during infancy, and throughout the period of childhood. The earlier observations and records were often based upon subjective data; however, refined techniques have resulted in more accurate data so that considerable information is now available relative to the child's development at different age levels and the influence of various factors and conditions on learning and development. These studies have reaffirmed the ideas propounded earlier by John Dewey and others that children vary considerably in their abilities and interests; but, because of the plasticity of children, opportunities for molding them according to certain preconceived general patterns are exceedingly great.

The biographical method has shown the effects upon the child's development of different methods of treatment. In one case, Johnny and Jimmy (twins) were studied from the age of twenty days until they were two years and seven months of age.[3] Johnny was chosen for the experimental subject, while Jimmy was the control subject. Johnny was, therefore, given special practice in the performance of various activities considered normal for a boy his age, while Jimmy was not permitted to take these exercises. Both were tested at various intervals to determine the effects of practice on various test performances.

The normative survey. The development of standardized measuring instruments for evaluating the development of children was accompanied by many studies of a survey type. These studies made use of standard instruments available for evaluating the developmental status of large groups of children of different age or grade levels. Studies of children at any age level reveal wide variations in any growth feature. By means of norms established on a large sampling of children of various age levels, one is able to determine the child's development in comparison with average children of different ages. Although there has been a shift toward the longitudinal method,

[3] M. B. McGraw, *A Study of Johnny and Jimmy* (New York: Appleton-Century-Crofts, 1935).

the normative cross-section approach has some distinct advantages. In the first place, considerable data about growth can be secured over a relatively short period of time. Secondly, the new samples drawn from the different age levels can be used as a cross-check upon the data from other age levels. Also, uniform sampling criteria can be established and applied from the beginning until the study is completed.

By means of norms obtained from the cross-section approach, one is able to compare a particular child with other children of the same age or grade level. This is perhaps the best standard method available for evaluating the extent of a child's development. The chief problem involved in conducting normative surveys is that of securing a representative sampling for the levels being studied.

Longitudinal versus cross-sectional measurements. It has already been suggested that during recent years there has been a continued increase in the use of the longitudinal approach. The normative-survey method furnished data that made it possible to construct growth curves for a number of developmental factors and tasks. However, with increased interest in child development, it became apparent that such cross-sectional data did not give an accurate picture of the growth of an individual child. Such curves obscured the cyclic periods found in individual growth curves by canceling out individual differences and cycles of development, thus producing smoothed curves.

Baldwin and others were among the early investigators who studied development by means of repeated measurements.[4] By this method, Baldwin was able to plot individual growth curves for boys and girls as well as average growth curves for different groups of individuals. While this method of studying physical development is not of so much immediate value, measurements kept over a period of time furnish a permanent objective picture from which the effect of various factors on development can be studied. Such measurements make possible both the scientific determination of how individuals grow and predictions about future growth.

The extensive growth studies conducted during the past quarter of a century indicate clearly that each child's development is unique in nature and should be interpreted in terms of his own tempo of growth, rather than with reference to averages based upon mass data

[4] Bird T. Baldwin, The physical growth of children from birth to maturity, *University of Iowa Studies in Child Welfare*, 1921, Vol. 1, No. 1.

from groups of children. Figure 1 shows the difference between the average and individual curves of growth in height.[5]

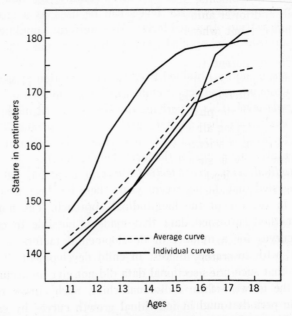

FIG. 1 Comparison of average and individual curves for growth in stature

(After Meredith)

In spite of the difficulties encountered in obtaining data and the time element necessary to complete a study, longitudinal growth data will tend to displace many of the mass methods used in the study of children. The increased use of permanent records in school, coupled with the increased attention being given to health and physical development, should provide much useful data for the study of the individual child. A number of longitudinal studies have been completed so that the general form of linear physical measurements is fairly well established.

The experimental method. An outgrowth of an attempt to get away from the subjective and limiting features of the introspectionists (best exemplified in the studies by Wundt and Titchener) was the development of laboratory procedures for studying and

[5] Howard V. Meredith, The rhythm of physical growth, *University of Iowa Studies in Child Welfare,* 1935, Vol. 11, No. 3, p. 112.

recording the reactions of individuals under controlled conditions. Many psychologists busied themselves with the development of procedures and instruments, and thus with laboratories for studying individuals and lower animals. This movement opened up new fields for psychology, but when carried to an extreme tended to close others.

It became apparent to most psychologists, as the field of psychology developed and applications of the principles and findings were made to different areas of life, that the strictly experimental approach found in the physical-science laboratories could not furnish the basis for studying all aspects of human behavior. Unfortunately for psychology as a science, the nature of the subject matter being studied objectively is such that wishful thinking and the influence of the personal self leads to a sort of speculation that tends to cause suspicion of psychology as a science.

a. *Single group.* There are two general types of experimental methods used in studying child development and growth—the single group and the parallel group. The former studies a single child or group of children under laboratory or controlled conditions. The effects of extra feedings upon the nervous habits of a child or group is a problem that would fall within the scope of this method. Other problems of child growth that might be studied by this method are the effects of adverse temperature conditions on reading comprehension, and the effects of motion pictures (some particular picture) on the attitudes and interests of a group of sixth-grade pupils.

b. *The parallel group* makes use of two or more groups in studying a problem. The parallel-group procedure may be used in studying many of the problems studied with single groups. The groups (parallel) should be equivalent except for the variable being studied. These groups are then compared in various ways in order to determine the effect of the differential imposed. Some problems of child development that would be studied by such a procedure might be the relative effects of nursery-school training on the intelligence of children, and the effects of democratic practices in the classroom on the study habits and attitudes of seventh-grade pupils.

c. *The co-twin control* represents a special type of parallel group, except studies of twins have been concerned with comparisons of two individuals. This has come into prominence in recent years as a method of studying the effects of certain practices or conditions on growth and development. This method presupposes one-egg twins completely similar, with all environmental factors held constant except for the one differential that is experimentally injected into the situation. The co-twin control procedure is applicable to many problems of child development and has wide possibilities. Concerning its possible uses Gesell has stated:

The method of co-twin control is peculiarly suited to the analytic study of the processes of child development and the genetic factors of life-career. If the instincts of an organism were only tinted pink and the habits robin egg blue, as Lloyd Morgan whimsically wished, then we might better grasp the relationships of nature and nurture, of endowment and environment. This differential stain has not been forthcoming; but with the aid of co-twin control studies we may glimpse the interrelations of learning and growth, the effects of specific training, the influence of attitudes and emotional patterns. The method may be fruitfully used to explore these intricate problems which are so resistant to absolute biometric approach. The method preserves the togetherness of the individual and affords more insight into the total integrated economy of performance and development.[6]

The individual case study. The case study is a method of evaluating all the significant facts that can be obtained about a child for the purpose of assisting him in his growth, development, and adjustments. The case history, on the other hand, consists of a collection of facts about the child from infancy up to the present stage of his development. The case study involves more than the history of the child's development, but includes clinical data available as well as interpretations that may be given to various aspects of his developmental history. There is a tendency for agencies to maintain records of the activities and accomplishments of the children with whom they are especially concerned. Some schools have developed rather complete cumulative records on the pupils. These include, in addition to the history of the child's development, data obtained from tests, rating scales, inventories, and samples of the child's work. Such records are most valuable in providing a better understanding of the child's development and problems.

The use of the case study method as a procedure in dealing with development and maladjustment among children may well be described as having three chief functions. These are:

1. It should serve as an instrument for securing a record of the child's development.

2. It furnishes a basis for studying the underlying factors connected with child development and adjustments.

6 A. I. Gesell, The method of co-twin control, *Science*, 1942, Vol. 95, p. 448.

3. It provides a comprehensive outline of the child's socioeconomic status and personality adjustment upon which an educational and treatment program may be planned.

Projective techniques. The projective techniques avoid direct questions and subjective ratings in an effort to arrive at the nature of a subject's personality. Rather, these procedures confront the subject with a stimulus for the purpose of so ordering his perception or response that it will reflect the dynamics and structure of the subject's personality. The best-known and most widely studied of the different projective techniques is the Rorschach Ink-blot Test.[7] This consists of a series of cards on each of which is an irregularly shaped blotch of ink. The subject taking the test is asked, "What might this be?" "What does this look like to you?" He then gives his own interpretation of it. The examiner notes the responses given, the number of different responses given, the quality and completeness of the responses, and the like. Needless to say, the value of such a test will depend largely upon the skill and ability of the examiner in his interpretation of the responses of the subject. This test has the distinct advantage over many other projective techniques in that the stimulus itself provides very little of the interpretation. The subject is required to bring his experiences to date into the test situation, and his responses are determined by his experiences and direction of emotional and mental reactions. This has been borne out by the wide range of responses obtained from subjects with different levels of maturity or cultural background.

There are certain important principles useful in the evaluation of projective techniques. Those generally listed include the following: (1) The method should be largely free from cultural limitations and directions. (2) The activity should be sufficiently simple to enable the child to reveal his characteristics. (3) The technique should not be used in situations that are so formal as to create tensions and inhibitions. (4) Tests requiring complicated or complex motor performances will be of little value if no motion-picture camera is available for recording such responses. (5) The stereotyping of a technique fails to elicit natural responses of one child, while the natural responses of another may be secured. (6) Materials secured from a projective technique should be of such a nature that they contribute to a better understanding of the child's development, personality, and adjustments.

[7] See M. R. Hertz, Rorschach: twenty years after, *Psychological Bulletin,* 1942, Vol. 39, pp. 529-572.

A child's interpretation of pictures and like materials is a most useful projective technique. Also, the child's drawings may furnish useful materials. These are easy to secure and furnish a permanent record for study. Margaret Mead has shown that there is a striking contrast between the drawings of children from totally different cultural backgrounds.[8] She contrasts the drawings of Balinese and Iatmul children. The drawings of the Balinese children are full of activity, with free-flowing lines; while those of the Iatmul are static, with little movement and no relationship between one element and another. These are in harmony with the differences in the culture of the two tribes.

The use of anecdotes. Considerable data have been gathered about the nature and characteristics of children by means of anecdotes. Anecdotes kept over a period of time have been found to be useful in showing behavior and growth trends in the life of a single individual. This method involves the observational procedure, and might well be classified as part of the observational method of gathering data. Prescott and his students have made considerable use of this method in their work at the Collaboration Center for Human Growth and Development at the University of Chicago and at the University of Maryland. Considerable use has been made of this method in school records and data on children obtained by teachers sometimes referred to as belonging to the progressive school of thought.

Certain features have been set forth which characterize useful and valid anecdotes. Some of these may be listed as follows: (1) They should be brief. (2) They should tell what actually took place, with only a minimum, if any, of interpretations presented. (3) They should not be confined to action in one type of setting, for example, a classroom setting. (4) They should be an outgrowth of the individual's own dynamics, not a response to some dictated situation. (5) They should deal with a single situation. (6) They should include descriptions of actual incidents in the individual's life activities.

Summary

Following the period of the Renaissance, there was a rapid development of knowledge and understanding leading in many directions. This accumulation of knowledge led one after another of the areas of study to break away from the mother philosophy and proclaim itself

[8] Margaret Mead, Research on primitive children, *Manual of Child Psychology* (New York: John Wiley and Sons, 1946), pp. 698-699.

a field of science. This represented a period of growing up or achieving independence on the part of various divisions of study. This assertion of independence was accompanied by a sort of rebellion against philosophy. Such a viewpoint was present among many educators at the beginning of this century, and was perhaps a necessary part of the growing-up process of education as a science.

Older concepts of child nature and development gave way to newer concepts introduced by Rousseau and his students. The theories thus propounded were carefully studied and tested by many of those interested in child study. These studies required the development of new techniques and the refinement of older techniques for studying children. Recent years have witnessed an increased use of the scientific method for studying child growth and development. The genetic-study procedure and longitudinal studies have provided valuable data on child growth. Other methods have been used more recently for these studies. Likewise, improved methods have been developed and used for gathering data on growth. These methods are not separate and distinct from those listed for studying child development, but in some cases supplement these methods, while in others they are a part of the method.

Questions and Exercises

1. Why has this age sometimes been termed "The Age of the Child?"
2. Evaluate the essentials listed for understanding the child. What other essentials would you list?
3. What were the general effects of the concept of the doctrine of innate depravity upon training methods used with children?
4. Show how parents sometimes regard the child as a miniature adult. Contrast the characteristics of the child when viewed as a miniature adult with those when he is viewed as a child.
5. What are the special merits of the genetic approach to studying children? What are some of the major difficulties encountered in the use of this method?
6. Contrast the normative-survey method and the longitudinal method of studying children. List two or three advantages of each of these methods.
7. What are some of the limitations of the experimental method of studying children? Suggest several problems of child growth and development which could be studied by this method.
8. Suggest ways in which anecdotes may be useful in studying the growth of children. What are some special precautions that should be observed?

9. What contributions do you think that infant biographies make to our understanding of child growth and development? What are the major weaknesses of studies of this nature?
10. Describe the genetic approach to child growth and development. In what ways are Gesell's studies examples of the genetic method? What are the practical advantages of this method?

Selected Readings

Anderson, J. E. "The methods of child psychology," in *Handbook of Child Psychology* (C. Murchison, ed.). Worcester, Mass.: Clark University Press, 1933. Chap. I.

Arrington, Ruth E. Time sampling in studies of social behavior, *Psychological Bulletin*, 1943, Vol. 40, pp. 81-124.

Bradbury, D. E. The contributions of the child study movement to child psychology, *Psychological Bulletin*, 1937, Vol. 34, pp. 21-38.

Brown, Francis J. *The Sociology of Childhood*. New York: Prentice-Hall, 1939. Chap. I.

Frank, Lawrence K. Research in child psychology: history and prospect, *Child Behavior and Development* (R .G. Barker et al., eds.). New York: McGraw-Hill Book Co., 1943. Chap. I.

Gesell, Arnold, Amatruda, Catherine S., Castner, B. M., and Thompson, Helen. *Biographies of Child Development. A Ten-Year Study from the Clinic of Child Development at Yale University*. New York: Hoeber, 1939.

Hurlock, Elizabeth B. *Child Development*. 2nd ed.; New York: McGraw-Hill Book Co., 1950. Chap. I.

Merry, Frieda K., and Merry, Ralph V. *From Infancy to Adolescence*. Rev. ed.; New York: Harper & Brothers, 1950. Chap. I.

Nagge, Joseph W. *Psychology of the Child*. New York: The Ronald Press Co., 1942. Chap. I.

Olson, Willard C. *Child Development*. Boston: D. C. Heath and Company, 1949. Chap. I.

Ragsdale, Clarence E. *Modern Psychologies and Education*. New York: The Macmillan Company, 1932. Chap. I.

Stoddard, George D., and Wellman, Beth L. *Child Psychology*. New York: The Macmillan Company, 1934. Chaps. I and II.

Thorpe, Louis P. *Child Psychology and Development*. New York: The Ronald Press Co., 1946. Chap. I.

2

Biological Inheritance
and Prenatal Development

Anyone interested in understanding the problems connected with child growth and development will be concerned with the principles and processes of heredity. The twentieth century brought forth biological research resulting in discoveries that are of profound importance in the understanding of child development. Snyder states:

This development includes not only the classical principles of the transmission of chromosomes and genes, but their physiological and biochemical activities, their evolutionary history, their distribution and behavior in populations, and the social, medical, and legal implications of many of the traits resulting from them. The understanding of these principles has given us the first clear insight into human individuality.[1]

Origin of the individual

The development of the child begins with the fertilization of the egg cell. In this case we have the fusion of parental germ cells—one from the male and the other from the female parent. When the individual is born, he is already a highly organized biological unit. Because of the integrated nature of this unit, he is capable of a considerable number of elaborate activities. The nature of the original material from which the individual child emerges must not be ignored in arriving at a better understanding of the child's development. What the child is at the various stages of life is determined jointly by the biological materials from which he is formed and the

[1] Lawrence H. Snyder, The genetic approach to human individuality, *Scientific Monthly*, 1949, Vol. 48, p. 166.

conditions under which he develops. This concept will be emphasized and enlarged upon later in this chapter.

The fertilized egg. Man is composed of two types of cells, somatic cells and germ cells. Somatic cells are body cells and are not involved directly in reproduction. The germ cells are specifically concerned with reproduction. The somatic cells divide so as to produce body growth and repair cells that have been destroyed.

The germ cells exist from the earlier fetal stage, but do not assume their special characteristics until after the period of puberty, when

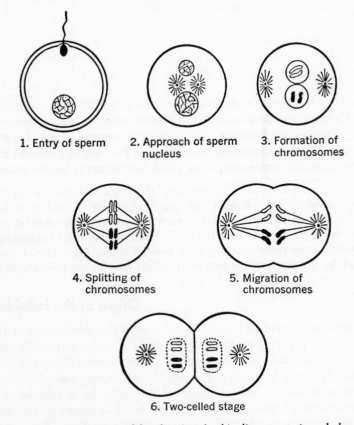

1. Entry of sperm   2. Approach of sperm nucleus   3. Formation of chromosomes

4. Splitting of chromosomes   5. Migration of chromosomes

6. Two-celled stage

FIG. 2   The mechanism of fertilization. In this diagram paternal chromosomes are represented as black, maternal as white. The number of chromosomes characteristic of the species illustrated is given as four.

(From H. E. Waters, *Genetics,* copyright 1913 by The Macmillan Company and used with their permission.)

reproduction becomes possible. The union of the germ cells of the male and female under favorable circumstances produces the fertilized egg, which may be thought of as the beginning of a new life. The male germ cells are called spermatozoa, while the female germ cells are known as ova. The ovum, oftentimes referred to as the egg cell, differs from the sperm cell in shape and size. Fertilization consists in the penetration of the outer membrane of an ovum by a sperm cell as, shown in Figure 2. Following this, a period of mitosis or cell division starts. The egg cell divides and redivides according to a schematic and sequential plan laid down by nature.

As shown in Figure 2, the process of mitosis begins after the sperm has penetrated the ovum and passed directly to the nucleus. The chromosome nuclei of the sperm and ovum come together and arrange themselves in such a way that the cell has its full complement of genes—one half from the sperm and the other half from the ovum. Thus, all cells are derived from both parents.

The theory of the gene. Within a species, all cells except those involved in reproduction will possess the same complement of chromosomes. These chromosomes appear in pairs in the fertilized germ cells. There are twenty-four pairs, one of each pair coming from each parent. These chromosomes contain a very large number of smaller units, the genes. These genes furnish the basis for the inheritance of unitary traits, referred to later in this chapter. Each trait is thus inherited through a gene or combination of genes. Like the chromosomes, the genes are also in pairs, that is, there is one gene for hair color in one chromosome and another gene for hair color in the homologous chromosome. These genes interact in a number of complex ways. The manner in which they react under normal growing conditions has been referred to as the law of heredity.[2]

The individual and his environment

Environment has been frequently envisaged as a passive place or *locus* in which the organism's behavior is said to occur. In other

[2] The publication of the experiments on hybridization by Gregor Mendel in the *Proceedings of the National History Society of Brunn* in 1866 was a new epoch in the advancement of the knowledge of heredity. His study was based upon experiments conducted during the previous ten years with many varieties of garden peas. It was from these experiments that he derived the *law of dominance.* This led to the *law of segregation,* which is based upon the concept that the individual is characterized by a number of unit characters. A complete description of Mendel's studies and more recent developments relative to the modes of transmission of genes will be found in recent texts in genetics.

words, the environment is considered a setting for behavior, rather than an active stimulating agent. From a modern psychological viewpoint, the environment consists of a myriad of specific stimuli that stimulate the dynamic organism to action. When heredity and environment are carefully studied in relation to the behavior of the organism, it will be observed that they are inextricably interwoven in their operation. Thus, the differentiation of heredity and environment becomes extremely difficult, and of doubtful value in the understanding of child growth and development. These problems will be described and illustrated in the following discussions.

Isolated operation of heredity and environment. The classification of behavior listed by psychologists during the early part of the present century into *habits* and *instincts* assumed the operation of heredity and environment in an exclusive manner. Habits were interpreted as learned ways of behaving and had no basis in hereditary drives and characteristics. Instincts, on the other hand, were thought to be transmitted forms of behavior from generation to generation through the germ plasm. Vast arrays of instincts were listed by certain students of human behavior. This theory of the transmission of certain behavior functions *in toto* has been discredited in more recent studies of child development.[3] Although this concept has been largely discredited, there is still much superficial and inconsistent thinking conducted in which functional behavior is classified as hereditary and acquired.

Interaction of heredity and environment. The most widely recognized principle of the operation of heredity and environment is that of the interaction between the two. Although early students of psychology attempted to classify all behavior as exclusively of hereditarian or environmental origin, it soon became apparent to many students in this field that the two were very closely related and that most behavior could not be classified as resulting exclusively from heredity or environment. This position is supported by observations of factors affecting the growth and development of children. The failure of the typical kindergarten child in the United States to distinguish between a motor bus and a train would be an indication of mental inferiority, while such a failure among typical children of India would be explained on the basis of the lack of opportunities to observe motor buses and trains. Varying conditions of either heredity

[3] An early exposition of the arguments against such a classification of behavior appears in Leonard Carmichael's article, Heredity and environment, are they antithetical? *Journal of Abnormal and Social Psychology*, 1925, Vol. 20, pp. 245-260.

or environment would have a pronounced effect upon one's selection of elements in his environment. The hard-of-hearing child would not be expected to select low soft music on the radio, while the child from New York would not have the same understanding and appreciation of the ranch as would a child from El Paso. Concerning the operation of heredity and environment, Anastasi and Foley have written as follows:

It is clear that any estimate of the relative contribution of hereditary and environmental factors to individual differences depends upon the range or extent of both hereditary and environmental differences within the population under consideration. But this is by no means the only sense in which the roles of heredity and environment are mutually interdependent. The nature and extent of the influence exerted by each type of factor depend upon the contribution of the other. In other words, any one hereditary factor would operate differently under different environmental conditions. Conversely, any environmental factor would exert a different influence depending upon the specific hereditary material upon which it operates.[4]

Inheritance of acquired traits. Theories have been presented throughout the centuries indicating a general belief in the inheritance of acquired traits.[5] The early Greek philosophers were concerned with this problem, and offered theories that indicated a belief in the inheritance of acquired traits, but in an indirect general manner.

The theory that was best formulated and received the most attention during the nineteenth century was presented by Lamarck in 1809, and is generally known as the Lamarckian hypothesis. This theory emphasized the importance of use or exercise in the development of traits which were passed on to the next generation. August Weissmann seriously challenged this theory in 1883, and offered the theory of the continuity of the germ plasm. This theory claims that the germ plasm (the bearer of heredity) continues to flow from one generation to another, and is neither produced by the body cells nor affected by their experiences. A number of studies have been designed to test the validity of the doctrine of the inheritance of acquired traits. The results of these studies present, in general, negative evi-

[4] Anne Anastasi and J. P. Foley, A proposed reorientation in the heredity-environment controversy, *Psychological Review*, 1948, Vol. 55, p. 241. Reproduced by permission of the journal and of the American Psychological Association.

[5] See T. H. Morgan, Human heredity and modern genetics, *Scientific Monthly*, 1938, Vol. 47, pp. 318-319.

dence for such a theory. Biologists and psychologists are therefore inclined toward the viewpoint that the germ cells are relatively independent of the body cells and of acquired traits. In this general connection, Kuppusawny describes the distribution of mental ability among the depressed classes and castes in India. He states:

... As is well known it is only the higher castes that were given the opportunities of education till recently. For some three thousand years or so the higher castes have been receiving education generation after generation in succession. The lower castes, particularly the lowest—the Panchamas, have received no education whatever for a similar period. The castes in India have been strictly endogamous. But in recent years, with a change in social outlook, when the Panchama boys and girls are given facilities to attend schools and colleges we find that they are responding well. They have been taking University degrees and holding responsible offices in civil and educational services. Among the front rank of Indian political and social leaders are to be found members of these castes. This great social experiment demonstrates that though among castes the literary habits have been cultivated for some thousands of years generation after generation, and in some other such habits were never cultivated, today when the boys and girls of the different castes are taught these habits we find that they are responding equally well.[6]

Prenatal development

Prenatal growth stages. Physical development takes place in two ways. There is growth by cell division and multiplication. This has been referred to as *hyperplastic* growth. The second method is through an increase in the size of the cells and is called *hypertrophic* growth. During the early fetal period, growth is almost wholly hyperplastic; after birth, hypertrophic growth becomes important. On the basis of the type of growth, embryologists have divided the prenatal life into several periods. The first period begins with the fertilization of the egg cell and continues until the ovum becomes attached to the mother. During this period there are important changes in the internal structure in that the fertilized cell divides and redivides until a globular mass of cells is formed. At the end of the ovum period, the outer layer of cells cuts through the uterine surface and becomes imbedded in the uterus. The outer membrane is at this time in contact with the mother, and the fetus exists and develops as a parasite.

[6] B. Kuppusawny, Laws of heredity in relation to general mental ability, *Journal of General Psychology*, 1947, Vol. 36, p. 38.

Food is taken from the mother through the blood stream; however, the fetus lives its own life and grows according to its own nature.

The period from the time the ovum attaches itself to the mother until the general form and structure of the body parts are formed is called the *embryonic period*. This lasts from the end of the second until the end of the tenth week. This period is one during which there is a rapid growth along with a differentiation of the bodily parts, so that at the end of the ten-week period the embryo has taken on the appearance of a human being. This does not mean, however, that the specific form of the infant now appears, but rather that the various parts of the body can be determined to more than 90 per cent of completion. The growth in size is also pronounced.

The development of the vertebrate embryo proceeds from the head downward. Thus, the arms and hands appear prior to the legs and feet, while the head takes on a significant size before the legs show their final shape. The general pattern of the nervous system is laid down early in the embryonic period, and shows a rapid development. By the fifth week, the principal structures are distinguishable as enlargements of the top of the neural tube. At an early embryonic stage the brain acquires all of its principal structural characteristics. However, the higher brain centers do not function effectively until some time after birth. The development of the nervous system appears to precede that of the muscles and sensory receptors, and proceeds from the head end of the neural tube down a sort of physiological gradient.

The third period of prenatal growth is known as the *fetus period*. This includes the time from the end of the embryonic period until birth, and is especially characterized by growth in size. It is during the latter part of this period that hypertrophic growth becomes more important. Throughout the fetal period there is a pronounced neural growth, nerve fibers growing out of the central nervous system. The advanced state of development of the nervous system as compared to other structures is significant in relation to motor and mental development.

The development of prenatal behavior. An understanding of the course of development of higher animals and man has been greatly facilitated through studies of fetal development of simpler organisms. The development of frogs and salamanders has been studied by direct observation, while investigations of bird embryos have been made through a "window" in the egg. Although direct observations of the development of the child have not been possible until recently, much knowledge has been gathered through reports of the mother on spontaneous movements, and to a certain extent through external observations in which various instruments were used for detecting the beating of the heart, special movements, and the like. Reports on operatively removed fetuses have given valuable information about the structural development at different stages. Through combining the evidences gathered from these varied sources and procedures, much has been learned about the prenatal development of structure and function. The results of the studies by Carmichael of guinea pigs during the fetal period present clear evidence in the case of locomotion movements that behavior development during this stage is of a sequential nature.[7] It is certain, from his studies, that there is a specific age range within which certain responses appear, and stimulation prior to this will be largely ineffectual.

Characteristics of early behavior. The early behavior of the fetus, whether it is animal or human, is generalized and mass behavior rather than local and specific in nature. It was once believed that complex forms of behavior emerged at various periods and were linked together to form a behavior pattern. Many of these patterns were believed to be formed during the prenatal stage and were referred to as "chain reflexes." Later developmental studies of fetuses and infants have shown that this is not the case. Rather than the independent development of the different parts of a behavior pattern to be linked together at a later stage, mass movements first appear. It is from these movements that finer and more specific movements are later formed.

Effects of diet. It has already been pointed out that after a period of about two weeks the ovum becomes attached to the mother and develops as a parasite—obtaining the required nutrition from the mother unless the maternal tissues are exhausted. Recent experimental and clinical observations have provided information about the effects of dietary deficiencies on the development of the embryo and fetus. The fetus appears to draw vitamin C from the mother as long as appreciable amounts of ascorbic acid are present in the maternal plasma.[8] Furthermore, studies indicate that the vitamin

[7] Leonard Carmichael, An experimental study in the prenatal guinea-pig of the origin and development of reflexes and patterns of behavior in relation to the stimulation of specific receptor areas during the period of active fetal life, *Genetic Psychology Monographs*, 1934, Vol. 16, Nos. 5 and 6.

[8] Josef Warkany, Dietetic factors in pre-natal development, *Proceedings of the Spring Conference on Nutrition in Relation to Child Development and Behavior of the Child Research Clinic of the Woods School*, Langhorne, Pa., 1948, pp. 26-30.

C content of the blood plasma of the fetus is higher than that of the mother. In the case of vitamin A, the fetal plasma is usually below that of the mother. However, if the mother's intake is low, the intrauterine development of the offspring is endangered. Malformations have been secured in cases of animals where the diet is poor in carotene and vitamin A. Congenital blindness and other visual abnormalities have thus appeared. It is clear from the studies of the development of the fetus that there is a close relation between the diet of the mother and growth. An adequate maternal diet is important for the development of a healthy normal child.

The effects of the Rh factor. In 1940, Landsteiner and Wiener presented a report on the nature of agglutinin.[9] This agglutinin, when tested with human bloods, demonstrated the presence of a new substance that is referred to as the Rh factor. This is a factor which causes the cells to clump when they come in contact with blood that does not contain the same factor. The presence of this factor in human bloods is designated as Rh positive; the 14 per cent in which this is not present are designated as Rh negative. The agglutinin is the destructive antibody responsible for the manifestation of erythroblastosis (a condition in which immature blood cells are found in the blood stream). When the blood of an unborn baby which contains the Rh factor comes into contact with the mother with a negative Rh, there is grave danger that the child's blood might clump. The possibility of such a danger exists when the child inherits the father's Rh positive blood.

Effects of congenital experiences. In every situation where the environment operates as a factor, there are "gremlins" or destructive forces at work. If the germ cell is injured before or after fertilization, the condition may be regarded as due to environmental forces or conditions. The most common sort of prenatal influences affecting the organism is that which operates within the body of the mother after the fertilization of the cell. Some of the congenital conditions which have an injurious effect during this period may be listed as follows:

1. Malnutrition of the mother during gestation, which deprives the developing organism from needed food from the maternal blood stream.

2. Infections from the parent, especially syphilis, which attack the

[9] K. Landsteiner and A. S. Wiener, Agglutinable factor in human blood recognized by immune sera for rhesus blood, *Proceedings of the Society of Experimental Biology and Medicine,* 1940, Vol. 43, p. 223.

nervous system. (The results from such an infectious condition may not be apparent at birth.)

3. Severe emotional strain or emotional shock on the part of the mother during festation, resulting in visceral changes that adversely affect the development of the fetus.

4. Severe prolonged wasting disease of the mother, such as cancer, diabetes, or tuberculosis, may affect the malnutrition of the fetus.

5. The position of the embryo and fetus during prenatal life may, in the case of abnormal conditions or circumstances, affect the growth and development of the organism.

6. Birth injuries, especially mechanical injuries resulting from difficulties encountered at birth.

7. There is considerable evidence that a relationship exists between maternal pituitary deficiency and mongolism.

8. Maternal toxemia contributes to anoxia (insufficient oxygen in the blood) in the newborn child. Analgesics, anesthetics, and drugs used during labor and at the time of birth increase the danger of anoxia.

The prematurely born child. The mental development of prematurely born children has not only been of vital interest to the physician, but has also interested those concerned with the educational and social development of the child. The topic is, therefore, of theoretical interest, since it provides opportunities for considering the effects of early care and treatment upon later personal and social development. Thus, a study of premature infants should throw light on child growth and development during the latter fetal period as well as on the social consequences of early birth. Arthur L. Benton has reviewed many studies conducted in this field since 1911. From these studies he has attempted to determine those conclusions that appear to be sound. He draws the following conclusions from his analysis of the studies reviewed:

(1) Prematurely born children show developmental retardation during the first two years of life.

(2) Premature birth does not lead to acceleration in developmental rate so that the child "catches up with" the full term child.

(3) As a group prematurely born children are not inferior to full term children in respect to intellectual development.

(4) It is suggestive that the incidence of mental defect is higher among the premature, but the question is open and deserves careful quantitative and qualitative investigation. The significance of certain

etiological factors (evidence of birth injury, type of delivery, hereditary factors) should be carefully evaluated.

(5) The fact of birth weight (within the range of 1,000-2,500
grams) is not of great significance in relation to the mental development of the children surviving the first year of life.

(6) It seems that the incidence of "nervous traits" or behavior
difficulties is definitely higher among the premature than among
full term children. However, a really well-defined and adequately
controlled investigation of this question is lacking. If these reports
were confirmed, a study of the responsible factors would be indicated.[10]

Summary and implications

In the act of conception, thousands of human varieties are represented, each in itself a possible hereditary pattern, but only one
hereditary organization ordinarily survives. This may be looked upon
as the first step in the emergence of the individual as a personality
with abilities and characteristics unique for the particular person.
During the fetal life many of the resources of the individual that
survived conception are modified or eliminated, so that at birth the
resources of the infant are much more restricted than they were
in the original hereditary endowment. Some elements in the hereditary constitution have been reinforced by favorable conditions, while
others have been weakened or destroyed by an unfavorable environment.

Studies of the nature and influences of heredity have suggested
the following:

1. Heredity includes all the resemblances between the child
and his ancestry that are not a result of environmental influences.

2. These resemblances may be separated into (a) those including
the general features of organization, and (b) its details.

The general features of organization include the phyla or class and
are dependent upon the characteristics of the living substance in the
fertilized germ cell. These characteristics are not restricted to the
chromosomes but also include the cytoplasm. The details refer to the
color of the eyes, baldness, etc., and correspond to the unit characters.
These are inherited in accordance with certain Mendelian ratios.

[10] Arthur L. Benton, Mental development of prematurely born: A critical review
of the literature, *American Journal of Orthopsychiatry,* October, 1940.

It has become increasingly apparent that the operation of heredity is inextricably linked with that of the environment, from the beginning of life with the fertilization of the ovum. The growth and development of the embryo and fetus follow an orderly sequence set forth in the hereditary constitution. This principle is enlarged upon in Chapter 4. However, the normal healthy development of the fetus toward its optimum condition will depend upon whether or not the prenatal environment is favorable for its development. Any attempt to separate the influences of heredity and environment in a study of prenatal development will be met with many difficulties. The localization and environmental conditions surrounding the chromosomes affect the genes in such a way as to produce modifications in structure. The interaction of heredity and environment is apparent from the beginning of life; however, the nature of the individual organism is restricted to the hereditary potentialities laid down in the germ plasm by the sperm from the paternal ancestry and the ovum from the maternal ancestry.

Questions and Exercises

1. Why is it very difficult to determine whether or not some physical trait in the newborn child is a result of heredity or some congenital experiences? What are some physical traits that are known to be determined by heredity?

2. Explain why, during the period of the child's fetal development, heredity and environment act together as a single factor in producing certain growth characteristics. What are the implications for this in the problems of child care at this stage?

3. In the light of our knowledge about gene inheritance, what predictions can be made about a particular child's probable physical characteristics? Can it be said in this connection that heredity tends to make children different as well as alike?

4. Give an illustration of a sex-linked trait. Of blended inheritance.

5. Differentiate the *embryonic period* and the *fetal period* of the child's development.

6. Have you heard of effects of congenital experiences other than those presented in this chapter? Evaluate these for thir scientific accuracy.

7. Give arguments for and against the inheritance of acquired characteristics. What bearing does an answer to this have on problems of education?

8. Explain the operation of the Mendelian Law. Why is it often difficult to determine whether some trait found in the human child is inherited in accordance with this law?

9. What is the hypothesis of gene recombination? Show how mutations are deep-seated in the individual's past generations.
10. Why is it unsafe to assume that a child inherits his "high temper" from one of his parents? What other factors should be considered before deciding that his temper is inherited?

Selected Readings

Breckenridge, Marian E., and Vincent, E. Lee. *Child Development.* 2nd ed.; Philadelphia: W. B. Saunders Co., 1949. Chap. IV.

Cook, R. C., and Burke, B. S. *How Heredity Builds Our Lives.* Washington: American Genetic Association, 1946.

Cruze, Wendell W. *General Psychology for College Students.* New York: Prentice-Hall, 1951. Chap. X.

Glass, B. *Genes and the Man.* New York: Teachers College, Columbia University, 1943.

Kingsley, H. L. *The Nature and Conditions of Learning.* New York: Prentice-Hall, 1946. Chap. X.

Merry, Frieda K., and Merry, Ralph V. *The First Two Decades of Life.* Rev. ed.; New York: Harper & Brothers, 1950. Chap. II.

Munn, Norman L. *Psychology.* Boston: Houghton Mifflin Company, 1946. Chap. V.

Scheinfeld, A. *You and Heredity.* New York: F. A. Stokes Co., 1939.

Shull, A. F. *Heredity.* New York: McGraw-Hill Book Co., 1938.

Snyder, L. H. *The Principles of Heredity.* Boston: D. C. Heath and Company, 1946.

Stone, Calvin P. Methodological resources for the experimental study of innate behavior as related to environmental factors, *Psychological Review,* 1947, Vol. 54, pp. 342-347.

Teagarden, Florence M. *Child Psychology for Professional Workers.* Rev. ed.; New York: Prentice-Hall, 1946. Chap. II.

Thorpe, Louis P. *Child Psychology and Development.* New York: The Ronald Press Co., 1946. Chap. II.

3

The Period of Infancy

Introduction: Some characteristics of infancy

Changed conditions at birth. Birth marks important changed conditions for the organism, but not the beginning of life. The true beginning dates back to the fertilization of the ovum by the sperm, discussed in Chapter 2. It has already been suggested that the structural characteristics and hereditarian pattern of traits are laid down in the germ plasm. According to Gesell, types of body build are prefigured: the round face, square shoulders, spindly framework, muscular build, and the like.[1] Also, certain modes of reaction characteristics related to specific varieties of physique are, according to some students of individual behavior, laid down in the germ plasma.

The early human fetal behavior has been termed "prereflex" behavior, since it occurs in the absence of a well-developed spinal cord with the connecting neurones essential for reflex behavior. At birth, however, many reflex patterns are ready to function. These aid in providing for the defense of the neonate as well as for certain biological needs. Concerning birth Carmichael has stated:

Birth makes many changes in the growing organism's patterns of behavior. Direct breathing produces a better oxygen supply for the blood, and the many new stimuli of the external world affect many changes in behavior. But birth does not suddenly alter the basic patterns of the nervous system. The patterns were growing before birth and continue to grow after birth. This growth is largely the result of processes which

[1] Arnold Gesell, *The Child from Five to Ten* (New York: Harper & Brothers, 1946), p. 10.

32

are in the last analysis dependent on heredity and not upon individual experience.[2]

Individual differences at birth. Before reviewing the results of investigations relating to the newborn child, it should be pointed out that individual differences appear at birth. The greatest differences will appear in premature and abnormal cases, although a wide range of abilities will be noted among the normal ten-lunar-month infants. Emphasis should therefore be given to certain general characteristics found among all children, the pattern of growth and development, and individual variations in the rate of growth and development. Variations appear not only in rate of growth but in the life dynamics of infants. Some infants are very active and respond to a much greater variety of stimuli than others. The intensity and duration of the responses will also vary with different infants.

Various studies have been made of the frequency and rhythm of sucking by infants. These studies indicate that bottle-fed babies suck in general more regularly than breast-fed babies. The observations by Michael Balint revealed individual differences among infants of the same age level. Normal infants appear to have a slow sucking rhythm, while the rhythm for those suffering from respiratory and digestive illness is somewhat longer. Slower rhythms, characteristic of the normal babies, are associated with a quicker finish, while higher rhythms are associated with a slower finish. More than one record was available for study from fifty-one infants. Balint concludes from this study: "Each infant seems to possess his individual rhythm (or rhythms) and keeps up its frequency even under widely varying conditions."[3]

Structural basis of infant behavior. Some students of child development have attempted to explain all infant behavior on the basis of learning. In the study by Morgan and Morgan,[4] fifty infants were given paired presentations of a visual stimulus and a puff of air in order to determine the age at which the conditioned wink reaction to the visual stimulus could be established. The results show that the normal infant cannot be conditioned to the visual stimulus before

[2] Leonard Carmichael, Growth of sensory control of behavior before birth, *Psychological Review,* 1947, Vol. 54, p. 322. Reproduced by permission of the journal and of the American Psychological Association.

[3] Michael Balint, Individual differences of behavior in early infancy, and an objective method for recording them: II results and conclusions, *Journal of Genetic Psychology,* 1948, Vol. 73, p. 110.

[4] John J. B. Morgan and Sarah S. Morgan, Infant learning as a developmental index, *Journal of Genetic Psychology,* 1944, Vol. 65, pp. 281-289.

the age of fifty-four days and that the normal child of over sixty-five days can be so conditioned. Wayne Dennis has pointed out that an explanation of behavioral development of the fetus in terms of learning must assume that the fetus is capable of learning long before the seven-month stage is reached, since surveys of the development of the fetus reveal that various forms of behavior appear at different ages. He states:

There is clear evidence of neurogenic movements in the third fetal month. Among the responses observed in this month are the patellar reflex, a slight grasp reflex, the suggested beginning of the sucking reflex, and toe responses similar to the Babinski. In the fourth month these responses become more precise and their areas of stimulation become somewhat more specific. A similar increase in definiteness of pattern occurs during the fifth month.[5]

One should not generalize, however, that all responses appearing at birth are a product of hereditary factors alone. Such responses as moving the limbs, swallowing, sucking, and grasping are elicitable before birth, and the response patterns have perhaps been affected by prenatal stimulating conditions. Any effort, however, to explain these and other response patterns wholly on the basis of learning must presuppose that learning may take place on a subcortical level, since many of these occur in an elementary form during the early fetal months when the cerebrum is absent. Thus, there is a need for re-examining the instinct versus learning theories in infant behavior. Dennis concludes from his analysis of materials bearing on this "that most of the behavior of the infant at birth is unlearned, and that fetal development is almost entirely a matter of maturation." [6]

John Schooland conducted an experiment to determine whether there is any innate basis for differences in cognitive abilities and behavior tendencies in ducks and chicks. He found "that chicks and ducks do give evidence of differentiated behavior tendencies and discriminatory abilities immediately after birth." The implications of this for child training and education are pointed out as follows:

We conclude, finally, that both human and animal behavior represent a developmental organization, in which bodily structure and function, adaptability, predisposition, and perceptual ability are integrally related, and we will do well in our educational practice to recognize that development is a continuing process in which all behavior must be regarded as the integrated expression of innate factors and environmental experience.[7]

Studying the newborn child. The biographical method was used in the early studies of infants. These were usually based on the observations of a single child. The main emphasis in these early studies was to present a description of the sensory and motor equipment of the newborn child. Many of these observations and records were made by parents, which accounts for some of the gross inaccuracies in the interpretations of the observed behavior activities. Studies were later conducted in Germany among infants in the maternity hospitals. These studies were largely concerned with the nature and state of development of the infant's sensory equipment. Wayne Dennis has compiled a bibliography of baby biographies published prior to 1936.[8]

In America certain students of psychology, following methods used in animal psychology, studied the child's equipment at birth. John B. Watson studied the reflex behavior, emotional development, and so-called "instinctive behavior" among infants at the Phipps Clinic of Johns Hopkins University.[9] Sherman and Sherman made use of kimeograph records for studying the leg movements of infants. Some results from this study appear later in this chapter. Two pronounced changes seem to have appeared in the methods of studying infants. In the first place, better controls have been established so that personal bias and associative factors do not influence so much the interpretations of data. Secondly, the observations have been carried on over a longer period of time. This is best illustrated in the studies conducted at Yale University, and may be regarded as the longitudinal approach. In the final analysis, however, it may be pointed out that practically all of the methods of studying children listed in Chapter 1 are applicable to the study of infants. This may be observed from a review of the experimental methods given by Richards and Irwin for studying infants.[10]

---

[7] John B. Schooland, Are there any innate behavior tendencies? *Genetic Psychology Monographs,* 1942, Vol. 25, p. 282.

[8] Wayne Dennis, A bibliography of baby biographies, *Child Development,* 1936, Vol. 7, pp. 71-73.

[9] See John B. Watson, What the nursery has to say about instincts, *Journal of Genetic Psychology,* 1925, Vol. 32, pp. 293-327.

[10] T. W. Richards and O. C. Irwin, Experimental methods used in studies on infant reactions since 1900, *Psychological Bulletin,* 1934, Vol. 31, pp. 23-46. A description of the experimental methods used in studying infant reactions from 1900 to 1934 is presented.

Physical characteristics at birth

General features. The bones of the infant are soft—composed chiefly of cartilage materials. The muscles are poorly developed, being soft and flabby. Those of the arms and hands are better developed than those of the legs. The neck of the infant is very short and the skin covering it seems to be in folds. The head is often covered by a

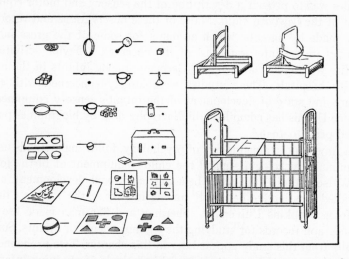

Materials and equipment for the developmental examination of infant behavior.

(Reproduced with permission from A. Gesell and C. S. Amatruda, *Developmental Diagnosis,* New York: P. B. Hoeber, Inc., 1949, p. 496.)

growth of fine-textured hair, and sometimes a soft downy growth of hair is found on the body, particularly the back. During the first few days after birth the infant usually loses weight. This is shown in Table 2, which presents the results from daily weight measurements of four infants during the first ten days after birth.[11] A further observation of the weight of these infants shows that there is a considerable variation in weight at birth. Baldwin's early studies showed that 85 per cent of infants weighed between six and nine pounds and were between seventeen and twenty-two inches tall.[12] More recent studies by Perlstein and Levinson gave an average birthweight of 7.13

[11] Orvin C. Irwin, The amount and nature of activities of newborn infants under constant external stimulating conditions during the first ten days of life, *Genetic Psychology Monographs,* 1930, Vol. 8, pp. 1-92.

[12] Bird T. Baldwin, Physical growth of children from birth to maturity, *University of Iowa Studies in Child Welfare,* 1922, Vol. 1, No. 1.

TABLE 2 The weight of infants in pounds on separate days
(after Irwin)

Age days	Infant No. 1	Infant No. 2	Infant No. 3	Infant No. 4	Average
1	6.80	8.56	6.39	7.63	7.35
2	6.40	7.93	6.03	6.91	6.82
3	6.25	7.72	6.05	6.87	6.72
4	6.34	7.70	6.16	6.91	6.78
5	6.36	7.78	6.19	6.92	6.81
6	6.31	8.01	6.23	6.93	6.87
7	6.27	8.09	6.31	7.00	6.92
8	6.25	8.18	6.52	7.09	7.01
9	6.27	8.25	6.50	7.14	7.04
10	6.29	8.25	6.53	7.13	7.05

pounds.[13] In this study, the average weight of male infants was found to be 0.2 pounds more than that of the female. The undernourishment in Rotterdam, Holland, during the winters of 1944 and 1945 was found to affect adversely the physical development of infants formed during this period. Smith [14] reports that there was a significant decrease in weight and a lesser decrease in length of babies born during this time. An improvement of the maternal diet tended to bring the weight and length of infants to the previous normal levels.

There is no one set of figures for height and weight that must be taken as normal for all babies at the time of birth. Children will vary in weight according to their biological heredity, the diet of the mother, emotional state of the mother during the period of pregnancy, and other factors. It has been suggested that there should be a gain in weight during the early months of from five to six ounces a week. The average weekly gain during the second half-year should be approximately from two and one-half to three ounces per week. The rate of gain after the first two years is considerably less than that during the early years.

Changes in body proportions. The child's head at birth is approximately one-fourth of the length of the entire body. There is a rapid growth of the head during the first two years, so that at two years of age the head girth is about 40 per cent greater than it was at birth.

[13] M. A. Perlstein and A. Levinson, Birth weight: its statistical correlation with various factors, *American Journal of Diseases of Children*, 1937, Vol. 53, p. 1645.
[14] C. A. Smith, Effects of maternal malnutrition upon the newborn infant in Holland (1944-45), *Journal of Pediatrics*, 1947, Vol. 30, pp. 229-243.

The growth of the head circumference from birth to two years is shown in Table 3 from studies conducted by Meredith.[15]

TABLE 3 Composite means of head girth for white infants of both sexes studied during the period 1927-1945 (after Meredith)

Age (months)	Number studied	Mean girth
Birth	2244	34.3
6 mos.	1098	43.0
9 mos.	1098	44.9
12 mos.	1103	46.2
18 mos.	805	47.8
24 mos.	682	48.8

The total height of an adult is about three and one-half times his stature at birth, but his head nearly doubles in length. The changes in relative size of the parts of the body in percentage of the total body volume at different age levels are shown in Table 4.[16] The infant's arms and legs are short and he is characterized by his top-heavy appearance. The head and neck comprise 32 per cent of the total body volume; the arms and legs comprise 8 and 16 per cent, respectively. The spinal column of the newborn infant has only one back curve, but two more curves develop at a later age. The vertebra and shoulder blades are cartilaginous, while the wrist bones are still absent. The changes in the proportions of the body and its parts are produced by: (1) differences in growth intensity for the different

TABLE 4 Changes in relative size of the parts of the body in terms of per cent of the total body volume (after Arey)

Age	Head and Neck	Trunk	Arms	Legs
Second fetal month	43	52	3	2
Sixth fetal month	36	44	7.5	12.5
Birth	32	44	8	16
Two years	22	51	9	18
Six years	15	50	9	26
Maturity	10	52	9	29

[15] Howard V. Meredith, Physical growth from birth to two years: II. Head circumference, *Child Development*, 1946, Vol. 17, pp. 1-61. See also Henry K. Silver and William C. Deaner, Graphs of the head circumference of the normal infant, *Journal of Pediatrics*, 1948, Vol. 33, pp. 167-171.

[16] Leslie B. Arey, *Developmental Anatomy* (Philadelphia: W. B. Saunders Co., 1946), p. 9.

parts of the body; (2) reduction of the early dominance of the anterior and posterior levels; (3) growth gradients; (4) differential functional demands of the various parts of the body; and (5) the effects of adjacent areas of the different parts of the body.

Changes in function at birth. In spite of the amazing growth and development prior to birth, the newborn child is still very immature. Although his respiratory system, digestive system, and circulatory system are evident several months before birth, they are not ready to function effectively until after birth. Birth, then, marks a stage in a change of function for many structures of the body. The sense organs are poorly developed at birth, and gradually come to function in relation to varied stimuli. The activities of the newborn child are largely reflexive in nature. There is evidence that many involuntary movements appear several months before birth; however, birth marks the beginning of a number of new and different forms of involuntary behavior. The birth cry, yawning, and sneezing are among the new forms of behavior that appear soon after birth.

Among the important changes in function at birth are those related to the lungs and heart. The lungs are relatively small prior to birth, but with the onset of respiration they gradually expand and occupy fully the space allocated to them. The pulmonary tissue, which was formerly of a compact nature, now becomes light and spongy. Inflation usually occurs during the three days after birth, and an increased amount of blood is admitted to the lungs. When the lungs become functional, there is an abrupt cessation of placental circulation. This transfer of the seat of oxygenation throws certain fetal passages and vessels into complete disuse, and there is a gradual but continuous obliteration of these anatomical passages. The heart increases in size and the oval window closes gradually in six to eight weeks' time.

Sensory equipment

Most of the activity of the infant during this stage may be accounted for through internal stimulation. The transition from fetal life to infancy involves a stepping up of internal stimuli and introduces many external stimuli not previously experienced. Internal stimulations during the fetal period are usually of fairly long duration. For example, pressure stimulation usually continues for some time. There may be a fairly long duration of the hunger state, during which there is almost incessant activity of the fetus. It has already been suggested that birth opens up new avenues of stimulation and increases the opportunities of the individual to explore and to react to the environmental forces and conditions about him.

Responses to touch and pain. Many investigators have reported "defense movements" in response to pressure stimulation. These range from localized responses to responses involving the entire self. The sense of touch is used by the infant to gain satisfaction by the time he is a month old. The baby's lips appear to be sensitive to touch from a very early stage. This is evidenced by the sucking movements set up in response to a slight touch on the lips. Likewise, the nose, eyes, fingers, and parts of the feet are sensitive to touch.

Sensitiveness to pain does not seem to be marked at birth, but develops gradually, with the head portion of the body leading in this development. This is especially true for skin pains. A number of investigators have found that scratches do not seem to bother the infant. For a given intensity of a given pain stimulus, the number of responses increases with age. Also, for a given age, the number of responses increases with the degree of intensity of the stimulus. The typical reaction to a pain stimulus (needle) applied to the face is a cross-flexion response of the arm—the opposite arm and hand being brought up to the point stimulated.[17]

Visual acuity. Although the infant is usually able to make some movements with his eyes from birth or soon thereafter, the vision of the newborn child is very immature. Chase observed the pupillary reactions and the movements of the eyes of infants in response to differences in brightness.[18] Although the age at which infants are able to sense differences in brightness is not known, the pupillary reflex increases in adequacy with age. For a given age, the adequacy of the reflex is greater in proportion to the intensity of the stimulus. A number of changes in the shape and growth of the eye occur after birth. The cornea and lens become less curved, the axis increases in length, and there is a gradual increase in the rods and cones in the retina. Pupillary action is present but slower than in adults. The earliest evidence observed by Wenger and others of the conditioned eyelid response was on the fifth day after birth, and followed three days of stimulation involving 124 pairs of stimuli.[19] Individual

[17] M. Sherman, I. C. Sherman, and C. D. Flory, Infant behavior, *Comparative Psychological Monographs*, 1936, Vol. 12, pp. 1-107.

[18] W. P. Chase, Color vision in infants, *Journal of Experimental Psychology*, 1937, Vol. 20, pp. 203-222.

[19] M. A. Wenger and others, An investigation of conditioned responses in human infants. Studies in infant behavior III, *University of Iowa Studies in Child Welfare*, 1936, Vol. 12, No. 1.

differences among infants were noted both with respect to the ease of establishing the response and the stability of the response once it is established. He concludes, however, that conditioning of the newborn is both unstable and difficult to secure.

The problem of the nature of color vision in children first aros' in 1877 when Darwin, as a result of observations of his own children concluded that color vision appears rather late in the child's general development. However, there is a lack of exact knowledge of color vision among young infants. The simplest reaction utilized in examining color vision among infants is that normal infants will follow moving objects with their eyes. In order to stimulate the infant to discriminate between colors, two colors must be presented simultaneously. They must be perceptually equal in brightness and intensity. They must be so arranged that one remains still while the other moves. The ability of the infant to discriminate between the two colors will then be determined by whether or not he will watch the moving color.

In the study by Chase, the infant tested was laid on a platform with a screen fifteen inches above him.[20] He was then tested for color vision by the method just described. The criterion for judging whether or not the infant followed the moving stimulus during the experimental period was this: if at any time during this period the subject definitely followed the moving stimulus at the rate at which it was moving, it was counted. The study was made with twenty-four infants, thirteen boys and eleven girls, as subjects. The age range was from fifteen to seventy days. From this experiment Chase concluded that young infants can distinguish between red and yellow-green, red and green, red and blue-green, yellow-green and blue-green, and green and blue-green.

Auditory sensitivity of the infant. The responses of the infant to auditory stimulation are unco-ordinated and diffuse. Thus, it is difficult to secure a reliable evaluation of auditory acuity at this stage. Some investigators believe the infant is deaf at birth, and that hearing ability develops gradually during the first several days of life. The wide differences in auditory acuity found among infants suggest that certain infants are born with some physical condition, such as gelatinous tissue in the middle ear, that contributes to the lack of auditory acuity during the first several days after birth. Irwin has pointed out that differences in the intensity and character

[20] W. P. Chase, Color vision in infants, *Journal of Experimental Psychology,* 1937, Vol. 20, pp. 203-222.

of the stimuli affect these reactions. He states: "The infant can discriminate gross intensities of sound, but its further ability in this direction and its recognition of finer differences of pitch develops late."[21] Studies show that hearing ability increases with the amplifications of the intensity or with an increase in the duration of the stimulus. Dorothy Marquis[22] was able to elicit the sucking reflex in the newborn infant in response to a buzzer by associating the sound of the buzzer with bottle feeding.

These and other investigations along with biographical data indicate that the structures responsible for hearing are not as well developed as those responsible for vision. Evidence shows further that the reaction of infants to sound is sporadic rather than timed and co-ordinated.

Gustatory and olfactory acuity. The results of investigations are not wholly in agreement about the acuity of the infant's sense of taste. Judging from their bodily movements, vocalizations, and sucking reactions to food from the mother or bottle, most infants react with a feeling of satisfaction to the taste of milk. Most infants appear to respond positively to sweet flavors and negatively to sour, bitter, and salt solutions.[23] The neonate displays facial responses indicative of unpleasant effects in response to a quinine solution. The responses of newborn infants to varying degrees of salt solutions were studied by Jensen.[24] Differentials to .900-per-cent salt solution were secured as early as the second day for five of fourteen infants tested. "The discriminatory reactions begin with a slight break in the curve, and increase up to the point where very rigorous avoidance movements are made and the child cries."

Differences of opinion have been expressed by investigators studying the presence of the ability of the neonate to distinguish olfactory stimuli. Stirnimann[25] has demonstrated that differential responses

[21] Orvis C. Irwin, Can infants have IQ's? *Psychological Review,* 1942, Vol. 49, p. 77. Reproduced by permission of the journal and of the American Psychological Association.

[22] Dorothy P. Marquis, Can conditioned reflexes be established in the newborn infant? *Journal of Genetic Psychology,* 1931, Vol. 39, pp. 479-493.

[23] See K. C. Pratt, A. K. Nelson, and K. H. Sun, *The Behavior of the Newborn Infant* (Columbus, Ohio: Ohio State University Press, 1930).

[24] Kai Jensen, Differential reactions to taste and temperature stimuli in newborn infants, *Genetic Psychology Monographs,* 1932, Vol. 12, Nos. 5-6, pp. 361-479.

[25] F. Stirnimann, Les réactions du nouveau-né contre l'enchainement, *Rev. franc. pediat.,* 1937, Vol. 13, pp. 496-502; ————, Le gout et l'odorat du nouveau-né: une contribution a la connaissance des réactions du nouveau-né, *Rev. franc. pediat.,* 1936, Vol. 12, pp. 453-485.

are evoked by various odorous stimuli. The neonate responds to some stimuli by throwing back the head, turning the head, or making facial grimaces indicating a disagreeable odor. These may be thought of as negative ways of responding. The response to other odors are of a positive nature accompanied by a sucking reaction, smiling, and licking the lips. These movements may be observed within the first hour after birth. Wide individual differences in the reactions of infants to olfactory stimuli were noted by Disher.[26] The ninety-one infants observed ranged in age from three hours to ten days and were subjected to violet, asafetida, sassafras, citronella, turpentine, pyridine, and lemon stimuli at three different saturations.

Motor activities

Moving-picture cameras as well as other technical devices have been used to assist investigators in studying the motor activities of infants. At birth, the infant is more than a living creature with bones, flesh, and various types of sensory equipment in a more or less immature stage. The newborn infant is an active creature. In fact, he was an active creature for several months prior to birth. Birth extends the scope of his activities and registers the beginning of vocalization in the birth cry. This is purely reflexive and results from air being drawn over the vocal cords and setting up vibrations in them.

Mass activities of infants. The first activity of infants are largely random and unco-ordinated. Thus, when sensory stimuli are applied to any part of the body, motor activity will occur throughout the entire body, but in a most pronounced form in the part stimulated. Observations of the responses of infants to a pressure stimulus revealed that some make pushing movements with their feet when pressure is applied to the chin.[27] Several subjects were observed to push at the experimenter's hands with their feet. Such foot action may be interpreted as part of the defense pattern of the infant. By means of kymograph records, the number of responses in a unit of time and the intensity or strength of the responses were determined. In relation to arm and leg movement, twenty-two infants made the strongest forward leg movements with the leg opposite that of the

[26] D. R. Disher, An experimental study of the reactions of new-born infants to olfactory stimuli, *Psychological Bulletin,* 1933, Vol. 30, p. 582.

[27] Mandel Sherman and I. C. Sherman, Sensori-motor responses in infants, *Journal of Comparative Psychology,* 1925, Vol. 5, pp. 62-65.

dominant defense hand, while seven of the infants made the strongest forward movements with the same side as the dominant defense hand. Twenty-five infants had both leg and hand dominance. The average number of significant leg movements of the right side was 3.4 for an infant from birth to 99 hours, 7.7 for infants 100 to 199 hours old, and 6.8 for infants 200 hours of age and older.

Using the stabilimeter-polygraph, Irwin measured the amount of motility of seventy-three infants.[28] With the exception of one case, the ages varied from birth to sixteen days. The most active infant was found to be about 290 times more active than the least active. The average number of oscillations per minute during periods when the infants were judged to be asleep and awake are presented in Table 5. It shows that during periods when infants are judged to be asleep, the average motility amounts to 8.7 oscillations per minute; the average number of oscillations per minute during the periods when they are judged to be awake was 51.5. The ratio of activity during waking and sleep periods was therefore about six to one.

TABLE 5   Comparisons of oscillations during waking and sleep periods (after Irwin)

	Infants	o/m	S. D.
Awake	71	51.5	43.3
Asleep	71	8.7	13.4
Difference		42.8	

Evidence has been offered from several studies by Irwin to substantiate the observations that newborn infants are more active just before than after nursing.[29] In one study, the motility of seventy-three infants was measured by means of stabilimeter continuously from 2:30 P.M. until 5:45 P.M. The mean oscillations per minute for each of the thirteen fifteen-minute periods are given in Figure 3. This also shows how motility is distributed between the two consecutive feedings. The distribution between two consecutive feedings represents mean values and does not show individual characteristics. Not all of the infants showed an increase in motility at the end of the experimental period. This is indicated from a comparison

[28] Orvis C. Irwin, The amount of motility of seventy-three newborn infants, *Journal of Comparative Psychology*, 1932, Vol. 14, pp. 415-428.

[29] Orvis C. Irwin, The distribution of the amount of motility in young infants between two nursing periods, *Journal of Comparative Psychology*, 1932, Vol. 14, pp. 429-445.

of the motility of each infant for the first hour with that of the last hour. This comparison reveals that forty-nine of the seventy-three infants show an increment, while twenty-four infants or approximately one-third show a decrement in the amount of motility. However, the average increment of the forty-nine infants showing increased motility is 3.5 times greater than the average decrement made by the twenty-four cases showing decreased motility.

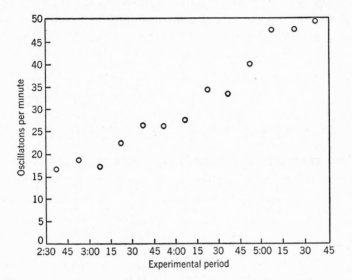

FIG. 3 Average motility of seventy-three infants between two consecutive nursings

(After Irwin)

Specific activities. Specific activities have been conveniently classified into (a) reflexes and (b) general responses. Many studies have been made of the reflexes appearing during the early weeks of life. More recently, a number of investigations have dealt with responses that involve a larger portion of the body than that encompassed in a reflex. These responses may be referred to as adaptive behavior. Much adaptive behavior evolves from these early mass movements. This is quite clear in the observations of the development of locomotion, which is described at a later point in this chapter and in a subsequent chapter. It should not be concluded, however, that the infant progresses from mass to specific movements suddenly or even smoothly. The movements of the hand toward an object are at first of a circuitous nature; later, these movements become more direct, but will often reveal many characteristics of a circuitous approach in the wavering of the arms and hands. Many lateral deviations may be observed before the infant's reaching and grasping evolve into a short and a more direct approach.

As the infant develops, the functions of the arm and hand are reversed. During the early stages, it is the arm that determines the movement of the hand. At this stage, as already suggested, movements are of a mass, diffuse nature. At a later stage, the hand determines the movement of the arm. The child at this stage grasps objects. Specialized functions appear as the thumb and forefinger assume more important places in the child's repertoire of activities.

Stimulation of crying. The stimuli which arouse the crying of infants come from the immediate environment or the physical condition of the baby. Aldrich and others have made continuous observations of over one hundred infants.[30] The causes of crying and the number of crying spells for each cause are presented in Table 6. The

TABLE 6   Number of crying spells for each cause

		CAUSES OF CRYING				
BABIES	DAYS	A *Hunger*	B *Vomiting*	C *Soiled diapers*	D *Wet diapers*	E *Unknown reasons*
50	8	2,760.0	45.0	737.0	1,630.0	3,295.0
50	1	345.0	5.0	92.0	203.8	411.7
1	8	55.2	.9	15.7	32.5	65.9
1	1	6.9	.11	1.9	4.07	8.2

most common cause of crying among these infants resulted from causes unknown to the observers, while hunger ranked second. However, the hunger cries were of longer duration than were those for unknown reasons. Mass activity of the infant's body accompanies crying, especially vigorous crying. No uniform cries for the different situations or conditions were noted among the newborn. The duration and intensity of the cries seemed to depend partly upon the vocal strength of the different infants and upon the nature of the stimuli which aroused them. Gesell and Ilg have suggested that they become more proficient in this ability if they are allowed to exercise it.[31] Furthermore, their proficiency appears to be promoted in the case

[30] C. A. Aldrich, C. Sung, and C. Knop, The crying of newly born babies. II. The individual phase, *Journal of Pediatrics*, 1945, Vol. 27, p. 95.

[31] Arnold Gesell and Frances L. Ilg, *Child Development* (New York: Harper & Brothers, 1949), p. 98.

of the hunger cries if their demands are met promptly and if the needs for food and sucking are insured.

Motor development during infancy. The scope and function of the ontogenetic changes during the first year of life have been summed up by Gesell and Ames as follows:

Head

The head lifts from the floor through an arc of 90° or more.

Arms

The arms, at first sharply flexed, extend forward; later they flex inward under the chest, and come to extension from shoulder to floor at right angles to the trunk which is at first supported on the forearms and in time on the hands.

Legs

The legs extend backward, lift; later they flex forward beside the trunk, and then under the trunk, supporting its weight on the knees. In time the legs like the arms come to right angle extension, supporting the trunk on the feet.

Trunk

The trunk, at first convex, flattens, concaves, then flattens again upon elevation above the ground surface. The trunk is in horizontal or oblique alignment until the assumption of the upright posture.[32]

They point out further that these changes of pattern come about gradually and concurrently. They state: "In deep perspective they may be envisaged as a single flow of postural transformations." And, although twenty-three stages have been characterized and described, these are not accurately separated as discrete stages. They state further: "During the course of a day, an hour, or indeed of a minute, he may display two or three closely related patterns or stages: (*a*) a pattern which he has almost outgrown but reverts to for pragmatic reasons; (*b*) the pattern which is most characteristic of him at his level of maturity; (*c*) the pattern which is so nascent that he uses or manifests it only sketchily and imperfectly."[33]

Ames conducted a study designed to compare the pattern of stair-climbing behavior with the pattern of prone progression.[34] Cinema

[32] Arnold Gesell and Louise B. Ames, The ontogenetic organization of prone behavior in human infancy, *Journal of Genetic Psychology,* 1940, Vol. 56, pp. 247-263.

[33] *Ibid.,* p. 254.

[34] Louise Bates Ames, Some relationships between stair climbing and prone position, *Journal of Genetic Psychology,* 1939, Vol. 54, pp. 313-325.

records of their stair-climbing behavior were taken in the majority of cases at monthly intervals. Records of the prone behavior of each child were compared with the prone behavior seen contemporaneously. Typical patterns of prone behavior and climbing behavior were then compared. A definite pattern in stair-climbing behavior was observed that was almost identical with that observed in the normal creeping stage. The typical stair-climbing pattern consists, as does the creeping pattern, of almost simultaneous forward movement of a contralateral pair of limbs, followed, after a short pause, by a forward movement of the other pair of limbs. The chief difference between the two patterns is that stair climbing often starts with a single foot movement of a pair of limbs. In the typical stair-climbing pattern the infant starts with the placement of the left foot on the first stair. The left hand is then placed on the second stair, and immediately afterward, the right foot on the first stair. There is a short pause at this point, then the right hand moves to the third stair and left foot to the second. After another short pause, the left hand and right foot move up one stair. Temporal analysis of these movements shows that the left hand and right foot move almost simultaneously, as do the right hand and left foot.

The ages at which the different children observed climbed smoothly up a flight of four or more stairs are listed as follows:

One child 48 weeks
One child 52 weeks
Six children 56 weeks
One child 60 weeks
Two children 80 weeks
One child 84 weeks

The mean age for this group for first pattern climbing is sixty-two weeks. In contrast, the mean age for first creeping is forty-four weeks. Thus, on the average, these infants crept about eighteen weeks before they were able to climb a flight of stairs.

The ability of the infant to reach for things develops through several stages. At first, he closes his fingers over any object that touches the palm of his hand. At three or four months of age, if someone offers him a toy, he moves his head, arms, and legs, and if either hand touches the toy, he grasps it. A month or so later, he is able to close in on the toy. Thus, the reaching of the arms for the toy is accompanied by fewer head and leg movements. More specialized movements are now developing out of the earlier mass move-

The Period of Infancy • 49

ments. By the age of nine months, he will probably be able to reach out with both hands, and with one hand leading, grasp the object that he wants. After this stage, there is a continuous development of co-ordination in reaching and grasping, but even at three and four years of age considerable awkardness in reaching for things beyond his arm's length may be observed.

Emotions during infancy

Investigations of the emotions of infants have been limited in number, but quite extensive in scope. Sherman and Sherman conducted some experiments with infants in an effort to determine whether or not the emotional responses of infants could be differentiated.[35] More recently, Gesell and others have attempted to describe the emotional characteristics at different age levels, beginning with infancy. There is evidence based on careful observations that infrahuman animals as well as infants react positively to stimulation that is beneficial, and negatively to stimulation that is harmful. The earliest differentiation of emotional responses would thus be closely identified with positive and negative reactions.

Emotional development during infancy. The development of emotional behavior during the first year of life comprises a number of changes. From birth onward, there is a gradual evolution of the emotions.[36] The earliest emotional reactions are very general in nature, involving the whole body in mass movements. With further development, the responses become better differentiated, muscular co-ordination improves, and more definite reaction patterns appear. Beginning, then, with general bodily excitement, there is an extension and differentiation of the emotions, so that by the end of the first year of life a number of different types of emotional reactions are discernible. Table 7 [37] shows the time of the first appearance of certain forms of behavior during emotional episodes. A study of the responses listed indicates that smiling, laughing, and other emotions present during pleasant states are absent from the list. This should

[35] M. Sherman and I. C. Sherman, The differentiation of emotional responses in infants, *Journal of Comparative Psychology*, 1927, Vol. 7, pp. 265-284.

[36] This is in harmony with the findings from Sherman and Sherman, who state: "When an infant below four or five days of age is dropped one or two feet it frequently shows no perceptible response." See M. Sherman and I. C. Sherman, *The Process of Human Behavior* (New York: W. W. Norton and Co., 1929), p. 71.

[37] E. W. Blatz and D. A. Millichamp, The development of emotion in the infant, *University of Toronto Studies: Child Development Series*, 1935, No. 4.

not be interpreted to mean that these are lacking at these age levels, but rather that they were not sufficiently intense to come to the attention to the observer. A number of factors may be given to account for their absence during experimental observations. The study by Washburn [38] furnishes evidence that smiling and laughing appear during infancy, so that by the end of the first year of life a number of different stimuli may provoke smiling and laughing.

TABLE 7 Different ages of appearance of different forms of behavior during emotional episodes (after Blatz and Millichamp)

1-4 Months	4-8 Months	8-12 Months	12-16 Months	16-20 Months	20-24 Months
Crying	Refusing and resisting	Stiffening	Running away	Hiding face	Slumping
Screaming		Throwing self back		Crying and saying "No"	Crying and asking
Restless	Holding out arms				
Struggling		Clinging			
Starting					
	Throwing	Crying and attempting			
	Crying and calling				

Startle movements. The startle pattern is typified by muscular flexion. There is a flexion of the arms at the elbow and of the fingers, the head moves forward, and the shoulders are raised. In the study by Bridges,[39] it was observed that on the presentation of certain strong stimuli the infants became agitated, their arm and hand muscles tensed, their breathing quickened, and their legs made jerky movements. The stimuli producing such an excitement were: bright sun directly in the infant's eyes, picking up and putting down the child on the bed, holding the child's arms tight by the sides, and rapping the baby's knuckles. A loud sound startled only four of ten one-and two-month-old babies. Those responding showed a mild general excitement of the nature just described. Children three or four months of age gave more of a jump and moved definitely in the direction of the sound.

Clarke studied the bodily reactions of fourteen infants to an

[38] *Op. cit.*
[39] K. M. B. Bridges, Emotional development in early infancy, *Child Development,* 1932, Vol. 3, pp. 324-340.

auditory startle stimulus.[40] A sudden intense auditory stimulus was produced by dropping a two-pound iron weight from a height of three feet on a hardwood surface. Infants were photographed and these photographs were analyzed and studied carefully by several persons working independently. The children were photographed within fourteen hours after birth and subsequently at one, four, eight, twelve, sixteen, and twenty weeks of age. Some results obtained may be listed as follows:

1. A bodily reaction was elicited from all fourteen infants.

2. There was an observable change in the general pattern of response with change in age level.

3. Responses most characteristic of the early weeks (reached a maximum of intensity at eight weeks) were the Moro reflexes (startle reflexes).

4. The relative intensity of the responses varied from individual to individual, and within each individual on different occasions.

5. The study showed a gradual breakdown of certain elements in the Moro reflex pattern first elicited.

Smiling of infants. In the study by Ruth Washburn, fifteen infants were used as subjects—nine girls and six boys.[41] No attempt was made to observe the infants before they were eight weeks of age, and no further observations were made after they were listed as one year old. Results from controlled observations were studied and analyzed. Although exact groupings could not be made, most of the fifteen infants could be placed in one of three classifications. The first of these groups consisted of subjects in whom two forms of expressive behavior (smiling and laughing, soberness or crying) were studied and analyzed. This group, referred to as *ambi-expressive,* was further divided into the *parvi-expressive* and the *multi-expressive.* The expressive behavior of the latter group was more exaggerated and occurred more frequently than that of the former group. A second group, called *risor-expressive,* was characteristically laughing and smiling individuals. The third group, called a *depressive-expressive* group, was characteristically crying or sober individuals. Seven of the infants were classified as ambi-expressive, five were classified as risor-expressive, and three were classified as depressive-expressive.

[40] Frances M. Clarke, A developmental study of the bodily reactions of infants to an auditory startle stimulus, *Pedagogical Seminary and Journal of Genetic Psychology,* 1939, Vol. 55, pp. 415-427.

[41] Ruth Wendell Washburn, A study of the smiling and laughing of infants in the first year of life, *Genetic Psychology Monographs,* 1929, Vol. 6, pp. 397-537.

The following summary describes the differentiating behavior in smiling which was most typical of the twelve-week and twenty-week age levels. Behavior common to all age levels is not described here.

Twelve weeks

Twitching of lips and other facial muscles preceding smiling.
Round open mouth.
Protrusion of chin (incidence and degree increasing up to 40 weeks).
Vocalizations monosyllabic—*ah* (decreasing up to 40 weeks).

Hands are moved up and down over center of body and come to rest in the mouth regions
Knees are drawn up toward the abdomen, with rolling of body.

These forms of activity are not confined to smiling, though typically present in the last stage of the smile.

Mobilized attention with reduction of bodily activity precedes smiling (decreasing up to 44 weeks).

Twenty weeks

Upward retraction of the corners of the mouth were frequent.
Crescent-shaped mouth first seen.
Shortened nose, wrinkled on bridge of nose first observed.
"Peach-stone" chin appears.
Disyllabic as well as monosyllabic vocalizations—"ha," "ah-gh," "ah-goo," "gargling," "squeals."
"Waving" of arms and successive kicking of legs, especially in the last stage of the smile.
Leaning toward source of stimulation begins (depending upon degree of development of eye-hand coordinations).[42]

Crying behavior. Crying as a type of motor response was discussed earlier in this chapter. It was pointed out that the crying of the infant was a response to some immediate condition or stimulation. However, crying during infancy is quite irregular. The two-month-old baby cries less than the one-month-old; but slightly discomforting stimuli appear to cause distress more frequently among these older infants. The three-month-old baby will cry and show other symptoms of distress when placed in an awkward or unusual position in his bed. The crying of the four- and five-month-old baby is extended to include a response to strange places and people. The five- or six-month-old baby will cry in connection with thwarting condi-

---

[42] *Ibid.*, p. 527.

tions. If an object that he has been playing with is taken from him, he may respond with crying. Thus, the extension of the response of crying is part of the child's total development. As his mental and physical horizon is extended, his emotional reactions come to include more conditions and situations.

Motor behavior which usually characterizes crying in the human infant involves body postures as well as traditional facial expressions earlier described by Darwin. Louise Ames [43] has pointed out from her studies that crying is especially characterized by increased leg movements. There is a marked flexor condition which may have a protective significance. The five forms of behavior that were found most commonly to accompany crying are presented in Table 8.

TABLE 8 Forms of motor responses accompanying crying (after Ames)

Crying behavior patterns	Number of times observed in crying	non-crying
1. More active than in non-crying	42	0
2. Legs more active than arms	33	2
3. Legs more unilateral than bilateral	41	6
4. Legs more flexed than extended	37	7
5. Foot to knee	15	6

Personal-social development. Gesell has pointed out that "The developmental progress of infant behavior can be envisaged as a series of advancing levels of maturity." Attention and fixation are indefinite at the age of four weeks. Although the infant responds to tactual stimulation from the beginning of his neonate state, he shows little regard for objects about him during the first week or ten days. There is much arm and leg movement during this time, but these movements are random and diffuse in nature. The development of personal-social behavior during infancy has been studied by Gesell and others.[44] Some observations of the personal behavior of infants are presented in Table 9. The materials presented show that personal behavior develops rapidly after the infant is eight weeks old. Prior to this time, his movements are not sufficiently co-ordinated for him to bring his hands together and to begin fingering.

At six weeks of age, infants begin to show facial brightening in response to a person's face, and to respond by smiling. Along with

[43] Louise Bates Ames, Motor correlates of infant crying, *Journal of Genetic Psychology*, 1941, Vol. 59, pp. 239-247.

[44] Arnold Gesell and Helen Thompson, *The Psychology of Early Growth* (New York: The Macmillan Company, 1938), p. 140.

this, they utter such syllables as *ah* and *uh*. Spitz found that children less than twenty days old do not respond to the smiling stimulation. She attributed this to the diffuse, unco-ordinated character of the infant's reactions, the inadequacy of their perceptions, and the lack of ability to focus the attention upon an object.[45]

TABLE 9   The development of personal behavior during infancy (after Gesell and Thompson)

Behavior Items	Age in weeks				
	4	6	8	12	16
Regards hand	0	3	15	73	80
Brings hands together	0	0	7	42	72
Hands active in mutual fingering	0	0	4	23	52
Pulls at dress	8	7	22	73	64
Pulls dress over face	4	0	4	31	52
Kicks off blankets	35	59	85	—	—
Kicks in bath	4	24	45	69	80
Likes sitting	0	0	3	50	57
Sits propped with pillows	0	0	4	42	63
Rests supine	0	0	3	15	36
Anticipates feeling on sight of food	0	0	7	42	68

At five months of age a baby vocalizes his delight in the form of such sounds as "uh—uh—ung." He also reveals his delight by laughing aloud, waving, or wriggling about. At eight months of age the child appears to take delight in self-initiated activities. At this time his behavior often shows much more purpose than earlier.

The infant's daily routine

It has already been suggested that certain reactions are present in the activities of the infant from birth. Some of these behavior patterns appear in a rather complete form. Some of the deep-seated reflexes that are elicited by external stimulation appear at birth. Likewise, many visceral responses, depending upon stimulation from within, appear at birth or soon thereafter. Many studies have been concerned with the development of behavior during the prenatal and neonatal period.[46] These studies have furnished valuable informa-

[45] Rena A. Spitz and K. M. Wolf, The smiling response: A contribution to the ontogenesis of social relations, *Genetic Psychology Monographs*, 1946, Vol. 24, pp. 27-125.

[46] For a survey of the literature on prenatal and postnatal activity from 1920 to 1934, see Evelyn Dewey, *Behavior Developments in Infants* (New York: Columbia University Press, 1935).

tion about the life activities of infants. The more recent studies by Gesell and others at Yale University have been invaluable in verifying the results of earlier studies and in some cases modifying some of the conclusions drawn from these earlier studies.

Sleeping schedule. All studies of infants agree that sleep plays an important role in their lives. The amount of sleep required and some of the characteristic postures found in the sleep life of infants change, but sleep during later childhood is similar in nature to that found during the early days after birth. According to the observations of Bryan, infants remain awake during the first several hours following birth.[47] The studies of Bühler reveal, however, that over twenty-one hours of the infant's day is spent in sleep or near-sleep.[48] The duration of the waking and sleeping states within a twenty-four-hour period is shown in Table 10. By the end of the first year the amount

TABLE 10 The duration of waking and sleeping states within 24 hours in per cent (after Bühler)

	Age in months				
	0-0	1-3	4-6	7-9	10-12
Sleep in per cent	80	60	55	53	49
State of waking in per cent	20	40	45	47	51
Total	100	100	100	100	100

of time spent in sleep and in waking is almost the same. Bühler also found that the length of the sleeping period of the infant was short and that these periods increased in length with age. One of the most complete studies of the spontaneous activities of infants is the one reported by Pratt, Nelson, and Sun, in which twenty-five infants were studied during the first seventeen days after their birth.[49] By means of a stabilimeter, movements were recorded in millimeters and seconds on a polygraph. They noted that sleeping infants were moving 21 per cent of the time, and those who were awake moved 42 per cent of the time. There was a decrease in the movement of the infants when they were dry.

The sleeping position of the infant has been given some attention. Kelting noted that bodily movements were of frequent occurrence.[50]

[47] E. S. Bryan, Variations in the responses of infants during the first ten days of post-natal life, *Child Development*, 1930, Vol. 1, pp. 56-77.

[48] Charlotte Bühler, *The First Year of Life* (New York: John Day Co., 1930), p. 130.

[49] *Op. cit.*

[50] L. S. Kelting, An investigation of the feeding, sleeping, crying, and social behavior of infants, *Journal of Experimental Education*, 1934, Vol. 3, pp. 97-106.

The head of the baby is usually turned to one side, the legs somewhat extended, the arms up, and the fingers usually extended. Changes in bodily posture were quite frequent.

Eating behavior. There is considerable evidence that the activity of infants is greater just prior to the eating period. Studies conducted by Pratt, Nelson, and Sun at Ohio State University, using a stabilimeter in an experimental cabinet, showed that babies taken shortly before their next feeding tend to be restless and fussy.[51] Chaney and McGraw found that all except one of one hundred neonates sucked when a nipple was placed in the mouth.[52] Of twenty-five infants less than one-half hour old, four made definite sucking movements, eight bit down on the examiner's finger, eleven gave no response, and the other two were not tested. Some observers have suggested that since sucking appears so early in the infant's life it is the one positive reflex act which appears from the beginning of postnatal life.

Charlotte Bühler observed the behavior of infants while they were taking nourishment.[53] The newborn child is so absorbed in taking nourishment that he gives no attention to things about him. Smacking of his tongue and sounds of joy usually accompany the taking of food. At the age of two months he holds his eyes open longer during the feeding period. At five months of age he observes those about him, shows unrest at the sight of his bottle, and clutches his bottle with both hands. These different ways of behaving are shown in Table 11. When the baby is satisfied, he stretches his body and turns the head aside. This may be observed by the end of the first month or by the second month. His satisfaction is further shown by his quiet, restful nature in contrast to the unrest displayed by the hungry child.

Davis and others have studied the effects of three types of feeding on sixty newborn infants.[54] These infants were divided into three groups of twenty each, based on types of feeding—breast feeding, bottle feeding, and cup feeding. The results of this study showed no significant difference in bodily activities. The breast-fed group yielded a significantly higher number of noneager feedings during the first

[51] K. C. Pratt, A. K. Nelson, and K. H. Sun, The behavior of the newborn infant, Ohio State University Studies, *Contribution to Psychology*, No. 10, 1930.

[52] L. B. Chaney and M. B. McGraw, Reflexes and other motor activities in newborn infants: a report of 125 cases as a preliminary study of infant behavior, *Bulletin of the Neurological Institute, New York*, 1932, Vol. 2, pp. 1-56.

[53] Charlotte Bühler, *op. cit.*, pp. 107-109.

[54] H. V. Davis, R. R. Sears, H. C. Miller, and A. J. Brodbeck, Effects of cup, bottle and breast feeding on oral activities of newborn infants, *Pediatrics*, 1948, Vol. 2, pp. 549-558.

TABLE II   Ways of behaving in taking nourishment (after Bühler)

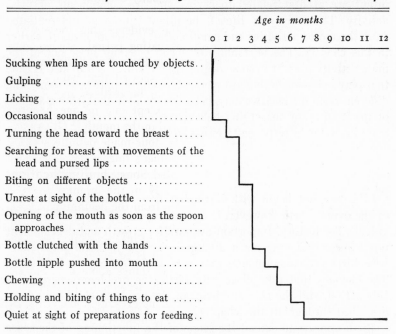

Age in months

	0	1	2	3	4	5	6	7	8	9	10	11	12
Sucking when lips are touched by objects..													
Gulping													
Licking													
Occasional sounds													
Turning the head toward the breast													
Searching for breast with movements of the head and pursed lips													
Biting on different objects													
Unrest at sight of the bottle													
Opening of the mouth as soon as the spoon approaches													
Bottle clutched with the hands													
Bottle nipple pushed into mouth													
Chewing													
Holding and biting of things to eat													
Quiet at sight of preparations for feeding..													

three days, and a slightly but insignificantly higher amount of crying and general bodily activity. The cup-fed group showed less sign of frustration or unsatisfied oral drive than did the breast-fed group. There is no evidence from this study that a long period of mothering evidenced by breast feeding is essential for healthy emotional development during infancy. This, of course, does not refute the infant's need for affection and security, which are given special consideration in Chapters 14 and 16.

Play behavior. According to Irwin, the activities of infants fall into two descriptive categories: specific movements and mass acivity. Rolling the head, flexion of the knees, and the like are examples of specific activities; the squirming of the body, rolling and the like tend to involve more than a single segment of the body and are termed mass activities.[55] As soon as the eating habits of the infant are well established, there is an increase in the movements of the infant. This usually takes a day or more, and during the first several days the

[55] Orvis C. Irwin, The activities of newborn infants, in *Child Behavior and Development* (Barker, Kounin, and Wright, eds.) (New York: McGraw-Hill Book Co., 1943), Chap. III.

activity level of the infant is relatively low. The vocal sounds of the infant are at first related to crying and are components of mass activity. The early play life of the infant cannot be differentiated from the motor activities and emotional responses referred to earlier in this chapter. The beginnings of social behavior arise out of the mass activity present to some degree from birth. It is also at this time that play behavior in its most elementary form appears as something different from the positive mass behavior found in the sucking actions of the infants, or the crying behavior which is a negative form of mass behavior in response to either external or internal stimulation.

Summary and implications

Life does not begin with birth, but dates from the fertilization of the ovum. Birth, however, is a most important epoch in the individual's life history. Important avenues for growth and development now appear that were not available during the prenatal state. Likewise, birth presents problems that were absent during the fetal state. The changes that take place with birth, the problems emerging at this period, and the characteristics of the newborn child have been described throughout this chapter.

Birth appears to extend the scope of the functioning of the sense organs. There is considerable evidence for the conclusion that certain types of stimuli affect the child before birth. Also, it is well known that the fetal child makes many adjustive responses. With birth, however, the range of stimuli affecting him is enlarged, and the scope of his movements is increased. There are behavior patterns that appear during the fetal period and others that appear at birth that seem to be the product of heredity and maturation. But it should be emphasized in the case of infant behavior as well as the behavior of the preschool and school child that heredity and environment are ever operating together in the development of different forms of behavior.

The growth of the infant is from the head downward and from the axis outward. At three months of age the baby is able to balance his head and may enjoy the rattle; at four months of age vocalizations of different sounds are becoming better established. The infant thus seems to grow in accordance with a pattern indicating an orderly sequence of development, although environment stimulation is essential for his growth and development. During the fifth month the infant usually learns to roll from his back to his stomach in a fairly successful manner. Some infants are able to sit up for a short time at this age. There is a discernible development of his sense of taste and smell. Evidence will be presented in a later chapter indicating that the child's taste should be given some consideration in connection with his dietary needs. During infancy there is a great need for a balanced diet, sufficient rest and recreation, and emotional care from the parents. These problems are far-reaching in their significance and will be given special consideration in subsequent chapters.

Those who would understand the infant must recognize his dynamic nature as well as his physical characteristics. Emotional changes occur during the first year of life which are important in relation to the personal-social development at this stage. These changes, like those involved in motor activities, are at first diffuse and undifferentiated. Through maturation and further activity they develop, and differentiation of emotions is manifested during the first year of life. This development is part of the development of the child as a whole and should not be regarded as a form of development unrelated to language growth, motor development, and the physical growth of the infant as a dynamic unified organism.

Questions and Exercises

1. What are the advantages of the long period of infancy found in the human species? What does this indicate relative to the presence of many ready-made ways of behaving at birth or soon thereafter?
2. What is meant by development from gross, undifferentiated behavior to specialized types of responses? Give examples to illustrate the nature of such a development in the case of the infant.
3. Describe the physical characteristics at birth. What are some of the most pronounced changes that take place during the first year after birth?
4. What are the outstanding changes in function at birth?
5. Describe the sensory ability of the child during the early weeks after birth.
6. How have the motor activities of infants been studied? How is the motility of the infant related to the period of nursing?
7. What do the studies reveal concerning the differentiation of emotional responses during infancy? What is the nature of the startle pattern? How is this related to the emotions?
8. What are the major causes of crying during infancy? To what extent is crying related to the expression of the emotions?

9. What is meant by personal-social behavior? What do studies indicate with regard to the development of personal-social behavior during the first year?

Selected Readings

Antonov, A. N. Physiology and pathology of the newborn. Bibliography of material for the period 1930-1940, *Monographs of the Society for Research in Child Development*, 1945, Vol. 10, No. 2.

Bakwin, Ruth M., and Bakwin, Harry. *Psychological Care During Infancy and Childhood*. New York: Appleton-Century-Crofts, 1942.

Bühler, Charlotte. An observational study of the first year, *Readings in Child Psychology* (Wayne Dennis, ed.). New York: Prentice-Hall, 1951. Pp. 73-84.

Carmichael, Leonard (ed.). *Manual of Child Psychology*. New York: John Wiley and Sons, 1945. Chap. II.

Cruze, Wendell, W. *General Psychology for College Students*. New York: Prentice-Hall, 1951. Chap. XI.

Dennis, Wayne. A description and classification of the responses of the newborn infant, *Psychological Bulletin*, 1934, Vol. 31, pp. 5-22.

Dewey, E. *Behavior Development of Infants*. New York: Columbia University Press, 1935.

Gesell, A., Thompson, H., and Amatruda, C. *Infant Behavior: Its Genesis and Growth*. New York: McGraw-Hill Book Co., 1934.

Gesell, Arnold. *Studies in Child Development*. New York: Harper & Brothers, 1948. Chaps. VI-X.

Goodenough, Florence L. *Developmental Psychology*. Rev. ed.; New York: Appleton-Century-Crofts, 1945. Chap. IV.

Munn, Norman L. *Psychology*. Boston: Houghton Mifflin Company, 1946. Chap. IV.

Nagge, Joseph W. *Psychology of the Child*. New York: The Ronald Press Co., 1942. Chap. II.

Pratt, K. C. The organization of behavior in the newborn infant, *Psychological Review*, 1937, Vol. 44, pp. 470-490.

Rand, Winifred, Sweeney, M. E., and Vincent, E. L. *Growth and Development of the Young Child*. 4th ed.; Philadelphia: W. B. Saunders Co., 1946. Chap. I.

Teagarden, Florence L. *Child Psychology for Professional Workers*. Rev. ed.; New York: Prentice-Hall, 1946. Chap. III.

Thorpe, Louis P. *Child Psychology and Development*. New York: The Ronald Press Co., 1946. Chap. IV.

4

Some Fundamental Principles
of Growth

Introduction

Need for understanding principles of growth. Anyone concerned
with the guidance and direction of children should have a clear
understanding of their growth and development. The parent who
recognizes that growth follows an orderly sequence will not attempt
to force the child in his motor, mental, and emotional development.
The teacher who recognizes individual differences in the rate of
growth among children will not be content with uniform assignments
and procedures for all the children of her grade. Willard Olson has
pointed out that children who differ in growth will also differ in the
experiences which they seek, and thus differ in the direction of their
achievement.[1]

It is the purpose of this chapter to give the student a better understanding of the principles of development. Some of the special problems which will be discussed are:

The importance of maturation in the child's development.

The relationships between maturation and training.

Specific growth principles which should operate as a guide for those
concerned with child growth and development.

The influence of various factors (heredity, glands, culture, nutrition, and psychological) upon child growth.

The implications of these principles to child guidance.

The nature of growth curves. The growth of the organism has been
described as a complex process, although it appears to follow a regu-

---

[1] Willard C. Olson, Experiences for growing, *Journal of the National Education
Association,* October, 1947, p. 503.

lar pattern. Individual growth curves have been plotted for various aspects of growth. These have brought valuable information about the nature of the child's growth. The growth curve that has the greatest usefulness is that which records the amount of growth in a unit of time under fairly constant conditions. Other growth curves would be obtained from data in which growth has been accentuated or retarded at some particular stage by such factors as nutrition, disease, injury, or some other special stimulation or deprivation. The growth of plants and animals as well as the growth of the individual physically, mentally, emotionally, or otherwise will follow this general pattern. This pattern is, therefore, similar for the child's growth in dentition and his growth in computational ability. An examination of this pattern of growth as presented by Courtis will clarify further the nature of growth under constant conditions.

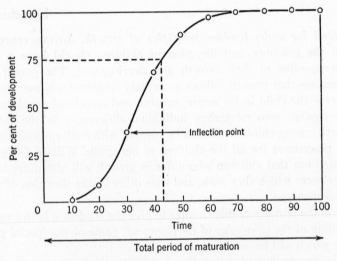

FIG. 4 **The universal growth curve**
(After Courtis)

The universal growth curve is presented in Figure 4. The vertical scale at the left represents the progress of maturation expressed in terms of percentage of development and extends to 100-per-cent maturity. The scale at the bottom represents the time period of maturation. The dotted lines extended in a perpendicular manner from the development and time columns will show the percentage of complete development at a particular phase of the total time required to reach maturity.

Maturation

Studies of the development of the newborn infant, discussed in Chapter 3, showed that the resemblances in the behavioral patterns were astonishingly numerous. The word *learning* has often been used in contrast to *maturation*. In an effort to differentiate the meaning of these terms, Carmichael has described learning as "the development of responses which can be demonstrated to be changed because of certain antecedent stimulus-released processes. In the growth or maturation of behavior on the other hand, the modification of the organism is a function of intrinsic or endogenous processes which, though not occurring in independence of external circumstances, are less directly related to specific antecedent external changes." [2]

Maturation and acculturation. It is generally stated that the individual comes into his biological inheritance through maturation, while he comes into his social inheritance through acculturation. Systematic studies of child development reveal, however, that there is a constant interaction of environmental and hereditary factors from the beginning of life, with the fertilization of the egg cell. Concerning the relation of learning and maturation, as early as 1936 Carmiachael wrote: "Therefore, in spite of the fact that the words 'maturation' and 'learning' can be given a valid meaning, physiologically the two processes do not seem to be wholly separable." [3] Studies in genetic psychology and cultural anthropology have provided much information about child development. When the results from these approaches are brought together in the study of child growth and development, a clearer insight is gained. Gesell has described the relationship as follows: "Growth is a unifying concept which resolves the dualism of heredity and environment. Environmental factors support, inflect, and modify, but they do not generate the progressions of development. Growth is an impulsion and as a cycle of morphogenetic events is uniquely a character of the living organism." [4]

The effects of culture are also reflected in the toilet training of children. Because of our cultural attitudes toward cleanliness, many

[2] Leonard Carmichael, A re-evaluation of the concepts of maturation and learning as applied to the early development of behavior, *Psychological Review,* 1936, Vol. 43, p. 465. Reproduced by permission of the Journal and of the American Psychological Association.

[3] *Ibid.,* p. 466.

[4] Reprinted by permission from *Manual of Child Psychology,* L. Carmichael, ed. (New York: John Wiley and Sons, 1946), p. 316.

parents insist upon toilet training at a very early stage, thus provoking a struggle that could largely be avoided if maturation were given more careful consideration. The effects of too early and too much insistence on the part of the mother in her efforts to train the child in regularly organized toilet habits may result in long-lasting emotional conflicts between the mother and child. At one time, the attitude of pediatricians and others followed the mechanistic approach, referred to in Chapter 1, to child feeding and toilet training. Many conscientious parents thus developed frustrations and conflicts in their children, and extreme anxieties in their own daily activities. Maurice Kaplan points out that "At present, the pediatrician is more inclined to take a tolerant view regarding toilet training, to consider individual differences in the rate of maturation and to suggest to the parents that they themselves observe and judge the child's readiness for training." [5]

Effects of restricted practice during infancy. Early experiments conducted with the pecking activities of chicks supplemented by later work of Cruze [6] have demonstrated conclusively that maturation is important in development. The appearance of unlearned behavior depends upon structural organization and development, achieved as a result of inner growth or maturation. Further data on maturation is offered in the work of Carmichael.[7] In his experiment, frog and salamander eggs were kept in his laboratory until the head and tail buds appeared. At this time, one group was placed in a dish of plain water and the other group was placed in a weak solution of chlorotone. This drug, while it does not interfere with growth, produces complete immobilization. Practice for this group was made impossible. These tadpoles remained in this solution until those in the plain water were swimming in a normal manner. After this time, the drug was washed from the anesthetized tadpoles and they were placed in plain water. The first movements then appeared within from six to twenty minutes, and within half an hour both the frog and salamander tadpoles were swimming so well that they could not be distinguished from those that had been swimming normally in plain water for five days.

[5] Maurice Kaplan, An approach to psychiatric problems in childhood, *American Journal of Diseases of Children,* 1950, Vol. 79, p. 800.

[6] For a review of the previous studies as well as a careful presentation of techniques and findings from his own study, see W. W. Cruze, Maturation and learning in chicks, *Journal of Comparative Psychology,* 1935, Vol. 19, pp. 371-409.

[7] L. Carmichael, The development of behavior in vertebrates experimentally removed from the influence of external stimulation, *Psychological Review,* 1926, Vol. 33, pp. 51-56.

An approximation to an experiment using the isolation and restriction of activity procedures with human infants is found in the work by Wayne Dennis.[8] Fraternal twins were subjected to conditions involving restricted practice and minimum social stimulation. These twins were secured for observation and study when they were thirty-six days old, and were confined to a nursery located in a second-floor room, where only the sky and the tree tops were visible. No pictures or decorations of any sort adorned the room and the door remained closed except when the experimenters entered the room to care for or observe them. However, sunlight, fresh air, and a balanced diet were provided and contributed to the health of the children. The behavior of the experimenters and visitors toward the children was indifferent at all times. Punishment and reward were avoided, while a feeding routine was maintained in a general but not extremely rigid way. Special caution was used in many ways to restrict practice and social stimulation.

A very complete record of observations was kept, with observations made approximately at each hour during the nonsleeping period. These records consisted of (a) spontaneous activities of the twins, and (b) their reactions to test situations. Many test situations were employed in securing developmental data. The order of appearance of the spontaneous responses was quite similar for the two subjects. During the early months, the subjects almost invariably developed the same responses, while in the later months each subject developed many behavior patterns that were not present in the other. On the basis of the data from these subjects combined with results obtained from other studies, Dennis has presented two general conclusions:

1. The first of these is that practically all of the common responses of the first years of life may be developed autogenously. That is, infants will develop these responses without encouragement or instruction, without reward or example. It follows that prior to the second year of life sociogenous responses, those which are learned through the intercession of other persons, are few and are relatively unimportant. If the well-being of the infant is assured, his behavioral development will take its normal course.

2. The second conclusion is that in the development of the autogenous responses of the first year learning plays an important part. The dichotomy of learned and unlearned responses is difficult to employ,

[8] Wayne Dennis, Infant development under conditions of restricted practice and of minimum social stimulation, *Genetic Psychology Monographs,* 1941, Vol. 23, pp. 143-189.

but if we are to apply these concepts the evidence indicates that there is little reason to believe the infant responses are made up exclusively of unlearned elements except in the case of very few reactions. However, responses which involve learning may at the same time involve instinctive contributions. As a corollary of this conclusion, it would follow that while maturation is a major factor in infant development its importance lies chiefly in making learning possible. Maturation in and of itself seldom produces new developmental items, but maturation of structures when accompanied by self-directed activity leads to new infant responses.[9]

Effects of delay on growth. Gesell and Thompson used the co-twin control method in studying the influence of practice and exercise on the appearance of stair-climbing and tower-building reactions. The results of their studies led to the general conclusion that the time of appearance of these abilities "is fundamentally determined by the ripeness of the neural structure." [10] Influenced by these studies and the likely inference that motor development was not perceptibly influenced by practice, and recognizing that practice does affect the performance of older children and adults, Myrtle McGraw conducted a study to determine the effects of practice on motor development at different age levels.[11] The subjects of her study were Johnny and Jimmy, referred to in Chapter 1. From the age of twenty-one days until he was twenty-two months old, Johnny was given the opportunity to practice certain motor activities which he was somewhat capable of learning, while Jimmy was denied this opportunity. His activities were restricted to remaining in a crib during the time of the experiment. The behavior development of these subjects was then compared from time to time, and was further compared to that of a group of sixty-eight children in whom these activities were being observed.

The activities studied were grouped into categories for special study and analysis: (1) those showing considerable susceptibility to practice, and (2) those showing very little or no susceptibility to practice. A study of these indicated that those showing the greatest fixity (less subject to the effects of practice) are controlled at the infracortical level and are considered phylogenetic activities—ac-

[9] *Ibid.*, p. 187.

[10] A. Gesell and H. Thompson, Learning and growth in identical infant twins: an experimental study in the method of co-twin control, *Genetic Psychology Monographs,* 1929, Vol. 6, pp. 1-124.

[11] Myrtle B. McGraw, *Johnny and Jimmy* (New York: Appleton-Century-Crofts, 1935).

tivities that every individual must acquire in order to function biologically as a normal human being, but activities not confined to
civilized man. Those activities showing the greatest effect from practice are controlled by higher structural connections of the nervous
system and are considered ontogentic in origin—activities that a
child may or may not acquire, depending upon conditions and circumstances related to his living conditions.

The results of the study by McGraw indicate that in the learning
of certain types of behavior, such as skating, bicycling, counting, etc.,
special training and practice would be influential. However, these
should be in harmony with the child's maturation and general state
of readiness. There is a certain time range within which a child may
be able to overcome any ill effects of delay; but if this is prolonged
the child's development will probably be adversely affected. One
activity tends to prepare for the next. A child who has not learned
to skip rope may be denied the opportunity to play with the group
that has developed skill in rope skipping. A boy who has not learned
to play baseball during the early teen years will not be chosen by
the captain of a team at some later stage in his development. Likewise, the social skills of teen-agers depend in part upon skills already
acquired. The child who lacks these skills will feel embarrassed and
will thus fail to enter wholeheartedly into the social activities. Thus,
we conclude that long delays in the development of certain important skills may seriously affect a child's later development and
adjustments.

Principles of growth

The longitudinal studies of growth that have been carried on during the past several decades have furnished a great deal of information about the nature of growth. The genetic studies of child
development have provided additional information about the general
principles of development during the early years of life. These studies,
supplemented by materials from related fields, form the basis for
the principles of growth presented here.

Growth is a continuous process. The fact that the various stages
of life are often divided into different periods, largely for the sake
of convenience in studying the stages of development, has led many
people to look upon growth as periodic or saltatorial rather than
continuous in nature.

What occurs at one stage of growth carries over and influences the subsequent growth stages. This process takes place at a slow regular pace, rather than by leaps and bounds. In man, as in infrahuman forms of life, it can be stated as a general principle that each stage in the development of the individual is an outgrowth of an earlier stage, not a mere addition to it. This is illustrated in the development of the teeth. The baby's teeth begin to develop before birth and will be affected by the diet of the mother during this period; however, they are not actually cut until about five months after birth.

The rate of growth is marked by fluctuations. Although growth is continuous, it is not even in tempo. For example, a child may speak three to five words at twelve months of age, but in the next three or four months acquire no additional words, since he is busy with the development of co-ordinations involved in locomotion. Furthermore, it has constantly been observed that muscular co-ordination does not keep pace with the accelerated growth in height during the early stages of adolescence. Individual curves of development in height, weight, strength, and motor co-ordination will show plainly that the rate of growth is marked by fluctuations. This will be discussed more fully in a later chapter dealing with physical and motor development.

Growth follows an orderly sequence. Although growth patterns are not absolutely uniform from child to child, there is good evidence from genetic studies of children that there is an orderly sequence for the emergence of special forms of behavior. Cinema-analysis records of creeping and stair-climbing behavior reveal the appearance of specific behavior patterns in a sequential order. Louise Ames observed the development of a patterned type of behavior for creeping in every one of a group of twenty cases studied.[12] The movement usually begins with a forward hand movement. At the time of the forward hand movement, there is a forward movement of the knee on the opposite side of the body. The movement of the hand is usually completed just before that of the knee. This movement may begin with either the right or left hand. In the case of stair climbing, a single pattern was observed in eleven of the twelve cases studied. This pattern is described by Ames as follows: "It starts with placement of the left foot on the first stair. The left hand is then placed on the second stair, and immediately afterward, the right foot on the first stair. There is a short pause, then right hand moves to the third stair and left foot to the second. After another short pause, the left hand and right foot move up again. And so it goes. Temporal analysis of

[12] Louise B. Ames, The sequential patterning of prone progression in the human infant, *Genetic Psychology Monograph,* 1937, Vol. 19, pp. 409-460.

this behavior shows that left hand and right foot move almost simultaneously, as do right hand and left foot." [13]

A comparison of the time for the whole pattern of identical twins shows that growth is of a gradual nature and follows an orderly sequence in its development and patterning from age to age. This is shown in Figure 5 for identical twins, T and C. It was observed that climbing behavior followed the type of prone progression manifested. That is, a child who creeps on both hands and one foot will make use of the same limbs in climbing. Climbing up stairs on hands and knees gradually gives way to two feet to a stair and then

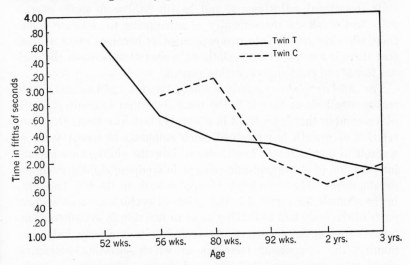

FIG. 5   Time for whole pattern, T and C compared

one to a stair as the child develops. Thus, creeping behavior was observed to appear on the average at forty-four weeks; patterned ascent of the stairs at sixty-two weeks; and patterned descent a few days later. The orderly sequence of growth is well illustrated in the case of the age-to-age progression of the child in movement and manipulation.

Children differ in rate of growth. Although children appear to follow an orderly pattern of growth and development, it should be emphasized that each child grows at his own unique rate. Thus, one child may begin crawling weeks before his cousin of the same age level. It is important to understand each child's growth pattern in

[13] Louise B. Ames, Some relation between stair climbing and prone progression, *Journal of Genetic Psychology*, 1939, Vol. 54, pp. 313-325.

order not to become disturbed by comparisons with other children or standards based upon group data. The timing of the early adolescent growth spurt varies considerably from person to person of the same sex.

The growth rate of each child is affected by many forces both within and without the body. The effects of some of these forces will be discussed in subsequent chapters. Some external factors influencing growth are nutrition, exercise, sanitary surroundings, the emotional climate, bacterial forces, and climatic conditions. Some internal conditions affecting growth are hereditary factors, the endocrines, health state, emotional adjustments, and health habits. A study of this classification shows the difficulty of attempting to separate conditions affecting growth into two categories. It becomes quite obvious that there is a constant interrelationship operating between the various forces and conditions affecting growth.

The child develops as a unified whole. Parents and teachers should realize at all times that it is the total child that is at play on the playground or that is involved in a learning task at school. The interrelation of growth has received much emphasis in recent years as a result of our increased knowledge of how the child grows and the introduction of the organismic concept in studying child growth and development. "The organismic viewpoint leads to the inference that in the struggle for survival in the course of evolution the component parts of the body had to develop so as to function in symphonic harmony of an optimal pattern. An organism is a closely knit community, the component members of which—nervous, endocrine, circulatory, excretory, digestive, and so on—co-operate in maintaining a dynamic steady state in the face of fluctuating external conditions." [14]

The interaction of the organism with its environment has been discussed in a previous chapter. A well-integrated organism may be described as one which, through continuous striving, has been able to maintain a balance in the behavior pattern which has best satisfied his needs for survival and development. The disorganized or disintegrated organism is one in which this balance has been destroyed and one in which harmonious patterns of reaction are no longer possible. A rather complete discussion of this will be presented in a later chapter dealing with the growing personality and personality disorders.

[14] Samuel Brody, Science and social wisdom, *Scientific Monthly,* 1944, Vol. 59, p. 205.

The fact that the child grows as a unified whole may very well be illustrated in connection with the growth in the ability to creep, crawl, and walk. This growth, in the case of the average child, will be accompanied by changes in interests, attention, mental outlook, and emotional manifestations. Furthermore, it can be shown that changes in interests and mental growth (related aspects of growth) are closely related to growth in walking and talking. This interrelation is sufficiently close so that when one is lacking or delayed the other will be affected—perhaps delayed. "The individual passes slowly and almost imperceptibly from stage to stage of his maturation, preserving a patterned integration of behavior throughout life. In other words growth and development are by patterns and not by accretion or by addition of minute increments." [15] Learning is not of a piecemeal fashion in which unrelated items are learned and somehow at some later date become fashioned into a unified pattern. Secondly, the entire child is involved in learning, as in learning to read, and not just his mental abilities. The child's emotional nature, social self, physical self, and other selfs are involved along with his intellectual self in learning to read and spell.

Habit patterns change with maturity. At any level of maturity, children display many forms of behavior that will be modified or abandoned in the course of time. If adults concerned with the guidance of growing boys and girls were better informed as to the developmental patterns of children and were patient enough to follow these more or less orderly sequences of growth patterns, the problems of being a parent or teacher would be more pleasant, and the child would be comfortable and secure. This principle of development includes the idea that behavior activities that are useful at one level of maturity are modified or abandoned at another stage of maturity in favor of activities more useful and harmonious with the child's organismic developmental level.

Factors influencing development

The rate and pattern of development can be influenced by forces and conditions within and without the body. A knowledge of the factors which influence development should be most helpful to those concerned with the stimulation and guidance of child development.

---

[15] Cecil V. Millard (Chairman, editorial committee), Child Growth in an Era of Conflict, *Fifteenth Yearbook of Department of Elementary School Principals,* Michigan Education Association, 1944, p. 13.

Some of these factors and conditions will be presented in the following discussion. These will be enlarged upon in the subsequent chapters dealing with different aspects of growth and development.

Hereditary factors. The nature and importance of heredity in relation to the development of the individual was presented in Chapter 2. Although the influences of heredity and environment cannot be entirely separated, there are gradations in the relative influence of these. Certain characteristics, such as the color of the eyes or pigmentation of the skin, can be attributed to heredity almost entirely; other characteristics, such as one's prejudices, attitudes, and values, are largely environmentally determined. However, even in the case of attitudes and understandings, certain potentialities for their development are provided for through the germ plasm.

Many studies of the effects of heredity upon intelligence have been conducted during the past two decades. Some of these will be referred to in a later chapter. The results of these studies indicate, however, that one's functional intellectual capacity as measured by intelligence tests is a result of the joint operation of heredity and environment. Studies of the inheritance of mental diseases, epilepsy, tuberculosis, and many other physical or mental conditions likewise indicate that both heredity and environment are involved. It appears that certain predispositions or tendencies are handed down through the germ plasm, but the development of the particular disease condition will depend also upon the type of experiences one encounters.

A further look at heredity furnishes valuable information about the selective nature of children's responses, which has important implications for child training and guidance. All children have certain needs, but the manner in which these are met will vary considerably. All children need food, but not the same amount. Children will even differ with respect to the kinds of food they need. Materials presented in Chapter 3 revealed that infants differed enormously in motility. They will also differ in their sleep requirements. Thus, the hereditary potentialities and requirements of the newborn child are such that it becomes impossible to fix standard requirements applicable to all children.

Glands of internal secretion. Recent studies in the field of endocrinology have shown the importance of the glands of internal secretion for the physical and mental development of the child. These glands affect development through the secretion of substances called *hormones.* The secretions from these glands act as regulatories for body growth. A deficiency of certain hormones, for example those produced by the parathyroid glands, will result in a calcium deficiency and thus in defective bone growth. Deficiency in the activity of the sex glands delays the onset of puberty, while hyperactivity results in precocious sexual development. Deficiency of thyroid activity during the growing years results in stunted development, and produces a condition which has been referred to as "cretinism." The pituitary gland secretes growth hormones. An excess of these hormones produces a condition of "gigantism," while a deficiency results in "dwarfism." It should not be inferred from the discussion here that all abnormalities of growth or that body size and body build can be accounted for through the endocrines alone. Studies in genetics show that body-size and body-build types tend to run in families and may be largely attributed to heredity.

Nutrition. During the period of growth, nutrition is of utmost importance for the normal development of the individual. It has been suggested that the baby needs to drink an amount of milk equal to one-seventh to one-sixth of his body weight per day. Tallerman points out that 25 calories and 1½ to 2 ounces of fluid per pound are needed throughout the first year.[16]

A number of studies have been conducted within recent years bearing on feeding schedules for infants. The results from these studies indicate that there is nothing mysterious about a three-hour or four-hour schedule. It appears rather that the schedule should vary with individual children. Careful observations on the part of the mother, combined with guidance from the family pediatrician, should provide the basis for a sound and functional feeding program. The suggestion made by F. H. Richardson seems to provide a safe guide. He states: "A regular schedule not too rigorously followed is probably the most sensible course to adopt; avoiding both unbending punctuality and the *laissez faire* self demand." [17]

Concerning the necessity of time limitations to avoid overfeeding the infant, Dr. Richardson states: "My own position is strongly against any arbitrary time limitations, which I believe to be the cause of many unnecessary weanings, especially the time-honored but evil hospital limit of twenty minutes. I have never seen anyone with patience and perseverance enough to overfeed a baby." [18]

[16] K. H. Tallerman, Common difficulties in breast fed infants, *Practitioner,* 1945, Vol. 154, p. 343.

[17] Frank Howard Richardson, Breast feeding comes of age, *Journal of the American Medical Association,* 1950, Vol. 142, p. 866.

[18] *Ibid.,* p. 865.

The food requirements will vary considerably among infants and growing children; however, a well-balanced diet rich in certain minerals is essential for the development of good bones and teeth, good skin condition, complete physical development, and other conditions that would contribute to healthy growth. The increased stature today as compared with earlier times may be traced in a large measure to improved diets. Closely related to good nutrition is the need for fresh air and sunlight. The desirable effects of fresh air and sunlight become obvious when comparisons are made between the growth of children from favorable environments with that of children reared in environments where fresh air and sunlight are lacking.

Differences in culture. In an attempt to determine the influences of culture on the infant's development, Dennis studied a group of Hopi and Navaho Indians of the southwestern section of the United States.[19] There is a marked difference in the treatment of the babies of these cultures from that of the white American culture. Among the Hopis the baby is bound to a board and spends most of his time in this position during the first three months after birth. Since he is tightly bound, there is little opportunity for random movements. Dennis studied the problem of whether the cradle board affected the age of walking. Thus, these children were compared for age of walking with those from Indian villages where the use of the cradle board has been abandoned but other child-rearing practices had remained about the same as those found in the villages where cradling is used. When comparing the two groups, Dennis and Dennis found that the average age of walking for those subject to the cradling practice was slightly less than for those who were not. Among both groups, however, the age of walking is significantly later than that reported by different investigators for white American children. However, the general patterns of response were strikingly similar. Indian infants may not cry as much, but their cries are similar. The sleep reactions of the Indian infants and the white American infants are the same, although different things may keep them from sleeping. The sleepy infant from all cultures tosses about, frets, and fusses. Dennis presents the following concluding remarks from his observations:

I would not deny that beginning roughly at one year of age the patterns of the infant do begin to vary in accordance with the cultures

[19] W. Dennis, Does culture appreciably affect patterns of infant behavior? *Journal of Social Psychology*, 1940, Vol. 12, pp. 305-317.

of the group. For one thing, language patterns which begin at about one year are definitely cultural patterns. Shortly after one year of age the child may also begin very simple dramatic play in which he imitates adult patterns which are distinctive of the culture group. . . . This corroborates the view that the characteristics of infancy are universal and that culture overlays or modifies a more basic substratum of behavior.[20]

Anthropologists, who have made comparative studies of the behavior and habits of white American and primitive peoples' children, have found evidence for the belief that such patterns as aggressiveness and competition among children are closely related to certain cultural practices. For example, Margaret Mead has pointed out that the children of New Guinea are extremely gentle and noncompetitive in nature, while children of the Western cultures are significantly more aggressive and competitive.[21] Likewise, Allison Davis has found evidence that personality development is significantly affected by the class status in which the child is reared. Materials bearing on certain aspects of this will be presened in a later chapter dealing with personality development.

Psychological factors. It is only within recent years that students of child development have come to recognize the importance of certain psychological factors in the development of the child. In this connection it should be noted that the infant's environment is quite restricted. His social environment is restricted largely to the mother or someone who cares for his physical needs. It has already been suggested that adequate nutrition is essential for the optimum development of the child. It was pointed out in Chapter 3 that the infant's response to psychological stimulation appears to present itself for the first time during the third month, when the baby smiles in response to the face of the mother or attendant. Somewhat later, displeasure is registered in response to certain types of psychological stimulation. The importance of this psychological stimulation for the development of the child during the first year of life was studied by Spitz.[22] Children from two institutions were compared. The institutions differed in one significant factor. In one of the institutions, the children were in a nursery but were reared by their own mothers. In

---

[20] *Ibid.,* p. 316.

[21] Margaret Mead *et al., Cooperation and Competition among Primitive Peoples* (New York: McGraw-Hill Book Co., 1937). See also G. Bateson and M. Mead, *Balinese Character* (New York: New York Academy of Science, 1942).

[22] Rene A. Spitz, The role of ecological factors in emotional development in infancy, *Child Development,* 1949, Vol. 20, pp. 145-155.

the other institution, the children were in a foundling home and were reared after the third month by overworked nursing personnel—one nurse cared for from eight to twelve children. The children appeared to be well cared for physically in each case but the emotional interchange between the child and the mother furnished the one inde-

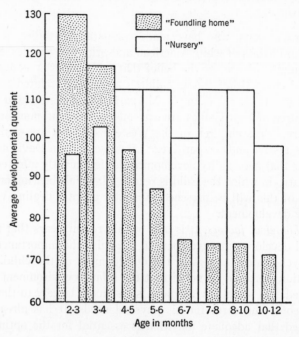

FIG. 6 Comparison of development in "Nursery" and "Foundling" home
(After Spitz)

pendent variable in the comparison of the two groups. The response to this variable was observable in many ways. The most comprehensive index of this response appears in the monthly averages of the development quotients that are presented in Figure 6. The developmental quotient consists of the development of six sectors of the personality: "mastery of perception, of bodily functions, of social relations, of memory and imitation, of manipulative ability, and of intelligence."

The contrast of the development of the two groups, presented in Figure 6, is very striking. A complete reversal of the developmental trend is noted in that the one group which seemed to be ahead during the first two months dropped to a developmental quotient of forty-five by the end of the second year. Another evidence for the disastrous effect of the lack of emotional interchange between the child and the mother is found in the comparison of the mortality rate for the two groups. The high mortality of the foundling-home group as compared to the nursery group is the most extreme consequence of the general decline, which was manifested by the children in various ways. Concerning this, Spitz presents the following generalization:

Consequently, barring starvation, disease or actual physical injury, no other factor is capable of so influencing the child's development in every field as is its relation with its mother. Therefore this relationship becomes the central ecological factor in infant development in the course of the first year. On the other hand, development, particularly in the emotional sector, provides an extremely sensitive and reliable indicator of variations in the mother-child relationship.[23]

Summary and conclusion

Before one can understand principles of development he must get a clear notion of what is meant or implied in this term. Development has been differentiated from growth in this chapter on the basis of its inclusiveness. Thus, we speak of child development, meaning the development of the child as a personality—a total self. Growth has been defined by Dewey as "a cumulative movement of action toward a later result." [24] In this chapter, growth has been described in terms of changes that take place as an individual passes from one age level to another. The nature of these changes will be presented in the subsequent chapters which deal with various aspects of growth.

The principles of growth that have been discussed in this chapter are: (1) growth is a continuous process; (2) growth is not even in tempo; (3) growth follows an orderly sequence; (4) growth is both quantitative and qualitative; (5) both the rate and pattern of growth can be modified by forces within and without the body; (6) growth patterns are not absolutely uniform from child to child; (7) the child develops as a unified whole; and (8) behavior patterns change with maturity. A knowledge of these principles is essential for the guidance and direction of children in their development. A parent who is familiar with these principles and uses them as a guide will recog-

[23] *Ibid.*, p. 151.
[24] John Dewey, *Democracy and Education* (New York: The Macmillan Company, 1922), p. 49.

nize the individuality of his child, and not make use of some artificial standard in directing and evaluating the child's growth.

Curriculum experiences should be adjusted in harmony with these principles of growth. When these principles are recognized and taken into consideration, a wide range of differences in readiness for learning will be found, differences in rate of learning will be observed; and educational growth will tend to follow an orderly process closely related to the maturational level of the child. The materials of instruction should be timed to the child's maturity level. When this is done, much time and effort will be saved and the educational growth of the child enhanced. The teacher who uses the developmental approach will recognize the child's potentialities and plan her materials and procedures in line with these abilities. Her prime concern will be the growth and development of the child in a desirable direction in harmony with his interests, needs, and abilities rather than the acquisition of skills and information that will probably be useful at some later stage in life.

Questions and Exercises

1. Describe briefly the general nature of growth curves as shown in Figure 4. What is the significance of this in relation to educational practices?
2. Contrast by definition and illustration the meanings of the terms *maturation* and *learning*. Review some study in which the co-twin method of experimentation was used in studying the problems of learning in relation to maturation.
3. What is meant by *acculturation?* How is this related to maturation? To learning?
4. Survey the literature in the field of child development for the past several years for case studies illustrating some of the principles of development discussed throughout this chapter.
5. What are the educational implications of the principle, *Growth is a continuous process?*
6. Show how the child's growth in ability to walk tends to follow an orderly sequence. What bearing does this have on stimulating the child to walk?
7. Study the height, weight, or some other measurement of a number of children of the same age level. What do you find relative to differences in their rate of growth?
8. What is meant by the statements referring to the interaction of the organism with its environment? How does this viewpoint affect the nature-nurture controversy?

9. What are some factors that influence the food requirements of the infant child?
10. What are some contributions anthropologists have made to the study of children?

Selected Readings

Bailey, E. W., *et al.* *Studying Children in School.* New York: McGraw-Hill Book Co., 1939.

Breckenridge, Marian E., and Vincent, E. Lee. *Child Development.* 2nd ed.; Philadelphia: W. B. Saunders Co., 1949. Chap. I.

Dearborn, E., and Rothney, J. *Predicting the Child's Development.* Cambridge, Mass.: Science Arts, 1941.

Gesell, A., and Ilg, F. L. *The Child from Five to Ten.* New York: Harper & Brothers, 1946. Chaps. I and II.

Hurlock, Elizabeth B. *Child Development.* 2nd ed.; New York: McGraw-Hill Book Co., 1950. Chap. II.

Jersild, Arthur T. *Child Psychology.* 3rd ed.; New York: Prentice-Hall, 1947. Chap. II.

Millard, Cecil V. *Child Growth and Development in the Elementary School Years.* Boston: D. C. Heath and Company, 1951. Chaps. II and III.

Olson, W. C., and Hughes, B. O. Growth of the child as a whole, in *Child Behavior and Development* (R. G. Barker *et al.*, eds.). New York: McGraw-Hill Book Co., 1943. Chap. XII.

Rand, W., *et al.* *Growth and Development of the Young Child.* 4th ed.; Philadelphia: W. B. Saunders Co., 1946. Chap. II.

Zachry, C. *Emotion and Conduct in Adolescence.* New York: Appleton-Century-Crofts, 1940. Chap. II.

II

Aspects
of Growth

5

Physical Growth
and Health

The physical growth and development of the child after conception may be divided into two periods: the period of life in the uterus, and the period from birth onward. The growth and development of the individual, however, are determined by his hereditary constitution and a multiplicity of environmental influences. Some of these environmental influences operate during the uterus period.

Factors affecting physical growth and development. Attempts to explain growth on the basis of some single factor have resulted in misconceptions and a lack of understanding of the forces affecting child growth. There is evidence that physical development is affected by various forces and conditions. Some factors for which some supporting evidence is available have been listed by Mabel Rugen.

1. Socioeconomic status is illustrated in improved standards of living.
2. State of nutrition and the particular value of milk as a growth food.
3. General state of health as determined by the physicians' examination supplemented by various measures of vital capacity, muscular strength, and nutritional status.
4. Physical defects when they are of such a nature as to produce strain or drain on the child.
5. Lack of proper medical care in time of illness and for the correction of handicapped defects.
6. Child labor and employment when under non-ideal conditions.
7. Sleep, rest, and relaxation.
8. Play, exercise, and athletics.

9. Health of parents and genetic stock.
10. Health of child during infancy.[1]

Longitudinal versus horizontal measurements. Most of the early studies of child growth made use of cross-sectional data in ascertaining height, weight, and other measures of large groups of children. The data from these measurements make it possible to construct representative average growth curves for a number of different developmental factors. The increased interest in child study brought forth many long-time studies. These studies introduced problems and data relative to individual growth curves. It soon became apparent that average growth curves failed to present an accurate picture of the pattern of child growth, since they tended to cancel out cycles of growth that are characteristic of individual growth curves. Furthermore, these cross-sectional data did not show individual differences which are prevalent in the rate of growth of children.

Baldwin and others were among the early investigators who made use of repeated measurements on the same group of children.[2] This method enabled Baldwin to plot individual growth curves as well as average curves for individual boys and girls and for various groups. While this method may not be of much immediate practical value, measurements kept over a period of time furnish a basis for determining the effects of various factors on growth. Furthermore, such measurements provide information concerning growth cycles and the nature of individual growth curves which should have practical value in the guidance and direction of the development of boys and girls. Cross-sectional measurements and longitudinal measurements serve somewhat different functions but are at the same time complementary. Cross-sectional data furnish information about growth tendencies in different groups, and thus provide a means of comparing age groups, races, different socioeconomic groups, and the sexes. By means of longitudinal studies, the growth of an individual at one stage can be compared with his growth at some previous stage, as well as with other members of the group with whom he may be associated.

Extensive growth studies conducted during the past two or three decades show that each child's development is unique, and that it

[1] Mabel E. Rugen, The physical growth of the child, in *Pupil Development and the Curriculum,* Bureau of Educational Reference and Research, University of Michigan, 1937-38, p. 75.
[2] Bird T. Baldwin, The physical growth of children from birth to maturity, *University of Iowa Studies in Child Welfare,* 1921, Vol. 1, No. 1.

must be determined in relation to his own rate of growth, rather than on standards based upon group averages. Roswell Gallagher emphasized this when he pointed out that there is no average boy. He stated: "Growth or maturation or obesity is not important, but too much interest and faith in tables and graphs breeds oversolicitude and anxiety. It is better to upset the scales than to upset the home."[3] The difference between the average and an individual growth curve for height is illustrated in Figure 1 of Chapter 1.

Although longitudinal growth data are more difficult to obtain and require careful measurements over a long period of time, this method of studying child growth and development is gradually displacing many of the mass methods frequently used in studying children. This does not mean, however, that all mass methods will be replaced by longitudinal studies. It has already been suggested that the two methods are complementary to each other. Students of child growth and development referred to throughout this and subsequent chapters have used both methods in gathering data on the various aspects of child growth and the factors that influence the growth and development of children. The more widespread use of complete permanent records in schools, coupled with the increased attention being given to the physical growth and health of children, should furnish much useful data for studying and guiding the physical development of the individual child. A sufficient number of longitudinal studies have been completed to provide fairly accurate information about the general nature of the physical growth of individual children. In connection with results from the twelve-year Harvard Growth Study, Rothney stated:

We can say with a great deal of assurance that growth is very rapid from birth to the age of two, that it tends to continue at a diminishing rate until a period of approximately three years before the advent of puberty, rises rapidly (more rapidly than previous cross-sectional studies have revealed) until puberty is reached, and then falls away quickly to end points (where the increase is smaller than the errors of measurement) at ages between seventeen and nineteen. The shape of the curve for both sexes is almost identical, but the timing of the adolescent spurt disturbs the parallelism of the growth curves.[4]

Measurements in terms of age units. Longitudinal and cross-

[3] Roswell V. Gallagher, There is no average boy, *Atlantic Monthly*, 1949, Vol. 183, pp. 42-45.
[4] J. W. M. Rothney, Recent findings in the study of the physical growth of children, *Journal of Educational Research*, 1941, Vol. 35, pp. 161-182.

sectional data have provided norms, thus furnishing a basis for interpreting the child's development in terms of ages. The *anatomical age* has been widely used in recent years in studying child development. A rather complete description of methods for determining the anatomical age along with growth factors related to anatomical development will be presented later in this chapter. The anatomical age has reference to the degree of physical development in terms of the eruption of the permanent teeth or the hardening of the bones. It represents the point at which the child has arrived in his physical development. It does not, however, have reference to size, weight, health, or strength. The *physiological age,* on the other hand, is used in connection with the development of the internal organs and especially the reproductive organs and sex glands. In general, three physiological ages are spoken of: the prepubescent, the pubescent, and the postpubescent.

Growth curves based upon single measurements show a great deal of fluctuation. In order to arrive at a clearer concept of the growth of the child as a whole, a combination of age units may be used as a basis for determining his growth. Olson and Hughes arrived at an *organismic age* by taking a number of different growth values of given chronological ages.[5] The organismic age of an individual child would be based on the average age unit obtained from various measures of growth. Such a measure is very important in determining a child's growth level. It thus provides a basis for evaluating growth and achievement in some specific direction. In terms of educational diagnosis, there is no reason to label a child a reading-disability case if his reading age is approximately the same as his organismic age. The question of what measures should be included in the organismic age cannot be answered with any high degree of finality. In most cases there are not a sufficient number of measures available to furnish a stable and conclusive organismic age. However, two measures are more likely to provide a better basis for determining a child's total growth than is one measure. Likewise, three or four measures would in most cases give a better basis for determining a child's total growth than would one or two. Olson and Hughes have stated: "Theoretically one would have determined a stable organismic age when no further additional values would cause it to fluctuate in a significant manner." [6]

[5] Willard C. Olson and Byron O. Hughes, The concept of organismic age, *Journal of Educational Research,* 1942, Vol. 35, p. 525.

[6] *Ibid.,* p. 526.

General features of physical development

According to the theory of longitudinal growth measurements, there are at least four distinct cycles of growth. These cycles involve changes in the rate of growth in height, weight, hardening of the bones, intelligence, interest in play, educational achievement, as well as other phases of growth. Furthermore, the cycles occur at different periods among individuals of the same chronological age. The four cycles referred to by Courtis [7] may be described as follows:

1. The first cycle covers the period of embryonic growth.
2. The second cycle begins with birth and extends to age four or five. During this period the sensory equipment develops and functions more completely. Also, the child learns to creep, walk, and talk.
3. The third cycle extends from age three or four to the beginning of adolescence as noted by the early indications of pubescence. During this period permanent teeth appear, the child learns to read, write, and understand some of the forces with which he is in constant contact.
4. The fourth period is referred to as the adolescent period. During this period appropriate sex hormones appear and the individual develops toward maturity.

Growth in height and weight. Any table of averages is likely to be misleading, especially in connection with children's growth periods. Tables of norms for height and weight disagree considerably from group to group upon which such norms are based. Thus, any table of averages should be interpreted with caution, not only because of the lack of agreement between different norms developed but also because of individual differences in tempo of growth. One of the most important uses to be made of norms is in connection with average growth figures for a group of children. In this case, norms serve as a point of reference for making comparisons.

Data bearing on the average weight of infants were presented in Chapter 3. One study was quoted in which it was pointed out that the average birth weight of infants was found to be 7.13 pounds. It was also suggested that the weight of the infant, although falling off during the first few days after birth, increases considerably during the first six or seven months so that at six months of age his weight is approximately twice his birth weight. The growth in height is not quite so marked, although the typical baby will average approxi-

[7] S. A. Courtis, Maturation as a factor in educational diagnosis, in Educational Diagnosis, *Thirty-fourth Yearbook of the National Society for the Study of Education,* 1935, pp. 177-178.

mately three-fourths of an inch of growth in height during each of the first nine or ten months after birth. In the study by Katherine Simmons, the average height of boys at age two was 34.03 inches, which is approximately one-half of the average found for sixteen-year-olds.[8] The average weight of the two-year-old was 29.13 pounds, which is slightly more than one-fifth of that for the average sixteen-year-old. However, the average height of the girl at two was 33.74 inches, which is more than one-half of that found among sixteen- or seventeen-year-old girls. The average gain in height and weight for boys and girls is shown in Figure 7. The enormous increase during the first year and the adolescent spurt are important characteristics of the data presented.

The averages for height and weight of seven-year-olds attending the University of Iowa experimental elementary school during the course of three decades is shown in Table 12.[9] These findings show an in-

TABLE 12 Comparison of the mean height and weight of seven-year-olds in three successive decades

Decade of data collected	No. of pupils	Mean height (inches)	Mean weight (pounds)
1920-27	219	47.8	50.6
1930-37	240	48.4	53.1
1940-47	170	48.9	55.1

crease in the mean height of 1.1 inches during the twenty-year period, and an increase in the mean weight of 4.5 pounds during this time. These findings are not confined to private-school children but have also been observed from a number of studies of children enrolled in the public schools.[10] The implications of these findings to growth charts based on charts constructed in the twenties are clear. The average ten-year-old of today would probably fall in the upper quartile in height and weight, based upon such charts.

Weight in relation to body build. There is considerable evidence

[8] Katherine Simmons, The Brush Foundation Study of Child Growth and Development. II. Physical Growth and Development, *Monographs of the Society for Research in Child Development*, 1944, Vol. 9, No. 1.

[9] Howard V. Meredith, Height and weight of private school children in three successive decades, *School and Society*, 1949, Vol. 70, pp. 72-73.

[10] See, for example, the results of the surveys of the height and weight of boys and girls attending the Toronto public schools in 1923 and 1939. Department of Trade and Commerce, Dominion Bureau of Statistics, *Survey of Toronto Elementary School Children 1939*, Ottawa, 1942.

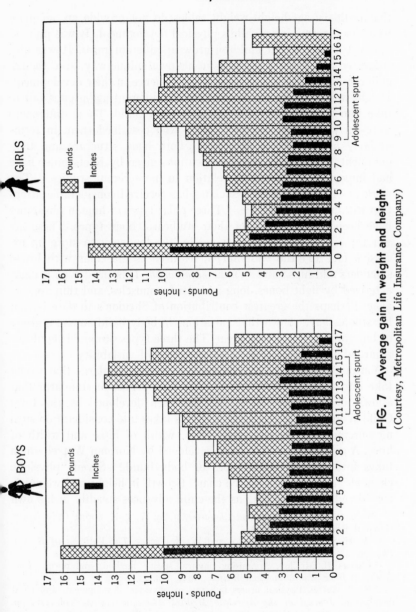

FIG. 7 Average gain in weight and height
(Courtesy, Metropolitan Life Insurance Company)

that ordinary age-height-weight tables do not provide an adequate basis for determining a child's physical development. It was pointed out in Chapter 4 that children grow at different rates. It was also suggested that each child grows in his own unique way, even though children do tend to follow an orderly sequence in their development. Height-weight tables established for the different age groups fail to take into consideration differences in body build. These differences were early observed by the Greeks, who described them in terms of body humors which determined both body structure and temperament. The studies and classifications given by Kretschmer have had important influences in relation to more recent studies.[11] The work of Sheldon and his associates has received considerable attention within the past decade.[12] Three polar types of human physiques have been developed out of their studies of body types. These are (1) the *endomorph,* characterized by the tendency to store up excessive fat; (2) the *mesomorph,* featured as muscular with broad shoulders and hips; and (3) the *ectomorph.* This third type is characterized by light bones, long and slender muscles, and thin appearance. Perhaps the greatest contribution of Sheldon's to date is that his studies have shown that variations in body build among a group of boys and girls are very great. The three types proposed should be regarded as dimensions on this large range of variability.

Various attempts have been made to set up standards that would take into account differences in body build. A set of standards that allows for differences in fatness has been developed by the Iowa Child Welfare Research Station.[13] This takes into consideration such measurements as height, chest girth, width of hips, and width of knee. A gridlike chart has been developed by Norman Wetzel which takes into account seven types of body build.[14] Seven "physique channels" are set forth on the chart. Growth in height and weight is considered normal as long as the child advances steadily in his own

[11] E. Kretschmer, *Physique and Character,* tr. by W. J. H. Sprott (New York: Harcourt Brace and Co., 1925).

[12] W. H. Sheldon, S. S. Stevens, and W. B. Tucker, *The Varieties of Human Physique* (New York: Harper & Brothers, 1940).

[13] Charles H. McCloy, Appraising physical status: methods and norms, *University of Iowa Studies in Child Welfare,* 1935, Vol. 15, No. 2.

[14] N. C. Wetzel, Physical fitness in terms of physique, development, and basal metabolism, *Journal of the American Medical Association,* 1941, Vol. 116, pp. 1187-1195. A *Physical Growth Record for Boys and a Physical Growth Record for Girls* has been prepared by the Joint Committee on Health Problems in Education of the N.E.A. and A.M.A., using data prepared by Howard V. Meredith of the University of Oregon. Copies may be secured from the American Medical Association or the National Education Association.

channel. When periodic examinations show cross-channel progress, growth progress is indicated. If the child deviates to the left channel, his weight is perhaps too great for his height; whereas if he deviates to the right of his channel, his weight is perhaps too little for his height. Such a chart should be useful to those concerned with evaluating the physical development of children. It should be especially useful in indicating the presence of growth problems and difficulties.

Changes in body proportion and size with age. Data were presented in Chapter 3 showing that the head of the infant comprised a large proportion of the total body weight. The legs of the infant are relatively short, while the neck is almost absent. Likewise, in comparison with other parts of the face, the chin and lower parts of the jaw are relatively small.

An investigation by Boynton and Parsons of the physical development of pupils attending the Peabody College Demonstration School shows the amount of growth in thirteen physical measurements between the ages of five and one-half and seventeen and one-half years.[15] The results based on annual retests of the children enrolled in the Demonstration School are presented in Table 13. An examination of the data will show that growth for the various parts of the body is very uneven. For example, while the boy at five and one-half years of age is 65 per cent as tall as he will be at age seventeen and one-half years, he weighs only 33 per cent as much and has attained only 18 per cent of the strength of grip he will possess at this later age.

The results shown in Table 13 indicate that there is an increase of over 50 per cent in arm span for boys after the age of five and one-half years, while the increase in head circumference is slightly less than 7 per cent. A further lack of uniformity in growth is in the development of lung capacity. Some features of physiological growth will be presented later in this chapter. Tests for strength, co-ordination, balance, and other aspects of motor development reveal an irregular but continuous growth. Materials bearing on various phases of motor development are presented in Chapter 6.

Appraisal of posture. The problem of what constitutes good posture should be the concern of every parent and teacher, since the effects of poor posture are pervasive and widespread. An examination of the child for good posture is not as simple as was once thought to be the case. In the first place, most teachers are not sure of just

[15] Paul L. Boynton and Rosa F. Parsons, Pupil analysis in the Peabody Demonstration School, *George Peabody College Bulletin,* 1933.

TABLE 13 Certain physical measurements for children of designated ages

Item Measured	Sex	5.5	6.5	7.5	8.5	9.5	10.5	11.5	12.5	13.5	14.5	15.5	16.5	17.5
Height Sitting	B	25.00	25.93	27.15	28.36	29.03	29.21	30.00	30.81	31.47	33.58	35.13	36.07	36.56
	G	24.88	25.82	26.88	26.91	28.45	29.05	30.17	31.29	32.65	33.15	33.38	33.72	33.56
Breathing Capacity	B	64.38	82.50	97.00	110.08	120.50	131.00	143.00	159.62	173.89	204.17	233.33	255.84	257.50
	G	64.50	73.75	87.50	93.44	107.50	117.50	135.00	152.06	166.67	180.42	180.42	181.80	186.67
Chest Circumf.	B	22.08	22.65	23.58	24.50	24.41	25.36	25.60	27.03	27.83	29.93	30.92	31.75	32.11
	G	21.46	22.14	22.82	23.18	24.13	25.15	26.25	27.88	28.69	29.59	29.71	29.70	29.56
Chest Width	B	7.48	7.55	7.93	8.16	8.21	8.45	8.79	9.16	9.27	9.95	10.32	10.74	10.71
	G	7.32	7.37	7.83	7.84	8.02	8.36	8.63	9.12	9.15	9.55	9.71	9.71	9.80
Chest Depth	B	5.51	5.68	5.81	6.05	6.16	6.12	6.29	6.48	6.71	7.15	7.31	7.52	7.49
	G	5.36	5.38	5.56	5.62	5.88	5.93	6.14	6.40	6.65	6.79	6.83	6.83	6.84
Head Circumf.	B	20.81	21.00	21.11	21.13	21.33	21.21	21.36	21.58	21.70	21.75	22.02	22.38	22.16
	G	20.30	20.39	20.68	20.65	20.90	20.98	21.05	21.15	21.46	21.49	21.62	21.65	21.65
Total Arm Span	B	44.75	48.00	49.79	53.55	55.33	56.43	58.17	60.00	63.00	67.17	69.30	71.07	70.50
	G	44.36	46.45	49.94	51.17	53.43	54.95	58.41	60.63	62.71	63.84	64.28	64.18	64.38
Shoulder Width	B	10.54	10.84	11.31	12.10	12.47	12.41	12.63	13.31	13.97	14.75	14.96	15.65	15.73
	G	10.58	11.05	11.32	11.50	11.75	12.33	12.68	13.50	13.54	14.06	14.13	14.06	14.00
Shoulder Front Wd.	B	9.44	10.10	10.35	10.75	11.23	11.42	12.05	12.32	12.93	13.78	14.38	14.91	14.88
	G	9.59	10.03	10.35	10.66	10.94	11.47	11.94	12.47	12.76	13.36	13.35	13.42	13.67
Hip Width	B	7.51	7.79	8.05	8.39	8.63	9.05	9.25	9.47	9.86	10.42	10.72	10.98	11.22
	G	7.43	7.71	8.06	8.20	8.54	8.86	9.28	9.58	10.22	10.75	10.98	11.04	10.99
Arm Length	B	18.55	19.04	19.90	21.23	22.17	22.56	23.43	24.28	25.47	26.95	28.16	28.69	28.03
	G	18.00	18.68	20.14	20.54	21.13	22.04	23.42	24.33	25.23	25.62	25.71	25.46	25.80
Abdominal Circumf.	B	21.25	21.80	22.75	23.63	23.20	24.00	24.21	24.75	25.35	26.41	26.94	27.46	27.78
	G	21.23	21.70	22.38	22.67	23.25	24.36	24.79	25.55	25.75	26.57	27.27	27.04	27.21
Ankle Circumf. R.	B	6.59	6.82	7.01	7.23	7.50	7.65	7.56	8.01	8.34	8.91	8.98	9.19	8.98
	G	6.23	6.52	6.74	6.96	7.25	7.57	7.71	8.05	8.15	8.19	8.11	8.13	8.10

Age in Years

what constitutes good posture, and may conceive of posture from a very limited viewpoint. Secondly, it should be emphasized that differences in body build must be taken into consideration. Where teachers are available—usually teachers of physical education or health—careful observations of individual pupils should be made in an effort to detect special posture defects. Where such teachers are not available, it should become the responsibility of someone especially concerned with the health guidance of children to make careful observations and secure a more accurate appraisal of the pupils' posture.[16] In general, such an appraisal should include standing posture, sitting posture, and posture while walking. The most important thing about standing posture is that the individual should stand erect, with the head, trunk, hips, and legs well aligned. Thus, children should be carefully observed for sagging shoulders, proper stance, correct manner of walking, and lateral curvatures. In order to understand more clearly the difference between good and poor posture, study the diagrams presented in Figures 8 and 9 along with the explanations. It should be pointed out, however, that few children during the preschool period hold their bodies exactly like the diagrams; small children often have more prominent abdomens, others have more curved backs.

Some causes of poor posture. Any effective program for the prevention of poor posture must have as its starting point a consideration of the major causes of poor posture among children. There is considerable evidence that the majority of cases of poor posture stem primarily from poor functioning between certain essential body parts, rather than from actual structural defects. Often, poor posture may be looked upon as a symptom of maladjustment in the child's daily program of activities. The following factors have been listed as conditions that contribute to good posture:

1. Good general health; good nutrition; freedom from fatigue; freedom from repeated or long-continued infections and from diseases that bring about deformities; good sight and hearing.
2. A well-balanced diet, including the foods that help to build bone and muscle—milk, fruit, green vegetables, eggs, and meat (and cod-liver oil for the child under 2).
3. Plenty of sleep and rest.

---

[16] See Charles H. McCloy, *Tests and Measurements in Health and Physical Education* (New York: Appleton-Century-Crofts, 1939), pp. 258-263. Many other sources may be found which will provide criteria for judging good posture and methods for evaluating posture.

4. Varied exercise outdoors—running, jumping, skipping, climbing. Encouragement by parents to take part in games and play that lead to symmetrical development of the body.

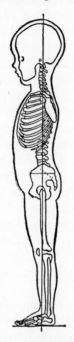 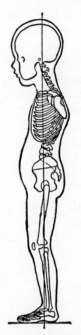

FIG. 8 Good posture	FIG. 9 Poor posture
This child stands at his full height, with his weight on the balls of his feet.	This child stands in a slumped position, with his weight on his ankles and heels.
He holds his head high, with his chin in.	He holds his head forward, with his chin out.
His chest is high, and his shoulder blades do not stick out in the back.	His chest is flattened and sunken and his shoulder blades stick out in the back.
His abdomen is drawn in.	His abdomen is relaxed and sags.
The curves of his back are slight.	The curves of his back are too great.
His knees are straight.	His knees are slightly bent.

(Courtesy, Children's Bureau, U. S. Federal Security Agency)

5. Wearing well-planned, well-fitting clothes and shoes, which put no strain on the bones or muscles or soft tissues of the child but let them develop naturally.

6. Sitting in a chair that supports the lower part of the child's back and that is low enough to let him keep his feet flat on the floor.

7. Sleeping in a bed that does not sag, with a firm, comfortable mattress and a flat spring; using no pillow, or a very small one, so that the child's neck is straight.[17]

Anatomical growth and development

Anatomical development. Anatomical development pertains primarily to the skeletal system, and especially to changes in the structure and composition of the bones. The hardening of the bones of the infant is in a very elementary stage. This is characterized by the softer, more pliable nature of the child's bones. The ligaments and joints are less firmly knit together. This gives the child increased flexibility in certain movements and accounts for the characteristic "double-jointedness" present in many children.

The hardening of the bones proceeds gradually and is rather far advanced prior to the onset of adolescence. Bone development has been studied by means of X-ray pictures of the hand and wrist.[18]

These X rays show the development of the ends of the bones, the epiphyses, the relative size of the different bones, and the progress toward the development of the ligaments and their attachment to the bony structures. After five or six years of age, girls show more advanced bone development than boys. This consistently advanced development of girls continues until maturity, and is evaluated by means of an *anatomic index.* An index of ten indicates that 10 per cent of the wrist shows hardening. At the age of thirteen, about 70 per cent of the area of the wrist shows hardening, and there is a considerable slowing down in the rate of anatomical development at this period.

Development of the teeth. As a rule, only six baby teeth appear prior to the first birthday, and the remaining fourteen come through during the year and a half following. Most children will have their temporary teeth by the age of two and one-half years or soon thereafter, and no more teeth appear until near the end of the fifth year. At this time the four permanent teeth and the sixth-year molars appear. Figure 10 shows the teeth of the six-year-old child, including the sixth-year molars.

The data on the eruption of deciduous teeth, presented in Table 14, are based on results obtained at the Harvard School of Public

[17] *Children's Bureau Publication No. 219* (Federal Security Agency, Washington, D. C., 1949).

[18] Changes in the hand and wrist have been found to be representative of the development of the bones of the entire body.

Health.[19] They are considered to be a representative sample of middle-class children. The presence or absence of a tooth was determined by a pediatrician at the time of the physical examination.

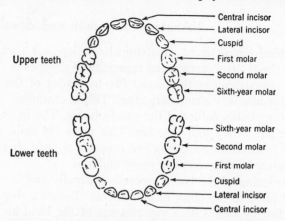

Upper teeth
— Central incisor
— Lateral incisor
— Cuspid
— First molar
— Second molar
— Sixth-year molar

Lower teeth
— Sixth-year molar
— Second molar
— First molar
— Cuspid
— Lateral incisor
— Central incisor

FIG. 10 Teeth of the average six-year-old child

These data do not reveal significant sex differences in the eruption of the deciduous teeth during the first three years. There is evidence, however, that beginning with the fifth birthday, girls begin showing an advanced state of development of their teeth over that shown by boys.

TABLE 14 Mean number of deciduous teeth erupted at different age levels (after Doering and Allen)

	Age in months (males)						
	6	9	12	18	24	30	36
Mean	0.43	3.27	5.99	12.48	16.75	19.25	19.88
S. D.	0.86	2.34	1.93	3.03	2.20	1.40	0.64
	Age in months (females)						
	6	9	12	18	24	30	36
Mean	0.34	2.82	5.52	12.43	16.64	19.07	19.91
S. D.	0.89	2.41	2.26	2.70	2.24	1.63	0.49

Dental caries. Dental caries appear to be a disease of civilization. They exist within a group in proportion to the use of modern tech-

[19] Carl R. Doering and M. F. Allen, Data on eruption and caries of the deciduous teeth, *Child Development,* 1942, Vol. 13, pp. 113-129.

nology in the preparation and handling of food. This has been shown from various surveys of dental decay among primitives and civilized peoples.[20] Scientific research during the past several decades has brought sufficient knowledge of the causes of tooth decay to indicate that its appearance is neither inevitable nor necessary. Since dental caries occur primarily as a result of bacterial action on tooth substance, any method of preventing the microorganisms from penetrating the enamel layer should be effective in preventing decay.

For every proponent of the protective-food-theory value of nutrition there appears to be an opponent with evidence that nutritional deficiencies of themselves do not increase dental caries.[21] Arvin Mann and others compared the caries incidence of a group of malnourished patients, particularly those suffering from a deficiency of vitamins A, B_1 (thiamine), and B_2 (riboflavin), with a group of patients free from nutritional deficiency disease. The results of this study offer good evidence that malnourishment alone is not significant in relation to dental caries. These investigators found a greater number of missing teeth and dental caries among the members of the control group than among the malnourished patients.

There is ample proof that low calcium, phosphorus, and vitamin D of the mother during the gestation period will adversely affect her own teeth as well as the development of the baby's teeth and bony structure. Of greater importance for the child, however, is an adequate diet for the child from birth until a complete dentition of the permanent teeth is attained. Philip Jay has reported the successful control of dental decay by dietary means without restricting the use of sugar.[22] Studies at the University of Michigan indicate that only the carbohydrate part of the diet is related to the control of dental decay. The carbohydrates, reaching the surface of the tooth, produce acid which decalcifies the tooth surface. The results of recent studies indicate that a large percentage of dental caries for both children and adults could be prevented by the formation of the habit of brushing the teeth and rinsing the mouth after each meal, and especially after eating foods containing a high percentage of sugar or starch. Of the various drugs and chemicals now being used

[20] See Paul H. Phillips, Relation of nutrition to good teeth, *Journal of the American Dietetic Association,* 1950, Vol. 26, pp. 85-88.

[21] For a review of studies bearing on this, see Arvin W. Mann and others, A comparison of dental caries activity in malnourished and well-nourished patients, *Journal of the American Dental Association,* 1947, Vol. 34, pp. 244-252.

[22] Philip Jay, Nutrition and dental caries, *Journal of the California State Dental Association,* 1947, Vol. 23, p. 37.

by the dentist to aid in the reduction of caries, local applications of sodium fluoride, administered to children between the ages of four and twelve, is proving to be a valuable agent.

Formation of malocclusions. A study of the dental development of 170 children, eighteen months to fifteen years of age, showed that occlusion (the fitting of the upper and lower teeth together while chewing food) may be affected by unevenness of growth.[23] The two jaws may not grow at the same rate, and thus the teeth fail to fit together in the chewing of food. Such a condition presents a threat to the child's health as well as personality development.

Studies bearing on the effects of thumb sucking on the formation of the teeth are not wholly conclusive. Lewis and Lehman observed that in cases of malocclusion associated with thumb sucking, the malocclusion continued as long as the habit persisted, and this tended to interfere with mastication. They further noted that in case the habit was broken before the child was five years of age, the child's teeth would tend to resume their normal position. Thumb sucking when prolonged after the fifth or sixth year may cause a protrusion of the upper front teeth and thus interfere with adequate mastication of food as well as present an unfavorable appearance of the mouth and teeth. Persistent abnormal pressure continued into the period of transition from the deciduous to the permanent teeth is likely to result in malocclusions. Concerning this, Klein has stated: "Some of the harmful pressure habits which cause malocclusions are thumb sucking, lip sucking, cheek sucking, blanket sucking, tongue biting, mouth breathing, as well as such external pressure habits as propping the chin on the hands, and leaning the face on the forearm or hands, either during the daytime or in an abnormal pillowing position at night. These are all pernicious habits which can either cause or aggravate malocclusion."[24]

Physiological growth and development

Evaluating physiological growth and development. The problem of determining the status of a child's physiological development is more difficult than that relating to height, weight, chest girth, and other physical features. In the first place, special techniques and instruments are required for gathering the necessary data. For ex-

[23] Samuel J. Lewis and I. Lehman, Observation on the growth changes of the teeth and dental arches, *Dental Cosmos*, 1929, Vol. 5, p. 71.

[24] E. T. Klein, Abnormal pressure habits, *Dental Survey*, August, 1950, p. 1081.

ample, metabolic changes are often used as a basis for determining energy requirements and physiological maturation. The basal metabolic rate cannot be observed and measured as readily as can physical measurements, and its ascertainment will require special laboratory materials and procedures. Furthermore, results obtained from physiological measurements are influenced by a number of variables. There is considerable evidence, for example, that the emotions are very important in relation to health and affect the metabolic rate. The metabolic rate is also affected by the time of day when the measurement is made, the effect of diet, the influence of exercise, the body position assumed, and other factors affecting the individual concerned. If reliable measurements are to be secured, the subject's activities and diet for a considerable time prior to the examination, and special conditions at the time, must be controlled. These difficulties, together with special techniques essential for obtaining accurate findings, make the evaluation of physiological development a problem for the average parent and classroom teacher.

Changes in pulse rate. A physiological measurement that is easy to make is that of pulse rate. This, however, has little value in the hands of the average person and is subject to misinterpretation when it is evaluated wholly on the basis of the norm or average for different age groups. The danger of the "force of the norm" appears again in connection with physiological measurements. There is a decreased pulse rate as the child develops toward maturity; however, comparisons of the rates of different children with averages or norms should be used with caution. A recognition on the part of the individual interpreting growth curves from pulse rate that wide differences appear should make one more cautious in drawing conclusions and in making generalizations from such curves. Figure 11 shows the average pulse rate of boys and girls taken under basal physiological conditions in connection with the Adolescent Growth Study at the University of California.[25] The more rapid pulse rate for girls continues from childhood until maturity. And, while there is a decrease in pulse rate during late childhood and early adolescent years, other physiological measurements may register an increase. There is, for example, an increase in blood pressure for both boys and girls, although the increase for boys is significantly more marked than that for girls.

[25] Nathan W. Shock, Physiological changes in adolescence, *Forty-third Yearbook of the National Society for the Study of Education,* Part 1, 1944, p. 59. Figure 11 is reproduced by permission of the Society.

Skeletal growth in relation to maturation. Investigations of the skeletal development of the same children over a number of years have furnished standards that allow for significant differentiation of skeletal maturity within similar age groups. This has provided some

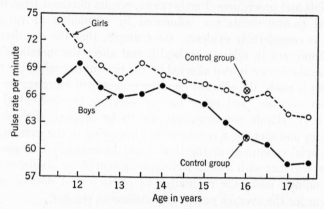

FIG. 11 Age changes in basal pulse rate. The vertical lines through each point indicate ± 1 S.D. mean. The control groups refer to test scores on groups other than the experimental groups obtained at the age of sixteen, in order to provide a comparison between the experimental groups of boys and girls and a sample without earlier experiences in the laboratory procedures used on the experimental groups.

(After Shock)

basis for the prediction of the kinds of growth changes that are likely to take place in a given child. In general, for both sexes, two factors may be listed as very important in connection with growth. These have been described by Bayley as follows:

(1) During childhood, the mere difference in velocity of maturation makes the rapid maturers large for their age and the slow maturers small. But (2) the longer the period of time a person is in the process of growing (that is, epiphysesopen and healthy growth factors operating), the more opportunity he has for growth. Therefore, though slow maturers are small for their age, they tend actually, to be large for their skeletal age, while the rapid maturers, though large for their chronological age, tend to be small for their skeletal age.

In girls some factors, probably related to the female sex hormones, stops growth rather abruptly after menarche. As a result we find that early maturing girls are usually large when young, slowing down to about average in height at 13 years, and completing their growth rapidly, to become small adults. Late maturing girls, conversely, are more often small when young, catch up to the average at about 13 and become tall adults.[26]

The skeletal age is usually measured by the formation of new areas of hardened bone and the changing outline of the bones. The hardening of the bones is rather far advanced at the beginning of

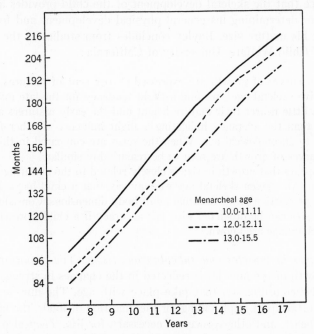

FIG. 12 Mean skeletal age of girls seven to seventeen years of age in three menarcheal age groups

(After Simmons and Grenlich)

adolescence. At the age of thirteen, about 70 per cent of the area of a girl's wrist shows hardening, and there is a considerable slowing down in rate of development at this period. The close relationship between skeletal age and menarche is shown in a study reported by Simmons and Greulich.[27] The skeletal development of three groups of girls similar in chronological age but differing in menarcheal age

[26] N. Bayley, Tables for predicting adult height from skeletal age and present height, *Journal of Pediatrics,* 1946, Vol. 28, pp. 49-64.

[27] Katherine Simmons and W. W. Greulich, Menarcheal age and the height, weight and skeletal age of girls 7 to 17 years, *Journal of Pediatrics,* 1943, Vol. 22, p. 518.

was studied from age seven to age seventeen. The skeletal development of these girls is shown in Figure 12. The growth curves indicate that there is a very close relation between skeletal development and sexual development. This correspondence may be noted as early as the seventh year. Skeletal age may, therefore, be used as a basis for predicting the sexual development of the girl. There is, furthermore, evidence that the skeletal development of the child provides a good basis for determining his general physical development and for predicting his mature size. Bayley concludes from studies at the Institute of Child Welfare, University of California:

When curves of growth are expressed as per cent of mature size at successive skeletal ages, we find a slight tendency for the late maturers to be a little nearer their mature height and the early maturers a little less so than the average—indicating a slight influence of other factors related to chronological age. When the sexes are compared in this way their curves of growth are seen to be remarkably similar.

It appears that growth in size is closely related to the maturing of the skeleton. At a given skeletal age we may say that a child has achieved a given proportion of his eventual adult body dimensions. Consequently, mature size can be predicted with fair accuracy if a child's present size and skeletal age are known.[28]

Changes in muscles and subcutaneous tissue. The importance of the growth of the muscles is reflected in the changes in strength and muscular co-ordination that take place with age. The muscles play an important part in providing for the digestion of foods, the beating of the heart, and other processes necessary for life. They also function in the maintenance of posture and equilibrium. The close relationship between the development of the bones and muscles has been observed from different measurements. This relationship is a necessary one, since the muscles, attached to the bones by means of tendons, hold the different parts of the skeleton in place.

There is a gradual and continuous increase in the relative weight of the muscles of the body from birth until maturity. At maturity, they constitute about forty times as much of the body weight as they did at birth. During infancy and the preschool years, they grow in weight largely in proportion to the weight growth of the individual. There is a very significant spurt of growth in muscle weight from ages five to six. The relative increase in muscle weight after age six

[28] Nancy Bayley, Skeletal maturing in adolescence as a basis for determining percentage of completed growth, *Child Development*, 1943, Vol. 14, pp. 44-45.

is gradual and continuous. At eight years of age it constitutes approximately one-fourth of the body weight; whereas at age sixteen it makes up approximately 45 per cent of the body weight.

A number of factors affect the thickness of subcutaneous tissue. Just as body build may be in a large measure a result of heredity, the thickness of the subcutaneous tissue may be, at least in part, hereditary, since there is a close relationship between body build and thickness of cutaneous tissue. This is, furthermore, related to the child's position in the weight range, which shows how closely his weight will approximate the average for his height and age group. The range of differences in thickness of subcutaneous tissue between individuals from different age groups is relatively greater than differences found from different measurements of most physical attributes. The changes occurring with age have been described by Stuart and Sobel as follows:

The thickness of subcutaneous tissue has been shown to increase rapidly up to 9 months of age, then to decrease abruptly and rapidly until 2½ years of age and more slowly until about 5½ years of age. The actual thickness at 5½ years is, on the average, about one-half that at 9 months. Between 5½ and 11 years of age the amount remains unchanged, but between 11 and 13 years of age there is a definite increase which appears to be the beginning of an adolescent accumulation.[29]

Caring for the child's nutritional needs

Nutritional needs of infants. Human milk is nature's diet for the infant, supplying all the nutritional essentials with the possible exception of vitamin D. It appears that neither human nor cow's milk supplies a sufficient amount of this vitamin. The need for supplying this from other sources exists from birth. The amount of vitamin D given should be considered in terms of *units*. The Food and Nutrition Board of the National Research Council has recommended 400 units as the daily allowance. Preparations of the D vitamins are commercially available in solutions that may be combined with the milk formula, in which it is perhaps more efficiently utilized than when presented in a more concentrated form. Cow's milk has quite frequently been substituted for human milk in the infant's diet, although these foods have different contents of the nutritional essentials and

[29] Harold C. Stuart and Edna H. Sobel, The thickness of the skin and subcutaneous tissue by age and sex in childhood, *Journal of Pediatrics,* 1946, Vol. 28, p. 646.

• have different effects on the growth and composition of the body.[30] Human milk is higher in sugar content but lower in total protein and casein than cow's milk. The greater protein content of cow's milk is reflected in a greater nitrogen content of the body of the artificially fed baby. The significance of any differences appearing is not clear. Furthermore, these differences disappear soon after there is no longer any differences in diet.

The lowered amount of calcium content in the human milk may be supplemented, if necessary, by calcium storage found in the bones of the healthy newborn baby. There is evidence, however, that the linear growth of artificially fed babies is related to the amount of calcium retained. Concerning this, Jeans has stated:

... Babies with poor retentions grow at average or less than average rates, while those with higher retention grow at rates greater than the average. Thus the higher calcium retentions would appear to be definitely advantageous to the artificially fed infant. On the other hand, the breast-fed baby has excellent linear growth despite a much lower calcium retention and grows at a rate definitely greater than that of the artificially fed baby who has the same calcium retention. It becomes obvious from these and other facts that factors other than those under consideration enter into the rate of growth and that probably it is inappropriate to state requirement standards for the artificially fed baby based on the requirement of the baby fed human milk.[31]

Self-selection of diets by young children. A number of interesting studies have appeared within recent years bearing on the effects of self-selection of diets by young children. These studies were motivated by the growing tendency in some circles to follow fixed formulas in the feeding of infants. and young children. These studies of self-selection of diets have, however, tended to support the theory of "the wisdom of the body" when the diets are provided under more or less natural conditions. The study of Clara Davis represents one of the best in this area.[32]

The subjects of the study reported by Davis consisted of infants from six to eleven months of age, who had never had supplements of the ordinary foods of adult life. A wide range of food of both animal and vegetable origin that would adequately provide all of the

[30] Philip C. Jeans, Feeding of healthy infants and children, *Journal of the American Medical Association,* 1950, Vol. 142, pp. 806-813.

[31] *Ibid.,* p. 807.

[32] Clara M. Davis, Results of the self-selection of diets by young children, *Canadian Medical Association Journal,* 1939, Vol. 41, pp. 257-261.

food elements known to be necessary for human nutrition was used.
The preparation of these foods was kept on as simple a basis as
possible. Food was not offered to the infant either directly or indirectly, the nurse's orders being to sit quietly by with a spoon in her
hand, but to make no motions toward the child or food. Only when
the child indicated a desire for certain food placed before him was
the nurse to offer it to him. The child was permitted to eat with his
fingers or in any· way he could, with no attention given to eating
manners. The results of the study were evaluated in terms of (1)
the health and nutrition of the fifteen children; (2) the adequacy
of the self-chosen diets as judged by nutritional standards; and (3)
the contributions of the study to our understanding of the appetite
and how it functions.

Some of the infants were in rather poor physical condition when
taken for the experiment; four were poorly nourished, and five had
rickets. Regardless, however, of their condition when received, within a reasonable time the nutrition of all, checked by different physical
and physiological measurements, came up to the optimal standard.
Checking of the diets of the fifteen children in their entirety (approximately 2,400 meals for each child) furnished some interesting
results. The daily calories of the diets were constantly found to be
within the limits set by scientific nutritional standards for the individual child's age, except for some of the undernourished who exceeded the standard during the early months of the experiment.
Davis concludes:

Such successful juggling and balancing of the more than thirty nutritional essentials that exist in mixed and different proportions in the foods
from which they must be derived suggests at once the existence of some
innate automatic mechanism for its accomplishment, of which appetite
is a part. The patterns of selective-diet appeared to develop as a result
of the sensory experiences with the food following a sort of sampling
process, which is essentially a trial and error method. Since trial and error
always involves the possibility of error, the most that can be expected
of careful nutrition in preference to the wide sampling is that of eliminating the possible error that may appear in the self-selection diet.

Symptoms of malnutrition. Inadequate dietaries came to man along
with improvements in various modes of living. The processing of
cereal grains and cane and beet sugar are examples of the ways
civilization has operated in providing the imbalance in our dietaries.
A survey of the nutritional status of children from Chicago was

conducted through the Elizabeth McCormick Memorial Fund.[33] The survey extended over two and one-half years and included 7,363 children from different socioeconomic groups. The income levels of the families ranged from relief status to annual incomes in excess of $10,000. The children ranged in age from two to eighteen years. The criteria used for determining nutritional failure were: "(a) the occurrence of certain physical abnormalities noted by the pediatrician which suggest deficiency states; and (b) dietary patterns which indicate a low consumption of protective foods." The results from this study give further evidence of the relationship between the socioeconomic status of children and their general health and diet patterns. Nutritional inadequacies were relatively common among those on relief, and was least frequent among those in better economic circumstances. Some specific conclusions reached were as follows:

6. Inadequate diets occurred frequently in all socioeconomic groups, but were most frequent at the relief level and least frequent in the higher groups—92 per cent at the lowest level, 41 per cent at the highest.

9. Dietary inadequacies were least often noted in the protein foods and most often in fruits and vegetables.

10. Consumption of fruit and vegetables, including potatoes, when compared with the yardstick for good nutrition, was found to be markedly low among both white and Negro children. The diets of 73 per cent of the white children were below the recommended allowances for fruits and vegetables, and in the poorest areas 98 per cent were below this standard." [34]

Malnutrition is not a disease that causes sufficient pain to demand immediate attention and treatment. There are, however, a number of symptoms that are helpful in identifying children suffering from malnutrition. These may be classed as *general symptoms*, including nervous habits, and *physical signs*. A list of such symptoms is presented in Table 15,[35] indicating those which might be observed by parents or teachers, those which might be observed by nutritionists or nurses, and those which physicians only would be expected to observe. Restlessness, inattention, irritability, forgetfulness, or definite

[33] Martha C. Hardy, and others, Nutritional and dietary inadequacies among city children from different socioeconomic groups, *Journal of the American Dietetic Association,* 1943, Vol. 19, pp. 173-181.

[34] *Ibid.,* p. 181.

[35] Recognition of early nutritional failure in infants, children, adolescents, and adults, *Journal of the American Medical Association,* 1942, Vol. 118, pp. 615-616.

mental retardation may distinguish a malnourished child from a well-nourished one. This relationship is evident from the results obtained in the experiment by Laird, Levitan, and Wilson.[63] They

TABLE 15 Symptoms and signs suggestive of early deficiency states in infants and children

Symptoms	*Physical Signs*
1. Lack of appetite (L)	1. Lack of subcutaneous fat (N)
2. Failure to eat adequate breakfast (L)	2. Wrinkling of skin on light stroking (N)
3. Failure to gain steadily in weight (L)	3. Poor muscle tone (D)
4. Late period of sitting, standing, and walking (N)	4. Pallor (N)
5. Aversion to normal play (L)	5. Rough skin (Toad skin) (N)
6. Chronic diarrhea (L)	6. Hemorrhage of newborn (D)
7. Inability to sit (L)	7. Bad posture (L)
8. Pain on sitting and standing (L)	8. Nasal blackheads and whiteheads (N)
9. Poor sleeping habits (L)	9. Sores at angles of mouth, cheilosis (L)
10. Backwardness in school (L)	10. Rapid heart (N)
11. Repeated respiratory infections (L)	11. Red tongue (D)
12. Abnormal intolerance to light, photophobia (L)	12. Square head, wrist enlarged, rib beading (N)
13. Abnormal discharge of tears (L)	13. Vincent's angina, thrush (D)
	14. Serious dental abnormalities (N)
	15. Corneal and conjunctival changes—slit lamp (D)

L = Those which parents or teachers might observe.

N = Those which nutritionists or nurses might observe.

D = Those which physician only would be expected to observe. The physician would take into account all other symptoms whether or not they have been previously observed.

conducted a controlled experiment with fifty-three children in grades one, three, and five of three elementary schools. The teachers had selected these youngsters as the most nervous in their class; also, they were free from malnutrition and other serious defects. One group was kept as a control; a second group was given a pint of milk daily at 9:30 A.M.; and a third group was given a special feeding at 9:30 A.M. daily, consisting of a calcium metabolism con-

[36] D. A. Laird, M. Levitan, and V. A. Wilson, Nervousness in school-children as related to hunger and diet, *Medical Journal and Record*, 1931, Vol. 134, pp. 494-499. There is considerable evidence that if one group receives special attention, such as that involved in special feeding during the morning hour, while another group does not receive this attention, this fact alone will result in a greater improvement of the former group over the latter. This fact should be kept in mind in the interpretation of differences between control groups and experimental groups.

centrate (containing calcium, phosporus, maltose, lactose, vitamin D, and some cocoa) added to the half pint of milk. Nervousness among the children was measured by the Olson's *Behavior Check List*. At the end of two weeks of the experiment there was an improvement noted for the control group of 2.3 per cent; for the group that received milk feeding, the improvement was 8.2 per cent; and for the group given the milk plus the concentrate, the improvement was 15.6 per cent. There was a marked improvement noted in 85 per cent of the children of the third group; in the case of fifteen traits, the improvement was 25 per cent or more. The experimenters concluded that many of the nervous symptoms manifested by pupils in the early years of the elementary school can be corrected merely by offsetting hunger pangs with a special feeding at school.

Nutritional needs of the preschool child. Nutritional needs at various age levels will vary from child to child; however, the differences are largely quantitative in nature, and are quite similar qualitatively. In general, these needs will vary considerably from child to child of the same age level. Concerning the desired diet of the child Boyd states: "Adequate nutrition involves adequacy of ingestion, digestion, absorption, utilization, and excretion."[37] Surveys of the diets of children from different socioeconomic groups in Georgia show that poor dietary practices may be found in homes where the weekly expenditure for food is ample. Furthermore, results from the survey (presented in Table 17) show that some of the greatest deficiencies exist in connection with the consumption of green and yellow vegetables and fruits, whereas one of the least deficiencies is in the use of meat. Green vegetables in particular can be grown in Georgia the year around in a small plot in the back yard, whereas meat is the most expensive of the foods consumed.[38] What seems to be most needed is an educational program that will function in the daily lives of growing boys and girls. This becomes in a large measure a program in parental education, if it is to affect the nutrition of the preschool child.

Special nutritional needs. Despite improvements in nutrition over the past quarter century, there is good evidence that the diets of a

[37] Julian D. Boyd, The nature of American diet, *Journal of Pediatrics*, 1938, Vol. 12, No. 2.

[38] A motion picture, The School Learned to Eat, developed under the joint sponsorship of the Nutrition Education Division, College of Education, University of Georgia and the State Department of Education, which was financed by General Mills, shows what can be accomplished when an educational program in nutrition is carefully integrated with the dietary practices of the home.

large percentage of children are still inadequate. Dietary surveys in families show an unequal distribution of food and nutritional essentials. The nutritions that are most commonly deficient are riboflavin, calcium, thiamine, and ascorbic acid. Protein and vitamin D deficiencies are also common during childhood. Many children receive an inadequate supply of sunshine during the summer, and very few receive an adequate supply during the winter months. Our indoor civilization should supply this needed sunshine vitamin throughout the growth period. Mothers appear more conscious of the needs of the infant for vitamin D than of those of the child. Without this vitamin, children vary enormously in their ability to use calcium and phosphorus.

Calcium is the chief mineral requiring attention during childhood, since most diets are likely to contain sufficient amounts of the other essential minerals. Milk, our only constant good food source of calcium, is seldom taken in sufficient quantity. During the early part of the preschool period, one pint of milk in addition to the usual diet is usually sufficient to meet the theoretical requirements. However, milk should not be regarded as a source of calcium only. It also contributes to the protein requirements. Concerning this, Jeans states:

... During the period when the calcium requirement is lowest the requirement for protein is high. Consequently it seems preferable to advise at least 1½ pints of milk after the period of infancy and up to the age of 10 years. The taking of a full quart throughout this period can be considered as beneficial, provided the larger quantity does not crowd from the diet other essential foods.[39]

Concerning thiamine, it appears that the solution of a deficiency found in many children lies in better food selection rather than in thiamine medication. The enrichment of flour and bread has done much to overcome this deficiency. A decrease in the amount of sugar used should prove helpful. Vitamin A is not needed in a special form, since a diet deficient in vitamin A will be otherwise deficient. What is most needed to insure a sufficient amount of this vitamin is a generally improved diet.

The calcium needs of preschool children have been studied in the home-economics laboratories of many of our universities and colleges. In a study conducted at the University of Illinois, the growth of seven normal healthy boys ranging in age from 2.7 years to 5.8

[39] *Op. cit.,* p. 812.

years was carefully studied for calcium requirements.[40] These boys were subjected to a forty-week experiment during which calcium balances at different levels of calcium intake were determined in order to assess the calcium requirements. The range of proposed daily requirements for dietary calcium of the seven boys was from 685 to 1,165 mg. Regarding the children's needs they conclude: "Assuming that children, under acceptable dietary conditions, could secure approximately 300 mg. of calcium daily from the non-milk foods which they eat and that such calcium is utilized to the same extent as is that of milk, the requirements of six of the children would have been met by a milk supplement no greater than 2 cupfuls. One subject would have needed as much as ¾ of a quart."[41] These results are in harmony with data obtained earlier at the laboratory from studies of five girls, from three to five years of age. It was pointed out in connection with the earlier study that these well-nourished children need less than one quart of milk daily to satisfy their calcium needs.

Nutritional needs of the school child. Any recommendations involving calorie allowances for children must take into consideration their energy expenditure. Most studies of the calorie needs of boys and girls are based upon food consumption in relation to gains in height and weight, with very little accurate information available on the energy expenditure at different ages. Thompson compared the energy expenditure of young girls during quiet play and during cycling with that of college girls (adults) engaged in the same activities under similar conditions.[42] The energy expenditure of the young girls at quiet play was found to be more than three times that of adults, and the difference in energy cost for cycling was in about the same order of magnitude. Further studies conducted in the nutrition laboratory, Teachers College, Columbia University, have revealed a higher energy consumption for boys and girls engaged in various activities than that of adults in similar activities.[43] The nutritional requirements recommended by the Food and Nutrition Board of the National Research Council is presented in Table 16 for special study.

[40] Dorothy Sheldon McLean and others, Further studies on the calcium requirements of preschool children, *Journal of Nutrition,* 1946, Vol. 31, pp. 127-140.

[41] *Ibid.,* pp. 138-139.

[42] E. M. Thompson, A study of the energy expenditure and mechanical efficiency of young girls and adult women, Doctor's dissertation, Columbia University, New York, 1940.

[43] See C. M. Taylor, M. W. Lamb, M. E. Robertson, and G. MacLeod, The energy expenditure of seven- to fourteen-year-old boys for quiet play and cycling, *Journal of Nutrition,* 1948, Vol. 35, p. 511.

TABLE 16   Recommended daily dietary allowances

REVISED, 1948

Food and Nutrition Board, National Research Council, Washington, D. C.

	Calories	Protein	Cal-cium	Iron	Vitamin A	Thia-mine	Ribo-flavin	Niacin (nico-tinic acid)	As-corbic acid	Vita-min D
		grams	grams	mg.	I.U.	mg.	mg.	mg.	mg.	I.U.
Man (154 lb., 70 kg.)										
Sedentary	2400	70	1.0	12	5000	1.2	1.8	12	75	
Physically active	3000	70	1.0	12	5000	1.5	1.8	15	75	
With heavy work	4500	70	1.0	12	5000	1.8	1.8	18	75	
Woman (123 lb., 56 kg.)										
Sedentary	2000	60	1.0	12	5000	1.0	1.5	10	70	
Moderately active	2400	60	1.0	12	5000	1.2	1.5	12	70	
Very active	3000	60	1.0	12	5000	1.5	1.5	15	70	
Pregnancy (latter half)	2400	85	1.5	15	6000	1.5	2.5	15	100	400
Lactation	3000	100	2.0	15	8000	1.5	3.0	15	150	400
Children up to 12 yrs.										
Under 1 yr.	110/2.2 lb. (1 kg.)	3.5/2.2 lb. (1 kg.)	1.0	6	1500	0.4	0.6	4	30	400
1-3 yrs. (27 lb., 12 kg.)	1200	40	1.0	7	2000	0.6	0.9	6	35	400
4-6 yrs. (42 lb., 19 kg.)	1600	50	1.0	8	2500	0.8	1.2	8	50	400
7-9 yrs. (58 lb., 26 kg.)	2000	60	1.0	10	3500	1.0	1.5	10	60	400
10-12 yrs. (78 lb., 35 kg.)	2500	70	1.2	12	4500	1.2	1.8	12	75	400
Children over 12 yrs.										
Girls, 13-15 yrs. (108 lb., 49 kg.)	2600	80	1.3	15	5000	1.3	2.0	13	80	400
16-20 yrs. (122 lb., 55 kg.)	2400	75	1.0	15	5000	1.2	1.8	12	80	400
Boys, 13-15 yrs. (108 lb., 49 kg.)	3200	85	1.4	15	5000	1.5	2.0	15	90	400
16-20 yrs. (141 lb., 64 kg.)	3800	100	1.4	15	6000	1.7	2.5	17	100	400

The numerous explanatory footnotes to the table are not included here, but will be found in the official printing which may be obtained from the National Research Council, 2101 Constitution Ave., Washington, D. C., or in the October, 1948, issue of *Nutrition Reviews*.

The major differences in the nutritional requirements of children with advancing age level are quantitative rather than qualitative in nature. With advancing age there is a need for increased calories. This is shown in Table 16 for all age groups with the exception of girls as they advance from the thirteen-fifteen age level to the sixteen-twenty age level. The sixteen-twenty-year-old boy is known for his great appetite. The requirements set forth by boys in this age category are greater than those for physically active male adults. Nutritionists are today emphasizing the importance of protein and amino acids in connection with health and disease. The value of blood proteins as plasma in the treatment of burns, the importance of amino acids in similar conditions and in peptic ulcer, as well as other discoveries, have shown the value of nutrition in relation to health. The proteins are capable of supplying the body with energy. Furthermore, proteins stimulate metabolism. There is good evidence that this is also related to immunity. "It has been estimated that there are 1,000 different proteins in the body. These consist of amino acids which are arranged differently in the various proteins." [44]

Nutritional needs are increased during the adolescent years (see Table 16) when there is an increased growth and enlarged activity program—especially among boys. Lack of an appropriate diet to permit the normal growth of the muscles tends to lessen physical activity. Summary studies of the diets of American children show that, despite advances that have been made, they are in a large percentage of cases inadequate. Table 17 gives a summary of diet studies of 5,642 unselected Georgia school children. An analysis of these diets was made for their adequacy, using the *Hatcher Check List of Food Needs*.[45] This analysis showed that 16.4 per cent of the diets was adequate, 28.5 per cent was fair, and 55.1 per cent was poor. A study of the growth and health of Belgian children conducted by Richard Ellis during the winter of 1944-45, three months after the liberation of Belgium, revealed that adolescents suffered more than the younger age groups from the inadequate diets. A study of 106 adolescent girls indicated "a retardation of puberty in a significant proportion of those living at home in a working-class environment." [46]

[44] See Ralph R. Scobey, Nutritional observations in pediatric practice, *Journal of the American Dietetic Association,* 1946, Vol. 22, pp. 1002-1006.

[45] The *Hatcher Check List of Food Needs* is published by the Burgess Publishing Company, Minneapolis, Minnesota.

[46] Richard W. B. Ellis, Growth and health of Belgian children, *Archives of Disease in Childhood,* 1945, Vol. 20, pp. 97-109.

TABLE 17 Summary of diet studies of 5,642 Georgia school children
(NUTRITION EDUCATION DIVISION, COLLEGE OF EDUCATION,
UNIVERSITY OF GEORGIA)

Food		Totals	Per cents
Milk	None	485	8.61
	1 cup	1495	26.54
	2 cup	1620	28.76
	3 cup	1274	22.63
	4 cup	758	13.46
Eggs	None	1553	25.86
	less than one	2527	42.08
	one or more	1925	32.06
Green and Yellow Vegetables	None	1063	18.82
	Less than ½C	2208	39.08
	½C or more	2378	42.10
Citrus fruit	None	1600	27.95
	Less than ½C	2015	36.85
	½C or more	2110	35.20
Other vegetables	None	920	16.33
	Less than ½C	1865	33.09
	½C or more	2851	50.58
Other fruits	None	1542	27.26
	Less than ½C	2056	36.35
	½C or more	2059	36.39
Meat	None	553	9.80
	Less than ½C	1101	19.51
	½C or more or 1 serving	3988	70.69
Meat Substitute	None	1784	31.76
	Less than ½C	2431	43.28
	½C or more or 1 serving	1402	24.96
Fats-Butter-Margarine	None	1502	26.64
	Less than 2 Tbs	2498	44.30
	2 Tbs. or more	1639	29.06
Whole grain or Restored Cereal: Whole Grain or enriched bread	None	725	12.89
	Less than 2 servings	2417	42.98
	2 or more servings	2482	44.13
Other breads and cereals	None	108	2.23
	Less than 2 servings	1261	26.08
	2 or more servings	3466	71.69
Other foods: Candy, sugar, jelly, syrup		1004	15.80
Preserves		1318	20.74
Cake, cookies		1659	26.10
Soft drinks, coffee, tea		2375	37.36
Meals not eaten: Breakfast		306	5.42
Lunch		457	8.10
Supper		546	9.68

General aspects of child health

Characteristics of the healthy child. Some of the features characteristic of the healthy child have been presented in the previous discussions. The characteristics of the healthy child may be conveniently classified into two major groups: (1) those relating to his personal appearance, and (2) those involving his general behavior. The following features have been listed by Norman Capon as characteristics of a large proportion of healthy children:

(1) The mucous membranes (e. g. the lips and palpebral conjuctiva) are definitely pink in colour.

(2) The facial expression is happy, often radiant; smiling is frequent, and, the eyes are bright and responsive.

(3) The skin is smooth, elastic, and covers a sufficient layer of subcutaneous fat to give the limbs a rounded appearance.

(4) The tissue targor is normal.

(5) The muscles are well-formed and their tonus is good.

(6) The limb muscles are almost straight.

(7) The stance is well balanced, erect, and graceful.

(8) The spine is straight and the shoulder girdles do not drop.

(9) The arches of the feet are well formed.

(10) The movements of limbs and body in walking and running, are characterized by elasticity, vigour and poise.[47]

Child mortality. Deaths from pneumonia, tuberculosis, and the contagious diseases such as measles, diphtheria, scarlet fever, and whooping cough have in the past two decades steadily declined, largely as a result of immunization and new drugs. Whooping cough is one of the most serious communicable diseases during the first two or three years. The high mortality rate among infants with whooping cough shows the necessity for beginning immunization by the time the child reaches three months of age. It has been observed that the production of tetanus antitoxin is as good in the early months of life as later, and this finding denotes that "the mechanism for the production of antibodies is well developed in young infants."[48]

While there has been a decline in the death rate among children, there are some diseased conditions in which there has been an in-

[47] Norman B. Capon, The assessment of health in childhood, *The Archives of Disease in Childhood*, 1945, Vol. 20, p. 54.

[48] Jean V. Cooke and others, Antibody formation in early infancy against diphtheria and tetanus toxoids, *Journal of Pediatrics*, 1948, Vol. 33, p. 146.

creased mortality. Childhood tuberculosis, rheumatic fever conditions, and cancer have replaced pneumonia and the contagious diseases as the child killers. Automobiles and other factors related to technology have also had an effect upon the mortality of children. Over ten thousand children between the ages of one and fourteen years are killed annually by accidents. Another large group is handicapped for life as a result of accidents. This has come to be the number-one killer of children, responsible for more than three times as many deaths in this age group as is pneumonia.

Tuberculosis in childhood. It is now generally agreed that childhood tuberculosis differs from tuberculosis during adulthood. It develops slowly, and since it is seldom accompanied by infection, it may not be detected during the early stages, except by X-ray tests or by some such means. The schools offer the most satisfactory opportunity for an early diagnosis of the tubercular predisposition. Various studies and surveys show a wide range of differences in the incidence of tubercular infection. There is a close relationship between living conditions and the frequency of tuberculosis among children. The best protection for the child against such infectious diseases is sufficient room to live in, sunlight, pure air, and favorable conditions for playing with other children. An early life of poverty that condemns children to a life of squalor and insufficient nutrition builds up a condition that protects the disease against the most intense efforts of the hygienist crusader. Since there has not yet been found a complete cure for poverty, the problem of protecting children against conditions that contribute to tubercular infection becomes a difficult one.

Tuberculosis presents a difficult problem to children, because of its abstract nature. When the child has measles, he has eruptions on his face; when he has whooping cough, he has spells of coughing; but when he has tuberculosis, he is sick but doesn't seem to have anything. This fact makes it more difficult for the child to accept his illness. Likewise, the treatment of tuberculosis is contrary to the child's drives and personality characteristics. Healthy children enjoy running, skipping, yelping, and physical activity in general. Severe conflict results from the variance of their desire for activity with the rest period prescribed for tubercular children. Tuberculosis furnishes a threat to the child's ego. He imagines other children referring to him as a TB case. He has the feeling that children will avoid him out of fear of contracting tuberculosis. He may so preoccupy himself with his condition, its causes, and the attitudes others are going to take toward him that recovery may not bring about a well-adjusted personality. Any treatment program, to be effective in caring for the whole child, must take into consideration these psychological factors so prevalent among the tubercular children.[49]

Heart disease—rheumatic fever. Heart disease is generally recognized as the greatest of all threats to the lives of American children. The toxins and antitoxins have aided in conquering diseases that were at one time feared by practically all homes. More recent discoveries have helped to dispel fears from any infectious diseases. "Heart trouble" among children is oftentimes looked upon with great fear, because it is either not understood or is misunderstood. As a result of this, some parents tend to restrict the activities of their children, others would direct them into special activities, while still others would control other aspects of their life activities. The most common form of heart disease among children is that associated with rheumatic fever. It has been estimated that in two out of every three cases there is some permanent impairment of the heart.[50]

Although rheumatic fever is a disease of all ages, preponderantly it involves children from the age of five to fifteen. It is the leading cause of heart disease between five and forty years of age. Rheumatic fever is an acute infection but the exact cause of it is unknown. It is known that 90 per cent of the cases follow or accompany "strep" sore throats, colds, and infection; that it usually appears in late winter and spring; and that poor nutrition seems to be a likely factor.

The most dangerous characteristic of the disease is its tendency to become chronic, with frequent, increasingly serious relapses. Susceptibility to the conditions that lead to the onset of rheumatic fever appears more common in some families than in others. A combination of poor appetite, persistent fever, increased pulse rate, and pain in the arms, legs, or abdomen should be looked upon as important symptoms of rheumatic fever. A child with these symptoms should be placed under the care of a physician as early as possible, since early care is closely related to recovery. Efforts should be made to keep the child in a cheerful mood, while he is under the care of the physician. Thus, the child should be kept occupied while at rest in bed. Usually his school work can be carried along satisfactorily after the acute stage of the disease has passed. Wholesome food and

[49] See Sara Dubo, Psychiatric study of children with pulmonary tuberculosis, *American Journal of Orthopsychiatry,* 1950, Vol. 20, pp. 520-528.

[50] Carl N. Neupert, Fighting rheumatic fever, *National Parent Teacher,* 1949, Vol. 44, pp. 7-9.

friendly treatment are especially important for the satisfactory recovery of the child.

Cancer during childhood. Cancer is usually thought of as a condition found only among adults. Although over 98 per cent of the
deaths from cancer occur among those over twenty, more than 2,800
deaths in 1947 occurred among children. This was more than ten
times the number killed by dreaded poliomyelitis.[51] More accurate
diagnosis of cancer in children and the recognition of leukemia as a
form of cancer has contributed to the increase in the number of
cases among children diagnosed as cancer. Perhaps 50 per cent of
cancer among youngsters appears as leukemia—a cancer of the bone
marrow which prevents normal blood formation. This condition has
sometimes been mistaken for anemia. Elmee Nash describes the case
of Marilyn, which illustrates such a condition.

Marilyn is responding to aminopterin, a drug discovered little more
than two years ago by two Boston doctors. Without aminopterin, little
leukemia patients usually die within two or three months. Since the drug
is so new, it's too early to judge whether its benefits are permanent or
only temporary. Up until a few months ago, aminopterin had to be administered by injections, but now it can be given by mouth.

Marilyn's case bears out a theory that leukemia often follows an infectious disease. After several weeks of intensive treatment in the hospital, she probably will be able to return home, feeling as well as a
normal child.[52]

Cancer among children develops more rapidly than among adults,
and is more likely to prove fatal. The fact that its symptoms are
recognized and that new methods are being used for its treatment
improves considerably the child's chances of recovery. Early discovery appears to bear the closest relationship to recovery. Thus,
children should be given regular and thorough examinations as a
means for checking on cancer as well as other disabling diseases.
If a lump or growth appears, the doctor's advice should be followed relative to its treatment or removal. The admonition of
avoiding quacks and home remedies is especially important in the
treatment of cancer at all ages. Educating the child about the symptoms and dangers of cancer is not especially important. It is the
parents' and teacher's responsibility to know about cancer, not the

[51] See the article, Is cancer a danger, *Woman's Home Companion,* March 1950,
pp. 34-35, 93.

[52] Elmee B. Nash, Your youngster can have cancer, *Better Homes and Gardens,*
February 1950, p. 141.

child's. This does not mean, of course, that the child should not be warned about aggravating lumps that appear or about following the recommendations of the doctor, but rather that undue concern on the part of the child may be more harmful than beneficial to his health and personal development.

Crippled children. The reported prevalence of crippled children will depend in part upon the criteria used in its evaluation. The *White House Conference Report* has summarized the results of a number of surveys. These surveys reveal that the prevalence varies considerably between different localities. Careful studies tend to agree that crippling conditions are most frequently found among the underprivileged children. Furthermore, crippling conditions at birth will be found more often among families that are constitutionally inferior. It might be stated as an explanatory principle that crippling conditions among children may be found among all family groups, but that they appear most often among the unfortunate and underprivileged. It was estimated by the United States Office of Education that in 1945 there were 336,040 children, aged five to nineteen, who were suffering from deformities or other crippling conditions.[53] Since 1935, when the Social Security Act was passed, the Children's Bureau has recorded information on the number and causes of cripples registered in the states and territories in accordance with that legislation. The number of children reported for the year 1944 for the different conditions is shown in Table 18.

It is significant that approximately four-fifths of these became crippled under six or seven years of age, and it is generally estimated that over one-half of these could be virtually cured if adequate treatment were given at a sufficiently early period. Infantile paralysis is responsible for almost one-third of the paralysis cases. This condition occurs more frequently with boys than with girls, and usually appears before the age of four or five. Figures from public health reports in North Carolina show the age distribution of the incidence of poliomyelitis there to be as follows:

Birth through five years 52 per cent
Ages six to thirteen years 25 per cent
Ages thirteen to eighteen years 8 per cent
Ages eighteen years and over 15 per cent [54]

[53] Romaine P. Mackie, *Crippled Children in School* (U.S. Office of Education Bulletin No. 5, 1948), p. 6.

[54] Beatrice J. Hurley, The handicapped child as a person, reprinted from *Understanding the Child,* 1949, Vol. 18, p. 9. Published by the National Committee for Mental Hygiene, New York.

TABLE 18   Number of crippled children as reported by the Children's Bureau for the year 1944

	Number of Cases	Per Cent of Cases
Poliomyelitis	62,373	18.3
Osteomyelitis	15,834	4.6
Tuberculosis of bones and joints	8,500	2.5
Cerebral palsy	33,380	9.9
Other birth paralyses	7,559	2.2
Cleft palate or harelip	14,899	4.4
Clubfoot	28,111	8.2
Congenital dislocation of hip	6,795	2.0
Spina bifida	4,644	1.4
Other congenital defect	26,414	7.7
Burn	7,521	2.2
Other injury	20,972	6.2
Rickets	13,684	4.0
Arthritis	6,601	1.9
Osteochondritis	4,327	1.2
Epiphyscolysis	2,525	.7
Scoliosis	10,419	3.1
Torticollis	3,981	1.2
Flatfoot	16,816	4.9
Muscular atrophy or dystrophy	3,367	1.0
Rheumatic fever or heart disease	5,499	1.6
All other definite diagnoses	28,647	8.4
Provisional diagnoses	8,154	2.4
Total	341,022	100.0

Other frequent causes of paralysis and palsies of different parts of the body may include birth injuries, hemorrhages, tumors and abscesses in the brain, or they may follow certain diseases such as diphtheria, typhoid fever, meningitis, and sometimes measles. Nerve and muscle paralysis usually follows accidents involving fractures, dislocations, or diseases affecting the bones, tendons, or joints.

Syphilis, tuberculosis of the bones, birth injuries, accidents, and malnutrition leading to rickets are some major causes of deformities of the skeletal frame. It was also suggested earlier in this chapter that certain posture habits and an unfavorable mental attitude tend to lead to bad posture and thus to deformities of the skeletal frame. All children should be observed for crippling conditions, and an examination given to those suffering from a physical deformity in order to ascertain more adequately the care and treatment that may be given the individual child.

Summary and implications

Growth begins with the fertilization of the egg cell, and birth extends the sphere of the activity of the individual. Heredity and environment interact to produce changes in the individual at each stage in his development. The physical growth of the child follows the principles set forth in Chapter 4. With the realization that growth follows an orderly sequence, that children grow at individual rates rather than according to group averages, that growth is characterized by periods of acceleration, and that different parts of the body grow at different rates, parents and teachers should provide opportunities for the child's growth and development and guidance in his development suitable to the individual child's physical status at the different stages in his growth.

There is a close relationship between the skeletal growth of the child and physiological development. This furnishes a basis for predicting the physiological development of the individual child. The development of the teeth and bony structure requires a diet that is adequate with respect to vitamin D. Dietary surveys show that the diets of many children are inadequate. Furthermore, these inadequacies are not confined to those in the lower income groups. There is a need for an educational program interrelated with the dietary habits of children at home, if such dietary deficiences are to be remedied.

Parents and teachers must recognize differences in body build in attempting to provide for the physical needs of children. Physical needs vary with children of the same age-height level. The differences in the needs are primarily quantitative rather than qualitative. Failure to recognize these differences in need leads to a variety of problems, among which are feeding problems during the early preschool years. Definite symptoms of malnutrition have been presented in this chapter. Parents and teachers can detect some of these symptoms, if they direct their observations toward them. As boys and girls develop into adolescence, their dietary needs increase. The needs continue to increase in the case of boys throughout the period of adolescence. Physical-education programs should take into careful consideration the dietary needs of pupils at different age levels, realizing at the same time that these will vary between individuals of the same age.

Posture has been discussed as a phase of the child's physical growth that should be given careful consideration. Bad posture usually results from a number of causes. Beneficial effects may be expected when these causes are understood, and when the individual concerned is motivated to improve his posture. Since the individual grows as a whole and all growth is interrelated (see Chapter 4), good posture, well-formed teeth, and physical health contribute to the development of all phases of the individual self.

Questions and Exercises

1. How early can individual differences in rates and patterns of growth be observed? Show how individual growth curves are helpful in observing these differences. What are some uses that may be made of such observations?
2. What are the different methods cited that have been used in studying the physical development of children? Give the advantages of each of these methods.
3. What items should be included in a complete examination of posture?
4. Compare the dietary needs of boys and girls at ages ten, twelve, and fourteen years. How would you account for the differences suggested for boys and girls?
5. What are the different methods for measuring anatomical development? What are some uses that can be made of anatomical measurements?
6. What factors might contribute to the dietary deficiencies of children from favorable income homes?
7. How do you account for the lack of attention and consideration given to childhood cancer? What cautions are suggested in this connection?
8. If data are available, study the five or six diseases that account for the greatest number of childhood deaths. How does the ranking here compare with the amount of attention given the different diseases?

Selected Readings

Breckenridge, Marion E., and Vincent, E. L. *Child Development.* 2nd ed.; Philadelphia: W. B. Saunders Co., 1949. Chap. VII.

Carlson, A., and Johnson, V. *The Machinery of the Body.* Chicago: University of Chicago Press, 1941.

Cole, Luella. *Psychology of Adolescence.* 3rd ed.; New York: Farrar and Rinehart, 1948. Chap. II.

Dearborn, W. F., and Rothney, J. W. M. *Predicting the Child's Development.* Cambridge, Mass.: Sci-Art Publishers, 1941. Chaps. I-VI.

Garrison, Karl C. *The Psychology of Exceptional Children.* rev. ed.; New York: The Ronald Press Co., 1950. Chap. III.

Garrison, Karl C. *Psychology of Adolescence.* 4th ed.; New York: Prentice-Hall, 1951. Chap. III.

Hardy, M. C., and Hoefer, C. H. *Healthy Growth: A Study of The Influence of Health Education on The Growth and Development of School Children.* Chicago: University of Chicago Press, 1936.

Hurlock, Elizabeth B., *Child Development.* 2nd ed.; New York: McGraw-Hill Book Co., 1950. Chap. V.

Johnson, R. L., and Kelly, H. G. Growth charts for use in pediatric practice, *Journal of Pediatrics,* 1945. Chap. 27, p. 215. Useful charts are given which will enable the advanced student to explore further their use in research and pediatric practice.

Keliher, A. V. *Life and Growth.* New York: Appleton-Century-Crofts, 1941. Chaps. VI-VIII.

McCloy, C. H. The child's physical characteristics, *Nineteenth Yearbook of the National Elementary Principal,* 1940. Vol. 19, pp. 260-272.

Meredith, Howard, The rhythm of physical growth, *University of Iowa Studies in Child Welfare,* 1935. Vol. XI, No. 3, 1935.

Olson, Willard C. *Child Development.* Boston: D. C. Heath and Company, 1949. Chap. III.

Simmons, Katherine. The Brush Foundation Studies of Child Growth and Development II. Physical Growth and Development. *Monographs of the Society for Research in Child Development,* 1944. Vol. 9, No. 1.

Thompson, Helen. *Physical Growth,* in *Manual in Child Psychology* (L. Carmichael, ed.). New York: John Wiley and Sons, 1946. Chap. V.

Thorpe, Louis P. *Child Psychology and Development.* New York: The Ronald Press Co., 1946. Chap. VII.

Vickers, V. S., and Stuart, H. C. Anthropology in the pediatrician's office. Norms for selected body measurements based on studies of children of North European stock, *Journal of Pediatrics,* 1943. Vol. 22, pp. 155-170. Norms are here presented which may be useful for those concerned with comparative scores.

For a very complete review of studies bearing on physical development see Growth and Development, *Review of Educational Research,* 1947, No. 5, Chaps. VI-VIII.

6

The Development
of Motor Skills

Sequence of motor and sensory development

The development of behavior patterns. The infant is a growing, dynamic individual. He is very immature, however, in his behavior patterns. As he develops, new behavior patterns emerge according to an orderly process, referred to in Chapter 4. Gesell suggests that these are "fundamentally determined by intrinsic growth factors that may be used as criteria for appraising the maturity and integrity of the nervous system."[1] By means of schematic observations of the behavior growth of a large group of infants at varying intervals, he was able to formulate developmental schedules. These were developed for four major fields of behavior as follows:

(1) *Motor behavior:* posture and locomotion; prehension and manipulation; gross and fine coordination.

(2) *Adaptive behavior:* self-initiated and induced behavior; learning; resourcefulness in adjusting to new situations; exploitive behavior.

(3) *Language behavior:* vocalizations, vocal signs; words, gestures; comprehension.

(4) *Personal social behavior:* relations to persons; response to gesture and speech; socialized learning; habits of self help.[2]

Normative behavior traits were codified in the form of a schedule. A schedule was then prepared for behavior at twenty-four weeks, twenty-eight weeks, and thirty-two weeks. A careful study of the behavior for different age levels makes it possible for the student to

[1] Arnold Gesell, *Studies in Child Development* (New York: Harper & Brothers, 1948). P. 183.
[2] *Ibid.*, p. 184.

understand the developmental characteristics of the average infant at the age levels represented. This is not, however, a psychological test that is numerically and mechanically scored. The schedule reveals a gradual and continuous growth in the complexity of behavior performed at these three age levels. The maturation process clearly operates in the development of better co-ordination and more specific forms of behavior. The development of behavior patterns is further illustrated in the achievement of erect locomotion in the human infant. The walking movements of infants were carefully studied by Myrtle McGraw with seven phases of the development of upright locomotion being noted.[3] These are shown in Figure 13. The first stage (A) has been characterized as *the newborn or reflex stepping phase*. This is followed by (B) *the inhibitory or static phase*. After this comes an important development referred to as (C) *the transition phase*. Stage (D) is the beginning of the stepping and is called *the deliberate stepping phase*. A progressive development of locomotion is shown in the next three stages. These are referrd to as: (E) *the independent stepping phase*, (F) *the heel-toe progression*, and (G) *the integrated or motive phase of erect locomotion*. According to McGraw, these progressive changes in locomotion development indicate that neuromuscular development involving cortical participation operates in the development of erect locomotion.

Sequence of motor development. Motor development does not occur in a haphazard manner, but rather according to fundamental principles of growth set forth in Chapter 4. It follows a developmental process and takes place in an orderly manner. Control first occurs in the head area, then in the arms and upper trunk, afterward in the lower trunk, and finally in the legs and feet. In this connection, it is interesting to note that motor development follows the same course as that presented in earlier chapters for physical development.

Experimental studies of children during the first years of life furnish a basis for determining the status of a child's motor development. The *California Infant Scale of Motor Development*, devised by Bayley, shows what one can expect in the way of motor skills of the average child during the first three or four years.[4] The materials presented in Table 19 show how his motor development begins with the control of the head. This growth in motor control gradually

[3] Myrtle B. McGraw, Neuromuscular development of the human infant as exemplified in the achievement of erect locomotion, *Journal of Pediatrics*, 1940, Vol. 17, p. 750.

[4] N. Bayley, The development of motor abilities during the first three years, *Monographs of the Society for Research in Child Development*, 1935, No. 1, p. 3.

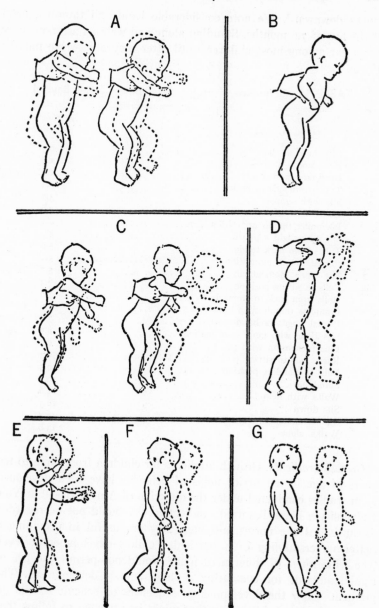

FIG. 13 Line drawings illustrating seven phases of the development of
erect locomotion

(After McGraw)

moves downward. We note considerable hand and thumb control at the age of 7.6 months. Standing alone and walking are not likely to appear among most children until after they are twelve months of age.

TABLE 19 Sequence of motor development (after Bayley)

Motor Performances	Age Placement in Months
Lifts head at shoulder	0.5
Head erect—vertical	1.9
Head erect and steady	2.9
Turns from side to back	3.4
Sits with support	3.5
Holds head steady	3.6
Beginning thumb opposition	4.1
Sits with slight support	4.6
Turns from back to side	5.0
Partial thumb opposition	5.1
Sits alone momentarily	5.7
Pulls to sitting position	6.2
Rolls from back to stomach	7.0
Complete thumb opposition	7.6
Partial finger prehension	7.8
Sits alone with good coordination	8.5
Fine prehension with pellet	9.3
Raises self to sitting position	9.4
Pulls to standing position	10.5
Stands up	10.6
Walks with help	11.6
Sits down	12.5
Stands alone	12.5
Walks alone	13.0

Growth gradients. Growth gradients for children from birth to ten years of age in ten major fields of behavior have been developed from studies conducted under the direction of Arnold Gesell at Yale University.[5] These itemized gradient levels should not be regarded as statistical age norms, although they are useful in providing a better understanding of a particular child's developmental level. The wide range of differences found would not permit the use of rigid standards for evaluating a child's motor development. The gradients show the developmental sequences of behavior—thus indicating the type of behavior that might be expected to follow that

[5] Arnold Gesell and Frances L. Ilg, *The Child From Five to Ten* (New York: Harper & Brothers, 1949).

manifested at some particular stage in the child's growth. The gradients may be looked upon as charts for interpreting the child's growth stage at a particular time.

At one year of age, the child walks, with the assistance of someone who holds one of his hands. By the age of two, he runs, nods his head, and shows certain rhythmical responses. He has also grown during this year in eye-hand co-ordination. At one year of age, he is able to place toys in a convenient container, whereas at two years of age he is able to fit toys together.

This gradual growth is further revealed throughout the succeeding years. At three, he walks erect, runs, gallops, and is able to erect things with blocks. At four years of age, he makes more complicated structures with his blocks, uses scissors, and enjoys manipulating more complex toys. By the age of five, his posture is predominantly symmetrical, with good co-ordination in reaching and grasping objects. By the age of six, when he enters school, he is normally very active—displaying good co-ordination. He may attempt things beyond his ability, and needs assistance and guidance in his motor development. He plays active games, skips to music, builds with blocks, and climbs on tables. Little sex difference is noted in children's general activity at this time, except where cultural forces have directed the sexes into specific play patterns.

Causes of retardation in walking. Peatman and Higgons conclude from an analysis of the ages for sitting, standing, and walking of 349 babies that age differences result primarily from internal rather than external conditions.[6] They point out further that after the muscular and skeletal development has advanced sufficiently for sitting, standing, and walking, the further course of the child's locomotor development will vary in accordance with other phases of learned activities. These differences are attributed to differences in the dynamics, needs, and responsiveness of the individual children. Bruch observed, however, that 72 per cent of 140 obese children were significantly below normal in their physical activity.[7] A large percentage of these children were lacking in the ability and drive to care for themselves.

Wayne Dennis has postulated the theory that there are multiple requirements for the onset of walking, and if any one of these re-

[6] J. G. Peatman and R. A. Higgons, Relation of infant's weight and body build to locomotor development, *American Journal of Orthopsychiatry*, 1942, Vol. 10, pp. 88-110.

[7] H. Bruch, Obesity in childhood. IV. Energy expenditure in obese children, *American Journal of Diseases in Children*, 1940, Vol. 60, pp. 1082-1109.

quirements is not met, walking will be delayed.[8] He further suggests that these different requirements are met at various times rather than simultaneously. Precocious walking, on the other hand, will not take place until all these requirements are met. The failure of gifted children to walk at an early age, although inferior intelligence is related to delay in walking, is cited as evidence for this postulate. There is good evidence that the following factors may operate to delay walking:

1. Rickets or other conditions which interfere with the hardening of the bones.
2. Prolonged illness appearing near the period when walking would ordinarily begin.
3. Unusual size in the form of excessive fat.
4. Low intelligence.
5. Sensory handicaps, especially visual and auditory, appearing from or near birth.
6. Severe restriction of practice.
7. Lack of motivation or incentive for walking.

The development of perceptual behavior. It has been observed from studies of the development of visual perception that children as young as two years of age can distinguish triangularity from a number of visual forms.[9] In this test the children succeeded in discriminating between very closely related figures. Gellerman points out that "The verbal behavior of the children indicated that they had formulated the problem verbally and that their behavior was partly controlled by verbal processes." Comparisons were made between the learning of these two-year-old children and two chimpanzees with estimated ages of five years and six years. In the main, identical procedures were used with all subjects. In this as well as in subsequent studies, involving the efficacy of form versus background in the discrimination of visual patterns, the children proved superior to the chimpanzees. The superiority of the children appears to be closely associated with their utilization of verbal behavior (symbolic processes) which enabled them to short-circuit the solution of problems. Thus, there is a rather clear indication of the development of perceptual behavior as early as two years of age.

An investigation of the occurrence and development of tactual

---

[8] Wayne Dennis, On the possibility of advancing and retarding the motor development of infants, *Psychological Review*, 1943, Vol. 50, pp. 203-218.

[9] L. W. Gellerman, Form discrimination in chimpanzee and two-year-old children, *Journal of Genetic Psychology*, 1933, Vol. 42, pp. 3-27.

form perception among preschool children was conducted by O'Neill.[10] In order to explore tactual skill in making form discriminations, and to compare it with visual skill in making the same discriminations, a number of pairs of wooden blocks of a type that the subjects could readily handle or regard visually were used. Thus, seven pairs of blocks were designed and fashioned: spheres, cubes, triangular prisms, cones, pyramids, hexagonal prisms, and cylinders.

Twelve subjects, six boys and six girls, were included in each of the age groups studied. The subjects ranged from three to six years of age. These subjects were divided into eight six-month age groups. The number of errors in tactual and visual discrimination made by the different age groups is shown in Table 20. O'Neill concluded from this study: "Among the younger subjects (three and four years) there is a considerable variation in the ability to discriminate tactually between various forms. ... By contrast there is but little variation among the older subjects since virtually all of them are skillful in either the visual or tactual discrimination of form at the level of difficulty presented by the present experiment."[11]

TABLE 20 Mean number of errors in tactual and visual discrimination of form (grouped by half-year intervals). N represents the number of subjects (after O'Neill)

Age	Boys			Girls			Both Sexes		
	N	Tactual	Visual	N	Tactual	Visual	N	Tactual	Visual
3-3	6	6.0	1.67	6	9.17	1.0	12	7.58	1.33
3-9	6	5.83	1.33	6	8.83	.33	12	7.33	.83
4-3	6	3.33	1.0	6	3.0	1.33	12	3.15	1.15
4-9	6	3.67	1.0	6	2.83	1.0	12	3.25	1.0
5-3	6	2.0	.17	6	2.17	.33	12	2.08	.25
5-9	6	1.33	.33	6	2.67	.17	12	2.0	.25
6-3	6	1.0	0	6	.67	0	12	.83	0
6-9	6	.33	0	6	.33	0	12	.33	0

The greater errors among the younger group in tactual perception over those in visual perception suggests that the development of tactual form perception lags behind the development of visual form perception. A difference was noted in the ways the subjects of different age levels handled the blocks. There was a gradual advancement from "simple closure" to "active rotation" with increased age.

[10] John Carroll O'Neill, The occurrence and development of tactual form perception in preschool children, Master's thesis, University of Oregon, 1948.
[11] Ibid., p. 54.

Growth in motor abilities

Eye-hand co-ordination. The increase in muscular co-ordination among nursery-school children is evident from observations over a short period of time. This thought was introduced in connection with the sequences of motor development. Reaching and grasping objects in one's environment require eye-hand co-ordination, or the working together of the muscles of the hands and of the eyes. This is not present in the random movements of the infant child, but appears during the first months, so that the child at seven or eight months no longer depends upon random movements to grasp his rattle or other objects about him.

The development of eye-hand co-ordination was studied by Watson and Watson by suspending a stick of candy within reach of the subject.[12] During the first four months the reaching and grasping of the infant child were poorly co-ordinated—the movements were slow, randomlike, clumsy, and without thumb opposition. A well-co-ordinated movement was noted, however, by the 171st day, and most infants at this time showed a preference for the right hand. Observations of the movements and posture of the infant child following the sixth month shows that the child is able to pick up objects that he reaches for. His movements are guided by his eye, which is kept on the object. The preferred hand takes the lead, with the other hand following, since he is reaching with both hands. Reaching-prehensile behavior of infants has been analyzed by McGraw.[13] The following six phases were observed:

1. The newborn or passive phase. A newborn infant will close the fingers and grip an object if it is placed in his hand; however there is no apparent connection between such grasping and the visual and neuro-muscular movements educed.

2. The object-vision phase. "Fixation convergence and accommodation without distinct neuro-muscular movements in the direction of the visual stimulus are the essential qualities which characterize this phase." At the onset of object-vision, there is an abatement of diffuse movements.

3. The visual-motor phase. The responses in this phase disclose visual and motor interaction without much evidence of purposeful activity.

---

[12] J. B. Watson and R. R. Watson, Studies in infant psychology, *Scientific Monthly,* 1921, Vol. 13, pp. 493-515.

[13] Myrtle B. McGraw, Neural maturation as exemplified in the reaching-prehensile behavior of the human infant, *Journal of Psychology,* 1941, Vol. 11, pp. 127-141.

The most important characteristic of the movements during this phase is their *autonomous* quality.

4. The manipulative and deliberate phase. This phase is especially characterized by "sustained attention upon the object during the reaching-prehension movements and the deliberate quality of the action. During the early stages the child may move his arm toward the object and draw the arm back without actually touching the object.

5. The visual release phase. This phase is an extension of the manipulative and deliberate phase in that the digits are more extended and sustained attention is no longer demanded in carrying out a motor performance, such as reaching for an article.

6. The mature phase. In this phase the child is able to appraise the location and nature of the object without giving undue attention to it. Both the visual and neuro-muscular aspects are reduced to the minimum essentials for the motor performance.

Age and reaction time. By means of the *Miles Reaction Board,* Florence Goodenough studied the speed of reaction to a predominantly auditory stimulus of subjects ranging in age from three and one-half years to adulthood.[14] The results revealed a marked degree of improvement with age. Goodenough points out that the improvement in voluntary control, shown in the reduction of useless accessory movements and decreased bodily tension, is even more marked than the increased speed of reaction. There was a slight sex difference found in favor of the males as early as three and one-half years of age; however, considerable overlapping exists.

A decrease in reaction time with age was observed in a study by Philip.[15] Boys and girls between the ages of nine and sixteen were used as subjects, and were tested for speed of reaction to light and sound. The boys were found to have a reaction time from 3 to 5 per cent faster than girls; however, there was a continuous improvement in average reaction time with age for both boys and girls.

Thirty-two carefully selected children, a boy and a girl at each six-month age level from two to seven years and at each age level from seven to twelve years, were used as subjects in a study of the behavior pattern of throwing.[16] Three overhand throws were executed

[14] Florence L. Goodenough, The development of the reactive process from early childhood to maturity, *Journal of Experimental Psychology,* 1935, Vol. 18, pp. 431-450.

[15] B. R. Philip, Reaction time of children, *American Journal of Psychology,* 1934, Vol. 46, pp. 379-396.

[16] Monica R. Wild, The behavior pattern of throwing and some observations concerning its course of development in children, *The Research Quarterly,* Oct., 1938, Vol. 9, pp. 20-24.

by each subject. These were filmed and carefully analyzed. Typical age patterns for the arm and body movements were observed. The trend was toward better mechanical means of projection and more advantageous timing. The age changes were closely related to developmental changes present in other forms of growth. Wild concludes: "Maturational factors are believed to be operative as the basic type patterns of throwing develop; learning, particularly after six years, greatly influences the skill pattern individuating out of and upon the basic growth stage; it may be the factor accountable for differences in performances, especially those so evident between the sexes."

Age and motor skills. Investigations of the development of motor skills among children show that ability at different motor tasks improves with age. A group of motor achievement tests was admin-

TABLE 21 Average scores obtained by five-, six-, and seven-year-old boys and girls in motor performances (after Jenkins)

	Five-Year-Olds		Six-Year-Olds		Seven-Year-Olds	
	Boys	Girls	Boys	Girls	Boys	Girls
Vertical Jump (Distance in inches)	2.52	2.22	4.02	3.48	4.98	4.28
Running Broad Jump (Distance in inches)	34.40	28.60	45.20	40.00	58.89	50.80
Standing Broad Jump (Distance in inches)	33.70	31.60	39.30	38.00	42.40	41.00
Thirty - Five - Yard Dash (Time in seconds)	9.30	9.70	8.52	8.84	7.92	8.02
Fifty - Foot Hop Without Error (Time in seconds)	10.82	10.33	9.20	8.89	8.81	7.59
Baseball Throw (Distance in feet)	23.60	14.50	32.80	17.80	41.40	24.40
Baseball Throw at 10-foot Distant Target (Error in inches)	8.87	16.90	5.40	13.17	4.28	8.50

istered by Jenkins to 300 white children enrolled in the public schools of Montclair and Englewood, New Jersey.[17] These children were distributed into age groups of five, six, and seven years. There were fifty boys and fifty girls in each age group. The results from the various tests are presented in Table 21. In the abilities tested, the

[17] L. M. Jenkins, A comparative study of motor achievement of children of five, six, and seven years of age, Teachers College, Columbia University, *Contributions to Education*, No. 414, 1930.

boys were, in general, superior to the girls, except for the fifty-foot hop. There was, furthermore, a gradual and consistent improvement observed during the three-year period. In the study by Espenschade, measurements were taken at six-month intervals, and averages determined for each half-year age level.[18] Boys and girls were tested during the period commonly referred to as adolescence. The results for the fifty-yard dash and the broad jump are given in Figures 14 and 15. On the fifty-yard dash there is a continuous increase from age 13.25 to and beyond age 16. The best performance

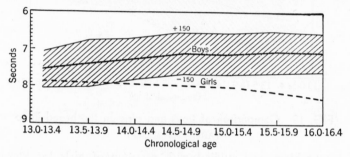

FIG. 14 Comparison of boys and girls on the fifty-yard dash
(After Espenschade)

for the girls was reached at 13.25 years of age. After this period there was a gradual decline; however, the decrease was slight during the next two years, and accelerated after the latter part of their fifteenth year. In the broad jump there is a significant increase in ability for boys from age 12.75 years to 16.5 years, with the most rapid increase during the ages of 14 and 15. A gradual and continuous decrease in this ability was noted for girls from ages 13 to 16.5 years. These activities are quite strenuous in nature, and this perhaps accounts for the lack of motivation and decrease of ability among girls during adolescence. This lack of motivation on the part of adolescent girls, combined with changes in body proportion, seems to provide a logical explanation for the continuous decline in these abilities among girls from age 13 through age 16.5.

Age and flexibility. It was pointed out in Chapter 3 that the plasticity of the bones of the small child provided for greater flexibility during the earlier years of life than that found in the individual as he progresses toward maturity. This is especially noticeable in the

[18] Anna Espenschade, Motor performance in adolescence, *Monographs of the Society for Research in Child Development*, 1940, Vol. 5, No. 1.

way that the baby can put his toes in his mouth and the position he oftentimes assumes while asleep. Thus, while strength and muscular co-ordination increases rapidly with age, in certain respects the bones of the body become less flexible.

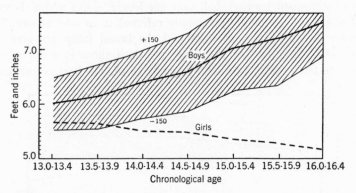

FIG. 15   Comparison of boys and girls on the broad jump
(After Espenschade)

This problem was studied with a group of girls by Florence Hupprich.[19] Her study had as its purposes, (1) to determine whether flexibility is a general or specific factor, and (2) to ascertain the trends in the development of flexibility of girls of the ages from six to eighteen years. Measurements of flexibility of twelve areas of the body were obtained from 300 girls from the public schools and the University of Oregon. The subjects ranged in age from five years and six months to eighteen years and six months and were grouped as follows:

Group I	100 cases	17 years, 6 months to 18 years, 6 months
Group II	50 cases	14 years, 6 months to 15 years, 6 months
Group III	50 cases	11 years, 6 months to 12 years, 6 months
Group IV	50 cases	8 years, 6 months to 9 years, 6 months
Group V	50 cases	5 years, 6 months to 6 years, 6 months

[19] Florence L. Hupprich, A study of flexibility of girls in five age groups, Doctor's thesis, University of Oregon, 1949.

The Leighton Flexometer was used for measuring flexibility. The reliability coefficients for the measurements used in this varied from .911 for leg abduction to .972 for trunk-hip flexion-tension. The data were analyzed statistically as well as through studies of individual cases to find evidence of the specificity or generality of flexibility as a characteristic. Only six cases of the 300 girls reached their respective age-group averages in all twelve measures of flexibility. A study of individual records showed that 25 of the 300 girls were very flexible in two or more joints and also very inflexible in two or more other joints. All age groups showed these extremes of flexibility. The ages at which the greatest specific range of movements were found and the degree of movement at each age level are presented in Table 22. The results from this study show that flexibility among girls does not increase after the age of twelve. Also, flexibility of the shoulder, knee, and thigh is greater at six years of age than at any of the later ages studied. Flexibility of head rotation seems to reach its peak at age nine.

TABLE 22   Ages in which the greatest specific range of movements are found (after Hupprich)

Joint	18 years	15 years	12 years	9 years	6 years
Hip			139.10°		
Trunk-hip			185.20°		
Side trunk			118.34°		
Head flex-extension			134.90°		
Elbow			157.42°		
Wrist			155.10°		
Ankle			76.94°		
Leg abduction			53.94°		
Head rotation				174.10°	
Shoulder					228.40°
Knee					130.62°
Thigh					111.78°

Strength and development. The total relative strength of the body has been found to correlate highly with results of medical examinations. Relative strength has been expressed in terms of a quotient, referred to as *physical fitness index,* which is the strength of an individual divided by the average strength of a group of persons similar in age, sex, and weight. Age and sex standards are available for elementary-school children. Many tests of strength are too expensive for general use. One of the simplest tests of physical abilities is that for strength of grip. The materials presented at a later point in this chapter show that the development of strength as measured by dynamometers is closely related to physiological development and maturity. Dynamometers have been devised for measuring the strength of arm pull, arm push, leg lift, back lift, finger grip, and the like.

A number of studies have shown a positive relationship between sexual maturing and strength. Harold Jones has presented data showing the total strength (a composite based on right grip, left grip, pulling strength, and thrusting strength) of premenarcheal and postmenarcheal girls.[20] These data are presented in Table 23 for girls of the same chronological age but different in sexual maturity. However, the early- and late-maturing girls reach similar strength levels at maturity, but through somewhat different growth patterns. These results give further support to the hypothesis that endocrine factors that tend to promote early pubertal growth also tend to bring about an early arrest of growth.

TABLE 23 A comparison of premenarcheal and postmenarcheal cases in total strength (after Jones)

| Age | N | Premenarcheal | | Postmenarcheal | | |
		Mean (kg.)	S. D.	N	Mean (kg.)	S. D.
12.25	63	86.0	16.30	15	100.6	15.55
12.75	44	92.0	16.35	24	105.6	15.30
13.25	25	93.0	16.20	37	108.8	16.35
13.75	20	97.1	16.35	54	105.6	16.50
14.25	17	100.7	19.50	63	107.9	18.00

Significant relations have been reported by investigators between dynamic and static strength and certain physical measurements. Dynamic strength has reference to the abilities involved in action such as running, jumping, and the like while static strength is usually measured by dynamometric tests. Correlations were obtained in a study by Bowers and reported by Jones between total strength and scores in track events, and such variables as chronological age, skeletal age, height, popularity, "good looks," and intelligence, based on average mental ages from two forms of a group intelligence

[20] Harold E. Jones, The sexual maturing of girls as related to growth in strength, *Research Quarterly*, 1947, Vol. 18, pp. 135-143. The data of Table 23 are based on materials from a Master's thesis by M. E. Caldwell, *On the Strength of Adolescent Girls*, Berkeley: University of California, 1940.

test.[21] These correlations are given in Table 24. An interesting feature of these results is that while chronological age and physical measurements correlate highest with total strength, popularity and "good looks" are more closely related to gross motor scores. This is to be expected, when one realizes the prestige value of motor performances among adolescent boys. The low correlation between motor performances and intelligence is also significant.

TABLE 24 Motor performance correlations with other developmental traits for boys (after Jones)

Variable	Total strength (grip, pull, thrust)	Gross motor scores (track events)
Chronological age	.29 ± .06	.18 ± .07
Skeletal age	.50 ± .035	.36 ± .06
Height	.65 ± .04	.40 ± .06
Popularity	.30 ± .07	.39 ± .06
"Good Looks"	.21 ± .07	.38 ± .06
Intelligence	−.17 ± .07	.05 ± .08

The mean scores for early-, average-, and late-maturing boys and girls for strength of grip of the right hand have been reported by Jones.[22] The results showed that the early-maturing boys and girls are significantly ahead in strength of grip during the early years studied. The average curves of growth in strength of grip for the three groups of boys are more or less parallel at all age levels, with the early-maturing boys remaining ahead and the average-maturing boys falling about midway between the early- and late-maturing group. This was not the case for the adolescent girls at all age levels. Although the early-maturing girls were ahead at the age of thirteen, they fail to maintain their superiority in the subsequent years, and actually drop below that of the average-maturing group. This is in harmony with results obtained relative to height and weight. Thus, precocious sexual development of girls appears to be associated with early arrest in physical and motor development; this is not true for boys.

Some sex differences. The data presented from the studies by Espenschade show that girls begin registering a decline in most track and field activities by the time they reach their fifteenth birthday, if the decline has not set in prior to this time. The development of

[21] See Harold E. Jones, *Motor Performance and Growth* (Berkeley and Los Angeles: University of California Press, 1949), Chap. II.
[22] *Ibid.*, p. 57.

physical fitness was studied by Jokl and Cluver among a group of boys and girls from five to twenty years of age.[23] Although no differences in performance were noted for the various racial groups involved, constitutional factors appeared to affect the physical ability of the children more than did the environmental. Endurance, measured by the 600-yard run, improved for both boys and girls during the six- to the thirteen-year-age period. There was little sex difference in improvement up to the age of thirteen. After this age, however, boys continued to improve, while the girls declined in efficiency, so that in the age-range from seventeen to twenty years the girls' mean ability was about that of the average six- to eight-year-olds. This decline in efficiency was reflected in their pulse rate, respiration, and fatigue as well as in their running time. The early interests of girls in social activities, and their desire to be "feminine" in nature no doubt affect their lack of interest in participating in athletics and in other forms of muscular activities.

The study of adolescent boys and girls by Espenschade, referred to on page 133, provides some interesting comparisons of sex differences. The tests comprising the *Brace Test* were given at school during the regular school day. The items making up this test are classified as: class I, agility; class II, control; class III, strength; and class IV, static balance. The Test consists of twenty items selected so as to include a wide variety of co-ordinations not frequently practiced. A comparison of the scores of boys and girls on the different test items showed that only slight differences appeared in total scores or in measures of the various classes before the age of 13.8 years. After this age, boys excelled in all events and their superiority increased rapidly at each age level. The most outstanding difference between the boys and girls was in the "push-up" test, which is classed as one of the strength tests. The greatest similarity was in the test, "sit, then stand again, with arms folded and feet crossed." This is classed under the control tests, and it is in this category that girls made their best showing. Their poorest showing was made on the tests of agility and strength. The following items are presented as a summary of the results:

1. The increment pattern for boys of total scores on the Brace Test battery is similar to that of adolescent growth in standing height. Scores for girls show little change after the thirteenth year.

2. The stunts of the Brace Test battery were placed in four general

23 E. Jokl and E. H. Cluver, Physical fitness, *Journal of the American Medical Association,* 1941, Vol. 116, pp. 2383-2389.

classes according to the predominant type of muscular action demanded. Additional elements necessary for performance were noted. "Dynamic balance," especially, is important in many events.

3. Boys show an increase in ability to perform events of all classes. The rate of growth is greater after 14 years of age than before and appears to be more rapid in "agility" than in "control."

4. The tests for boys in which "dynamic balance" is a factor show a marked "adolescent lag." . . .

5. Girls improve in "agility" up to 14 years, then decline. In "control" and in "flexibility and balance," little change can be seen over the age range studied. . . .[24]

Hand dominance and motor development

The usefulness of the hands in the performance of various motor activities is well known; however, the average person does not realize the potentialities for training in motor performances residing in the hands and in man's neuromuscular structure. The modern school program had its beginning as a reading school, with special emphasis being given to the reading of the Scriptures. Very little attention has been devoted to training in motor skills. As a result, the majority of boys and girls fail to develop a large percentage of their potential abilities for motor skills.

Laterality of function. Various theories have been presented dealing with the causes of hand dominance. Schiller presents a rather complete review of studies conducted prior to 1936.[25] A study by Dennis of laterality of function in early infancy dealt with laterality aspects of the behavior of two infants.[26] These infants were restricted and supervised in their activities from an early age. Nevertheless, laterality preferences developed and these were attributed to responses to particular situations rather than to some general trait resulting from cortical asymmetry. Gesell points out that these appear very early in life as part of the individuality of the child. On the basis of cinema-analysis observations he states:

Every infant seems to have what may be called a motor habitude or characteristicness which expresses itself in postural demeanor and modes of movement. . . . One of the most accessible of these is laterality, and

[24] Anna Espenschade, Development of motor coordination in boys and girls, *Research Quarterly,* 1947, Vol. 18, pp. 30-43.

[25] A. Schiller, Theories of handedness, *Journal of Applied Psychology,* 1936, Vol. 20, pp. 77-92.

[26] Wayne Dennis, Laterality of function in early infancy under controlled developmental conditions, *Child Development,* 1935, Vol. 6, pp. 242-252.

even this presented wide variation among the five individuals. By laterality we mean right or left predilection or predominance in motor adjustment. One of our infants (Girl A) showed unmistakable left-handedness as early as twenty-eight weeks. She has remained definitely left-handed for five years. . . . Boy A showed a less marked tendency to left-handedness. Boy D has been emphatically right-handed. Foot dominance was determined by a careful study of the preferred foot used in prone progression. Boy D showed a right-foot dominance at thirty-six weeks; Boy A, left-foot dominance at forty weeks; Girl B and Boy B left-foot dominance at forty-eight weeks. This dominance is a well-established trait, but we do not know how late in life it persists.[27]

Gertrude Hildreth offers evidence to show that right-handedness is a product of the development of civilization and particularly of the development of the use of tools and mechanical devices. She states:

. . . Effective motor adjustments require an active hand and an auxiliary hand. Uneven handedness, and complementary manual co-ordination, with one hand in the dominant rôle, is considered to be practically the only certain test of civilization, and may be regarded as a social symbol.
There are two kinds of manual skill in which hand dominance is a factor: (a) Skills performed entirely or largely with one hand alone; unimanual skills such as using a spoon, eating pie with a fork, shaking hands, writing, turning a key in a lock; (b) bimanual skills that demand the complementary use of both hands, with one hand dominating. Most handedness tasks, even writing, are two-handed, for the right-handed writer uses his left to steady the paper or to push it along.[28]

There is a common tendency to classify people as right- or left-handed. Studies of the laterality of individuals in the performance of different tasks show handedness varies with situations and circumstances, and must be regarded as relative rather than exclusive in nature. When the teacher speaks of a girl's being left-handed, she usually means that the girl writes with her left hand; whereas her big brother is regarded by his peers as right-handed, since he throws a ball with his right hand. Even the normal right-handed person develops skill in the use of his left hand for doing certain tasks. One boy observed recently was definitely right-handed, but

[27] Arnold Gesell, Early evidences of individuality in the human infant, *Scientific Monthly*, 1946, Vol. 45, pp. 221-222.

[28] Gertrude Hildreth, The development and training of hand dominance: I. Characteristics of handedness, *Journal of Genetic Psychology*, 1949, Vol. 75, p. 199.

dealt playing cards with his left hand. Women usually button their clothes with their left hand. Driving an automobile requires the use of both hands. In playing musical instruments, raking leaves, and other activities requiring the use of both hands, each hand learns to play its particular role. The hands may be said to complement each other; their particular roles are learned as part of the total behavior act.

Developmental difficulties associated with handedness. Hildreth has suggested that the handedness habit displayed in early childhood becomes the pattern the child is likely to have as an adult. This notion finds support from the fact that with age there is an increased strengthening of hand preference due to habit formation and cultural influences. Prejudice against left-handedness has persisted since earliest times; however, this has tended to become less within recent years. Just a few decades ago, parents and teachers were concerned with trying to change over all left-handed writers to righthanders. Due largely to some speech difficulties that seemed to emerge from this, there was a strong reaction among certain groups against changing handedness. The more recent emphasis in child development on allowing the child greater freedom in his choices and actions has tended to permit more children to use the hand they prefer. Thus, the number of left-handed children has increased during the past two decades. There are, however, a number of reasons why handedness deserves attention in child training. These have been listed by Hildreth as follows:

1. Achieving handedness is essentially a learning process involving habit formation, spontaneous reactions, postural adjustment, expression of choice, and responding in social situations.

2. The learning and adjustment process begins in infancy and is not completed until adulthood.

3. Emotional conflicts may arise due to the type of training the child receives.

4. There are physiological, neurological, and motor factors to be considered in handedness.

5. Individual differences are very great.

6. Conflicting theories influence training practices.

7. The question of whether handedness is hereditary or environmentally conditioned has never been satisfactorily answered.

8. There appears to be a connection between handedness and speech, as well as between handedness and learning to read, write, and spell.

Dr. Gesell believes this phase of growth is so important that it should be included in every clinical examination.

In this industrial age with greater demands being made on manual dexterity and with greater liability to manual incapacity, training the hands for fullest performance becomes a matter of great concern to employers. All clinicians, psychologists, and vocational counsellors should be prepared to give advice on this subject.[29]

Inconsistent hand dominance, or conflicts resulting from efforts to change dominance after handedness has been established, may result in emotional or motor difficulties. Bryngelson and Rutherford have presented statistical data from seventy-four stutterers and seventy-four nonstutterers, showing the histories of handedness. They show "four times as much ambidexterity in the stuttering group as in the control group, and approximately eight times as much shifting of handedness is experienced by the stutterers."[30] In a nervous child any interference with immature habits may result in special nervous difficulties, such as that encountered in stuttering. Such difficulties are more likely to arise during the early childhood years when motor development is relatively immature and many new adjustments are being made. The manner in which the change is made is especially important in this connection. Where the change is accompanied by continuous reminders, nagging, and mental confusion, nervousness and other ill-effects may result.

Ocular dominance and laterality. According to the studies by Gesell, eye movements develop during infancy ahead of hand movements. The infant, therefore, gains control over eye movements before he achieves control over the movements of the hands. Hildreth contends that eye dominance develops as a function of maturity in relation to activities involving eye-hand co-ordination. Eye dominance, like handedness, tends to increase with age, but unlike handedness it is not significantly affected by culture and tends to persist. Eye dominance is significant in man's development, since eye-hand functioning is involved in various motor adjustments, manual skills, writing, and perhaps reading and speech. There is no significant relation between the strength of one eye and eye dominance. Eyedness appears to be a matter of motor control and probably has its beginning with the child's earliest eye-hand co-ordinations.

The relationship between eye dominance and handedness is not very close and appears to diminish with age. This diminished relation-

[29] *Ibid.,* pp. 210-211.

[30] B. Bryngelson and B. Rutherford, A comparative study of laterality of stutterers and non-stutterers, *Journal of Speech Disorders,* 1937, Vol. 2, pp. 12-16.

ship stems from several possible sources. In the first place, many children are trained to use their right hand, whereas training has little if any effect upon eye preference. Secondly, during the early manipulative stage eye-hand co-ordination is most important. The preferred hand and preferred eye for grasping an object came from the same side of the body, since these were closer together and could more conveniently and accurately be used together than the hand and the opposite eye. Eye dominance is perhaps not so essential in skilled activities as is manual dominance. Lack of agreement between hand and eye dominance is referred to as "mixed dominance." According to Hildreth, from 20 to 40 per cent of the population show this characteristic.[31] It would appear, however, that superior manual performances involving skill would result from hand preference and eye preference from the same side of the body.

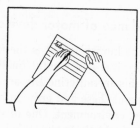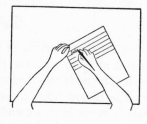

FIG. 16   Showing the position of the paper and hands for left-handed and right-handed pupils in writing

(After Hildreth)

The left-handed child at school. The question of how to deal with the left-handed child at school baffles many teachers. Continued interference with left-handedness may create difficult emotional and adjustment problems and result in the left-handed child's acquiring less skill than his right-handed classmate in corresponding acts. The one-arm chairs at school are usually built for right-handed pupils, the ink wells of the desks are placed in a position appropriate for right-handed pupils, lighting arrangements have been established for the right-handed, and the teachers are usually ill-prepared to deal with the problems growing out of left-handedness.

The left-handed child is placed in an awkward situation when he tries to write like the other children. He is forced to move in a direc-

[31] Gertrude Hildreth, The development and training of hand dominance: III. Origins of handedness and later dominance, *Journal of Genetic Psychology*, 1949, Vol. 75, pp. 255-275.

tion that is unnatural to him. When the paper is placed in the same position as it would be for right-handed writing, he is then compelled to place his pen above the line of writing and to move the entire arm a number of times while writing across the page. When writing is performed in this manner, it is invariably cramped and illegible, and is an awkward as well as laborious process for the writer. The paper in left-handed writing should be placed just opposite to the position for right-handed writing (Fig. 16). This makes it easier for the left-handed child to do his writing with the hand and pen below the line of writing as is the case for the right-handed writer under normal conditions. Since most teachers are right-handed, it will be necessary for them to give special attention to the position of the paper for the left-handed pupil. An attempt on the part of the pupil to imitate the teacher will only lead to confusion.

Guidance of motor development

An outstanding characteristic of the human infant is the fact that he is equipped at birth with the physical and mental qualities for rapid growth. The activities during his intrauterine life are of such a nature that he is now ready to expand these and grow in harmony with his bodily needs in an expanded environment. One of the most outstanding achievements that follows birth is the acquisition of behavior patterns involving bodily control which leads to crawling, walking, skipping, hopping, and various motor skills involving the entire body. The growth of some of these skills was traced in the previous discussions of this chapter. This growth is not of a haphazard nature; neither should it be left to chance. Some of the factors affecting the development of motor control will be described throughout the subsequent discussions.

Maturation and growth in motor skills. From the developmental viewpoint, the correct timing of motor skills is very important. Although research is not available to furnish safe guidance for all learning, there is ample evidence that certain motor skills, such as walking, using the spoon in eating, hopping, skipping, and the like, appear according to a sequential order of development. A detailed investigation of the climbing behavior of identical twins was made by Gesell and Thompson.[32] The purpose of their study was to deter-

[32] Arnold Gesell and Helen Thompson, Learning and growth in identical infant twins. An experimental study by the method of co-twin control, *Genetic Psychology Monographs,* 1929, Vol. 6, pp. 1-124.

mine the effect of practice on such an activity as stair climbing. To this end, one twin (T) was trained in the behavior of climbing the stairs from age forty-six weeks to age fifty-two weeks. The second twin (C) was given no such training during this period but was given a brief and delayed training period from age fifty-three weeks to age fifty-five weeks. It was concluded that training and practice neither altered the total developmental complex nor hastened to any marked degree the manifestation of climbing. Twin T was also given daily practice in cube behavior. It was impossible to detect any significant influence of training upon the cube behavior pattern of twin T when compared with twin C after two weeks of training beginning at the age of fifty-three weeks.

In a study by Josephine Hilgard, two groups of ten children each, aged twenty-four to thirty-six months, were equated for chronological age, mental age, sex, and approximately equal initial abilities in three skills: buttoning, cutting with scissors, and climbing.[33] The practice group was given twelve weeks of special practice in these three skills, with retests at two-week intervals. The control group, on the other hand, was given no special practice during the twelve-week period, but was given four days of intensive practice at the end of this period. At the end of the thirteen weeks covered by this study, the outstanding result is the marked similarity of the two groups in these three skills. Though the practice group leads in the gains made in cutting with scissors and buttoning, the gains are practically the same in climbing. The rapid gains made by the control group during the four days of extensive practice suggests that factors other than the amount of practice contributed to the development of these three skills. One cannot infer from this that the control group received no practice. In ordinary life activities, children get practice in doing things related to cutting with scissors and buttoning. Thus maturation, general motor activities performed daily, and practice at the appropriate time provide the basis for growth in motor skills. These results have been supplemented by many studies. The results of these studies lead to the generalization that training cannot transcend maturation. However, training in harmony with maturation will provide for the optimum growth.

The value of practice in the performance of a simple act of motor skill was carefully observed by Margaret Curti in a study of an

[33] Josephine R. Hilgard, Learning and maturation in preschool children, *Journal of Genetic Psychology,* 1935, Vol. 41, pp. 36-56.

infant grasping a rattle.[34] The strong reflex grasp of the infant has been observed by many investigators. In the study by Curti, tests were begun at the age of 129 days. The rattle was held directly above and in front of the infant for a period of one minute, or until it was grasped. The early trials revealed considerable diffuse activity of the whole body, with waving of the arms and kicking of the legs very much in evidence. Progress was measured by recording the number of kicks of the legs involved in the performance of a single grasping of the rattle, and is shown in Figure 17. There was an ap-

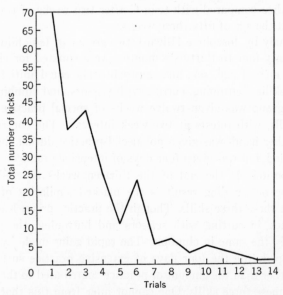

FIG. 17 Curve showing the progress of an infant in grasping a rattle
(After Curti)

parent decrease in general-bodily activity with learning. The main features of the early grasping consisted of squirming, wiggling, movements involving the whole body; after nine or ten trials, the infant was able to grasp the rattle promptly with a minimum of bodily movements as measured by kicking behavior.

Guidance of early motor development. The development of walking changes the whole life of the child. Some of the factors that retard walking were presented earlier in this chapter. Those con-

[34] Margaret W. Curti, *Child Psychology* (New York: Longmans, Green & Company, 1938), p. 95.

cerned with the guidance of the child's development should provide opportunities and incentives for the child to develop the skills involved in walking. To ignore the child is not sufficient, neither is it highly desirable to try to force the child's development. The relationship between maturation and the development of walking should be recognized.

The child should be praised and encouraged in different ways when he begins to walk; however, he should not be encouraged to do things he is not ready to do or things that require the protection of one of the parents. At the age of sixteen months, the baby's energy reaches a new height. There is an increase at this time in his ability to use large and small muscles. The growth gradients of child development show that after this age there is a continued development of better co-ordination of the hand, wrist, and finger movements. At two years of age, he is reaching for objects and pulling things down from tables and shelves. There is a need for directing these newly developed abilities so as to insure their continued growth. The second year has often been given as the end of infancy and the beginning of the preschool period. Certainly this period represents for the average child the beginning of greater motor control and increased power over his environment.

The purpose of the study by Theresa Jones was to investigate the child's motor development and his use of certain play materials.[35] Repeated observation were made on a group of twenty-four children beginning at twenty-one months of age and thereafter from month to month for one year, and again at thirty-six months and forty-eight months. She draws the following conclusions from her study:

First the successive levels of performance which were studied seem to be in large part, functions of increasing maturity as distinguished from experience or practice alone. The qualitative play activities of the children appear to be largely dependent upon intrinsic factors related to growth and development. Further data from controlled experiments would be necessary, however, to provide a definite statement regarding this matter.

Second, it appears that minimum performance, such as that represented by the ability to use the pedals of the kiddie kar for propelling, may occur when a child has reached a given degree of neuromuscular maturation, but the development of the skill into graceful coordinated performance depends upon continued practice.

[35] Theresa D. Jones, The development of certain motor skills and play activities in young children, Teachers College, Columbia University, *Child Development Monographs*, No. 26, 1939.

Third, sex differences appeared even greater when opportunities for similar experience were provided as evidenced by a significant difference between sexes of the higher socio-economic group in terms of age of performance at Level III. In the non-locomotor activities there was great similarity between sexes in initial ages of performance, although the boys showed more interest in manipulation of parts and the girls in combination of materials.

Fourth, in the locomotor activities, the opportunity to have experience with materials appears to be the most important extrinsic factor influencing progress in the development of skill.

Fifth, certain conditions in the home environment of these children appeared to be related to progress in play activities as evidenced by ages of reaching the various levels of performance. A home environment, including (1) a playmate from one to three years older than the subject; (2) no full-time maid or relative other than the parents living in the household; (3) availability of a variety of play materials; and (4) outdoor play space which gives opportunity for freedom of locomotor activities seemed to foster the kind of adjustment that is conducive to greater use of materials in play activities.[36]

Guidance of motor development of the elementary-school child. There is considerable evidence from studies of motor development of children that the elementary-school child possesses motor skills and potentialities for development in advance of that provided for him in the ordinary elementary-school program. Gutteridge has pointed out that there is a lack of scientific standards for the motor education of young children, and that the slowing down of motor development among preschool and primary-school children may be partially accounted for by a lack of environmental stimulation and opportunities for the child's motor development.[37] Every first-grade teacher has observed some children who have had experience with hammers, saws, scissors, crayons, and other materials that provided for their motor development; while other children had had little experience with such types of materials.

The six-year-old throws a ball with his whole body, making unusual facial expressions as well as awkward bodily movements. The learning of a new skill is very satisfying to him, and the confidence, satisfaction, and motor development resulting from such learning are valuable outcomes. Thus, he should be encouraged in such learning; but the principle of maturation, referred to in Chapter 4 and

[36] *Ibid.*, pp. 148-149.

[37] M. A. Gutteridge, A study of motor achievement of young children, *Archives of Psychology*, No. 244, 1939.

discussed further in this chapter, should be taken into consideration in the guidance of these youngsters in their motor development. Activities that require the use of large muscles should be stressed throughout the sixth and seventh years. Opportunities should be provided for climbing, swinging, running and jumping, and for free active play involving group activities. The six-year-olds like to push and pull. The boys engage in activities involving wrestling and tumbling. Their physical skills are not yet well co-ordinated, and they are just learning to bat a ball and jump rope. These skills grow rapidly during the course of the next year or two. A well-developed child of this age may perform quite well on the trapeze, while others, not yet ready for such motor skills, prefer to engage in activities requiring less muscular co-ordination and strength.

Writing skills, involving finer movements, are developed beginning with grade three. Girls as well as boys are able, after the age of eight or nine, to use the hammer and saw with a reasonable amount of skill, provided they have had the experience needed for the development of these skills. Changed customs and manner of dress have liberated the elementary-school girl so that she is encouraged to engage in more rigorous physical activities to her benefit. Furthermore, changed emphasis in our social and recreational activities has had its effects upon the skills developed by boys. Camp activities as well as some phases of the elementary-school program provide opportunities for boys to learn to cook, mend, wash dishes, and engage in other activities closely related to homemaking. There is no evidence that girls are more adept at the performance of these skills or that boys are more adept at the performance of skills involving the use of shop tools, provided their previous experiences have given them equal practice in these performances.

Strength and participation. A number of investigations have indicated an interrelationship between motor skills and favorable personal and social adjustments.[38] Skill in walking, running, hiking, swimming, and handling simple tools are important activities in the lives of growing boys and girls. The ability to achieve competency in these activities, plus the ability to learn new skills, requires strength and co-ordination, as well as a minimum of agility, rhythm, speed, and accuracy. There is considerable evidence that a significant positive relationship exists between muscular strength and co-ordination,

[38] See Harold E. Jones, The development of physical abilities, in *Adolescence, Forty-third Yearbook of the National Society for the Study of Education*, Part I, 1944.

especially among boys during the preadolescent and adolescent years. This, of course, would be truer for some activities than for others. In a study reported by Carl Willgoose, a group of 500 boys ranging in age from twelve to eighteen years were tested for speed in the 50-yard dash.[39] The Rogers Strength Index was also available on each of these boys.[40] The mean distribution of speed scores for the 50-yard dash according to the various Strength Index groups were as follows:

Strength Index	50-yard Dash
under 1,000	7.9 seconds
1,000 -1,400	7.3 seconds
1,400 -1,800	7.0 seconds
1,801 -2,200	6.8 seconds
2,201 -2,600	6.6 seconds
2,601 -3,000	6.3 seconds
over 3,000	6.0 seconds

A variability in the Strength Index may be noted between age groups, just as there is a considerable variation in motor performances between age groups. Also, there is considerable variation within a particular age group. A sixth-grader with a higher Strength Index is likely to have better motor co-ordination than a seventh-grader with a lower Strength Index. Willgoose concludes, "It seems safe to say, in general, that adolescent motor coordination, as measured by tests of motor performance, improves with an increase in physical power brought about by development of muscular strength." [41]

Dalen reports a study of the participation of adolescent boys in play activities. Strength tests [42] were administered to 342 boys in the seventh, eighth, and ninth grades. The median age of the boys was 13.4 years with a range from 12 to 16 years. Strength Index for the boys was determined from the results on the strength test, while the Physical Fitness Index was derived from comparing an Achieved Strength Index with the norm based upon the individual's age and

[39] Carl E. Willgoose, The relationship of muscular strength to motor coordination in the adolescent period, *Journal of Educational Research*, 1950, Vol. 44, pp. 138-142.

[40] The Rogers Strength Index items of grip strength, back and leg strength, chin ups, push ups from the parallel bars, and the height-weight multiplier were used.

[41] *Ibid.*, p. 141.

[42] D. B. Van Dalen, A differential analysis of the play of adolescent boys, *Journal of Educational Research*, 1947, Vol. 41, pp. 204-213.

weight. This, then, is a measure of the immediate capacity of an individual for physical activity.

A comparison of the frequency and amount of participation of the high and low Physical Fitness Index groups showed that the boys in the high groups engaged in more play activities and devoted more time to play than did the low groups. This was true for all types of activities except for the reading and constructive categories. The high Strength Index groups also engaged more frequently as spectators at physical activity events than did the low groups. Boys of the low strength groups participated in games of a more individualistic nature and of a lower degree of organization than activities participated in by boys from the high strength groups. Boys of the high strength groups participated more frequently in games requiring muscular strength and large-muscle co-ordination in comparison to the games participated in by the boys of the low strength groups.

Interrelations of motor achievement. The materials presented relative to the relationship between strength and certain motor skills indicate that a child high in strength is more likely than not to excel in the 50-yard dash. In the study by Bayley, sixty-one children were tested from infancy up to three years of age. From a careful analysis of the growth of these children in various motor functions, she states: "There remains the possibility that the motor functions measured during the first three years are actually less discrete and independent than are the motor skills measured at later ages." [43] In such a case, there would be a gradual and continuous increase in the functional independence of motor skills during the growing years. A study conducted by McCaskill and Wellman was concerned with the growth and interrelations of certain motor achievements at the preschool age level.[44] The tests devised for the study were given to ninety-eight children from two to six years of age in the preschool laboratories at the University of Iowa. The selected activities were: ascending and descending ladders, ascending and descending steps, hopping, skipping, jumping, balancing on path and circle, ball throwing, ball catching, and ball bouncing. Scores were assigned the various stages of each skill according to their difficulty of performance as evidenced by the percentage of children of each age who accomplished them. The different skills were combined into partial score

[43] Nancy Bayley, The development of motor abilities during the first three years, *Monographs of the Society for Research in Child Development,* 1935, No. 1.

[44] Carra Lou McCaskill and Beth L. Wellman, A study of common motor achievements at the preschool ages, *Child Development,* 1938, Vol. 9, pp. 141-150.

groups in order to obtain a range of scores sufficiently large to give significant correlations, under (1) steps and ladder activities, (2) ball activities, (3) jumping, and (4) hopping, skipping, and balancing activities.

The correlations between these partial scores for each sex are presented in Table 25. The correlations between these skills are high and statistically reliable. The correlations between the scores on the tests made by the girls tend to run higher than those between the scores on the tests by the boys. A further study of the scores made by the different age groups showed a significant gain in ability from one age level to another. Boys appeared to be somewhat

TABLE 25 Correlations between scores on various motor achievements of preschool children (after McCaskill and Wellman)

	Boys		Girls	
Measures Correlated	Number	Correlation	Number	Correlation
Total Group				
Steps and ladders with ball activities	50	.54 ± .10	48	.72 ± .06
Steps and ladders with hopping, skipping, etc.	50	.69 ± .07	48	.79 ± .05
Ball activities with hopping, skipping, etc.	50	.69 ± .07	48	.74 ± .06
Younger Group (26 to 53 months)				
Steps and ladders with ball activities	16	.40 ± .21	29	.66 ± .10
Steps and ladders with hopping, skipping, etc.	16	.72 ± .12	29	.72 ± .09
Steps and ladders with hopping, skipping, etc.	16	.69 ± .13	29	.75 ± .08

superior on steps and ladders and ball activities, while the girls were superior on hopping and skipping. Since these differences are in harmony with the activities most frequently engaged in by boys and girls during this period, it would appear that practice may be offered as a partial explanation for these sex differences. The findings from this study further corroborate other evidences for a significant interrelationship of motor skills and achievement during the early childhood years.

Summary and implications

Intrinsic growth factors operate in affecting the orderly sequence of motor development of the infant child. The sequences for walking and for prehension illustrate the operation of the maturational processes. In the case of the infant's development, it has been pointed out that motor functions follow structural development and that mass activity precedes specialized activities. Schedules of normal behavior activities have been established, and provide a guide for determining the stage of a child's development. These should not, however, be used as norms for making specific comparisons.

There is a continuous growth in speed of reaction with age, with the average for the boys being slightly faster than that for girls of the same age level. Results from different tests of motor skills likewise show an improvement with age. The boys were superior to the girls (averages) at all ages studied beyond the six-year level. After the onset of adolescence, girls register a decline of interest and ability in most motor performances. This is not the case for boys. The differences here may be accounted for in a large measure by the different values and emphasis placed on motor activities by boys and girls. There is a continuous growth in strength with increased age. This is especially noticeable among boys as they develop physiologically. Both boys and girls who are physiologically more mature than the average for their age register a greater strength index than those who are average or below average in rate of physiological maturation. Strength has further been shown to be related to participation in play activities requiring physical exertion. Boys with a low strength index are likely to prefer reading activities and other pursuits that do not require physical exertion.

Hand dominance is definitely related to the performance of motor skills. It appears that eye-hand co-ordination begins early in life, and perhaps accounts for eye dominance. Parents and teachers should encourage children in the development of motor skills and in the use of their hands for finer co-ordinations. There is good evidence that most children are not given training commensurate with their abilities and needs in this connection. The left-handed child should be guided in his development so as to develop the needed skills in writing, sawing, etc. Too often the major handicap that may result from left-handedness is an outgrowth of the teacher's inability to help the child in the performance of such acts as writing and the like.

The guidance of the child's development of motor skills should be an integral part of the elementary-school program. The principles of learning applicable to other aspects of the school program will be applicable to the learning of motor skills. These include (1) choosing activities in harmony with the child's maturational level, (2) capitalizing on interests already present, (3) setting forth purposive learnings and goals, (4) giving the child some opportunities to explore as well as guiding him in his pursuits, (5) keeping criticism to a minimum, and offering constructive suggestions, (6) encouraging the child in his efforts and helping him to evaluate his growth and development, and (7) providing through the motor skills the all-around development of the child.

Questions and Exercises

1. Observe a physical education program in some elementary school of your acquaintance. Is the play equipment suitable for the children for whom it is intended? What suggestions would you make for the improvement of such equipment?
2. List some activities that might be engaged in by both boys and girls in the third grade which would provide for their motor development. What differences would you suggest for the sexes?
3. How is strength related to play participation?
4. What are the major conclusions presented in this chapter about the problem of handedness in the school program? Look up further materials bearing on this problem. Do these materials corroborate the suggestions set forth in this chapter?
5. Of what value are the materials presented in Table 20 for the nursery-school teacher?
6. Present several generalizations based on the materials presented in this chapter relative to maturation and development.
7. List motor skills that may be successfully learned by the average child at the following age levels: 2 years; 3 years; 5 years; 7 years.
8. What are the general conclusions about sex differences during the preschool period? What are the implications of these conclusions to nursery-school training? To kindergarten training?

Selected Readings

Averill, Lawrence A. *The Psychology of the Elementary-School Child.* New York: Longmans, Green & Company, 1949. Chap. IV.

Breckenridge, Marian E., and Vincent, E. Lee. *Child Development.* 2nd ed.; Philadelphia: W. B. Saunders Co., 1949. Chap. VIII.

Espenschade, Anne. *Motor Performance in Adolescence.* Society for Research in Child Development, National Research Council, 1940.

Garrison, Karl C. *Psychology of Adolescence.* 4th ed.; New York: Prentice-Hall, 1951. Chap. IV.

Gesell, Arnold, *et al. The Child From Five to Ten.* New York: Harper & Brothers, 1946. Chap. II.

Gutteridge, M. A study of motor achievement of young children, *Archives of Psychology,* 1939, No. 244.

Hurlock, Elizabeth B. *Child Development.* 2nd ed.; New York: McGraw-Hill Book Co., 1950. Chap. VI.

Jersild, Arthur T. *Child Psychology.* 3rd ed.; New York: Prentice-Hall, 1947. Chap. IV.

Jones, Harold E. *Development in Adolescence.* New York: Appleton-Century-Crofts, 1943. Pp. 81-88.

Lindsey, L. *The Nature and Conditions of Learning.* New York: Prentice-Hall, 1946. Chap. XI.

Millard, Cecil V. *Child Growth and Development in the Elementary School Years.* Boston: D. C. Heath and Company, 1951. Chap. V.

National Society for the Study of Education, *Forty-third Yearbook,* Part I. Chicago: Department of Education, University of Chicigao, 1944. Chaps. VI, VII.

Shirley, Mary M. *The First Two Years.* Vol. I: *Postural and Locomotor Development.* Minneapolis: University of Minnesota Press, 1931.

Thorpe, Louis P. *Child Psychology and Development.* New York: The Ronald Press Co., 1946. Chap. X.

7

Emotional Growth
and Control

The child, because of his unique physiological and psychological constitution, responds emotionally as well as physically to various forces and conditions. Two children from the same family brought up in a very similar environment will respond differently to conditions about them. The unique constitution possessed by each child will determine in part the nature of his responses. However, in our discussion of the emotional growth of the child, it must not be inferred that emotional growth is distinct and separate from other aspects of growth. It was pointed out in Chapter 4 that all growth is interrelated, and that the child grows as a whole. The distinctions made between the different aspects of growth are given in order to focus the attention of the reader upon certain phases of the child's growth, and thus lead to a better understanding of the nature, characteristics, and importance of that phase of the child's development.

The genesis of emotional behavior

The nature of emotions. The word emotion was derived from the Latin word *emovere,* to move out. It is usually defined as a stirred-up state or condition. Genetic studies of child development show that differences in emotionality appear during the first months of life. However, the concept that the emotions are themselves causal agents is open to serious question. Such a notion likens the emotions to instincts, as conceived of several decades ago. If one proposes the question: "Why does the small child cry and withdraw when the dog appears?" and received an answer, "Fear makes him do that," no clear explanation has been presented. One may well reply: "Just what is this fear that makes the child behave in such a manner?" The crying and withdrawing behavior are responses to stimulating conditions. This stirred-up state of the child is part of that total complex which we define as the emotion.

The emotions have also been defined as dynamic drives to action. This again places the emotions in the role of causal agents. Furthermore, such an idea presents something of an animistic explanation of behavior. If the emotions are responses to stimulating situations, they cannot serve as causal agents or basic drives. The materials presented in the subsequent discussions of the genesis of emotions and the growth and development of emotional behavior give a more complete description of the emotions as responses developing through the continuous interaction of the child's innate constitution and environmental forces and conditions. Any attempt to explain emotional behavior as a result of either heredity or environment alone fails to recognize the importance of the interaction of the organism and environmental conditions from the very beginning of life in the uterus.

Early indications of emotional behavior. According to Paul Young, the first definite sign of emotional behavior in the human infant is its general excitement to intense stimulation.[1] This diffuse excitement of the infant is analogous to the undifferentiated emotional excitement that appears in human adult behavior. A number of investigators have studied the extent to which infants displayed differential emotions in their facial expressions and other reaction patterns. One of the earliest of these was the investigation by Sherman, in which the ability of observers to name infant emotional responses without a knowledge of the nature of the stimulation was studied.[2] This study made use of motion pictures of babies responding to various types of stimulation. Sherman concluded that the emotional responses of infants to the different stimuli employed could not be differentiated with any significant degree of success by the observers, who were graduate students in psychology.

The results of Sherman's study have been confirmed by other investigators. Katharine Bridges failed to find such well-defined emotions as fear, rage, or love among infants during the first three

[1] Paul T. Young, *Emotion in Man and Animal* (New York: John Wiley and Sons, 1943), p. 159.

[2] Mandel Sherman, Differentiation of emotional responses in infants, *Journal of Comparative Psychology*, 1927, Vol. 7, pp. 265-284.

months of age.[3] Differential patterns of responses appeared later as a result of the progressive development of the child. According to Bridges, the earliest emotional response of the infant is a general agitation or excitement produced by a large variety of stimulating conditions. During this state of excitement, the young infant's arm and hand muscle are tensed; the breathing is quickened; the legs make jerky kicking movements; the eyes are opened as if gazing into the distance; and the upper lid is arched. Out of this diffuse excitement, specific forms of emotional behavior appear to emerge.

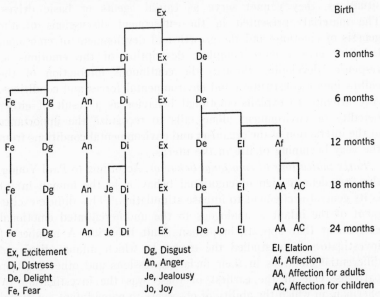

Ex, Excitement
Di, Distress
De, Delight
Fe, Fear

Dg, Disgust
An, Anger
Je, Jealousy
Jo, Joy

El, Elation
Af, Affection
AA, Affection for adults
AC, Affection for children

FIG. 18 The approximate ages of differentiation of the various emotions during the first two years

(After Bridges)

The gradual differentiation of the emotions during the first two years has been described by Katherine Bridges from observations of this age group of children. According to the materials presented in Figure 18, *distress* and *delight* appear around the third month. Recognizable responses indicative of fear, disgust, and anger on the one hand and elation and delight on the other appear at the six- and twelve-month levels.[4] Goldfarb has pointed out that, as

[3] K. M. B. Bridges, Emotional development in early infancy, *Child Development*, 1932, Vol. 3, pp. 324-341.
[4] *Ibid.*, p. 340.

early as six months, one observes the beginnings of sentiments. These appear in the form of attachments to a particular person or limited number of people within the family circle. He states: "Close attachment to specific adults considerably before the end of the first year thus appears to be a fact." [5]

Early development of affectionate behavior. The earliest indications of affectionate behavior in the infant involve excessive activity directed toward an object or person. It is characterized by out-going activity. In the beginning stages, the arm and leg movements are poorly co-ordinated. With growth in motor co-ordination, the infant's reactions become better organized and oriented toward the person or thing to which the baby is attracted. As the ability to vocalize develops, the infant's affectionate behavior includes smiling and gurgling sounds denoting pleasure. Observations of more than nine hundred infants by Katharine Banham showed that babies varied as to the beginnings of the manifestations of affectionate behavior. She points out that these signs usually begin around the age of four months, and that between the ages of five and six months babies usually come to distinguish between familiar people and strangers. Concerning the development after this age, Banham states:

The child responds reciprocally to affectionate cuddling. It reaches out for the mother's face and mouth. Possibly, it would feed her if it could. Later, as a toddler, it does try to feed its dolls, carry them about, wrap them warmly, and rock them to sleep. Affectionate behavior even in its beginnings, as all through life, is that of cherishing, protecting, giving of the self to and caring for another person. Attention is directed outward and not inward to bodily sensation. [6]

As the child develops, he begins to anticipate the arrival of his mother. If he has been well cared for by his mother, this anticipation is one of pleasantness. He displays delight and joy at her arrival. The growth and development of the child is also characterized by an increased ability to distinguish between familiar persons and strangers. If his relationship with strangers is pleasant, any fear that he might have had of strangers will probably be dispelled. During the second year, following the development of the ability to walk and adjust to a larger environment, he discovers

[5] William Goldfarb, Effects of psychological deprivation and subsequent stimulation, *American Journal of Psychiatry,* 1945, Vol. 103, p. 18.

[6] Katharine M. Banham, The development of affectionate behavior in infancy, *Journal of Genetic Psychology,* 1950, Vol. 76, p. 284.

himself as a discrete person with certain powers and an increased degree of independence. It is at this stage, according to Banham, that some children turn their affection to an increased degree toward themselves. This is explained as follows:

Learning from experience that their mothers are not always ready to receive and reciprocate their affectionate embrace, they become temporarily subdued, and eventually find substitute objects of interest toward which to direct their activity. When the young child finds he has a diminished share of mother's attention, particularly after the arrival of a new baby, and an increase in interference with his explorations and loving advances, he develops antagonistic and negative rather than approaching and affectionate behavior toward her.[7]

Beginning around the second year, different responses are made to men and women, and to children of different age levels. The child's actions toward these different types of people will depend upon the ways he has been treated by them. If his father is impatient and demanding, he will react with fear and in other negative ways toward men. If he is required to take a subdued form of behavior before older children, he might be expected to assume this form of behavior when older children appear. It is in this connection in particular that a jealous and unfavorable attitude toward older brothers and sisters may develop.

Conditioning of emotional behavior. The methods used by Pavlov for conditioning the salivary response of the dog to the sound of a bell were early applied to the study of the behavior of infants and children. Pavlov's contribution, then, to child study was his discovery that when two stimuli—meat, which natively stimulated the flow of saliva, and the ringing of a bell, which elicited no salivary response—are presented simultaneously a number of times, the ringing of the bell comes to evoke the salivary response. The principle, when applied to child study, would indicate that when a conditioned stimulus is associated with an original stimulus a number of times, the conditioned stimulus will come to evoke the response originally produced by the original stimulus. Many of the early studies with children as subjects were conducted in Russia by pupils of Pavlov.[8] The early results indicated that, in general,

---

[7] *Ibid.*, p. 285.

[8] See G. H. S. Razran, Conditioned responses in children: a behavioral and quantitative critical review of experimental studies, *Archives of Psychology*, 1933, No. 148.

the infant's behavior has the flexibility to be modified through learning, involving the conditioning process. Probably the most widely publicized experiments on emotional conditioning are those conducted by Watson and associates at Johns Hopkins University. The results from observations of Albert B., an even-tempered eleven-month-old boy, is of interest in this connection.[9] In this study, Albert, who was originally not afraid of a white rat, was taught to show a fear response at the sight of the rat. After it was ascertained that Albert displayed withdrawal and crying responses to a loud noise produced by striking a heavy steel bar, Albert was shown the white rat at the same time that a loud noise was evoked. After this was done a number of times, Albert displayed fear reactions at the sight of the rat alone. This reaction to a stimulus-object that has not previously produced such a response has been labeled the *conditioned response*. From this and similar experiments the conclusion is reached that many early fears are learned responses. The conditioned response furnishes an explanation of the genesis of many intense fears for specific objects and situations, established during infancy and early childhood.

Changes of emotional behavior with age

A systematic account of the changes of emotional behavior with age will require further research; however, much data are available relative to the emotional characteristics found among children at different age levels. As the child grows and develops, he comes to respond differently to specific situations. This change in the nature of his responses is reflected in the emotional changes that take place with age. Not only does the child respond differently at the different age levels to specific stimuli, but certain stimuli which formerly produced an emotional response no longer produce such a response, or if they do, the response is very weak; while other stimuli, which formerly produced no emotional response, produce emotional responses of varying degrees of intensity.

Crying of children. It was pointed out in Chapter 3 that the crying of the six-week-old baby is a result of internal causes, hunger usually leading the list. By the time the infant is four months old, the crying behavior may be set off by outside conditions, such as handling by strangers. Parents may observe that the child cries

[9] John B. Watson and R. Rayner, Conditioned emotional reactions, *Journal of Experimental Psychology*, 1920, Vol. 3, pp. 1-14.

at this time in order to get the attention that he has become accustomed to receiving.

There is not only a change in the nature of the stimulus that provokes crying during the early months of life, but there are changes in the nature of crying as well. It has already been suggested that the child cries less with the body as a whole as he develops. Crying at one year of age may take the form of fussing or vocalizing, as a means of indicating a desire for attention. The influence of culture and feeding practices upon crying may be noted from a comparison of the crying of Hopi and American children. American culture is filled with many restrictions and prohibitions that tend to produce frustrations and prolonged crying behavior. In contrast, there is no feeling among the Hopi that crying is to be expected among infants, and there are very few prohibitions and little adherence to routines.[10] The American child soon after birth is placed on a rigid schedule of feedings. Many infants begin crying some time before the exact time for their next feeding. The Hopi infant, on the other hand, is nursed as soon as he becomes restless and begins crying. He may, therefore, cry more frequently than the American child, but his crying will be of far less duration. A significant observation, related to the crying of the American and Hopi infant, is that the different cultures may determine some of the conditions that provoke crying and may affect the pattern of the responses. Dennis noted that the reactions of the Hopi and American children were indistinguishable. The hungry infant frets, fusses, shows excess bodily movements, and cries, regardless of his culture.

As children progress into the preschool years, social pressure tends to reduce the amount of crying. This is particularly true of boys. The child who has spent a year in the kindergarten is not likely to cry as a result of some conflict with a playmate when he reaches the first or second grade in school. Children also learn to abstain from crying because of some physical injury. Crying among primary-school children is more likely to be an expression of anger. When the kindergarten or first-grade child has a sudden outburst of temper, violent crying may result.

The eight-year-old child is not likely to display his emotions and feelings by crying. Social pressure by this time is very strong, and keeps children from crying and being referred to as "babies" by

[10] See Wayne Dennis, *The Hopi Child* (New York: Appleton-Century-Crofts, 1940).

their classmates in school. At this age, the child may state that he feels like crying, but exercises a reasonable amount of self-control by refraining from showing his tears. The continued growth in restraint from crying characterizes the child as he passes beyond his eighth-year level into preadolescence and on to adolescence.

The development of interpersonal smiling. Studies of interpersonal smiling responses of infants show personality differences during the first year of life.Washburn's studies revealed further that smiling responses occur earlier than laughter and are less stereotyped in nature.[11] An important study of laughing and smiling behavior manifested by children during the preschool period was conducted by Ding and Jersild.[12] The subjects for their study consisted of fifty-nine Chinese children ranging in age from two to five years. They found a slight tendency for both laughter and smiling to increase from two to five years of age. Relative to conditions provoking laughing and smiling, they concluded that "laughing and smiling of children from two to five occur predominantly in connection with general physical activity."

During the preschool years, laughter is associated largely with physical contacts such as rolling and tossing, bodily activity, opportunities for self-assertion, feelings of well-being, and play stimulation from others. In one study reported, laughter appeared among nursery-school children when a special problem that had created tension was suddenly solved.[13] This appeared to bring forth the feeling of satisfaction to the *ego*. A study conducted by Louise Ames was designed to determine whether or not definite age trends appear during the preschool years in the amount and source of laughter and smiling. Observations were made over a two-year interval of children during the regular activities in the Guidance Nursery of the Yale Clinic of Child Development. Records were obtained of the spontaneous smiling and laughing behavior from eighteen months to four years of age. From three to seven children were observed on each of the 150 observation periods. An analysis of the data indicated that definite age trends appeared in the ratio of smiles to laughs, the stimuli that elicited smiling, and the individ-

[11] R. W. Washburn, Personality differences in the smiling and laughter of infants, *Childhood Education*, 1932, Vol. 8, pp. 239-245.

[12] G. F. Ding, and A. T. Jersild, A study of the laughing and smiling of preschool children, *Journal of Genetic Psychology*, 1932, Vol. 40, pp. 452-472.

[13] W. E. Blatz, K. D. Allin, and D. A. Millichamp, A study of laughter in the nursery school child, *University of Toronto Studies in Child Development*, Series No. 7, 1936.

ual toward whom the smiling was directed. The age trends observed are here presented.

Eighteen Months

The child smiles most at his own activity; and the type of own activity which amuses him most is his own gross motor. Second most smile-provoking are his own social approaches to the teacher.

Twenty-One Months

Smiles in relation to the teacher lead, particularly child's own social approach to teacher, without verbalization. Child's own gross motor comes second.

Two Years

Smiles in relation to the teacher still lead, but now it is a verbal-social approach to the teacher, not merely a social approach. Smiles in relation to child's own activity come second.

Two and One-Half Years

Here there is a marked shift. Verbal-social approaches to teacher still lead as smile producers but now behavior in relation to other children (social approach without verbalization) comes second, rather than child's own activity in relation to himself.

Three Years

As at $2\frac{1}{2}$ years, verbal-social to teacher produces the most smiles; but now, the second leading behavior is verbal-social in relation to other children, not mere social alone.

Three and One-Half Years

Another major shift takes place. Now for the first time child-child behavior evokes the most smiles, verbal-social to other children being the outstanding category. Next most smiles are caused by child's verbal-social approaches to teacher.

Four Years

Verbal-social to other children still leads, but now for the first time child's behavior in relation to teacher produces the least smiles of any type of behavior, and child's own activity unrelated to others comes second.[14]

The fears of children. If one will observe carefully the conversation of children, he will hear expressions of fears of concrete things. The fears prevalent during early childhood are mostly personal and pertain to things prevalent in the child's immediate environment. An early study of childhood fears by Jones and Jones revealed that prior to the age of two years children displayed no fear of a

[14] Louise Bates Ames, Development of interpersonal smiling responses in the preschool years, *Journal of Genetic Psychology,* 1949, Vol. 74, pp. 289-290.

live snake.[15] The changing nature of fear manifested with increased age is interwoven with other aspects of the child's development.

An experimental study of the nature of children's fears during infancy and early childhood, reported by Jersild and Holmes, shows that certain fears tend to decrease while others increase during the first five years of life.[16] The fear responses of preschool children to experimentally created fear situations were recorded. The results are presented in Table 26. In four of the eight fear situations there is a definite and consistent decrease with age in the frequency of fear. When the responses of all eight fear situations are combined, a definite and consistent decrease in the display of fear with age is noted. It is noticeable that there are no fears of loud noises and snakes recorded for the two-year-old children. Fear of a dark room, high boards, falling boards, and being left alone appear at all ages studied.

TABLE 26   Number and percentage of children at yearly age levels who showed some slight degree of fear in response to the various experimental fear situations (after Jersild and Holmes)

| | Age in months | | | | | | | |
| | 24-35 | | 36-47 | | 48-59 | | 60-71 | |
Situations	NO. OF CHIL-DREN	PER CENT	NO. OF CHIL-DREN	PER CENT	NO. OF CHIL-DREN	PER CENT	NO. OF CHIL-DREN	PER CENT
Being Left Alone	33	6.1	45	8.9	14	7.1	12	8.3
Falling Boards	33	12.1	45	8.9	14	7.1	12	8.3
Dark Room	32	18.6	45	11.1	14	7.1	13	23.1
Strange Person	32	9.4	45	15.6	14	21.4	13	23.1
High Boards	31	16.1	45	8.9	14	0	13	23.1
Loud Sound	31	0	45	2.2	14	0	13	0
Snake	23	0	36	2.8	14	7.1	13	0
Large Dog	21	14.3	28	28.6	7	0	—	—
Total	236	10	334	10.2	105	6.7	89	12.4

As the child passes from the nursery period into the kindergarten stage, his fear of darkness, being left alone, and animals tends to disappear. His awareness of and reaction to social situations tend to have an impact upon him. Gesell found that six-year-old children

[15] H. C. Jones and M. C. Jones, A study of fear, *Childhood Education,* 1928, Vol. 5, pp. 136-143.

[16] Arthur T. Jersild and Frances B. Holmes, *Children's Fears* (Teachers College, Columbia University: Bureau of Publications, 1935).

were afraid of physical dangers, such as storms, fire, thunder, witches, and ghosts.[17] There is some indication that rural children may show greater fear of animals than do urban children. Such fears, however, would probably be more realistic in nature and would not involve elephants, tigers. Those listed were related to animals, although these fears tended to decrease with age and fears of inanimate things to increase.[18] Girls listed more fears than boys; however boys gave more different fears. Also, girls gave more fears of insects and spiders; while boys listed more often fears of wild animals.

There is good evidence that fear of animals and other concrete things in the immediate environment appears to decrease as the child develops from age five to age twelve, while fear of the dark, of being left alone at night, and the like increases. With growth into adolescence, fears of a social nature come to be very important. A study by Hicks and Hayes shows that 50 per cent of a group of 250 junior-high-school students reported they were afraid of something.[19] Some of their fears, in order of frequency reported, were of snakes, dogs, the dark, storms, accidents, high places, strange noises, and being alone at home. This indicates that many childhood fears persist into adolescence, and there is good evidence that they tend to persist throughout life. Older children and adolescents become much concerned over peer approval, failure in school, fear of being disliked, and other fears related to gang and friendship relations.

Expressions of anger. Infants respond with anger to minor physical discomforts, interference with physical activity, or removal of attention. As part of his display of anger, the infant arches his back, thrusts his arms and legs into the air, displays muscular tension, and cries in a forceful manner. According to Gesell, a tantrum of the first magnitude may appear at eighteen months.[20] In this case, the child hits, pushes, kicks, struggles, and cries with all his force and power. Resistant behavior, which will be discussed further in Chapter 15, appears as part of the anger response around the age of twenty-one months or two years. Objections to routine physical

[17] Arnold I. Gesell and Francis Ilg, *The Child from Five to Ten* (New York: Harper & Brothers, 1946).

[18] Karl Pratt, A study of the fears of "rural" children, *Journal of Genetic Psychology,* 1945, Vol. 67, pp. 176-194.

[19] J. A. Hicks and M. Hayes, Study of the characteristics of 250 junior-high-school children, *Child Development,* 1938, Vol. 9, pp. 219-242.

[20] Arnold Gesell and Frances Ilg, *Child Development. II. From Five to Ten* (New York: Harper & Brothers, 1949), p. 280.

habits, such as dressing, bathing, eating, and the like, account for slightly more than one-fourth of all the anger outbursts observed in two infants by Goodenough.[21] Problems of social relationship involving a general desire for attention and involving minor physical discomforts were in the opinion of the parents responsible for 50 per cent of all cases. During the second year of age, she found a large percentage of anger responses arising in connection with the establishment of routine habits, or with problems of social relationships, particularly with playmates. Gesell, however, found anger responses at two and one-half years due chiefly to interference with physical activities or with the child's possessions. In his reactions he is likely to be more violent and sometimes shows evidence of destructiveness. Difficulties with playmates, as a source of anger, reach a maximum between three and four years of age. Language begins to take the place of physical aggressiveness as an anger response at this time.

By the time the child is five or six years of age, he may call his playmates by some undesirable name,* or may make some verbal threat as a part of his display of anger. In groups of preschool children who have been together long enough to form a social group, one form of showing resentment against a particular child is to exclude him from the group. During the school years, this remains a frequent means for disciplining an individual by the group, and thus serves to maintain conformity to group standards. Anger outbursts among children after the age of four years are less frequent than prior to this time. This is shown in Figure 19, based upon studies by Florence Goodenough.[22] The outbursts appear to reach their peak after the child is one year of age—after he has developed a reasonable amount of independence. These anger outbursts are often a means of asserting his independence in a manner which, he has learned, appears to work fairly well.

Gesell observed a period of less aggressive expressions of anger at age five, followed by a renewal of violent methods of expression at age six, with hitting and kicking as typical behavior. At seven, however, less anger aggressiveness seems characteristic, although kicking and throwing stones were observed. The child may at this time remove himself from groups rather than try to force the withdrawal of others. By eight and nine years, the "hurt feelings" expression of anger appears. In the normally growing child, physical aggressive-

[21] Florence L. Goodenough, *Anger in Young Children* (Minneapolis: University of Minnesota Press, 1931).
[22] *Ibid.*, p. 72.

ness is almost at an end by this time. By the age of five, children begin arguing, calling names, or making disagreeable remarks. These forms of expression become more subtle as the child develops and tend to be used increasingly, while physical aggressiveness tends to disappear. As children grow older, during the early school years,

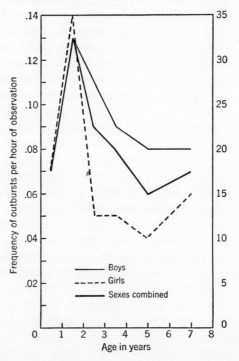

FIG. 19 Age and sex differences in frequency of anger outbursts
(After Goodenough)

anger reactions become more directed toward a single person and take the form of attempts to hurt the feelings rather than to injure the body of the offender. After-reactions, such as sulking and resentment, increase during the school years.

There are fewer controlled studies of the development of aggresiveness or anger in children of elementary- and secondary-school ages than of the preschool age. There are, however, many clinical findings from the observations of psychologists and psychoanalysts that help in furnishing a better picture of the successive sequences of the development of anger throughout the elementary-school period. In

general, it has been observed that children pass through an elementary-school period of loudness and boasting, or sauciness toward
adults and others. To some observers this may indicate a means by
which the child keeps up his courage, to others it may be regarded as
a means of asserting his growing self. Faced with adjustments to
the school program, competition in the classroom and on the playground with his classmates, and being beyond the reach of his
parents when he is faced with such difficulties, frustration and tension frequently appear. They, thus, "woof," boast, and yell at each
other, often finding that the louder they bluster the greater is their
success with their peers. To the observer they may sound tough.
Underneath the child's aggressiveness, which has been considerably
aggravated by our competitive society into which he is suddenly
thrust, we find a growing individual with his loves, fears, likes, and
dislikes. He is faced with needs, which will be presented in a later
chapter, and when these needs are not being met with a fair degree
of adequacy, emotional outbursts may frequently be expected.

Age and affection. Goldfarb has pointed out that "As early as six
months and possibly even somewhat before, one observes the beginnings of sentiments, particularized attitudes, and attachments to a
particular person or limited number of people within the primary
family circle." [23] This is most important in the care and treatment
of infants and preschool children. Placement observations of babies
separated from their parents at this age reveal that such children
experience a prolonged psychological shock. The child's capacity for
affection and love develops gradually out of this early association,
in which he displays a close attachment (something certainly closely
akin to affection) to his mother or nurse. This early affectionate behavior may be looked upon as "outgoing" in nature, which is somewhat contrary to the idea that the infant and preschool child is
primarily egocentric in nature. His growth in capacity for affection
and love will be greatly influenced by the love shown him by his
parents. Love seems to be a two-way affair and grows best when it
is both given and received. A constant rejection in the home may
leave the child's capacity for giving forth affection undeveloped, or
may cause him to seek affection from individuals outside the home.
Overaffection and indulgence may have as undesirable effects as lack
of affection or rejection. While affectionate home conditions are helpful in the development of a feeling of security, which is essential for
good personal and social growth, overindulgence may operate to

[23] *Op. cit.*, p. 18.

produce a feeling of lack of security outside the home situation. There is, therefore, the danger that overaffection for one or both parents will tend to exclude affection for children of the child's age level. The child must make contacts outside the home and establish favorable affectionate relations with other children as part of the growing process as well as make preparation for the maintenance and assertion of himself as a unique personality.

Age and the development of jealousy. Jealousy should be looked upon as a response to situations established as a result of certain frustrations and inhibitions. It is a response usually directed at persons or objects that threaten to take away something, share something, or interfere with that which is felt to belong to oneself. Although the idea may be an obsession, taking possession and controlling the thoughts and behavior of the individual concerned, it is dynamic in nature and should be reckoned with as real insofar as it affects the thoughts and feelings of the particular individual. It may be of a prolonged nature, residing in the thoughts of the individual, or it may appear only when the situation or condition that produces it is present. The feelings caused by jealousy are difficult to describe. Responses similar to those of fear are present in the inability to face the issue and those of anger are aroused in the desire for revenge. The most frequent emotional combinations are feelings of anger, fear, self-pity, and grief.

Many children have the feeling of jealousy for the new baby, or when one child appears to be more favored by the parents than the other. Sometimes the response will take the form of aggressiveness in which they try to hurt the baby, or the unfavored child will show his feelings of anger in his relation with his toys and objects encountered in his play life. The jealous child may resort to infantile habits to gain the attention he desires, attention that is being denied him because of the appearance of the new baby, or some other condition. As the child grows older, the feelings of jealousy will be shown in other ways. Sometimes aggressiveness at school may be attributed to jealousy on the part of the child. He may turn to dirty expressions, or lying and cheating. He may become a loud-mouthed show-off or a very "good" child. Many forms of maladjustments are rooted in jealousy.

Changes in emotional behavior. It has already been suggested that many of the fears found among preschool children tend to lose their potency as the child matures and encounters new experiences. This is especially true in connection with fears of imaginary things.

and fears relating to animals. As the child matures and meets new situations, new fears appear. Experiments show that children quite quickly outgrow temper tantrums. Sometimes they develop more subtle ways of reacting to frustrating conditions. The development of

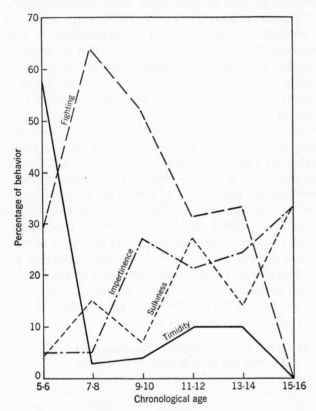

FIG. 20 Changes of behavior with chronological age for school pupils

emotional control and the elimination of many of the early childhood fears are closely related to growing up; the lack of such developments is symptomatic of infantilism. Some of the changes in behavior that have been observed and recorded by investigators are shown in Figure 20.[24] Changes in four types of behavior are shown here. Fighting seems to reach its peak at ages seven and eight and

[24] W. E. Blatz, S. N. F. Chant, and M. D. Salter, *Emotional Episodes in the Child of School Age.* University of Toronto Studies, Child Development Series, No. 9, 1937.

declines rapidly thereafter. However, the extent to which this form of behavior is found among a group of boys depends in a large measure upon the culture in which these boys are reared. Boys from the lower socioeconomic groups in the United States are taught by their parents as well as their peers that "one must fight for his rights." Timidity reaches its peak during the early adolescent years, and is no doubt closely related to the development of social consciousness and the desire for social approval that are associated with the beginning of adolescence. Sulkiness and impertinence are somewhat subtle ways of showing one's dislike for something or of meeting a frustrating situation. These continue to develop throughout the period of adolescence.

Worries of preadolescents. A number of studies have dealt with problems and worries of adolescents. Some of the problems of adolescents are presented in Chapter 17. In a study conducted by Pintner and Levy, a worries inventory was administered to 540 children in grades five and six of New York City.[25] The inventory consisted of fifty-three items. When these were grouped into eight categories, it was found that both sexes worry most about family and school situations and conditions. Next as sources of worry were those items grouped under personal adequacy, economic problems, and health problems. Little concern was noted for the imaginary and ornamental categories. The ten items ranking highest for the boys and the ten ranking highest for the girls are presented in order of frequency of worries reported in Table 27.

TABLE 27 Items from the "worries" inventory most frequently reported by boys and girls, in order of frequency

Boys	*Girls*
Failing a test	Failing a test
Mother working too hard	Mother working too hard
Being blamed for something you did not do	Mother getting sick
Father working too hard	Being late for school
Having a poor report card	Getting sick
Being scolded	Father working too hard
Spoiling your good clothes	Being scolded
People telling lies about you	Being blamed for something you did not do
Getting sick	Doing wrong
Doing wrong	Father getting sick

[25] R. Pintner and J. Levy, Worries of school children, *Journal of Genetic Psychology*, 1940, Vol. 56, pp. 67-76.

A careful observation of these sources of worry shows that fear is the foundation of the tendency to worry. As the child passes from the preschool to the school period, considerable anxiety related to failure in connection with different school situations appears. It has already been suggested that the earlier fears relate to bodily injury; but as the individual grows in understanding and meets different conditions and situations, he develops anxieties and fears relative to his status in the group. This does not mean that the earlier fears relative to bodily injury are suddenly eliminated. Rose Zeligs noted that sixth-graders were most frequently worried about matters pertaining to bodily injury, health, grades, and promotion in school.[26] Growth into and through adolescence is accompanied by anxieties connected with appearance, popularity, and inadequacies related to the sex role. Boys are fearful that they may not have the muscular physique that brands them as the male. They also attempt to show their strength and motor capacities. The girls feel the need to play the role of lady. It was pointed out in Chapter 6 that they register a decline in interest and ability on various motor tasks. There is some evidence that the freer expressive lives of girls may effect some change here. Also, the increased participation of members of both sexes in different types of social and recreational activities promises to give new values and concepts to specific sex roles. Boys in the middle-class culture are displaying an increased interest in the arts, while girls in all cultures are showing an increased interest in sports, both as participants and spectators. In many recreational activities where both boys and girls participate, the roles are differentiated so that one tends to complement the other.

Direction and control of emotional behavior

The capacity for emotional expansiveness on the part of the growing individual is limited; however, the range of possible development of emotional expressions will depend to a very large extent upon environmental experiences. Healthy social development requires that the child's emotions be controlled and channeled into worth-while activities. The subsequent pages furnish materials bearing on ways of directing the emotional growth of the child toward emotional maturity and healthy childhood and adulthood.

Understanding and accepting the child's feelings. One of the most

[26] Rose Zeligs, Social factors annoying to children, *Journal of Applied Psychology*, 1945, Vol. 29, pp. 75-82.

common methods used by parents and teachers in dealing with the child is that of attempting to reason with him as to how he should behave and to persuade him to behave in a manner acceptable to the parent or teacher. The child may be asked, "Why did you do this?" If the reason appears undesirable, an effort is made to show him that he should have responded on the basis of some other reason more acceptable to the adults. The assumption back of such an approach is that the child's behavior was deliberate and based upon reason.

The child may be given another reason for action or shown where his reasoning is not sound, and then persuaded to behave according to the new reason set forth. Such a process conceives of behavior resulting primarily from deliberation and thinking, and assumes that almost complete changes can be brought about through reasoning with the child and showing him inconsistencies in his ways of behaving, and by leading him to see that his behavior is inappropriate and undesirable. The results from this approach are sometimes effective; however, in many cases, the apparent effectiveness of this approach is not real. Simply learning the ideas and wishes of the parent or teacher and accepting these uncritically is not likely to be desirable. Furthermore, such an acceptance does not lead to growth in character development or to a responsible self-directive individual. In many cases, behavior outcomes show that this reasoning approach is far from effective. The statement is commonly made by parents and teachers, "I've talked and talked with *the child* about this but it doesn't seem to do any good."

With the development of the dynamic concept of the child, teachers and parents are coming to view child behavior as motivated by conditions and forces deeper and more inclusive than those of thinking and reasoning. There is a trend toward attempting to understand the child's feelings—viewing his behavior in terms of these feelings. When this approach is followed, much behavior that was conceived of by the teacher as inconsistent becomes more consistent and behavioral expressions are better understood in relation to actual situations. The importance of considering the child's own feelings about a situation is recognized, with the teacher indicating a willingness to evaluate behavior in terms of such feelings. The importance, then, of understanding how the child feels becomes paramount to any effective guidance in this connection. When such an approach is followed, the teacher or parent will show a less critical attitude toward the child; will reveal a real desire to understand his feelings about the situation; and will demonstrate a vital interest in helping im resolve conflicts and arrive at desirable means of adjusting to he situations with which he is confronted.

Helping the child meet frustrations. Emotions arise primarily as result of the blocking or frustration of some dynamic need of the child. If the child's needs for affection are frustrated, the result will be disorganized emotional behavior. The maintenance of emotional control will, therefore, depend in a large measure upon the extent to which these fundamental needs are realized. Since many frustrations appear during infancy, emotional maladjustments often have their onset in child-rearing practices. This, then, should be the beginning point for helping the child to meet frustrations. This does not mean that the child should be confronted with no frustrating situations, but rather that he should be taught satisfying and desirable ways of meeting such situations. Some conditions that contribute to the development and maintenance of emotional control during childhood may be described as follows: (1) *Secure home life.* The child who feels that he is wanted in his home and receives normal affections from his parents will tend to develop stable emotional outlooks and desirable emotional habits. (2) *Adequate physiological needs.* If the child receives adequate nourishment, sleep, and recreation, his chances for the development of emotional stability and control will be considerably enhanced. The need for recreation presupposes the possession of sufficient play materials to furnish him with opportunities for the satisfaction of his needs for activity. (3) *Achievement and status.* From infancy onward, the child is constantly facing problems. Continuous failure in his efforts to solve these problems will only lead to feelings of inferiority and loss of status. Children at all age levels should be provided with situations and conditions which they can meet satisfactorily. (4) *Protection from excessive emotional stimulation.* Traumatic emotional experiences, such as being bitten by a dog, or frightened by some movie experience, may be a tragedy in the emotional development of the child. Children should not be pushed into intense emotional situations. This does not mean that the child should be protected from all emotional situations, but rather the growing child is neither mentally nor emotionally prepared to meet intense or prolonged emotional situations without disastrous results. The child brought up in a home where there are continual bickering and emotional episodes will probably develop symptoms of nervousness and emotional instability. (5) *Social experiences with peers.* Young children should be provided with opportunities for playing with children of their age level. It is through happy experience with one's peers that many needs are met and emotional stability established. Through these experiences, children learn to express their feelings and at the same time control emotional behavior that proves to be undesirable and ineffective. The socially oriented child learns to respect the rights and feelings of others, he comes to think more about the welfare of others and give less consideration to his own self. This is a definite indication of growth in emotional control.

Some school situations productive of unpleasant emotional reactions of the elementary-school child are: interference with habitual self-expressive activities; the requirements of a difficult school task; unfamiliar and dominating demands of the teacher; unfamiliar requirements relative to personal habits; being left out in special tasks of an agreeable nature; being scorned or frowned at by the teacher; lack of status with classmates; and other conditions associated with the satisfaction of fundamental needs. Certain frustrations are likely to occur when a child goes to school for the first time. A case recently came to the attention of the writer which illustrates this.

Betty went to school for the first time with her cousin. The school was a traditional five-room school with poor physical facilities and teachers not very well trained, especially in the understanding of children. During the first day at school, Betty refused to come to the front and take a seat with several other children when she was requested to do so by her teacher. The teacher interpreted this as an act of stubbornness and threatened to punish Betty by spanking her with a ruler. This frightened Betty and she began crying. The teacher, then, passed her up for the day, but assured her that if she didn't do what she was told to do the next day she would really spank her. The next day Betty went into a very nervous state and cried profusely when the time came for her to go to school. It was at this time that Betty was brought by her parents to the attention of a clinical psychologist.

Special attention will be given in Chapter 16 to the practice of many schools today in meeting the mental-hygiene problems of children. Such practices tend to contribute to the development of emotional control among the pupils. The less rigid activities of the school provide opportunities for the satisfaction of certain fundamental needs. Friendly attention from the teachers, companionship with other children, and success in school tasks call forth emotional reactions of an agreeable nature and contribute to the healthy emotional growth of the child.

Controlling fear in children. Parents and teachers should recognize that fear as such is normal, and when properly directed is highly desirable. The child who has no fear of falling from high places is all too likely to bring injury to himself. The child lacking fear of automobile traffic would soon be killed if left alone on the streets. Fear, therefore, is something to be respected, and, in the case of the child lacking in the normal amount of fear for certain things and conditions, something to be cultivated. The child must be taught how to react to dangerous situations so as not to bring injury to himself or to others. When he has learned to meet such situations satisfactorily, his fear with regard to them will largely disappear. This is well illustrated in the case of the child's fear of drowning. Such a fear tends to disappear as the child learns to swim. The first rule, then, of coping with the child's fear is that of *teaching him to respect dangerous situations and at the same time develop sound methods and techniques for dealing with them.*

Perhaps the starting point in controlling the development of undesirable fears is that of *watching for early indications of undesirable fears and training the child to face the fear situation.* If the child begins showing signs of fear of dogs, he should be favorably conditioned toward dogs, providing the parent does not want these fears to grow and develop. The technique for handling a fear situation will best be learned under pleasant conditions or surroundings. According to the conditioning process, pleasure is connected with the experience of overcoming or breaking down the fear.

A third suggestion for controlling fears of the growing child is *never force the child to meet the fearful situation.* Sometimes parents use social exertion rather than physical exertion to get the child to meet a fearful situation. By forcing the child to recite in class in order to please the teacher, one may develop a sort of timidity that becomes difficult to eradicate. Forcing the child is likely to aggravate the particular fear or develop other fear states more harmful than the one that the parent or teacher is attempting to eliminate. Intense fear of parent or teacher, or intense fear of social disapproval, may be more subtle in nature than some other manifestations of fear, but perhaps more harmful to the development of the growing child.

The small child in particular learns a great deal from imitation. If the parent displays an intense fear of darkness, the child will in all probability develop a like fear. The principle of *avoiding an in-*

tense display of fear in the presence of the child is most important in connection with the development of favorable fear habits in the child. The mother's explanation that nothing will injure the child in the dark will be of little avail if she herself persists in displaying a strong fear at the appearance of darkness. A fifth rule for handling fears in children is that of *not playing upon the fears or referring to them further after the child has learned to handle the fearful situation*. A parent should not continue to give a child candy or some other reward every time he displays no fear of darkness, simply because he has learned to handle his fears in such a situation. If these satisfactions are continued, the child will come to expect them. If they should then fail to be forthcoming, the fear tendencies are likely to reappear.

As a child grows and develops toward maturity, he should develop an increased interest in others and less interest in the self. A sixth rule for the child in controlling fear is that of *arousing motives of self-sacrifice and interest in the welfare and happiness of others*. The child who is afraid of the dark may be motivated to protect his baby sister by looking after her welfare after she is asleep in a dark room. The child afraid of the rain may be motivated to meet his mother with an umbrella and thus shelter her from the rain and storm.

Certain fears are not justified by reality and do not yield to the reassurances coming from experiences and learning. These fears have at times been termed *neurotic fears* or neurotic anxieties. When such fears are observed, the parent or teacher should realize the necessity for securing specialized help. Teachers and parents should not be expected to understand the nature, bases, and treatment of such fears. A sympathetic attitude toward the child and his problems will, in such a case, be more beneficial than one of blame and exhortation. Some of the problems concerned with these fears will be given further consideration in Chapters 15 and 16.

Summary

The early emotional reactions of the child tend to be relatively diffuse and undifferentiated. As the child develops, the generalized excitement found in crying, laughing, and other emotional expressions tends to become less vigorous and involves less of the body as a whole. As the child develops, there are pronounced changes both in the nature of the stimulus which is effective in the arousal of the emotion, and in the manner of expression on the part of the individual concerned. Young children's emotions center around particular things, objects, or situations; the older child shows fears of happenings, social situations, and failure. The extent to which the child's emotions have moved out from *the self* to a consideration of the activities, feelings, and welfare of others is a rather good measure of growth toward emotional maturity.

Another sign of emotional maturity is emotional control. The emotionally mature person does not resort to childlike tactics and ways of expressing his feelings when confronted with an emotional situation. As children grow older, they will, if given adequate help by adults and if their lives have not been filled with frustrations, tend to outgrow certain infantile fears, angers, jealousies, and similar emotional features. This does not mean that emotions will cease to exist. Emotional control and direction mean the direction of emotions into satisfying activities and in ways harmonious with group welfare and group co-operation. Some factors that have been found to be helpful in aiding the child to meet frustrations of needs and desires are: (1) secure home life; (2) adequate physiological needs; (3) achievement and status; (4) protection from excessive emotional stimulation; and (5) social experiences with peers.

Questions and Exercises

1. Draw a diagram illustrating emotional conditioning in a child. What are the important features of such a diagram?
2. List as many different sources of fear in children as you are able. If convenient, use children whom you have observed to exemplify these.
3. Compare several first-grade children with several sixth-grade children for the effects of maturation upon the control of overt emotional expression. What are some of the subtle ways the sixth-grade children used for expressing their emotions?
4. Point out some of the ways children acquire fears—from parents, at school, home experiences, neighborhood experiences. How can parents guide the preschool child in the development of fears?
5. What is the significance of the changes in emotional manifestations with age presented in this chapter?
6. Distinguish by illustration between the *suppression* and *direction* of one's emotions.
7. Evaluate the methods suggested in this chapter for directing the child's emotional behavior. What other suggestions would you offer?

Selected Readings

Averill, Lawrence A. *The Psychology of the Elementary School Child*. New York: Longmans, Green & Company, 1949. Chap. II.

Breckenridge, Marian E., and Vincent, E. Lee. *Child Development*. 2nd ed.; Philadelphia: W. B. Saunders Co., 1949. Chap. III.

Gesell, Arnold, and Ilg, Frances L. *Child Development. II. The Child From Five to Ten*. New York: Harper & Brothers, 1949. Chap. XIII.

Goodenough, Florence L. *Anger in Young Children*. Minneapolis: University of Minnesota Press, 1931.

Hurlock, Elizabeth B. *Child Development,* 2nd ed.; New York: McGraw-Hill Book Co., 1950. Chap. VIII.

Jersild, Arthur T., and Holmes, Frances B. *Children's Fears*. New York: Bureau of Publications, Teachers College, Columbia University, 1935.

Jersild, Arthur T. Emotional Development; Chap. XV in Carmichael, L., *et al., Manual of Child Psychology*. New York: John Wiley and Sons, 1946.

Jersild, Arthur T. *Child Psychology*. 3rd ed.; New York: Prentice-Hall, 1947. Chaps. VII and VIII.

Mahler, M., Child Analysts, a chapter in Lewis, N., *et al., Modern Trends in Child Psychiatry*. New York: International University Press, 1945.

Millard, Cecil V. *Child Growth and Development in the Elementary School Years*. Boston: D. C. Heath and Company, 1951. Chap. XI.

Olson, Willard C. *Child Development*. Boston: D. C. Heath and Company, 1948. Chap. X.

Prescott, D. A. *Emotion and the Educative Process*. Washington: American Council on Education, 1938.

Thorpe, Louis P. *Child Psychology and Development*. New York: The Ronald Press, 1946. Chap. IX.

8

Intelligence:
Growth and Manifestation

There has been a continuously mounting tide of research on the nature of mental development; however, these studies have failed to bring forth a clear-cut set of principles relative to the nature of intelligence. This fact has made the problem of evaluating mental growth a difficult one—a problem around which much controversy still exists. The vast amount of research in this area of child development has brought forth information about the nature of mental growth and some of the identifiable factors affecting it which should be useful in understanding the characteristics of the growing child. The materials of this chapter will be especially concerned with the implications of research findings dealing with the following aspects of mental growth and development: (1) the nature and measurement of intelligence; (2) characteristics of mental growth; (3) factors that influence mental growth; (4) growth toward mental maturity; and (5) mental growth and child guidance.

The nature and measurement of intelligence

Concepts of intelligence. Concepts of the nature of intelligence held by students of psychology at the beginning of the present century were quite simple. Intelligence was regarded as a general mental power, or as a multiplicity of mental powers, that could be measured on a vertical scale by a single score. These scores were further transmuted into mental ages.[1] The IQ (intelligence quotient) was then

---

[1] A child's mental age, according to the early Binet tests and revisions, is his test score expressed in terms of the average age of children making that test score.

obtained by dividing the mental age by the chronological age. This was, therefore, a measure of the rate of growth of mental ability from infancy. Any significant changes in the individual's IQ from year to year were regarded as exceptions. Thus the theory of "the constancy of the IQ" was developed and generally accepted.

The concept of intelligence which has most influenced the development of group intelligence tests for school use is that based upon the ability of the individual to learn. This concept was somewhat in harmony with that advanced by Alfred Binet, the father of mental tests. Binet regarded intelligence as the ability *to comprehend, to follow directions,* and *to carry on autocriticisms.*[2] A definition of intelligence, consistent with the one presented by Binet, is that based upon the individual's *ability to adjust to novel situations.* "Intelligence is," according to William Stern, "a general capacity of an individual consciously to adjust his thinking to new requirements: it is general mental adaptability to new problems and conditions of life."[3] This is a broader idea than that based upon the subject's ability to think in abstract terms, which largely means the ability to learn materials from books and lectures. Stern's definition has been amplified and clarified by a number of students of educational psychology. Stoddard's definition furnishes a functional and more precise characterization of intelligence as the ability to perform activities which are characterized by "(1) difficulty, (2) complexity, (3) abstractness, (4) economy (speed), (5) adaptiveness to a goal, (6) social value, and (7) the emergence of originals (inventiveness), and to maintain such activities under conditions that demand a concentration of energy and a resistance to emotional forces."[4]

After reviewing many definitions of intelligence and analyzing what happens as a result of intelligence, Goddard arrived at what appears to be a sound and functional definition, which reads as follows: "Intelligence is the degree of availability of one's experiences for the solution of immediate problems and the anticipation of future ones."[5] This definition, like the one given by Stoddard, does not confine intelligence to one aspect of life activities; neither does it

[2] Joseph Peterson, *Early Conceptions and Tests of Intelligence* (Yonkers, New York: World Book Company, 1925).

[3] William Stern, *Psychological Methods of Testing Intelligence* (Baltimore: Warwick and York, 1914), p. 3.

[4] George D. Stoddard, On the meaning of intelligence, *Psychological Review,* 1941, Vol. 48, p. 225. Reproduced by permission of the *Review* and of the American Psychological Association.

[5] H. H. Goddard, What is intelligence? *Journal of Social Psychology,* 1946, Vol. 24, p. 68.

make of intelligence a simple ability that can be measured by means of a single test that would be applicable to all individuals, without regard to their past experiences.

Early manifestations of intelligence. Parents and social workers are intensely interested in ascertaining those characteristics exhibited by infants that are indicative of their level of intelligence. Eager parents observe certain activities of their child, and regard these as evidence that the child is superior in intelligence. A number of investigators, among whom are Gesell,[6] Bühler,[7] Shirley,[8] and Cattell,[9] have attempted to measure the mental ability of children less than two years of age.

By means of a developmental schedule, Gesell has been able to classify the behavior of children from the age of four weeks to three years. He has suggested the use of the DQ (developmental quotient) as a basis for evaluating the child's development.[10] The developmental quotient is found in a manner similar to that used for finding the intelligence quotient. It shows what percentage of normal development is present at a particular age level. Gesell's technique furnishes a basis for evaluating the child's development in four separate areas, namely, adaptive, motor, language, and personal-social behavior. Studies have shown that some of these have greater predictive value for future mental ability than do others. Furthermore, the earlier the tests are made, the less exact are such predictions. The intelligence of the one-month-old child cannot be estimated with as great an accuracy as that of the six-month-old child. At one month of age, the child will not show the same amount and variety of responsiveness to his environment as he will at six months of age. What responses are made must, therefore, be given greater weight in the evaluation of his intelligence than would the same responses made at a later period. Certain tests have been developed, however, which give significant correlations with IQ's obtained at a later period in the child's development. Such tests have provided a basis

[6] A. L. Gesell and Helen Thompson, *The Psychology of Early Growth* (New York: The Macmillan Company, 1938).

[7] Charlotte Bühler, *The Mental Development of the Child* (New York: Harcourt Brace and Co., 1930).

[8] Mary M. Shirley, *The First Two Years* (Minneapolis: University of Minnesota Press, 1933).

[9] Psyche Cattell, *The Measurement of Intelligence of Infants and Young Children* (Rev. ed.; New York: The Psychological Corporation, 1942).

[10] Arnold Gesell and Catherine S. Amatruda, *Developmental Diagnosis* (2nd ed.; New York: Paul B. Hoeber, Inc., 1947).

for observing early manifestations of intelligence. In this connection it should be realized that at all stages in the child's development the nature of his mental activities will be conditioned by such factors as (1) his hereditary constitution; (2) his physical and emotional well-being at the time; (3) his background of experiences; and (4) the nature of his needs, wants, and aspirations—child dynamics.

A study conducted by Shotwell and Gilliland was designed to ascertain which infants from the Cradle in Evanston should not be placed for adoption because of mental deficiency.[11] Generally, in case there are no mental or physical defects, the infants at the Cradle are placed by the age of three months. Test items were first selected which met the following criteria: (1) objectivity in giving and scoring; and (2) suitability as a measure of *adaptability*, rather than of physical structure of reflex behavior. Other criteria used in the final selection of test items were (1) age progression, (2) variability, (3) agreement of each item with the total score, and (4) correlations with IQ's secured from other standard tests of intelligence given at a later date. Upon the basis of these methods of validation and the age at which each of the test items was passed by approximately 75 per cent of the infants, a tentative battery of tests was assembled for the ages of four weeks, eight weeks, and twelve weeks. A careful study of these test items will show the nature of the child's manifestation of intelligence during the first three months of life. The following list shows the items in the battery for the four-weeks and eight-weeks age level.

4-weeks: first eleven items are given with child in supine position (necessary apparatus is indicated in parentheses)

1. Listens to Voice
2. Focuses on Object (metal tape)
3. Follows Tape Horizontally (metal tape)
4. Blinks or Averts Eyes (flashlight)
5. Closes Eyelids at Touch
6. Moves Abdomen at Touch of Alcohol (alcohol and applicator)
7. Reacts to Pain Stimulus (blood-sample instrument)
8. Opens Hands at Touch of Rattle (rattle or ring)
9. Closes Fingers about Rattle (rattle)
10. Diminishes or Ceases Activity at Sound of Music (music box)
11. Startles at Loud Sound (door bell)
12. Lifts Head to Zone 1 (head is raised from blanket)

[11] Anna M. Shotwell and A. R. Gilliland, A preliminary scale for the measurement of the mentality of infants, *Child Development*, 1943, Vol. 14, pp. 167-177.

13. Lifts Head to Zone 2 (head is raised between 45 and 90 degrees)
14. Compensates Head When Pulled to Sitting Position
15. Holds Head Erect Momentarily

8-weeks: first fifteen items are with child in supine position

1. Responds to Adult's Glance
2. Listens to Voice
3. Babbles
4. Follows Moving Person
5. Focuses on Object (metal tape)
6. Follows Tape Horizontally (metal tape)
7. Follows Tape Vertically (metal tape)
8. Follows Tape Circularly (metal tape)
9. Holds ring with Thumb Assisting (embroidery ring)
10. Makes Searching Head Movements (rattle)
11. Investigates Paper on Face (cellophane paper)
12. Reacts to Crumpling of Paper (cellophane paper)
13. Moves Head in Flight Movement (cotton applicator)
14. Reacts to Ringing of Bell (door bell)
15. Reacts to Changing Tone of Voice
16. Lifts Head to Zone 2
17. Lifts Head to Zone 3 (head is raised more than 90 degrees)
18. Compensates Head When Pulled to Sitting Position
19. Holds Head Erect

Measuring mental development during childhood. Binet's tests of general intelligence are especially important because of their influence in stimulating and guiding students in other countries in the development of instruments for measuring intelligence of preschool and school-age children.[12] His tentative scale of 1905 passed through a process of revision and finally culminated in a set of standards arranged at age levels. (Note the nature of this test as presented in Chapter 1.) The best-known American revision of the Binet scale is the Stanford Revision by Terman. The Binet test materials, along with others, were tried out on approximately a thousand children. Certain tests were dropped, others added, and after considerable study and revision the *Stanford Revision of the Binet Tests* was developed.[13] For more than two decades this remained a standard instrument for use in clinical psychology, psychiatry, and educational counseling. A further revision of this scale was published by Terman

---

[12] Joseph Peterson, *op cit.,* Chap. XI.
[13] Lewis M. Terman, *The Measurement of Intelligence* (Boston: Houghton Mifflin Company, 1916).

and Merrill in 1937.[14] This was standardized on more than three thousand cases and so extended that it would be useful for testing individuals of all ages from very young children to superior adults. Excerpts from the various age levels indicate the types of tests used as well as the typical performances of children from the different age groups.

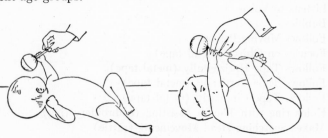

The four-week-old (left) merely grasps the rattle; the forty-week-old shakes it somewhat enthusiastically.

(Reproduced with permission from A. Gesell and C. S. Amatruda, *Developmental Diagnosis,* New York: P. B. Hoeber, Inc., 1947.)

Stanford Revision of the Binet Tests (Terman and Merrill Revision, 1937)

Year II

1. Identifies by name such objects as cat, button, thimble, cup.
2. Identifies parts of the body such as mouth, ears, and hands.
3. Builds tower using twelve 1-inch cubes.

Year III

1. Builds bridge using twelve 1-inch cubes.
2. Copies a circle.
3. Repeats three digits.

Year IV

1. Names such objects from memory as automobile, shoe, dog, spoon.
2. Completes drawing of a man.
3. Identifies common objects from cards with pictures.

Year V

1. Defines the words "ball," "hat," and "stove."
2. Copies a square.
3. Counts four objects such as blocks, or beads.

[14] L. M. Terman and M. A. Merrill, *Measuring Intelligence* (Boston: Houghton Mifflin Company, 1937).

Year VI

1. Locates missing parts in mutilated pictures.
2. Counts three, nine, seven, and five blocks.
3. Traces maze paths with pencil.

Year VII

1. Gives similarities between two things such as "wood" and "coal."
2. Copies a diamond-shaped figure.
3. Repeats five digits.

Year VIII

1. Gives similarities and differences between two things such as "baseball" and "orange."
2. Repeats sixteen-syllable sentence.
3. Notes absurdity in sentences, such as, "An engineer said that the more cars he had on his train the faster he could go."

Year IX

1. Finds words that rhyme with "head," "tree," etc.
2. Makes change, such as 10 - 4.
3. Repeats four digits reversed.

Types of intelligence tests. Intelligence tests have at times been classified as *individual* and *group* tests, depending upon whether they are designed to be administered to only one or to more than one person at a time. The *Stanford Revision of the Binet Scale* is one of the best-known examples of the individual intelligence test; the *California Test of Mental Maturity* and the *Thurstone Test of Mental Alertness* are examples of the group intelligence test. The chief advantage of the group test lies in the economy of time involved in administering the test to a number of individuals. Furthermore, it appears that less training is needed for administering and interpreting results from group tests. The advantage usually claimed for the individual intelligence test are (1) its greater reliability and validity and (2) its value in affording clinical data. The first-named advantage is certainly questionable. The reliability coefficient of most group intelligence tests is about as high as that of individual tests, such coefficients ranging from .82 to .92. There is no absolute criterion whereby the validity of an intelligence test may be determined, but when school marks are correlated with intelligence test results, the correlation coefficient is as high with the group test as with the individual test. Individual tests probably have their greatest advantage in testing (1) preschool children, (2) "problem" children, and (3) abnormal and defective persons.

The California Test of Mental Maturity, Pre-Primary S-Form is a group test designed for use with children from four to seven years of age. Tests 1 and 2 of the Short-Form reveal orientation in and ability to utilize space relationships. This perceptual ability is an important factor in mental abilities. Three tests in this S-Form reveal evidence of the more complex forms of intellectual activity found in reasoning or problem-solving behavior. The language tests consist of the following types: numerical quantity, inference, and vocabulary. The Elementary Form of the *California Short-Form Test of Mental Maturity* is designed for grades four through eight. A diagnostic profile of a twelve-year-old boy on this test is shown in Figure 21.[15] This shows graphically the status of the individual subject in language, nonlanguage, and total mental ages. Although the IQ may be obtained from the results of this test, its major purpose is to furnish information bearing on the nature and organization of the mental abilities of a given individual, so that such information may be used in the guidance and training program. The nonlanguage feature of such a test makes it possible to determine whether or not the individual being tested is mentally retarded as a result of some language handicap and particular retardation in reading. Thus, mental tests may be classified as *language* and *nonlanguage* tests.

Some criteria for selecting intelligence test items which would not discriminate significantly between children from different socioeconomic groups may be listed as follows:

1. Most of the problems should be equally common to the different socioeconomic groups.

2. Those words unfamiliar to any one socioeconomic group should be eliminated from the direction as well as from the test items.

3. The test should be a test of power rather than a test of speed. The time element should be unimportant.

4. Problems should be selected which require reasoning and problem solving without too much consideration being given to some special branch of knowledge or an accumulation of facts.

5. Creative and critical thinking should be introduced, when this can be done without discriminating in favor of or against any socioeconomic group.

6. Efforts should be made to see that all subjects tested are highly motivated. The testing program should not be too closely related to the school achievement program.

7. The examiner should have an understanding of the background of

[15] *Manual, California Short-Form Test of Mental Maturity,* Elementary, 1950 S-Form. Figure 21 is reproduced by permission of the California Test Bureau, Los Angeles, California.

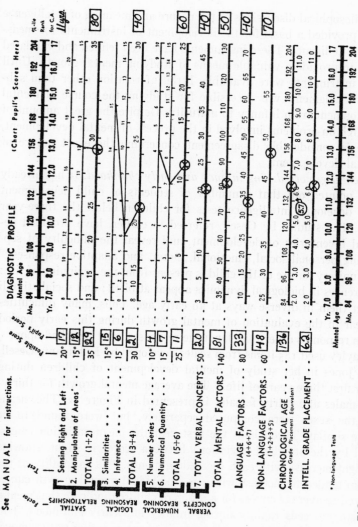

FIG. 21 A diagnostic profile of an eleven-year-old boy on the California Short-Form Test of Mental Maturity, Elementary 1950 S-Form

all the children tested and organize the program so as to provide a suitable psychological setting for all groups.

Characteristics of mental growth

Philosophical discussions of the nature and meaning of intelligence have provided a basis for the development of instruments for measuring intelligence. These instruments have been refined and validated so as to provide a valuable means of studying mental growth. Until such instruments were available, little information other than subjective judgments was accessible for studying the course of mental development from infancy to maturity. Despite the great amount of research on problems involved in the process of mental development, there is considerable disagreement concerning the exact nature of mental development.

Mental growth during infancy and early childhood. It has already been pointed out that a number of students of child development have developed intelligence tests for children below the three-year level. The studies by Gesell, referred to earlier, have provided detailed inventories of development, and reveal the difficulty of separating personal-social, emotional, motor, and adaptive responses.[16] The unitary nature of the child is present from the beginning of life; differences in biological dynamics appear at birth; and social stimuli affect them in diverse ways at an early age. Thus, many difficulties appear in the evaluation of mental growth during this early period when responses other than language responses must be relied upon.

Bayley used 185 items from scales developed by Kuhlmann, Gesell, and Jones in her study of mental development of children during their first three years of life.[17] The average mental growth for thirty-one males and thirty females is presented in Figure 22. The means for the sexes were computed separately, but were found to be quite similar. Throughout the first year the mean variation (measured by the standard deviation) between scores is slight, showing a slight increase with each succeeding month. The variability of the group tended to increase with age. Individual mental growth curves as well as average curves for a group of children indicate that mental growth proceeds rapidly during infancy and early childhood. This growth is evidenced both in the improvement of earlier performances

[16] Arnold Gesell, *Infancy and Human Growth* (New York: The Macmillan Company, 1928).

[17] Nancy Bayley, Mental growth during the first three years, *Genetic Psychology Monographs,* 1933, Vol. 14, pp. 1-92.

and in the increase in the variety of responses. Thus, mental growth from the beginning may be thought of as both quantitative and qualitative in value.

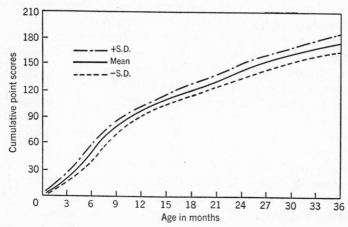

FIG. 22   Mental growth curve in terms of cumulative point scores
(After Bayley)

In general, intelligence tests given at the preschool level are less trustworthy than those given at a later age. This was shown in a study of the mental growth of 252 children in the guidance study at the University of California.[18] These children were given mental tests at specified ages between twenty-one months and eighteen years. The scores obtained were analyzed to show the extent of stability of mental test performances during this period. The constancy of mental test performances appeared to depend largely upon the age at testing and the interval between tests. That is, prediction was good over short age periods, with the predictive value of test scores increasing after the preschool years. However, the correlation between tests given at age two and at age five (r = .32) is not indicative of much stability in test performance at this age level.[19] When test scores earned at twenty-one months and twenty-four months are correlated (r = .71), a significant amount of stability is observed.

[18] M. P. Honzig, J. W. Macfarlane, and L. Allen, The stability of mental test performance between two and eighteen years, *Journal of Experimental Education*, 1948, Vol. 17, pp. 309-324.

[19] A perfect correlation would be a correlation coefficient of 1.00. A correlation of 0 signifies that no statistical relationship exists between the variables; while a minus correlation indicates a reverse relationship. For a more complete understanding of these and other statistical terms the reader is referred to any recent textbook on statistical methods applied to education or psychology.

The constancy of the IQ. During recent years there has been a great deal of controversy over the extent to which the IQ fluctuates. It was pointed out in the preceding paragraph that low correlations are found between IQ's obtained during the first three years of life and those secured later. Correlations between intelligence test scores obtained one or more years apart are far from perfect. Significant fluctuations are likely to occur in a large percentage of cases. The extent of these changes will depend largely upon the varying circumstances that have appeared in the child's life during the interim. In case few changes have appeared, fluctuations may be expected to be small. Most of the early studies were conducted with children from rather stable educational, cultural, and economic backgrounds. These studies yielded high correlations between IQ's obtained from successive tests. Many of the more recent studies have been conducted among children for whom significant changes had taken place in some aspects of their environment. These studies have revealed important changes in the IQ's obtained from test scores found at various intervals.

The Berkeley growth study is primarily based upon results obtained for children from socioeconomically superior homes. This study is especially useful, since forty children tested as infants were continuously tested until they were eighteen years of age. The data from these testings have been analyzed by Nancy Bayley.[20] She found that the IQ during early childhood is a poor indicator of later intelligence. The IQ's of these forty subjects were most variable at one month of age and again around nine to eleven years of age. The variability tends to diminish as maturity is approached. She gives the following interpretation to this variability:

It thus seems likely that the test scores are reflecting actual changes in variability which are inherent in the process of development of any given function. During growth of a structure or function variability increases, in part because of increasing individual differences in capacity, and in part because of individual differences in the speed with which the maturing process takes place. These two factors are known to be operative in physical growth, and it seems reasonable to expect that they may be characteristic of many growth processes. During the stage of development when both factors operate freely, the variability of measures or scores will become greater with the general increments in the structure or function concerned.

[20] Nancy Bayley, Consistency and variability in the growth of intelligence from birth to eighteen years, *Journal of Genetic Psychology*, 1949, Vol. 75, pp. 165-196.

The study by Honzig, Macfarlane, and Allen indicated a considerable stability of mental test performance between six and eighteen years of age; however, a study of individual cases showed that the IQ's of almost 60 per cent of the group changed fifteen or more points.[21] The IQ's of 9 per cent changed thirty or more points. Thus, predictions of IQ's at age eighteen, based on mental test scores obtained at age six, should be made with extreme caution. The University of Iowa Studies in Child Welfare have furnished some valuable materials bearing upon the fluctuations of the IQ and some factors associated with these fluctuations. Studies reported by Marie Skodak, Skeels, and others are of interest in this connection. Significant increases in IQ's are reported for children placed in superior environments, while continued decreases were observed for those placed in an inferior environment. The conclusions presented by Skodak emphasize the importance of a stimulating environment in raising the IQ level of children during the growing years.[22]

Certain broad generalizations may be made from an analysis of the various studies bearing on IQ changes. In the first place, intelligence test scores obtained during the first three years of life show a smaller correlation with test scores obtained five or six years later than do test scores obtained at age seven and age twelve or age thirteen. Secondly, the longer the interval existing between the tests, the lower the correlations found between the scores obtained from the two testings. Thirdly, intelligence test scores are affected by changed environmental conditions to a greater degree than had been supposed by the early investigators. Fourthly, varying factors related to the mental and emotional life of the child have an important bearing on his performance on mental test items. Some of the major factors affecting mental growth and thus the constancy of the IQ will be discussed at a later point in this chapter.

Mental growth curves of individuals. Individual age curves of intelligence scores have been plotted by Nancy Bayley.[23] These curves provide valuable information about the nature and stability of mental growth of individuals. An examination of the curves show that only a fifth of the forty-eight children had maintained approximately the same relative position throughout the first nine years. Some had successive periods of rapid and slow growth, while others

---

[21] *Op. cit.,* p. 315.

[22] Marie Skodak, Children in foster homes, *University of Iowa Studies in Child Welfare,* 1939, Vol. 16, Series No. 364.

[23] Nancy Bayley, Consistency and variability in the growth of intelligence from birth to eighteen years, *Journal of Genetic Psychology,* 1949, Vol. 75, p. 189.

showed a fairly consistent trend in fast or rapid growth over a longer period of time. Examples of individual trends for subjects during the entire eighteen-year period are presented in Figures 23 and 24.

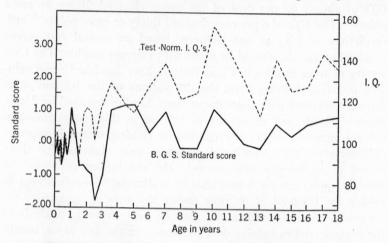

FIG. 23 Standard score and I.Q. curves for Case 3 M
(After Bayley)

The mental growth curves for the two children presented are plotted in terms of standard scores (sigma scores) and IQ's. The IQ's were derived from the published norms for the tests used. The standard scores were computed from the means of the mental ages for the group. This is a statistical measure of the child's relative status in his own group, which in this case is the Berkeley growth study group.

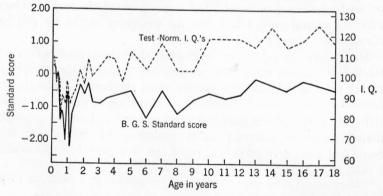

FIG. 24 Standard score and I.Q. curves for Case 15 F
(After Bayley)

The curves show considerable variability of scores during the first year or two, regardless of whether the curve is based upon one's status in his own group or norms from the test used. This variability tended to decrease after four, five, or six years of age. An inspection of the curves of different children show that some maintain fairly constant growth rates while others showed wide shifts. These shifts may occur at any age level and over a wide range of mental functions.

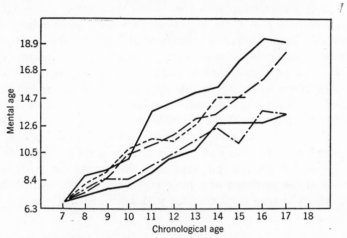

FIG. 25   Variability in mental growth of five boys whose mental test scores were equivalent at age seven

(After Dearborn and Rothney)

The principle that children grow in mental ability according to their own special pace is shown in the case of the growth curves of five children, shown in Figure 25.[24] Each of these children had an IQ of 92 at age 7 ; however, by the age of 17 one of the children had a mental age of almost 19, while two had a mental age of 13.6 years. These growth curves show the vast differences that may be observed in the rate and amount of mental gowth, a fact that must be borne in mind by all students concerned with the growth, development, and guidance of children.

Various explanations have been offered for the variations in IQ's of children as they grow older. In this connection, it seems likely that no single explanation will suffice for all cases. An explanation, in harmony with one of the principles of growth presented in Chapter 3, suggests that these irregularities may be due to differences in tempo

[24] Walter F. Dearborn and John W. M. Rothney, *Predicting the Child's Development* (New York: Sci-Art Publishers, 1941), p. 329.

of growth toward maturity. Mental growth curves do indicate that some children reach their peak of mental growth at an earlier age than others. This explanation, it would seem, operates, in part at least, in producing irregularities in the periodic IQ's obtained from children who vary from the average in their tempo of mental growth.

Another explanation would attribute these variations to the nature of tests used, that is, the kinds of intellectual abilities being tested. Some tests are made up largely of verbal tests, others are weighted heavily with various types of performance tests, while others may consist of a large number of mathematical items. Ideally, the testing situation should test the same group of children under constant conditions from early childhood to maturity, and these children should be given a single test applicable over the entire age period being studied. However, since the mental ability of the preschool child is so different from that of the preadolescent, it becomes very difficult to develop such a test, except perhaps in a very narrow function. An examination of the nature of a group of mental abilities suitable for testing mental growth indicates that the growth of intelligence consists of the maturing of a large number of closely related functions which become more complex with advanced maturity.

The upper limits of mental growth

The problem of when mental maturity is reached has practical as well as theretical implication. The answer to this problem is of special interest to students of adolescent psychology as well as to educators concerned with the training program for adolescent boys and girls. Some questions with which these students of education and psychology are concerned include: When does the average boy and girl reach the upper limit of mental growth? What factors affect the period of the cessation of mental growth? Is the upper limit of mental growth similar for individuals of different grades of intelligence? Do the upper limits of mental growth vary with different types of activities?

The cessation of mental growth. Students of educational psychology are not in agreement on the question of when mental growth or the ability to solve increasingly complex problems is reached. The age of sixteen was early set forth by Terman as the period when mental growth had reached its limit. This notion was arrived at as a result of his studies in which the *Stanford Revision of the Binet Test* was standardized. As a result of research conducted in connection with the revision of his test, the age of fifteen was arrived at as the upper limit of mental development. This is in harmony with the view earlier presented by Spearman in which he points out that studies indicate "that the growth of *g* (the general factor in intelligence) certainly does not continue to any appreciable amount after the age

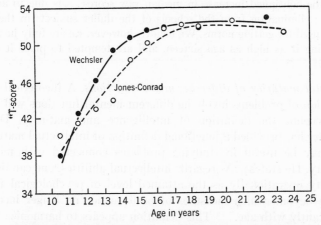

FIG. 26 Mental growth curves in terms of T-scores
(Reproduced from H. E. Jones and H. S. Conrad, "Mental development in adolescence," *Adolescence, Forty-third Yearbook of the National Society for the Study of Education,* Part 1, Chap. VIII.)

of fifteen or sixteen, and perhaps even ceases some years earlier. A person is thus adult in respect of *g* long before he is in respect of physical stature." [25]

In contrast to these conclusions, Jones and Conrad as well as others have furnished data indicating a later period for the cessation of mental growth.[26] Their results (see Fig. 26) indicate that in relatively homogeneous populations mental test scores increased up to age eighteen and in some cases beyond this age level. Retests of college students have also shown impressive gains. In the study by Livesay [27] of college students ranging in age from fifteen and a half to twenty-seven and a half, every individual studied registered a gain on the retests. One cannot say with certainty how much these

[25] Carl Spearman, *The Abilities of Man* (New York: The Macmillan Company, 1927), p. 364.
[26] H. E. Jones and H. S. Conrad, The growth and decline of intelligence: a study of a homogeneous group between the ages of ten and sixty, *Genetic Psychology Monographs,* 1933, Vol. 13, pp. 233-298.
[27] T. M. Livesay, Does test intelligence increase at the college level? *Journal of Educational Psychology,* 1939, Vol. 30, pp. 63-68.

gains may be attributed to practice on such tests and how much to the college environment. In his 1936 revision of the Kuhlmann-Binet test, Kuhlmann concludes from his findings:

Age median scores increase up to eighteen, apparently indicating that development continues well beyond this point. We do not know how much the continued increase in median raw scores... is due to an increasing elimination from the schools of the duller subjects in the age groups used for getting norms. We believe, however, we are fully justified in placing it as high as age sixteen, and are tempted to place it even higher.[28]

Mental maturity of different mental functions. A theoretical consideration of problems involving different mental functions will take into account the definition of intelligence and maturity. David Wechsler has provided a functional definition of intellectual maturity that may be useful in studying problems connected with mental maturity. He states: "As regards intellectual abilities, one can define maturity operationally as the attained level of psychological functioning beyond which measures of performance no longer increase significantly with age."[29] This definition appears to harmonize with the assumption underlying most objective measures of intellectual functioning.

An important observation, from the point of view of maturation, is that different abilities emerge and mature at different times. This is shown in Table 28 for scores on the different items of the *Wechsler Intelligence Scale for Children.* The scale consists of twelve equated tests, which may be said to involve as many different abilities, with some overlapping between the different tests. The data of Table 28 are based upon test results obtained from a single group of children whose ages are from five to fifteen years. Since the tests have been equated, it is possible to appraise maturity levels in terms of the age for attaining maximum performance in each of the abilities measured. Curves of growth obtained from plotting the weighted scores for the different tests show that the age at which maturity is reached for each of the abilities varies considerably.

Intelligence level and mental maturity. William Stern set forth at the beginning of this century the hypothesis that the age of cessation of mental growth varied markedly with the grade of intelli-

[28] F. Kuhlmann, *Tests of Mental Development* (Philadelphia: Educational Test Bureau, 1939).

[29] David Wechsler, Intellectual development and psychological maturity, *Child Development,* 1950, Vol. 21, p. 45.

TABLE 28   Weighted scores at mean of each age when base of comparison is equivalent standard score of 15-4 to 15-7 (after Wechsler)

Inf.	Com.	Ar.	Sim.	Voc.	D.Sp.	Test Age	PC	PA	Bl.D.	O.A.	Code	Maze
½	1	½	1	¾	2	5- 2	3	½	½	½	—	2
½	1	½	1	¾	2	5- 6	3	1	½	1	—	2
1	1	1	2	1	2	5-10	3	1	½	2	—	2
1	1	1	2	1	2	6- 2	3	1	½	3	—	2½
2	2	1	2	1	4	6- 6	4	2	2	3	—	3
2	2	2	3	2	4	6-10	4	2½	2	3	—	3
2	2	2	3	2	4	7- 2	4	3	3	4	—	3½
2	3	2	3	2½	6	7- 6	5	3	3	4	—	4
3	3	3	3	3	6	7-10	5	4½	4	4	—	4
3	4	3	3	3½	6	8- 2	5	5	4	4½	3	4½
4	4	4	4	4	6	8- 6	5	5½	4½	5	3	5½
4	5	4	4	4	6	8-10	5	6	5	5	3½	5½
4	5	4	5	4	7	9- 2	6	6	5	6	3½	7
4	5	5	5	5	7	9- 6	6	6½	5½	6	4	7
5	5	5	5	5	7	9-10	6	6½	5½	6	4½	7
5	6	5	6	5	7	10- 2	7	7	6½	6½	4½	8
5	6	6	6	5½	7	10- 6	7	7	6½	6½	5	8
5	6	6	6	6	7	10-10	7	7½	6½	6½	5	8
6	7	7	7	6	9	11- 2	8	8	7½	8	6	9
6	7	7	7	6½	9	11- 6	8	8	7½	8	6½	9
6½	7	7	7	7	9	11-10	8	8	7½	8	6½	9
7	8	8	8	7½	9	12- 2	8	8½	8	9	7½	9
8	8	8	8	8	9	12- 6	8	8½	8½	9	7½	9
8	8	8	8	8	9	12-10	8	8½	8½	9	7½	9
9	9	9	9	8½	9	13- 2	9	9	8½	9	8½	9
9	9	9	9	8½	9	13- 6	9	9	9	9	8½	9
9	9	9	9	8½	9	13-10	9	9	9	9	8½	9
9½	9½	9	9½	9½	10	14- 2	9	9½	9½	10	9	9
9½	9½	9	9½	9½	10	14- 6	9	9½	9½	10	9½	9
9½	9½	9	9½	9½	10	14-10	9	9½	9½	10	9½	9
10	10	10	10	10	10	15- 2	10	10	10	10	10	10
10	10	10		10	10	15- 6	10	10	10	10	10	10

gence, the idiot grade ceasing to develop rather soon after birth.[30] A number of students of testing have furnished information supporting such an assumption. The results of re-examinations of 639 cases

[30] See William Stern, *The Psychological Methods of Testing Intelligence* (translated from German by G. M. Whipple, 1914).

from the grade of idiocy to nearly average normal intelligence have been reported by Kuhlmann. The *Kuhlmann-Revision of the Binet Scale* was used. The subjects were divided into four groups: idiots (35 per cent); imbeciles (23 per cent); morons (12 per cent); and borderline (2 per cent). The mental growth in terms of mental ages

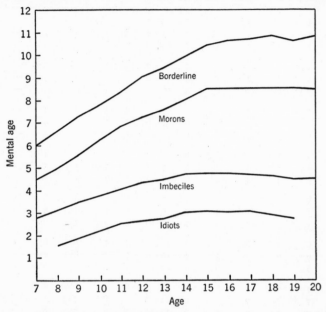

FIG. 27. The mental growth of children representing different degrees of mental retardation

(After Kuhlmann)

for the four groups is presented in Figure 27. These curves show that the mental ages of these subjects increased with age in proportion to the degree of mental ability present. On the whole, the mental ages cease to increase between the ages of fifteen and eighteen, the idiot grade ceasing to develop further about three years earlier than the borderline group. Kuhlmann points out further: "The lower grades lose more frequently in mental age than the higher grades."

The various studies agree that there is a deceleration in the rate of mental growth with age and that mental maturity is reached gradually. It is most likely that a careful analysis of individual growth curves will show that the upper limits are not reached at the same time by all individuals. Since growth in the more complex functions appears to continue longer that that in the simpler functions, one would expect growth among intellectually superior children to continue longer than growth among the mentally handicapped or perhaps average children. Additional research will be needed before this hypothesis can be completely verified. There is considerable evidence, however, that when the individual is stimulated by a rich and favorable environment, mental growth will continue beyond the age of fifteen or sixteen and perhaps into the twenties.[31]

Factors that influence mental growth

A great many studies have been conducted bearing on the relationship between mental development and various aspects of the child's environmental and hereditary constitution. The question of heredity versus environment constantly appears in an evaluation of the results of these studies. Although these studies have not brought forth an answer by means of which certain things may be attributed to heredity while others may be attributed to environment, they have shown how closely the child's hereditary nature and environmental forces and conditions are interrelated from the very beginning of life. These studies have furnished the bases for generalizations about the factors that influence growth, factors which will be presented in the subsequent discussions.

Hereditary factors. The nature of the child's hereditary nature was discussed at length in Chapter 2. It was pointed out there that certain fundamental principles of heredity operate in producing the embryo and the infant child. These principles do not operate, however, independently of environmental factors and conditions. The effects of environment begin to operate with the fertilization of the ovum and continue to operate until death. Since one's ability to perform any task is a result of both hereditary and environmental factors, one can never say just how much each contributes. At one time, intelligence was defined as one's "innate ability to learn." Many psychologists looked upon intelligence as an inherited capacity that could not be affected by adverse physical conditions and unfavorable environmental factors. There were others who would discount the influence of heredity. John B. Watson once stated:

Give me a dozen healthy infants, well formed, and my own specified world to bring them up in and I'll guarantee to take any one at random and train him to become any type of specialist I might select—doctor,

[31] See D. Wechsler, *The Measurement of Adult Intelligence* (Baltimore: William and Wilkins, 1939).

lawyer, artist, merchant-chief, and yes, even beggar man and thief, regardless of his talents, penchants, tendencies, abilities, vocations, and race of his ancestors.[32]

There is good evidence, however, that individual differences in mental performances appear during the first year of life. Genetic studies of child development reveal that some children are born with structural deficiencies that make it impossible for them to acquire the personal and social skills necessary for daily living. The widespread recognition of individual differences, even within a relatively homogeneous social and economic group, furnishes further proof that much of what we term individuality arises from constitutional differences.

It seems relatively safe to say that heredity sets rather broad limitations to one's achievements. Whether or not the capacity will be developed depends on a number of factors in the child's environment and experiences. It seems probable that few if any individuals ever develop their full potentialities; however, some develop theirs to a much greater degree than do others. It would seem that *good genes* and *favorable conditions for their development* are both essential to the production of an intelligent individual.

Although children with defective intelligence may be found in all cultural levels and from families with normal or superior intelligence, the preponderance of feeble-minded will be found among the degenerates, and in families with a history of mental deficiency. Recent statistical studies of blood groups in mentally defective children and their mothers suggest that the Rh factor bears some relationship to mental deficiency.[33] Not all children regarded by their teachers as feeble-minded are actually feeble-minded, although their reactions may be on the level of those of a feeble-minded child. There is a difference between children whose potential mental abilities are extremely low and those who are functioning on a very low plane. Some conditions, listed by Grace Arthur, that can lower the reaction level of an individual to the feeble-minded level in spite of normal intellectual endowment include the following:

(1) Physical handicaps such as impaired vision, impaired hearing, impaired mechanisms for motor coordination, etc. that interfere with academic learning and with success on some scales for measuring intelligence.

[32] *Behaviorism* (New York: W. W. Norton and Co., 1925), p. 82.
[33] See Peter Gruenwald, Mental deficiency of prenatal origin: A challenge to preventive medicine, *American Journal of the Medical Sciences,* 1947, Vol. 214, pp. 605-611.

(2) Brain injury which occurred at birth or from later accident that interfered with some kinds of intellectual activity but not with others.

(3) Severe early illness that delayed but did not prevent mental development.

(4) Delayed speech that extends far beyond normal limits, but has not prevented development of non-verbal abilities.

(5) Intellectual idiosyncracies that act as special intellectual disabilities until they are diagnosed and given appropriate treatment, and frequently are confused with general mental deficiency.[34]

The relation between physical and mental development. The problem of the relationship between physiological and anatomical structures and intellectual and other personality factors has received the attention of a number of investigators during the past two decades. Some of the early anthropological studies by Franz Boas and others showed that the proportions of the body are not stable, but that children may differ considerably in bodily form from their parents. The significant increase in stature among American children, assumed to be the effect of improved standards of living, is evidence of the changes that may occur within a generation. A study of these changes has led to the problem of the relationship between physical changes and mental growth. Shuttleworth's studies indicated a relationship between mental age and the period of maximum physical growth.[35]

The studies conducted by Franz Boas furnish some worth-while information on this problem. Mental and anatomical measurements were made on the children at the Lincoln School of Teachers College, Columbia University. Boas concludes from an analysis of the data gathered:

A study of the data collected shows an unexpectedly high relation between intelligence quotient and stature. Children short for their age had an intelligence quotient markedly under the norm, those tall for their age, one above the norm. The groups short and tall contain a hereditary element that is probably less pronounced in the tempo of ossification. The latter shows the same type of relation to intelligence quotient. Retarded children have a lower intelligence quotient than those accelerated. . . . The close correlation between anatomical and psychological traits in childhood must be interpreted as due to the influence

[34] Grace Arthur, Some factors contributing to errors in the diagnosis of feeble-mindedness, *American Journal of Mental Deficiency,* 1950, Vol. 54, p. 497.

[35] F. K. Shuttleworth, The physical and mental growth of girls and boys aged six to nineteen, *Monographs of the Society for Research in Child Development,* 1939, Vol. IV, No. 3.

of the tempo of physiological development over the body and its functions.[36]

Two factors should be borne in mind in connection with generalizations from the conclusions reached by Boas. In the first place, it is always dangerous to generalize from averages to individual cases. Thus, the tall child need not be above average in intelligence, and the short child need not be below average in intelligence. Secondly, one should not confuse causation with association. It seems likely that certain factors that cause children to be healthy and larger than other children may result from conditions which also affect mental growth. There are, on the other hand, factors that cause other children to be tall which have no bearing on the intelligence quotient. Tallness tends to run in certain families. Likewise, superior intelligence tends to run in certain families. The two traits or conditions may or may not appear in the same family.

There is evidence that physical defects are often associated with mental retardation. In a study of 900 educationally backward children of Los Angeles, Goldwasser reports a higher incidence of physical defects than that found among 2,700 mentally normal children.[37] Other studies have verified this positive relationship. In interpreting the results from these studies, it should be pointed out that the relationship is not high. Furthermore, many physically handicapped children are also handicapped by adverse environmental circumstances. This may result in such a child with normal intelligence being judged as subnormal. The case of Dick shows how defective sensory equipment may be a handicap to a child's mental development.

Dick was a feeble twelve year old boy. His speech had the quality of that of a deaf person. His work was slow and careful. He had had a succession of intelligence tests. His last Binet test had yielded an IQ of 51. This failed so completely to state his reaction level, that a non-verbal examination was indicated. On Form I of the Point Scale of Performance Tests, that can be given without any speech on the part of either the patient or the psychologist, Dick earned an IQ of 89. An audiometer test showed a hearing defect severe enough to demand special training. A more careful diagnosis was the starting point for a change in treatment, and type of training that should result in

[36] Franz Boas, The relation between physical and mental development, *Science,* 1941, Vol. 93, pp. 339-342.

[37] M. Goldwasser, Physical defects in mentally retarded school children, *California and Western Medicine,* 1937, Vol. 47, pp. 310-315.

a return to normal community living when his schooling is completed. At the State School for the Deaf, Dick made a happy and successful adjustment. Under the teaching provided there, he began to learn, as he had not been able to do in classes for hearing pupils.[38]

The home environment. The influence of the family upon the intelligence of the children has been a subject of considerable controversy and research. The fact that siblings are in general more alike in intelligence than children selected at random has been offered as evidence of the influence of heredity. Studies conducted at the Iowa Child Welfare Research Station have provided some interesting and worth-while results bearing on the influence of the family. In one of these studies, Harold Skeels investigated the mental development of children with known inferior social histories who were placed in adoptive homes during infancy.[39] Three groups of children were used in this study. One group consisted of 87 children who had IQ's of 75 or less. A second group consisted of 111 children whose fathers were unskilled or slightly skilled laborers. The third group consisted of 31 children, who were included in both of the other groups, with mothers mentally retarded and fathers classified low on the occupational scale. The mental ability of these children was studied after they had resided in their foster homes a number of years. Skeels found that the children with inferior social histories attained a mental level that equals or exceeds that of the population at large. He further concluded from this study that inferior mental ability did not appear among these children any more than among the population at large, while superior mental ability appeared more often than would be expected, based on that found in the population as a whole.

Another study conducted at the Iowa Child Welfare Research Station was concerned with the extent to which adopted children in the same family resembled each other in mental ability.[40] All of the adopted children had had four or more examinations in which the 1916 revision of the Stanford-Binet test was used. A correlation coefficient of $.65 \pm .06$ was found between the IQ's of the pairs of adopted children tested at approximately the same ages in their preadolescent years. Most studies of siblings give a correlation co-

---

[38] Grace Arthur, Some factors contributing to errors in the diagnosis of feeblemindedness, *American Journal of Mental Deficiency,* 1950, Vol. 54, pp. 497-498.

[39] Harold M. Skeels, Children with inferior social histories: their mental development in foster homes, *Psychological Bulletin,* 1941, Vol. 38, p. 594.

[40] Marie Skodak, Mental growth of adopted children in the same family, *Journal of Genetic Psychology,* 1950, Vol. 77, pp. 3-9.

efficient of approximately .40 to .60.[41] Skodak concludes, "The patterns of mental growth on repeated examinations show a similarity between pairs of children growing up in the same family."

The social-class structure. There is evidence that continued exposure to differential environmental conditions found in different social-class groups favors the development of certain abilities, while it discourages the development of other abilities. The tasks to be learned at school are more closely related to the background of the middle-class group than of the lower-class group; consequently, middle-class children tend to excel on these tasks. This was shown in the study by Janke and Havighurst.[42] All available sixteen-year-old boys and girls in a Midwestern community were given the *Revised Stanford-Binet* intelligence test, the *Performance Scale* of the Wechsler-Bellevue Adult and Adolescent Scales, the *Iowa Silent Reading Test*, the *Minnesota Form Board*, the *Minnesota Mechanical Assembly Test,* and the *Chicago Assembly Test for Girls.* They conclude:

(2) Boys and girls from families of higher social status tended to do better in all the tests than boys and girls of lower social position, with the exception of the Mechanical Assembly Test, where there was no reliable social class difference between the boys.

(3) Urban boys and girls tended to do better than rural boys and girls, but not statistically so.

(4) No significant sex differences were obtained.

A large percentage of intelligence-test materials is taken from the cultural environment of the higher social and economic groups. This is especially evidenced by the type of vocabulary used and the total situation in which tests are given. The school program promotes middle-class values and rewards those children who are successful in attaining the things regarded by the middle class as superior. Thus, it is obvious that the lower-class child is at an extreme disadvantage on most intelligence tests used in connection with school situations. Recognizing this condition, Allison Davis and Robert Hess set forth to develop a test which would appeal equally well to all occupational

[41] See E. Ebert and K. Simmons, The Brush Foundation study of child growth and development, I: Psychometric studies, *Monographs of the Society for Research in Child Development,* 1943, Vol. 8, No. 2: E. L. Thorndike, The resemblance of siblings in intelligence test scores, *Journal of Genetic Psychology,* 1944, Vol. 64, pp. 265-267.

[42] L. L. Janke and R. J. Havighurst, Relation between ability and social status in a midwestern community, II: Sixteen-year-old boys and girls, *Journal of Educational Psychology,* 1945, Vol. 36, pp. 499-509.

groups.[43] One of the new tests they developed is known as the *Davis-Hess Individual Test of Intelligence.* The type of problems included in this test dealt with: "(1) the understanding of physical principles; (2) the classification of objects into categories selected by the child; (3) memory processes; (4) the drawing of inferences from given relationships; (5) imaginative processes involved in mentally grasping and manipulating objects in their spatial relations; (6) perception and description; (7) discrimination; (8) critical processes and the ability to verify solutions; (9) ability to discover possible arithmetical combinations and possible permutations in ordered objects; and (10) general inductive and deductive reasoning." The results from this test do not show the lower socioeconomic white children to be inferior to the upper socioeconomic group. One girl referred to as Nancy was listed as having an IQ of 90. On the Davis-Hess test, her IQ equaled that of the upper socioeconomic group whose average IQ was 110.

The results of such studies as the one referrred to by Davis and Hess are not intended to show that average differences in intelligence among children from different class structures may be wholly accounted for on the basis of the type of materials used in the tests. These results do indicate, however, that, in general, intelligence-test scores are seriously affected by a child's experiences, and that most intelligence tests have been constructed so as to favor the child from our middle- and upper-class groups.

The influence of schooling. The question with which this topic is concerned is: Is the child's intelligence quotient affected by systematic or formal schooling? If the intelligence quotient is increased through schooling, does this mean that the general level of one's capacity to learn, to reason, and to cope with novel situations has been raised beyond what it would have been without such a program of schooling? Or, does this mean that a stock of information and skills has been acquired that enable him to make a better score on intelligence tests? There is a distinct difference between raising the general mental level of the individual and that of developing certain skills and mastering information encountered through formal school experiences. The question here raised may be thought of as another aspect of the nature-nurture controversy, referred to earlier in this chapter. Many students have been concerned with the problem of the effects of schooling on the IQ and considerable data

[43] Allison Davis and Robert D. Hess, What about IQ's? *Journal of the National Education Association,* 1949, pp. 604-605.

have been gathered bearing on this. Some of the representative studies of recent date will be reviewed briefly in this connection.

A number of investigations, most prominent of which are those conducted at the University of Iowa, have been concerned with the effects of attendance at nursery school upon the intelligence quotient.[44] The results of these studies have been summarized by R. L. Thorndike as follows:

(1) The Binet IQ of children from generally superior homes rose markedly during a period in nursery school, but did not rise during the summer spent in the general home environment.

(2) Performance on the Merrill-Palmer test showed some residual gain, after nursery school attendance, over and above apparent adaptation effects, but the influence was not as marked as for the Binet.

(3) The gains in Binet IQ were maintained by a sample of children located and tested after several years of attendance at other than University schools.

(4) The gains in Binet IQ were further added to by a sample of children who remained in the University schools and were tested at a later time.

(5) Length of attendance at the University schools was related to intelligence test score in high school and at college entrance.

(6) Gain from attending preschool was not related to the occupational level of the parent.

(7) The greatest gain in preschool was for those who originally received the lowest scores, and the smallest gain for those who received the highest (regression effect).[45]

The Iowa studies have been severely criticized by a number of psychologists.[46] It has been pointed out that many of the children used in the Iowa studies came from underprivileged homes and had not had the opportunities for mental growth which would be found among children upon whom mental tests have been developed and standardized. In a study of the effects of nursery-school attendance, Olson and Hughes used as subjects children from average or superior home environments. They found that nursery-school children from such home backgrounds did not differ significantly in their mental

[44] See the *Thirty-ninth Yearbook of the National Society for the Study of Education*, 1940, Part II.

[45] R. L. Thorndike, Constancy of the IQ, *Psychological Bulletin*, 1940, Vol. 37, p. 178. Reproduced by permission of the *Bulletin* and of the American Psychological Association.

[46] See especially the criticism by Quinn McNemar, A critical examination of the University of Iowa studies of environmental influence upon the IQ, *Psychological Bulletin*, 1940, Vol. 37, pp. 79-92.

growth from non-nursery-school children from similar home backgrounds.[47] It appears that an environment which provides for mental stimulation and opportunities for mental development in harmony with the maturational level tends to provide for the optimum mental development of the child. Thus, the improvement of an environment beyond a certain point may be valueless insofar as its contribution to mental growth is concerned.

The question may be raised as to what constitutes a superior environment. An allied question is: Will an environment that is superior for one child necessarily be superior for another child? The problem of what constitutes a superior environment is difficult to describe, except in very general terms. It has already been suggested that an environment that provides for stimulation and optimum opportunities for mental growth might be regarded as a very good environment. Since children differ in needs and in abilities, it seems most likely that an environment that would provide stimulation for one child may actually frustrate another. Studies of the effects of schooling show that some schools appear to affect changes in IQ's whereas other schools produce very little if any change. A modern school would provide for the needs and abilities of all the pupils and thus produce changes in IQ's among those who were formerly handicapped by an unfavorable environment. Findings in a study by Lorge support this viewpoint.[48] A number of boys who were tested in 1921-22, when they were in the eighth grade, were tested again in 1941, twenty years after the first testing. These boys were grouped in terms of the highest grade completed at the time of the 1941 testing and in terms of scores earned in 1921-22. The findings showed that schooling made a difference in the IQ's. The further the person had gone in schooling in terms of grades completed, the greater the increase in scores over the original scores in 1921-22. However, not all individuals registered gains in proportion to their schooling. Gains appeared to be somewhat relative to the earlier scores. A few children who made high scores at the initial testing but did not continue their schooling beyond the eighth grade made greater gains than some who made low scores on the original testing and remained in school two or three more years. These findings support the hypothesis earlier presented. *An environment which*

[47] W. C. Olson and B. O. Hughes, Subsequent growth of children with and without nursery-school experience, *Thirty-ninth Yearbook of the National Society for the Study of Education,* 1940, Part II, pp. 237-244.

[48] I. Lorge, Schooling makes a difference, *Teachers College Record,* 1945, Vol. 46, pp. 483-492.

challenges the individual and furnishes opportunities for mental growth in harmony with his limitations is the optimum environment for the development of one's intelligence.

Effects of bilingualism. The difficulty of obtaining reliable estimates of the intelligence of lower-elementary-school children from homes of low socioeconomic status or from homes in which a foreign language is the medium of conversation is well known. Since a large number of children may fall in some such category, this fact should be borne in mind by those concerned with measuring the intelligence of children from such a background. In a study of Goldin and Rothschild, the *Pintner-Cunningham Primary Mental Test* was administered to a group of school children of whom 99 per cent were of Italian home background.[49] The predominant language in the homes of these pupils was Italian, and the children had little literary or cultural background. Correlation coefficients obtained between intelligence quotients from children at the first three or four grade levels indicated that the IQ was so unstable that intelligence tests should be given annually, if up-to-date intelligence quotients are to be available for these pupils.

In the study by Natalie Darcy of the effect of bilingualism upon the measurement of the intelligence of preschool children, 106 monolingual children were matched with 106 bilingual.[50] These children were matched for age, sex, and socioeconomic status. Two individual intelligence scales were administered to each child of the two groups. The 1937 *Revision of the Stanford-Binet Scale,* Form L was used as a verbal test and the *Atkins Object-fitting Test,* Form A was used as a nonverbal measure of intelligence. Some of the conclusions from this study are summarized by Darcy as follows:

1) There were significant differences between the mean IQ's achieved by the monolingual and bilingual subjects on the *Stanford-Binet Scales.* These differences were consistently in favor of the monoglots when divided according to age and sex and also when the age groups and sexes were combined.

2) Conversely, when the differences in the mean IQ's were determined for both language groups on the *Atkins Test,* significant differences in favor of the bilingual group were found. . . .

[49] Myron R. Goldin and Seymour Rothschild, Stability of intelligence quotients of metropolitan children of foreign-born parentage, *Elementary School Journal,* 1941-42, Vol. 42, pp. 673-676.

[50] Natalie T. Darcy, The effect of bilingualism upon the measurement of the intelligence of children of preschool age, *Journal of Educational Psychology,* 1946, Vol. 37, pp. 21-44.

3) ... In every age and sex division, the mental ages of the monoglots surpassed those of the bilinguists on the *Stanford-Binet Scale,* while on the *Atkins Test,* the performance of the bilinguists was consistently superior to that of the monoglots.

Effects of conflicts and maladjustments. Case studies of children suffering from some emotional shock show that the IQ may be adversely affected. In a study conducted primarily with nursery-school children at the University of Georgia, 28 per cent of 130 children tested and retested, at later intervals had lower IQ's on the retest. A case reporting a loss in IQ indicates some of the conditions that may adversely affect a child's intelligence test score on retests.

A loss of 22 I.Q. points was recorded for a little girl who was tested at the age of three years three months and retested at five years eight months. The Merrill-Palmer Scale was used for the initial testing and the Terman-Merrill for the second testing and this may account for some of the change. It seems possible, however, that the maladjustment arising from jealousy of an infant brother may have had some influence. Until the birth of the sibling the subject was the center of attention, and numerous relatives showered her with affection and gifts. The arrival of a competitor brought about a distinct personality change. The subject showed sullenness, negativism, and timidity. Her mother stated that her play tended to be more solitary and quiet in type. The second test was given during the period when the maladjustment was an acute problem in the home. In the test situation the child seemed to be reasonably cooperative but somewhat cool and aloof. It should be stated that after much effort the parents have succeeded in improving the adjustment of the subject.[51]

Mental growth and child guidance

A better understanding of the nature and principles of mental growth is especially important to those concerned with the guidance and training of preschool and school-age children. The development and use of mental tests have furnished much information about the mental development of children at different age levels. Such tests have considerable value in the hands of one who understands their limitations as well as their possibilities. The fact that the various studies referred to throughout this chapter do not agree on many items connected with mental growth is in itself evidence that intelli-

[51] Mary E. Allan and Florene M. Young, The constancy of the intelligence quotient as indicated by retests of 130 children, *Journal of Applied Psychology,* 1943, Vol. 27, p. 56. Reproduced by permission of the *Journal* and of the American Psychological Association.

gence tests are not infallible and that the results obtained from administering them should be used with caution.

Need for quantitative analysis of test performance. Results from tests are usually expressed in a quantitative score, with too little consideration given to the nature of the mental performances involved in securing such a score. Two children may make the same score on an intelligence test, but be quite different in what might be termed general mental structure. The one child may be able to complete all of the items involving memory and show a long memory span but make a poor record on items involving completions; the other child may show the reverse abilities. Thus, the abilities making up the composite score, although different in general structure, furnish the same total score.

Another factor that should be borne in mind by those interpreting test results grows out of the quest for objectivity. We have no more reason for believing that a child's capacity to practice good health habits, or his ability to produce some worthy piece of art, can be measured by means of a single score from an objective test than that the IQ of the child will reveal his full mental resources. The problem of determining one's level of mental ability is just as complicated as that for determining other levels of performance. An objective test, although highly reliable, may not be valid. The problem of testing the validity of an intelligence test is extremely difficult, since scores must be compared with other mental performances, all of which will be conditioned by varying environmental forces and conditions.

Present-day guidance procedures seek to avoid certain weaknesses that have characterized much counseling during the past two or more decades. The development of tests designed to evaluate more accurately the traits and characteristics of individuals is among the first prerequisites for guiding them in their educational and social activities. Tests alone, however, are insufficient. In fact, these are not the most important element in a guidance situation. An understanding counselor is essential not only for evaluating the quantitative score but for determining and evaluating the qualitative elements. These qualitative elements present in individual testings are difficult to evaluate, and are thus oftentimes omitted. The notion that those items that cannot be objectively evaluated should be omitted from any consideration of the child's mental growth may lead to the omission of some of the most important elements. The converse of this would be to include items because they are objective.

Photographic observation done with examination crib.
(Courtesy of Dr. Arnold Gesell)

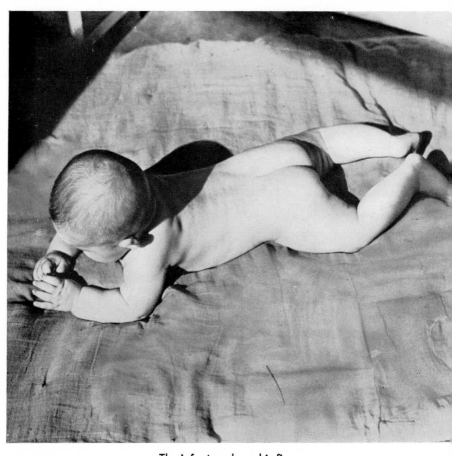

The infant explores his fingers.
(Courtesy of the Metropolitan Life Insurance Company)

Each stage of the baby's growth is accompanied by certain changes in behavior—the child grows as a whole.

(Courtesy of Gerber's Baby Foods)

The child's development follows an orderly sequence, but it is at all times conditioned by the forces and conditions around him.

(Courtesy of the Metropolitan Life Insurance Company)

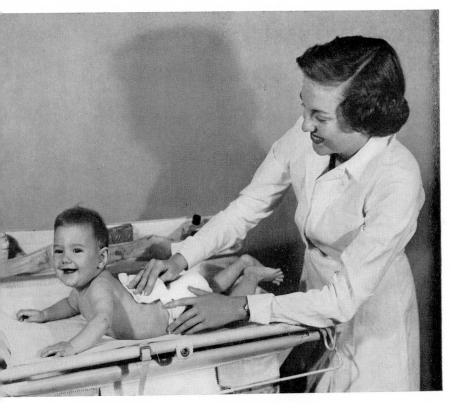

The child displays delight at an early age.
(Courtesy of the School of Home Economics, University of Georgia)

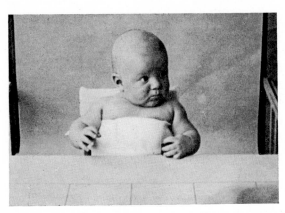

A sixteen-week-old infant seated in an examining chair of the clinic crib.
(From Gesell *et al., Vision: Its Development in
Infant and Child*, Harpers, 1949)

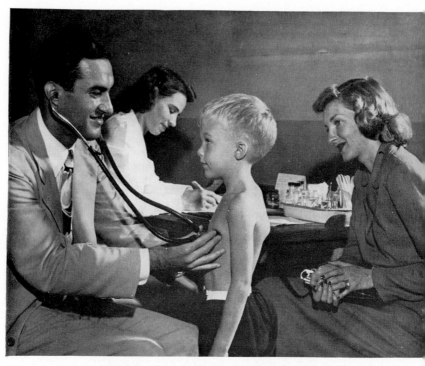

Checking the child's physical development.
(Courtesy of the New York City Department of Health)

**The effects of malnutrition on the growth and health of
Belgian children.**
(From *Archives of Disease in Childhood,* September, 1945)

Differences in body build of three girls all eight years old.
(Courtesy of the U.S. Bureau of Human Nutrition and
Home Economics)

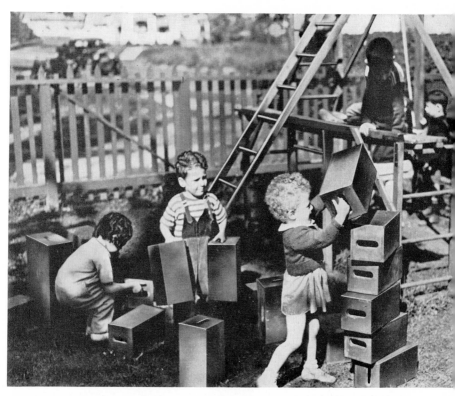

Wholesome personality development begins in childhood.
(Courtesy of the Metropolitan Life Insurance Company)

Jimmy finds that using a man-sized saw requires coordination and strength.
(Courtesy of the McCall Corporation)

The make-believe world approaches reality as the child rolls out cookies.
(Courtesy of the School of Home Economics, University of Georgia)

**The needs of children are satisfied through wholesome and
pleasant experiences.**
(Courtesy of the School of Home Economics, University of Georgia)

Language growth is enhanced through social and educational experiences.
(Courtesy of the Fulton County Board of Education)

The reading interests of rural children are enriched through the bookmobile.
(Courtesy of the State Board of Education, Atlanta, Georgia)

The old jalopy becomes a source of joy. Through group activities,
preadolescents learn to get along with each other.
(Courtesy of the McCall Corporation)

The early adolescent years are characterized by enthusiasm and vitality on the part of both boys and girls.
(Courtesy of the McCall Corporation)

Boys and girls learn roles that complement each other.
(Courtesy of the McCall Corporation)

School achievement in relation to intelligence. It has been pointed out throughout this chapter that intelligence is not something that develops in isolation, apart from the daily activities of the individual concerned. Furthermore, intelligence is not revealed in a barren

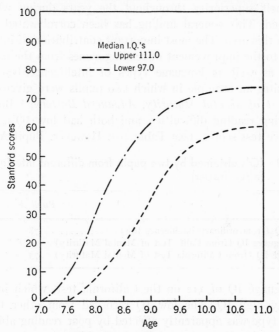

FIG. 28 **Comparison of reading performances of two groups of boys at different I.Q. levels**

environment. The opportunities for the expression of one's intelligence and incentives for mental activity are important in connection with the effective use of intelligence. A good school situation will provide genuine problem situations that will offer opportunities for mental growth on the part of the pupils. The child who feels emotionally secure at home and at school who encounters problem situations within the limit of mental capacities, and who is spurred on by intense interest and an endless stream of curiosity will grow in his achievements in harmony with his hereditary constitution and maturational level.

Many studies of the effects of intelligence upon reading performances have been conducted.[52] These studies reveal a high correla-

[52] See, for example, Donald D. Durrell, *Improvement of Basic Reading Abilities* (Yonkers, New York: World Book Co., 1944).

tion between reading achievement scores and intelligence test scores. The reading curves of two groups of children differing in intelligence are indicated in Figure 28.[53] The children in the upper intelligence group were advanced in their reading ability at age seven and maintained their superiority throughout the years during which they were tested. This general finding has been corroborated by many studies in this area. The most important contribution of intelligence-test data to the improvement of reading comes from the use of non-language as well as language types of intelligence tests. Arthur Traxler cites an example in which two pupils were given the *California Test of Mental Maturity, Advanced Battery*.[54] Both pupils were having reading difficulties, and both had low IQ's, based on intelligence test scores. (see Table 29). However, Pupil A obtained

TABLE 29   IQ's obtained by two pupils from different intelligence tests (after Traxler)

	Pupil A	Pupil B
1. Total IQ (from ordinary intelligence test)	78	76
2. Non-language IQ (from Calif. Test of Mental Maturity)	112	79
3. Language IQ (from California Test of Mental Maturity)	73	74

a nonlanguage IQ of 112 on the California test, which indicates a reasonably high IQ. The low IQ recorded from other tests of a language type was apparently affected by poor reading ability.

Most studies show an overlapping achievement between individuals with varying degrees of intelligence. Correlations between achievement- and intelligence-test scores usually range between .45 and .60. Although these studies indicate that a significant relation exists between achievement and intelligence, there is evidence that school achievement is dependent upon a number of factors, some of which are quite intangible and unpredictable. The relationship between intelligence and teachers' marks of 1,500 junior- and senior-high-school students from Philadelphia was studied by William Bradley.[55] Correlations ranging from .33 ± .06 to .64 ± .04 were obtained. The relationship of marks and intelligence is clearly re-

[53] The materials of Figure 28 are taken from Albert J. Huggett and Cecil V. Millard, *Growth and Learning in the Elementary School* (Boston: D. C. Heath and Company, 1946), p. 122.

[54] Arthur E. Traxler, A study of the California Test of Mental Maturity, Advanced Battery, *Journal of Educational Research,* 1939, Vol. 32, No. 5.

[55] William A. Bradley, Correlates of vocational preferences, *Genetic Psychology Monographs,* 1943, Vol. 28, pp. 99-169.

vealed by a comparison of the percentage of pupils from the different intelligence levels assigned marks of A with those assigned marks of D. This comparison is shown in Table 30. Although it is well known that teachers' marks are not highly reliable, the results show that

TABLE 30 Relationship of high and low marks to the mental ability of high school students (after Bradley)

IQ	Per cent of pupils	Per cent of A's	Ratio of per cent of A's to per cent of pupils	Per cent of D's	Ratio of per cent of D's to per cent of pupils
140-149	.2	3.2	16.0	0	0
130-139	1.3	10.6	8.1	0	0
120-129	7.5	25.5	3.4	0	0
110-119	22.5	35.1	1.6	0	0
100-109	32.5	18.1	.6	13.7	.5
90-99	25.3	4.3	.2	36.8	1.5
80-89	9.7	3.2	.3	42.3	4.3
70-79	1.0	0	0	5.3	5.3

high-school students with an IQ in excess of 110 are not likely to be assigned marks of D, while those with an IQ below 100 are not likely to be assigned marks of A.

Learning characteristics of the mentally retarded. The question may be asked: What are the learning characteristics which distinguish the mentally retarded from the average? The fact that intelligence is defined in terms closely related to learning ability would answer the question in a general way. The concept of mental age developed by Binet and closely followed by other students of child development during the early part of this century was based on the premise that a child of twelve or thirteen years of age whose score on a mental test gave him a mental age of ten years would have the same mental ability as the average ten-year-old. That this is only partially true is shown by a number of studies. A comparison of the ability of mentally retarded children to understand certain arithmetic processes with that of normal children of the same mental age was made by Cruikshank, in order to furnish information relative to this problem.[56] Two groups of mentally retarded boys made up the experimental group; the control group consisted of boys of average mental ability. A comparison of the two groups shows that they were equated for mental age and arithmetic age.

[56] William M. Cruickshank, Arithmetic work habits of mentally retarded boys, *American Journal of Mental Deficiency,* 1948, Vol. 52, pp. 318-330.

	C. A.	M.A.	Arith. A.
Experimental group average	14.29	10.06	9.73
Control group average	9.09	9.96	9.84

The *Buswell John Diagnostic Chart for Fundamentals in Arithmetic* was administered to determine differences in types of errors made during the solution of simple arithmetic problems. An analysis of the results showed that as the process becomes more complicated, the difference in the performance of the mentally retarded and that of normal children became more pronounced, the mentally retarded being inferior in each of the four fundamental processes. Four general types of errors were prominent among the mentally retarded subjects. These are listed as, (1) habits including certain primitive or immature procedures, such as counting on fingers, making marks on paper, and the like; (2) habits of a technical nature: outstanding among these habits are those showing a lack of proficiency in the use and manipulation of combinations involving zero; (3) carelessness, manifested in such activities as adding carried numbers, forgetting to carry, guessing, and the like; and (4) errors in reading. The major poor habit demonstrated by the control group is that of carelessness. Concerning these Cruickshank states:

They hurry, omit digits, forget to add the carried numbers, use the wrong operation by not thinking of what they are doing, and in multiplication make errors in the position of partial products. On the other hand, the normal subjects tend to use aids which facilitate accuracy in their problem solving. . . . They show themselves capable of abstract thinking in the addition process by almost universally mentally retaining the carried number to be solved.[57]

In harmony with the findings of Cruickshank, McElwee has found that performance ability continues to develop in adolescent moron cases after development on the Binet scale has ceased.[58] The difficulty of the mentally handicapped appears to be a general defect that prevents the development of adequate concepts. The subnormal is more successful in dealing with problems of a concrete nature, problems in which symbols do not play such an important role for their solution. This characteristic of the problem-solving ability of the mentally retarded was noted earlier by Robson. He stated:

[57] *Ibid.*, pp. 329-330.
[58] E. W. McElwee, The constructive ability of subnormal children, *Journal of Juvenile Research,* 1935, Vol. 19, p. 25.

He can work with actual things, and sometimes with models, though he cannot deal with maps or plans. He may be quick at grasping spatial relations, but only in connection with concrete things. He cannot copy movements of a person opposite to him, for this depends mainly on the ability to generalize a spatial relation to grasp that "left" and "right" are relative and not absolute positions in space.[59]

Composite portrait of the gifted child. The large-scale Stanford study begun in 1921 under the direction of Lewis Terman was designed to determine the physical, mental and personality traits characteristic of gifted children.[60] The standard set forth for the inclusion of subjects in the gifted category was 140 for the Binet-tested subjects and 135 for those tested by the Terman group test. Both Terman and Hollingworth regarded the intelligence test as the best means of selecting gifted subjects.[61] Hollingworth regarded the intelligence scale in the hands of a competent person as the best tool for use in measuring intelligence, with those rating within the top centile as the superior group.

The gifted children of the Terman study were found to be accelerated on a three-hour achievement test about 44 per cent of their age. The advanced achievements were not equally high in all school subjects. Of the subject areas tested, the gifted group was most advanced in reading, language usage, arithmetic reasoning, science, literature, and the arts. Although there was an unevenness of development of individual children, the amount of unevenness on the achievement tests did not differ significantly from that found among unselected children.

An outstanding characteristic of gifted children is the number and variety of their hobbies. Although reading activities rate high with them, they make various collections. The diaries and collections of gifted children reveal greater variety and complexity than the simple collections of average children. Also, their questions are not only likely to be more numerous but are also more intelligent in nature. These questions reveal the greater insight of gifted children into problem situations, as compared to the insight of unselected children.

[59] G. M. Robson, Social factors in mental retardation, *British Journal of Psychology*, 1931-32, Vol. 22, p. 133.

[60] Lewis M. Terman, *Genetic Studies of Genius, Vol. 1. Mental and Physical Traits of a Thousand Gifted Children* (Stanford: Stanford University Press, 1925).

[61] See Leta S. Hollingworth, How should gifted children be educated, *Baltimore Bulletin of Education*, 1931, Vol. 50, p. 195.

Summary and educational implications

The problem of the general nature of intelligence has challenged the thinking of educational psychologists and others to intensive study and research during the course of the past several decades. The early work by Alfred Binet was conducted among school children of Paris. He was concerned with the problem of determining those children who were mentally retarded in order that appropriate remedial measures could be used. This problem has motivated many of the studies dealing with the construction and use of intelligence tests throughout the period following the early, pioneer work of Binet. During the past two decades, a number of tests have been developed for measuring the intelligence of children during their first three years of life. The validation of these tests has provided interesting and useful information about the mental ability of the average child at different stages during the first three years. The difficulty of evaluating the mental ability of the preschool child is increased because of his limited experiences and lack of a variety of responses for making such evaluations.

The various studies of mental growth agree that growth is rapid during the preschool period. Most of the intelligence tests designed for school-age children make use of language. Thus, mental growth has been closely identified by some students of child development with language development. The child who has been handicapped because of his environmental background in the acquisition and use of language will tend to make a low score on such intelligence tests. There is a need to consider the child's ability on performance as well as upon language tests, if an accurate estimate is to be made of his mental ability.

Studies of the upper limit of mental growth are not wholly in agreement as to the time of cessation of the growth of intelligence. There is considerable evidence that some abilities reach their upper limit earlier than do other abilities. Some abilities seem to continue to develop beyond the fifteen- or sixteen-year level, although mental growth after age fourteen is very slow. The mental growth curve, therefore, is by no means a straight line. It shows a rapid acceleration during the first six or seven years with a gradual deceleration in rate after that time. The deceleration becomes greater around thirteen or fourteen years of age. Much controversy has taken place regarding the "constancy of the IQ." Again, studies are not wholly in agreement. The various studies conducted at the University of Iowa have made use of adopted children. These studies have offered considerable evidence that environmental conditions have an important bearing on changes in the IQ. Although the physical conditions of the child are not as important in this connection as some of the early students of this problem would have indicated, there is good evidence that the IQ is not as fixed as the early studies seemed to indicate. Some factors that have been listed which affect the constancy of the IQ are: (1) the home environment; (2) the social-class structure; (3) bilingualism; (4) conflicts and maladjustments.

There is a significant correlation between intelligence-test scores and school achievement. This stems in part from the fact that intelligence has been defined largely in terms of ability to learn the types of materials included in the school program. Nevertheless, intelligence-test scores are useful in the hands of teachers who recognize their limitations as well as their values. There is a need, however, to develop a school program that will be in harmony with the abilities of all the children enrolled in school. If the elementary school is to function effectively in a democratic society, it must first of all be democratic. It will provide opportunities for growth of all the children commensurate with their abilities. The teachers, supervisors, and principals will be concerned with the wholesome development of every child. The program of work, procedures, and evaluations will be carried out in a democratic spirit; pupils as well as teachers will participate in planning activities and assuming responsibilities. Such a school conceives of the pupils as citizens of a democratic school community. All of this has been well stated by Lousdale as follows:

In such a school the belief that school experiences prepare children for living is superseded by the belief that school is life. The school recognizes its responsibility (1) to provide experiences which will maintain and insure the physical fitness of each individual, (2) to provide experiences which will help individuals understand the world in which they live, (3) to provide experiences which will help individuals acquire the skills and attitudes necessary for effective participation in a democratic society, (4) to provide experiences which will help individuals to grow in esthetic appreciation and creative expression.[62]

[62] Bernard J. Lousdale, The characteristics of a good elementary school, *Nineteenth Yearbook of the California Elementary School Principal's Association,* 1947, p. 12.

Questions and Exercises

1. Why is it difficult to determine the factors responsible for individual differences among children four, five, or six years of age?

2. What are the major difficulties involved in attempting to evaluate the intelligence of a child two years of age? Observe some child of this age level and attempt to make a subjective evaluation of his or her intelligence. What are some of the problems you encounter in attempting to make such an evaluation?

3. Trace the development of mental testing. What prompted Binet to develop his first test of intelligence? What was the nature of this test?

4. Elaborate upon the ideas suggested in this chapter relative to the importance of considering the qualitative aspects of test performances as well as the quantitative. What errors arise when one insists upon complete objectivity?

5. Show how two children may have the same IQ's but be very different in their general mental structure. What is the educational significance of this?

6. In what ways do tests oftentimes favor the urban child? The child from a rich cultural environment?

7. What are the general implications of the findings from Skodak relative to adopted children referred to in this chapter? What are some factors that might account for the similarity of adopted siblings in a family?

8. Give arguments in favor of the claim that mental growth ceases at the age of fifteen. Give arguments in favor of the notion that mental growth continues until the age of nineteen or later. Can these viewpoints be reconciled?

9. Cite studies relative to the relationship between intelligence and school achievement. Can you offer evidence from your observations where superior intelligence was associated with average school achievement? What are some factors that might account for such a condition?

10. Compare the definitions of intelligence from various sources. On the basis of this comparison, how would you define intelligence?

11. What is meant by the statement that "heredity sets broad limitations to one's mental development"?

12. Contrast the learning characteristics of mentally retarded and mentally superior children.

Selected Readings

Bayley, Nancy. The role of intelligence, *Thirteenth Yearbook, Department of Supervisors and Directors of Instruction*, National Education Association, 1941. Chap. III.

Bayley, Nancy. Mental growth in young children, *Thirty-ninth Yearbook of the National Society for the Study of Education*, Part II, 1940. Pp. 11-47.

Cornell, Ethel L., and Gillette Annette. Construction and educational significance of intelligence tests, *Review of Educational Research*, 1950. Vol. 20, pp. 17-26. A review of sixty-three titles is here presented.

Cronbach, Lee J. *Essentials of Psychological Testing*. New York: Harper & Brothers, 1949.

Gesell, Arnold and Amatruda, C. S. *Developmental Diagnosis*. New York: Paul B. Hoeber, 1941.

Goodenough, Florence L. The measurement of mental growth in childhood, *Manual of Child Psychology*, L. Carmichael, ed. New York: John Wiley and Sons, 1946. Chap. IX.

Goodenough, Florence L. *Mental Testing: Its History, Principles, and Applications*. New York: Rinehart and Co., 1949.

Jersild, Arthur T. *Child Psychology*. 3rd ed.; New York: Prentice-Hall, 1947. Chap. XV.

Jones, Harold E. Environmental influences on mental development, *Manual of Child Psychology*, L. Carmichael, ed. New York: John Wiley and Sons, 1946. Chap. XI.

Mursell, James L. *Psychological Testing*. 2nd ed.; New York: Longmans, Green & Company, 1949.

Olson, Willard C. *Child Development*. Boston: D. C. Heath and Company, 1948. Chaps. V and VI.

Sherman, Mandel. *Intelligence and Its Deviations*. New York: The Ronald Press Co., 1945. Chaps. I-IV.

Stephenson, William. *Testing School Children*. London: Longmans, Green & Company, 1949.

Wood, Ben D., and Haefner, Ralph. *Measuring and Guiding Individual Growth*. New York: Silver Burdett Company, 1948.

Witty, Paul, ed. *The Gifted Child*. Boston: D. C. Heath and Company, 1951.

Thorpe, Louis P. *Child Psychology and Development*. New York: The Ronald Press Co., 1946. Chap. VIII.

9

Language Growth
and Development
by Florene M. Young,
University of Georgia

Speech is perhaps the most valuable adjustment mechanism that man possesses. He uses it in giving vent to his feelings, in his social contacts, and in bringing about action on the part of his fellows. By means of it he is able to communicate with others and leave meaningful records for future generations. Marked inefficiency or inadequacy of speech implies an impaired adjustment. The daily employment of language is affected by and related to the total, unified functioning of the integrated mechanism. The far-reaching influence of this instrument is obvious when it is realized that, as Lewis indicated, "it subserves all the purposes of human activity—practical, scientific, aesthetic, and religious alike." [1]

Garrison and Garrison early pointed out that "The ability to acquire language must be thought of in terms of the neuro-muscular coordinations made possible by the biological nature of the individual. The organism in its development in response to stimuli is able to coordinate the movements of the various organs which function in speech and produce a unified response." These authors emphasize the fact that the ability to acquire language is innate, while the language one learns is a result of environment. Thus, if several children were isolated from civilization so that they never heard any speech, they would learn to communicate with each other by simple sounds and signs. Moreover, it would probably take thousands of years for such children and their descendants, having absolutely

[1] M. M. Lewis, *Infant Speech: A Study of the Beginnings of Language* (New York: Harcourt, Brace and Co., 1936), p. 8.

no contact with a well-developed language, to develop one of their own.[2]

In our society, language is ready for the child and it provides the most important means whereby he can learn the prevailing culture. It is the key to his participation in social life and without it he remains aloof from it and ignorant of his cultural heritage.

Language is a uniquely revealing type of behavior. It identifies a person with amazing effectiveness. Language habits reflect one's past life, the geographic area where childhood years were spent, grammatical errors copied from uneducated associates, and the critical or kindly attitude of the speaker.

The genetic development of speech

Prelinguistic utterances of infancy. The machinism for the production of vocal sounds is ready to function considerably before birth.[3] The neonate's first vocalization is the birth cry. Its function is physiological, having to do with the establishment of normal respiration and the oxygenation of the blood.

Bühler found that crying during the first months of life often is traceable to (1) pain, especially when related to digestion or elimination, (2) strong stimuli, as bright lights, sharp noises, heat, or cold, (3) abrupt changes of posture or uncomfortable positions, (4) strong disturbances during sleep, (5) fatigue, (6) hunger, (7) failure of the intended reaction, such as inability to move due to restricting clothes or covers, (8) loss of playthings (from the fifth month), (9) fear (from the eighth month), and (10) when contact with others is withdrawn (from the third or fourth month.)[4]

Gesell, in speaking of development during the first four months, says "... the major task of the mother is to be alert to all forms of crying and fussing, to read their meaning and to give as prompt attention as possible." He indicates further that "punctual attention to crying in the early weeks reduces the total amount of crying...."[5]

[2] S. C. Garrison and K. C. Garrison, *The Psychology of Elementary School Subjects* (New York: Johnson Publishing Co., 1929), pp. 208, 211.

[3] Dorothea McCarthy, Language development in children, *Manual of Child Psychology*, L. Carmichael, ed. (New York: John Wiley and Sons, 1946), pp. 488-489.

[4] Charlotte Bühler, *The First Year of Life* (New York: John Day Co., 1930), pp. 26-34.

[5] Arnold Gesell and F. L. Ilg, *Infant and Child in the Culture of Today* (New York: Harper & Brothers, 1943), p. 87.

For forty babies observed by Irwin during the first ten days of life, phonetic recordings revealed that vowels were clearly predominant over consonants. The one vowel sound used by all forty babies was that of the "a" as in *sat*. The most frequently used consonant was "h," which comprised 64 per cent of all the consonants employed by them. It seems probable that the direction of progress in the development of vowels is from those that are formed with the front part of the mouth to those that are formed with the back of the oral cavity; and that consonant formation progresses from the back part of the mouth to the front.[6]

Lewis says that the origin of certain vowels and consonants lies almost entirely in the expression of hunger and its satisfaction. He emphasizes that the vocalizing of discomfort is well established before the comfort-sounds appear. He thinks it "inevitable that any utterance made by the infant in connection with feeding should become shaped by the movements of feeding." Gradually, the child "transforms into babbling both these comfort-sounds and also those which are expressive of discomfort."[7]

By the third month, most observers of infants report cooing and babbling, which continue until approximately twelve months of age, when the first words are heard. Gesell and Thompson have stated that at eight weeks, 42 per cent of the babies cooed, and three-quarters or more did so at the age of twelve and sixteen weeks.[8] The vocal behavior observable during the period of infancy from four to fifty-six weeks of age is presented in Table 31.

By the age of five months, according to Shirley, some babies are combining vowel and consonant sounds and repeating them several times in succession, as "uggle-uggle," "erdah-erdah," "oddle-oddle," "bah-bah," "hey-hey," and the like. Among the utterances of the infants studied by this investigation were "squeals of delight, strong grunts of pain or disgust, grunts with the rising inflection of a question, and gutteral barking growls...."[9] Gesture language, including efforts to take, avoid, or reject, also serves as a means of communication prior to the time when the child can use words.

[6] O. C. Irwin and T. Curry, Vowel elements in the crying vocalization of infants under ten days of age, *Child Development*, 1941, Vol. 12, pp. 99-109.

[7] Lewis, *op. cit.*, pp. 36, 58.

[8] A. I. Gesell and Helen Thompson, *Infant Behavior: Its Genesis and Growth* (New York: McGraw-Hill Book Co., 1934), p. 249.

[9] M. M. Shirley, The First Two Years: A Study of Twenty-five Babies. Vol. II. Intellectual Development, *Institute of Child Welfare Monograph Series* (Minneapolis: University of Minnesota Press, 1933), No. 7, pp. 50-51.

TABLE 31 The development of vocalization in infancy (after Gesell and Thompson)

	Weeks of Age														
	4	6	8	12	16	20	24	28	32	36	40	44	48	52	56
1. Face brightens	40	68			24										
2. Chuckles	0	0	36	42											
3. Smiles	22	65	96	100	100										
4. Laughs	0	0	7	31	38										
5. No vocalization heard	45	31	21	15	28										
6. Vocalizes small throaty noises	84	72	3	4	4										
7. Vocalizes ah-uh-eh	40	96	82	96	67										
8. Coos	0	3	42	88	76										
9. Blows bubbles	0	0	3	42	44										
10. Gurgles	0	0	10	42	56	7	7	18	59	64	63	62	69	67	59
11. Vocalizes da					0	11	26	43	47	51	60	52	60	64	64
12. Vocalizes ma or mu					5										
13. Two syl., 2nd rep. first, ma-ma, ba-ba, etc.					14	11	7	25	66	70	80	83	86	79	91
14. Makes "d" sound					0	7	22	21	66	64	69	62	88	67	73
15. Makes "m" sound					5	11	26	43	47	58	63	55	60	64	64
16. Makes "ē" sound (at end of word)					0	4	7	7	16	12	14	35	46	48	64
17. Makes "b" sound					9	4	15	14	22	24	32	41	32	57	64
18. Says no word					100	100	100	93	88	79	66	31	23	12	5
19. Says one word or more							0	7	12	21	34	69	77	88	95
20. Says two words or more							0	4	0	3	3	28	34	67	86
21. Says three words or more											0	10	26	40	68
22. Says four words or more											0	7	9	26	36

Development through imitation. How does babbling become transformed into words? Several writers have accepted the view that new sounds are not learned by imitating the language of others, but that they emerge in the child's vocal play as a result of maturation, and that the baby imitates only those sounds that have already occurred in his spontaneous babbling.[10]

Several writers report that by the age of nine to twelve months the baby seems capable of imitating the speech of others. The significance of imitation in language development is obvious when one realizes that the child learns his native tongue, the language of his environment. The fate of the deaf child who does not learn to talk because he cannot hear others is further evidence of the importance of imitation.

No one expects the baby of three months of age to walk or talk. Much growing, much maturation must take place before the child is capable of these activities. Experimental illustration of the significance of maturation is given in Strayer's work. He found that a given amount of language training at eighty-nine weeks of age was more efficacious than similar training at eighty-four weeks. The twin, who at eighty-nine weeks was still untrained, acquired within twenty-eight days a vocabulary which equaled that of the twin who had had five weeks of training previously. Moreover, the pattern of response was more mature. Strayer concludes that "A maturational difference of even five weeks has a definite influence on the effectiveness of training."[11]

Simultaneous with his apparent ability to imitate is the development of the ability to comprehend. At thirty-six weeks of age the baby "adjusts to words" and by twelve months he "adjusts to simple commands" and says two words or more.[12]

The dawning of comprehension has been dramatically described by Helen Keller: "Some one was drawing water and my teacher placed my hand under the spout. As the cool stream gushed over one hand she spelled into the other *water*, first slowly, then rapidly. I stood still, my whole attention fixed on the motions of her fingers. Suddenly I felt a misty consciousness as of something forgotten—a thrill of returning thought, and somehow the mystery of language was re-

[10] McCarthy, *op. cit.*, p. 495.

[11] L. C. Strayer, Language and growth: The relative efficacy of early and deferred vocabulary training studied by the method of co-twin control, *Genetic Psychology Monographs,* 1930, Vol. 8, pp. 209-319.

[12] Gesell and Thompson, *op. cit.*, p. 258.

vealed to me. I knew then that *water* meant the wonderful cool something that was flowing over my hand." [13]

Comprehensible speech. As shown in Table 32, 69 per cent of the babies said one or more words at forty-four weeks of age. The variations among the infants are noteworthy. For instance, 12 per cent used one or more words at thirty-two weeks, yet at fifty-two weeks some babies had not spoken. Usually, the first word is a monosyllable or a reduplicated monosyllable as: *bye-bye, mama, bebe, tick-tick,* and the like. If the child uses *mama* in his babbling, the parents may interpret it to designate the mother. Actually, it is necessary to observe over a period of time to see that the sound is not used in any other situation, before deciding that the child is using the word with comprehension.

Since comprehension is not based alone on the interpretation of the words heard but on a response to the facial expressions and gestures used in accompaniment to the words, comprehension is an easier task than speaking. Young children learn to react to many commands because of the facial expression, the gestures, the tone of voice, and also the association of the word with the act. The recognition vocabulary, which refers to the comprehension of speech, is always greater than the spoken or active vocabulary.

The apparent growth of vocabulary between twelve and eighteen months seems relatively slow. The immaturity of the child is one possible factor. It has been suggested that the baby's concentration upon walking at that age consumes much of his energy and attention, leaving little for language development. Arlitt speaks of this period as a plateau and thinks that perhaps the "lower-order habits are approaching their maximum development, but are not yet sufficiently automatic to leave the attention free to attack the higher-order habits." [14]

Age and talking. The real spurt in talking does not usually occur until after the child is eighteen months old. McCarthy found that at that age only 26 per cent of the utterances were comprehensible, while nearly all that the child said at fifty-four months was understandable.[15]

[13] H. Keller, *The Story of My Life* (New York: Doubleday, Page and Co., 1903), p. 23.

[14] A. H. Arlitt, *Psychology of Infancy and Early Childhood* (New York: McGraw-Hill Book Co., 1946), p. 379.

[15] D. A. McCarthy, The language development of the preschool child, *Institute of Child Welfare Monograph Series* (University of Minnesota Press, 1930), No. 4, p. 51.

As the child develops in ability to use comprehensible speech, he tends to cry less. Young reported a consistent decrease in crying with age, the greatest rate of decrease being indicated by respective means of 5.1 and 0.1 syllables at thirty and sixty months.[16] In the preschool groups which were observed, boys cried approximately twice as much as girls. Such behavior was particularly characteristic of boys from the lower socioeconomic levels. It was this group whose comprehensible speech was retarded in comparison with all other groups. The marked decrease in crying with age, and the better records of girls, may indicate the significance of maturation. Seemingly, girls have a faster rate of maturation than boys in many aspects of development.

In a study of the social behavior of young children, Murphy found a marked predominance of verbal over active responses in two of the older preschool groups. She thought it likely that individual abilities and patterns of responses were more significant than age trends. Murphy states that "... children who develop motor control more rapidly than mastery of language will express sympathetic responses in active ways, while children who develop verbally may depend more heavily upon verbal techniques in their social relations, including responses to distress situations." [17]

Coincident with increase in age there is usually an increase in comprehensible vocalization. This was found to be true of both sexes, and also of children from fortunate and unfortunate socioeconomic groups, as may be seen in Table 32. At each age, the children from the upper socioeconomic groups talked more than those from less fortunate families. At all ages, girls were more talkative than boys.

Closely related to the increase of vocalization with age is the expansion of the vocabulary. Jersild found that when matched children were compared, there was approximately a fivefold increase in loquacity and a fourfold increase in active vocabulary.[18] In other words, a child's verbosity is likely to increase with age at a faster rate than his vocabulary.

The number of words a child knows determines in large measure his school progress, and failure to progress normally has far-reaching significance. Words are the means by which the child learns about his world. If his knowledge of words is grossly inadequate, the interpre-

[16] F. M. Young, Social indices in the language of preschool subjects, *Journal of Genetic Psychology,* 1942, Vol. 61, pp. 109-123.

[17] L. B. Murphy, *Social Behavior and Child Personality* (New York: Columbia University Press, 1937), p. 152.

[18] A. T. Jersild, *Child Psychology* (New York: Prentice-Hall, 1940), pp. 122-123.

TABLE 32 Number of comprehensible words spoken per 10-minute period by age, group, and sex (after Young)

Age (mos.)	Boys			Girls			
	REG.[1]	REL.	ALL	REG.	REL.	ALL	ALL CASES
30	22.1	14.6	18.4	27.4	17.9	22.7	20.6
36	37.7	22.5	30.1	43.2	35.3	39.3	34.7
42	55.4	37.2	46.3	61.7	50.7	56.2	51.3
48	61.9	45.5	53.7	78.4	62.1	70.3	62.0
54	74.6	58.7	66.7	84.9	75.2	80.1	73.4
60	50.4	43.9	47.2	72.1	64.6	68.4	57.8

[1] *Reg.* refers to the regular group of children from homes of moderate or superior socioeconomic level. *Rel.* refers to children from homes receiving Federal Emergency Relief.

tation of his environment will be correspondingly so. In an age of radios, television, films, rapid transportation, and world relationships, the child needs to know many words and to be able to use them. Failure tends to result in impaired social adjustment.

As shown in Table 31, 69 per cent of the infants said one or more words at the age of forty-four weeks. After the age of two years, language growth is rapid. There is evidence that the child adds five hundred to six hundred words per year to his vocabulary, between his second and sixth birthdays.

Many vocabulary studies have used small samples of words. Seashore and Eckerson [19] have shown that the larger the dictionary used as a basis for sampling, the larger the estimated vocabulary will be. These authors have constructed an *English Recognition Vocabulary Test* from a sampling of Funk and Wagnalls' *New Standard Dictionary of the English Language.* The use of this test by Smith [20] yielded larger vocabularies than those obtained in many investigations. For the first grade, the average number of basic words known was 16,900, with a range from 5,500 to 32,800. For grade twelve, the average number of basic words known was 47,300, with a range from 28,200 to 73,200. The results indicate a fairly steady growth of vocabulary through the school years. Smith's findings for

[19] R. H. Seashore and L. D. Eckerson, The measurement of individual differences in general English vocabularies, *Journal of Educational Psychology,* 1940, Vol. 31, pp. 14-38.
[20] M. K. Smith, Measurement of the size of the general English vocabulary through the elementary grades and high school, *Genetic Psychology Monographs,* 1941, Vol. 24, pp. 311-345.

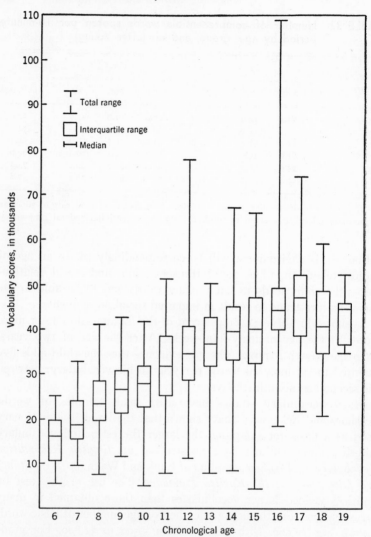

FIG. 29 Basic vocabulary scores by chronological age groups
(After Smith)

ages six through sixteen are shown in Figure 29. Terman likewise observed that the growth in vocabulary was remarkably regular.[21] He found that the curve of medians for the successive mental ages was almost a straight line.

[21] L. M. Terman, The vocabulary as a measure of intelligence, *Journal of Educational Psychology,* 1918, Vol. 9, pp. 452-466.

Parts of speech. Although the first words are usually spoken of as nouns, they are most often used as whole sentences and function for a time as one-word sentences. For instance, the word "wah-wah" (water) may mean "I want water." When the child is in the "naming stage" of language development, he attempts to learn the names of objects, of people, of colors, in fact, of everything possible. He asks repeatedly, "What's that?" When he is told, he may say the name over several times, as "carrots, carrots."

Considering these characteristics of the young child, it is not surprising that McCarthy found that nouns predominated at the age of eighteen months, the proportion being 50 per cent.[22] At two years, the proportion was 39 per cent. By the age of fifty-four months, however, nouns constituted only 19 per cent. Other parts of speech showed an increase with age, the most rapid changes occurring at the lower age levels.

Using children of thirty to sixty-five months of age, Young found that the period of greatest change, that is, prior to thirty months, had passed. At the ages mentioned, the proportions of nouns, pronouns, verbs, adverbs, adjectives, and infinitives changed relatively little. However, there was a noticeable increase in the proportions of articles, conjunctions, and prepositions and a decrease in the use of interjections.[23] As soon as the child begins to use complete sentences which are grammatically correct, the percentages of the various parts of speech become more or less set by the conventions of the language.

Boyd ascribed significance to the incidence of certain pronouns, as follows: "The diminishing of the *I* and the growing use of the other pronouns, especially of the *we* and *you,* is a significant revelation of the process by which the self-centered child is transformed into a social being." [24] Another investigator found that the use of *I* and *me* constituted an even larger proportion of the total pronouns at sixty months than at thirty months of age, respective percentages being 39.5 and 35.5. Concurrently, the use of *we, us,* and *you* increased markedly with age. There is, then, a definite growth in social consciousness coincident with a less obvious development of the self-

[22] McCarthy, *op. cit.,* 1930, p. 114.

[23] F. M. Young, An analysis of certain variables in a developmental study of language, *Genetic Psychology Monographs,* 1941, Vol. 23, pp. 88-89.

[24] W. Boyd, The development of a child's vocabulary, *Pedagogical Seminary,* 1914, Vol. 21, pp. 95-124.

reference. The use of the impersonal *it* occurred proportionately less in the records of the older children.[25]

Egocentric versus socialized speech. Piaget emphasized what he termed egocentricity in the child's language and life. In egocentric speech, as Piaget defines it, the child "does not bother to know to whom he is speaking nor whether he is being listened to." Moreover, "he feels no desire to influence his hearer nor to tell him anything." In contrast, he considers socialized speech as that "in which the child addresses his hearer, considers his point of view, tries to influence him or actually exchanges ideas with him." In socialized speech he includes: adapted information, criticism, commands, threats, requests, questions, answers. Piaget stated that about 38 per cent of the children's remarks fell in the egocentric category.[26]

McCarthy studied a much larger number of children than Piaget and concluded that egocentric reactions comprised only 3.6 per cent of the responses of her preschool subjects. The marked difference in findings has occasioned considerable controversy. McCarthy has summarized numerous studies concerning the problem and concludes: "... it appears that the controversy over egocentrism is more apparent than real...." She further states that "... the enthusiastic statements one occasionally finds regarding *predominance* of egocentrism in the speech of young children is quite unfounded." [27]

Using a different approach from that of Piaget, two investigators studied the spontaneous remarks of college students and unselected groups and found that 40.7 per cent were ego-related. They concluded that "These percentages of ego-related remarks are similar to those found in the studies of children's conversations." [28]

Before conclusions are drawn concerning the relative proportions of self-reference material in child and adult conversations, it will be necessary to make studies upon both groups employing the same techniques and the same frame of reference.

Sentence length. Experts have long regarded sentence length as one of the most valuable indexes of language development. By the time a child is two years of age, he combines words into short sentences which attempt to express, with the help of gestures, a complete

[25] F. M. Young, Development as indicated by a study of pronouns, *Journal of Genetic Psychology,* 1942, Vol. 61, pp. 126.

[26] J. Piaget, *The Language and Thought of the Child* (New York: Harcourt, Brace and Co., 1926), pp. 9-10.

[27] McCarthy, *op. cit.,* 1946, pp. 533, 539.

[28] M. Henle and M. B. Hubbell, Egocentricity in adult conversation, *Journal of Social Psychology,* 1938, Vol. 9, pp. 227-234.

thought. Sample sentences of this period are: "Want milk." "Shut door." "Why him fall?" "Daddy car go."

In Table 33, typical findings concerning sentence length are summarized. It is clear that with advancing age the length of sentence tends to increase, although there may be periods of little or no progress. In general, girls tend to have slightly longer responses than boys. Children from the upper socioeconomic levels almost always surpass those of less fortunate groups. One investigator has pointed out, however, that "The effects of sex and socio-economic status do not adequately explain the differences existent in the length of response, since the findings are not consistently indicative of a positive relationship." [29]

TABLE 33   Mean length of verbal response as reported by McCarthy, Smith, Young, and Davis

Age	McCarthy [1]		Smith [1]		Young [1]		Davis [2]	
	BOYS	GIRLS	BOYS	GIRLS	BOYS	GIRLS	BOYS	GIRLS
18 mos.	1.0	1.3						
24	1.4	2.1	1.3	2.2				
30	3.2	3.1	2.2	2.4	3.1	3.3		
36	3.1	3.8	3.3	3.5	3.3	3.9		
42	4.2	4.4	4.4	3.8	4.2	4.6		
48	4.3	4.4	4.1	4.4	4.6	4.8		
54	4.6	4.7	4.8	4.7	4.7	5.0		
60			4.7	4.6	4.9	5.5		
5½ yrs.							4.5	4.6
6½							5.1	5.5
9½							6.4	6.7

[1] D. McCarthy: Language development in children, *Manual of Child Psychology*, L. Carmichael, ed. (New York: John Wiley and Sons).

[2] E. A. Davis: *The Development of Linguistic Skill in Twins, Singletons with Siblings, and Only Children from Age Five to Ten Years* (Minneapolis: University of Minnesota Press, 1937), p. 46.

Usually, only simple sentences, if any, are used at eighteen months of age. At four and one-half years, complex and compound sentences are employed but constitute only a small part of the child's conversation. Before the age of six, a child whose language development is normal is using practically every form of sentence structure. This achievement is noteworthy when we consider that it takes place in six short years in a period when he is relatively immature.

Imagination and language. Most children speak fluently by the time they are three years of age, and enjoy using their verbal skill.

[29] Young, *op. cit.*, 1941, p. 47.

Since they are immature and inexperienced, the statements of pre-school and primary children are sometimes incorrect and even far-fetched. If they find that their tall tales attract notice and cause amusement, they will naturally continue to secure attention by this device. Usually, it seems best not to suppress completely this form of language expression, but to teach the child to differentiate between the real and the imaginary. Undoubtedly, much legitimate pleasure may be derived from the imaginary and the important point is to help the youngster to label it is "make-believe." The normal child gradually learns to recognize the folk tale or fairy story as fanciful. Eventually, he comes to admit that his imaginary playmate is fictitious and not made of flesh and blood. By the time he finishes the second grade, he is fairly proficient in detecting the realistic from the imaginary.

Soon after the child has reached the stage where he can usually distinguish between reality and fantasy, he may become interested in a code language and in communicating in such a manner as to baffle adults and all who do not belong to his inner circle of friends. This type of language may involve considerable effort, yet some children become adept in the use of "pig Latin," "double Dutch," and secret codes. This causes considerable concern when it is associated with undesirable gang behavior. Provision for wholesome recreation, supervised by understanding leaders, is usually helpful with this problem.

Factors affecting speech development

Reference has already been made to the influence of age and maturation upon language development. There has also been mention of the verbosity and the longer responses of girls, and of children from more fortunate backgrounds.

Intelligence and language development. Intelligence and language development also are related. Terman obtained a correlation of .91 between the results of a vocabulary test and mental age.[30] He further observed that "children of a given mental age have approximately the same vocabulary regardless of chronological age."

Two investigators who examined 2,500 mental defectives found that only one-third spoke normally.[31] The lower the mental rating, the lower was the amount of normal speech.

[30] Terman, *op. cit.*, p. 465.
[31] J. Sirkin and W. F. Lyons, A study of speech defects in mental deficiency, *American Journal of Mental Deficiency,* 1941, Vol. 46, pp. 74-80.

Fisher's subjects showed marked linguistic superiority according to the usual criteria.[32] The average IQ of these young subjects was 132.

From comparisons of preschool children whose intelligence ratings were average or superior, Young found that the latter surpassed the less capable in amount of speech and in the length of sentence. It was noted, however, that marked inconsistencies from comparisons of some of the subgroups indicated that "intelligence as a possible causal factor did not exert a uniform influence."[33]

The positive relationship between vocabulary and general achievement in the elementary school has long been recognized. Traxler found that a close relation exists between knowledge of word meaning and over-all achievement in grades four through eight.[34] Correlations ranging from .78 to .88 were found between word-meaning scores and total scores on the *Stanford Achievement Test*. These correlations are presented in Table 34. The correlations are perhaps slightly higher than one would ordinarily find, since the word-meaning test was taken from the Stanford test and was a factor in determining the total score.

TABLE 34   Correlation between word-meaning scores and total scores on Stanford Achievement Test (after Traxler)

Grade	Cases	Correlation	Probable Error
IV	105	.839	.020
V	104	.877	.015
VI	120	.809	.021
VII	97	.780	.027
VIII	67	.827	.026

Influence of siblings. Davis compared twins, singletons, and only children and indicated that twins were retarded in their language (Table 4).[35] They partially overcame their handicap by the age of 9½ years if they were fortunate enough to come from a good environment.

[32] M. S. Fisher, Language patterns of preschool children, *Child Development Monographs*, No. 15, pp. xvi + 88.

[33] Young, *op. cit.*, 1941, p. 53.

[34] A. E. Traxler, The relationship between vocabulary and general achievement in the elementary school, *Elementary School Journal*, 1944-45, Vol. 45, pp. 331-333.

[35] E. A. Davis, *The Development of Linguistic Skill in Twins, Singletons with Siblings, and Only Children from Five to Ten Years* (Minneapolis: University of Minnesota Press, 1937), p. 135.

During the preschool years, twins play together and evidentl; imitate each other's immature speech, rather than that of an olde child. In such instances, facial expressions, gestures, and grunts seem to take the place of conventional language.

It is interesting to note that the famous Dionne quintuplets a thirty-two months of age appeared to be seriously retarded in lan guage development. Blatz concluded that their backwardness wa due to: "(1) the care which they received, in which most demand; were met before the need for asking arose, and (2) their intercom munication among themselves, which was sufficiently skilled withou the use of language." [36]

Emotional maladjustment. Insistence upon impossible or unrea sonable standards of speech may so discourage a child as to cause difficulty. Janet's parents, wishing for her to use perfect English frequently corrected her mistakes in pronunciation and grammar At the age of thirty-two months, she suddenly stopped talking. When taken to the home of her grandparents, she resumed normal speech It was several weeks before she would talk freely in the presence of her parents. Usually, it is better to overlook some bad grammar than to develop a morose and uncommunicative child.

Kanner has described a type of maladjustment in children that is characterized by marked inability to relate themselves to other people. The children seem to have little need for language, some remaining mute, though evidencing good intellectual ability. Kanner noted that very few of the parents of these children were "really warmhearted fathers and mothers." [37]

Ribble has described cases of apparent maladjustment known as "marasmus," that disease of wasting away through no known cause other than lack of individual, affectionate attention or "mothering." In some hospitals it has become a rule that every baby shall be picked up, patted, and rocked for a short time each day. Ribble emphasizes that "the appropriate stimulation of the senses leads to getting a sense of self and of the world of physical objects, as well as to begin-ning to feel a sense of personal relationships." [38] The bringing of feeling and perspective life into action is regarded as a significant

[36] W. E. Blatz, M. I. Fletcher, M. Mason, *Early Development in Spoken Language of the Dionne Quintuplets,* University of Toronto Studies, Child Development Series (University of Toronto Press, 1937), No. 16, p. 13.

[37] L. Kanner, Early infantile autism, *Journal of Pediatrics,* 1944, Vol. 25, pp. 211-217.

[38] M. A. Ribble, *The Rights of Infants* (New York: Columbia University Press, 1943), pp. 4, 9.

aspect of infantile mental development, which includes language development.

A bilingual environment. Smith measured the vocabularies in both languages used by thirty bilingual children who knew Chinese and English words. In either language, the group was found to have below-average vocabularies for children of their age. When the vocabularies of the two languages were combined, two-fifths of the subjects exceeded the norms for monolingual children; but when words of duplicate meaning were subtracted, only one-sixth of them did. Smith pointed out the inadvisability of starting any "but children of superior linguistic language ability in a second language during the preschool years." [39]

Smith also studied 1,000 preschool children of varied racial background and varied amounts of bilingualism in Hawaii.[40] The bilingual groups were seriously retarded in the use of English, using shorter sentences, and fewer complex and compound sentences. They were also retarded in the use of connectives and pronouns.

Influence of hearing defects. Language retardation is almost certain to result if the child is deaf. Since he cannot hear the speech of others, learning to use the language of his environment is difficult. The possibility of deafness should always be investigated if a child's speech is not developing normally.

If hearing acuity is greatly reduced, the child will not only be unable to hear the sounds of the world about him but he will be unable to hear even his own speech. Since speech appears quite early in the life of an individual, the delay of special help for the hard-of-hearing child imposes unnecessary hardships upon him and development is retarded correspondingly. Because of his handicap, such a child is often regarded as stubborn and disobedient. When he enters school, his defect is frequently overlooked and he may even be erroneously classified as dull or feeble-minded.

Congenital deafness is probably inherited deafness in most instances, although prenatal accidents or birth injury are sometimes named as likely causes. Childhood diseases are rightly blamed for some cases of impaired hearing. In fact, any disease accompanied by high fever and infection of nose, throat, or brain is a potential cause of deafness. Children who are victims of severe colds and

[39] M. E. Smith, Measurement of vocabularies of young bilingual children in both of the languages used, *Journal of Genetic Psychology,* 1949, Vol. 74, pp. 305-310.

[40] M. E. Smith, Some light on the problem of bilingualism as found from a study of the progress in mastery of English among preschool children of non-American ancestry in Hawaii, *Genetic Psychology Monographs,* 1939, Vol. 21, pp. 121-284.

infected ears sometimes lose enough of their hearing to interfere with the proper development of speech.

Without realizing it, some deaf children make peculiar noises, thus attracting unfavorable attention. Knowing little of what is going on around them, hard-of-hearing children tend to become suspicious, shy, depressed, resentful, or seclusive. Parents and teachers may prevent or reduce these undesirable patterns of behavior. Early diagnosis, followed as soon as possible by special training, should be emphasized. The use of hearing aids, and supervised contacts with normal children, will also help the child with impaired hearing.[41]

Speech problems

Incidence of speech disorders. The report of the White House Conference gives statistics based on forty-eight cities having populations of over 10,000. The proportion of children having speech defects ranged from 1.0 to 21.4 per cent, and the average was 5 per cent. The variations probably were due in part to differences of opinion as to what constituted a speech defect.

The White House Conference found that articulatory defects (sound substitution, oral inactivity, dialectal) were the most frequent type of disorder.[42] The next in frequency was stuttering. Defects due to structural causes, voice disorders, and the aphasias were relatively rare.

Types of speech disorders. The major speech problems are divided by Louttit into five types:

(1) Delayed speech. The child does not start to talk until much later than average age.

(2) Articulatory disorders. These include the production of improper sounds because of structural or training defects.

(3) Rhythmic disorders. This group is characterized by poor temporal coordination in the operation of the speech apparatus, giving rise to the condition called stuttering.

(4) Voice disorders. These include cases whose speech shows an abnormal phonation such as hoarseness, nasality, etc.

(5) Symbolic disorders. In this type the difficulty is in the ability to

[41] H. K. Baker, How important is speech? *Crippled Child* (Chicago: National Society for Crippled Children and Adults, October, 1948).

[42] White House Conference on Child Health and Protection, Sect. III F, Committee on Special Classes, *Special Education. The Handicapped and the Gifted.* (New York: Appleton-Century-Crofts, 1931).

place words in acceptable grammatical relationship. The various types
of disorders in this group are called aphasias.[43]

Delayed speech is frequently due to low mentality, but not every
child who is slow to talk is feeble-minded. The possibility of other
causes should first be investigated. These include deafness, sickness,
extreme fright, and lack of normal stimulation for language development.

Articulatory disorders are more frequent than any other type. In
this classification are such speech defects as lisping, lalling, clut-
tering, sound-substitutions, and "baby talk." These speech patterns
tend to diminish with age, probably as a result of educational training and maturation. Some cases improve after correction of structural
organic defects such as tongue-tied condition, or deformed teeth,
palate, lips, or jaws.

Prevention of speech disorders. Prevention of articulatory and
other types of speech disorders in young children is emphasized by
Fishbein, as follows:

1. Do not correct the child's pronunciation or enunciation. Applaud
that which is right. Do not stress that which is wrong.

2. Do not imitate the child's baby talk. If you keep on talking English, he will too, as soon as he can—and naturally.

3. Never talk down to babies and little children.

4. Do not nag, coax or raise your voice in an effort to get the baby
to talk. Speech will come naturally.

5. If the baby's uncle and aunt stammer, or if you stammer your-
self, give the baby a chance to learn how to talk from someone else.

6. Give the child a chance to talk and listen to him when he talks.
This will encourage him.

7. Tell the child to listen. Do not ignore him but include him in the
conversation wherever possible.[44]

Stuttering. Much more common in boys than girls is stuttering.
Figures range from a male preponderance of two to one up to estimates as high as ten to one. Furthermore, there seems to be no
correlation between intelligence and stuttering.

Explanatory theories of stuttering are numerous and varied, as
described by Hahn.[45]

[43] C. M. Louttit, *Clinical Psychology* (New York: Harper & Brothers, 1947),
p. 456.

[44] M. Fishbein, The baby's growth, *The American Home*, November, 1946, p. 101.

[45] E. F. Hahn, *Stuttering; Significant Theories and Therapies* (Stanford University: Stanford University Press, 1943).

Some authorities believe that stuttering is the reaction of certain children to excessive pressure, heavy demands, or marked frustration. The inco-ordination seems to be greater in specific social situations than in others. For instance, some children are able to talk with relative normality when alone with playmates but stutter when faced by someone in authority.

Johnson *et al.*[46] emphasize the fact that nonstuttering children and adults exhibit occasional hesitations and repetitions in their speech but they talk nonfluently as calmly as they talk fluently. For the stutterer, the thought of being nonfluent in speech arouses panic. He prizes fluency so highly that the thought of hesitating speech causes him to be emotionally disturbed. Johnson cites instances in which stuttering in young children apparently was caused by the anxiety, nagging, and critical attitudes of relatives or teachers. To label the child a "stutterer" increases his tension. In straining to speak in a manner to please the adults about him, the stuttering becomes worse. Obviously, it is best not to call the child's attention to the interruptions in his speech. He should not be made more self-conscious about his language. The problem of stuttering is often temporary if handled wisely. The general treatment consists of giving the child a sense of security, eliminating undue pressure, and aiding him to relax and to enjoy life.

Further evidence that stuttering is psychogenic in origin is found in Blanton's report [47] that many stutterers showed their first symptoms of speech disorder when in the first grade. It is assumed that the difficulty of adjusting to the new environment is an important factor. The problem of preparing a child to enter school is discussed in a later section in connection with reading readiness.

Johnson [48] points out certain things a teacher will be careful to do and not to do, in working with a child who is defective in speech: "She will not criticize a pupil's speech in such a way as to embarrass him. In case of doubt, she will give him a smile, a friendly pat, or a word of praise for the speaking he does."

According to the authorities just cited, stuttering is like stage-fright in being an emotional disturbance. There is no necessity to assume any neural pathology or disorder of cerebral control to explain it.

[46] Wendell Johnson, S. F. Brown, J. F. Curtis, C. W. Edney, and J. Keaster, *Speech Handicapped Children* (New York: Harper & Brothers, 1948), pp. 179-257.
[47] S. Blanton, Speech disorders, *Mental Hygiene*, 1929, Vol. 13, pp. 740-753.
[48] Johnson, *et al., op. cit.*, p. 30.

Other experts believe that stuttering is the inevitable consequence of any disturbance of cerebral dominance. According to these writers, which hemisphere of the brain happens to be dominant is not of much importance, provided it is dominant. Failure to establish such dominance might interfere with speech control, since there might then be a conflict between the hemispheres, thus affecting the neuromuscular patterns of speech. This theory is discussed by Hahn.[49]

The problem of handedness is closely related to the question of cerebral dominance. There is increasing evidence that dextrality is a matter of degree. There is likewise evidence that some cases of stuttering seemingly occurred as a consequence of forcing the child to change from the use of the preferred left hand to the use of the right hand. The theory of cerebral dominance is supported by certain studies in electroencephalography.[50]

All the known methods of treatment of stuttering have produced both successes and failures. Each case must be investigated individually and treated in terms of the most probable etiological factors. It is probable that stuttering arises out of different combinations of causes in different individuals.

Treatment usually includes programs of physical and mental hygiene, and special remedial techniques. In general, the aim of psychotherapy is to remove crippling fears and restore the child's self-confidence. Friendly, affectionate treatment tends to build up a sense of security that counteracts fear. Unreasonable demands and serious frustrations should be reduced to a minimum. Distraction of the child's attention from himself to wholesome recreational and work activities may prove beneficial. Finally, it is helpful to provide acceptable outlets for aggression and hostility, and reasonable satisfaction of basic needs.

Reading, an aspect of language development

Importance of reading. In the preschool years, language is oral in type, but when the child enters the public school he is expected to learn to read. Of all school subjects, this seems to lead in importance, forming a basis for much other school work. It is generally regarded as an invaluable means for securing greater and more

49 Hahn, *op. cit.*

50 J. R. Knott and T. D. Tjossem, Bilateral electroencephalograms from normal speakers and stutterers, *Journal of Experimental Psychology,* 1943, Vol. 32, pp. 357-362; L. C. Douglass, A study of bilaterally recorded encephalograms of adult stutterers, *ibid.,* pp. 247-265.

accurate knowledge concerning self, others, and the world. In a democracy, it has special value with reference to the duties and privileges of citizenship.

Gates remarks that "Failure to learn to read makes one socially conspicuous in an unfavorable way. Children are likely to experience very severe frustrations if they do not get along well in reading. These circumstances alone may set up a variety of nervous and emotional symptoms which are not the cause of the reading difficulty but, on the contrary, the result of it." [51]

The general practice is for the child to enter the first grade at the age of six years. Actually, some are not ready for this step and cannot learn to read at this age because of physiological and mental immaturity. When a child is pushed beyond his level of maturation, failure or inadequate adjustment is almost inevitable because the nervous system is not yet ready for the new tasks. It is contrary to the laws of nature that children should advance lock-step through the grades. They achieve at widely differing rates.

Reading readiness. There are signs of maturation which indicate that the child is ready to go into the first grade. Some of these indications of readiness should be familiar to all who try to help young children. For instance, it is obvious that the child should have developed the health and stamina to undergo the strain of the school day. He must be willing to stay at school, away from his mother, or homesickness will interfere with learning. Unless the beginner speaks clearly enough to be understood and has an adequate vocabulary, he is not fully prepared to read. This is understandable when it is recalled that reading is itself primarily a language skill.

Ability to differentiate between forms is of great value in learning words and letters. A limited experiential background often handicaps the child in reading. Most first-graders are expected to be able to sit quietly and attend to school activities for periods of ten to fifteen minutes. Gesell adds that the child should have normal (or corrected) vision, normal hearing, and a general mental level of six to six and one-half years. [52] Some children whose chronological age is six years are mentally retarded and have mental ages of five years or even less. Such children are not ready to learn to read.

Reading-readiness tests are useful in finding those who, on the

[51] A. I. Gates, *Improvement of Reading* (New York: The Macmillan Company, 1947), p. 108.

[52] A. I. Gesell *et al.*, *The First Five Years of Life* (New York: Harper & Brothers, 1940), p. 209.

basis of their test performance, may be expected to encounter difficulties in learning the basic skills. Monroe has devised one of the best tests for this purpose, namely, the *Reading Aptitude Tests* for determining reading readiness. In these tests are included: memory of orientation of forms, ocular-motor control and attention, visual memory, motor speed, motor steadiness, auditory discrimination of words, sound blending, vocabulary, auditory memory, word articulation, speech facility, extent of vocabulary through association, sentence length and use of language, motor test of handedness, and laterality tests of hands, feet, and eyes.

The composite score on the Monroe test correlated .75 with reading achievement at the end of the first grade.[53] The test provides an analysis of a child's achievement on each of the subtests, thus revealing specific needs which may be met.

Beginning to read. Most children now are taught to read by associating the actual object, or the picture of the object, with the whole word. For instance, the word "house" is shown the beginner and the teacher pronounces the word, pointing to the picture of a house. In like fashion, more words, or even short phrases, are presented, either with or without pictures. The child finally develops a good basic vocabulary from associating the printed word with the familiar oral word or with the picture. This is called the word-recognition method.

It should be emphasized that the entire word is presented to the beginner. This method has been found to be superior to the older method of teaching the alphabet first. One reason is that the child is already familiar with the names of objects and is more interested in them than in the letters of the alphabet, most of which have little meaning when presented singly, as "d," "s," "t," and the like. Experts emphasize the need for teaching the alphabet, but not in the early stages of learning to read.

Some children do not learn to read by this method, however, and other approaches should be tried. Dr. Gesell says of this problem: "There are multiple methods—visual, auditory, manual, and phonetic, which should be used freely and variously and separately and in combination to suit the fluid psychology of this school beginner, and to do justice to the individual differences which prevail among all school beginners." [54]

---

[53] Marion Monroe, *The Reading Aptitude Tests* (Boston: Houghton Mifflin Company, 1935).

[54] Gesell and Ilg, *op. cit.,* 1946, p. 379.

Hildreth found significant interrelationships between reading and the other language arts.[55] Some of the investigations cited show that the key factor in silent reading is language or thought, and that many of the difficulties in reading are due to inadequate language comprehension.

Emotional factors in reading. Psychologists and teachers generally recognize the importance of emotional factors in cases of reading disability. Some children prefer to be read to and therefore resist the learning of personal skills that would deprive them of the pleasure of being entertained by the reading of others. Overanxiety of a parent or teacher concerning reading, unfortunate comparisons of pupil progress in this subject, and embarrassment over mistakes frequently contribute to the child's emotional tension. In fact, the first-grader may even refuse to go to school because of some unpleasant experience.

The case of Jim is illustrative. The boy was eleven years old when brought to the clinic for testing. He was in the fifth grade but was reading at the third-grade level. Jim's trouble, as revealed during several sessions, seemed to begin in the first grade. There his teacher tried to control him with harsh punishment and with sarcasm. The boy reacted with aggression and hostility. His behavior became worse and finally he was sent to a private school for three years. This Jim interpreted as rejection by his family. He said, "They sent me off to school to get rid of me. I guess I did give 'em a lot of trouble." At private school, with the help of understanding teachers, Jim eventually began to make a better adjustment and his reading improved correspondingly.

Frequently, the child is concerned over home conditions and ceases to make progress in reading and in other school work. This was the case with Edna, a quiet, retiring little girl in the second grade. Her teacher observed that she seemed preoccupied and that her attention was not on classroom activities. Even the Halloween program failed to arouse her interest. The child made little progress in reading and in November her teacher called at Edna's home to talk with her mother. Inquiry revealed that the child's father was serving a prison sentence and the little girl was deeply troubled over his fate. She was devoted to her father and it is not surprising that her grief and anxiety affected her school work.

Axline describes a follow-up study on twenty-four nonreaders for

[55] Gertrude Hildreth, Interrelationships among the language arts, *Elementary School Journal*, 1948, Vol. 48, pp. 538-549.

whom a therapeutic approach to reading was used. Five years after the therapy sessions ended, each child was asked to write the one thing he remembered best about the semester of help. Some of the comments written by the children were: "I found out I could make friends and I stopped being afraid of everything." "Everybody was nice to one another." "I lost my feeling of being lonesome and I felt that I wasn't all bad, and that some people liked me and didn't shove me away." "I remember how I came to feel like I was worthwhile." "I was afraid of everything and everybody but I got over being an afraid person, because I wasn't afraid of anybody in there like I used to be." "We could move without being yelled at, and do things kids like to do." "I loved the paints and clay and the stories." "I learned to read." [56]

The children whose comments were quoted by Axline had many disturbing emotional and social factors in their lives. As they improved their adjustment, their reading improved. Gains on standard reading tests in the three and one-half months of the experiment averaged about five months.

Growth in reading ability. After the learner has mastered the fundamental skills in reading, he enters what Gates calls the "intermediate reading stage." According to this writer, the average child reaches this stage in the latter part of the third grade and continues in it through grades four, five, and six. Gates described this stage as "characterized by greater speed, more advanced techniques, and greater flexibility. Word recognition in reasonably familiar material has now become so effective that the pupil can and does give his mind more fully to the thought."

Gates indicated that the next stage, that of "mature reading," is characterized by "gradual improvement in efficiency, increased skill in word recognition, in working out the pronunciation and meaning of new words, in recognizing words during reading on the basis of increasingly superficial clues, better phrasing and organization, higher speed, and greater flexibility." [57] Superior children may reach the mature reading stage as early as the third grade and there is evidence that some geniuses have achieved it even earlier.

Psychological principles. After an examination of many research studies, Russell summarized six important psychological principles pertaining to reading:

[56] V. M. Axline, Play therapy experiences as described by child participants, *Journal of Consulting Psychology,* 1950, Vol. 14, pp. 53-63.

[57] Gates, *op. cit.,* 1947, pp. 34-39.

(1) All children go through similar stages of development as their reading abilities mature.

(2) Development of reading abilities is a continuous and gradual process.

(3) Although children go through similar patterns of continuous development there is a wide variation in the times individuals reach certain points in reading achievement.

(4) Although reading is a continuous development, at various levels different needs and interests tend to accelerate certain phases of growth in reading abilities and attitudes.

(5) In general, there is a positive relationship between reading achievement and general physical, mental, and social development, and among the various reading achievements themselves.

(6) The effect of environmental influences related to reading varies with the stage of maturation reached by the child.[58]

Selection of reading materials. Reading material has appeal if it is based upon the interests of the child at a given stage of development. The growth in reading interests is developmental in nature; hence, it is important to appraise the level of maturation that the child has attained. Inasmuch as children of a given chronological age vary greatly, a wide variety of reading materials should be made available, with the purpose of appealing to each child.

Cole has recognized the psychological problem of individual differences in the following realistic statement: "It would be very nice if all children liked good literature from the start. The fact is that they do not. A teacher can force a small child to sit still and look at a book, but she cannot force him to read it. The only thing one can do is to build on whatever interests are already in existence, trying to raise the level as quickly as possible." [59]

Kindergarten children usually delight in animal and nature stories, here-and-now narratives of everyday doings, and stories that contain repetitive phrases. Young children enjoy accounts that cause them to recall familiar sights, sounds, odors, and tastes. In the primary grades, the preference is usually for stories of the local environment, and many children of this age delight in stories that feature toys, games, and home and school activities.

There is an apparent exception to the interest in local material

[58] D. H. Russell, Reading and child development, *Forty-eighth Yearbook of the National Society for the Study of Education,* 1949, pp. 10-31.

[59] L. Cole, *The Improvement of Reading* (New York: Rinehart and Company, 1938), p. 303.

in the choice of fairy tales. These are enjoyed by many children in the upper primary years, and by others in the intermediate grades. For some children, there is a real need for narratives that temporarily carry them away from their actual environment into a world of drama and imagination. Some editions of fairy tales prove to be quite disturbing to certain children. This may likewise be true of mystery and adventure stories. In such instances, the child will usually accept guidance in choosing less terrifying material. In general, a child who is developing normally will tend from year to year to be less upset by the presentation of exciting or frightening stories. The use of ridicule or force in such cases is most unfortunate. Understanding and kindly guidance are needed when fear is present.

Terman and Lima found that by nine years of age, sex differences in reading were evident: "Boys turn sharply from the fairy and fantastic to the realistic. . . . Girls begin to care for more sentimental fiction than do boys." These authors further noted that boys demand plenty of adventure and vigorous action, while the human interest is "so uppermost in the girl's nature that nothing seems to interest her more than the everyday life of a loving, happy family." [60] It is worthy of note that although boys rarely read girls' books, girls show a decided liking for boys' books.

The years from nine to twelve usually are characterized by a widening of reading interests and an increase in the amount of material which is read. Many children peruse an astonishing number of books but there are some who read little. Books about boys and girls are popular. Nature stories and books on science, mechanics, and travel also rank high. The subjects now are less in the present and less local. They may cover the nations of the world in extent, and the centuries of the past in time.

Some girls at this age enjoy the classics, but boys are inclined to postpone romantic books. Biography is selected frequently by children at this level of maturation.

Rankin found that books about careers for girls were quite popular. She states that "The combined average yearly circulation of career books for girls is much greater than that of books dealing with any other theme." Stories of aviation appeared prominently in the books chosen for boys. The highly popular books for boys were "almost without exception stories of physically strenuous adven-

[60] L. M. Terman and M. Lima, *Children's Reading, A Guide for Parents and Teachers* (New York: Appleton-Century-Crofts, 1931), p. 36.

ture." [61] The findings of this study are supported by the results obtained by May Lazar and presented in Tables 35 and 36.[62] Mystery, adventure, and detective stories led the list preferred by boys in the different mental ability groups.

Witty reports that the amount of time devoted to reading by the gifted child increases with age and the quality of his choices is superior.[63] He noted that, as in the case of mentally average children, the girls read more than the boys. For average children, a decline in the amount of reading tends to occur after age thirteen, but for the gifted there is a steady increase up to age seventeen.

TABLE 35 Five kinds of books liked best by boys (after Lazar)

Per Cent Bright		Per Cent Average		Per Cent Dull	
Adventure	33.0	Mystery	23.4	Mystery	30.8
Mystery	19.7	Adventure	22.1	Detective	29.2
Detective	14.2	Detective	18.1	Adventure	9.8
Science	10.4	History	13.6	History	7.9
History	7.0	Invention	8.2	Nature & Animals	7.9

TABLE 36 Five kinds of books liked best by girls (after Lazar)

Per Cent Bright		Per Cent Average		Per Cent Dull	
Mystery	27.1	Mystery	32.3	Fairy tales	38.3
Adventure	21.0	Fairy tales	21.1	Mystery	21.8
Fairy tales	14.4	Adventure	14.1	Detective	8.6
Novels	9.6	Home & School	7.0	Adventure	7.6
Home & School	9.3	History	6.2	Home & School	6.6

Language and thinking

Interrelationships. Thinking and language development are so closely interrelated that it is difficult to study the development of one to the exclusion of the other. In this connection, it has even been

[61] Marie Rankin, *Children's Interest in Library Books of Fiction* (New York: Bureau of Publications, Teachers College, Columbia University, 1944), No. 906, pp. 130-131.

[62] May Lazar, Reading interests, activities, and opportunities of bright, average and dull children, Teachers College, Columbia University, *Contributions to Education,* No. 707, 1937, p. 56.

[63] Paul Witty, *Reading in Modern Education* (Boston: D. C. Heath and Company, 1949), p. 44.

pointed out: "All of the data for every kind of reasoning experiment so far reported suggest that reasoning increases by small increments as a function of age. Since reasoning and language are so closely related, this improvement may be largely linguistic." [64]

Words in themselves are not significant. It is what the words mean, or stand for, that is important to thinking. Words and gestures are substituted for the original situations and the original object or situation no longer has to be present. Words may suffice, since they are representative in function.

Importance of early months. The importance of mothering in the early months of life as emphasized by Ribble has been mentioned previously.[65] Gross failure to provide adequate physical and psychological care may result in crying habits, exaggerated sucking, or even in the states of inanition, shock, or hypertension. In such children, serious physical and mental retardation may occur. The same writer further says that "When the baby has achieved the ability to imagine his mother's presence when she is not there, we may say that his mental functioning is well under way." [66]

Somewhat akin to this response is that described by Gesell as "adaptive behavior," in babies of nine to twelve months of age. The examiner takes a "small red cube and casts it upon the table to entice the child's attention. While the attention of the child is directed to the cube, the examiner swiftly covers it with an inverted enamel cup." Many infants recover the cube, sometimes several times in succession.[67]

Dewey says that "Thinking begins as soon as the baby who has lost the ball he is playing with begins to foresee the possibility of something not yet existing—its recovery, and begins to forecast steps toward the realization of this possibility, and, by experimentation, to guide his acts by his ideas and thereby also test his ideas." [68]

Importance of activity. Basic to thinking is the tendency to explore, to manipulate. The young child is exceedingly active and in his ceaseless movements he builds up a host of perceptions, both physical and social. Through recurrent experiences he gradually develops, for instance, the understanding of *indoors* and *outdoors*, of

---

[64] N. L. Munn, *Psychological Development: An Introduction to Genetic Psychology* (Boston: Houghton Mifflin Company, 1938), p. 358.

[65] Ribble, *op. cit.*, p. 9.

[66] *Ibid.*, p. 94.

[67] A. Gesell, *The Mental Growth of the Preschool Child* (New York: The Macmillan Company, 1925), p. 113.

[68] J. Dewey, *How We Think* (Boston: D. C. Heath and Company, 1933), p. 89.

up and *down*, of *in* and *under*, of *big* and *little*. These and oth·
concepts continue to expand as new associations are made.[69]

The concept *ball* may be limited at first to an object that wi
roll. Lifting and squeezing the ball may give some notion of i·
weight and its softness. As the child obtains more experience, th
term *ball* will also include baseballs, basketballs, and footballs, an·
the concept will be immeasurably richer and more complex.

Judgments of distance are difficult for young children and can b·
learned only through experience. The child must learn to regard th·
clearness of outline and of color, and notice the definiteness of detai·
as clues to perception of distance. He has to find out that "the littl·
baby sheep" in the distant meadow are full-grown animals, and tha·
objects and animals in the distance appear to be small.

Experiences with tricycles, wagons, ladders, form boards, an·
puzzles help the child to develop more accurate space perception.

The world for the five-year-old is still local. It usually is limite·
to his neighborhood and kindergarten. Gesell says that by age si·
there may be some interest in the sun, the moon, and the planets·
and there is a marked interest in Heaven and Hell. There is ·
"minimal, picture-book type of interest in children of other lands."[7]
For the ages of eight and nine years, school curricula provide fo·
study of cultures outside their own and they are interested in detail·
of life in foreign countries, and in earlier periods of history.

Importance of questions. Children obtain much of their informa·
tion by means of questions, and their inquiries reveal the inadequacy·
of their concepts. These questions, asked by preschool subjects who·
were studied by Smith, are illustrative: "How many minutes is ten·
o'clock?" Mary, aged forty-two months, asked concerning her·
shadow, "Why Mary walk on the floor?" A girl of forty-one months·
inquired: "Who made God?" Eugene, aged forty-six months, asked·
concerning a firecracker: "How would it went bang."

In this investigation, Smith studied 3,095 questions asked by pre·
school children and found that the largest proportion of questions·
concerned human action and intentions, the total being 46 per cent.·
Questions of time, fact, and invention increased with age and com·
posed 14 per cent. Questions regarding place constituted 13 per cent,·
and causal inquiries 8 per cent.[71]

[69] Gesell and Ilg, *op. cit.*, 1949, pp. 21-27.
[70] Gesell and Ilg, *op. cit.*, 1946, pp. 442-443.
[71] M. E. Smith, Influence of age, sex and situation on frequency, form and function of questions asked by preschool children, *Child Development*, 1933, Vol. 4, pp. 201-213.

Significance of maturation. Maturation as well as experience affects the concept which the child has. The effects of these two factors are well illustrated by Gesell's analysis of the concept of Santa Claus at various ages:

"The 4-year-old is a true believer and accepts every detail of the myth. The 5-year-old embraces the realism of Santa's clothes, his laugh, his reindeers. The 6-year-old hears doubtings, but he fiercely repels all suspicion. His belief is more emotional; his enjoyment more intense. Reflective seven has moments of skepticism; or we should say, moments of constructive criticism. At age eight, the notion of Santa Claus is more etherealized, but it is by no means surrendered. The spirit of Christmas is taking shape as an observed and felt reality. By the age of nine or ten, the Santa myth has been generally abandoned; but who can doubt that it may play an enriching role in the development of personality?" [72]

Further evidence of the influence of maturation and experience may be seen in the studies of animism. Piaget asserts that children between four and six believe that everything is alive. Children of six and seven call that which moves alive, in contrast to what is inert. From eight to ten years, a new distinction arises: to be alive is to move oneself. Finally, at about eleven, the child reserves life to animals and plants, or even to animals alone.

Russell investigated Piaget's theory, using 774 children as subjects. He concluded: "It is probable that individuals pass sequentially through the series of concepts with increasing mental and chronological age." He found, however, that it was impossible to limit the age range of the stages as Piaget attempted to do. [73]

Limitations resulting from immaturity and lack of experience. The child's concepts often show inaccuracy due to failure to notice differences. Errors of generalization are quite common. A small child seeing a fur neckpiece for the first time may call it "kitty." It is not unusual for babies to call any and all men "daddy." To advance from such inadequate concepts, observation and reinforcement are necessary. Meaning has all degrees, from the vaguest general appreciation of some experience to the fullest scientific comprehension of an object. Fuller meaning comes from hearing or seeing a word used in a number of concrete applications, each of which helps to clarify

[72] Gesell and Ilg, *op. cit.,* 1946, p. 437.
[73] R. W. Russell, Studies in animism: II, The development of animism, *Journal of Genetic Psychology,* 1940, Vol. 56, pp. 353-366.

the total meaning. As Sapir expresses it, we think in terms of symbols, symbols which represent concepts.[74]

As he develops, the child becomes capable of comparing and seeing relationships. It is as important for him to see similarities as it is for him to observe differences. In fact, it is on the basis of similarities that he generalizes. Hazlitt presented to young children four trays holding, respectively: Dog and bird; dog and pig; dog and cow; dog and sheep. She asked: What have all the trays got? Very few of the children under five years of age could pick out the common elements.[75]

Terman and Merrill, as part of their scale for measuring intelligence, test the ability to perceive similarities and differences. For instance, at the designated ages these questions are asked:

Age 7: In what way are wood and coal alike? Apple and peach? Ship and automobile? Iron and silver?

Age 8: In what way are a baseball and an orange alike and how are they different? Airplane and kite? Ocean and river? Penny and quarter?

Age 11: In what way are a snake, cow, and sparrow alike? Rose, potato, tree? Wool, cotton, leather? Knife-blade, penny, piece of wire? Book, teacher, newspaper? [76]

Experiences basic to successful problem solving. Combinations of concepts into rules and principles will occur as the child develops. For instance, he evolves a set of concepts which relate to safety, another set concerning behavior at the table, and still another regarding playground codes. These groups of concepts guide his thought and constitute a useful frame of reference. At times, the child may refer to the wrong set of concepts and thereby draw wrong conclusions.

Unless the child has had some experience or experiences that furnish meaning, he is confused and unable to solve the problem. His ability to understand terms and his failures in reasoning often stem from this lack of background experience. It is quite futile to urge him to think when he has had no prior activity comparable to the one which faces him. Home and school must therefore conspire to furnish him with a wealth of experiences, using pictures, stories, pets, toys, books, creative materials, excursions, opportunity for manipula-

[74] E. Sapir, *Language: An Introduction to the Study of Speech* (New York: Harcourt, Brace and Co., 1921), p. 17.

[75] V. Hazlitt, Children's thinking, *British Journal of Psychology*, 1930, Vol. 20, pp. 354-361.

[76] L. M. Terman and M. A. Merrill, *Measuring Intelligence* (Boston: Houghton Mifflin Co., 1937), pp. 97, 101, 109.

tion and exploration, answers to questions, and contacts with persons of various ages.

As long as life proceeds along familiar channels where no new actions are demanded, habit is sufficient. Whenever a strange situation arises, habit is insufficient and the child is faced with a problem. Thinking seems to occur, when the individual, confronted by a problem, endeavors a solution based upon relevant past experiences. The steps in such problem solving are as follows:

1. Location of the problem and realization of its nature.
2. Survey of possible solutions.
3. Choice of the most suitable solution.
4. Trial of the selected solution.

Experiments in problem solving have been attempted with very young subjects. For instance, Richardson studied the reactions of infants, aged twenty-eight to fifty-two weeks, to a toy attached to a string. The latter was always within reach but the toy was not. The experimenter attracted attention to the toy by tapping it, rocking it, squeaking it, and the like. The reactions of the infants varied and Richardson states that two types of behavior evidenced incomplete insight: awareness of lure and string without purposive utilizing of the string, and experimentation. He claimed that success with insight was manifested by those infants who definitely utilized the string to bring the toy into reach. Responses with insight increased in frequency with age.[77]

Language aids problem solving. The significance of language in the development of generalizations has been shown by a multiple-choice experiment reported by Pyles. A child was told: "One of these shapes has a toy under it. See if you can find which shape has a toy." One series of experiments had nonsense figures which were not named; in a second series, the figures were named; in a third series, well-known animal forms were used. A series was considered as learned when the correct choice was made four times in succession. Results showed that verbalization helped the subjects, who were two to seven years of age, in the problem solving. The more familiar material was mastered most quickly.[78]

[77] H. M. Richardson, The growth of adaptive behavior in infants: an experimental study of seven age levels, *Genetic Psychology Monographs*, 1932, Vol. 12, pp. 195-359.

[78] M. K. Pyles, Verbalization as a factor in learning, *Child Development*, 1932, Vol. 3, pp. 108-113.

Factors that inhibit thinking. It is important to know what factors are inhibitory to thinking. Alpert, in a study of forty-four children, noted many types of behavior associated with inferior problem solving. She used nine different problem situations. For instance, an attractive toy was placed so far away from the child, who was in a playpen, that it could be obtained only if the two halves of a fishing rod were properly combined as a tool. Some of the following factors seemed to be responsible for partial or complete inhibition of insight:

1. Self-consciousness. The uneasiness which is a natural concomitant prevents the subject from carefully surveying the field. He is not inclined to commit himself to action lest it result in failure, of which he is afraid and ashamed.

2. Lack of confidence. The subject prefaces all action with a look at the experimenter—manifestly a plea for approval or encouragement—and is inclined to interpret the absence of response as disapproval or permission withheld.

3. Fixation. To the extent that the child permits one assumption to usurp attention, to the exclusion of all others, he lessens his chance to see the problem in the right perspective.

4. Lack of interest. This is often a chronic lack of enthusiasm on the part of the subject, causing him to "give up" too readily.

5. Discouragement. Sulks and tears, in any case a withdrawal of attention and cessation of activity, cut out the possibility of solution.

6. Excitability. When the problem solving is too eager, or energetic, or excitable, attention is not directed to any one thing at a time, with the result that excellent "clues" are often unheeded.

7. Lack of observation. This is present in all degrees, from a total unawareness of surroundings to its opposite, a minute investigation of all details.

8. Emotional immaturity. This presents a picture of inactivity, almost immobility. Under the circumstances insight is surely interfered with, if not completely inhibited.[79]

Is thinking subvocal talking? Young children vocalize with little restraint. Even as they play alone they often engage in much conversational activity. Piaget has emphasized this type of egocentric behavior.[80] In the normal development of language and thinking, as exemplified in the child, there is a gradual transition from overt to implicit speech.

[79] A. Alpert, The solving of problem-situations by preschool children, Teachers College, Columbia University, *Contributions to Education*, 1928, No. 323, pp. 58-63. A more complete description of the method used by Alpert is presented in Chapter 10.

[80] Piaget, *op. cit.*, p. 35.

There have been many attempts to identify thinking as internal speech, but decisive experiments were performed by Jacobson. Wire electrodes were placed in the muscles of the tongue and under-lip. The subjects were asked to imagine counting; telling a friend the date; recalling poems or songs; thinking of abstract matters such as "eternity," "electrical resistance," and the like. Jacobson concluded that "The series of vibrations occur in patterns evidently corresponding with those during inner speech." *During absence of these patterns in (approximately) complete relaxation, no thinking occurred.*

This demonstrated only that to some forms of thinking inner speech is indispensable. Jacobson's investigations included other forms of thinking as well. His investigations showed that visual forms necessarily include muscular movements or steady tensions of the eyes and that still other forms of thinking can be objectively confirmed. Acts of imagination in some subjects, for example, included actual but invisible movements of bodily parts as if the subject were actually engaged in the imaginary experience but on a minature or microscopic scale.

Jacobson concludes that thinking never takes place exclusively in the brain, but necessarily involves muscular action. Thinking subsides when specific muscular patterns are relaxed, but he does not interpret this as favoring the traditional "motor theory of thinking." [81]

Summary and generalization

Speech is man's most important means of adjusting. A surprisingly large part of life involves speaking, writing, listening, or reading. Without language, it would have been impossible for man to organize into national groups. But for written language, there would have been relatively little transmission of the cultural achievements of past generations to succeeding generations.

A baby is born into a society that is ready to give him its special type of communication, for instance, French, German, English, or Chinese. He learns the language of his environment. He comes into the world, however, equipped with the structural basis for speech. The mechanism is ready for use. In the normal child, the intellectual ability is adequate for the gradual mastery of the language of his

[81] E. Jacobson, Electrophysiology of mental activities, *American Journal of Psychology,* 1932, Vol. 44, pp. 677-694. *Progressive Relaxation* (Chicago: University of Chicago Press, 1938).

people. Language is the result of innate factors as well as environmental stimulation.

As maturation continues, the child tends to improve in his language skills. He talks more and in longer and more complex sentences. His vocabulary increases by leaps and bounds.

Speech is a reliable indicator of the normality or abnormality of adjustment or development. Failure of normal progress may be due to feeble-mindedness, to physical defects, to lack of opportunity or need, or to traumatic causes.

When he enters school, the child is expected to learn other language skills, reading, spelling, and writing. As with oral language, failure to make satisfactory progress is often associated with mental retardation, physical handicaps, inferior environmental opportunity, or emotional maladjustment.

There is increasing recognition of the need for early diagnosis of the cause or causes of language retardation. There is also more widespread realization that normal language development is basic to normal personality development.

Questions and Exercises

1. What are the causes of crying in infancy, according to Bühler?
2. Discuss the viewpoint of Gesell concerning crying of infants during the first four months after birth.
3. Describe the types of vocalization that occur during the first year. Are these learned?
4. How does babbling become transformed into words?
5. What factors may cause the vocabulary development at twelve to eighteen months to be relatively slow?
6. Preschool girls are more talkative than boys. Name several other factors, besides the sex of the child, that seem to be associated with more rapid language development.
7. The proportion of nouns at the age of two years is 39 per cent, but at fifty-four months the proportion has dropped to 19 per cent. What explanation can you give for this change?
8. Give several reasons for the close relationship that exists between vocabulary and general school achievement.
9. Explain why twins are often retarded in language development.
10. Do you advocate beginning a foreign language during the preschool years? What did Smith advise from her study of bilingual children?
11. Discuss this statement: "Basic to thinking is the tendency to explore, to manipulate."

12. Give several illustrations showing the importance of maturation in the development of language and thinking.
13. Name some of the most significant factors which Alpert found to be associated with inferior problem solving by young children.
14. Identify each:
    1. Recognition vocabulary.
    2. "Naming stage" of speech.
    3. Egocentric speech.
    4. Ages for code languages.
    5. Marasmus.
    6. Reading readiness.

Selected Readings

Anderson, John E. *The Psychology of Development and Personal Adjustment*. New York: Henry Holt and Company, 1949. Pp. 153-176.

Arlitt, Ada Hart. *Psychology of Infancy and Early Childhood*. New York: McGraw-Hill Book Co., 1946. Pp. 370-400.

Breckenridge, Marian E. and Vincent, E. Lee. *Child Development*. 2nd ed.; Philadelphia: W. B. Saunders Co., 1949. Pp. 393-426.

Cole, Luella, and Morgan, J. J. B. *Psychology of Childhood and Adolescence*. New York: Rinehart & Co., 1947. Pp. 319-351.

Gesell, A., et al. *The First Five Years of Life*. New York: Harper & Brothers, 1940. Pp. 189-237.

Gesell, A., et al. *The Child from Five to Ten*. New York: Harper & Brothers, 1946. Pp. 395-399, 382-386, 444-447.

Hubbard, Elizabeth Vernon. *Your Children at School: How They Adjust and Develop*. New York: John Day Co., 1942.

Hurlock, Elizabeth B. *Child Development*. New York: McGraw-Hill Book Co., 1950. Pp. 203-246.

Jersild, Arthur T. *Child Psychology*. New York: Prentice-Hall, 1947. Pp. 321-348.

Landreth, Catherine, and Read, Katherine H. *Education of the Young Child*. New York: John Wiley & Sons, 1942. Chaps. XIII, XVI.

Lee, J. Murray, and Lee, Doris May. *The Child and His Curriculum*. New York: Appleton-Century-Crofts, 1940.

Rand, Winifred, Sweeny, Mary E., and Vincent, E. Lee. *Growth and Development of the Young Child*. Philadelphia: W. B. Saunders Co., 1946. Pp. 304-322.

Strang, Ruth. *An Introduction to Child Study*. New York: The Macmillan Company, 1938.

Witty, Paul. *Reading in Modern Education*. Boston: D. C. Heath and Company, 1949. Pp. 21-79, 142-175.

10

Growth in Knowledge
and Understanding

The growth and function of memory

The statement has been made: "Childhood is the golden age for memory." This statement is very misleading, since there is an inference that memory ability reaches its peak during childhood. Some questions related to memory during childhood may be listed as follows: When does memory begin in the development of a child? What is the general nature of the growth curve for memory? Do growth curves vary with different types of materials? What differences exist between the memory span and memory ability at different levels of growth? What is the effect of experience upon memory? Some of these questions will be answered in the following discussions.

Early manifestations of memory. It was suggested in Chapter 3 that the child may be conditioned during the early weeks of life; however, memory not based upon physical comfort and conditioning does not appear in most children prior to the fourth- or fifth-month age level. Bühler found that five-month-old infants could remember for a few seconds a smiling face and a game played.[1] Children of fifteen to seventeen months could remember for eight minutes, while children of twenty-one to twenty-four months could remember for seventeen minutes. These findings have been verified by subsequent studies in Germany and the United States. This is shown in the bibliographical records of memory in preschool children as observed by Hurlock and Schwartz. As a result of their studies, they present

[1] Charlotte Bühler, *From Birth to Maturity: An Outline of the Psychological Development of the Child* (London: K. Paul, Trench, Trubner and Co., 1935).

the following developmental schedule of memory during the first several years of life:

1. Memory, of an impressionistic kind, appears in the first half year of life. The first instances of true remembrance appear by the end of the first year.

2. Memory, in the first year, is only aroused by a sensory stimulus, but, by the end of the second year, a sensory experience is no longer necessary to reinstate memory. It has developed into a more ideational type of experience.

3. During the first two years, memory is stronger for persons and objects than for situations. But, in the years from three to six, persons and objects in situations have become the significant factors in the child's memory.

4. Unusual events and things which are interesting to the child have a longer latency period than neutrally toned events. The emotional quality of the impression influences the memory of it.

5. The child recognizes and remembers colors and forms in the second half of the third year.

6. At the age of three years, the child is able after a few days to recount a story heard, and give detailed information about past experiences.[2]

The development of memory ability. The speed with which children acquire vocabulary (see Chapter 9) after the eighteenth-month period provides some basis for determining the nature of memory at this age and its development during early childhood. Memory may be classified as *immediate* memory and *delayed* or long-time memory. Most of the memory of children during the first two or three years for happenings, based upon their ability to recall the incident, would be classed as immediate memory. *The Stanford Revision of the Binet Tests of Intelligence,* as well as other revisions, have made use of the immediate-memory span for digits in measuring intelligence. The normal immediate span for the two-and-one-half-year group is two digits, with three digits for the three-year-old group, four for the four-and-one-half-year olds, five for the seven-year-olds, and six for the ten-year-olds. Gesell found children two years of age able to repeat a sentence of three to four syllables.[3]

In a study conducted by Stroud and Maul, the problem of the influence of age upon the learning of poetry and nonsense syllables

[2] E. B. Hurlock and R. Schwartz, Bibliographical records of memory in pre-school children, *Child Development,* 1932, Vol. 3, p. 238.

[3] A. I. Gesell *et al., The First Five Years of Life* (New York: Harper & Brothers, 1940).

was studied.[4] The subjects comprised 172 grade-school children, 2[?] ninth-grade students, and 23 college freshmen. The average chrono-logical ages ranged from 7.7 years to 18.1 years. The groups were approximately equal in average IQ. The growth with age in the ability to memorize poetry is presented in Figure 30. The memory

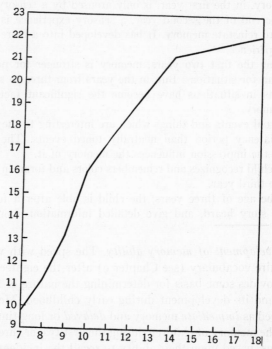

FIG. 30 The relation of age to memorizing poetry
(After Stroud and Maul)

curve for nonsense syllables is similar in nature to that given for poetry. These curves show a continuous increase with age in the ability to memorize poetry and nonsense materials. A high correla-tion was obtained between memory ability and mental age. No rela-tion, however, was found between age and retention as measured by the savings scores. This study, supported by subsequent studies of growth in memory ability, disproves the old adage that "Child-hood is the golden age of memory."

[4] J. B. Stroud and Ruth Maul, The influence of age upon learning and retention of poetry and nonsense syllables, *Journal of Genetic Psychology,* 1933, Vol. 41, pp. 242-250.

The development of percepts and concepts

It was once believed that children were born with equipment which through maturation provided for most elementary meanings. Studies of the development of the sense of space, time, weight, and the like reveal that individuals at maturity differ in the possession of such abilities. Furthermore, these differences are closely related to the backgrounds of experiences of the persons concerned. No two children have had the same experiences, and no two experiences may be expected to get the same meaning from environmental stimuli. Each child will tend to interpret things about him in terms of his pattern of experiences, which are entirely his own.

Perception of space and distance. The perception of space and distance is such a commonplace part of everyday life that adults are oftentimes inclined to consider this as part of our hereditary equipment. Children are slow to develop binocular vision with depth perception. Thus, the perception for depth is poorly developed in the five- or six-year-old child. To the preschool child, the automobiles on the street, when viewed from the window of a ten-story building, are toy automobiles. Through experiences with standard objects in the distance, he comes to learn that objects appear much smaller when they are far away. Through additional experiences he learns to use other cues in the judgment of distance. Adults are often misled in their judgment of distance because of a change in conditions which brings about a change in the use of cues for judging distance. Children grow through maturation and experiences in their ability to estimate distances correctly. The immature child may be seen placing his cup very close to the edge of the table. This sometimes accounts for accidents and breakage of cups and plates on his part. He may incorrectly estimate distances when he is at play, and may be seen to give a big step downward when a small step is sufficient, or to jump from a high place thinking that it is not so high.

The study by Ames and Leonard was concerned with the development of the child's verbalized manifestations of the sense of space, not with the total concept of space.[5] Two methods were used for gathering data bearing on this problem. There were (1) observations of children in the Guidance Nursery at the Yale Clinic of Child Development; and (2) questioning the children individually about various aspects of space. The types of questions asked were as fol-

[5] Louise Bates Ames and Janet Leonard, The development of verbalized space in the young child, *Journal of Genetic Psychology*, 1948, Vol. 72, pp. 63-84.

lows: Where do you live? Where do you sleep? What is under the floor? The results revealed that complete mastery of any one space concept is not acquired all at once; rather, there are several different levels of attainment. Individual differences were quite conspicuous; however, a relatively uniform sequence in the development of the major concepts of space was observed. Table 37 summarizes the age sequences typical of the children observed in this study.

TABLE 37 Age trends in the development of space concepts (after Ames and Leonard)

---

1 year

Gestures for *up*.
Wriggles for *down*.

18 months

Spontaneously uses *up, down* and *off*, dealing chiefly with his own basic movements in space. *Come, go* and *gone* also refer to his own activities or the presence or absence of objects in which he is directly interested.

No space words commonly used in answers to questions. Child may merely look in a direction indicated. He can, in examination, obey two directions with ball, putting it on chair and giving it to mother.

21 months

Still no space words in answer to questions, but *up, down, on* and *off* are all used spontaneously; also the size-word, *big*. Also, most characteristic of this age are *all gone*, expressing interest in absence or departure of an object, and *here,* suggesting the "here and nowness" of this age. Child frequently merely looks in a direction indicated.

24 months

Uses space words both spontaneously and in answer to questions. Although 2 years is not a particularly expansive age, note the expansion from earlier "here and nowness" implied in the use of such words as: *there, where, other side, outdoors, up stairs, up high.*

The more complex notion of container and contained comes in with *in* and *out.* *In* is used more than any other word in answer to space questions. *All gone* is still strong. There is great interest in having things in their proper places.

The child can answer such space questions as "Where is Mummy?", "Where is Daddy?", "Where do you sleep?" He can obey four directions with ball: putting it on chair, on table, and giving it to mother and to examiner.

30 months

At this age the use of space words is very much in keeping with the rigid, patterned, exact behavior of the age. Many of the space words are rigid, exact words and many appear at this age only. Thus we have: *right, right here, right there, right up there, right home, right down, right in.*

Also note at this age for nearly the first time two space words combined to give more exactness to the location indicated: *way up, up in, in here, in there,* in addition to those listed above. *Near* represents a definite advance over the earlier *in* or *at.* A beginning interest in more distant places is expressed by *far* and *far away.*

Further, the most new space words are added in the 6-month period from 2 to 2½ years of any 6-month period under consideration, both in spontaneous verbalization and in answer to space questions. (In contrast to the addition of the most new "time" words between 2½ and 3 years.)

Also, of questions asked in this investigation, the largest number of questions becomes answerable in this 6-month period of any other period studied. (See Table 5). Such questions deal chiefly with customary location of common objects or activities.

Words used most are: *in, on, up in* and *at.* There is great interest in and marked insistence upon having objects in their proper places.

36 months

Most of the space words used at 2½ years are continued in use except for a few of the more exact and rigid words, such as *right there, right up there,* etc. A few of the new words which come in, though not as exact as the 2½ words, express an increased refinement in space perception: *back, corner, over, from, by, up on top, on top of.*

A new and marked interest in space detail and direction detail comes in at this age, particularly in answering questions. In telling how to get somewhere the child may give an actual direction, i.e., *turn left and then turn right.* In telling where his daddy is he no longer says merely, "At his office" but spontaneously describes where the office is. In telling where he sleeps he may tell where his crib, or bedroom, is located. *To,* with a city name, shows increasing expansion of space interest.

The 3-year-old can tell what street he lives on though usually not the number. He can put a ball *on* and *under* a chair. New questions answered at this age deal chiefly with where people live and how to get to certain places.

In, on, at and *to* are the words used most.

42 months

Next to, under and *between* all mark increased interest in new dimensions of space. *Go* (meaning belong) and *find* (or found) express interest in appropriate places for objects. Interest in comparative size is indicated by *littlest, bigger, larger. Way down, way off, way far* express expanding but also exact interest in location.

In answering questions, the 3½-year-old uses actually less different words than the 3-year-old; in spontaneous vocalization, a few more. He can now put the ball *on, under* and *in back of* a chair. *In, on, to, home* and *up in* are words used most.

48 months *

The space verbalization of the child of this age includes most of the words used before plus a few new ones. Outstanding at this age is the use of expansive space words characteristic of the out-of-bounds expansive tendencies of the 4-year-old. Some of these words have been used before but are especially noteworthy as a group at this age. Thus: *on top of, far away, out in, down to, way up, way up there, way far, out, way off.* A new dimension is suggested in use of the word *behind.*

The child can now tell both on what street and in what city he lives. He can put a ball *on, under, in front of* and *in back of* a chair.

In, on, up in, at, and *down* are space words used most.

---

* For ages above 4 years, see pages 441-443 in Gesell and Ilg, *The Child from Five to Ten.*

Development of a sense of time. The development of the sense of time in young children was studied by Louise Ames through observations of their verbalizations and by means of a series of questions

asked each child individually.[6] Marked individual differences were
found in the children's orientation in time. The age at which 50 per
cent of children correctly answered the questions asked in the interview is presented in Table 38. In the spontaneous verbalizations,
words dealing with the present appear first; next, those indicating
the future; and finally, those indicating the past. The complete mastery of a single time concept was a gradual process. The time at
which some event happened appears in its relation to other events.
"A rather elaborate expression of temporal order occurs as early as
30 months of age, but words which imply duration do not as a rule
appear till 36 months."

**TABLE 38   Age at which 50 per cent of children answered correctly
questions about time (after Ames)**

2.5 years

Where is mummy?
Where is daddy?
Who comes for you?

3 years

What is your name?
How old are you?
What will you do tomorrow?
When do you go to bed?
What do you do at Christmas?
What do you do in winter?

3.5 years

When do you take your nap?
What do you do in summer?
What do you do at Easter?

4 years

When is your next birthday?
When do you get up?
When do you have breakfast?
When do you have supper?
When does daddy come home?
What did you do yesterday?
What do you do on Sunday?
Is it AM or PM?
When does PM begin?
What did you do at Halloween?

5 years

How old next birthday?
What day is today?

[6] Louise B. Ames, The development of the sense of time in the young child,
Journal of Genetic Psychology, 1946, Vol. 68, pp. 97-125.

Name days of week.
What day does daddy stay home all day?
What day comes after Sunday?
What day do you like best?

6 years

What time do you go to school?
What do you do in spring?
What do you do in fall?
How long do you stay in school?
What grade are you in?

7 years

What time is it?
What season is it?
What month is it?
How many minutes in an hour?

8 years

What day of month is it?
Name the months.
What year is it?
What does time mean?

The study by Bradley was concerned with the growth of the ability of elementary-school children to understand ordinary time words and the development of a concept of the universal and continuous nature of the time scheme.[7] Four tests were administered to a group of urban school children aged five to thirteen. The purpose of the first test was to trace the growth of an understanding of ordinary time words used in everyday life, while that of the other three was to explore the development of the child's grasp of the time scheme extending into the past and future. In the first test, thirty questions were asked of each child, such as: What is your age? Is it afternoon or morning now? What season is it?

The results showed that growth in understanding time words was gradual and continuous. By the age of five years, distinctions between the present, past, and future seems to have been established. The first time words used after this stage were those referring to natural phenomena and personal activities. In general, the ability to understand the conventional time scheme and to use particular time words appeared later than was generally believed. Nine- and ten-year-olds were able to comprehend a long period of years. Twelve- and thirteen-year-olds could answer questions which were mainly

[7] N. C. Bradley, The growth of the knowledge of time in children of school-age, *British Journal of Psychology*, 1947, Vol. 38, pp. 67-78.

concerned with duration. A definite order appeared in the acquisition of time knowledge. This is well shown in Figure 31 with the per cent correct at each age level on the temporal-absurdity test.

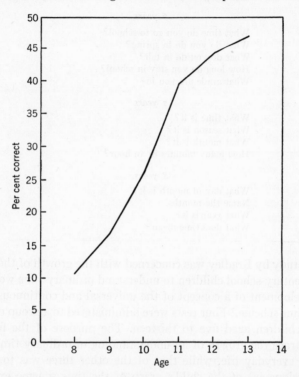

FIG. 31 The percentage of correct responses made by the different age groups on the temporal absurdity test
(After Bradley)

The results of a study by Friedman of the time concepts of elementary-school children suggests that the child's background of time concepts is developed largely outside of organized school instruction.[8] Approximately one hundred pupils from each grade from kindergarten through grade six were given tests consisting of questions dealing with some aspect of time, such as: Is this morning or afternoon? How old are you? Ideas of the future were found to be less definitely developed than those related to the past. Classification of responses according to sex showed little sex difference, while a higher

[8] K. G. Friedman, Time concept of elementary-school children, *Elementary School Journal,* 1944, Vol. 44, pp. 337-342.

percentage of correct answers was given by those with higher IQ's. This trend, however, was not nearly so marked or so constant as were the increases in the percentage of correct responses given by pupils of successively higher grades.

Importance of cues. Although cues are important in determining the responses the child will make, they must always operate within the framework of the child's experiences. Thus, there will be a growth in the meanings attached to cues, in harmony with the child's maturation, experiences, and motivation. Perception of distance, size, time, shape, and the like are all improved through training. It is through experiences involving size and shape that the child learns to react to cues which enable him to react more accurately to objects varying in size and shape. Guidance in the functional relationship of a particular cue to size or shape facilitates the growth in perception in this connection.

Studies show further that when the same general response is made to two distinct situations in which there is a common cue, a sort of equivalent response may be elicited. For example, a child may be taught that a knife will cut. At a later date when this equivalent "cut" is applied to scissors, a somewhat similar response may occur. It is in this manner that transfer takes place, based upon generalized experiences with a single perceptual cue.

The converse of this would be the development of separate and distinct perceptual responses to situations that have similar elements. In such a case, the child learns to respond to specific perceptual cues which are different in the two situations despite the fact that certain perceptual cues in the two situations are similar in nature. This may be noted in the example of the growth of the child's responses to scissors and knife. It is further observed in connection with his responses to different kinds of fruit juice. A two-year-old child, as a result of perceptual cues observed in his feeding experiences, may react quite differently to milk that comes from a bottle and milk that comes from a can. Labels attached to these differential perceptual cues are useful in the development, fixation, and extension of specific responses to these varied perceptual cues.

Number concepts of the preschool child. Number concepts grow through maturity and favorable opportunities for their development. The contribution of the nursery school and kindergarten is to furnish children with many such favorable opportunities. Through being with other children, working with different things where numerical terms are employed, meanings are gradually developed and become a part of the total self. Materials are available for stimulating the growth and clarification of number concepts. The children working at a particular table or on a special problem are counted, shovels for the sand pile are counted, fire engines are available, doll carriages are introduced in some small quantity. Such situations and opportunities furnish the stimulation needed for growth in number concepts. The three-year-old may be heard counting 1, 2, 5, 10, etc. He may be heard going through such a process without the numbers having any special meaning to him. Children of three and four tend to comprehend simple quantitative relationship, as evidenced by a child getting enough spoons and cups for the family of four. The nursery-school child may be seen bringing enough chairs to the table for her group of four or five children. The child will realize when there are enough chairs without necessarily knowing how many chairs were brought out.

Growth in memory ability, experiences with numerical situations, and added opportunities for experiences with numerical problems provide for an increase in the child's numerical concepts. The child of six has learned to count to a certain degree, depending in part upon his experiences. Haste at this point in abstract learning of symbols will retard the development of an understanding of numerical concepts.

In a study conducted by Long and Welch, 135 children ranging in age from thirty to eighty-three months were presented with three tasks: (1) discrimination of ten marbles from a varying number of marbles; (2) matching a group of marbles varying in number from two to ten; and (3) selecting the larger and smaller groups of marbles, when four groups of marbles were presented.[9] The purpose of this study was to study the effects of chronological age and mental age on the ability of children to discriminate and match numbers. The summary of the average scores obtained on the three tests, the scores of the individual tests, as well as the average of the three tests, indicate that performance varies in a regular and systematic manner with age. The youngest children found the tasks too difficult, while the flattening of the growth curve at the upper age limits suggests that the major development in the abilities involved in these tasks has occurred by the age of six or seven years.

Successful development of mathematical abilities requires an

[9] Louis Long and Livingston Welch, The development of the ability to discriminate and match numbers, *Journal of Genetic Psychology,* 1941, Vol. 59. pp. 377-387.

understanding of the growth of these abilities in children at different age levels. A child should learn to count before he memorizes the sequence of numbers. He should have concrete experiences with situations involving numbers before he is taught to count, and he should have concrete experiences with simple fractional parts before being confronted with a formal presentation of such fractions. The abstract mathematical symbols should be associated with mathematical concepts already formed. Opportunities should be given for the child to study and solve problem situations in which simple numbers are used in harmony with the child's experiences and maturation. Mathematical thinking, like other forms of thinking, should grow out of experiences and become an integral part of the child's experiences and habit patterns.

The development of concepts of causal relations. One aspect of children's thinking is that of the development of their concepts of causal relations. The work of Jean Piaget aroused considerable interest in the nature of the child's thought processes.[10] Through the individual testing method he arrived at a systematized classification of children's concepts of causality, including seventeen types of explanation. These represented three stages of development. The first two of these stages were present during the first seven years and were regarded as precausal. The third stage appeared around the seventh or eighth year, and involved a mechanical type of explanation. These stages are further related to the development from egocentrism to socialization in the child's language activities, discussed in Chapter 9.

In the study of children's concepts by Jean Marquis Deutsche, two types of analysis of children's causal thinking were made— quantitative and qualitative.[11] Questions of causality were selected and tried out with children as subjects. From these preliminary trials, final forms of the tests were developed. Form I consisted of questions based upon demonstrations of experiments in the classroom. Form II consisted of questions without experiments. The children were requested to answer each of the twelve questions the very best they could, and as quickly as possible. Quantified scores were derived for each of the questions. These were based on the adequacy of the answer as an explanation of the phenomenon. The

---

[10] See especially Jean Piaget, *The Child's Conception of Physical Causality* (New York: Harcourt, Brace & Co., 1930).

[11] Jean Marquis Deutsche, *The Development of Children's Concepts of Causal Relations* (Minneapolis: University of Minnesota Press, 1937).

mean quantified scores increased with age on each question of the two forms. The increase was greater, however, on some of the questions than on others. The increase was especially marked on the questions:

What makes the wind blow?
What makes the frost on the window panes?
What makes water boil?

The difference in the amount of increase is undoubtedly related to the difficulty of the exercise or question. The drop in the mean scores for the two forms at the fifteen-sixteen age level is perhaps a result of the selection of subjects for the study.

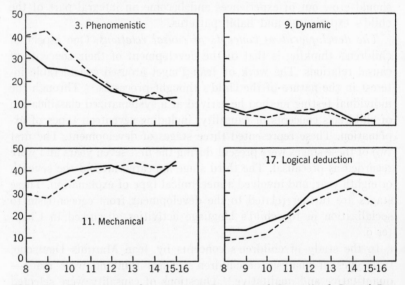

FIG. 32 Percentage of answers on Form I and Form II of Causal Relations Questions falling into several classifications, according to age

(After Deutsche)

A qualitative analysis of the scores showed considerable variation from question to question in the percentage of answers falling into each type of causal thinking. Four types of causal thinking are represented by fairly high percentages. These include: phenomenistic causality, 20.8 per cent, found on all questions; dynamic causality, 6.3 per cent, found on nine questions; logical deduction, 23.4 per cent, found on all questions; and mechanical causality, 38.9 per cent, found on all questions. The age curves for the two forms of the tests are given in Figure 32 for these four types of causal thinking. An examination of these results shows that while phenomenistic answers comprised from 30 to 40 per cent of the answers at age eight, they included approximately 10 per cent of the answers at the fifteen-sixteen age level. There was, on the other hand, a striking increase from age eight to age fifteen-sixteen in logical deduction answers. Very little change with age is noted in dynamic causality and mechanical causality answers.

Growth of the concept of God. Groups of children from various age groups were studied by Ernest Harms in order to determine the development of their concepts of God.[12] These children were asked to try to imagine what God or the highest being they thought to exist would look like to them if they were to picture Him in their minds. They were requested to picture on paper what had come to their minds. Older children and adolescents were presented with a problem of somewhat wider scope.

The drawings were analyzed and studied with respect to differences appearing among different age groups. Harms noted that the normal development of children studied in this experiment passes through three stages of religious development. These are described as follows:

1. *The fairy-tale stage.* This stage appears among preschool children and is consistent with their thoughts and fears. The small child's concept of God is quite similar to his concept of other unknowns, except in the case of God a sort of awe and respect appears to a much greater degree.

2. *The realistic stage.* This stage appears when the child enters school and encounters realism in his relation to the teacher and other pupils. At this time, the child's concept of God turns from the fairy-tale notion to that of God as a reality. Angels are at this time represented as human beings with wings. God may be pictured as an all-powerful man. As the child advances through this period, he appears to adapt himself to religious institutions, accepting the ideas and practices of his family. He also comes to symbolize God through some form or sign such as the crucifix or the Jewish star.

3. *The individualistic stage.* The individualistic stage of religious concepts and the concept of God appears among a large percentage of children in the United States. However, many children never expand beyond the realistic stage, and thus accept blindly a form of teaching and concepts from the home or other sources. There are

12 Ernest Harms, The development of religious experience in children, *American Journal of Sociology*, 1944, Vol. 50, pp. 112-122.

three degrees of this stage recorded by Harms. The first is a form of religious imagination expressed in the conventional manner. This may be merely an expansion of the realistic stage. The second type involves a greater degree of originality, resulting from the development of the individual as a person with increased independence and social consciousness. Here the uniqueness of individual development is brought forth in the concepts presented. The third type involves an increased amount of originality. In this case, the adolescent may display concepts far removed from those encountered in his earlier environment. Perhaps the more intelligent child is likely to follow such a course in his imagination and in his conceptual growth.

The child's concept of the world is further reflected in his theories of death. The problem of the child's notion of the nature and significance of death was studied by Maria Nagy.[13] Written compositions, drawings, and discussions were used in securing data from children of different ages. Three stages in the child's development were noted. The first stage is characteristic of children between three and five years of age. Death is looked upon as a departure, or change of abode, at this stage. As a final process, death is denied. The attitude concerning death at this age corresponds with fairylike concepts of God, already referred to in this chapter.

In the second stage, in general between the ages of five and nine, death is regarded as an eventuality. Fantasies are less frequent at this age than formerly. Death at this age is personified, not a universal occurrence. The word death is frequently employed in the same way as dead. There is no answer as to the why of death, since death is not yet regarded as a process that takes place as a result of certain conditions and happenings. This period is closely identified with the egocentric nature of the seven- and eight-year-old child. In the third stage, generally beginning around the age of nine, death is recognized as a process which takes place, and death comes to be regarded as inevitable. The conception of death at this age is in harmony with the child's concept of the world. Cause and effect relations are recognized, and death is looked upon in a more realistic manner.

The development of problem-solving behavior

Problem-solving behavior as an educational objective. A fairly recent study of children's explanations of natural phenomena by

[13] Maria Nagy, The child's theories concerning death, *Journal of Genetic Psychology,* 1948, Vol. 73, pp. 3-27.

Mervin Oakes furnishes evidence that the kindergarten child is able to offer solutions and methods of solving problems within the grasp of his maturity and experiences.[14] This and other studies point to the importance of providing opportunities and guidance to children at all age levels for the solution of problems. Kindergarten and primary-school children can deal with problems of the world about them, and by so doing they learn to think more clearly and avoid the use of make-believe and irrational solutions to simple everyday problems of their physical world.

Problem-solving behavior of primary-grade children should not be confined to things in their physical world. There is plenty of evidence from the experiences of elementary-school teachers that children are capable of problem solving in the realm of people. Two children at play with large blocks in the kindergarten may find that there are not enough of a certain kind of block for each of them to build the train that he is trying to build. The kindergarten teacher should guide them in arriving at a reasonable and sound solution to such a problem. The boys are capable of suggesting several possible solutions (hypotheses), and through guidance and suggestions reach an agreement whereby one of the possible solutions is followed.

The teacher should be concerned with helping children to improve their thinking and acting in order that they may be able to control more completely the conditions about them and the situations with which they are constantly being faced. Traditionally, the elementary school was conceived of as an institution where the three R's were taught, along with information that could be recited back to the teacher. Problem solving was believed to be a higher mental process that should be deferred until later grades when advanced arithmetic, algebra, and general science would be studied. The changed concept of the nature of the child has brought the realization that problem solving develops according to fundamental principles found in all growth. Kindergarten and elementary-school children should be guided in the development of problem-solving ability if they are to be expected to solve more difficult problems as they reach maturity. Furthermore, children at all ages are faced with problems. They need to be able to attack these problems in such a manner that sound conclusions may be reached, if they are to adjust satisfactorily to the everyday situations with which they are confronted. These concepts

---

[14] Mervin E. Oakes, *Children's Explanations of Natural Phenomena* (Teachers College, Columbia University: Bureau of Publications, 1947).

have been related to child growth in an industrial-technological society as follows:

Clearly, our type of society requires a creative and problem-solving approach by people. Patterns of thinking and acting that have gone before are not sufficient to the requirements of an adaptive society. Children are marginal people in the sense that they have not internalized the old patterns. ... Nevertheless, they very quickly make their adjustment to social conditions by adopting the ways of their parents and other adults *unless* the elementary school uses a problem-solving approach. ... If the disposition for using a problem-solving approach—the approach of science—is to be acquired, its cultivation must start early and continue through the entire period of formal education.[15]

What are the characteristics of problem solving? It was suggested in Chapter 9 that problem-solving behavior begins early in life. A careful analysis of the nature of problem solving shows that although children are limited by experiences and mental maturity, the processes through which they solve problems are logical in nature. Perhaps one of the best studies that illustrates this is the classic one conducted by Susan Isaacs, who kept a detailed record of the questions and answers of a group of children, ranging in age from two to five years. These children asked sound and timely questions about cooking, weather, snow and ice, electric light, plant growth, and the like. They also formulated hypotheses and suggested ways of testing them out. She concludes: "These instances of direct interest in the physical world and mechanical causality in young children ... suggest strongly that the *extent* to which they do appear and are sustained must in large part be a function of the environment, and of the degree of response which they meet with in influential adults."[16]

The act of problem solving has been formalized from time to time in an orderly sequence of steps. These steps usually include: (1) statement or definition of the problem; (2) formulation of hypotheses or ideas relative to the solution of the problem; (3) testing the hypotheses through reasoning; (4) test or experimentation of the hypothesis judged to be satisfactory; (5) generalizing the affirmed hypothesis and making applications to other problems of a similar nature. This order of the solution of a problem may appear to be

---

[15] Max R. Goodson, Problem-solving in the elementary school, *Progressive Education*, 1950, Vol. 27, p. 147.

[16] Susan Isaacs, *Intellectual Growth in Young Children* (New York: Harcourt, Brace and Co., 1930), p. 82.

that of the mature adult following a logical course. The rudiments of problem solving will be found in much of the thinking of children. This is illustrated in the study conducted with forty-four nursery-school children, ranging in age from nineteen to forty-nine months, as subjects.

Using problem situations comparable to those used by Köhler with apes, Alpert studied the methods used by these nursery-school-age children in solving problems.[17] Nine problem situations were chosen for special study. The problems required the child to make use of objects in his immediate environment in reaching some desired goal. In one case, the child was placed in a play pen and two halves of a fishing rod were placed inside the pen. An attractive toy was placed so far away that it could not be reached with either half of the rod. If the two halves were fitted together at the metal ends, the joined stick would be long enough to enable the child to reach the toy which is outside the pen and beyond the reach of the child.

Individual differences were observed in the method of attacking the problems, although the nature of the problem situation was the most important factor determining how the subject would attack the problem. Exploration and elimination, characteristics of problem-solving ability at all age levels, were found to be the most frequent type of responses, and yielded the greatest number of solutions. This same observation was noted by Köhler in the problem-solving behavior of apes.[18] Children lacking in self-confidence and children overreliant upon adult approval are likely to be handicapped in the exploration of techniques useful in the solution of problems. This study shows further that children at all age levels are capable of solving problems involving insight, provided such problems are not too complex in nature.

The place of memory in problem solving. Problem solving is more than mere recalling of past experiences. This is well illustrated in the case of a child confronted with a problem in arithmetic. He does not simply remember something and thus solve the problem. What else he does may be difficult to define. The solution of the problem will require him to see relations in the situation with which he is confronted that are similar in nature to other situations with which he has been confronted. The seeing of relations between this situation

[17] Augusta Alpert, The solving of problem-situations by preschool children, Teachers College, Columbia University, *Contributions to Education*, No. 323, 1928.

[18] W. Köhler, *The Mentality of Apes* (New York: Appleton-Century-Crofts, 1925).

and a number of different situations he has been confronted with in the past involves an element of reasoning. Memory, however, is present in the act of problem solving. He must not only see that the problem situation is related to a fromer situation or parts of several situations, but he must also remember what he did in the former

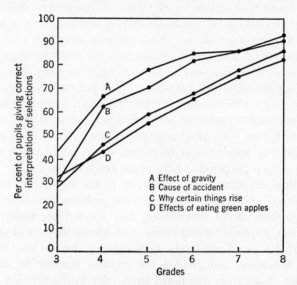

FIG. 33 The development of literary reasoning capacity among children in grades three to eight, inclusive

(After Pyle)

situation. Johnson found that a child's vocabulary is a potent factor in problem solving in arithmetic.[19] This is perhaps to be expected, since words are our vehicles of thought, and the better the vehicle, the better the thinking. Also, the better the thinking, the better will problem solving be carried on.

The growth of problem-solving ability. It has already been suggested that problem-solving behavior may be found at all age levels. Millia Almy has recently suggested that "even babies solve problems."[20] She gives as an illustration of problem-solving behavior the case of the six-month-old baby, lying on her back, confronted with the light of a candle which she cannot see. Her struggles to

[19] J. T. Johnson, On the nature of problem-solving in arithmetic, *Journal of Educational Research,* 1949, Vol. 43, pp. 110-115.

[20] Millia Almy, Are they too young for problem solving?, *Progressive Education,* 1950, Vol. 27, pp. 148-151.

change her position so as to see the source from which the light is coming illustrates problem-solving behavior in which experimentation and testing are used. The problem is solved, tension is reduced, and the struggles cease when she has managed to turn herself in a position where she can look directly at the flame from the candle.

The study by Oakes showed that while the understanding of essential relationships tended to increase with age, some kindergarten children gave better answers to questions about natural phenomena than some of the sixth-graders. Tests of reasoning ability of children in grades three through eight reveal that there is a constant and continuous growth in their literary reasoning capacity. The tests used at the different grade levels were designed to determine their capacity to give the correct interpretation of different literary selections. The results of the tests, in terms of the per cent of pupils at each grade level giving correct interpretations, are given in Figure 33.[21] These results show continuous development from the third grade through the eighth, although there was considerable overlapping of the abilities of the pupils at the different grades.

General educational growth

Growth in school achievement. The development of objective tests for measuring achievement in the school subjects was early extended to cover all the major subjects of the elementary-school program. Batteries of tests were developed, which consisted of a number of different tests measuring achievement in the different school subjects combined in a single booklet. The *Progressive Achievement Tests* are illustrations of batteries of tests designed for different grade levels. The *Progressive Achievement Tests—Elementary Battery* is a diagnostic-survey group test in the fundamental skills combined in a single booklet. The tests are designed to measure pupil growth in reading vocabulary, reading comprehension, arithmetic reasoning, arithmetic fundamentals, and language in grades four, five, and six. These five major areas are differentiated into nineteen subareas so as to provide a basis for diagnosis of a pupil's growth and difficulties. Norms, based on data from over 25,000 tests given in many areas throughout the United States, are available. These norms give the typical performance of unselected groups of

[21] W. H. Pyle, An experimental study of the development of certain aspects of reasoning, *Journal of Educational Psychology*, 1935, Vol. 26, pp. 539-546.

children of different age and grade levels. The age norms for the children given the *Progressive Achievement Tests* are given in Figure 34.[22] This graph shows the nature of growth in the mastery of the fundamental school subjects, based upon raw scores from this test. One should not expect every child to conform to this chart of

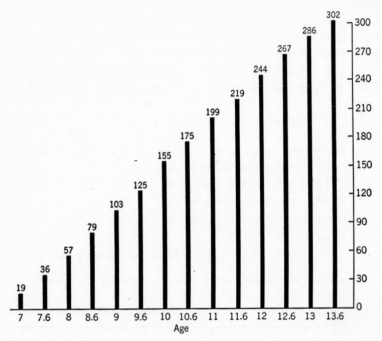

FIG. 34 Growth in elementary-school subjects based upon norms for the progressive achievement tests (1943 revision)

growth. Individual differences within a single group will affect the educational growth of the individual pupils. Furthermore, differences in methods of instruction, courses of study, time allotments to the different areas, and special emphasis on certain skills may account for deviations from the test norms by a particular group of pupils.

Qualitative aspects of vocabulary growth. It was pointed out in Chapter 9 that there is a continuous growth in the size of the child's vocabulary at all age levels. Studies of the qualitative aspects of the vocabulary of children at different ages reveal also a growth in the

[22] *Manual of Directions,* Progressive Achievement Tests—Elementary Battery. Los Angeles: California Test Bureau, 1943 Edition.

character of the word definition as well. The quality and completeness of word definitions given by children of different ages was studied by Feifel and Lorge.[23] The vocabulary test of Form L, *Stanford Revision of the Binet Tests* was chosen for use, and the definition given by the subjects studied for their completeness and qualitative nature. The subjects tested consisted of 900 school children ranging in age from six through fourteen years. The children used as subjects were slightly above the average in intelligence at all age levels except at age fourteen.

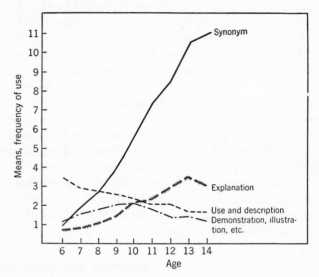

FIG. 35 Mean frequency of use of four qualitative categories by age
(After Feifel and Lorge)

A graphic presentation of the results is presented in Figure 35. It is apparent that children at the six- and seven-year age level give the use and description type of response most often. This would indicate a response to the word "orange" as "something to eat." The explanation type of response is used very little at this age, and appears to grow slowly but continuously in use until the thirteen-year age group. The drop noted at age fourteen may be partially accounted for on the basis of the lower intelligence suggested for this age group in comparison to that of the other age groups. The synonym type of response, although seldom used by the six- and

[23] Herman Feifel and Irving Lorge, Qualitative differences in the vocabulary responses of children, *Journal of Educational Psychology,* 1950, Vol. 41, pp. 1-18.

seven-year-olds, comes to be used quite widely by children around the ages of nine or ten and continues to grow in use throughout the age periods studied. The demonstration and illustration type of response grows in use until ages nine or ten and then declines. This decline may be accounted for by the growth in the child's vocabulary and in his ability to symbolize things in terms of opposites and similarities.

Need for guidance in problem solving. Problem-solving behavior is a learned type of behavior. However, the notion that children are too immature to solve problems is not supported by our knowledge of child growth. More consideration is being given to this in the present-day educational program. Allison Davis has pointed out in this connection: "The greatest need of education is for intensive research to discover the best curricula for developing children's basic mental activities; such activities, that is, as the analysis and organization of observed experiences, the drawing of inferences, the development of inventiveness." [24] The present curricula are often stereotyped and arbitrary selections passed down from middle- and upper-class cultures. Their lack of a functional relationship to present-day life and the daily problems there encountered is evidence of their archaic nature and structure. The assumption that the development of reading skill and arithmetical abilities will develop reasoning abilities and the abilities to solve problems of everyday life is without foundation and proof.

Summary and generalization

There is some evidence that memory for a short duration is manifested during the first six months of the child's life; while fifteen- to seventeen-month-old children are able to remember a smiling face or a satisfying activity for eight minutes. The development of memory ability follows the principles of growth set forth in Chapter 4 and illustrated throughout Chapters 5-9. The perception of time and space is such a commonplace occurrence to adults that they oftentime fail to appreciate the element of learning in the acquisition of these perceptions. Studies of the development of such percepts show that the child is slow in acquiring binocular vision with depth perception. By the age of four years, he has, however, developed verbalized space so that he uses such space words as *in front of*,

[24] Allison Davis, Education for the conservation of human resources, *Progressive Education*, 1950, Vol. 27, p. 220.

back of, way off, on top of, and the like. The understanding of time words develops in harmony with his understanding of space words.

Number concepts, like the development of word concepts for space and time, grow through maturity and favorable opportunities for learning. The child of six, if provided with favorable experiences, will have learned to count. Haste, however, in the learning of abstract symbols and problem solving involving abstract symbols will retard rather than aid further growth. Successful development of mathematical concepts requires a consideration of the child's maturation at the various stages in his development. A study of the causal thinking of children shows that logical deduction does not appear until the eleventh year, while phenomenistic answers comprised the largest number of types of answers given by seven- and eight-year-old children. The growth of the concept of God appears to pass through several fairly well defined stages, although these stages cannot be completely separated from each other. Neither is the growth from one stage to another a sudden change. The growth of concepts in various areas will be closely interrelated. The child's concept of God will be affected by his concepts of space, time, and causal relations. This becomes very apparent as he develops and reaches a realistic stage. This realistic stage will be little beyond that of the fairy-tale stage for children who have had limited experiences and who have been brought up in an environment where some such idea of God prevails.

The importance of problem-solving behavior in a democratic society has caused educators to give special consideration to the guidance of children in the development of problem-solving techniques. Increased consideration is being given to this problem with the general recognition that children can be guided and stimulated to solve problems from a rather early age level.

The importance of individual growth curves in connection with the guidance and stimulation of the child's educational growth is effecting a change in the use of age and grade norms. The educational growth of the child follows the principles of development set forth in Chapter 4. A recognition of this and an understanding of this principle should form the basis for educational guidance.

Questions and Exercises

1. Give an illustration showing how the child acquires the concept of some number or object. To what extent would such a concept be affected by limitations of the child's experiences?

2. Trace the growth of memory ability among children. How is age related to *immediate* memory? To *delayed* memory?
3. If children must learn through experience, what values may be derived from educational guidance?
4. Show how the growth of the child's concept of God is interrelated with other aspects of his growth.
5. Explain the meaning of the statement, "Words mean only what they represent in one's experiences." What is the significance of this statement in relation to the development of concepts?
6. What are some of the major difficulties encountered by children in problem solving?
7. What general conclusions would you draw regarding the problem-solving behavior of primary-grade children?
8. Show how problem-solving behavior among children is similar to and how different from that found among adults.
9. What relationship may be said to exist between maturation and educational growth? What factors might affect such a relationship?
10. What uses can be made of individual growth curves for achievement in the school subjects?
11. What generalizations would you make relative to the use of standards and norms in the educational guidance of the individual child?

Selected Readings

Dewey, John. *How We Think*. Boston: D. C. Heath and Company, 1933.

Gates, Arthur I., Jersild, Arthur T., McConnell, T. R., and Challman, Robert C. *Educational Psychology*. New York: The Macmillan Company, 1948. Chap. XI.

Hurlock, Elizabeth B. *Child Development*. 2nd ed.; New York: McGraw-Hill Book Co., 1950. Chap. XI.

Jersild, Arthur T. *Child Psychology*. 3rd ed.; New York: Prentice-Hall, 1947. Chaps. X and XI.

Munn, N. L. Learning in children, *Manual of Child Psychology*, L. Carmichael, ed. New York: John Wiley and Sons, 1946. Chap. VIII.

Piaget, Jean. *The Child's Conception of the World*. New York: Harcourt, Brace and Co., 1929.

Thorndike, Robert L. How children learn the principles and techniques of problem-solving, *Learning and Instruction, Forty-ninth Yearbook of the National Society for the Study of Education*, Part I, 1950. Chap. VIII.

Thorpe, Louis P. *Child Psychology and Development*. New York: The Ronald Press Co., 1946. Chap. XII.

11

Growth in Creative Expression

Introduction: The nature of creative activities

It has been suggested that every child has "an inborn creative spirit." The notion that creative ability is to be found only among the gifted is erroneous. Creative expressions are found in the daily activities of children at all age levels and with varying degrees of abilities. The descriptions and illustrations of these presented in the following discussions should clarify the nature and meaning of creative activities.

Some special characteristics of creative expression. The notion, frequently expressed, that creative ability is limited primarily to the activities of gifted individuals results perhaps from one's concept of what constitutes creative expression. The idea that creative ability may be found among children of varying degrees of ability may be better understood from an examination of child experiences involving creativeness. A small boy was recently observed by the writer at play. He suddenly grabbed a stick, ran into the woods, placed himself behind a large fir tree and began pointing the stick from one side of the tree, making the sounds pow, pow, pow, pow-pow, etc. He then moved forward to another tree and there performed similar movements and made sounds similar to those made when he was behind the first tree. He was apparently experimenting with slight variations in the movements and sounds. Some changes were noted in the dramatic play, the movements, and the rhythmic sounds produced, indicating an increased attitude of bravado and improved rhythm in the sounds produced. When he was questioned concerning these actions, he said:

"I was shooting bears."

"There were lots of bears."

"I shot some of them three times, and one of them twenty times."

"I killed most of them."

A bear had been observed in that area a few weeks prior to this incident. The four-year-old boy had been told about it. This provided the stimulating condition (dynamics) for his actions. There is discernible in this behavior some of the important characteristics of creative expression. These include the following:

1. Prolonged attention related to some absorbing experience.

2. Heightened motivation to discover, test, or interpret for one's self the meaning related to the experience.

3. Expressive behavior resulting from the heightened motivation.

4. Variations in behavior as an outgrowth of experimentation to discover ways of expressing one's self.

5. Tension reduction through successful experiences in creating ways of expressing one's self.

Applied to the play life of the five- or six-year-old, any activity into which children enter wholeheartedly will probably have some characteristics of creative expression. In situations in which imagination, initiative, and orignality exist, creative expression will be found. Thus, creativeness in play connotes a quality which may pervade almost all play experiences. A parent or teacher who realizes the nature of creative expression may observe it in the daily activities of children.

Play and make-believe. Make-believe play activities constitute a more indirect method used by children to construct a real world from their experiences and the things about them. Through this procedure they explore and experiment with things about them—drawing upon various aspects of their experiences. These activities give meaning and expression to their feelings and worries. Thus, a small girl playing in the yard with another child says: "The milkman has brought some milk for my baby. You stay here. I'll get the milk and come right back."

The little girl is here drawing upon her experiences about the milkman. The fact that no milkman appeared is of little consequence to the child, since through her own explorations she invents a milkman and a baby. She here conceives of herself as a woman with a baby to be fed. Likewise, when little boys play with toy horses, guns, and fire trucks, they recreate the world as they see it. This world is recreated out of their experiences, and is constructed so that they and others can see it. When the creative product is unsatisfactory or fails to represent the world as he sees and feels it, the child changes various parts of it to fit into the world that he sees and feels. Satisfaction results from the creation of products that reflect things that harmonize with his world. These things may be created in a make-believe manner or constructed in a miniature form that is a sort of a make-believe object, since it represents aspects in the child's world of experience.

The dance. Another medium of self-expression is the dance. The dance also serves as an outlet for pent-up energy resulting from frustrations. Under favorable conditions and with proper stimulation, children grow in their ability to express themselves intelligently through the dance. The development of various dances throughout the ages was the outgrowth of the creative expression of different groups.

The development of self-expression does not take place through the application of rigid rules or a formalized curriculum. To devise a rigid curriculum for the dance is similar to the approach to vocal music by note learning. To so limit the bounds of the dance is to destroy initiative and creativeness through this medium. The skills used by primary-grade children will be simple rhythm. At this period, the time and rhythm of simple music should be stressed. The skills used by children of the intermediate grades (ages ten to thirteen) are more highly specialized, requiring more advanced maturation, understanding, and experience. Concerning the organization of these dance experiences Huggett and Millard have stated:

> ... The dance is not a thing set apart; instead, it is but part of the whole. Children often, for example, secure their stimulation from music, social studies, reading, or science. Indian dances, motivated by the reading period, are very common. Negro spirituals serve as stimulation for dances embodying the hopelessness and everlasting sorrows of slavery. The story of snowflakes fluttering down in the first storm of winter may encourage a dance. Certainly one does not dance unless he feels, and he does not feel unless he has had experiences. Experiences may be actual or they may be gained vicariously through reading, art, discussion or music.[1]

Other creative expressions. Many forms of creative expressions are observable in the art activities of children. On one occasion, a first-grade child, when requested to draw a man, drew a house with one

[1] Albert J. Huggett and Cecil V. Millard, *Growth and Learning in the Elementary School* (Boston: D. C. Heath and Company, 1946), p. 254.

window and one door. When the teacher asked where the man was, the child replied, "He was behind the window, but he has gone away." The understanding teacher will take advantage of such a situation for directing the growth of creative ability, rather than discouraging creative expression by demanding conformity in the various activities being pursued. The beating of the tom-tom by James may show all the characteristics of creativeness, when he is allowed to beat out the frenzy of an Indian war dance, or the fury of the approaching storm.

Self-expression may be contrasted with imitation. In the case of self-expression, the child's responses are in terms of his own ability and age level, motivated by his own feelings and ideas. This does not mean, however, that there is no place for suggestions and guidance from others. Materials bearing on this will be presented later in this discussion. In the case of imitation, the child's responses are patterned after the expressions of others. Small children have been observed trying to imitate their parents in the performance of some parts of a folk dance. The teacher may have the children reproduce through drawing some picture hanging on the wall. Viktor Lowenfeld [2] has presented the following contrasts of self-expression and imitation:

Self-Expression	*Imitation*
Expression according to child's own level	Expression according to strange level
Independent thinking	Dependent thinking
Emotional outlet	Frustration
Freedom and flexibility	Inhibition and restriction
Early adjustment to new situations	Going along set patterns
Progress, success, happiness	Leaning toward others, dependency, stiffness

Development of creative abilities

Hazards to growth in creative ability. One of the greatest hazards to the growth of creative expression on the part of the growing child is the standard set forth by the school and community for the encouragement of pupils in art, music, dramatics, and the like. This is

[2] From Viktor Lowenfeld, *Creative and Mental Growth.* Copyright 1947 by The Macmillan Company and used with their permission.

also observable in special school exhibits. If the teachers and parents can be brought to realize that the purpose of such activities is to reveal the growth of individual pupils in creative expression rather than the production of a finished product, this hazard would be eliminated. Where parents have been aided by capable teachers and pupils in arriving at this idea about the purpose of activities and exhibits, excellent results have been obtained in developing ability in creative expression and appreciations among the pupils.

At six years of age, children enjoy using their hands and feet. They are, however, quite clumsy or awkward, and are unable to make the co-ordinations essential for the most skilled performance. Even if their muscular co-ordination and precision were better, they lack the experience essential for producing perfect products. Also, their short interest periods would hinder them in completing a product requiring continuous effort over a long period of time. Their work, therefore, is likely to be somewhat crude in nature rather than finished. This is to be expected in connection with creative products, and children should not be discouraged in their creative efforts by the holding up to them of standards and models of perfection.

Freedom of choice is important in developing creative expression. Studies show that when children are allowed to make choices of what they wish to paint, they produce a variety of pictures.[3] Perhaps only one out of ten could be classified as creative in the sense that something new, unique, or vital and worth-while has been produced. The fact, however, that the child explores, experiments, and recreates a world or some experience according to his own feelings and understanding is of prime importance. He has thus been able to express his own thoughts and feelings, rather than following in a somewhat blind manner the directions given by adults. Too much interference on the part of parents and teachers becomes a dangerous hazard to the development of creative expression.

A third hazard results from the lack of stimulation. The child living a drab, routine life will not be stimulated to discover and try out new experiences. The absorbing interests necessary for creative expression do not develop in a vacuum, and will be lacking. A school program organized in a formal manner will not provide the dynamics essential for creativeness. A teacher lacking in enthusiasm and originality is not likely to be a stimulating force in the development of creativeness among her pupils.

[3] N. C. Meier, *Art in Human Affairs* (New York: McGraw-Hill Book Co., 1942), pp. 35-39.

Color preferences of children. Ruth Staples studied the color preferences of twelve infants between the ages of five and one-half and twenty-four months.[4] The colors red, yellow, blue, and green were matched for brightness and paired with each other. Every color was shown along with every other color, and the choices determined by the child's attention to the color. The results are shown graphically in Figure 36. The preference for red is the outstanding finding

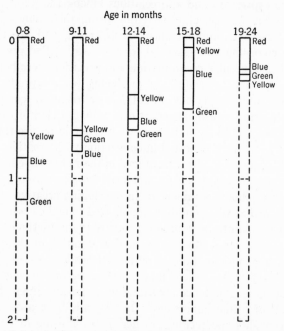

FIG. 36 Color preference of infants at different age levels. The distance between the positions of the colors on the bars indicates the extent to which the infants agreed in their preference for the colors. Wide spacing indicates fairly general agreement; narrow spacing shows general disagreement

(After Staples)

of this study. With advancing age, from five and one-half to twenty-four months, the differences between the colors liked best and those liked least become less. This means that individual differences in attention given to the different colors become more pronounced as the child develops. With the younger child, red leads by a clear

[4] Ruth Staples, The responses of infants to color, *Journal of Experimental Psychology*, 1932, Vol. 15, pp. 119-141.

majority for all children, but at the upper age range studied, the choices showed greater variation.

As early as 1926, Peppino Mangravite challenged the practice of many writers of elementary-school textbooks because of the types of illustrations used.[5] She expressed the idea that true creative vision of children is crippled by the use of pictures in books and trips to museums and galleries. Recent years have brought some noteworthy trends in the illustrative materials to be found in readers. An early study conducted by Bonnie Mellinger is worth while in this connection.[6] Using as subjects 821 children from the first-, third,- and fifth-grade levels, she studied children's choices of certain elements contained in pictures. Three subjects were used in the pictures: an animal (elephant), a pine tree, and a child (girl). Two styles were shown each child, realistic and conventionalized. (The conventionalized style was obtained by omitting certain curves and other details found in the realistic style.) Each of the pictures was shown in black and white, two colors, and three colors.

Individual differences in choices were noted at all grade levels, although certain trends were quite noticeable from the results obtained in tabular form. At all grade levels the pictures were more frequently chosen in color than in black and white. Also, the children at all grade levels chose the pictures in realistic style more frequently than those in the conventionalized style. Of the three subjects, the pine tree showed the greatest percentage in favor of the conventionalized style. Of the three grade levels studied, the first grade, although preferring the realistic style, showed the greatest percentage choosing the conventionalized style. The following grade choices were noticeable:

a. The first grade chose more frequently the picture of the child (girl) in three-color (black, red and yellow), the pine tree in two-color (black and green), and the animal in two-color (black and gray).

b. The third grade chose more frequently the picture of the animal (elephant) in three-color (black, gray, yellow), and the child (girl) in three-color (black, red, yellow), but the pine tree in two-color (black and green).

c. The fifth grade chose more frequently the picture of the animal (elephant) in three-color (black, gray, yellow), the child (girl) in

[5] Peppino Mangravite, The artist and the child, *Progressive Education,* 1926, p. 124. The author makes a plea to bring children closer to nature and life if creative expression is to be obtained.

[6] Bonnie E. Mellinger, Children's interests in pictures, Teachers College, Columbia University, *Contributions to Education,* No. 516, 1932.

three-color (black, red, yellow), and the pine tree in two-color (black and green).[7]

Observations of three- and four-year-old children, reported by Staples and Conley, revealed that in general children at this age level tend to use all colors freely, showing little or no preference for specific hues.[8] Twelve colors were used by Ann Gale in a study of the preference of elementary-school children for a single color.[9] The results of the tests given to children in grades three to eight inclusive are presented in Table 39. The children showed a preference

TABLE 39   Number of choices for single colors in grades three through eight (after Gale)

Grade	Yellow-Orange	Blue-Violet	Violet-Green	Yellow	Red-Violet	Orange	Blue	Blue-Green	Green	Red-Orange	Violet	Red	Total No. of choices	No. of choices possible
III	20	44	11	18	40	52	28	12	13	20	10	26	312	315
IV	18	22	20	10	35	42	25	7	28	12	12	15	246	246
V	30	38	15	13	40	76	20	1	11	14	12	11	291	291
VI	30	24	15	15	34	42	25	4	33	8	0	21	260	264
VII	17	13	16	12	45	55	36	5	14	15	5	13	246	246
VIII	16	21	12	5	31	38	36	6	15	7	5	10	201	201

for orange, red-violet, and blue in the order named. The position of blue and red-violet, a variation of red, among the colors preferred is supported by other studies. Although the composite number of choices for all grades shows that orange, red-violet, and blue are the first three preferences, the distribution of choices varies with the different grades. Orange and red-violet have first and second choices in all grades except the eighth, where blue has second place. The greatest variation comes in the place given to blue. In grades three, four, and five, blue has fourth place, while grade six placed it in the fifth position. The colors with the fewest number of choices were blue-green, violet, and yellow in the order listed. If one compares the choices of the warm colors with those of the cool colors,

[7] *Ibid.*, p. 35. Black is used in this study as a color.

[8] Ruth Staples and Helen Conley, The use of color in the finger painting of young children, *Child Development*, 1949, Vol. 20, pp. 201-212.

[9] Ann Van Nice Gale, *Children's Preference for Colors, Color Combinations and Color Arrangements* (Chicago: University of Chicago Press, 1933).

it will be observed that the choices for the warm colors (red and yellow) outnumber those for the cool (green and blue).

In the case of the tests for complementary colors, there was a decided preference for blue and orange over yellow and blue-violet, and red and blue-green. This preference was constant throughout the grades. No positive relationship was found between color combinations preferred at full intensity and color combinations preferred in a harmonizing print.

Early activities involving paper and crayon. Creative activities involving crayon and paper reveal levels of behavior at different stages of the child's development. These levels are in harmony with the development of neuromuscular co-ordinations, and furnish a perspective of the child's neuromuscular maturation. This development has been described by Gesell from observations of children during the first five years.[10] During the first month, the infant merely clasps the crayon without any regard as to marks that may be made on a piece of paper. By the end of the first year, however, he tends to bring the crayon and paper into a sort of functional relationship with each other. His marks are of a banging or wavering nature.

Growth in the use of crayons after the first year is of a gradual and continuous nature during which the child shows ability to imitate more complex strokes and to copy more difficult materials. By the age of five years he is able to copy a cross, a square, and like objects. Thus, there is a gradual emergence of more complex forms of activity out of the simpler, less co-ordinated movements. It was pointed out in Chapter 6 that by the time the child reaches six years of age and is enrolled in the first grade at school, his muscular co-ordinations are sufficiently advanced for him to use crayons and pencils to express himself in various ways.

Creative potentialities in music. Although one should expect to find vast differences among children in their performances involving music, research studies show (1) that creative ability in music is closely related to the child's stage of maturity; (2) that children who have been exposed to a rich musical environment show a greater and earlier ability to carry a melody than those children from a poorer musical environment; and (3) that early training in harmony with the child's maturation will have a beneficial effect on certain musical skills.

The ability of children to produce tones in the voice range was

---

[10] Arnold Gesell, *Infancy and Human Growth* (New York: The Macmillan Company, 1928), p. 216.

studied by Jersild and Bienstock.[11] The results, presented in Table 40, show a continuous increase from two years to maturity. These results should not be interpreted as norms; they do, however, show that the growth of the ability studied follows the developmental pattern described in earlier chapters. In another study, Jersild observed that children tended to improve in proportion to their initial ability.[12] Of all the abilities studied, he noted that the ability to sing is the one that was most strikingly affected by training.

TABLE 40 Increase of tone reproduction in the voice range (after Jersild and Bienstock)

Age in Years	Number of Tones	Age in Years	Number of Tones
2	5	7	14
3	7	8	15
4	9	9	16
5	10	10	16
6	13	Adults	20

These findings have been verified by a study conducted with preschool children by Updegraff, Heiliger, and Learned.[13] The subjects, consisting of sixty-six children ranging in age from three to six years, were arranged in matched groups at each age level. One of the groups was subjected to an intensive training program while the other served as a control group. After a period of thirty days of training, the two groups were compared. It was found that the experimental group had doubled their initial scores, while the control group showed no marked improvement. Thus, a program of instruction based on scientific findings related to the maturational level of children should prove fruitful in the development of musical ability and creative expressions in activities involving music.

Drawings of the human figure and age. The drawings of the human figure by kindergarten children usually shows the figure in full face, but around the age of nine or ten, sometimes earlier with bright children, profiles are drawn. It appears that boys change to the

[11] A. T. Jersild and S. F. Bienstock, A study of the development of children's ability to sing, *Journal of Educational Psychology*, 1934, Vol. 25, pp. 481-503.

[12] A. T. Jersild *et al.*, Training and growth in the development of children, Teachers College, Columbia University, *Child Development Monographs*, 1932, Vol. 10.

[13] R. Updegraff, L. Heiliger, and J. Learned, The effect of training upon singing ability and interest in music of three, four, and five year old children, *University of Iowa Studies in Child Welfare*, 1936, Vol. 14, pp. 85-131.

profiles earlier than girls. The reason for this is not wholly clear; but it may be associated with boys' greater interest in physical activity. It is easier to show a person in action through profile drawings. Many errors appear in the drawings of the backward child. There may be a lack of arms, or just one arm shown on the full-face drawing. The neck is seldom shown as distinct from the head or body. The head or arms are likely to be very much out of proportion to the rest of the body. Sometimes both eyes are on the same side of the face, the nose is out of position, and the body in general lacks symmetry. These observations led early to the use of children's drawings of the human figure as a means for evaluating this intellectual development.

The drawings of bright, average, and dull kindergarten children are presented in Figure 37, those of eight-year-olds are shown in Figure 38.[14] A comparison of the two groups shows a distinct de-

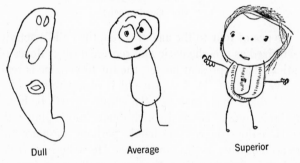

Dull   Average   Superior

FIG. 37 Drawings of a man by kindergarten children of varying degrees of intelligence

(After Goodenough)

velopment in the inclusion of the various parts of the body in their correct perspective from age five to age eight. The bright five-year-old child does distinctly better than the backward eight-year-old and almost as well as the average eight-year-old.

Organizational changes and age. The child at the age of two or three normally engages in activities of a random, disorganized nature. The fact that these activities appear disorganized to the adult does not mean, however, that they are disorganized and meaningless to the kindergarten child. The scribbling of the child may represent

[14] From *The Measurement of Intelligence by Drawings* by Florence L. Goodenough. Copyright 1926 by World Book Company. Reproduced by special permission.

to him a rather complete grouping of objects and events. These meanings must be detected and understood by adults, if they expect to be able to guide the child in the development of his creative abilities.

Dull   Average   Superior

FIG. 38   Drawings of a man by eight-year-old children of varying degrees of intelligence

(After Goodenough)

From the age of four to the age of seven, the child's activities may be characterized as preschematic and representative. Boxes represent houses, sticks may represent horses, the toy fire engine is real to him. The creative work of the five-year-old is observable in his rhythm and song. He likes to chant songs. Sometimes he will be heard chanting a rhythmic song of his own which relates to his play activities at the time. He enjoys the rhythm band—perhaps the noise and action of others are effective in this connection. He sometimes develops his own rhythm in keeping time to music and enters into rhythmic games with much enthusiasm.

The next stage has been referred to by Viktor Lowenfeld as the schematic stage.[15] This includes ages seven to nine years. During this age, space concepts are revealed. Likewise, time concepts and color relationships are used. However, much phantasy and make-believe still appear in the creative activities during this period.

The age of artistic development during the period from nine to eleven years of age is known as the drawing-realism stage. This is characterized by an increased awareness of the self. There is an increased tendency toward realism in representation, and the use of overlapping planes is noted at this stage. During this period the

[15] *Op cit.*, pp. 284-286. Copyright 1947 by The Macmillan Company and used with their permission. Lowenfeld has developed a chart showing the growth from one stage of development to another in the realm of shape, space, color, and design. Some of the more important features of this chart are reproduced in Table 41.

child finds expression in a variety of materials such as paint, chalk, clay, wood, and metal. With increased awareness of the self, there is often present an egocentric attitude and a lack of co-operation. The need for being worth something appears at this time, and the creative work in the arts provides a splendid opportunity for the satisfaction of this need.

The preadolescent stage follows. This has been referred to as the age when reasoning is manifested to a greater degree, and covers ages eleven to thirteen. During this stage there is an increased tendency toward realism. The individual is not satisfied with a make-believe substitute. The boy wants a real bicycle, not a make-believe one made of stone, lumber, and metal pieces. The girl is likely to discard her dolls, and begins showing an increased interest in the opposite sex. Further materials bearing on the changes of interest manifested at this stage will be presented in Chapter 13. In the field of art there is a greater sensitivity to proportions and to three-dimensional forms at this stage. This period is also characterized by love for the dramatic. Thus, this is an important period in the child's development, since it represents the beginning of a fundamental transition in all areas of life. Since there is an increased interest in realism and a greater sensitiveness to the elements that make up good productions, there is usually a falling off of interest in creativeness. The child will not draw, or perform at some task, since he feels that his production or behavior is inefficient, inferior, and childish. The more he has been prepared during the earlier period to use his own resourcefulness, and to follow approaches in his work that will provide for growth along favorable lines, the smoother will be the transition into this stage of development without a pronounced loss of interest in creative activities.

Creative expression and personality development

The daily life of the child is beset with many problems. The child does not have years of experience to guide him in meeting these problems as does the adult. Each new experience is therefore a vital one and often a crucial one. He resorts to various methods in meeting and interpreting these experiences. In his creative expressions, adults exert little control; therefore, he is free to experiment and to express his feelings, thoughts, and needs—in fact, the *total self*.

Creative products as diagnostic aids. Children use indirect as well as direct methods for revealing their worries and feelings. The

TABLE 41 Developmental stages in the realm of space, color, and design (after Lowenfeld)

Stage	Representative of space	Representative of color	Representative of design
Scribbling (two to four years).	None.	No conscious use. Color used to distinguish between scribblings.	None.
Pre-Schematic (four to seven years).	No order in space. Relationship according to emotional significance.	Emotional use according to appeal. No relationship to reality.	No conscious approach.
Schematic stage (seven to nine years).	First difficult space concept: base-line. Discovery of being a part of environment. Subjective space representation. Space-time concept.	*Definite* relationship between color and object. Through repetition: color, schema.	No conscious approach. Design characteristics received through urge for repetitions.
Dawning Realism Pre-Adolescent (Crisis nine to eleven years). Gang Age.	*Removed* from base-line concept. Overlapping. Discovery of plane. Difficulties in spatial correlations due to egocentric attitude.	*Removed* from objective stage of color. Subjective color experiences with emotional significant objects.	First conscious approach toward decorations. Use of materials and their function for design.
Pseudo-Realistic Stage. Stage of Reasoning (eleven to thirteen years).	Urge for three-dimensional expression. Diminishing sizes of distant objects. Horizontal line (visually minded).	Changes of color in nature (visually minded). Emotional reaction to color (non-visually minded).	First conscious approval to stylizing. Symbols for professions. Function of different materials.

	Visual type	Visual type	Visual type
The Stage of Decision. Crisis of Adolescence (thirteen to seventeen years).	Perspective representations. Apparent diminution of distant objects. Atmosphere. Appearance. Mood. Three-dimensional qualities. Light and shadow.	Appearance of color in nature. Color reflections. Changing qualities of color environment, with regard to distance and mood. Analytical attitude. Impressionistic.	Aesthetic interpretation of form, balance, and rhythm. Decorative design. Emphasis on harmony.
	Haptic type	*Haptic type*	*Haptic type*
	Perspective of value with relationship to self. Value relationship of objects. Base-line expressions.	Expressive, subjective meaning of color when insignificant. Color changes with regard to emotional significance. Psychological meaning of color.	Emotional design of abstract quality. Functional design. Industrial design.

use of projective techniques, referred to in Chapter 4, illustrates the use of indirect procedures for evaluating personality characteristics and adjustments. The shy and repressed child is most likely to show his feelings and problems through activities involving his own free expressions. The simple play of the child may be very revealing about his thoughts and feelings. The boy's construction and manipulation of fire engines reveals a re-creation of the world as he sees and wants it to be. As he develops, he creates his world through more complex designs and introduces new media.

The pictures and stories of third- and fourth-grade children show the problems and feelings of the individual children.[16] A child's distinct like or dislike for a particular color may be an indication of the affective nature of his association with that color. For example, a child might prefer blue because his father, with whom he is closely associated, usually wears blue ties, or he may dislike red because some neighbor's "old mean dog" is red.

An interesting study of the animal drawings of children revealed a close relation between the type of animals a child draws and his personality.[17] Sometimes these drawings give an index of the child's home or school life. A child that persists in drawing ferocious animals may have a punitive father or teacher. A child who prefers to draw birds is again revealing certain personality characteristics. From a comparison of the free drawings of American and Indian subjects, Taylor concludes that the cultural background of the subject was closely related to certain aspects of his drawings.[18] This provides further support to the place and value of a child's drawings in revealing personality characteristics.

Creative expression and personality adjustments. The development of creative ability is closely related to personal adjustments. The child's freedom to express himself in art, music, rhythm, and other activities provides a splendid outlet for pent-up feelings and wishes. The mental-hygiene value of free expression is continuously being given further consideration by mental-hygiene and child-guidance clinics. The child who has been unable to succeed in his physical performances or in academic pursuits is in need of oppor-

[16] W. E. Henry, The child tells about himself through his creative products, *Fostering Mental Health in Our Schools. 1950 Yearbook of the Association for Supervision and Curriculum Development*, p. 243.

[17] Lauretta Bender and Jack Rapport, Animal drawings of children, *American Journal of Orthopsychiatry*, 1944, Vol. 14, pp. 521-527.

[18] William S. Taylor, A note on the cultural determination of free drawings, *Character and Personality*, 1944, Vol. 13, pp. 30-36.

tunities for self-expression through which he gains self-recognition and satisfaction. Caroline Zachry has emphasized this in connection with the arts. She states:

> The artist asks of the individual that he make an order out of chaos, that he take what he perceives in imagination and convey relationships of ordered form and content within some given medium. The mental hygienist asks of the individual that he make a related order out of the disintegrated experience of which his life is composed, and through his action or behavior find the fulfillment of his growing experience. Both have the same struggle for coherence in an incoherent society. Both seek the same fulfillment.[19]

If creative ability is to function in wholesome personal adjustment, certain fundamental principles must be adhered to, among which are the following:

1. Every individual must be conceived of as having some creative ability.

2. Creative ability may be expressed through a variety of experiences.

3. Every child has the right to use the medium for expressing himself that is in harmony with his interests and abilities.

4. Success as measured through standard instruments is less important than the experience in the creative activity.

5. The introduction of new techniques and skills should be based upon the needs of the individual, rather than upon demands for improved patterns or better practices.

6. Training and guidance should have as their goal the development of appreciations, self-evaluations, and interests rather than superior skills as such.

Therapeutic values of creative activities. Creative activities furnish the child with opportunities for experimentation, self-expression, and release of tensions. In the construction of a train and railroad, the child is able to gain satisfaction through self-expression and exploration of things only partially understood. The child's attempt at the solution of some conflict resulting from frustration or the lack of fulfillment of some basic need is likely to be more satisfactory than that of the adult's, if he is allowed to express himself in some area of creativeness. A need for "belongingness" may be reasonably satisfied through play activities in which make-believe characters are

[19] Caroline B. Zachry, *Art Education Today* (New York: Teachers College, Columbia University, 1937), p. 31.

introduced, or through painting of construction where people and things from his environment are developed. Concerning the therapeutic value to be derived from creative activities, Henry has stated:

> In an impersonal world of paints and blocks and make-believe, experimentation with mixed-up feelings of love and resentment can go on safely—safely for the adults, in that the child does not actually act out his resentments; and safely for the child, in that the playing out does not arouse the retribution of the outside world, nor arouse his own guilt of having feelings of which his parents disapprove. This very explanation also helps the child recognize and express his feelings. Many of his hostile feelings tend to disappear once he has acted them out in his creative products.[20]

Evaluating growth in creative expression

When the child is guided in expressing his abilities in such a way that his own creative self is not blocked, learning will be satisfying and pleasant. The development of a composition bearing on the planning for the observance of some occasion can be a pleasant and stimulating experience, when the creative nature of the pupils is given reasonable expression. The materials may provide fruitful experiences for creative self-expression. The arrangement of flowers, the choice of colors, the rhythmic motions in games and dances provide for self-expression.

Difficulties of evaluation. The problems involved in the evaluation of growth in creative expression are more abstract and complex than those found in evaluating physical growth or growth in understanding. Objective tests or scales have been developed for measuring different aspects of growth. Some of these have been widely used in measuring certain aspects of growth. Since standard instruments are not available for measuring self-expression or creative productions, objectives and criteria must be set up by the person concerned with the evaluation process. Some of the special difficulties involved in evaluating creativeness may be listed as follows:

1. The difficulty of determining just what products of the child are creative.

2. Should the quality or quantity of creative expression be measured?

3. Should emphasis be given the end products or the intensity of expression by the child?

[20] *Op. cit.,* p. 258.

4. What shall be the criteria for good, average, and poor creative expression?

5. What types of behavior samples shall be used in making the evaluations?

6. How are these behavior samples to be rated or scored?

Once these problems have been partially answered, those concerned with evaluations will be in a better position to evaluate creative expression. Since practically all attempts at evaluation of creativeness have been concerned with the quality of the end products, evaluations may be more harmful than good. It was pointed out earlier in this discussion of creative expression that such use of evaluations presents one of the important hazards to growth in creative ability. If evaluations are to function in the promotion of growth in self-expression, they should first be made on the basis of comparisons with the individual's own record, rather than comparisons made with some average child used as a standard. Secondly, the evaluations should be concerned with the development of the whole child, rather than a specific skill. The degree to which evaluations based on these principles may be made will depend largely upon the resources of the teachers, materials available, and the educational philosophy of the teaching and administrative staff.

Evaluating growth in creativeness in art. An informal procedure that gives much insight into a child's growth in creative expression and appreciation in art is that of noting his responses to the painting of other pupils. The teacher may ask the child to tell the things he likes about the painting in question. Secondly, she may ask the often-used question: Why does he like certain features of the painting? One child observed by the writer seemed to enjoy a snow scene in New England. When asked why, she remarked that it reminded her of Christmas and made her happy. Another child observing the same painting enjoyed the beautiful trees covered with snow. When asked why, she spoke of the different-sized trees which gave depth to the picture. Here we note different types of reactions and different degrees and directions of appreciations. Grimes and Bordin have proposed that creative expression in art should lead to the development of certain personality traits.[21] These traits would be evaluated by the teacher through observations of the child at work and conversations with him. Such a process would be guided by a check list of personality traits. If the teachers of a particular school

[21] James W. Grimes and Edward Bordin, A proposed technique for certain evaluations in art, *Educational Research Bulletin,* 1939, Vol. 18, pp. 1-5, 29.

were to make a check list, as a result of co-operative studies of this problem, the results would be more desirable in terms of promoting pupil growth.

Evaluation of children's verse. The increased recognition of the value of the development of creativeness in poetry has led to the need for evaluating a child's growth in verse writing. The building up of criteria by which children may judge their own work is an important phase of the teaching process, and is especially applicable to growth in creativeness in literary as well as other activities. Lela Ward has developed some worth-while criteria by which children may judge poetry, including their own verse.[22] The essential factors in the business of evaluation, then, seem to be, according to Ward: (1) the ability to tell poetry from prose, (2) an understanding of imagery, (3) the realization that rhythm but not rhyme is essential, (4) the ability to recognize good rhyme, and (5) the placement of a premium on originality of thought and expression."

Evaluation in music. A pupil's reaction to his own performance is of value in the evaluation and motivation of work in music. However, the bright pupil is more capable of autocriticism than is the case for the average pupil. A fifth-grade pupil, after practicing at the piano for a short while, was heard to remark; "I can't play this piece today. Let me play the number that I played for you when Mr. Smith was here last week. I like that number much better." Actually, according to the instructor, there was very little difference in the difficulty of the two numbers; but the child liked the melody of the other number very much. This is an informal evaluation of the nature of her music appreciation, and should be noted by the teacher and recorded in her current individual file for this pupil. A pupil's likes and dislikes in any area of activity, including music, reveal something about his interests and appreciations.

Summary

It has been suggested throughout this chapter that every child has some creative ability. Furthermore, it has been pointed out that this creative ability appears very early in the child's life and is expressed through his play activities, conversation, and free expression in his make-believe world.

Creative behavior is characterized by free expression as opposed to

[22] Lela Ward, Writing original poetry, *Twentieth Yearbook of the National Elementary Principal*, National Education Association, 1941, Vol. 20, p. 359.

copying or reproducing the behavior of others. The following were listed as characteristic of creative expression. (1) prolonged attention around some absorbing experience; (2) heightened motivation related to the experience; (3) expression. In situations where imagination, initiative, and originality exist, creative expression will be found. In this connection, self-expression is contrasted on page 286 with imitation.

Certain conditions have been found helpful in the development of creative expression, while some of the methods used in the homes and schools provide hazards or obstacles to the development of creativeness. Opportunity for experimentation, freedom of choice, heightened motivation, and guidance in the form of encouragement and a minimum of suggestions are helpful in the stimulation and growth of creative ability. Although optimum conditions may be provided for the growth of creative ability, it should be pointed out again that training and practice cannot transcend maturation. This is clearly shown in studies in which the child is asked to draw the human figure. Studies of the drawings by children at different age levels show that there are continuous growth and organizational changes with age. This developmental concept of the child's growth is further shown in the realm of space, color, and design.

The child appears to express his *total self* through his free expressions. These activities are tension-reducing devices, and have mental-hygiene value. They are also symptomatic of personal difficulties and problems. The evaluation of growth in creative expression is very difficult, and perhaps should not be the first consideration of those concerned with the guidance of the individual child. Some of the special difficulties involved in evaluating creative expressions have been listed as follows: (1) the difficulty of determining just what is creative; (2) qualitative versus quantitative aspects of creativeness; (3) the point of placement of emphasis (the end products or the intensity of the child's expression); (4) specific criteria for good, average, and poor; (5) types of behavior samples to be chosen for use; and (6) method of scoring such samples. In any consideration of the evaluation of creative expression, such evaluations should be looked upon as means toward more remote and worth-while ends, rather than looked upon as ends in themselves.

Questions and Exercises

1. Compare the stages of a young child's drawing with his use of language. What relationships might be expected here?
2. How can a teacher use children's creative imagination to help them acquire number combinations?
3. What are some of the characteristics of creative expression? Illustrate these in the play life of a three- or four-year-old.
4. What are some of the major barriers set up by the school in the development of creativeness?
5. What are the color preferences of preschool children? Upon what do these preferences depend?
6. What are some of the special characteristics of the drawings of the human figure by a four- or five-year-old child?
7. Point out how one's creative expressions are means of expressing the personality.
8. What methods have been used for evaluating growth in creative expression? What are the major difficulties encountered in making such evaluations?
9. Observe a group of children in their creative expressions. For example, you may wish to observe some children doing creative work in art, music, dramatics, or some other activity. Are the activities of these children indicative of creativeness? Are these activities consistent with findings from research studies bearing on the creative expressions of children of the ages observed?
10. Teachers often lament the fact that the older children show less spontaneity and imagination than do the younger children. Does this signify that creativity has been lost? Or, has it been channeled into pursuits not observed by the teachers? Or, is it covered up by changed attitudes toward the self and others? Or, is the individual more inhibited as he grows older?

Selected Readings

Alschuler, Ruse H., and Hattwick, LaBerta W. *Painting and Personality: A Study of Young Children,* 2 vols. Chicago: University of Chicago Press, 1946.

Biber, B., *et al. Child Life in School.* New York: E. P. Dutton Co., 1942.

Breckenridge, Marian E., and Vincent, E. Lee. *Child Development.* 2nd ed.; Philadelphia: W. B. Saunders Co., 1949. Chap. X.

Cole, Lawrence E., and Bruce, William F. *Educational Psychology.* Yonkers, New York: World Book Co., 1950. Chap. XV.

Forest, Isle, *Early Years at School*. New York: McGraw-Hill Book Co., 1949. Chap. XI.

Hartman, Gertrude, and Shumaker, Ann (eds.). *Creative Expression*. New York: John Day Co., 1933.

Henry, William E. The child tells about himself through his creative products, in *Fostering Mental Health in Our Schools. 1950 Yearbook, Association for Supervision and Curriculum Development*, 1950. Chap. XV.

Jersild, Arthur T. *Child Psychology*. 3rd ed.; New York: Prentice-Hall, 1947. Chap. XII.

Lee, J. Murray and Lee, Doris May. *The Child and His Curriculum*. New York: Appleton-Century-Crofts, 1950.

Lowenfeld, Viktor. *Creative and Mental Growth*. New York: The Macmillan Company, 1947.

Millard, Cecil V. *Child Growth and Development in the Elementary School Years*. Boston: D. C. Heath and Company, 1951. Chap. VIII.

Mursell, James E. How children learn aesthetic responses, *Learning and Instruction, Forty-ninth Yearbook of the National Society for the Study of Education*, Part I, 1950. Chap. VI.

Schaefer-Simmern, Henry. *The Unfolding of Artistic Activity: Its Basic Processes, and Implications*. Berkeley: University of California Press, 1948.

Williams, J. N. Interpretations of drawings made by maladjusted children, *Virginia Medical Monthly*, 1940. Vol. 67, pp. 533-538.

Case studies are presented showing a relationship between the free expression of children through drawings and experiences or conditions related to the maladjustments of the different children studied.

12

The Development of
Social Behavior and Attitudes

by Florence Heisler,
Brooklyn College

A hermit has little need for social skills. For the rest of us, how-ever, the ability to get along with others is extremely important. Sometimes, how much and how easily a child learns is determined more by his social adjustment at home and at school than by his mental capacity. Physical health, too, may be affected by one's ability to give and take with his associates. Even vocational success depends to some extent on a person's ability to get along with his fellow workers. Occasionally, a well-trained and well-educated per-son finds that he does not make progress in his chosen field because people do not care to work with him. Nearly every phase of one's life is altered in some way by his ability to get along with people.

Social effectiveness may vary with the situation. One may find that he is comfortable with his associates in his home and when engaged in leisure-time activities, but during a business contact he may find himself ill at ease. One person may prefer to be with his contemporaries; another may be happier with his elders. An indi-vidual may have an enjoyable time when associating with an in-timate group of friends. If the group were enlarged, this same person might become uneasy. A child may play nicely with the other children of the neighborhood during morning play periods, but he may become shy and nonco-operative when these same children appear at his birthday party.

How well a child or an adult adjusts to others at any particular time depends to a large extent upon his personal development and his past experiences. Age, mental and physical development (including health conditions), family relationships, social status of the family, sex, race, type of school and home atmosphere, and school and community associates all have an influence on an individual's social development.

Some people are appalled at the great number of forces that tend to affect a person's social behavior. It would seem that parents, teachers, and others who work with children should not be discouraged when they consider the great number of influences, but, instead, be encouraged because there are so many avenues through which help can be given to the socially incompetent child.

Sequence of social development

The first year of life. Practically from the time of conception, the child has an influence upon those about him. Even before he is born, family ties are being established. During his first year of life, he changes from a passive member of the family who receives much attention, but gives little in return, to one who initiates social contacts. This development is slow. At four weeks, he stares at faces that are close to him. A few weeks later, he cries to be picked up and placed where he can see lights, hear voices, and see people moving about.[1] This desire to be with others continues and expands. At seven months, he differentiates between the people of his home and demands more attention from the one who feeds him. He enjoys being bounced on the knee of a friend but may become shy when a stranger approaches. At forty weeks, he bids for still more attention. Playing peek-a-boo, having someone hold his hands to walk him, and being given carriage rides afford considerable enjoyment. About the time the first birthday is reached, the child is delighted when he can play hide-and-seek behind chairs or is chased as he hurriedly creeps away. He now occasionally waves "bye-bye" at the proper time.[2]

From age one to six. The child's competency in adjusting to social situations varies greatly in the years between the first birthday and the time of entering school. At eighteen months, he is "into everything." He knows where things are kept and can get and return them if he wishes. When walking, he darts in and out of corners and up and down steps, refuses to allow anyone to hold his arm, and en-

---

[1] Arnold Gesell and Frances L. Ilg, *Child Development* (New York: Harper & Brothers, 1949), p. 99.

[2] *Ibid.*, pp. 115-130.

joys turning knobs and handles that catch his eye. If inhibited in any way, he may strenuously resist.[3] Six months later, his increased understanding of the property rights of others helps him to be a much more acceptable member of the household. He "gets into" fewer things around the house and can really be a help in running errands. He has arrived at the age when he likes to have someone hold his hand while he walks on a wall or a high curb. Father is a favorite, but the child will run to his mother when he is in trouble. The companionship of children is enjoyed. He may play well with older children, especially if this play is of the parallel type.[4] At two-and-a-half, the youngster becomes quite domineering. He often insists on managing the affairs of all the members of his family. He will order adults around and, at times, is unreasonable in his demands. Household tasks must be routinized. Deviations are not tolerated. One little girl who had been in the habit of dusting the furniture in the living room was so disturbed when she came home to find her task had been done that she sprinkled dirt from the street on the tables so that she could remove it. Another tot went into a tantrum because her mother hurriedly took off her socks. The socks had to be replaced so the child could whisk them off by pulling the toes just as she had become accustomed to doing every night. A three-year-old is less demanding and will do chores around the house. He can play nicely out doors with another three-year-old for twenty or thirty minutes. However, if no supervision is given after a time, he may withdraw from the play situation or become very aggressive. Just as earlier, he gets along better when playing with older children. When the child is four, his interest in other children becomes so strong that he prefers their company to that of adults. But, in spite of this strong attraction to children and away from household activities, the four-year-old still has strong family ties. He will boast about his parents and hold them up as authorities.[5] The kinder-gartener wholeheartedly enjoys his play. He still needs supervision when with a friend for longer than a half or three-quarters of an hour, however. A child at this age may get along better with a younger child, an older one, a child of his own sex, or one of the opposite sex; but, in any case, he gets along better with one child at a time. When three play together without the advantage of an adult onlooker, two are apt to "gang up" on the third.[6]

[3] *Ibid.*, p. 151.
[4] *Ibid.*, pp. 167-168.
[5] *Ibid.*, pp. 209, 233.
[6] *Ibid.*, p. 81.

The elementary-school child. The first-grader has a difficult time at home, in school, and with his friends. He seems either to love or hate intensively. Often he is domineering and cruel to younger siblings and playmates. It is not beyond him to take delight in telling of the misdeeds of other children and of his own accomplishments. At seven years of age, the child is more easily influenced. He is co-operative and seems to enjoy doing simple household tasks. His demand for friendship is not as great as it was previously. He can spend time happily by himself, but he does want to feel that he has a place in the playground group and at home. He may acquire a girl friend and become quite serious with her.[7] It is on about the third-grade level that the child acquires a bosom pal with whom he spends a considerable amount of time. School, now, seems important because his friends are there. During school and home play time, very loosely organized clubs are formed with the intention of following some current interest. Most of these spontaneously formed groups last only a short time, sometimes only a day or two. At home, the eight-year-old is a more intimate member of the family. He shares his school and play experiences with his mother and other members of the family. There is difficulty, however, in getting things done on time. Now, as earlier, praise is more effective than blame in bringing about the desired behavior. Company manners are being acquired, and the child is able to get along well when he is away from home.[8] The nine-year-old does not have the close connection with his home and family that he had formerly, but when he is home, he is pleasant and helpful. He may have to be reminded to do his chores, but, generally, he complies easily and rather promptly. Boys and girls seem interested in each other, but they do not play together, and they occasionally make derogatory remarks about one another. Organizations become more closely knit. A nine-year-old may even enjoy membership in such clubs as the Boy Scouts, Girl Scouts, or Camp Fire Girls. At ten, the child has gained poise and social graces. He is more relaxed and casual in his relationship with people. A boy enjoys wrestling and "horseplay" with his best friend, but a girl wants to walk arm in arm with her chum and talk over events that took place in or out of school. Now, more than ever before, a youngster likes to have a secret with a friend. Notes are exchanged, often in code which is understood only by those "in the know." Secret societies exist, complete with passwords and "clubhouses." Parents and

---

[7] *Ibid.,* pp. 120, 150.
[8] *Ibid.,* pp. 179-180, 204.

teachers occasionally become concerned over the child's impulse to stress secrecy. Generally, this is only the youngster's way of satisfying a great need to "belong." [9] The hero worship and the discussions on appearance, social customs, etc., that take place in these groups do much to develop standards of behavior. If, of course, adequate supervision and good environmental conditions are not provided, delinquency may result.

The preadolescent. During this period, interest in learning the niceties of social behavior continues. When teaching on the junior-high-school level, the author placed several books on etiquette in the library. She noticed that the books were checked out regularly, but she never saw the books taken or returned, nor did she see a child reading one. It seems that the child at this age prefers to get such information with as little adult guidance as possible. These niceties, regardless of how they are acquired, are most generally used when associating with adults; however, a preadolescent is becoming aware of and is responding to the pressures of the group. It is important for this child to be invited to parties and social get-togethers, which are quite popular at this age.[10] There is a continual effort made to be as grown up as possible. This youngster resents being dressed like a "child." In spite of this desire to be mature, boy-girl relations may take peculiar form. A boy may hide his girl friend's notebook, untie her shoe, or take her locker key. "Crushes" on age mates and on adults, too, occur frequently now.

Family conditions which affect social behavior

The above sequence gives some of the social characteristics of the various age levels. Anyone who has observed children, however, knows that many do not follow this pattern. Some six-year-olds are quite mature socially and seem to have few of the annoying characteristics of their age level. Others, regardless of their age, have difficulty when they associate with children or adults. Some of this variation in behavior may be the result of environmental influences and some may be caused by the individual's unique make-up.

The family into which the child is born provides much of the environment that affects social development. Relationships that exist between the family and community, between the father and the

---

[9] University School Series, No. 3, *How Children Develop* (Columbus, Ohio, The Ohio State University, 1946), p. 32.

[10] *Ibid.*, p. 47.

mother, between the parents and the child, between siblings, continually influence the behavioral pattern of every member of the family.

The place of the family in the community. The socioeconomic status of the family into which the child is born determines to some extent the kind of social adjustment that will be made. Children brought up in homes where there is a considerable amount of space for everyone and where the necessities of life and a few luxuries are provided, with little sacrifice on the part of the parents, surely have less cause for conflict than those who must share sleeping facilities and clothing with siblings. It is true that children brought up in the homes of the well-to-do may have other conditions that disturb them, such as lack of intimate contacts with their parents, but they do have some opportunities that are not available to their less fortunate contemporaries. Macdonald, McGuire, and Havighurst in their study of ten-, eleven-, and twelve-year-olds found that "there were systematic class differences in participation in organized recreational groups, and in certain individual activities, such as taking music lessons. The middle class children took part mainly in Scouts and Y.W.C.A. while the lower class children took part mainly in two centers or clubs for underprivileged children."[11] This difference in the home and recreational activities seems to make the middle- and upper-class child a more acceptable member of society. Neugarten used a sociometric technique with fifth- and sixth-grade children and found that "membership in the upper class group carried with it a kind of insurance that one's reputation will be favorable—certainly never unfavorable," and that "membership in the lower class is almost certain to result in unfavorable reputation among one's peers."[12] Bonney ranked third-, fourth-, and fifth-grade children according to their family's socioeconomic status, averaged a social status score for each quartile, and discovered "that the most popular children, as a group, came from homes which were decidedly superior to those of the other children in cultural, social, and economic factors" (see Table 42).[13] How much of this popularity is the result of

[11] Marcherita Macdonald, Carson McGuire, and Robert Havighurst, Leisure activities and the socio-economic status of children, *American Journal of Sociology,* 1949, Vol. 54, p. 519.

[12] Bernice Neugarten, Social class and friendship among school children, *American Journal of Sociology,* 1946, Vol. 51, p. 313.

[13] Merl E. Bonney, Relations between social success, family size, socio-economic background, and intelligence among school children in grades III to IV, *Sociometry,* 1944, Vol. 7, p. 32.

TABLE 42 Relation of socioeconomic home background to social behavior (after Bonney)

Quartiles on Basis of Home Background *	Average Social Status
4	4.61
3	2.35
2	1.99
1	2.03

* Each quartile consists of 22 cases.

good social adjustment on the part of the financially more fortunate child, and how much can be attributed to the desire of children to associate with members of the well-to-do family, is hard to say. It seems, however, that the child from the better home environment has greater opportunity for social contact, and, as a result, learns to get along with others better than do his less fortunate contemporaries.

Children of minority groups, whether the groups be racial, national, or religious, may have few contacts with other children of the community. This separation may be the result of the parents' desire to continue customs peculiar to their group, or it may be caused by the attitude in the community toward the minority faction. Some of these families require their children to attend classes for religious or language instruction at a time when the children of the neighborhood get together for play. Prejudice, too, against a race or religious group may exclude children from social situations, and, as a result, limit opportunities to learn to get along with others.

The influence of interparental relationships. The type of adjustment made by parents to each other is often reflected in the social behavior of their children. Parents who have common interests, and who have much pleasure when together, will have a home which is comparatively free from tensions and quarreling. Youngsters raised in such an environment will not only have little cause to be unhappy, but will get the habit of being pleasant. Many of us know that it is difficult to be disagreeable when near some people. A good disposition is often contagious. On the other hand, parents who find it hard to understand and adjust to each other's attitudes and feelings have homes in which tensions and misunderstandings are common. These tensions, according to a study made by Baruch, may be related to the behavior problems of children. Her findings on nursery-school children were as follows:

1. The tensions in the parents which were significantly related to the problems of the children were those over ascendance-submission, sex, friends, relatives, overwork, health, extramarital relations, and tensions over lack of ability to talk over differences, to cooperate in bringing up the children, to be considerate, to express affection.

2. The tensions which were most closely related to the children's adjustment problems were those over sex and ascendance-submission.

3. The tensions which were related to leisure pursuits, criticalness of the partner, financial difficulties, and differences in taste seemed not to be related to the behavior of the children.

4. Certain relationships which existed in the premarital family life of each parent were significantly related to the adjustment problems of the children. They were: compensation for, or prolongation of a premature status in the family when this compensation or prolongation was followed by friction in marital relations; premarital attachment or antagonism of the mother to her father; premarital antagonism of the father to his mother; and the degree of harmony which existed between the mother's parents.

5. Behavior difficulties in the children seemed to be more closely related to problems in the mother's background than they were to the father's.

6. There were no constellations discovered in the behavior of the children.

7. Neither the premarital attachment of the father to his mother, the antagonism of the father to his father, the antagonism or attachment of the mother to her mother, nor the degree of harmony which existed between the father's parents seem to have any significant relationship to the children's behavior. Changes in social status which came about as a result of marriage, also, seem not to affect the adjustment of the children.[14]

As bad as it may be for children to be brought up in a broken home, such a home may be more wholesome than one that is psychologically broken by continuous quarreling. Children who live with unhappy, bickering parents lack security. They never know how their parents will react to one another and how this reaction will affect their relationships with their parents. Often, children like their parents equally well, but are prevented from giving or receiving

[14] Dorothy W. Baruch, A study of reported tension in interparental relationships as co-existent with behavior adjustment in young children, *Journal of Experimental Education*, 1937, Vol. 6, pp. 202-203.

affection from one because of restrictions imposed by the other, either subtly or outwardly.

When homes are broken by death, sickness, incarceration, or the inability of the parents to live together, an unnatural home environment results. Even when the separation of the parents has removed the cause of many disturbing problems, the children are likely to have inadequate living conditions. They may be placed with their grandparents, they may live with one parent or take turns living with each parent, they may be put in a foster home, they may live with one parent and his or her new spouse. In any case, security and completeness in the home may be lacking. Grandparents seldom have the vitality and understanding to make a good home for a young child. Parents often find it difficult to understand the reasoning of their children's generation. Think of the difficulty encountered when elderly people are called upon to understand children who are two generations younger! Living with one parent deprives the child of relationships with both sexes, and spending part of a year with each parent involves the necessity of continually adjusting to new situations. Neither the child nor the parent will be exactly the same after a considerable interval of separation. These changes occur in people when they are not separated. The change, however, is so gradual that it is hardly noticeable when people live together constantly. Being forced to live with a parent who has remarried causes a situation which may increase in complexity as time passes. There could be "his" children, "her" children and "their" children in the same household. Foster homes may or may not be an answer to the children's needs. Unless the home is unusual and the child is very young when he is placed, feelings of intruding and not belonging are felt by the child.

Situation alone, of course, does not cause social maladjustment. There are children who have developed fine attitudes and social demeanor in conditions that seemed intolerable, while other children have experienced difficulty in a seemingly good environment.

The influence of parent-child relations. The young couple who look forward to the birth of a child with much joy, and who are stimulated by the new responsibility which is to come to them, generally provide a more wholesome environment for their children than do parents who are not eager to have children because it will necessitate the sharing of time and money with the newcomer, or because it will mean that the mother will have to give up a career, and that the father will have to readjust his family and social life.

Parents have many adjustments to make. If there is no one in the home other than the parents to share the responsibility of caring for the child, this young couple will need to change their entire mode of living. They must remain at home most of the time because the baby's things are there, and he is more easily cared for in his own room. The townspeople, too, do much to change the customs of young parents. They expect certain characteristics to accompany parenthood.[15] Unsolicited advice and criticism come freely from the lips of some well-meaning folk and exert a pressure on the couple. Then, such little things as getting accustomed to being called "Mother" and "Daddy" require an adjustment. Some married couples declare they will never use these terms when referring to another. The majority, however, use these names as they see the father and mother stereotype emerge in the other spouse.

Parents, because of their past experiences and their present feelings, vary greatly in their method of responding to their children. In some families, the parents and the child have a high level of verbal contact. There is explanation for family rules, a lack of arbitrariness on the part of the parents, and a quiet, permissive atmosphere. At the other extreme, there are families in which rules and regulations are decided upon by the parents and clearly conveyed to the child. There is little discussion or friction over disciplinary decisions. Most families, of course, fall somewhere between these two extremes. They are neither entirely democratic (the first description) nor entirely controlled (the second description). In spite of difficulties one encounters in classifying individual families, Baldwin[16] attempted to determine the effect of these two methods of management on the social behavior of nursery-school children. The democratic, he found, seemed to produce an active, aggressive, fearless, and planful child who had leadership characteristics but who, also had a tendency to be more cruel than the average child. He was apt also to be (nearly statistically significant) more curious, nonconforming, and disobedient. The controlled home, on the other hand, produced a quiet, nonresistant, well-behaved, and unaggressive child with restricted curiosity, originality, and fancifulness. Baldwin concluded that it is difficult to get a child to conform to cultural demand and, at the same time, retain the personal integrity that will allow him to satisfy

[15] James H. S. Bossard, *The Sociology of Child Development* (New York: Harper & Brothers, 1948), p. 90.
[16] Alfred L. Baldwin, Socialization and the parent-child relationship, *Child Development,* 1948, Vol. 19, p. 129.

his curiosity and carry out his own ideas. Authoritarian control obtains conformity but limits freedom to grow creatively. Democracy frees the child to explore and experiment, but does little to help him to conform to cultural demands.

The activity level of the home is another characteristic that seems to influence the behavior of the child. Baldwin discovered that his families differed not only in the amount of interaction that occurred between the parents and the child, but also in the form the activity took. Interaction may take one of several forms. It may appear as a well-ordered schedule, a continuous flow of criticism and suggestion, in child-centeredness of activities, or in special training for the child and attempts at acceleration. When children from active homes are compared with those from inactive homes, regardless of the form of the interaction, it seems that the child's level of activity is raised along with his rebelliousness and nonconformity. Activity and democracy in the home seem to have similar effects upon the child. It is, however, possible to differentiate between them. Activity seems to affect the characteristics that are more related to the child and his emotions, while democracy affects such variables as curiosity and planfulness.[17] The children from active democratic homes are described as being aggressive, competitive, quarrelsome, and resistant, with some curiosity, emotional excitability, impatience, and cruelty. Those from an inactive democratic home are more detached from their parents, with the level of verbal interchange more lethargic and spasmodic. In these homes, the effects of democracy are less marked than in homes where there is a higher level of activity.

The results of the Baldwin study lead us to believe that there must be in the home of the child a certain amount of democracy, control, and activity. How much of each of these is necessary to produce a child who has curiosity, fearlessness, planfulness, aggressiveness, and still is fit to live with, depends, it seems, upon the nature of the particular child. Some children are able to manage more self-direction and activity than others. They take responsibility in their stride, while less fortunate individuals flounder and make decisions that get them into difficulty. The age and background, too, determine the amount of parent-child planning and activity that a youngster can absorb without harm. Little children have neither the maturity nor the experience which will help them select the more advantageous of two alternatives. Wise parents realize this and help their child

[17] *Ibid.*, pp. 134-135.

by explaining just those relationships that the child can understand and by limiting both the number and kinds of choices. As the child increases in age and experience, more explanation and greater opportunity to select a course of action are provided.

In spite of the fact that parents seem to have a characteristic way of reacting to their children, there are variations in their attitude toward and treatment of individual children of the family. Even those parents who try to be impartial in their relations do not react the same toward each of their children. The circumstances under which a particular child was born and the physical, mental, and emotional make-up of the individual child account for much of this variation.

The circumstances under which the child is born affect to some extent the attitude his parents will have toward him. The child who comes when parents are young and happy to start a family, the child who has been long awaited, and the child who arrives at a time when his parents are incompatible and prefer not to remain together, all have a different set of parental attitudes with which to cope. These attitudes will affect the child-parent relationships for a considerable length of time. The child born to the young couple who are happily married and desirous of having a child has a good chance of living in an environment made pleasant and wholesome by his parents. The child born to parents who have waited years for him may be overprotected. He may be so sheltered that he does not have an opportunity to participate in normal childhood activities. Such toys as bicycles and skates may not be made available for him. If they are given to him, he may be so closely supervised that he derives little pleasure from them. An unwanted child may be neglected by his parents, and, as a result, deprived of many opportunities for socialization, or he too may be overprotected. Overprotection often accompanies a feeling of guilt on the part of the parents.

Some parents see in the birth of their child a second opportunity to satisfy a desire once cherished. Some children are required to take music lessons because a parent was frustrated in his attempt to become a singer or pianist.

A father who brought his fifteen-year-old son to the psychological clinic complained because the boy was doing poor school work and was having adjustment problems. It seemed that the father had wanted to be a physician, but was unable to get the required amount of education necessary for such a vocation. When his son was born, the father declared that nothing would prevent the child from going to medical school. Now that the boy was a sophomore in high school, it was quite evident that he would not have the academic standing to be admitted to a college for premedical training. While discussing the background of the case, a clinician asked the father to indicate the activities in which the child had achieved success. The father could think of no area in which the boy excelled. Later, it was discovered that the youngster had learned to grow orchids and was at the present time conducting a thriving business after school. Either the father was so intent on preparing his son for medical school that he had not noticed the extent of this enterprise, or he did not see the value of such an occupation to the child.

Occasionally, parents are determined to have their children follow a pattern of behavior which meets the needs of the parents but which totally disregards the child's learning potentialities and personality. School principals throughout the country have a difficult time every September persuading certain parents to wait until their child has reached the appropriate age before entering him in first grade. It seems that the satisfaction gained from knowing that their child is one of the younger members of his class is more important than the well-being of the child.

The influence of the child's own status. Children of the same family live in different environments. The first-born, the middle child, the baby, the only boy in a family of girls, the only girl in a family of boys, the bright child, the dull child, the one who resembles Uncle Charlie, etc., all evoke different feelings and, as a result, different reactions from parents, siblings, and neighbors.

Whether the child is the first-born, one of the middle, or the youngest child seems to make a difference in the child's status. This position in the family brings with it certain responsibilities. Parents and adults outside the home are quite conscious of the order in which the children appeared and continually refer to it when evaluating the behavior of the various siblings.

The first-born has certain experiences before and after the birth of his siblings that will not be experienced by other members of the family. He, like an only child, has to learn to adjust to a household in which there are only adults. His parents are inexperienced at this business of rearing children. They may vary their methods from time to time in an effort to discover satisfactory techniques of coping with this new member of the family. He may be cared for by his grandparents. If he is the first grandchild, he may be the favorite of his aunts and uncles as well as of his grandparents.

When the second child arrives, the first-born may or may not be prepared for his coming. Even when a child is well prepared for his new sibling, and even when he is given every consideration during his period of adjustment to the baby, his changed status in the family will affect his behavior.[18] He probably will leave no method untried in his attempt to regain his former position in the family. He may revert to infantile behavior, refuse to eat, become constipated, or try any of a dozen techniques to get the attention of his parents. A few older children may express their resentment by hurting the newcomer. One youngster seldom passed the carriage of his baby sister without reaching in to twist a toe!

Sooner or later, however, most of the first-born children assume the role of the big brother or sister. They soon realize they are the first to have new experiences and privileges. They enter school first and in many ways set the pace for those who are to follow. They are expected to be, and generally are, because of their age, superior in mental ability, physical skills, and general achievement. Often, as parent surrogates, these children are given the responsibility for the actions and safety of younger children.

There are reasons to believe that the first-born, especially in a large family, has training that will develop certain specific traits. His experiences at the time the second and each succeeding child is born, and his understanding the feelings a younger child has when he suddenly finds he is no longer the baby of the family, gives the oldest child an insight into life and family relationships. The responsibility given the first-born by parents and other members of the community, along with the fact that younger children soon learn to expect this older brother or sister to be superior and to know the proper action to take in every situation, more or less forces the first-born into a leadership role. As leader of his small group, he may learn to help immature siblings, to settle disagreements, and to inspire good behavior in other children. The standards for the first-born are set high; if he can live up to them, he will get experiences that will be invaluable to him throughout life.

The second child, unlike the first-born, never has the full attention of his parents. He always has a larger, stronger, and more capable person with whom he must contend. He does receive for a short time the intimate attention parents must give a baby, but

[18] Anonymous, Ambivalence in first reactions to a sibling, *Journal of Abnormal and Social Psychology,* 1949, Vol. 44, pp. 541-548.

even this is more routinized now that the parents have had a second child.

His relationship with his older sibling can be quite difficult, for even the best-adjusted older child will resent his young brother and sister occasionally. Seldom, indeed, is an older child not held as an example for the other children. It may take this form: "When Billy was your age, he could tie his shoelaces." On the other hand, the second child may not be held responsible for his actions. Such comments as "You saw your little brother go toward the flower bed. Why didn't you stop him?" are made to the older child in the presence of a younger sibling. These home relations, along with the normal amount of ridicule and defeat that a child experiences when associating with the children of the neighborhood, make it necessary for each child to try to regain prestige. The older child can pass on derogatory comments and other abuse to his younger sister or brother. The younger child can retaliate by tattling and attempting to place the older child in bad with his parents.

The middle child has a continual struggle to become an individual. Most of his clothing and many of his toys are handed down to him from his older siblings. In school, his achievement is continually compared with that of the older children of the family. If the older youngsters did well, he will be expected to succeed also. If the older children did poorly, little will be expected of him. He will be introduced as Jim's brother and may even be called Jim on occasion. In such a situation, the middle child has two alternatives open to him. He may put forth much effort and equal or exceed the achievement of his older sibling, or he may settle back to the level of his younger brother or sister. If this middle child has superior capacity and stamina (superior, that is, for his family), he generally follows the first course of action.[19]

The last-born child has still a different set of circumstances with which to cope. He is born into a family situation that is considerably more complex than it was when his siblings were born. He has not only the personalities of his parents but also those of his brothers and sisters to adjust to. Then, occasionally, he must contend with the desire on the part of his parents and the older children of the family to have him remain young and helpless.

This "baby" of the family, if well accepted, has advantages that the other youngsters did not have. First, he never has to relinquish

[19] James H. S. Bossard, *The Sociology of Child Development* (New York: Harper & Brothers, 1948), p. 114.

his place in the family to another child. Second, he continues to receive much protection and affection from all members of his family throughout his life. Third, he generally receives the advantages of a better financial position. His parents in middle age may have increased means or, if this is not the case, older brothers and sisters now working may remember how they appreciated an allowance and give the baby a considerable amount of spending money. Fourth, the youngest child has the advantage of a higher cultural level. The older children by their various activities have made the home richer in its educational and social contributions.

There are disadvantages in being the youngest member of a family. The parents, now older, may not assume the responsibility for this child's rearing, and, as a result, various members of the family contribute rather haphazardly to his upbringing, or the parents, now less sympathetic with the problems of childhood, may be quite severe with this youngest child. Then, because the members of his family continue to consider him a baby, he may find it easy to play the role of an immature person and not accept the responsibility for his self-improvement and self-discipline.

Children who are considerably older when a younger child is born may not have the intense feeling of insecurity that younger children experience; they may, however, have quite definite feelings toward the baby. Some are delighted with the newcomer and do everything in their power to make life pleasant for him. Sometimes, the good intentions of the older children take the form of overprotection. If this is the case, the "baby" has an atypical home situation, since he finds himself with, not two, but many playing the parent role for him. Other grown children resent the coming of the new baby. Some are ashamed of their parents because they are having a child so late in life. They feel that the burden of the child's support and rearing will fall on them. In either situation, the youngest child will have unusual adjustment problems. He may have all the problems of the only child along with those peculiar to his own situation.

Some children who are born within a year or two of each other may enjoy each other's companionship so much that they will not seek other friends, and, as a result, they learn little that will help them in larger social groups. Two such children may feel that they are expected to reach the same standard of achievement. Sometimes the younger child tries to match the accomplishments of the older sibling. Sometimes the older gives up and is satisfied with the standard set by the younger. Learning capacity determines to some extent which course is taken. In any event, comparisons result even in the best-regulated homes and schools.

The only child, like every other child, has problems. He may be overprotected and limited in his contacts with other children. He does, however, have many advantages.[20] Generally, he receives the benefits of a better socioeconomic position, which brings with it better medical care, more toys, more travel, and more education.

Characteristics other than place in the family enter into the social adjustment of youngsters. While riding in a subway recently, the writer noticed two sisters of about four and five years of age. One was rather a plain-looking child with straight, mousy-colored hair and light-blue eyes. Her sister, the younger of the two, had dark brown curly hair, dark-brown eyes, and nice features. Do you suppose that when neighbors forget the names of these girls, one is referred to as the "good-looking child"? Children are quick to notice the reactions of others. Will the older child find a way to compensate for her appearance, or will she just refuse to compete? History is filled with examples of people whose handicap in one situation served to motivate them to outstanding success in another. The older youngster's own potentialities and her environmental relationships will influence her reactions. In any event, the behavior of the two will be colored somewhat by their individual characteristics.

Other characteristics such as level of intelligence, special talents, physical ability, body build, health, racial traits, and abnormalities influence not only the reactions of the child affected but also those of his siblings.

The sex of the child, too, is an important factor in determining reactions of the children and parents. The fact that to some parents the sex of the child is very important has already been stated. Our society and some families more than others demand that girls be brought up according to a pattern that is quite different from the pattern considered correct for boys. The writer remembers quite vividly how disturbed she was when, on the way to the beach, the car in which some neighborhood boys, her parents, and she were riding was stopped because of an accident ahead. The boys and her father

[20] Merle E. Bonney in his study of the relationship between social success and family size, socioeconomic status, and intelligence among intermediate-grade children, points out that the only-child families have a slightly higher representation than normal expectancy in the two upper social-status quartiles, and are definitely below normal expectancy in the two lower groups, especially the lowest one.

jumped out quickly to see what had happened. The writer, however, was told to return to the car when she started to follow. It was not proper for a girl to see an accident. Boys and girls are given certain prerogatives that are considered proper for their sex. Girls, for example, may cry if hurt or sad without disgrace; boys, however, are not very old when they learn that "men" do not cry. Differences which are not always reasonable and which are often quite limiting are made in the rearing of boys and girls. These, too, play a part in the development of social relations.

A crippled, deformed, or mentally deficient child in the home produces situations that influence the behavior of every member of the family. Parents may feel guilty or resentful because such a child exists. A young mother of a mongolian idiot felt that she had sinned and that God was punishing her by placing this feeble-minded child in her care. To atone for her sins, she enslaved herself to this child, while allowing the needs of two normal children to go unheeded. The siblings of an atypical child are required often to give time, which under other circumstances would be used for play, to this unfortunate youngster or to household tasks which the mother can not do. Then there is the feeling of embarrassment brought about by the attitude of neighbors toward such a child. Many people do not understand that feeble-mindedness or deformity can be the result of causes other than inheritance, and that, if it is the result of hereditary influences, the siblings are not responsible. This ignorance on the part of others can limit the social activities of a home. Children and parents are reluctant to bring friends to their home if a handicapped child is in evidence. Invariably, a crippled or deformed child has needs that require the expenditure of the parents' finances. When the family is in the middle or lower income bracket, such expenses may deprive siblings of necessities that in turn restrict the number of social contacts.

Social acceptability and social development

The outsider. Generally, children begin to make social contacts with other children in the second half of their first year of life. A six-month-old baby when placed near another child will try to attract the attention of the other child. He may touch him, make sounds, or interfere with his activities.[21] His success in establishing contact

---

[21] Charlotte Bühler, The social behavior of the child, in *A Handbook of Child Psychology,* ed. Carl Murchison (Worcester, Mass.: Clark University Press, 1931), chap. 12, p. 396.

depends largely on his level of motor co-ordination. The youngster who sits easily and moves readily has an advantage over his less active associate. As the infant becomes stronger and more agile, he also becomes more aggressive in his social contacts. By the time he is old enough to enter kindergarten, he wants to associate with several children at the same time. There are children, however, who are apparently aware of other children, but who seem not to be interested in making social contacts with them. The percentage of such children decreases with age. Bühler reports the findings of a study by Wislitzky which gives the percentage of solitary children as being 8 for those between the ages of three and four, 5 between four and five, 2 between five and six, and 0 between six and seven.[22]

Northway [23] studied nursery-school children who made few social contacts and who seemed to be least acceptable to their age mates. Her findings lead her to believe that innate temperamental differences which seem to be associated with the vitality, readiness for social contact, and adaptability to change, influence the success of children in social situations. Some youngsters appear to be "enclosed within themselves, resistant to change in routine," and unresponsive to other children. Teachers found them to lack the basic personality organization that comes from affection and social guidance in the home.

In an effort to determine those children who were and who were not attractive to their classmates, Moreno [24] asked every child in a kindergarten and elementary school to select the boys and girls whom he would like to remain in his grade and sit near him. The results, shown in Figure 39, revealed that there were between 15 and 35 per cent of the children in every grade not selected by anyone. These may not be solitary children, since many of them probably made contact with other children outside of school.

There are fewer isolates in classrooms where the teachers make an effort to help the new child find his place in the group, where the teacher considers each child's social as well as academic needs when grouping children for activities, and where the teacher considers social guidance a part of her teaching. Children who can learn to help themselves and others become more acceptable members of a group.

[22] *Ibid.*, p. 397.

[23] Mary L. Northway, Outsiders—a study of the personality pattern of children least acceptable to their age mates, *Sociometry*, 1944, Vol. 7, pp. 10-25.

[24] J. L. Moreno, Changes in sex groupings of school children, in *Readings in Social Psychology*, ed. Theodore M. Newcomb, Eugene L. Hartley, and others (New York: Henry Holt and Company, 1947), pp. 383-387.

Socially accepted children. Parents, teachers, and even children occasionally say, "Well, I don't see what John sees in that boy." Evidently, John sees much that the onlookers do not see. It may be that "that boy" lives close by and is more accessible than other children. Propinquity plays an important part in the selection of a

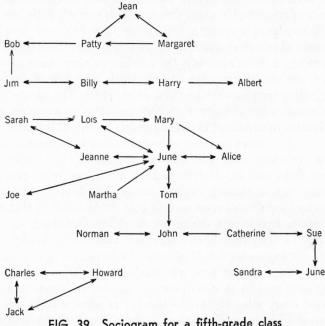

FIG. 39 Sociogram for a fifth-grade class

companion. A youngster who lives where there are few children, or who is separated from neighborhood boys and girls (because of religious differences, or attendance at a private school, or some other factor) may have difficulty in acquiring friends. There are, however, factors other than nearness which bring children together. The children may be of about the same socioeconomic status, may have a similar family background, or belong to the same racial stock. Many of these factors operate within our culture to bring certain children together.

Children have various kinds of friends. One pair may go together because they live near each other, another because of a common interest, a third because neither is accepted by other children, and still another for the help each gives the other. Sometimes a younger child cherishes a friendship with an older boy or girl because it makes him feel important. The older child, on the other hand, may when associating with this younger child get a much-needed feeling of superiority.

The age of the child itself seems to have some influence on the amount of time and the kind of social relations a child will have. It has been found that before the age of two, children give little evidence of co-operative play. Two-year-olds spend a little less than half, three-year-olds spend a little more than half, and four-year-olds spend about three-quarters of their play time associating with other children. It is not only the amount of time spent in social contact, but also the number of individuals who join in the social group, which increases as the child grows older. The nature of the social organization changes with age, too. The spontaneous group participation of preschool children consists mostly of dramatic play. Primary-grade youngsters engage in games that have more organization and in which each child gets his turn to be "it." Upper-grade children like games in which there are a number of quite specialized positions, such as pitcher, catcher, center, goal keeper, etc., and in which there are a number of specific rules.[25] And so it is that social relationships change with the age of the children involved.

Other characteristics that make one child more attractive to another are more complex. Challman [26] observed seventeen nursery-school boys and sixteen girls who ranged in age from twenty-seven to fifty-nine months to determine the number of times each child contacted every other child. The number of times a child was with another child gave an indication of the strength of the friendship between the two children. Those who seemed strongly attracted to each other were compared in order to discover similarities in characteristics that might account for this attachment. Similarities in sex, chronological age, mental age, IQ, height, personality, degree of extroversion, sociality, physical activity, and laughter were compared with strength of friendship. The findings were as follows:

1. As boys grow older, they have a tendency to form stronger friendships with boys. This is not the case in friendships of girls with girls or boys with girls.

2. Children of the same sex tend to form friendships within their own sex.

[25] John E. Anderson, The development of social behavior, *American Journal of Sociology,* 1939, Vol. 44, p. 84.

[26] R. C. Challman, Factors influencing friendships among preschool children, *Child Development,* 1932, Vol. 3, p. 158.

3. Of the similarities investigated, only chronological age seemed to have an influence on the friendships between boys and girls.

4. Boys with boys friendships seemed to be influenced by similarities in chronological age, sociality, and physical activity in the order given.

5. Girls with girls friendships seemed to be influenced by similarities in social participation, chronological age and sociality in the order given.

6. The other characteristics, mental age, height, extroversion, attractiveness of personality, IQ, and frequency of laughter, seemed to have no influence on either the boy's or girl's friendship at this age.

Grossmann and Wrighter [27] attempted to determine the relationship of such characteristics as intelligence, achievement, and personality to a selection-rejection score obtained for each of 117 sixth-grade children from a sociometric instrument. They found that level of intelligence and of reading achievement was important in determining the acceptability of a child up to a certain point—normal intelligence and average reading ability—but that beyond this level it seemed not to affect the selection-rejection scores. Personality scores of those children who were most popular with their classmates were considerably higher than those of children who were not so acceptable to their associates.

When the children themselves were asked to give reasons for selecting their three best friends, Austin and Thompson [28] found that sixth-grade youngsters considered such characteristics as being cheerful and friendly the most important reasons, with availability and similarity of interest and taste coming next. After an interval of two weeks had passed, Austin and Thompson asked these same children to indicate changes that had been made in their best friends and found approximately 40 per cent had made no changes. Among those who selected new best friends, factors such as lack of recent contact, quarreling, replacement by another child, and incompatibility were given most frequently as the reason.[29]

How much or how little boys and girls associate with each other probably depends upon family, school, and community attitudes, the age of the youngsters, and the social attractiveness of both the boys

[27] Beverly Grossmann and Joyce Wrighter, The relationship between selection-rejection and intelligence, social status, and personality amongst sixth grade children, *Sociometry*, 1948, Vol. 11, pp. 346-355.

[28] M. C. Austin and G. G. Thompson, Children's friendships: a study of the bases on which children select and reject their best friends, *Journal of Educational Psychology*, 1948, Vol. 39, p. 110.

[29] *Ibid.*, p. 112.

and the girls to children regardless of their sex. Some adults do much to discourage social contacts young boys or girls may wish to make by remarks designed to provoke fun. Schools and homes that make a definite distinction between the type of activity suitable for a boy and a girl do much to make it difficult for children of opposite sexes to become friends. In some homes, dishwashing is always the girl's chore, while tending to the garden is the boy's. Many schools never consider courses in cooking for boys or manual training for girls, in spite of the fact that many boys enjoy cooking and many girls like to work with a hammer and saw. Whether the age of the child in itself is a factor that affects the attractiveness of a pre-adolescent boy for a preadolescent girl and vice versa is difficult to say. Surely, interests which a child might have at a certain age affect the choice of a friend. Moreno, without going into influences other than age, determined, by asking children to choose from their class those whom they would like to have remain in their group and sit near them, the per cent of boys who selected girls and girls who selected boys at the various grade levels.[30] He found that approximately 25 per cent of the kindergarten and first-grade children selected a child of the opposite sex to be near them. The results presented in Table 43 show that this percentage decreased considerably in grades three, four, and five. Throughout these grades there was very little choice by either sex for members of the opposite sex.

If a child is to get along well with his contemporaries, he must,

TABLE 43 Quantitative analysis of choices between the sexes in the grades of a public school (after Moreno)

Of all choices made	Boys chose girls, per cent	Girls chose boys, per cent	Both Sexes per cent
Kindergarten	10.0	15.0	25.0
1st Grade	19.0	8.0	27.0
2nd Grade	10.0	6.5	16.5
3rd Grade	3.5	5.0	8.5
4th Grade	1.5	1.0	2.5
5th Grade	1.0	4.5	4.0
6th Grade	2.05	2.05	3.5
7th Grade	2.0	1.0	3.0
8th Grade	4.0	4.0	8.0

[30] J. L. Moreno, Changes in sex groupings of school children, in *Readings in Social Psychology,* ed. Theodore M. Newcomb, Eugene L. Hartley, and others (New York: Henry Holt and Company, 1947), pp. 383-387.

of course, enter into the activities of the group, be alert, and reasonably active. Some children will be popular in one group but not in another. This may be the result of the child's interests. He may not comprehend the activities of one group or he may be so advanced intellectually that their activities seem silly to him. A very brilliant and physically mature seven-year-old was placed in the first grade. After two days of trying to get along with her classmates, she went to the teacher to report that it was just impossible for her to play or work with the "children." The second grade also failed to meet her need. By the end of the first year, the school authorities had put the child in the fourth grade. In spite of the fact that she now was about a year and a half younger than the average child of this class, she was accepted into the social activities and was quite happy.

Leadership. From the time that children begin to make social contacts, differences in methods of approach are quite obvious. Some children are quick to take the initiative in getting some type of activity started. If quite young children are placed together, one may dominate the other by taking the toys, sharing the toys, or by making more physical contacts with his companion.[31] Children who are active in social situations often become leaders of their group. At first, this leadership is felt by the one or two playmates who associate with the child; later, during nursery school, a small group may be influenced; and still later, the entire class as a unit may work with one or two children.

There are several types of leaders. Some lead in outdoor activities, while others lead in scholastic pursuits. Some children hold attention by their forceful and aggressive ways, while others are diplomatic in their relationships.[32] Generally, the child who is a leader is slightly above average in the area in which he leads. He may not be the most outstanding, but he has practical suggestions that children can follow. Occasionally, a quite dull child is found to have a quite prominent position in his group. One such child frequently was made chairman by his eight-grade class. He himself had few ideas for organization, but he seemed to have a knack of being able to select outstanding children for important tasks and of being able to give sincere praise to those who helped. He was not aggressive and seldom lost his temper. Children who are quite forceful in their demands for

[31] Bühler, *op. cit.*, p. 400.
[32] Rosemary Lippott, Popularity among preschool children, *Child Development*, 1941, Vol. 12, p. 331.

the leadership role may dominate simply because the group finds it easier to let them lead than to make them follow. Such children, however, cannot be considered true leaders. Sooner or later they will be replaced by more capable children. A true leader displays such characteristics as fairness and social responsibility to the group.

The amount of direction given by a diplomatic leader is not always obvious. Furthermore, such indirect forms of leadership appear early among children. One nursery-school girl continually managed the affairs of several children in quite an indirect way. This incident was observed: One little boy had a new drum and a whistle that he insisted on using by himself. Shirley (diplomatic leader) wanted to play with the drum. She had seen several other children refused the use of it. Finally, the drum was placed on the ground, and the owner wandered around blowing his whistle. Shirley was heard to announce, "That's a fine idea. You lead the parade, and I will follow with the drum." Off the two went, the drum owner quite pleased with "his idea."

Various studies conducted among different groups of junior-high-school-students indicate that leaders generally are superior to the group in many characteristics. The interraction of the group tends to bring the more brilliant individual to the front. Outstanding children, however, are not always leaders. This may be because they have not had enough social contact with their group, because of their innate make-up which makes them prefer not to be active in a group, or because their personality is not attractive to other children.

Sometimes, children make unwise choices in selecting leaders for their activities. Partridge [33] found that youngsters who lived and worked together for a considerable length of time were better able to select competent leaders than those who were together only a short time. He found that social interaction developed leaders and brought children with leadership qualities to the attention of the group. When children make poor choices in the selection of leaders, it may be that the school has not provided enough time for group participation to develop leaders or bring them forward.

Competition and co-operation. In spite of the fact that co-operation and competition seem to be anithetical terms, they often are motivated by the same drives and are often experienced at the same time. A child as he works on his own project may compete with his

[33] E. Dalton Partridge, Leadership among adolescent boys, Teachers College, Columbia University, *Contributions to Education,* No. 603, 1934, p. 92.

classmates for the satisfaction that comes from achieving and for the approval which he receives, or he may work co-operatively with a group on a project for the same satisfaction and approval. In sports, a player may co-operate with his teammates to the limit of his ability in order that his team may be successful in a competitive match. Generally, when a child competes, he is working for his own interests entirely; when he co-operates, he is working for others as well as for himself.

Signs of competition become noticeable as children increase in age. Leuba [34] brought children aged two to six years individually and in pairs into a room. Each child was given a peg board with which to play. No comment or attention was directed toward the children after the preliminary instructions were given. Records were made by an unseen observer of each child's reactions and comments as he placed the pegs in the holes. The children who were approximately two years old did not seem to be affected by the presence of another child. Those in the three-four-year-old bracket were aware of what the other child was doing and made remarks of a competitive sort. Some, however, used words such as "beating" with apparently little or no understanding of their meaning. Fewer pegs were inserted when these children worked in pairs than when they worked alone. The presence of another child distracted attention and caused pauses in the work. Nearly all the five-year-olds inserted more pegs when paired with another child. Every child of this age level except a foreign-born child gave evidence of rivalry at some time during his peg-board experience. There were no sex differences in the expression of rivalry at any age level.

Maller [35] carried out an experiment in which fifth-, sixth-, seventh-, and eighth-grade children were asked to do simple addition combinations under four different conditions: unmotivated, working for themselves, working for the group, and working for themselves or the group, whichever they wished to do. The children while working for themselves and for the group were further encouraged by being told that the papers were to be ranked and that prizes were to be given to the individual or group, whichever was concerned, for high scores. It was found that both the group and individual motivation were effective in increasing scores, but that children of these age

[34] Clarence Leuba, An experimental study of rivalry in young children, *Journal of Comparative Psychology*, 1933, Vol. 16, pp. 367-378.

[35] Julius E. Maller, Cooperation and competition: an experimental study in motivation, Teachers College, Columbia University, *Contributions to Education*, No. 384, 1929.

levels accomplished more when working to win a prize for themselves than they did when working for a class prize.

How much of this rivalry that children possess is the result of home and community urging is difficult to say. It is interesting to note that the foreign child mentioned in Leuba's study who was brought up in an environment that differed markedly from that of our American children showed no signs of rivalry in her peg-board performance.

We observe daily the many ways in which competition helps children improve in achievement. Youngsters who dawdle and refuse certain foods when eating at home often eat rapidly and without comment that which is placed before them at school or camp. Those who need to be coaxed to do chores at home seem more than eager to help when visiting. Whether the rivalry is forced upon the individual or is self-imposed, it seems to have an influence on behavior.

There are times, however, when competition retards rather than accelerates achievement. A younger brother followed his two sisters through the grades of a small-town elementary school. The sisters were honor students. The brother was superior in intelligence but was not so brilliant as his sisters. Five years of "When your sister was in this class, she would never have handed in a paper like this," etc., brought the boy's achievement to such a low level that it seemed desirable to send him to a boarding school. If there is a chance to succeed occasionally, competition may encourage a child.

Then, it seems that so much emphasis can be placed on competing that values other than those of doing the task quickly and correctly are lost. One wonders if children who are encouraged through competition to read rapidly and without error learn to enjoy reading for the pleasure and information that come from such a skill. This type of reading instruction may develop interest in the competition rather than in the reading.

Generally, children are interested in competing because success in a competitive venture brings approval of others and a feeling of accomplishment. Excessive competition, however, may eliminate these satisfactions. People are not interested in individuals who continually strive to be first. Social progress can be impeded by too much competition.

Quarreling. Quarrels, like friendly contacts, increase as the child becomes more mobile and able to communicate to others. The active child who has many social contacts with his contemporaries also has many altercations. Green [36] found that the preschool child quarreled more frequently with his friend than with other children. The friend, of course, is the one with whom the child does his social experimenting.

The cause of quarreling may be quite simple, like accidentally bumping into another child, or it may be complex. Forest,[37] after observing nursery-school children, concluded that quarrels were the result of (1) an accident, (2) children working at cross purposes in play, (3) the desire of the child to feel powerful, and (4) a need to release emotional tensions. Appel [38] found that approximately 36 per cent of preschool conflicts centered about the possession of property, and that another 23 per cent were the result of intrusion or rejection of companionship.

Jersild [39] believes that combativeness may be the result of poor social adjustment or improved social relations. One child may not know how to get the attention and co-operation of the other children. He may try various methods. He may hit a child, push himself between two children who are playing, or attempt some other equally ineffective way of gaining recognition. Another child may be shy and have no quarrels until he improves his social relations. An example of the latter came to the attention of a first-grade teacher. Jimmy, a very timid child, often sat by himself in the corner playing with blocks. Children occasionally interfered with his play by running through his constructions. One day when a child deliberately knocked down his "garage," Jimmy started to fight with the child. This was the first time he had asserted himself—a big step in the improvement of his social relations.

Little research on the causes of quarreling is available on the elementary-school level. Attempts have been made, however, to discover any relationship that may exist between the kind of adult leadership provided for children and children's behavioral reactions. Lippitt and White [40] in a study to determine the effects on group

[36] E. H. Green, Friendships and quarrels among preschool children, *Child Development,* 1933, Vol. 4, pp. 221-248.

[37] Ilse Forest, Amey E. Watson, and Madeleine H. Appel, Nursery school quarrels, *Childhood Education,* 1934, Vol. 10, pp. 314-318.

[38] Madeleine H. Appel, Aggressive behavior of nursery school children and adult procedures in dealing with such behavior, *Journal of Experimental Education,* 1942, Vol. 11, pp. 185-199.

[39] Arthur T. Jersild, *Child Psychology* (New York: Prentice-Hall, 1947), p. 148.

[40] Ronald Lippitt and Ralph K. White, An experimental study of leadership and group life, in *Reading in Social Psychology,* ed. Theodore M. Newcomb, Eugene L. Hartley and others (New York: Henry Holt and Company, 1947) pp. 315-330.

and individual behavior of three types of leadership—authoritarian, democratic, and laissez-faire—found the adult leader role to have a strong influence on the social interaction of a group of children. Those children who were subjected to an authoritarian leader built up frustrations that were channeled into aggressive behavior toward the less acceptable children of the group. This aggression often took the form of blaming and rejecting. In the democratic and laissez-faire atmosphere, the children seemed not to need a scapegoat upon whom to express their aggressions.

Fighting and obvious quarreling seem to be less evident as the children grow older. This may be due to the fact that the activities of the elementary- and junior-high-school children are more routinized and supervised than those of the nursery-school child. Games have specific rules, are often played during the school or club recreation periods, and may be refereed by an adult. After-school activities often include club participation during which there is adult leadership. When the children are not in school, at Boy Scouts, Camp Fire Girls, a church group, or whatever, they are often taking or practicing music lessons, delivering newspapers, or doing odd jobs. Many preadolescents lead a busy life. Sometimes there is little time for unrestricted play. Then, too, these children are becoming more and more aware of social pressures. Parents and townspeople frown upon quarreling and fighting. Those children who have aggressive feelings soon find methods other than quarreling and fighting to express them.

Teasing and bullying may take the place of open conflict. Teasing is a mental attack on another person, sometimes to belittle and conquer him without actually fighting. It generally takes the form of name calling. Bullying is the more open form of attacking. It may involve physical contact with the child, such as pulling hair, pushing, pinching, etc. Generally, boys tease and bully more than girls. Older children are more apt to tease or bully younger children, especially if the younger child is a sibling.

The development of attitudes

A three-year-old was heard to say, "Little boys are to play with little boys, and little girls are to play with little girls. You go home." This attitude seemed to be firmly established. Someone quite close to this child had directly or indirectly influenced her feelings. Surely these conclusions were not the result of careful deliberation.

The source of children's attitudes. Attitudes, such as the above, expressed by preschool and elementary-school children are the result of influences of the general culture, the family, the teacher, other children, and the environment.[41]

Of the factors presented above, the general culture is of basic importance in forming attitudes. Through the other forces, it exerts a tremendous pressure on the feelings of every individual. Those white, Protestant, American-born youngsters who are brought up in areas where there is little feeling against people of different races and religions can rather easily develop a pride in their cultural heritage. They may find it easy, too, to respect the racial and religious backgrounds of others. Children of minority groups born into communities where many tensions exist may acquire quite fundamental attitudes that will color their entire outlook on life.

Attitudes that come as a result of the general culture are first brought to the child through his parents. Frequently, we are amused at the definite opinions held by a preschool youngster. If we know the parents, we can predict many of the child's reactions.

The teacher is one of the first very potent nonfamily influences that will affect the child's attitudes. Teachers by their comments and manner alter to some extent the reaction pattern of children. The influence of any one teacher may have little permanent effect on the child's attitudes, but whether the changes in feelings be permanent or temporary, they appear quickly. Special teachers who work with children from various classes learn to expect certain characteristics to be expressed by the children who are taught by certain teachers. The majority of the children from a class may, year after year, be co-operative and sympathetic when they see a classmate in difficulty, while children from another room may appear to be uninterested and even cruel in a similar situation.

The influence of the neighborhood gang, too, leaves its imprint on youngsters. How much of a force this will be depends upon the background and the age of the child. Preadolescent and adolescent children, because of their strong desire to be accepted by their contemporaries, seem to be more susceptible to the influences of their associates than do younger children.

Characteristics of the community itself affect children's attitudes. Neighborhoods where there is an interest in providing adequate school and recreational facilities, where there is enough civic pride

[41] Lawrence A. Averill, *The Psychology of the Elementary-School Child* (New York: Longmans, Green & Company, 1949), pp. 52-57.

to maintain help and equipment to keep parks and streets clean, and where there is a respect for law and order provide an environment that will do much to encourage wholesome attitudes in their young people.

The intermingling of these forces continually modify the attitudes of the younger generation. These forces are not of equal importance at any time during the child's life, but, if the child is allowed to associate freely with the members of the community, all will exist and play some part in forming attitudes.

Characteristics of attitudes. In the beginning, the attitudes of children are very specific. Feelings about honesty may apply to just one phase of being honest. For example, a child may be trustworthy in matters that involve money, but he may not hesitate to take another child's writing paper or eraser. Another child may have difficulty in understanding that every one has a right to worship as he pleases. A Protestant child may, after associating with a Jewish boy of the neighborhood, feel that it is perfectly all right for a child to be Jewish, but he still may not see that another child has the right to be Catholic. In order to get a child to generalize, it is necessary to give him a great number of experiences and then to help him see relationships.

Attitudes are tinged with emotions. A child's ability to be tolerant and unprejudiced depends not only on his understanding of the issues involved, but also on his emotional stability. Feelings of fear and resentment may hinder social acceptance of some children. Often one's own hurts may drive him to hurt others. Emotions sometimes even more than understanding determine our attitudes.

Favorable attitudes toward an activity or cause may motivate a youngster to action. The preadolescent who really believes that we should help the children of war-torn Europe will work tirelessly with his Junior Red Cross group to collect food and toys to send abroad. The boy who believes that to be a football hero is the most important thing in the world will be careful to select a well-balanced diet, will go to bed early, and will for long hours practice skills needed for the game. No amount of persuasion on the part of the parents has ever made such a drastic change in the child's behavior. If parents and teachers can evoke favorable attitudes toward a desired course of action, more than half the "battle" is won.

Those who work with children and young adults know that attitudes change. Whether this change will be for the better depends upon the effort that is made by parents, teachers, and members of the community to provide a wholesome environment and good instruction for children.

Summary

Social development, like other forms of development, follows an orderly process. The child's first social reactions appear when he comes to distinguish between animate and inanimate things about him. When the child distinguishes the mother or nurse from other members of the family, he is showing signs of social development. Social development is more than mere gregariousness. Social development implies responsiveness. As the child grows socially, he comes to pursue the friendship of some individuals and to reject the friendship of others.

Home relationships and environmental conditions do much to help or hinder the development of good social behavior. Factors such as the adjustment of parents to each other, position in the family, characteristics of the individual child and his siblings, acceptance of the family in the community, and racial and religious background, all influence the social development of an individual child.

Some children are more acceptable to their age mates than others. This was shown by plotting a sociogram of a fifth-grade group. Such children usually rate higher than their less acceptable classmate in personality and they have at least average intelligence and reading ability. Children, when asked to give reasons for selecting certain children as friends, considered such characteristics as being cheerful and friendly as the most important, with availability and similarity of interest and taste coming next.

Very young children seem not to be competitive. Older children are motivated by competition, especially if it is for their own individual gain and if there is an opportunity to succeed. At the preschool level, quarrels are frequent but of short duration. In many cases, these are a result of accidents, social experimentation, or the need to release emotional tension. As the child grows older, his aggression may take forms other than open conflict.

Questions and Exercises

1. Young children seem to pass through stages of behavior. What steps can parents take to make some of the more difficult periods as "painless" for the child and the parents as possible?

2. What can the classroom teacher do to help the child who has no friends become more socially acceptable?

3. Children from authoritarian homes are often so inhibited that it is almost impossible for them to express themselves creatively. What can a classroom teacher do to "free" these children?

4. In what way does a sibling or a lack of a sibling affect the social relations of the child?

5. What is the place of competition in a school situation?

6. Adult leadership may vary from democratic to authoritarian. Do you believe the age of the child has a relationship to the amount of democracy or autocracy that should be provided in this adult leadership?

7. What are the characteristics of a school that wishes to develop good social adjustment in its pupils?

8. How, other than through direct instruction, can a teacher help to develop wholesome attitudes in children?

Selected Readings

Averill, Lawrence A. *The Psychology of the Elementary-School Child.* New York: Longmans, Green & Company, 1949. Chap. III.

Bossard, James H. *The Sociology of Child Development.* New York: Harper & Brothers, 1948.

Gesell, Arnold, and Ilg, Frances L. *Child Development.* New York: Harper & Brothers, 1949.

Hurlock, Elizabeth B. *Child Development.* 2nd ed.; New York: McGraw-Hill Book Company, 1950. Chap. IX.

Jersild, Arthur T. *Child Psychology.* 3rd ed.; New York: Prentice-Hall, 1947. Chaps. V and VI.

Merry, Frieda Kiefer, and Merry, Ralph Vickers. *The First Two Decades of Life.* New York: Harper & Brothers, 1950. Chap. X.

Moreno, J. L. *Who Shall Survive? A New Approach to the Problems of Human Interrelations.* Washington, D. C.: Nervous and Mental Disease Publishing Co., 1934.

Newcomb, Theodore M., Hartley, Eugene L., and others, eds. *Readings in Social Psychology.* New York: Henry Holt and Company, 1947. Chaps. III, VI, VII, VIII, IX, and XI.

Olson, Willard. *Child Development.* Boston: D. C. Heath and Company, 1949. Chap. VIII.

Teagarden, Florence M. *Child Psychology for Professional Workers.* New York: Prentice Hall, 1946. Chaps. VII, VIII, and XIII.

Thorpe, Louis P. *Child Psychology and Development.* New York: The Ronald Press Company, 1946. Chap. XIII.

III

Personality
Development

13

Change of Interests
with Age

Introduction: The growth and significance of interests

In the course of the child's development, interests and habit patterns change with age. At any level of maturity, a child will display interests and behavior acts that will be modified or abandoned in the course of time. The growth and development of interests cannot be separated from other aspects of growth. Furthermore, the principles of development presented in Chapter 4 and subsequent chapters are applicable to the development of interests. These include the idea that behavior activities and interests that are useful at one level of maturity are abandoned at another stage in favor of activities and interests that are more useful and in greater harmony with the organismic developmental level.

The significance of interests. Even though the existing interests of the child may be faint or limited in scope, they provide the basis for possible expansion so as to embrace other more distant experiences. Thus, a child who displays an interest in Indians, even though his knowledge is only that which he has gained through the movies, has already acquired a focal point for the development of further knowledge and understanding of the life and activities of Indians of the past as well as of the present. When children develop an interest in the growth of flowers or some other plant life, their attention and understanding can be guided more readily into the acquisition of an increased knowledge of plant life and culture. During some of the elementary experiences with the growth of plants around the school or at home, other more highly technical interests may be developed that can be followed into an ever-enlarging sphere to enrich their educational development.

The job of the teacher is to find some ways of connecting worth-while information and skills with existing interests. Through this connection, education becomes personal, worth-while, and meaningful to the child. It might be stated that the presence of interest in any school activity is an indication of educational health, while its absence is a sign of a lack of adjustment between the child and the school program. The teaching of counting becomes a simple process for the boy or girl when this provides a means of determining how many school days there are until Christmas. Studies of learning in the sciences show that meanings, interests, and increased knowledge and understanding go along together. The learning of chemistry is well-nigh fruitless for the girl, if the formulas and facts are unrelated to things with which she is somewhat familiar. In substance, personal interests might be called the starting point of instruction, a readiness for learning and growth in an increased understanding and widened interests.

The role of learning. Oftentimes, teachers and others point out the need for basing instruction upon the child's interest, as if interests exist as some separate entity that can mysteriously be found in the child's life and used as a basis for all learning. Actually, interests are learned as truly as is the case for any other learning. Furthermore, they are not learned as something separate and apart from the acquisition of skills, information, attitudes, and habit patterns. An educational policy of utilizing a child's interest in learning new materials may be misleading. The learning process involved in the acquisition of understandings should include the growth of interest. Under favorable conditions, growth in understanding and interests would take place simultaneously as phases of the total growth of the individual child.

A question may be raised at this point as to how interests develop. In this connection, it might be stated that a child's interests are closely related to his needs. Factors or conditions conducive to the satisfaction of needs will contribute to the development of interests. It may be stated further that interests are based on experiences—experiences conducive to the satisfaction of needs. Such experiences should be meaningful, significant, and successful. For a situation to be interesting to the child, it must have meaning for him. This does not mean that he must understand the complete operation of all the elements of the situation. Also the child may not have an exact understanding of the situation as it exists; nevertheless, he is able to give his interpretations to certain elements of the situation. Other phases of the situation may not be understood, and curiosity is attached to such elements. The situation stimulating the child's interest is also significant. He sees some elements of importance and value in it. These values are of course interpreted in terms of his own needs and satisfactions; but to him they are very real. Success is involved in connection with interests, in that the child must be successful in the interpretation and understanding of the situation, and, if the interest is to grow, must be successful in reaching a better understanding of the situation and in attaining satisfaction from the pursuance of activities related to it.

Factors limiting a child's interests. It has already been implied that a child's interest in a particular object, condition, or situation will be limited by his ability to understand and interpret it in accordance with certain values and needs he may have. A child reared in an urban environment will have had very limited experiences with animals. His conception of animals may be based on experiences with animals seen through cages and fences at the zoo and circus. Thus, his interest in the small colt on the farm will be colored by fear and curiosity. He may look with awe and suspicion at the colt as it follows its mother into the fields and over the hills; but he will not have the abiding interest and admiration for the colt felt by the boy on the farm who understands and appreciates the habits of the horse.

Again, interests are going to be seriously limited by one's constitutional equipment. There will be an enormous difference in the nature and depth of interest in music of two boys with somewhat similar experiences, but differing considerably in constitutional ability to learn, understand, and appreciate various aspects of music. This was recently observed by the writer in the case of two boys from the same family. Although no claim is made here that their experiences with music were identical, those experiences were sufficiently similar to discount efforts to ascribe all differences in interest in music to environmental conditions and opportunities. Although neither boy was given training in music, as children, one showed considerable interest in music whereas the other boy showed very little interest in music. The interest of the one boy was manifested in such ways as the choice of radio programs, the phase of the movie and type of movie liked best, singing games and other activities pursued at home and in the neighborhood, special school activities, participation in the choir at church, and the like.

The development of an interest appears to be the result of the interaction of many forces and conditions in the life of a single child. It cannot be explained on an all-or-none principle. Neither can it be explained on the basis of so many separate forces acting independently. The interests of a child may be restricted by the absence or limitations of any forces or conditions which affect its development.

Play activities

Play and development. The growth of the child physically, mentally, and socially is reflected in the nature of his play. Play at first is quite simple, consisting primarily of random movements of the arms and legs. It was pointed out in Chapter 6 that out of these random movements skills develop. There is a close relationship between the development of skills and the play life of the child. The importance of practice in harmony with the maturation level of the child has been emphasized throughout previous chapters. The play of the infant child is reflected in his touching, pulling, and pushing things around him. This is his means for exploring the world of things, and such experiences broaden his interests and extend his range of muscular skills. The play of the child after the stage of infancy is gradually but continuously extended into other areas and involves other people. There are four different forms of play engaged in by young children: (1) random movements and activities that are not directed toward any particular goal; (2) free play of an individualistic nature, which may or may not involve others, directed toward the fulfillment of certain goals; (3) make-believe play that ascribes attributes to things with which they are playing, attributes which they do not actually possess; and (4) constructive play which takes on added meaning and significance with the child's growth and development.

It has already been suggested that random movements, gurgling, and the like characterize the play life of the infant. With increased development, the infant's movements are better co-ordinated and he is able to make use of simple toys in his play. The spontaneous play life of the baby at this stage is characterized by an exploratory nature. He pulls at his toys, twists them, bites them, and thus unintentionally breaks them. By the time the child reaches his second birthday, his attention is likely to be directed toward meaningful elements of toys. The toy is now used not merely for exploring but as an object or thing with certain simple attributes. The doll is animated and personified. The toy dog may bark. Two or three blocks become a train. The make-believe play of the child is based on the culture around him. On the farm, sticks may become horses and cows. The fire engine becomes prominent in the make-believe play of the urban child. Make-believe play increases with age after the second birthday so that the four-year-old gives evidence of being very creative. The nature of the creative ability of the preschool child was described in Chapter 12. The play material used by the four- and five-year-old child is considerably more complicated than that used by younger children. The blocks are now used to make a house, or some other structure, rather than merely given some make-believe names with assigned attributes.

Some forms of make-believe play. It has already been suggested that through make-believe play children tend to mirror the culture of their community and to some degree the spirit of the particular period. The changed nature of the make-believe play of children during World War II illustrates the effects of the spirit of the age on play. Both boys and girls showed an intense interest in make-believe play involving soldiers, guns, tanks, airplanes, and other activities and mechanisms related to war.

In the study of play among preschool children, Parten found that "playing house" was very popular among children as early as two years of age.[1] The size of the play group increases with age so that at five or six years of age they play in groups of three or four. Their play at this stage is still largely unisexual, although in much of their make-believe play a recognition of the sexes is evident. Both boy-baby dolls and girl-baby dolls are to be found in their playhouses. The girl may play the role of a mother with lots of children. The boy may be seen playing the role of a cowboy, riding and shooting.

Age differences in toy preferences. Toy manufacturers have been interested in devising toys suitable for the different age levels. Toys have been developed not only for different age levels, but also in harmony with the special interests of boys and girls of different ages. Rattles and other toys that make a noise seem to be enjoyed during the first two years. Children, after the first year of life, enjoy blocks that can be handled, and pile one on top of another. They en-

[1] M. B. Parten, Social play among preschool children, *Journal of Abnormal and Social Psychology*, 1933, Vol. 28, pp. 136-147.

joy playthings that they can bang, and simple two- or three-piece toys that can be taken apart and put back together.

Toddlers like to play with toys that can be pushed around or handled. The little girl enjoys the doll carriage with her doll, while the little boy prefers the cars, airplanes, wagons, and the like. This was shown in a study conducted a number of years ago by Harold Benjamin.[2] The toy preferences of young children aged two to six years was studied by observing their choice of toys from a group of six toys. These toys were selected on the basis of similar size, cost, color, and general attractiveness for subjects of the particular age group, and consisted of a car, girl doll, horse, powder (a cylindrical vanity case), airplane, and boy doll. Toy preference was studied by the amount of time each toy was played with and by each child's special choice of a toy. The girl doll was most commonly chosen by the girls, although the boy doll was most frequently chosen at the fourteen- to twenty-one-month level. The airplane was frequently chosen after the third-year level. The car and airplane were selected an equal number of times by the boys, although the airplane was most frequently chosen at the ages forty-six to fifty-three months and fifty-four to sixty-one months. The boy doll was chosen by two of the boys at the fourteen- to twenty-one-month level. It appears that with age an increased sex differential in preference appears. This is no doubt in line with the training and conditioning afforded by our culture. The boys turn more and more toward automobiles, airplanes, and soldiers as they reach their fifth birthday, while the girls develop more elaborate techniques for caring for their dolls and playhouse equipment.

The kindergarten years provide opportunities for boys and girls to play together, and their activities are oftentime somewhat complementary to each other, although there is still little sex differentiation in connection with activities of a competitive nature. Interest in group play is manifested after the age of six. Clay, paints, and other materials of this nature are useful for their development. Boys are definitely interested in wheel toys and construction sets. Both boys and girls enjoy active games. Girls become particularly interested in jumping rope, and, as suggested in Chapter 6, have developed sufficient co-ordination to engage in such activities along with hopping and skipping. Both boys and girls find skates an endless source of fun. There is good evidence that toys at this age need

[2] Harold Benjamin, Age and sex differences in the toy preferences of young children, *Journal of Genetic Psychology,* 1933, Vol. 41, pp. 417-429.

not be expensive or elaborate. Boys and girls may improvise see-saws, swings, and other means for engaging in physical activity, if they are given the opportunity and the meager materials necessary for such activities.

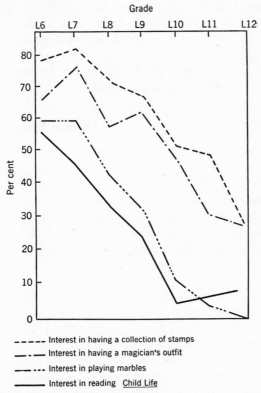

FIG. 40 Changes of four childhood interests with change of grade status

(After Jones)

The *Lehman Play Quiz* was used by Lehman and Witty for studying periodicity in play for the ages seven and one-half to nineteen and one-half years.[3] No single age was found at which there was an abrupt change in the nature of interests. They concluded from their studies that the change of play interests that characterize a given age group appears to be gradual in nature, in harmony with other growth changes taking place. This is further shown in the

[3] H. C. Lehman and P. A. Witty, Periodicity and play behavior, *Journal of Educational Psychology*, 1927, Vol. 18, pp. 115-118.

study reported by Jones, in which the *University of California Interest Record* was administered to a group of boys beginning with the high sixth grade.[4] A group of activities in which there is a decided decline in play interests is shown in Figure 40. These curves show that beginning with the seventh-grade boys, there is a rapid and continuous decline in early childhood interests in marble playing, collecting stamps, the magician's outfit, and reading *Child Life*. The extent to which these interests are replaced by more mature interests is a good measure of the social development and sexual maturation of the adolescent boy and girl.

Wishes, likes, and dislikes

The play life of the child usually reflects his wishes, likes, and dislikes. If we were able to penetrate the motives and feelings of the child in his everyday activities, we would get a much better notion of the nature and problems of the child. Child psychologists, psychoanalysts, and psychiatrists have endeavored to arrive at interpretations of the free expressions of children. Some of the results from such efforts have led to projective techniques for studying personality, and to an interpretation of the dynamics of children at different age levels.

Age and sex differences in wishes. The *Wishes and Fears Inventory,* formulated by Martin L. Reymert, has been used for a number of years at the Mooseheart Laboratory for Child Research. Twelve inventories for boys and twelve for girls were selected at each of three age ranges—from seven years to eight years, from eleven years to thirteen years, and from fifteen years to seventeen years. In each group of twelve selected for study, six were selected from children with IQ's ranging between 90 and 110, three from IQ's ranging below 90, and three from IQ's ranging above 110. Responses to the inventories were obtained during a personal interview with each child after rapport had been established. The responses were then tabulated and the frequency of each type of response determined. A summary of the significant age and sex differences to the "Wishes" is presented in Table 44.[5]

The wish "to be someone" was mentioned significantly more by the

[4] Harold E. Jones, *Development in Adolescence* (New York: Appleton-Century-Crofts, 1948), p. 104.

[5] James B. Winkler, Age trends and sex differences in the wishes, identifications, activities and fears of children, *Child Development,* 1949, Vol. 20, pp. 191-200.

TABLE 44   Significant age and sex differences in the wishes of children (after Winkler)

Categories of Wishes	Percentage of Responses				
	7 & 8	11 & 12	15 & 16	BOYS	GIRLS
To have material things	88.4	48.3	23.2	50.3	52.5
To be someone	0	16.7	21.4	12.8	8.1
For toys	47.8	18.3	3.6	26.7	23.2
For vocation	0	5.0	14.2	7.0	5.1

fifteen- and sixteen-year-olds than by the younger groups, while the wish "to have material things" was mentioned most frequently by the younger group. This is in harmony with findings by Jersild and others, who have pointed out from their studies that there is a marked decline with age in wishes for specific materials, objects, and possessions.[6] This decline, accompanied by the rise in interest in being someone relatively important, is a reflection of the concept of the child's idea of what provides for status. It is also a reflection of the child's mental and social development.

A study closely related to the one conducted by Winkler was made with second-, fourth-, and sixth-grade pupils as subjects.[7] This study was primarily concerned with the fears and ideals of 344 elementary-school children. An analysis of the ideals of these children showed that characters from movies, comics, and the radio were more often listed as ideals by fourth-grade children than by either older or younger children. Table 45 shows the extent to which boys and

TABLE 45   The per cent of boys and girls from different grades choosing as ideals masculine and feminine characters (after Stroughton and Ray)

	Grade 2		Grade 4		Grade 6		All Grades	
	BOYS	GIRLS	BOYS	GIRLS	BOYS	GIRLS	BOYS	GIRLS
Masculine characters	85	11	95	11	94	7	92	9
Feminine characters	10	86	5	87	5	92	6	89

[6] A. T. Jersild, F. V. Markey, and C. L. Jersild, Children's fears, dreams, wishes, daydreams, likes, dislikes, pleasant and unpleasant memories, *Child Development Monographs*, 1933, No. 12.

[7] M. L. Stroughton and A. M. Ray, A study of children's fears and ideals, *Journal of Experimental Education*, 1946, Vol. 15, p. 157.

girls chose masculine and feminine characters as ideals. Both boys and girls tended to choose as ideals characters from their own sex; however, girls in each of the grades studied chose a larger percentage of ideals from the opposite sex than did the boys.

The University of California Inventory I: Social and Emotional Adjustment was given seven times to groups of adolescent boys and girls in April or May of each year, beginning in 1932 with groups in the high-fifth and low-sixth grades.[8] Some of the items dealt with fears and wishes. Table 45 gives the percentage of boys and girls wishing for certain items from a list of thirteen. The desire to be grown up and to get away from home was not manifested by many boys or girls and showed little change with age. The desire to be bigger was expressed by a majority of the girls at each age level. This desire appeared to increase among the boys with advance in age level. "To be better looking" was not one of the foremost wishes among boys, but was indicated by a large percentage of girls at each age level and appeared to increase with advanced age. The desire to be bigger and the desire to be stronger are closely associated with masculine aspirations during the growing years. After the fifth- and sixth-grade levels, very few girls wished to be stronger and larger. The need for money seems to be felt by both boys and girls as revealed in their wishes at all grade levels, although this was not the paramount wish of this group of boys and girls.

Some race differences in wishes. Susan Gray compared the wishes of Negro elementary-school children with those reported by Boynton for white school children.[9] The children ranged from grades one to six in a fairly large Negro school in Nashville, Tennessee. Each child was asked the question: "If you could have anything in all the world that you might want, just *anything,* what would you ask for?" Sufficient records were available on 820 pupils for inclusion in the study. The desire for a bicycle is clearly shown for both boys and girls throughout the preadolescent and adolescent years.

A comparison of these results with those obtained by Boynton revealed some differences; however, the basic similarities of the wishes of the two groups at the different age levels overshadowed

---

[8] *U. C. Inventory I: Social and Emotional Adjustment.* Revised Form for Presentation of the Cumulative Record of an Individual, with Group Norms by Items for a Seven-Year period. Two forms are available, one for boys and the other one for girls. This was prepared by Caroline M. Tryon.

[9] Susan Gray, The wishes of Negro school children, *Journal of Genetic Psychology,* 1944, Vol. 64, pp. 225-237.

TABLE 46 The percentage of girls and boys expressing certain wishes at different grade levels from the H-Fifth and L-Sixth to the H-Eleventh and L-Twelfth Grades in school

		Years						
Wishes		'32	'33	'34	'35	'36	'37	'38
To be grown-up and get	Boys	6	4	0	3	1	3	3
away from home	Girls	0	1	1	3	6	4	6
To be brighter than I am	Boys	46	61	59	51	58	63	68
now	Girls	61	69	68	53	57	61	56
To be better looking	Boys	10	18	13	11	13	18	11
	Girls	41	37	50	54	49	58	54
To be bigger than I am	Boys	23	20	18	27	31	25	25
now	Girls	18	15	18	12	8	11	7
To have more money to	Boys	24	17	15	20	28	34	32
spend	Girls	18	18	18	31	32	34	49
To be stronger than I am	Boys	80	75	76	66	48	54	55
now	Girls	39	25	12	6	15	8	10

these differences.[10] This similarity supports the idea presented earlier in this chapter about the origin of interests out of experiences that are meaningful and significant to the individual concerned. Some race differences noted are listed as follows:

1. The Negro children gave more wishes related to the home.
2. White children gave slightly more wishes related to animals, and especially the wish for a pony.
3. Negro children, specifically girls, gave more wishes for a piano.
4. There were less scattering of responses in the wishes of the Negro children than of the white children.

Age differences in identifications of wishes and fears. When the seven- and eight-year-olds of the study by James Winkler were asked whom they would like to be like, more than one-half of them named someone in their family.[11] The results from this question and the question concerning whom they would not desire to be like are shown in Table 47. The eleven- and twelve-year-olds were more interested in being like someone who plays a general role in our society, such as an athlete, a movie star, a cowboy, or a policeman; however, more

[10] Paul L. Boynton, The wishes of elementary school children, *Peabody Journal of Education*, 1936, Vol. 13, pp. 165-174.
[11] *Op. cit.*, p. 195.

than one-fourth of this age group showed a greater interest in being like some particular well-known person. The fifteen- and sixteen-year-olds reflected in their answers to this question the "hero worship" complex, which is somewhat characteristic of adolescence. This hero worship has at times been explained as a process of identification, in which the adolescent is trying to identify himself with the hero in question. In choosing someone outside the family whom they would like to be like, the fifteen- and sixteen-year-olds are showing their growing independence, which is one of the roles the adolescent must learn.

TABLE 47 Age differences in the types of identifications on the wishes and fears inventory (after Winkler)

Age Differences	Type I GENERAL ROLES	Type II WELL-KNOWN PERSON	Type III FAMILY	Type IV PERSON-ALLY KNOWN	Type V SELF
Positive Identifications					
7 and 8	33.3	12.1	51.5	3.0	0
11 and 12	50.0	27.5	20.0	2.5	0
15 and 16	15.6	43.8	12.5	18.8	9.4
Negative Identifications					
7 and 8	31.6	0	10.5	57.9	...
11 and 12	61.5	30.8	0	7.7	...
15 and 16	56.3	31.3	0	12.5	...

A study of the negative identifications is also of interest. The negative identifications of the seven- and eight-year-olds centered to a large degree around persons whom they knew outside the family circle. These choices reflect the experiences of these boys and girls. Older children, since their experiences are broader, are acquainted with various types of people and with certain well-known people whom they do not wish to be like. And, although many of these differences are not statistically reliable, they denote trends that are in harmony with results from other studies as well as general hypotheses and conclusions presented from different sources about child nature. Winkler concludes with regard to sex differences: "Girls in this study showed greater identification with those people in face-to-face contacts where social relationships are of prime importance while the boys were more interested in people who had important roles and status in our society."

Parental preferences of children. Closely related to the wishes, likes, and dislikes of children is the problem of parental preference. Considerable interest has been manifested, both theoretical and practical, in the problem of which parent a child prefers, and why. According to certain psychoanalytic interpretations, there is an inherent inclination for the child to prefer the parent of the opposite sex. This theory is an expression of the Oedipus complex, which claims that there is an innate unconscious sexual desire among sons for their mothers, and among daughters for their fathers. Studies of preferences of children in different cultures indicate that such a choice does not necessarily occur.

In our own culture, there has been provided some evidence for the Oedipus-complex theory. Most studies, however, indicate a mother-preference for the majority of both boys and girls. Margaret Simpson reports preferences in favor of the mothers from 500 children, five to nine years of age, using indirect means of ascertaining filial preference, such as reactions to pictures and stories.[12] She reported that 70 per cent of the girls and 61 per cent of the boys favored the mothers. Similar findings were reported by Jersild and others from a study of 400 children between the ages of five and twelve.[13]

The craving of the infant is for satisfaction rather than a particular person. Case studies show that he will become affectionately attached to a nurse, if she provides him satisfaction. Furthermore, studies of adopted children show that they become closely attached to their foster parents and this moves out and embraces their foster grand parents, when conditions are favorable for the development and expansion of such affectionate relationships. If the child prefers the mother, the explanation appears to lie in her relationship with him in satisfying his needs, rather than some genetic sex-linked determiner. Restrictive discipline and companionship have been offered by Meyer Nimkoff as two important factors in determining the child's reactions to his parents.[14] Evidence is offered by Nimkoff from studies of preferences of children reared in different cultures. He cites the cases of the Marquesans and the Manus children who,

[12] Margaret Simpson, Parent preference of young children, Teachers College, Columbia University, *Contributions to Education*, No. 652, 1935.

[13] Arthur T. Jersild, Frances V. Markey, and Catherine T. Jersild, Fears, dreams, wishes, daydreams, likes, dislikes, pleasant and unpleasant memories, *Child Development Monographs*, No. 12, 1933.

[14] Meyer F. Nimkoff, Child's preference for father or mother, *American Sociological Review*, 1942, Vol. 7, pp. 517-524.

because of certain customs, come to prefer the father to the mother. Further cases are cited where there is training from early childhood for nondependence, and children show little affection for either parent. Biographies are analyzed and studied in relation to parental preference. The conclusions from these studies support the hypothesis that discipline and companionship are two most important factors affecting these preferences. In most cases the mother, beginning early in life, provides for the child's needs and furnishes companionship for him. Where discipline and companionship are both present, it appears that companionship exerts the greater influence. A parent may be the disciplinary power in the home, but if such a parent administers the discipline in a spirit of fairness and affection, and retains the companion relationship, the child will continue to love the parent and show preference for such a parent.

Interests related to school life

Change of reading interests with age. The reading of the kindergarten and elementary-school child tends to follow a more or less definite pattern. In general, small children like small books with attractive pictures and short stories about animals and other children. The boys at this age care less for the fairy stories than do the girls. During middle childhood, boys seem to like adventure stories related to war, hunting, fishing, and daring escapades, while girls continue some interest in fairy stories and show a distinct interest in tales of home and school life. In order to determine which books

TABLE 48 Book favorites—kindergarten children

Author	Title	Rank
	Little Golden Book of Fairy Tales	1.0
Flack	Angus and the Ducks	2.0
Bannerman	Little Black Sambo	4.5
Gruelle	Raggedy Ann	4.5
Lindman	Snipp, Snapp, Snurr books	4.5
Potter	Tale of Peter Rabbit	4.5
Flack	Ask Mr. Bear	10.5
"	Story about Ping	10.5
Friskey	Seven Diving Ducks	10.5
Huber	I Know a Story	10.5
Lowrey	Poky Little Puppy	10.5
Grimm (illustrated by Wehr)	Hansel and Gretel	10.5
Bishop	Five Chinese Brothers	10.5
Flack	Restless Robin	10.5

are favorite with pupils, Witty, Coomer, and McBean studied the books preferred by kindergarten children and children at different grade levels.[15]

In the kindergarten and in the first three grades, the children simply listed the stories they liked best. Their teachers reported the choices of the pupils. The titles most commonly listed as favorites by the kindergarten and primary-grade children are listed in Tables 48 and 49. These choices show a fairly close relation to standard book lists insofar as grade level is concerned. The kindergarten children named books, of course, which had been read to them but which appealed to their interest.

TABLE 49   Book favorites—primary grades (I-III)

Author	Title	Rank
Salten (Disney version)	Bambi	2.0
Bannerman	Little Black Sambo	2.0
McCloskey	Make Way for Ducklings	2.0
Lang	Cinderella	4.0
Collodi (Disney version)	Pinocchio	5.0
Anderson	Billy and Blaze	6.5
Austin	Peter Churchmouse	6.5
Gag	Snippy and Snappy	8.0
Piper	The Little Engine That Could	9.5
Barnett	They Hunted High and Low	9.5
Disney	Donald Duck and His Nephews	12.0
Huber	It Happened One Day	12.0
Grimm	Fairy Tales	12.0

In the study by Witty and Coomer, 7,879 children from grades four through eight were asked to list the five books they had read and enjoyed during the year. The titles most commonly listed are presented in Tables 50 and 51. Each title was listed from 18 to 195 times. It is significant that poetry finds such a small place among the children's interests. Only one book of poetry, *Little Brown Baby,* was found among the composite list of titles given at the different grade levels, and this did not merit consideration among the most frequently selected. This may be a result of the way in which poetry is usually presented to the child. Perhaps an increased interest in poetry may result from the experimental procedures of encouraging children to write their own poetry—free expression. The creative

[15] Paul Witty, Ann Coomer, and Dilla McBean, Children's choices of favorite books: a study conducted in ten elementary schools, *Journal of Educational Psychology*, 1946, Vol. 37, pp. 266-278.

ability of the child, discussed in Chapter 11, when expressed in writing poetry, should provide for greater interest and increased appreciation for materials of this type.

TABLE 50 Book favorites of the intermediate grades (IV-VI)

Author	Title	Rank
Knight	Lassie Come Home	1.0
Atwater	Mr. Popper's Penguins	2.0
Sewell	Black Beauty	3.0
Clemens	Adventures of Tom Sawyer	4.0
	Fairy Stories (no edition given)	5.0
Rains	Lazy Liza Lizard	6.0
McCloskey	Homer Price	7.0
Grimm	Fairy Tales	8.0
Estes	Moffat books	9.0
Brooks	Freddy the Detective	10.0
Geisel	The Five Hundred Hats of Bartholomew Cubbins	11.5
O'Brien	Silver Chief	11.5
Lofting	Dr. Dolittle books	13.0
	Arabian Knights Entertainment	14.0
Spyri	Heidi	15.0

TABLE 51 Book favorites—upper grades (VII-VIII)

Author	Title	Rank
Knight	Lassie Come Home	1.0
Estes	Moffat books	2.0
Boylston	Sue Barton books	3.0
Tunis	Keystone Kids	4.0
O'Brien	Silver Chief	5.0
Terhune	Lad: A Dog	6.0
Tunis	All American	7.0
Brink	Caddie Woodlawn	8.0
Sperry	Call It Courage	9.0
Stevenson	Treasure Island	10.0
Sewell	Black Beauty	11.0
Tunis	Kid from Tomkinsville	12.0
Forbes	Johnny Tremain	13.0
Clemens	Adventures of Tom Sawyer	14.5
Seredy	The Good Master	14.5
Beals	Davy Crockett	17.0
O'Hara	My Friend Flicka	17.0
Tunis	Champion's Choice	17.0

Things liked best in school. A study of children's interests reported by Jersild and Tasch showed that, at all grade levels, items in the category that includes study and academic subject-matter areas were mentioned most frequently when children stated what they liked best in school.[16] Nature study and the natural sciences were not listed by primary-grade children, were mentioned infrequently by nine- to twelve-year-old children, and showed a gain in popularity at the junior- and senior-high-school levels—grades seven-nine and ten-twelve (See Table 52.) Sports ranked third in interest for chil-

TABLE 52   What I like best in school (after Jersild and Tasch)

Category	Ages 9–12		Ages 12–15		Ages 15–18	
	BOYS	GIRLS	BOYS	GIRLS	BOYS	GIRLS
Sports, games, physical education	13.3	9.5	30.6	33.2	34.8	34.4
Areas of study, subject matter	69.7	76.3	44.4	60.1	41.3	45.5
Art activity or appreciation: music, painting, drawing	11.1	14.8	10.0	15.9	16.2	13.8
Crafts, mechanical arts	.3	0	19.8	0	15.5	.4
Discussion clubs, student council	1.3	.8	1.0	.5	3.6	6.4
People: both pupils and teachers	2.5	6.1	4.1	5.6	6.0	11.4

dren in grades 1-3, while a continuous growth of this interest with advancing grade is revealed in Table 52. The results of this study show a decline of interest in the academic areas and art activities, which reach their highest point in grades 1-3, and an increased interest in sports, games, discussion clubs, student council, and the category of people. This is to be expected, since with growth and development the child reaches into a larger area of meaningful and significant experiences and finds new and enlarged interests in his new-found abilities and experiences.

The California growth study furnishes data about things in school disliked by boys and girls at different periods of their development.[17] An inventory consisting of fifty items, entitled "Things You Do Not Like About School," was checked annually by a group of boys and girls for seven consecutive years. The responses of these students to items involving teacher-pupil relationships are presented in Table 54. The number of students checking each of the seven items listed at the first checking (H5 L6), the fourth checking (H8 L9), and the

[16] A. T. Jersild and Ruth J. Tasch, *Children's Interests* (Teachers College, Columbia University, Bureau of Publications, 1949).
[17] *Op. cit.*

TABLE 53 Percentage of boys and girls from grades 1-3 choosing various things liked best in school (after Jersild and Tasch)

	Boys	Girls	Total
Areas of study	69.5	66.9	68.2
Art activities, etc.	13.2	17.4	15.3
Sports, games, etc.	11.5	8.0	9.8
People	1.6	1.8	1.7
Physical plant and facilities	1.1	1.8	1.5
Assembly	.4	2.2	1.3
Miscellaneous school demands	1.2	.8	1.0
Monitor duties	.2	1.0	.6
Movies, theater	0	1.1	.5
Self-improvement	.4	.2	.3
Crafts	0	.4	.2

seventh checking (H11 L12) are presented as a basis for showing changes in things disliked with advancing grades. At each of the stages shown, there is a strong dislike for activities on the part of the teachers regarded as unfair. All the items listed, with the exception of the one dealing with being made to feel embarrassed, were checked more frequently by the boys at all grade levels than by the girls. This indicates that, in general, there are more boys than girls who find displeasure in their relations with teachers at school. The changes with advancing grade are not significant.

TABLE 54 Aspects of the school situation disliked by adolescents: Teachers and discipline

Aspect	H5 L6 *		H8 L9 *		H11 L12 *	
	BOYS	GIRLS	BOYS	GIRLS	BOYS	GIRLS
Being punished for things you do not do	69	58	69	56	59	36
Teachers who are not interested in their pupils	30	26	38	33	34	44
Teachers who make one feel embarrassed before the class	51	46	54	67	46	60
Teachers who mark you down because they do not like you	49	39	68	65	58	54
Examinations that are unfair	35	25	65	51	62	49
Too many teachers' pets	61	42	49	39	38	22
Teachers who have the wrong opinion about you	30	28	52	51	51	36

* H5 refers to high-fifth; L6 refers to low-sixth; and likewise for H8, L9, H11, and L12.

Items from the inventory bearing on attitudes toward classmates which were most frequently checked are presented in Table 55.[18] There appears a gradual and continuous decline from the high-fifth

TABLE 55   Aspects of school life disliked by adolescents: Attitudes toward classmates

	H5 BOYS	L6 * GIRLS	H8 BOYS	L9 * GIRLS	H11 BOYS	L12 * GIRLS
Classmates who plan games or hikes or parties and then won't let others in on the fun	45	32	20	25	15	7
Groups or gangs or crowds that won't have anything to do with pupils outside of these groups	42	31	21	26	11	26
Having some of the pupils start a club which they won't let others into	39	31	17	14	8	6
Having the classmates you like most turn out to be stuck-up	45	44	24	22	30	11
One's classmates are snobbish and stuck-up	39	44	27	37	30	21
Having certain pupils run everything in the school	61	49	38	43	37	46
Classmates whispering and making fun of one behind one's back	55	47	20	26	23	10
Having a few pupils in the school make fun of some of the other pupils	46	42	18	25	10	15
Being laughed at when one recited in class	29	35	35	35	23	21
Being called nicknames	18	11	3	8	0	0

* H5 refers to high-fifth; L6 refers to low-sixth; and likewise for H8, L9, H11, and L12.

to the eleventh and twelfth grades in per cent of boys and girls who checked items connected with the tendency of cliques to form and exclude certain people from them. Boys dislike the practice of closed groups, cliques, and other forms of exclusions more than do girls.

[18] For a further discussion of these items and a method for using the inventory for studying the development of an individual during the preadolescent and adolescent years, see H. R. Jones, *Development in Adolescence* (New York: Appleton-Century-Crofts, 1948).

Special interests at school. It has already been suggested that children show a widespread interest in study activities, art, and sport events during the elementary-school period. The potency of some of these interests changes with age and grade status. A study of the grade trends in the interests of elementary-school children was conducted by William McGehee at North Carolina State College.[19] The purpose of the study was twofold: (1) to determine whether interests in certain hobbies decrease or increase as the grade level changes; and (2) to find out whether certain types of interests, (a) social or nonsocial, (b) sedentary or nonsedentary, and (c) intellectual or nonintellectual, increase or decrease as the child advances in school.

One thousand children of each sex at each grade level (grades four through eight) were selected at random from 455 schools in 310 communities in 36 states. The teachers of these children were sent a list of twenty-one hobbies and requested to designate the hobby or hobbies of each child selected for study. The hobbies of these children were then tabulated by grade and sex. No clear-cut trend was noted in the change of interest for boys or girls with advancing grade in the hobbies of reading novels, quiet games, sewing, and religious activity. There were no pronounced changes with grade for boys in listening to the radio and dramatics. Boys' interest in housework showed a decrease, while girls' interest in make-believe increased. Both boys and girls showed an increased interest with grade in working, social clubs, and scouting. There was an increased interest noted for the boys in reading comics, while girls showed an increased interest with grade in active games, playing musical instruments, listening to the radio, going to the show, traveling, collecting, and driving a car. This increased interest on the part of girls for a wide range of activities is closely associated with their expanding environment. The environment and activities of the boys at the time they are in the fourth grade are usually not so limited as that of the girls. This may account, in part at least, for the lack of any pronounced changes with advancing grade status in the interests of boys in the activities listed. These findings indicate that there are changes in interests in certain hobbies with change in grade status. These changes appear to be functions of certain hobbies rather than general types of interests. The boy who is interested in "Superman" when in the fourth grade will perhaps show an interest in the

[19] William McGehee, Change in interest with change in grade status of elementary school children, *Journal of Educational Psychology,* 1941, Vol. 33, pp. 151-156.

comics and other materials of a similar type at a later stage. This change follows the idea set forth earlier that interests grow out of interests, and that the growth of interests tends to follow orderly sequences.

With respect to the second question with which the study by McGehee was concerned, no clear-cut trends in change of types of interests were found. Furthermore, when an interest in one category registered a decrease, such as nonsocial, there was not found to be a corresponding increase in the opposite category (in this case, social). There is some support here for the principle of development of interests being gradual and continuous in nature. A child who is inclined to be nonsocial is quite likely to remain nonsocial. This does not mean that changes in types of interests cannot be made, but rather that such changes are not likely to be made. The likelihood of such changes will be conditioned by the age of the child, changes in types of situations with which he is confronted, changes in treatment, and other factors related to his growth and development.

Out-of-school interests

Change of interests in movies with age. The young child's interest in movies is at first very similar to that involved in reading, in that he prefers comics and animated films. At a later stage, children become interested in Western movies and adventure stories. According to the material presented in Table 56 from studies reported by Gesell and Ilg, boys at nine years of age like action, war, cowboy, and Indian pictures.[20] At this age neither boys nor girls show an intense interest in love stories.

Around 50 per cent of boys and girls at ages eight to eleven attend at least one show per week and another 35 to 40 per cent attend occasionally. It is evident that the motion picture is an item of importance in the activities and interest of the elementary-school child. Small children get lots of ideas about games from what is seen in pictures. This is reflected in their social games, dress, and cowboy and Indian activities.

Children's interests and tastes in movie entertainment develop and change in harmony with changes found in their reading tastes. Children's Entertainment Films, a British organization, recently obtained the support of British theater managers in surveying the

[20] Arnold Gesell and Frances L. Ilg, *The Child From Five to Ten* (New York: Harper & Brothers, 1946), pp. 372-373.

TABLE 56 Change of interest with age in music, radio, and cinema (after Gesell and Ilg)

2 years

Dances to radio or phonograph music.

Prefers phonograph to radio because it repeats and he can watch it turn.

3 years

Likes to watch and listen to phonograph. Little interest in radio. Can recognize several melodies. May have favorites.

Gallops, jumps, walks, runs in time to music.

4 years

Still prefers phonograph to radio. Some can run phonograph themselves.

Likes to experiment with the piano.

A few can sing songs correctly; can identify simple melodies.

Likes to dramatize songs.

Occasionally listens to children's programs on radio and may be susceptible to admonitions delivered on these programs.

5 years

May pick out tunes on the piano and learn to play a few familiar, simple melodies.

Prefers phonograph records to radio. Likes to play them over and over and to sing or dance to them.

Some listen to scattered radio programs. Likes a combination of music and talking.

May like the advertising jingles on the radio which are repetitive.

A few listen to one or two special programs, favoring those directed to very young children.

Some have attended an occasional child's movie.

6 years

Enjoys own phonograph records.

Radio becoming a great favorite with most. Spends several hours a week listening.

Likes talking programs with some music.

Most have one or two preferred programs to which they listen regularly; prefer adventure stories of children.

Anxious not to miss his particular programs. Asks, "Is it time for my program?"

Likes short home movies about nature, animals or his own life.

Attends cinema occasionally. May become restless, close eyes or cry.

7 years

Craving for piano or dancing lessons. Likes to use various percussion instruments.

Radio now a part of daily diet. Dislikes to miss set programs.

Many listen to late afternoon programs of adventure and shooting. Beginning of interest in Westerns. Likes to have radio turned on loud.

Slight interest in news broadcast; little in music.

Some attend cinema weekly. Others occasionally.

Likes musicals, dancing, singing and animal pictures. Some like adventure movies while others are disturbed by them. Dislikes love stories.

8 years

Less desire to practice on piano. May like to change a passage in a piece to one of own invention. Likes to have an audience as he plays. Also enjoys duets.

Marked interest in radio programs. Most listen to several regular programs each day and do not like to miss these.

Likes late afternoon adventure stories, slap-stick comedies, mysteries, quiz programs and dramas of domestic life.

Frightening programs may influence dreams. Can turn radio off if it becomes too frightening.

Great interest in cinema. Most attend weekly, usually on Saturday.

Boys like action pictures: Westerns, baseball, war. Girls like musicals.

Both like animal and adventure stories and those about children. All dislike love stories.

If movie is too exciting, close eyes, hide heads or go to back of theatre.

9 years

Really applies himself in practical music. Touch is lighter with girls but surer with boys. Enjoys executing staccato or legato notes.

Beginning to be interested in composers.

Listening to radio is constant from late afternoon to bedtime with some.

Knows time and station for programs. Likes teen age serials; detective, mystery, quiz, information, and adult comic programs.

Individual differences with cinema. Some go to weekly cinema, others go on occasion. May want to see one picture several times.

Girls like musicals. Boys like action, war, cowboy, Indian pictures.

Both sexes like animal stories and dislike love stories.

---

reactions of elementary-school children to films.[21] This survey was made with specially prepared questionnaires on which to record the findings. Some of the major findings from this survey are presented for further study:

(1) Pleasing patterns of light and shade and good picture composition give a sense of satisfaction to most children. They all appear to like bright and well-lighted scenes, since these are easy to understand.

(2) Nearly all children enjoy colour, but crude, bright colours may be over-stimulating. Soft pastel shades will often produce little "ohs" and "ahs" of pleasure and are evidently preferable.

(3) A child often finds a scene in a film difficult to understand quickly. For this reason, scenes must be left on the screen long enough for the audience to absorb them. At the same time, action must be brisk and the story must not be allowed to slow down.

(4) Long shots seem to puzzle children. If there are many objects on the screen at once, it is not easy for them to pick out the ones that are essential to the story.... Children find close-ups easy to understand and absorbingly interesting.

(5) It has become increasingly clear that any violent action should take place in a long view and never in a close-up.... Fights viewed from a distance are too remote to be real and frightening.

21 Children prefer close ups ... audience survey shows, *Canadian Film News*, 1950, Vol. 2, No. 1.

(6) A children's audience does not like surprises. It prefers to know what is going to happen and then having the satisfaction of seeing its expectations realized, and its sense of importance increased by knowing more than the characters of the screen.

(7) Children identify themselves so much with what is happening on the screen, if it is within their comprehension, that the greatest care needs to be taken not to over-tire them.

(8) Natural sound, especially bird song, appeals to children. So does music which is so fitted to the picture that the eye and ear are satisfied simultaneously.

Another British study, conducted in the Greater Birmingham area, was concerned with the film choices of boys and girls between the ages of thirteen years and sixteen years and eleven months.[22] Data were gathered from choices made, among showings of nearly three-hundred films, by 2,069 boys and girls and upon data derived from essays written by 979 of these subjects on the topic, "The Best Film I Have Ever Seen." An examination of age trends indicated few changes that may be regarded as significant. There was some tendency among the boys not attending grammar schools to mention excitement less as they get older, and a like tendency to mention violence, horror, and mystery to a greater degree. Realism and the appeal of some particular star showed some increase with age. Among grammar-school boys, excitement and violence were mentioned less frequently after age thirteen. With the possible exceptions of a decline in the mention of sentiment, color, and excitement, few differences were indicated by the grammar-school girls through the age range studied.

Radio interests and age. Studies of the types of radio programs preferred by children of different ages show that these preferences follow rather closely those listed earlier for reading and the movies. This is rather clearly shown in the studies reported by Gesell and Ilg and presented in Table 56. At two years of age the child dances to radio or phonograph music, showing his interest and delight. The preference at this age and for several succeeding years is for the phonograph and certain melodies from the radio. By the age of five, some children begin to listen to certain radio programs, and prefer a combination of talking and music. The interest in particular radio programs develops rapidly after this age, so that by the ages of seven and eight they dislike missing their favorite radio programs. This

[22] W. D. Wall and E. M. Smith, The film choice of adolescents, *British Journal of Educational Psychology*, 1949, Vol. 19, Part II, pp. 121-136.

interest varies with children and with the range of interests present. A study of the interest of boys and girls from grades five, eight, ten, and twelve reported by Brown showed that mystery plays were liked by a very large percentage of students at all grade levels, with the possible exception of the twelfth-grade girls. These results are presented in Table 57.[23] Comic dialogues and skits and dramatic plays

TABLE 57   Types of radio programs liked best by boys and girls of different grade levels by per cent choosing each type (after Brown)

Type of Program	Fifth Grade		Eighth Grade		Tenth Grade		Twelfth Grade	
	BOYS	GIRLS	BOYS	GIRLS	BOYS	GIRLS	BOYS	GIRLS
	%	%	%	%	%	%	%	%
Mystery plays	94.0	97.1	94.3	95.1	84.9	76.0	66.7	39.4
Comic dialogues and skits	86.4	96.2	92.0	98.5	87.9	93.0	76.8	78.3
Dramatic plays	88.0	90.0	82.8	84.7	67.1	86.2	55.0	89.8
Popular dance music ..	47.3	70.2	63.4	81.3	83.5	95.2	94.2	98.7
Popular song hits	45.1	53.6	52.4	60.2	78.1	81.3	70.5	82.4
Semiclassical music: orchestra and band ...	44.4	60.0	78.3	81.4	60.8	57.2	17.2	32.4
News, including sports..	12.3	46.4	47.5	31.3	55.3	52.6	54.8	26.1
Political speeches	6.6	2.0	46.4	19.6	51.2	33.0	45.2	18.0
Classical music, including opera	5.7	10.2	16.4	25.0	12.3	23.1	10.8	20.2
Educational talks	1.4	3.6	11.5	8.1	22.0	12.2	13.4	13.4

were also high on the list of types of radio programs liked by preadolescents and adolescents. An increased interest in political events and educational programs developed with an increase in age and maturity of these subjects. However, the small percentage of boys and girls reporting an interest in the educational type of program presents a challenge to educators.

Reactions of 505 children to different types of radio programs have been reported by Clark.[24] These children were representative of the white-school population in Washington, D. C., the rural children in Fairfax County, Virginia, and the boys from the National Training School for Boys. The study showed the importance of the local radio programs, in that most of the listening habits were built

[23] Reprinted by permission from The Sociology of Childhood by Francis J. Brown. Copyright 1939 by Prentice-Hall, Inc.

[24] W. R. Clark, Radio listening habits of children, Journal of Social Psychology, 1940, Vol. 12, pp. 131-149.

up around programs broadcast from Washington radio stations. Some interesting age differences were noted. The increased interest in the popular and novelty type of dance with advanced age and social maturity is in harmony with findings presented in Chapter 12 relative to the development of attitudes and social behavior. Also, the decline of interest in children's radio programs after age twelve is to be expected, since by this time the child is beginning to look to adult ways of doing things and begins to assume an ever-increasing interest in adult activities. Again, it should be pointed out that the changes observed in types of radio programs listened to will be affected in a large measure by opportunities; however, there are gradual and continuous changes operating throughout the growth period that reflect the total changes taking place in the child as he advances toward maturity.

Interests in comic strips. That children are interested in comic strips is a common observation. This is usually the part of the newspaper first read by a very large percentage of children at all grade levels from the fourth through the twelfth. The interests of the children are oftentimes developed out of the existing interests among the parents. Bessie West noted in her study of the interests of preschool children in comic strips that in 90 per cent of the families there was some member who enjoyed comic strips appearing in the daily newspapers.[25] The study by West as well as an earlier study by Verletta Hearn revealed that the major source of preschool children's interest in comic strips was the parents and older brothers and sisters.[26] The parents reported a larger percentage of girls than of boys interested in comic strips at the age of two years. There were no pronounced differences among the age groups in preference for particular comic strips during the preschool period. Comic books were available in some of the homes of the children studied by West, and in some cases were owned by the child. More boys than girls owned or had access to comic books and more of the boys asked to have the books read to them. Although the number of cases used in these studies is small, they do indicate that many children show an interest in comic books during the preschool period. There was also evidence that these did not hold the first interest in reading materials at this age, especially when desirable story books were

[25] Bessie Maurie West, A study of the interest of thirty-one preschool children in the comic strips, Master's thesis, University of Tennessee, 1949.

[26] Verletta Hearn, Study of the interest of fifty-two preschool children in the daily comics, Master's thesis, University of Tennessee, 1934.

available. An exploratory study of children's interests in comic strips was undertaken by Hill and Trent in order to obtain objective information about the nature of these interests.[27] A questionnaire, previously tried out on a group of 240 elementary-grade pupils, was administered to 256 children in the fourth, fifth, and sixth grades. These children were also given a thirty-item multiple-choice test covering facts about these comics which were most popular. Seven comics were common to the twelve ranking highest in interest for both boys and girls. The greater preference of girls for comics of romance and family life is shown by their favoring *"Blondie, Toots and Casper, Dixie Dugan, Maggie and Jiggs,* and *Tillie the Toiler.* (These are not in the list of twelve ranking highest among the boys.) The boys choices of *Tarzan, Joe Palooka, Little Joe, Henry,* and *Tailspin Tommy* revealed their attraction to action, adventure, fighting, feats of strength and daring, aviation, and the like. (These were not listed among the twelve ranking highest among the girls.) The sex differences in interests are clearly manifested in this study. Eight of the twelve comics most popular among boys are stories of adventure, while only four of the comics most popular among girls are adventure stories, three portray family life, two are burlesque (although one of these, *Maggie and Jiggs,* portrays a sort of family life), and two are animated cartoons. These interests are very similar to those presented in reading, the radio, and the movies.

A comparison of the comics read by white and Negro elementary-school pupils shows little difference.[28] Data have been reported by Witty and Moore on 207 Negro pupils from the fourth, fifth, and sixth grades of Chicago bearing on the extent and nature of their interests in comics. The Negro pupils displayed a greater interest in the reading of comics than did the white pupils. This may be attributed to the greater lack of varied reading materials available for the Negro pupils. Mean frequency of reading comic strips for the different grades is shown in Table 58.

Ruth Strang advocates moderation rather than total abstinence in the reading of comics.[29] Parents and teachers should be con-

[27] George E. Hill and M. Estelle Trent, Children's interests in comic strips, *Journal of Educational Research,* 1940, Vol. 34, pp. 30-36. The term "comic strip" is used by these investigators to identify the cartoon story of the newspaper.

[28] P. A. Witty and D. Moore, Interest in reading the comics among Negro children, *Journal of Educational Psychology,* 1945, Vol. 36, pp. 303-308.

[29] Ruth Strang, Why children read the comics, *Elementary School Journal,* 1943, Vol. 43, pp. 336-342.

TABLE 58 Mean frequency of reading comic strips (after Witty and Moore)

Grade	Mean Number Read Regularly	Mean Number Read Often	Mean Number Read Some
IV	13.00	2.85	5.06
V	14.24	5.65	5.78
VI	13.50	5.69	6.81

cerned with the reasons for a particular child's intense interest in comics, rather than with the bare fact that such an interest exists. Comics serve different purposes for different children. Some children find an escape from unpleasant conditions and situations through the process of identifying themselves with certain personalities and adventures of the comics. Others find this a means of satisfying certain felt needs which are not otherwise satisfied, such as the need for attention or the need for status. Comics may be used, however, to motivate a child in the development of a reading skill. The principle of developing new interests out of existing interests may operate in this case in developing reading interests and lead to the acquisition of reading skills and additional information and understanding. Educators may also make use of the methods and procedures of comics for teaching reading skills, understandings, attitudes, and fundamental character qualities. Strang states: "He should work with, rather than futilely against the comic-strip artists and thus mold this naturally attractive medium to educative purposes."

Special interests outside of school. Although the family culture and class status influence the child's interests from the earliest stages of his development, there are certain significant changes which occur with age that are important in connection with the education and guidance of boys and girls. It has already been pointed out that interest in certain types of movie and radio activities characterize children at different age levels, although it was further suggested that individual differences within a particular age group may be expected at all ages. Data on children's interests outside of school show that at all age levels those activities falling in the category of sports, games, and play lead in popularity. This has been shown from the results obtained by Jersild and Tasch. Results bearing on this are presented in Table 59.[30]

[30] *Op. cit.,* pp. 158-159.

The high degree of interest in sports and games appears, according to the results reported by Jersild and Tasch, to reach its pinnacle during the age period nine-twelve. There is a gradual but continuous increase in interest in the radio from the six-nine age level to the twelve-fifteen age level, while the interest in the performance of chores and special duties registers a decrease throughout these age periods. Although no pronounced changes are noted in the amount of interest displayed in people, one would expect a qualitative change here, since the individual makes a wider range of acquaintances and friends with development from early childhood into adolescence. Interests in people would, in all probability, move away from the home and immediate environment to other homes and a larger neighborhood, or perhaps to other neighborhoods.

TABLE 59 What I like best outside of school (after Jersild and Tasch)

Category	Ages 6–9		Ages 9–12		Ages 12–15	
	BOYS	GIRLS	BOYS	GIRLS	BOYS	GIRLS
Material things, specific objects, toys, food, shelter, pets, dress	1.0	3.6	1.9	3.4	3.1	3.2
Sports, play, games, outdoor activities, driving car	64.3	56.1	73.5	68.0	56.4	51.9
Miscellaneous places of recreation, parks; travel, camp, resort	1.9	3.9	2.4	5.7	5.2	8.5
Radio, movies, theater, comics	4.0	5.3	5.5	9.5	9.8	16.7
Social activities, organizations, parties, Scouts, DeMolay	0	0	1.5	1.0	1.3	8.0
Areas of study, reading, school subjects	3.5	2.6	4.3	3.9	5.3	13.3
Art activity or appreciation: music, painting	2.0	1.8	.6	3.1	2.4	5.5
Crafts, mechanical arts	.9	0	3.5	1.7	4.5	.7
Self-improvement, understanding, including vocational placement or competence	.9	1.3	3.3	3.6	.8	5.0
Chores, duties, everyday routines	7.2	7.3	1.2	5.0	2.2	3.9
People: both relatives and non-relatives	5.1	11.2	3.9	4.8	3.7	8.9

Sex interest patterns

Sexual interests during infancy and the preschool years. At one time, the infant child was considered nonsexual, and any interest manifested in sex was looked upon as evil. Recent studies of child development have revealed that sex feelings and sex attitudes, although considerably stimulated by glandular conditions during puberty, have their beginnings in the earliest months of life. A recognition of this has produced a changed attitude toward the child's interest in sex during the period of infancy and early childhood. Today, parents are approaching problems involved in sex information and attitudes more realistically than ever before. Observations by Gesell have revealed that the child's interest in his own body increases rapidly during the first two years.[31] Since the body is ever present, it becomes an object for him to explore. With the development of increased muscular ability and better co-ordination, the infant child is able to touch and handle various parts of the body. When undue attention is given by parents to the infant when he touches parts of the body concerned with sex, the problem is likely to become an aggravated one. Exploration of the genitals on the part of the child should be treated in a somewhat similar manner to that of the exploration of other parts of the body. When this is done and the child is supplied with toys to manipulate, no problem related to "sex" is likely to appear.

The development and patterning of "sex" interests are not different from the methods and principles involved in the development of other interests. The newborn child has no special interest in matters relating to sex. Such interests are the product of the interaction of the maturing self and everyday experiences. It has already been suggested that during the first year the child makes considerable strides in discovering his physical self through exploration with the hands. In the period from one to two years, there is an increased amount of exploration. Growth gradients involving sex interests and activities have been charted by Gesell and Ilg, from their observations of children during the preschool years.[32] At two years, the child is aware of differences between boys and girls based on manners of dressing and style of haircut, but shows little interest in any physiological differences. With the development of some knowledge about physiological differences, the child is likely to go through a stage of "show" and name calling. This does not usually last long, and in our middle-class culture is ordinarily suppressed at the first sign of its appearance.

[31] A. L. Gesell and F. Ilg, *The Child from Five to Ten* (New York: Harper & Brothers, 1946).

[32] A. Gesell and F. Ilg, *Child Development, Part II* (New York: Harper & Brothers, 1949), pp. 322-325. The student will find here a splendid outline of sex behavior and interests characteristic of children at different age period from eighteen months to sixty months.

(The nature of such a suppression sometimes has an undesirable effect upon the growth of a healthy emotional attitude toward sex.) Among most children after three or four years of age there is an increased modesty. Their attitude at this time toward sex is impersonal in nature—lacking the morbid curiosity commonly found among preadolescents and adolescents.

A study conducted by Katharine Hattendorf [33] was directed toward answering the questions: (a) Do young children, in general, ask questions about sex? (b) If so, at what specific ages are they likely to appear? (c) What information do they seek? The questions were gathered from parents whose children were between the ages of two and fourteen years. There were 1,763 questions

TABLE 60   Rank of interest of children in different age groups for sex questions (after Hattendorf)

	Age in years		
Classification of questions	2 TO 5	6 TO 9	10 TO 13
Origin of babies	1	1	2
Coming of another baby	4	2	1
Intra-uterine growth	7	7	8
Process of birth	5	3	5
Organs and function	3	4	3
Physical sex differences	2	4	6
Relation of father to reproduction	6	6	4
Marriage	8	8	7

reported by parents representing 981 homes with 1,797 children. The questions were tabulated by age groups for boys and girls. The rankings of the sex interests for the different age groups, based on the frequency of questions asked, are presented in Table 60. The origin of babies and physical sex differences ranked first and second among the preschool children. The rank of interests for the different age groups indicates the existence of a developing interest from simple inquiries concerning the origin of babies, through the physiological processes of conception and birth, toward the place of the members of the family in the reproduction process.

Sex antagonism. From six to twelve years, and in the case of boys often extending into the teen years, there is a gradual development of an antagonistic attitude toward members of the opposite sex.

[33] Katharine W. Hattendorf, A study of the questions of young children concerning sex: a phase of an experimental approach to parent education, *Journal of Social Psychology,* 1932, Vol. 3, pp. 37-63.

Boys and girls who played together on almost the same level during the kindergarten years begin pulling away from each other around the age of seven and play to a greater and greater degree with members of their own sex. Boys at this age level begin showing similar interests and regard many of the play activities of girls as "sissy," while the girls look upon the boys as rough and too much given to scuffling and fighting. This antagonistic attitude is reflected in the reactions of boys toward girls shown in Figure 41.[34]

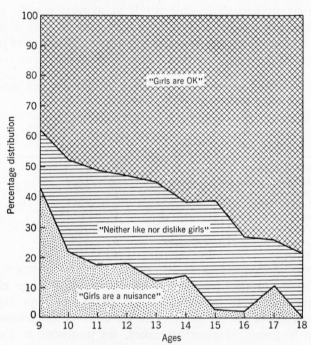

FIG..41. Anonymous reactions of seven hundred boys, aged nine to eighteen, to questions about their attitude toward girls
(After Sollenberger)

A large percentage of boys, however, regard the girl as OK, but would prefer to play with boys. By the age of eighteen, very few boys regard girls as a nuisance.

The effects of puberty. Some pronounced changes of interests appear with the onset of adolescence. The earlier interest in the

[34] F. K. Shuttleworth, *The Adolescent Period,* Monographs of the Society for Research in Child Development, 1938, Vol. 3, No. 3. This is based upon unpublished data by R. T. Sollenberger and is used by permission of the Society.

secret code, the secret message, and the mystery associated with gang activities are considerably less. These interests are retained longer among boys than among girls, partially because of the later maturity of boys. The more mature youngsters begin showing an increased interest in members of the opposite sex at an earlier age than the less mature ones. The girl will miss a scout meeting for a date, and this is accepted by the other girls as a matter of her choice. Boys, however, retain a loyalty code much longer, and this code is at all stages in their development stronger than like codes found among girls.

The interests and attitudes of 1,000 girls from two large junior high schools of Berkeley, California, were studied for the purpose of determining the influence of menarche [35] on their development. [36] These girls were matched with respect to chronological age and social status, but were significantly different in physiological development. This made it possible to compare the attitudes and social development of premenarcheal and postmenarcheal girls. These comparisons revealed that postmenarcheal girls favor interests and attitudes that are more mature in nature than those favored by the premenarcheal girls. The postmenarcheal girls expressed a significantly greater interest in those things related to the opposite sex and showed a more favorable attitude toward boys in general than was the case for the premenarcheal girls. In harmony with findings already presented relative to the decline of interest in sports and games around the tenth grade, it was observed that the postmenarcheal girls were less interested in engaging in physical activities and games than were the premenarcheal girls. This often presents a difficult problem for the physical education instructor in high school. The postmenarcheal girls engage in daydreaming and imaginary activities to a greater degree than do the premenarcheal girls. Their increased interest in adornment, greater desire for independence, and awakened interest in boys thus appear as a result of forces associated with the menarche.

The psychological differentiation of the sexes at this stage furnishes an interesting and significant feature of the development of

[35] Onset of the menstrual period denotes neither the beginning nor the end of the pubescent period. Even prior to the menarche, there are noticeable changes present in the contour of the girl. The menarche does furnish an excellent basis for determining the physiological maturity of the girl.

[36] Calvin P. Stone and Rogers G. Barker, The attitudes and interests of premenarcheal and postmenarcheal girls, *Journal of Genetic Psychology,* 1939, Vol. 54, pp. 27-72.

boys and girls. This has been described by Stolz, Jones, and Chaffey as follows:

The girl feels a necessity to prove to herself and to the world that she is essentially feminine; the boy needs to demonstrate that he has those masculine qualities which will require others to recognize him as a man. This characteristic accounts for the girls' spending a large part of their leisure time in shopping and in personal adornment. This is the secret of the manicured nails, painted red to match vivid lips. This is why they must wave and curl their hair, and, having perfected the process, must pin into it ribbon bows, bits of lace, or flowers. This is the reason for the boy's urge to learn to drive a car and for his willingness to move heaven and earth to borrow or own one. Along with this development, also, we are told by our group that a girl to be popular must be modishly pretty, keep herself clean and neat, be a good mixer. A boy, on the other hand, must be aggressive and must excel at sports. He must have the ability to dance and to talk easily with girls, and in addition he must show that he can compete readily with other boys; that he can achieve and master. This picture of adolescent development is often disturbing to adults, but it should be reassuring to know that, once the girl has arrived at the status in the group to which she has aspired, or has learned to adjust herself to a version of the universal feminine model which suits her own personality, she will be a happier person and a pleasanter one to teach or to have around the house. Likewise, once the boy feels that he is accepted as a man, he can go on with the important business of preparing himself for a job or for college. We have repeatedly noticed that those boys and girls who have acquired some understanding of their personal relations to others and have made a place for themselves in a mixed group, have become more stable and predictable.[37]

Summary and generalization

The significance of *interests* in the life and development of the child has been stressed throughout this chapter. It has been suggested by some students of child growth that interests are by-products of learning and development. That interests are also dynamic and affect the child's development is well known by teachers and others concerned with child guidance. Interests develop out of experiences. This does not mean that all children with similar experiences would have similar interests. There are factors

[37] H. R. Stolz, M. C. Jones, and J. Chaffey, The junior high-school age, *University High School Journal*, 1937, Vol. 15, pp. 63-72.

inherent within each child that will affect the nature and amount of interest developed in relation to some special experience. The strong child may be expected to develop a greater interest in activities requiring physical strength than would the weak child. The play interests of children are conditioned by such factors as mental maturity, physical development, adult culture, climatic factors, the physical environment, and other factors that relate to play opportunities.

The wishes, likes, and dislikes of children change with age. The most noticeable change found is that related to the wishes of the small child for material things, although this wish persists to a marked degree throughout childhood and adolescence. Pronounced age differences are found in ideals preferred. Both boys and girls of the early elementary-school grades choose as ideals characters from their home and immediate environment. Hero worship is observed as the boys and girls develop into the preadolescent years. Some interesting sex differences are found in this connection. Girls more often choose someone whom they encounter in face-to-face situations, while boys choose characters who have attained status and prestige in our society.

There are changes in reading interests, movie interests, and interests in radio programs with age. These changes are closely interwoven and interrelated. At ages six and seven, children prefer stories and books dealing with animals and other children. They enjoy stories of animals in which the animal is personified. With advancing age, they come to like stories of other lands, adventure, and action. Girls develop an interest in love stories at a fairly early age, due in part to their early physiological maturity. These reading interests are reflected in the choice of movies by children at different age levels. The appeal of the Western movie is indicated by the large attendance of children at the movies over week ends, when such pictures are featured at many of the movies. The radio programs involving adventure and excitement also appeal to boys during the early elementary-school period. The change of interests found in this connection, as children grow toward adolescence, is part of the growing-up process. New experiences, wider social contacts, increased understanding and knowledge, and a changing physiological self affect changes in interests as the boy and girl grows from early childhood into late childhood and adolescence.

The early interest of the child in sex is not an abnormal occurrence, and should be faced realistically by parents and dealt with in a frank manner as other matters might be treated. The child's pre-school years are taken up with learning things about himself as well as the world about him. It is natural that he should be interested in himself as a sexual person. He soon learns that there are two types of children—one type wears dresses and has fairly long hair, while the other type wears trousers and has short hair. At a later date, he learns that there are differences in physiological structure, and especially those structures related to sex. This new learning provides for increased interest in sexual differences. This interest may be guided in a wholesome manner or directed into unwholesome questionable attitudes and feelings. Sex interests manifested by children at different age levels present difficult problems to many parents. There is some evidence that these problems are often aggravated by a lack of understanding and an overcritical attitude on the part of parents.

At all stages in the child's development, interests are being manifested in various ways. These interests should be looked upon as guides and symptoms relative to various aspects of growth. Furthermore, it should be realized that interests at all stages are products of a child's experiences and thus follow the principles of growth and development which have been presented through the chapters of Part II.

Questions and Exercises

1. Observe the play of a group of kindergarten children. What are the major characteristics of the play activities observed? Are these in harmony with those presented in this chapter?
2. Point out how the child's interest in animal life may be limited by his experiences. By his mental ability.
3. How would you account for the age differences in the wishes of children shown in Table 44. What is the significance of this to parents?
4. Study the tables showing the books preferred by children at different grade levels. How would you account for certain books appearing at several different grade levels? What are the major characteristics of the books preferred at each of the grade levels listed?
5. What is the significance of the materials presented in the table showing things about the school situation most disliked by pupils? What do these materials suggest relative to the nature and characteristics of pupils?

6. Note the age differences presented in Table 57 for interests in the radio programs. Do these results coincide with your observations?
7. Using the materials presented in this chapter bearing on interests at different age levels in reading, movies, and the radio, what general conclusions or generalizations can be drawn?
8. What are some of the most common mistakes made by parents in dealing with the sex interests of three- and four-year-old children?
9. Show how with growth into adolescence interests of boys and girls tend to complement each other.

Selected Readings

Averill, L. A. *The Psychology of the Elementary-School Child.* New York: Longmans, Green & Company, 1949. Chap. V.

Cole, Luella. *Psychology of Adolescence.* 3rd ed.; New York: Farrar and Rinehart, 1948. Chap. XIV.

Dale, E. *Children's Attendance at Motion Pictures.* New York: The Macmillan Company, 1935.

Eisenberg, A. E. *Children and Radio Programs.* New York: Columbia University Press, 1935.

Garrison, Karl C. *Psychology of Adolescence.* 4th ed.; New York: Prentice-Hall, 1951. Chap. VII.

Gessell, Arnold, and Ilg, F. *Child Development.* New York: Harper & Brothers, 1949.

Harris, Dale B. How children learn interests, motives and attitudes, *Learning and Instruction. Forty-ninth Yearbook of the National Society of Education,* Part I, 1950. Chap. V.

Hurlock, Elizabeth B. *Child Development.* 2nd ed.; New York: McGraw-Hill Book Co., 1950. Chap. XIII.

Jersild, A. T. *Child Psychology* 3rd ed.; New York: Prentice-Hall, 1947. Chap. XIV.

Nagge, E. *Psychology of the Child.* New York: The Ronald Press, 1942. Chap. XI.

Skinner, C. E., Harriman, R. L., *et al. Child Psychology.* New York: The Macmillan Company, 1941. Chap. XIV.

Thorpe, Louis P. *Child Psychology and Development.* New York: The Ronald Press, 1946. Chap. XIII.

14

Personality Development:
Its Nature and Evaluation

Introduction: The nature of personality

The twentieth century has been, to a considerable extent, the century of child study. This idea was emphasized in Chapter 1. The environmental conditions under which an American child grows and develops today are radically different from those under which he was reared a half-century ago. Many of the traditional methods of child-rearing have been challenged and more attention is being given to the effects of early childhood experiences upon personality development.

The meaning of personality. The term "personality" was derived from the Latin word "persona," meaning a mask worn by an actor while speaking and performing on the stage. The wearer of the mask revealed himself through his speech and actions. This concept of the actor bears some relationship to the notion of personality held by many psychologists today. What a person thinks, how he feels, what he does in response to various situations, all tend to reveal the individual's personality. According to Merry and Merry, personality may be defined as "the complete and unified outcome of all developmental processes through which the individual has passed." [1] Woodworth (1947) has referred to it as the "quality of the individual's total behavior." The totality concept has been emphasized within recent years. J. C. Raven has defined personality in terms of the characterization given an individual by

[1] Frieda K. Merry and Ralph V. Merry, *From Infancy to Adolescence* (New York: Harper & Brothers, 1940), p. 277.

378

an observer as a result of his capacities, training, and interests. He states: "For this reason, I propose to use the word 'personality' to mean *'the qualities of a person's thought and conduct as they are apprehended by another person.'* " [2]

Longitudinal study of personality. Each individual has his own unique history. There is a continuity to the development of the process, so that the effects of each day affect the behavior of the future. A recognition of the uniqueness of the personality of each child, and the principle of continuity in his development, will enable the teacher to better understand the child, his problems, and his needs. Thus, an essential element in the study of a child is to observe his behavior over a period of time and to note the recurring behavior patterns. This makes it necessary that anecdotes and other material and data be collected on each child. It is necessary, however, for the teacher, parent, or other person concerned with the child's welfare to be able to interpret the data gathered on the child. The staff of the Division on Child Development and Teacher Personnel has presented the tasks that should be performed by the teacher in the interpretation of cumulative observations and other materials on a particular child. These are listed as follows:

1. Arranging the facts in accord with an organizing framework for information.

2. Checking the facts.

3. Looking for clues and uncovering blind spots.

4. Identifying and listing recurring situations and patterns of behavior.

5. Spotting significant unique events.

6. Forming a series of hypotheses to account for particular patterns of behavior.

7. Relating hypotheses about different patterns of behavior to each other in order to understand the child as an organized whole and as a developing personality.

8. Checking hypotheses against an organized framework of explanatory principles in order to discover contradictory, oversimplified, or biased interpretations.

9. Planning practical ways of helping children.

10. Evaluating hypotheses and plans on the basis of the effects of practical attempts to help the child. [3]

[2] J. C. Raven, The comparative assessment of personality, *British Journal of Psychology—General Section,* 1950, Vol. 40, p. 115.

[3] Staff of the Division on Child Development and Teacher Personnel, *Helping Teachers Understand Children* (Washington: American Council on Education, 1945), pp. 188-193

Hereditary basis of personality. Heredity has often been used as a convenient basis for explaining behavior and personality—disputed but not readily disproved. With the advances made in the biological and genetic sciences, one may speak with greater certainty about the relative effects of heredity and environment. The nature of heredity and its influence upon the growth and development of the individual child were discussed in Chapter 2. It has also been pointed out throughout the previous chapters that the influence of heredity and environment are so interrelated that one cannot safely take an all-or-none attitude toward the development of various aspects of personality.

Some of the most noteworthy and interesting experiments in this area have been carried out with identical and fraternal twins as subjects. Most studies show that identical twins are more alike in various personality traits than are fraternal twins. Studies conducted by Newman and others made use of fifty pairs of twins reared separately and fifty pairs of twins reared together.[4] Several cases

Case 1. Two young women, separated for twenty years, found to be practically identical physically and in intelligence but extremely different in temperament and other personality traits.

Case 2. Two young women, one reared in England and the other in Canada, found to be similar in temperament and personality traits, but the Colonial was in much better physical condition and much more intelligent.

Case 3. Two young women separated for twenty years, reared in about the same kind of physical and social environment, but one given more educational privileges than the other, found to be extraordinarily alike in physical and temperament qualities, but the educated one showed more intelligence.

One cannot conclude from these case studies that any one aspect of personality is fixed by heredity and thus not amenable to environmental forces and conditions. The Dionne quintuplets were uniovular and were brought up in much the same environment, yet early in life they displayed distinctly different personalities.[5] From a consideration of the quintuplets we would conclude that neither hereditary nor environmental factors operate in a separable manner but rather that their interaction produces different personalities.

[4] H. H. Newman, F. Freeman, and K. Holzinger, *Twins: A Study in Heredity and Environment* (Chicago: University of Chicago Press, 1937).
are cited to show the effects of separation on twins.

[5] Gardner Murphy, *Personalities* (New York: Harper & Brothers, 1947), p. 60.

Gardner Murphy suggests in this connection that there is no such thing as a trait that is primarily hereditary or a trait that is primarily environmental; every trait is a product of the interaction of the hereditary constitution and the environment. The task of one who would explain the development of a child's personality is that of showing the individual's hereditary potentialities and the ways in which the forces and conditions in his environment have affected the development of these potentialities. The limitations set by heredity for an individual constitute a rather definite boundary, but this boundary is far less limited than many students of child development would admit. At the same time, personality differences resulting primarily from the hereditary constitution manifest themselves during the early days of life after birth. Environment, however, begins operating from the very beginning of life and thus interacts with hereditary potentialities.

The stability of the personality pattern. Genetic studies of infants show that differences in personality characteristics are manifested from the beginning of life. This was indicated in the discussion of the hereditary basis of personality. The question has been proposed as to whether or not personality patterns are subject to change as individuals grow and develop. Also, if changes do occur, how much change can be expected and in what direction will such changes occur? Further questions of special importance to teachers and parents are concerned with the factors that influence such changes and methods that may be used for producing such changes.

In a study reported by Roberts and Fleming, twenty-five college women were selected from a list of one hundred.[6] Detailed life histories of these college women indicate that the home relationships were most important in the development of personality traits, and that although some personality traits in a given personality may change as the individual develops, there is a central core or focus that remains quite stable. The studies by Shirley conducted with two infants as subjects provide good evidence for the stability of the personality pattern.[7] Shirley noted that one of the infants consistently displayed a more irritable nature than the other one. As the infants developed, it was observed that certain forms of behavior would wane, only to be followed by some other behavior somewhat

[6] Katharine E. Roberts and Virginia Fleming, Persistence and change in personality patterns, *Monographs of the Society for Research in Child Development,* 1943, Vol. 8, No. 3, Serial No. 36.

[7] M. M. Shirley, *The First Two Years; Vol. III, Personality Manifestations* (Minneapolis: University of Minnesota Press, 1933).

consistent with the earlier behavior activities. Profile charts showing ratings and scores for each baby on a number of personality characteristics indicated a definite consistency in these personality characteristics at different ages.

Despite the fact that these early studies have been supported by more recent studies at Yale University as well as by a number of minor studies, one should not generalize that personality cannot be changed. There is considerable evidence for the following conclusions relative to the stability of personality:

1. Personality is less stable in nature than is physique, or even intelligence.

2. The central core around which certain habits, attitudes, and emotions are organized becomes stabilized rather early in life.

3. Habits and attitudes that become firmly established early in life tend to persist.

4. The personality pattern is less stable during the period of childhood than during a later period.

The fact that there is a central core of personality that tends to persist is important in connection with the guidance and training of children. This central core furnishes a working balance and provides for unity in an individual's personality. Attempts to change certain aspects of an individual's personality may be dangerous to the unity of such a personality. Due regard must be given to the nature of the habits, attitudes, and emotional characteristics of the individual. These should function in a harmonious manner.

The early studies by Jack [8] at the Iowa Child Welfare Research Laboratories show that personalities may be changed during the preschool period. A group of four-year-old children were paired with a group of other children. Each child was carefully observed for dominant behavior. It was noticed that the chief difference between the ascendant and nonascendant child was in the amount of self-confidence displayed by each child in the test situation. The nonascendant children were then trained in some skills such as block construction. After the nonascendant children had developed some of these skills, they were again observed for dominant behavior. Only one of these children trained in some special skills failed to show a significantly higher dominant score. This child had a serious speech defect, which is closely related to certain emotional qualities.

[8] L. M. Jack, An experimental study of ascendant behavior in preschool children, *University of Iowa Studies of Child Welfare,* 1934, Vol. 9, pp. 17-65.

The implications of this study for the parent and teacher are clear. Specific habits or attitudes can be changed. By changing a habit pattern such as lack of confidence to an increased self-confidence, desirable changes may be produced in the child's personality. The timid child in the classroom may become more confident and show leadership qualities if he is able to develop some skills that give him the self-reliance badly needed by him. Various studies have shown that the manifestation of such a trait as dominance is specific rather than general in nature. Children may be dominant in one situation and somewhat submissive in another. The possession of a number of skills furnishes the child with a range of capabilities that contributes to the child's self-confidence in relation to a number of different situations.

Physiological factors affecting personality development

While the organismic conditions may or may not be inherited, they are important in the determination of personality. Almost any physical defect, if observable, will have a bearing on the child's personality development, particularly when he begins to mature socially. Conditions caused by the malfunctioning of certain glands affect the child's development or may affect his mental and emotional functioning. The nervous system, with its intricate network of neurons and synapses, may be affected by disease or childbirth injury. Indeed, the prenatal condition of the mother has much to do with the health, strength, and vitality of the offspring. The influences of heredity are doubtless more significant for the human being during the germinal and embryonic period than in the fetal, and before birth than after. Development from conception until death is always dynamic, altering relationships between the internal states of the individual and his environment.

Size and physique. Children become conscious of their size at an early age, and reveal considerable interest in their height and weight. To be taller than someone else of the same age is an admired characteristic. It was pointed out in Chapter 13 that boys in particular wish to be larger and stronger, while girls wish to be more beautiful. As the girl develops socially, she becomes especially interested in the development of the appropriate physique as well as in appearing attractive. During the growing years, unless the child is very tall for his age, tallness is usually advantageous, since it is associated with being older, stronger, and more agile than smaller children. Excessive thinness or excessive fatness is a disadvantage to the child in his activities and social relations. There is. however, a tendency for children to be critical of those who deviate considerably from the average in height, weight, and body build. The child who falls short of acceptable standards is likely to be given a nickname indicative of his special characteristic.

The relationship between body build and special personality characteristics has been studied by Sheldon and others. They have produced some evidence indicating that such a relation does exist. The best evidence appears to be found among cases of the extreme types. Bayley found no significant relationships between body build and special personality characteristics among young children.[9] She noted that many chunky children were not phlegmatic and placid, in keeping with the characteristics attributed to chunky children; and that many thin children were not nervous and irritable—characteristics assigned to thin children.

The energy level. The energy level of a child is extremely important in determining his behavior patterns and personality characteristics. Every individual inherits certain developmental potentialities; however, environment may alter these in many ways. The strong, physically active child will react to restrictions placed upon him at home quite differently from the way a child with a lowered energy level would react. An example given by Sontag illustrates this.

R. H. Is a slender, stringy, undernourished girl, the daughter of a prominent manufacturer and his former secretary, whom he had married when he was forty. The mother's doubt as to her ability to have a child at her somewhat advanced child-bearing age, plus her determination that the child by its perfection should justify her own elevation from the status of secretary to that of wife of her wealthy employer, were important factors in her handling the child. The concern for the child's nutrition was marked, and R. H. appeared to learn rapidly that refusal of food was a potent tool and bargaining weapon for privilege. Poor eating habits and food refusal were followed by underweight, which in turn increased the mother's anxiety and made her most solicitous of her child. As a result of this poor nutrition, R. H.'s energy and strength were probably less adequate and her adjustment to competitive situations less aggressive.[10]

[9] N. Bayley, *Studies in the Development of Young Children* (Berkeley: University of California Press, 1940).

[10] L. W. Sontag, Some psychosomatic aspects of childhood, *The Nervous Child*, 1946, Vol. 5, p. 298.

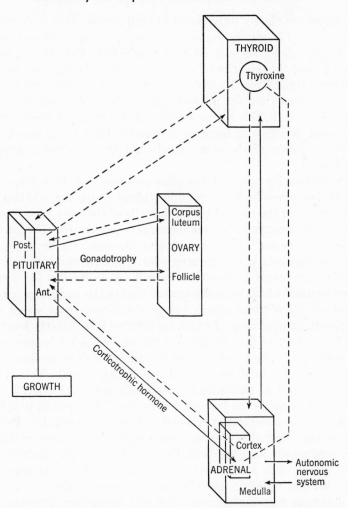

FIG. 42   The interrelations of the endocrine glands responsible for growth and its limitations and their relation to the autonomic nervous system through the medulla. (Solid lines represent stimulation; broken lines represent inhibition.)

(After Margolese)

Glandular conditions. The secretions from the endocrine glands go directly into the blood stream. The chief role of these glands is the control of growth and reproduction, and the maintenance of certain chemical balances. These glands do not function independently, but rather are closely interrelated in their action. This is shown in Figure 42.[11] The pituitary gland has sometimes been referred to as the master gland, since it (the anterior lobe) produces a growth hormone and the posterior lobe produces a stimulating hormone for the other glands. This aids in maintaining a balance, since the stimulating hormone from the pituitary gland affects the glandular hormones so as to inhibit the production of the trophic hormone. Any significant deviation in hormone production by any one gland will affect the action of the other glands and thus produce a general imbalance.

The maturation process takes place as a result of the influence of growth hormones from the pituitary gland. With the addition of hormones from the thyroid gland, the cells of the body become specialized and eventually become bones, nerves, skin, etc. The advent of the sex hormone inhibits growth and stimulates the development of various secondary sex characteristics. Children whose sex glands function improperly or insufficiently will fail to develop the sexual characteristics which normally appear during the early teen years. Hyperactivity of these glands brings about precocious sexual development, extreme cases of which are referred to as *puberty praecox*. The best-known of the endocrines is the thyroid gland, located near the windpipe in the lower part of the throat. Iodine, produced by this gland, is essential for physical and mental growth. This gland also has the task of regulating the metabolic process. A sluggish and apathetic manner results from an underactive thyroid, while irritability and nervousness appear when the thyroid is overactive. Pediatricians have been able to correct thyroid deficiency among children more adequately than has been the case for the other endocrines. Since these glands are related to physical growth, sexual development, nervous stability, and the metabolic process, they are recognized as most important in connection with personality development. Any imbalance of any one of the endocrine glands will have its effect upon personality development.

At the Fels Research Institute in Yellow Springs, materials have been gathered bearing on the relation of certain physiological variables to conditions of stress and strain. Longitudinal studies have been made in which physiological variables, such as skin resistance,

[11] M. Sydney Margolese, Mental disorders in childhood due to endocrine disorders, *The Nervous Child*, 1948, Vol. 7, pp. 55-77. A splendid discussion, with illustrations, is presented.

blood pressure, and heart rate, have been measured before, during, and after stresses. These studies have revealed definite sex differences in the stress response patterns. These patterns are furthermore of different magnitude in different systems, indicating widespread differences in different autonomic nervous systems. Studies have been reported by Sontag and Jost indicating that these autonomic patterns tend to approximate each other in proportion to the closeness of kinship. The autonomic scores for monozygotic twins and triplets are very much alike, while the scores for siblings are more similar than those for nonsiblings. Sontag concludes: "These findings, while not conclusive, suggest that the patterns of organ response of the individual are in part an inherited characteristic, subject to modification, of course, within the limits of physiological capacty of the individual."[12]

The influence of the home

Institutional versus home care. Among the basic needs of the child are affection, a feeling of security, and recognition. These needs will be given further consideration in Chapter 15. The close relationship between the satisfaction of these and other basic needs and the development of a wholesome personality has been shown in many studies.

The baby ordinarily receives considerable attention and affection from his mother or the person in charge of his care. The importance of this has been stressed recently in connection with changed concepts concerning child care during early infancy. The child needs to see the same face often so that he will not be frustrated by having to adjust to many different people. The home provides for this need, and the child early becomes attached to the person responsible for providing for his needs. There is evidence that the younger a child is when deprived of this source of security and affection, the more serious will be the effect on his personality.[13] Affection during the first two or three years of life is most important. The study by Goldfarb has provided valuable information on the relative effects of the foster home and institution on the personality of the growing individual. Two groups were studied. One group had spent the first

[12] L. W. Sontag, Physiological factors and personality in children, *Child Development,* 1947, Vol. 18, pp. 185-189.

[13] William Goldfarb, Effects of early institutional care on adolescent personality, *Journal of Experimental Education,* 1943, Vol. 12, pp. 106-129.

two or three years in an institution, while the other group had been in a foster home from the beginning. The institutional group showed a greater evidence of problem behavior than did the other group. These are some of their personality traits or "problems": restlessness, inability to concentrate, temper display, impudence, destructiveness, failure to regard property rights, cruelty without cause, and affective impoverishment. They were also less secure, more isolated from others, and less capable of good personal relationships. Institutional children seemed to have poorer adjustment in foster homes, as evidenced by a significantly greater replacement record. These children also showed greater speech deficiency, more school difficulty, and more mental retardation.

Some institutions and adoption agencies are realizing how important it is for the child to make satisfactory adjustments in life. The feelings, attitudes, and parent-child relationships are recognized by social workers as most important elements in relation to wholesome personality development. The emotional and social needs are more frequently the focus of attention rather than are merely physical needs. Before future plans for the child are made, careful studies are made of the home situation in relation to the special characteristics and needs of the particular child.

Those interested in adopting a child may find it more difficult through legal agencies, but the chances of securing a child that will fit into the pattern of the home are much greater. Preparing the foster parents for the child is very important, since the parents must adjust to changed conditions when the new member is brought into the home. Foster parents seek a child because they want the child. Thus, adopted children are not likely to be rejected. There is a much greater danger that foster parents will be overprotective or overindulgent in their care of the foster child. Again, the attitudes of foster parents are most important. Foster parents may be too eager about the growth, development, and success of the foster child. Such parents will need counsel, lest they become frustrated or set up conditions whereby the child feels insecure. Foster parents must be brought to realize that their task is not that of molding the child according to some preconceived pattern. The child must be allowed to grow up as a distinct personality, influenced, of course, by the teaching and example of the foster parents.

The influence of parental attitudes. The emotional attitude of the parents and the extent to which they offer the child affection and security are of utmost importance for wholesome personality development.[14] Rautman and Rautman have emphasized the importance of early home training in the development of character education. They state:

> A recognition of the fact that the solid core of human personality has its beginnings in the first few years of life reemphasizes the need for good breeding from babyhood on, this time from a psychological point of view. It is during the nursery years that we lay the foundation for our pleasant and unpleasant personality traits; it is at this point that our well-adjusted or maladjusted and neurotic individuals are made.[15]

The attitudes of parents toward their children are often a result of their own experiences during childhood. If a boy's experiences with his father are unpleasant and the father is very strict with him, the boy is likely to be unfavorably conditioned toward such treatment on the part of a father toward a son. Thus, he will tend to be very lax and perhaps overindulgent or overprotective of his own son. Lotz [16] made a study of the environment of a group of problem children eight to fourteen years of age. In approximately half the homes represented by these children were found neurotic behavior tendencies on the part of the parents. The parents tended to quarrel frequently with each other, denounce the school attended by their children, criticize the teachers and city officials, and speak disparagingly of their employers and their work. Four factors should be given special consideration in a discussion of this topic.

First, *the balance of behavior.* It is decisive for the formation of the child's personality whether the relationship of the father and mother to each other is harmonious or full of tension; also, whether the attitudes and aspirations of the father and mother toward the child tend to be similar. If one parent tends toward overindulgence and protects the child in all of his activities, while the other one assumes the role of punishing the child for behavior that is not harmonious with the parents' standards, conflicts and anxieties arise in the child's personality. The stimulation of opposite projections from the parents lays the foundation for the development of unstable and frustrated personalities among the children.

[14] See Alexander Reid Martin, A study of parental attitudes and their influence upon personality development, *Education,* 1943, Vol. 63, pp. 596-608. Unfavorable parental attitudes are listed as: rejection, deprivation, overprotection, and exploitation.

[15] Emily W. Rautman and Arthur L. Rautman, Is your child well-bred? *Mental Hygiene,* 1950, Vol. 34, p. 239.

[16] E. R. Lotz, Emotional status of the parents of problem and psychopathic children, *School and Society,* 1933, Vol. 42, pp. 239-240.

Second, *the consistency of behavior*. Parents whose behavior is unpredictable delay the development of consistent behavior trends on the part of the child, which are based upon a feeling of stability and security. When parents discharge their moods upon the child, the child tends to develop unstable habit patterns, and character traits characterized by moodiness and nervousness.

Third, *respecting the child's personality*. For many parents the child is an object of their own projections. They attempt, therefore, to project their own unfulfilled ambitions and likes upon the child. A mother may treat her child like a doll, an object to love and play with and thus a means of overcoming boredom. The child is not allowed to develop himself or even be himself. A father may try to develop his son into the person he always wanted to be, imposing upon him ways of behaving that do not fit into the son's personality framework. Parents should respect the child's characteristics and abilities. He should be guided in the development of these along socially acceptable lines. Attempts to mold the child in accordance with fixed standards and ideals on the part of parents will result in the development of a child beset with anxieties and frustrations.

Order of birth. Contrary to rather widespread belief, there is no one position in the family circle that might be regarded as the ideal. Each position in the family circle involves special problems as well as certain advantages. Many studies have been conducted bearing on this problem, but the results from these studies are by no means conclusive. This is to be expected, since so many variables enter into the family situation. The age of the parents, the financial conditions of the home at various stages, and the influence of relatives will also affect the personality development of the growing child.

There is some evidence from studies of only children that more dominance exists among these children than among those with siblings; however, these only children more often show superior characteristics and leadership qualities.[17] According to the study by Kawin, a preponderance of socially maladjusted children are found to be only children.[18] Certainly the only child is in a hazardous position. Since many parents are inclined to be overprotective or oversolicitous, the only child is likely to become the victim. In families consisting of several children, the parent will not be able

[17] R. B. Guilford and D. A. Worcester, A comparative study of the only child, *Journal of Genetic Psychology*, 1930, Vol. 38, pp. 411-426.

[18] E. Kawin, *Children of Pre-school Age* (Chicago: University of Chicago Press, 1930).

to give so much attention to any one child. This may, however, operate to the advantage of the only child when parental attitudes are more favorable and opportunities are afforded for wholesome personality development.

The effects of order of birth on the child's behavior was studied by Wile and Jones.[19] Correlations were obtained between order of birth and behavior disorders, based upon data from 125 histories of children under eight years of age. These children were divided into five ordinal position groups—only children, older children from two-child families, middle children from families of three or more children, younger children from two-child families, and the youngest children from families of three or more children. The behavior found to be most frequent for each of the five groups is presented in Table 61. No one type of behavior seemed to characterize any one group, as evidenced by the fact that fewer than 48 per cent of the children holding similar positions in their families exhibited the same behavior disorders. According to the data presented, older children frequently quarreled with others, while the youngest child seldom quarreled with the others. This, however, may be attributed to maturity, since investigations show that quarreling among children tends to increase throughout childhood into the early stages of adolescence. The conclusion from this and other studies of the effects of ordinal position supports the theory of multiple causation that has been emphasized throughout the previous chapters. While order of birth does have its effects, one must look beyond this into other factors in the home situation for a more complete explanation of any differences observed.

The emotional climate. The emotional climate of the home is distinctly related to the attitude of the parents. The importance of well-balanced affectional relations in the home was emphasized in connection with parental attitudes. The child should feel that he is a part of the home, that someone cares for him and is interested in his welfare. Some parents become so involved with activities and events about them that they become indifferent to the needs and values of their children. On the other hand, a parent may be so over-indulgent with his children that they develop such undesirable traits as selfishness, self-concern, or a total disregard for the rights and feelings of others.

Emotional displays on the part of parents, or violence, can be

[19] I. S. Wile and A. B. Jones, Ordinal position and the behavior disorders of young children, *Journal of Genetic Psychology*, 1937, Vol. 51, pp. 61-93.

TABLE 61 Behavior disorders most frequently found in the different ordinal position groups (after Wile and Jones)

Only (25)	Older (25)	Middle (25)	Younger (25)	Youngest (25)
Restlessness (12)	Restlessness (9)	Temper tantra (9)	Temper tantra (10)	Restlessness (9)
Food fads (10)	Quarrels with siblings (9)	Intellectual retardation (9)	Quarrels with others (9)	Food fads (9)
Vomiting (9)	Temper tantra (8)	Enuresis (7)	Fears (8)	Temper tantra (8)
Temper tantra (7)	Quarrels with others (8)	Speech defect (6)	Restlessness (6)	Disobedience (8)
Enuresis (6)	Food fads (6)	Unmanageable (6)	Converted sinistral (5)	Converted sinistral (7)
Fears (6)	Cries easily (5)	Quarrels with sibling (6)	Enuresis (4)	Vomiting (7)
Quarrels with others (6)	Nail biter (5)	Disobedient (6)	Vomiting (4)	Mother dresses and feeds (6)
Mother overprotection (6)	Mother dresses and feeds (5)	Quarrels with others (5)	Food fads (4)	Quarrels with others (6)
Destructive (5)	Vomiting (4)	Restlessness (5)	Quarrels with others (4)	Enuresis (5)
Speech defect (4)	Fears (4)	Swears (5)	Unmanageable (4)	School problem (5)
Converted sinistral (4)	Disobedience (4)	Mother feeds and dresses (4)	Swearing (3)	Nail biter (5)
Mother dresses and feeds (4)	School problems (4)	Tic (3)	Sleeps badly (3)	Unmanageable (4)
Intellectual retardation (3)	Destructive (4)	Cries easily (3)	Destructive (3)	Speech defect (4)
	Unmanageable (3)	Nail biter (3)	Irritable (3)	Tic (3)
	Tic (8)	Stealing (3)		Masturbation (3)
	Masturbation (3)	Fears (3)		Cries easily (3)
	Converted sinistral (3)			Fears (3)

disastrous to the young, impressionable child. While the trait of aggressiveness is somewhat characteristic of our culture, this becomes extremely undesirable when it is directed toward selfish ends. Such a trait should be guided and controlled. The child should be guided at an early stage to rely upon understanding in determining his course of action. Dunbar has emphasized the importance of the mother's emotional attitude on the infant.[20] The emotional climate of the home begins functioning at a very early stage of life and affects the individual's development in many and diverse ways. A case of a nine-year-old boy reported by Phyllis Blanchard illustrates the operation of jealousy and hositility toward a brother because of the feeling of lack of affection from the mother.

A nine-year-old boy had never learned to read in spite of attempts at remedial reading at school. He was also quarrelsome with other boys and antagonistic to the teachers. Just before he entered school, his older brother had died. Jealousy and hositility toward the brother, who seemed to him to retain more of the mother's affection in death than he, the living son, possessed, were evident in his interviews.

At first he dwelt on his wishes to be good, to love people and never to hurt any one. But soon he began to accuse the therapist of preferring other boys who were her patients and to engage in play and phantasies dealing with destructive and sadistic impulses directed toward these other patients and the therapist. He told of how the teachers, in his view, treated other pupils better than him. Later, he admitted the real feeling (which he had transferred to the teachers and other boys at school, just as he had transferred it to the therapist and her other patients) that his mother cared more for his dead brother than for him. He described her weekly visits to the grave, how she wept over it, decorated it with flowers, and so forth. He told how his mother always was talking of the dead brother, how good he had been and how bright in school work. "But I think he was a sissy; he couldn't fight, even if he could read," said the living brother, in angry criticism. He then went on with phantasies, previously repressed because of his guilt over them, telling how he would like to dig up his dead brother's coffin, which would contain his skeleton, and remove it to a grave so far away his mother would never be able to find it, or burn it up and completely destroy it. He hoped that then she would forget the dead brother and love him.

Unfortunately, the treatment was broken off by the mother, after only ten interviews, while it was still incomplete. One other significant

[20] F. Dunbar, Effect of the mother's emotional attitude on the infant, *Psychosomatic Medicine*, 1944, Vol. 6, pp. 156-159.

statement had been made during the interviews, however. The boy had recalled and described one of his first attempts at reading. He related that one of the first books he had tried to read was full of stories about war and people being killed. He had cried when he looked at this book and at last had torn it up so that he would never have to think of it again.[21]

Social and institutional factors

Parental versus peer controls. Our society, according to Kinsley Davis, ascribes to infants certain statuses in a somewhat blind manner, and at a time when the least is known about the child's potential value to the society.[22] This description is made on a meager basis of age, relationships, and kinships. After having been given his status, the child finds two categories of people from whom he gets his beliefs, sentiments, knowledge, and the ways of his culture. These persons and the interactions of life with them are the means of socialization. These two groups are the child's peers and those who have authority over him. A third group may be listed as those children in a different class status, i.e., in a lower or higher class status. In many cases, however, contact with these during the growing process is not sufficient to have a pronounced effect on the personality development of the child. Both authoritarian and equalitarian relationships contribute to the socialization process and personality development of the individual.

The authoritarian element is closely associated with morality and justified by the fact that behavior patterns are not innate, but are often actually contrary to biological drives. Hence, there is a need for those in charge of the socialization of the child to use their power of coercion when other means of guidance fail. The problem of societal morality is not a matter of rational understanding but a felt obligation on the part of those in authority—be they parents, educators, ministers, or others—as representatives of the society of which they are a part.

In the lives of preadolescent and adolescent boys and girls two types of culture may be said to operate. Boys and girls develop a culture of their own that shields them from adult interference and provides them with status in their own group. This is reflected in the slang of the group, and in the cliques that are formed. Through

[21] Phyllis Blanchard, Reading disabilities in relation to difficulties of personality and emotional adjustment, *Mental Hygiene,* 1936, Vol. 10, pp. 405-406.

[22] Kinsley Davis, The child and the social structure, *Journal of Educational Sociology,* 1940, Vol. 14, pp. 217-229.

these peer cultures, barriers are provided against customs and ideas that adults would impose. This provides ways of doing things different from the ways used by the older generation when it was growing up. Recently, a group of adolescents were observed who had adopted the letters *iss* as part of their speech and culture. They were very apt in the use of this. The letters *iss* were thrown into many of the key words used in their conversation. The statement, "Have you studied your lesson?" would be written and spoken with the letters inserted somewhat as follows: "Haveiss you sisstudied youriss isslesson?" These expressions provide for the protection of these boys and girls and for the promotion of their activities within their own peer group. The strong desire to be with their own group and the importance of peer culture must be recognized by those who would guide the activities of growing boys and girls.

Influence of play. The influence of play on the formation of personality is clearly recognized by students of child development. Margaret Mahler has suggested that "One of the most vulnerable stages of any child's developmental process is the one around the age of $2\frac{1}{2}$-3, when he has gradually to give up his belief in his own magic omnipotence. More or less suddenly he has to become aware of and accept a shockingly different state of affairs, namely, that the world around him is gigantic compared to his own relative and absolute smallness and weakness." [23] Thus, through play the child is able to enter into a make-believe world and convert the threatening reality demands into a pleasant aspect of his life, in which he becomes the mover of forces and master of certain conditions. He makes the stick horse carry him over the hills. He drives tanks against enemies and annihilates them. The little girl places her dolls in bed and makes them sleep at her bidding. Children tend to repeat in their play those phases of the adult world that have made a deep impression upon them.

As the child moves out of his early parallel play, he comes to share his activities and toys with others. He learns to co-operate with others, to consider the wishes of others, and to carry on certain activities as common undertakings. Play represents for most American children the first and most vital lessons in learning to live with others.

In the gang the child acquires a sort of "we" feeling, which is

[23] Margaret S. Mahler, Play as a learning process, *The Exceptional Child in Infancy and Early Childhood.* Proceedings of the Annual Spring Conference on Education and the Exceptional Child. The Woods Schools, 1950, p. 30.

most important in the satisfaction of the need for belongingness. Through group action and participation he receives valuable lessons in co-operation, and comes to recognize the importance of giving consideration to the welfare of the group. Through group activities boys and girls acquire training for democratic ways of living. The moral and educational value of play should not be overlooked. When the play activities of growing boys and girls are directed according to worthy ideals and standards, they become means for developing character qualities that will carry over into later adult activities. The boy who has learned to play a clean and an honest game is quite likely to follow some such procedures in dealing with adults in a business and professional manner at a later date. It is well known that habits and ideals acquired transfer to other situations to a much greater degree than do factual materials learned from textbooks.

Furthermore, many skills are acquired through play activities. These skills have an important bearing on one's personality during adolescence and adulthood. The increased interest in recreational pursuits and the outdoor world makes play activities all the more important. The boy who is able to pursue games, who is agile in his everyday movements, and who has developed good muscular co-ordination and balance will be in a better position to meet social, recreational, and vocational situations than will the boy who is deficient in these physical abilities. Through playing with fire engines, airplanes, and other toys the child is learning things about the adult world, and is getting ready for the activities that he will be observing or doing in a more realistic manner at a later date.

Names and nicknames. There is some evidence that the name given a child may be a psychological aid or a psychological barrier to his socialization. Around the third year of life, the child begins to realize that names are significant. Names that lend themselves to distortions or those that are extremely difficult to pronounce or are frequently mispronounced present hazards to the child's personality development. On the other hand, names that denote admiration and give the child a feeling of belongingness and a reasonable degree of recognition are favorable to his development. A study of first names, conducted by Allen and others, indicated that certain names are handicaps.[24]

[24] L. Allen, L. Brown, L. Dickinson, and K. C. Pratt, The relation of first name preference to their frequency in the culture, *Journal of Social Psychology,* 1941, Vol. 14, pp. 279-293.

Nicknames are usually verbal descriptions of the individual. They may come from an adaptation of the child's own name, when such an adaptation provides a description of the individual. The study by Orgel and Tuckerman [25] showed that nicknames fall into the following classifications: "pet" names, such as Dollie; nationality or place of birth, such as Birmingham for the boy born in Birmingham but is now living in Seattle; distortion (often shortening) of the real name, such as Bill for William; nicknames from the individual's initials, such as "Casey" from K.C.; nicknames from physical conditions, such as "Skinny;" and nicknames based on personality characteristics, such as "Sissy."

When nicknames denote a description of the individual that undermines his status and well-being, they are disliked. Oftentimes they are liked by the child, since they denote endearment or close friendship. The nature of the nickname given a child and the use made of it may, therefore, have a profound effect on the development of his personality. A child who can muster up the courage to laugh at the personal trait or nickname about which he is sensitive will get relief from the tension thus aroused. Once he comes to accept it as a distinction, it is no longer a source of difficulty and embarrassment to him. This is illustrated in the case of Tom.

Tom, a boy of twelve, came home from school one day in great distress, and told his mother that he wished he were dead, since he was ashamed of his red curly hair, which was the source of his being teased by some of the boys. The mother listened patiently to Tom, as he related his feelings, but said nothing to him at that time about how to cope with the situation. At a later time she made it a point to talk in a casual manner about some activities in which he excelled and drew Tom into the conversation. This seemed to give a boost to Tom's ego, which had been somewhat seriously hurt by the teasing at the hand of his peers. Gradually, a suggestion was dropped now and then that led the lad to feel differently about his hair. He and his father entered into some activities together, and the father proudly boasted of the achievements of "Red." Tom's attitude toward his red hair gradually changed, and he began to look upon this as a mark of individuality to be pleased with rather than to be ashamed of. After several months he dubbed himself "Red," and encouraged his friends to address him by that name.

The school. When the child enters school for the first time, he is faced with problems of adjusting to many new conditions and situa-

[25] S. Z. Orgel and J. Tuckerman, Nicknames of institutional children, *American Journal of Orthopsychiatry*, 1935, Vol. 6, pp. 276-285.

tions. In the first place, there are many other children to be considered. If the child has been accustomed to being the center of attention and affection, he must soon learn that the attention and affection of the teacher must be shared with other children.

As he develops further, he will find himself competing with others for success and recognition on the playground and in the classroom. It is at this point that many maladjustments have their origin, and they may become more serious as a result of continued failure to achieve success and thus the satisfaction of certain needs that normally accompany achievement. The indiscriminate use of report cards has often been a source of serious harm to the personality of the growing child. The failure of parents and teachers to realize the limitations of the child may produce a strain on him that leads to serious emotional conflicts. Such conflicts become more pronounced with increased maturity, since competition is likely to become greater as one's social awareness matures. Such a condition may develop among normal as well as subnormal children. It is more likely to appear among families from the middle class or the upper lower class, where there are greater anxieties existing about their own achievements and the achievements of their children. Abel and Kinder cite a case of a subnormal adolescent girl who came from such a family.

Elizabeth, a young girl of fourteen, was brought to a psychiatric hospital because she had become mute, rigid, and indifferent to her surroundings. After a few months in the hospital she slowly began to take an interest in the people around her. Elizabeth was particularly fond of sewing and embroidering, but lapsed into her former depression at the least suggestion of doing academic work or reading a book. Records revealed that at the age of seven, when she was in the second grade, her IQ was 73. The intelligence level of her two sisters and brother was considerably higher, no one having an IQ below 110. Elizabeth's school record was poor, and she had repeated a grade in school on two occasions. Apparently neither her parents nor her school realized the nature of her limitations, and they tried to drive her to keep up with normal standards of intellectual achievement. This girl had the misfortune, for her, to come from a home where there was an aspiration level beyond her capacity, and where there was no understanding of any line of conduct other than that of doing well in school.[26]

[26] T. M. Abel and Elaine F. Kinder, *The Subnormal Adolescent Girl* (New York: Columbia University Press, 1942), p. 36.

The school situation brings boys and girls of the same age level together and provides opportunities for them to grow and develop in harmony with certain ideals set forth in the philosophy of the school and the community. Methods in use for personality and character training may be classified as: (1) incidental, (2) formal, and (3) planned functional. The first of these has no planned activities, but the fact that a favorable environment for growth is provided will insure that the individuals concerned will gradually absorb worthy ideals and desirable ways of behaving. The second type depends upon verbal instruction and upon the development of an understanding of the facts and principles found in the school curriculum. The concept that the school should concern itself with verbal learning alone has in general been replaced with a much broader concept of education, although one should not deny the values of knowledge and understanding in the solution of problems and in relation to character and personality development. The planning of activities in the classroom and in the clubs, as well as on the playground, that will contribute to personality development is extremely important, but oftentimes difficult to develop. The schools are turning their attention toward educative experiences in connection with all phases of the school program and even to certain types of out-of-school activities. The activities of the school can best function in personality development when its entire program is integrated in a functional manner with other aspects of the lives and activities of growing boys and girls.

Religious activities. It was pointed out in Chapter 10 that the child's concept of God grows and expands from that of a fairylike notion to more individualistic concepts in which God is looked upon as a more intangible force or being. A reverent attitude is displayed by the child in his religious activities at a fairly early age. This results from his experiences, both at home and at church. This attitude is further enhanced as a result of his experiences elsewhere when God is discussed, when prayers are given, and when the Bible is used. To the small child, religion may be tied in with other aspects of his egocentric nature. This is revealed in the prayers of the child in which he seeks help, security. and things that he is wishing for in his everyday life.

The religious life of the child becomes formalized in connection with the institutions with which he is associated. The child learns to say certain things, to have regard for religious phrases, to recite a special creed, and to do other things fostered by the church with which his parents are identified. These are oftentimes meaningless to the child, but they serve to identify him with certain groups and practices that have an important bearing on his character and personality. Two things stand out in the child's early interests in religious activities. It has already been stated that the preschool child is egocentric in his religious zeal and practices. This may be observed in the attitudes of primary-grade children toward Christmas and Easter. The following dialogue illustrates the egocentric nature of a first-grade child.

"Daddy don't you think that it is bad the way they nailed Jesus to that cross?"

Father replying, "Yes son, I think that was real bad."

Child, "But, if they hadn't done that we wouldn't have Easter eggs, would we?"

A second characteristic of children's interests and attitudes at this stage is that they are interested in happenings and persons, but show little interest in doctrine as such. Children display a keen interest in the childhood of Jesus, and manifest an interest in such characters as Samson, Moses, Joseph, and David.[27] This is in harmony with facts presented in Chapter 13 relative to the concrete nature of children's interests and their interest in children and in action.

Although the growing child has many needs and functions in common with lower animals, he has insights, aspirations, and goals that are distinctly unique and human. Ideals of justice and fair play, of humility and reverence, and of love and understanding are learned through experience. These ideals represent spiritual values that are fostered in religious teaching and experiences, and are promoted in a complete and functional educational program. Although these values may not be observable, they have important bearings on the child's conduct and relations with others. Where such spiritual values prevail, love and co-operation become more than platitudes. They become an integral part of the self and affect behavior in an all-inclusive manner. A child who has developed worthy social and personal habits will function as a co-operating member of a class in worth-while undertakings. Such a child initiates

---

[27] Note the study of G. E. Dawson, Children's interest in the Bible, *Pedagogical Seminar,* 1900, Vol. 7, pp. 151-178. Although this is an early study of this problem, the findings are in harmony with those obtained from various sources bearing on children's interests.

activities that are in harmony with these ideals, and exercises self-control in an effort to reach certain goals. Thus, it makes a great deal of difference whether a child has or has not developed worth-while ideals, and whether the child is guided by ideals and values that promote the welfare of the group as well as of the individual self. The church plays an important role in the development of stable and worth-while ideals among growing boys and girls.[28]

Democratic versus autocratic leadership. There is evidence from the study of the early social climate of adults that aggressive behavior and instability are related to an early life dominated by authoritarian control. Where the father or mother was the dominating (authoritarian) force in the home, the children obeyed, but their lives were filled with tension and frustration. Lewin, Lippitt, and White have conducted a number of investigations of this general problem.[29] Their studies have furnished considerable evidence for the conclusion that the nature of the experimentally created social climate (autocratically or democratically controlled) affects the behavior of children.

In their first experiment, two clubs of ten-year-old boys engaged in theatrical mask-making for a three-month period were studied. The group leader treated one group in an authoritarian manner, while the other group was handled in a democratic procedure.[30] The leader later changed his philosophy of leadership for each club. The behavior of the boys was carefully studied by four observers. In the club meetings the authoritarian-club members developed an increasingly aggressive, domineering attitude toward each other and an attitude of submission toward the leader. The behavior of the democratic-club members toward each other was characterized by friendliness and fact-finding. This group was more spontaneous in its responses and assumed a free and friendly relation with its leader. On the one item of overt hostility, the authoritarian group was much more aggressive than the other, the ratio being 40 to 1. The authoritarian-group members displayed greater hostility toward

[28] For a splendid discussion of the development and importance of spiritual values in the lives of elementary-school children, see *Spiritual Values in the Elementary School, Twenty-sixth Yearbook of the Department of Elementary School Principals*, National Education Association, 1947.

[29] Kurt Lewin, Ronald Lippitt, and Ralph K. White, Patterns of aggressive behavior in experimentally created social climates, *Journal of Social Psychology*, 1939, Vol. 10, pp. 271-299.

[30] Ronald Lippitt, An experimental study of the effect of democratic and authoritarian group atmospheres, University of Iowa, *Studies in Child Welfare*, 1940, Vol. 16, No. 3, pp. 43-195.

each other, used more attention-getting devices, showed hostile criticism, and lack of fair play.

In the second experiment by Lewin, Lippitt, and White, five democratic, five autocratic, and two "laissez faire" atmospheres were established. In the laissez-faire groups the leader sat around and left things to the club members. There was less than half as much participation by him as in either of the other types of groups. The influence of the leader's personality was controlled by having each of four leaders play the role of autocratic and of democratic leader at least once. Relative to tension created, they point out the following:

An instance where tension was created by *annoying* experiences occurred when the group work was criticized by a stranger (janitor). There were two cases where fighting broke out immediately afterwards.

In the autocratic atmosphere the behavior of the leader probably annoyed the children considerably (to judge from the interviews)....

In addition there were six times as many directing approaches to an individual by the leader in autocracy as in democracy. It is probably fair to assume that the bombardment with such frequent ascendant approaches is equivalent to higher *pressure* and that this pressure created a higher tension.[31]

The problem of the factors associated with aggressive behavior among preschool children was studied by Muste and Sharpe.[32] Their study was based upon observations of thirty children ranging in age from two years and ten months to five years and four months at the time of the first observation. In order to have comparable data on the children, special situations were devised in which the play materials and the children present could be controlled. They observed aggressive behavior at some time or another in all the children, although it appeared more often in some children than among others. Also, the nature of the aggressive act varied with different children. The young child, lacking in ability to perceive a situation except from his own point of view, directs his activities toward his own ends or goals. Occasionally, children appeared to show in their aggressiveness a sort of social interplay based upon certain experiences that they had had at home or at some other point. Boys at all age levels displayed more aggressivness than did

[31] *Op. cit.*, p. 291.

[32] Myra J. Muste and Doris F. Sharpe, Some influential factors in the determination of aggressive behavior in preschool children, *Child Development*, 1947, Vol. 18, pp. 11-28.

the girls. Also, less aggressive behavior was observed among the children from the more strictly controlled nursery than from the freer nursery. The controlled-nursery children likewise showed less social interchange. In a controlled environment, children are likely to be more inhibited, and when aggressive behavior does appear, it is of a dominant compulsive nature rather than that of vigorous participation involving the social element. The latter type of aggressive behavior appeared also as a function of age and is related to mental, emotional, and social growth.

Class and cultural status

Cultural differences are important in the development of personality traits of boys and girls, since parents attempt to direct the behavior of their children in harmony with certain cultural patterns. Every culture has its own patterns of behavior which are approved for boys and girls. Margaret Mead has pointed out in this connection that "sexual behavior patterns" vary with different tribes, according to the cultural ideals of the tribe.[33]

The social class of a child's family determines not only the neighborhood in which he lives and the play groups he will have, but also the basic cultural acts and goals toward which he will be trained. There are three major types of cultural systems in the United States. These include

1. the general system of cultural behavior, such as language, manner of dress, and the like,
2. the social-class cultures, and
3. the ethnic-group cultures.

The ethnic-group culture refers to a culture different from that of the general culture, such as the culture of an Oriental of the first generation residing in the United States.

Class status. Studies conducted by Davis and Havighurst in Chicago among different social-class groups show that these differences operate from the very beginning of the child's life and are reflected in child-rearing practices of mothers from the different class groups.[34] Guided interviews were held with fifty mothers of young children from each of four groups: white middle-class.

[33] Margaret Mead, *Sex and Temperament in Three Primitive Societies* (New York: Morrow, 1935).

[34] Allison Davis and Robert Havighurst, Social class and color differences in child rearing, *American Sociological Review,* 1946, Vol. 11, pp. 698-708.

white lower-class, Negro middle-class, Negro lower-class. The principal factors used in making the classifications were occupation of parents, property ownership, membership in churches and other associations, and section of the city in which they lived. Middle-class families were found to be more rigorous than lower-class families in their training of children for feeding and cleanliness habits. Also, the middle-class families are less permissive. They require their children to take naps at a later age, and to be in the house earlier at night. In general, the middle-class families supervise their children more closely and permit less free play of the impulses of their children. The more orthodox middle-class practices make the children overly anxious and thus lead to greater frustration on their part. Closely related to this, thumb sucking was found among three times as many white middle-class children as among white lower-class children.

Comparisons were made by Norton Springer of the scores on the Brown *Personality Inventory for Children* made by children from different sociocultural environments.[35] The scores of the experimental group of 327 boys and girls from grades four through nine from an unfavorable neighborhood were compared with those of 473 boys and girls from middle-class families in a good residential neighborhood. The mean neurotic scores of the experimental group were significantly higher than that of the control group, indicating more emotional instability among children from poor neighborhood conditions. An item analysis of the inventory revealed neurotic responses pertaining to physical symptoms, general social adaptation, home conditions, school adjustments, and dreams.

Membership in a minority group. As children develop, they become aware of race and cultural differences. Such an awareness is not apparent among kindergarten and first-grade children, and this tends to create pronounced anxieties among many parents of children in the majority group. This awareness brings with it a changed attitude toward the self and a changed attitude toward others. These changed attitudes affect behavior and thus personality. Studies show, however, that there is no personality pattern that differentiates the elementary-school child from most minority groups. Results from a comparison of Amish and Negro second- and third-grade children with a control group on the *California Test of Personality* showed more maladjustments among the Amish and Negro chil-

[35] N. Norton Springer, The influence of general social status on the emotional stability of children, *Journal of Genetic Psychology,* 1938, Vol. 53, pp. 321-328.

dren.[36] Amish boys were less well adjusted on the items dealing with sense of personal freedom, while the girls were less well adjusted on the items dealing with a sense of personal worth and feelings of belongingness. Both Negro boys and girls were more antisocial than the control group. Both Amish and Negro children were more sensitive to being mistreated than were children of the control group. There was perhaps some basis for this last-named feeling on the part of these children.

Cultural patterns and values. Commerical forces of various kinds have limited the free activity of children and provided for an early coercion into a set cultural pattern. Children in all cultures are limited in part by the coercions of the customs and mores of the group. John Whiting noted that in the Kwoma community aggression toward younger brothers and sisters on the part of older siblings was approved by the parents, provided it did not result in bodily harm.[37] This practice would no doubt affect the adjustments of children. It was observed that aggression in the play activities of five- and six-year-old children led to retaliation by older and larger children. As a result of this, the younger children adopted a submissive response as the most usual and adaptive way of behaving in the presence of larger and stronger members of the group.

Cultural conditions, reflected in well-planned yards and lawns and household furniture selected for its appearance rather than home use, become coercive at all age levels. For the child, such coercions produce tension and frustrations. His activities are seriously limited by the amount and quality of play space outdoors and by the values placed on "good taste" and appearance within the home. Lois Murphy has pointed out the ways in which standards of living tend to limit the expression of the child's individuality as follows:

The decreasing size of families, which means that we seldom now see a home in which children outnumber the grownups, has helped make it possible for grownups to maintain the artificial standards of appearance. It is only a home in which grownups outnumber children that finds it possible to put appearance first. Where grownups outnumber children the results are apparent in the way the child works, talks and acts generally. He is more apt to be a carbon copy—a little adult—instead of the romping, happy-go-lucky, puppy-like creature that the

[36] T. L. Engle, Personality adjustments of children belonging to two minority groups, *Journal of Educational Psychology,* 1945, Vol. 36, pp. 543-560.

[37] John W. M. Whiting, The frustration complex in Kwoma society, *Man,* 1944, Vol. 44, pp. 140-144.

child between three and ten generally is when he lives in a child culture.[38]

Not only do cultural patterns and values operate to produce frustrations among children, but these produce tension among preadolescents and adults. The interests and values of preadolescents are not directed toward aesthetic and social prestige values of the home and furnishings. The early adolescent would prefer a chair whose arms he can throw his legs over to one made according to some recognized colonial design. The informal, carefree, impulsive nature of the adolescent is hampered by the home when aesthetic and social-prestige values are given priority over utilitarian and socially useful values. When such conditions exist, the children seek other places for fun and recreation—places where they will not be so seriously blocked in their ordinary group activities. These cultural patterns and values found in the home and neighborhood become important forces in molding well-adjusted or poorly adjusted personalities.

In a study of child-rearing practices, Davis and Havighurst found there were more class differences than color (white versus Negro) differences.[39] Negroes of both classes appear to give girls earlier training for responsibility in dishwashing, going to the store, and dressing themselves. Negro mothers were found to be more permissive than white mothers in feeding and in weaning of children but more rigorous than the white mothers in toilet training. Among the middle-class Negroes, there was a tendency noticed to attempt to protect the preadolescent girl as evidenced by the fact that she was not allowed to play across the street and go to the movies alone as early as middle-class white girls.

The adjusted personality

Personality types. Individuals are constantly being divided into types for the purpose of cataloguing and classifying personalities. These efforts have resulted in an oversimplification of personality, and have furnished a number of two-way classifications, such as the following:

introverts — extroverts
dominant — submissive
theoretical — practical

[38] Lois Barclay Murphy, Cultural factors in the development of children, *Childhood Education,* 1946, Vol. 23, p. 58.
[39] *Op. cit.,* pp. 706-708.

Careful studies show, however, that most people represent a mixed type, and do not fall into either of the extreme groups. Furthermore, variations between individuals of a group are continuous in nature, falling at all points between the two extremes.

The concept of types based on body build has received emphasis in recent years. The early classification of Kretschmer [40] provided a basis for classifying personality into the following types based upon physical structures:

Body Build	*Personality Characteristics*
Asthenic or slender build	Withdrawal tendencies
Pyknic or broad build	Volatile, outgoing, assertive tendencies

Sheldon's studies followed those of Kretschmer, but furnish a different classification.[41] He has brought forth a tripolar classification parallel to his three large groups of body-build types. His first group, the *viscerotonia,* is characterized by general relaxation, liking for people, desire for comfort, a high degree of sociability, and love of affection. The second group, the *somatotonia,* is largely a muscular type and is characterized by vigorous bodily activity, strength, and energy. The third group, the *cerebrotonia,* is secretive in nature and is especially characterized by its inhibitory nature. Subjects of these three types may be rated on a seven-point scale for each of the primary body builds. Other types have been listed, such as intellectual, sexual, and so on. Marked agreement between body structure and personality characters have been reported by Sheldon.

The Grant Study, conducted by the Department of Hygiene at Harvard University, has made studies of the relationship between body structure and certain personality types.[42] Somatotype ratings were given to 260 individuals included in this study. In the case of subjects where there was a somatotype dominance, there was a pronounced amount of cerebrotonia dominance. The association here was found to be 84 per cent dominant somatotype, whereas dominant viscerotonia was typical of only 2 per cent of those classified as ectomorphs. This study offers evidence that there is a close relation-

---

[40] E. Kretschmer, *Physique and Character* (New York: Harcourt, Brace and Co., 1925).

[41] W. H. Sheldon, S. S. Stevens, and W. B. Tucker, *The Varieties of Human Physique* (New York: Harper & Brothers, 1942).

[42] Carl C. Seltzer, F. L. Wells, and E. B. McTernan, A relationship between Sheldonian somatotype and psychotype, *Journal of Personality,* 1948, Vol. 16, pp. 431-436.

ship among the extremes. In the case of the less extreme types, the association does not appear so clear.

Personality adjustments. Life has been described as a continuous process of change and adjustment. It was pointed out in Chapter 3 that the newborn infant is faced with many adjustment problems as he emerges from the sheltered life within the mother to an expanded social and physical environment. As he develops out of the stage of infancy, new problems arise that call for adjustments and readjustments in his behavior. His first adjustments are concerned with life activities in his home environment. These early home adjustments are of utmost importance in connection with later adjustments. Personality conflicts growing out of home conditions will be discussed in Chapters 15 and 16. As the child grows and develops, his world becomes enlarged and adjustments must be made to people and conditions beyond his home environment. These transition or adjustment periods are crucial points in the development of the individual, since it is in connection with such conditions that conflicts arise.

It is the home, however, that furnishes security to the child during the early years of life. In the home, the child under normal circumstances receives affection and learns to give affection.

Qualities of the "poorly adjusted" child. A number of criteria can be set forth for evaluating the qualities of the "poorly adjusted" child. In the first place, children may be evaluated in terms of their responses to various situations listed on personality tests, referred to earlier in this chapter. Many studies have been made of personality development based upon tests validated by carefully devised techniques. The items from such tests may be used as a basis for determining the qualities of a poorly adjusted child. Another method of determining the qualities of poorly adjusted children, is to consider qualities found in their behavior that are satisfying to those with whom they come in contact. This procedure differs from the first in that in this case emphasis is placed upon the effects of the child's behavior on others, while in the former procedure greater emphasis is given to the behavior as indicative of frustrations in relation to certain needs.

A study by Del Solar emphasized the effects of the child's behavior on parents and teachers.[43] A check list, consisting of thirty-five propositions, chosen from a group of "satisfactions" and "problems"

[43] Del Solar, *Parents and Teachers View the Child* (Teachers College, Columbia University: Bureau of Publications, 1949).

that had been reported during interviews with parents and teachers was prepared. The propositions described some aspect of the child's way of behaving, his attitudes, or his abilities.

A comparison was made between the appraisals of the children who differed, according to their teachers' opinions, with respect to their school adjustments. Both parents and teachers placed considerable emphasis on the "problems" confronting them in dealing with children. It appears that the poorly adjusted child is likely to be judged in terms of whether or not his behavior is satisfying to the individual making the appraisal. A marked similarity was noted in the problems reported by parents of "poorly" and "well-adjusted" children; however, the parents of the poorly adjusted group reported significantly more problems in the categories involving difficulties in social relationships, not being well-groomed, and having poor work habits. The teachers described the poorly adjusted children as lacking in self-confidence, tense, fearful, and unable to work persistently or to use their abilities to full advantage. They report few strong points, while the parents of the poorly adjusted seem to appreciate certain characteristics which do not appear in the teachers' observations. They agreed more on what was wrong with the child than on what was right.

Summary and generalization

A study of the meaning of personality as defined by students of psychology shows a widespread emphasis upon the individual as a unified whole. The infant child is more than a composite of many separate physiological and psychological factors: he is a dynamic personality functioning as an organism in his ever-expanding environment. Explanations of the development of a child's personality have within recent years emphasized the interaction of hereditary factors and environmental forces and conditions. Attempts to set off heredity and environment as two forces operating independently fail to explain personality differences appearing under varying circumstances and conditions. The hereditary nature of the child affects his reactions to environmental conditions about him and the environmental conditions about him affect his hereditary potentialities.

Everyone whom the child meets and to whom he responds and every group and institution with which he is identified leave their marks upon him. The parents and childhood friends, with whom he is in close contact, have the most lasting effects upon his personality development. The development of a well-adjusted personality is not the result of accident, but rather of forces and conditions that are favorable for personality development. If a child is encouraged to participate in social activities where mutual interests are respected, if he is fortunate in being reared in a home where the parents are well adjusted, if he is given a reasonable amount of guided liberty, rather than authoritarian control, he will probably develop desirable personality traits. But if his life is circumscribed with limited activities and superficial satisfactions, he will be unable to respond to a well-balanced program of living when he reaches maturity. The roots of most inferiority feelings are laid in the insecurities of childhood. The growth of personality begins in the cradling practices of the home. The child may be truthfully said to be a part of everything that he has experienced. The attitudes of the parents, the values and pattern of the home, his class membership, the composition of his playmates, the nature of his community, the quality of the school he attends, and his own constitutional make-up are factors that operate in an interrelated manner in affecting the growing personality.

Questions and Exercises

1. Look up several definitions of the term personality. Show how one's definition of the term will affect his treatment of the subject.
2. Cite cases from your observations, readings, or experiences in which glandular conditions have affected a child's personality.
3. Show how size might affect one's personality. How would oversize likely affect the personality of a child in the first grade at school?
4. Contrast the general effects on the personality of a child of being reared in a high and low sociocultural status.
5. The question has sometimes been raised: What's in a name? How would you answer this in the case of nicknames? Can you cite instances in which a child's nickname might have been an influential factor in his personality development?
6. Contrast the effects of an autocratic and democratic environment on the behavior of a group of nine- or ten-year-old children.
7. Why is it very difficult to measure personality? What experiences have you had with personality evaluations? What cautions should be observed in connection with results from such evaluations?
8. What are some of the outstanding features of a home situation which tend to provide for good personality adjustments among the children of the home?

9. The volume by Ruth Benedict, *The Chrysanthemum and the Sword: Patterns of Japanese Culture,* published by Houghton, Mifflin Company (1946), provides splendid material for a report on the effect of early cultural influences upon personality development. Read it and comment on it.

Selected Readings

Anderson, John E. Personality organization in children, *Readings in Child Psychology,* Wayne Dennis, ed. New York: Prentice-Hall, 1951. Pp. 476-490.

Beverly, Bert I. *Psychology of Growth.* New York: McGraw-Hill Book Co., 1946. Chap. III.

Breckenridge, Marian E., and Vincent, E. Lee. *Child Development.* 2nd ed.; Philadelphia: W. B. Saunders Co., 1949. Chap. XII.

Cattell, Raymond B. *Description and Measurement of Personality.* Yonkers, New York: World Book Co., 1946.

Forest, Isle. *Early Years at School.* New York: McGraw-Hill Book Co., 1949. Chap. XII.

Garrison, Karl C. *Psychology of Adolescence.* 4th ed.; New York: Prentice-Hall, 1951. Chap. XV.

Goodenough, Florence L. The appraisal of personality, *Psychological Review,* 1949, Vol. 56, pp. 123-131.

Hurlock, Elizabeth B. *Child Development.* 2nd ed.; New York: McGraw-Hill Book Co., 1950. Chap. XV.

Lewin, Kurt. Behavior and development as a function of the total situation, *Manual of Child Psychology,* L. Carmichael, ed. New York: John Wiley and Sons, 1946. Chap. XVI.

Millard, Cecil V. *Child Growth and Development in the Elementary School Years.* Boston: D. C. Heath and Company, 1951. Chap. XIII.

Murphy, Lois B. Childhood experiences in relation to personality development, in *Personality and the Behavior Disorders,* J. McV. Hunt, ed. New York: The Ronald Press Co., 1944.

Olson, Willard C. *Child Development.* Boston: D. C. Heath and Company, 1949. Chap. VII.

Thorpe, Louis P. *Child Psychology and Development.* New York: The Ronald Press Co., 1946. Chap. XIV.

15

Personality Development: Conflicts and Adjustment

Introduction: Problems of adjustment

The source of maladjustments. It has been suggested by some students of psychology that "life is beset with conflicts." As soon as the individual becomes adjusted in one respect, he appears to be maladjusted in some other way. These maladjustments result from thwarting of basic needs or conflicts between certain needs. Thus, it appears that personality adjustment is dependent upon a balanced satisfaction of these needs. Prescott and others have emphasized the importance of meeting the emotional needs of children, if wholesome personality development is to be attained.[1] These needs have been listed and studied under three interrelated interacting categories: structural needs, social needs, and ego-integrative needs. The structural needs have to do with with physical needs for oxygen, appropriate foods, liquids, proper elimination, normal sexual activities, appropriate rhythm of exercise and rest. The social needs include need for affection, belonging, and satisfactory human relations. The ego-integrative needs involve personal worth, status, and security. Louis Raths has emphasized the need for meeting the basic needs in order to avert maladjustments and to improve human relations. He recognizes eight basic human needs: (1) love and affection, (2) belonging, (3) achievement, (4) freedom from fear and aggression, (5) economic security, (6) sharing and participation, (7) freedom from guilt, and (8) world understanding.[2]

[1] Daniel A. Prescott, *Emotion and the Education Process* (Washington: American Council on Education, 1938).

[2] See the measuring instrument by Louis E. Raths, *The Wishing Well* (Columbus, Ohio: Bureau of Educational Research, Ohio State University).

Authorities are not in complete agreement about these basic needs, especially those that may be termed personality needs and must be met by the interaction of the individual with environmental conditions. There is good evidence from anthropological studies that the personality needs are not similarly manifested among all children. In fact, these needs appear to vary with different socioeconomic groups. To the extent that these are interrelated with the biological nature of the maturing individual, they would appear in some form among all children.

Child dynamics and conflicts. Throughout this study, the child has been described as a dynamic individual, growing and developing in accordance with the various forces and conditions of his environment. Child dynamics has been considered by some students of child growth in terms of basic needs, the importance of which have been described by Daniel Prescott:

These needs are the basis of permanent adjustment problems which all of us face. They are more or less continuously with us. Our behavior is patterned in accordance with what experience has shown us to be the most satisfactory way of working them out, but, as conditions around us vary and change, we are continuously under the necessity of modifying our behavior. These needs become sources of unpleasant effect and even of serious personality maladjustments if they are not met adequately. Furthermore, our society is rich in circumstances which deny to individuals the fulfillment of one or several of these needs and quasi needs for periods of varying length—this is what has happened to thousands of maladjusted children. There is a serious disharmony between the needs which they feel to be vital to themselves and the experiences in life as they meet them.[3]

The actions of a maladjusted child are directed toward social integration just as truly as is the case for the adjusted. The well-adjusted child, however, tends to conform to the requirements of the social group in which he lives and thus attains social acceptance. Disturbing behavior, according to Rudolf Dreikurs, is directed toward one of four possible goals.[4] In order to establish a satisfactory place in the group he tries to "(1) gain attention; (2) demonstrate his power or superiority; (3) punish or get even; or he (4) gives up in complete discouragement." The same child may display "attention-getting behavior" in his peer group, while he resorts to a

[3] Prescott, *op. cit.,* pp. 111-112.
[4] Rudolf Dreikurs, The four goals of the maladjusted child, *The Nervous Child,* 1947, Vol. 6, p. 322.

different sort of behavior at home. The attention-getting behavior is usually fostered in our middle-class culture, and is ordinarily present among young children from middle-class homes.

Changes with age. Parents are often heard to say, "Mary is so annoying. She was no trouble at all when she was three years of age, which was just two years ago." The question might well be raised as to why this is true. When Mary was obedient and easy to manage, she had not learned the possibilities of expressing herself in so many different ways as she is able to do at the age of five years. When she learned that she could through her own initiative and self-assertion do many things for herself, she attained one of the most important lessons in "growing-up." This was indeed a small but important step toward the achievement of independence. However, such a step might be most annoying to a mother who had earlier been able to handle Mary by direct suggestions and directions. At the earlier stage, there were no arguments, few questions, and little if any discussion relative to things to do. Perhaps Mary has changed. The trouble is all too often that parents who are responsible for guiding children fail to realize that this change has come about. The failure of parents to realize that the child is growing up may be listed as one of the outstanding causes of problems among preschool children.

Closely connected with the problem of parents' failure to realize that the child is growing up is the failure to guide and prepare the child for the next stage of development. It has already been pointed out that the growth of the preschool child is gradual in nature. If the child of five is going to be able to skip and jump as other children of this age level, he must have had opportunities for play and the development of self-assurance and initiative that are essential for the performance of many more complex motor skills. The development of self-assurance is only indirectly related to maturation. Thus, while the child of five may be sufficiently mature to learn to skip and jump, he may fail to develop skills of this type because of the lack of those experiences that would give him the initiative, self-assurance, and desire for learning such skills. Johnnie's quietness around the house or at the nursery, which leads the teacher and parent to comment favorably about his conduct, should not be regarded as a favorable symptom of adjustment. Such a child may actually be more in need of attention than the "naughty" child who is a continuous source of annoyance. From infancy onward, children have their moments of activity and their moments of quiescence. The child who refrains from all activity should be regarded as a problem needing special attention.

Fundamental needs of the child

Meaning and significance of needs. "Needs" are often a source of confusion because of the different usages of the word. One person will emphasize the biological needs, another a group of social needs, while another may emphasize psychological needs. Also, needs are sometimes designated for different stages in life. In such a case, the needs for the infant and preschool child would be quite different from those for adolescents and adults. Concerning the meaning and significance of needs of nursery-school children, Lawrence Frank has stated the following:

The child's needs may be seen as arising from his biological and physiological functions and, more significantly, from the series of life tasks that he faces in the required socialization of his impulses and his behavior. These requirements create acute needs that are generally ignored or denied, because we are usually more interested in using the child for various purposes that we value more than the integrity of the child. The fundamental needs of the child are the basic requirements for a desirable social life.[5]

Organic needs. All children need food, rest, sleep, and play; but they vary widely in the amount of each of these needed. Since some children are much more active than others, they will need more food to provide for the energy used in various activities. Some do not grow as rapidly as others and so do not require as much food. Some children will need more sleep than others. Sometimes it is wiser to forego a nap because of the adverse psychological effect that a forced nap may have on the child. Furthermore, there is always the question of just how much rest a particular child needs.

Nutritional needs. The food that a child eats from birth until he is six years of age will be an important factor in determining his physical health and emotional well-being. Furthermore, since later development is so largely dependent upon what has gone on before, the early diet will have an important bearing upon the child's growth and development toward maturity.

Table 62 shows the main kinds of food that are usually given

[5] Lawrence K. Frank, *The Fundamental Needs of the Child,* Paper presented at the conference of the National Association for Nursery Education, Nashville, Tennessee, October 22, 1937.

to children of the preschool age and the amount required by such children of average size. metabolic rate, and appetite.[6] Except for a few foods that are not suitable to the preschool child, the diet of the adult is much the same as that of the young child. Children of the preschool age should eat at least part of their meal with the family, and their food should increasingly be prepared and planned as part of the family meal as they grow from one to six years of age. However, parents should be warned against impatience and overanxiety in dealing with the child's eating. Many feeding problems have their origin at the time the baby first starts playing with his food. The child's experiments in stirring and otherwise manipulating the food with his spoon are part of the process of growing up in which the child is making new discoveries and finding new skills. These actions try the patience of the anxious mother who desires to see her child eat a well-balanced meal and not get gravy all over his face, the tray, and his high chair.

Happy children, who are not forced to comply with tightly drawn food rules and eating habits, do not present difficult feeding problems. Many children, however, rebel against the impatience and domineering attitude of the mother or nurse. The child will eat a sufficient amount to satisfy his small appetite, an amount which gives him sufficient nourishment to exert himself. From that point, he battles his mother over eating more food. There are many different ways in which he wages this battle. Sometimes he knocks the plate of food to the floor. He is especially apt at dawdling and spilling things. As he grows older, he may find that an upset stomach is a great weapon against forced feeding. In any case, the parent should be concerned about the reason for his refusal to eat all of his cereal, or drink his milk or orange juice. Meeting the mealtime calmly and with patience and recognizing that better eating habits will not be developed suddenly will go a long way toward improving the eating habits of the child whose eating habits offer a problem.

Need of acceptance. The discussion of the child's organic needs indicates that all children cannot be treated in the same manner. Each baby must be recognized as a unique living organism with its own hereditary characteristics. Furthermore, these characteristics become still more unique as a result of differences in experiences from the very beginning of life. The child is not an image of either parent, neither is he ordered according to their peculiar likings. The

[6] This table is reproduced from *Your Child from One to Six,* U.S. Children's Bureau, Federal Security Agency, 1945, Publication No. 30.

TABLE 62 The foods commonly given to preschool children and the amounts that the average healthy child may be expected to eat

Family meal	Two-year-old child	Five-year-old child
Morning		
Orange (1). Oatmeal (½ cup) with cream. Whole-wheat toast (2 slices). Butter. Milk or coffee (1 cup).	Orange juice (4-6 table-spoonfuls). Oatmeal (3-4 tablespoon-fuls) with milk. Whole-wheat toast (½ slice). Butter. Milk (1 cup).	Orange (1). Oatmeal (½ cup) with milk. Whole-wheat toast (1 slice). Butter. Milk (1 cup).
Noontime		
Egg salad. Potato (cooked in jacket). Peas, fresh (½ cup). Whole-wheat bread (2 slices). Butter. Fruit cup (⅔ cup). Milk (1 cup).	Hard-cooked egg or beef ball. Potato (cooked in jacket). Sieved peas (½ cup). Whole-wheat bread, stale or toasted (½ slice). Butter. Pear, cooked and mashed (4 tablespoonfuls). Milk (1 cup).	Hard-cooked egg (1). Peas, fresh (½ cup). Potato (cooked in jacket). Whole-wheat bread (1 slice). Butter. Fruit cup (⅔ cup). Milk (1 cup).
Evening		
Beef balls with spa-ghetti. String beans (½ cup). Carrot and cabbage salad. Whole-wheat bread (1-2 slices). Butter. Apple Betty. Milk or coffee.	Well-cooked whole-grain cereal (4 tablespoon-fuls) with milk (2-4 tablespoonfuls). Stale bread (1 slice). Butter. Apple sauce (¼ cup). Milk (1 cup).	Beef balls (1). String beans (½ cup). Carrot strips (3 pieces). Whole-wheat bread (1 slice). Butter. Apple Betty (½ cup). Milk (1 cup).

Note.—Fortified margarine may be used in place of butter.

parents must accept the child born from the union of the sperm and ovum, even though it may not meet their wishes or standards. From the very beginning, parents should recognize the individuality of the baby and accept the child that was born, encouraging the development of his abilities and potential characteristics. Failure to accept the child as he is leads to many difficulties. In the first place, the real child becomes in some respects an unwanted child.

The child may try to be like one of his parents in order to please the parent, or he may try to live up to the parental ideal in order to win approval. However, this does not provide for wholesome personality development.

Need for affection. The child, from the very beginning, needs love and affection. It is at this point that the child in a happy home has a great advantage. Babies need to be cradled and loved, especially when they are being fed. As the child grows older, cuddling should perhaps be diminished gradually and love shown in other ways. In this connection, parents should be careful lest they smother the growing child with too much affection. Sometimes the mother who actually rejects the child displays an excess of affection in an effort to prevent the child and others from realizing that he is rejected. As the child grows older, affection can be shown by avoiding criticism and by praise and encouragement. In all forms of affection there exists to some extent the coming together of two or more personalities. W. C. Menninger has stated: "Among the basic requirements for healthy development of personality, probably the most difficult lesson that every child needs to learn—and many adults should, but have not learned—is how to love and be loved." [7] The child's need for love and affection must be satisfied if he is to develop a healthy personality and feel secure in meeting life's problems in a troubled world. A child who feels that he is not wanted or loved often becomes a problem. He attempts to attract attention by aggressive behavior or some other means. If he knows that he is loved, he develops an outgoing, generous, and trusting attitude toward others.

Another source of difficulty comes from divided attention. The child may show jealousy when a newborn sister or brother arrives. Unless a child has been prepared beforehand, the arrival of a new baby may cause anxiety or stimulate jealousy or hatred of the baby. The child faces a baffling situation; not only the mother's time and attention, but also much of her affection and interest, are transferred to the baby. Many ill-effects may result from such a condition. This situation can be avoided if the child is told that he may expect a new brother or sister and that the new baby will require considerable care and attention because he is too young to care for himself. If the child is old enough, he can be given some responsibility in helping with the baby.

[7] W. C. Menninger, Mental health in our schools, *Educational Leadership,* 1950, Vol. 7, pp. 510-523.

Need for a feeling of security. Closely related to the need for affection is a need for security. The small child needs to feel that he is wanted, that he belongs to someone and some place, and that he is closely identified with that place. As he develops, he comes to feel more keenly that he has a definite place to fill in his small environment. The cuddling of the child, important in connection with the need for affection, likewise aids in providing a feeling of security. During the weaning process, the child needs additional comfort and reassurance to prevent acute feelings of insecurity and anxiety.

Sometimes a feeling of insecurity is caused by discord between the parents, by frequent moves from one place to another, or by a broken home condition in which the child is shifted from one home base to another. Economic insecurity in the home may have its effect upon the child at a fairly early age, since he senses certain fears and anxieties of his parents.

Closely related to the need for a feeling of security is *a feeling of achievement or success.* This need may be conceived of as an outgrowth and combination from the other needs listed. The child needs to feel at an early age that he has a role to play, that his contribution to the home is worth while, and that he is needed and wanted. Desirable ways of eating and toilet training, when begun before the child is sufficiently mature, tend to discourage him and build up a feeling of failure. Here again, patience and understanding on the part of the parents are most important. During the toilet-training period, the child needs constant reassurance and encouragement. Frequently, enuresis results from the methods used during this training period. Tenseness, anxiety, and fear should be avoided, while self-assurance and a feeling of success should be encouraged. This can best be done by providing the child with opportunities to do things in harmony with his maturation and needs and encouraging him when he shows an indication of achievement.

Needs related to social demands. The child needs guidance, reassurance, and understanding if he is to accept his own sex and the fact that the differences between boys and girls is a matter to be expected and accepted. He needs enlightenment on problems that may arise in connection with birth. However, such an enlightenment should not go beyond the child's interests and ability to understand.

The small child must learn at a fairly early age that there are some inviolables. A child may not understand why it is all right for him to handle certain objects at his own home but not while he is visiting. He may not understand why he may have a cookie from a plate on the table in his own home but must wait until offered one when he is at someone else's home. He may not understand why it is all right for him to box his older brother at home but why he must not hit larger boys when he is away from home. He will need to learn that adults other than the members of his family do not wish to be caressed by him. He will need toleration, assurance, and guidance while he learns to follow customs and accept certain inviolables.

Adjustment problems of the child

When the attainment of a need is thwarted or progress toward a goal is blocked, an adjustment problem appears. The child faced with such a condition becomes tense, and this tension persists until an adequate response is made. For one reason or another, the need may diminish in importance; otherwise, it may be said to have been satisfied when the desired goal or a substitute has been reached. If there is nothing to hinder the child from reaching the goal, action directed toward it will occur and no adjustment problem will appear.

Child dynamics and adjustment. The child's needs are continuously being blocked by varying circumstances and conditions in his environment. This does not mean that personality disturbances are ever-present in his life. Neither does it imply that the satisfaction of all of the child's needs would result in a well-developed personality. It would appear rather that the child will grow best as a result of help or guidance in meeting difficult situations rather than in provisions whereby difficult situations are never met. Materials bearing on this will be presented in Chapter 16. The extent to which the blocking of needs will lead to maladjustment will depend upon a number of factors, such as "(1) the dynamic nature of the need that is blocked, (2) the extent to which it is blocked, (3) the possibilities of providing a substitute goal, and (4) the extent to which the child is fortified by affection, security, and a feeling of personal worth." [8] The child who is unwanted or apparently not loved by any particular person will reveal characteristics of instability and general lack of self-control. When the need for affection seems to be denied, the child might resort to stealing, exhibitionism, lying, or other forms of behavior in an effort to adjust to such a condition. Lawrence Lader has described a case of a child's lying in order to adjust to a need for affection.

[8] Karl C. Garrison, *The Psychology of Exceptional Children* (rev. ed.; New York: The Ronald Press Company, 1950), p. 402.

At the age of eight, Jane was continually fibbing. When her class-mates talked about ponies, Jane insisted that she had one. When they talked about chickens, she told them about her chicken coop. One day she insisted her father was an aviator; the next day that he was a policeman. Her teacher warned her that if she didn't stop, she would be punished. But the fibbing continued.

One day the teacher visited Jane's home. She found that Jane had a younger brother who had been the family pet since his birth two years before. Although unjustifiably, Jane had built up the idea that her parents were no longer interested in her. What Jane needed, the teacher realized, was not discipline but affection. Since her own world wasn't fulfilling her needs, she was creating an artificial one.

The teacher persuaded Jane's parents to give her more attention and suggested buying her a dog. In class, the teacher gave Jane a new sense of importance by putting her imagination to work through school plays, and introduced real adventure into her life with trips to museums and zoos. In a few months, Jane's fibbing ceased.[9]

Parental attitudes. Too often an overambitious parent is the major factor responsible for maladjustment. From a study of the incidence of emotional symptoms in elementary-school children, Cummings found that overprotected children revealed a preponderance of nervous difficulties, while neglected children were more aggressive in their behavior, along with being given to lying, stealing, and cruelty to a greater extent.[10] The early development of destructive and negatively directed patterns of behavior presents clinical psychologists and psychiatrists with baffling problems. Especially is this true when no glandular or other organic basis or traceable psychogenic factors from unfavorable environmental influences are noted. The label "constitutional type" has been given to this group; however, such a label does not offer an explanation for the develop-ment of such behavior patterns, but rather substitutes a name for the understanding of the origin of these patterns in terms of child dynamics. Frederick H. Allen presents the case of the development of psychopathic behavior in a child through the operation of projec-tion on the part of the mother.

This boy (age nine) was described as completely unmanageable at home and at school. He was said to be a well-organized boy with a veneer of good manners and with normal intelligence, and with the capacity

[9] Lawrence Lader, Warning to parents, *This Week's Magazine,* Sunday Magazine, April 30, 1950, p. 5.

[10] John D. Cummings, The incidence of emotional symptoms in school children, *British Journal of Educational Psychology,* 1944, Vol. 14, pp. 151-161.

to create irritations everywhere he went. The mother gave a description of stealing, six attacks on his young sister, and other evidence that he was setting himself against all authority and defying everyone to change him.

The early beginnings of this problem are important for discussion. . . . She (the mother) had a satisfying job when she was married, and was deeply disturbed when she became pregnant, one month after marriage. She tried to reconcile herself to this by building up in her mind a picture of the kind of child she wanted. This child, even before birth, became a symbol of her own frustration and of standing between what she wanted for herself and what was required of her as a parent.

Her first experiences as a mother were strongly influenced by her own conflicts. The early feeding experience, for example, probably brought out some of the normal reactions of a healthy vigorous infant in his first aggressing. She recalls the vigorous way he went for her breast. Her emotional reactions to these first demands of her child on her as a mother could not help influencing the way she responded. Her husband was away for the first weeks which added to her anxiety and irritation. Her breast milk became scarce, the infant became more demanding out of natural demands, and by the end of eight weeks she had a fretful, demanding, crying infant, who vomited nearly every time she tried to feed him. . . .

Here we see the beginning of a projection—the mother, starting with partially disguised hostility, finds in the child's behavior the cause for more hostility. Wanting to find a way of expressing the positive feeling for the child, she found herself constantly correcting behavior which became the justification for her not being able to love him.

At six months the boy began to show a more organized pattern of aggression. His physical development was rapid and with the aid of a "toddler" he could move about the house. Everything he could reach was attacked and broken. Out of the ensuing struggles he developed rapidly as an individual, but as one who was organized against society and determined to get what he wanted on his own terms. At eighteen months he was collecting milk bottles in the neighborhood and selling them. He began running away at four; through his beguiling manner he could always get money by begging in order to get back home.[11]

This case reveals the operation of a dynamic individual in an environmental situation where his needs are thwarted by the projections of his mother. The aggressive behavior pattern developed out of this interaction between forces and conditions essential for growth on his part and the needs and aspirations of the mother, which

[11] Frederick H. Allen, Psychopathic behavior—fact or projection, *American Journal of Orthopsychiatry*, 1950, Vol. 20, pp. 238-239.

are in this instance operating in opposition to each other. The child becomes labeled a "bad boy," and this is referred back to his constitutional nature for an explanation. The fact that the opposing forces operate in an insiduous way makes it difficult to understand their psychogenic origin, and provides the way for an explanation based on the constitutional make-up of the individual.

Home environment. Many children are brought up in home situations characterized by emotional turmoil and difficulties. Sometimes the child is caught between dissension on the part of the parents. Each one, then, attempts to win his love and admiration by various methods. Again, the child may be brought up in a home where a balanced sense of values does not exist. All the energies and activities of the parents may be directed toward the attainment of certain social aspirations. Genuine understanding, affection, and a balanced program of living will be lacking. A child, absorbing such attitudes, will find himself a misfit with his peers at a later date. Kanner presents the case of Donald, a seven-year-old boy brought to the clinic by his mother, who complained about his progress in school, his conduct at home, and his general depravity. The mother apparently wanted the clinic to remake Donald. The home situation is described as follows:

Donald is the second of two children, the family, therefore, consists of four people. There is no affection between them. The mother resents her husband, is constantly quarreling with the 15-year-old daughter, and patently hates Donald, who has been subject to incessant scolding and whipping. She blames her husband for "being too calm with the boy." This calmness is not the result of particular fondness for Donald, but of an artificial pachydermatoris which he has developed as the only escape available to him from his wife's persistent nagging.[12]

School adjustments. Another focal point in the adjustment of boys and girls is the school. When a child enters school for the first time, he is faced with the problem of adjusting to many new conditions. In the first place, there are many other children to be considered. Regardless of his desire for attention, he must share his experiences and activities with others. At home he received the attention and recognition usually given to children of his age level. He was not called upon to share this special attention with others, while at school there will be many of his age level, each having a felt need for recognition and affection.

[12] Leo Kanner, The role of the school in the treatment of rejected children, *The Nervous Child*, 1944, Vol. 3, pp. 236-248.

As he passes out of the nursery-school period, he will find himself competing with others for success and recognition in the various tasks of the school. It is in this connection that a number of maladjustments have their inception, or that certain maladjustments already present become aggravated. The failure of parents and teachers to recognize a child's limitations may produce a strain on the individual that leads to serious emotional conflicts. If the child is successful in making adjustments in school, and if the balance between success and failure in school activities is in favor of success, he will develop habits of self-confidence and self-realization important for his personal and social adjustment. In this connection, the kinds of report cards that are carried home may be a source of confusion and difficulty. The effects of these report cards become more grave as the individual passes through the grades and develops an increased social sensitiveness about his shortcomings. They also appear to be a source of great conflicts at the junior-high-school age than during the earlier years. This is illustrated in the case of a seventh-grade student, referred to as Anne, who came to the writer's attention.

Anne's report card, which she carried home, was what has generally been termed quite poor. The father was very much irritated over the poor showing in mathematics and social studies, and made some strong threats. Certain week-end privileges were taken from the girl, and she was required to spend more time with her studies. The girl seemed to withdraw from her classmates and indulged in considerable daydreaming. Little improvement was noted in her grades, and the father became all the more concerned and proceeded to visit the school principal about the matter, as he had earlier threatened to do. The principal looked up her record on the cumulative records and noted that she had never made good grades. He also observed that on one intelligence test she made a score which gave her an IQ of 86 while on a later test her IQ was listed as 82. The principal reminded her father that the girl's past work was not superior, and that he was perhaps expecting too much from her. The mother appeared to sense the problem better than the father, and brought the case to the attention of a psychologist. The below-normal intelligence was verified from administering the *Stanford Revision of the Binet Tests* to the girl. Tests of reading ability revealed a low comprehension score. The mother was told that the girl was definitely not of the academic type and should not be expected to make good and superior grades in school. A second visit to the psychologist by the mother, accompanied by the father, cleared up some points of confusion created from the traditional report card sent to the parents.

Various studies have shown a close relationship between disorderly behavior in school and maladjustments. A recent study by Frances Mullen was designed to ascertain what physical, educational, personal, and social factors were closely associated with truancy and with disorderly classroom behavior.[13] The data for this study were secured from the records of the Bureau of Child Study of the Chicago Board of Education. A comparison of the truants and classroom disorderly groups showed the truants to come more often from broken homes, to have a more checkered school career, to have engaged in lying or stealing to a greater degree, and, more often, to have a parent or sibling who is a delinquent. The classroom discipline cases, on the other hand, are more often nervous and hyper-

TABLE 63   Behavior and personality factors cited in the case histories of discipline problems in school compared with those found among the total group (after Mullen)

Behavior and Person- ality Factors	Preadolescent Classroom Disci- pline Problem Group (N-511)	Adolescent Classroom Disci- pline Problem Group (N-231)	All Children Examined in 1946 (N-8679)
Poor work habits	52.5 per cent	51.9 per cent	10.6 per cent
Nail biting or thumb sucking	8.6	10.8	7.0
Lack of self-confidence	8.6	13.4	6.0
Nervousness, hyperactivity .	18.6	19.5	5.6
Social immaturity	5.9	7.8	5.1
Aggressive, antisocial behavior	27.4	27.7	3.5
Attention-getting devices ..	16.9	19.0	2.4
Habits of lying or stealing	6.5	4.8	1.9
Withdrawn, unsocial nature	2.9	4.8	1.8
Temper tantrums	3.3	6.1	.7

active, antisocial, and characterized by poor work habits. The percentage of children displaying classroom discipline problems characterized by certain personal and social factors is presented in Table 63. A comparison of these discipline problem groups with all the children shows that poor work habits, nail biting or thumb sucking, nervousness, hyperactivity, aggressive antisocial behavior, and temper tantrums are found much more frequently among both the pre-

[13] Frances A. Mullen, Truancy and classroom disorder as symptoms of personality problems, *Journal of Educational Psychology,* 1950, Vol. 41, pp. 97-109.

adolescent and adolescent discipline problem groups than among the total group. Lack of self-confidence appears to increase with the onset of adolescence.

Physical irregularities. Feelings of inferiority manifest themselves in children in many ways and in varying degrees. One of the most common causes of such feelings results from the child's comparison of himself with others in some physical characteristics. The results of such a comparison may not be accurate; however, if they appear unfavorable to the individual concerned, feelings of inferiority are likely to result. Among boys, physical deformities, lameness, and physical weaknesses are common causes, while girls more often develop feelings of inferiority if they are regarded as unattractive or homely. The case of J. B. shows how a feeling of inferiority may develop and operate in a boy who was superior in mental ability.

J. B.'s IQ was 116 when he was ten years old, 121 when he was eleven, 136 when he was twelve, and 132 by the percentile rank method when he was sixteen and in the upper high school. J. B. was a bright, merry little fellow of nine when a terrible accident left him permanently and conspicuously maimed and incapacitated for boyish sports. As a little boy his language work was less good than his mathematics, and there was a very slight, rather attractive, lisp in his speech. As the yearly examinations progressed, vocabularly and other verbal tests tended to lag behind, though not to fall below the mental level. But as full realization of his physical handicap dawned upon the growing boy, he shrank more and more within himself till it became almost impossible to get whole sentences out of him; all through high school he fell back upon his courteous manner and bright smile, seldom voicing a rounded sentence, although there was no real speech defect. The tests yielded good results in reasoning, memory, mental representation, and so forth, but he never regained spring, zest, joy in life. He explained that he was working hard and that the teachers did not blame him, but he "just lacked ability." Perhaps I was able to show him that he was allowing a physical defect to assume undue domination of his life, even to the extent of an apparent mental incapacity quite contrary to fact. We all desire normally to be like our fellows, but his grief over the thwarted herd-instinct had extended his unavoidable physical deviation into an unnecessary mental and behavior deviation. There was a decided awakening and happier outlook, but it required all the skill at the command of the school to lift the sense of mental inferiority which had spread from his physical inferiority.[14]

[14] Anna Gillingham, Educating the gifted child, *American Review*, 1923, Vol. 1, pp. 403-404.

Symptoms of maladjustment

The symptoms of personal and social maladjustments will vary from child to child. Some symptoms will appear, however, more often than others. Likewise, some are more readily observed than others. For example, Jane, who enjoys reading and much solitary play, may be regarded as a model, whereas, in actuality she is beset with many conflicts and is definitely maladjusted. On the other hand, Jim, a troublemaker in school, seems to enjoy pulling Jane's pigtails or pinching one of the classmates when his back is turned toward him. The teacher stamps Jim as a troublemaker and maladjusted boy at once. She may overlook the symptoms of maladjustment manifested by Jane. The inexperienced teacher, in particular, and the poorly prepared teacher may not recognize symptoms of maladjustment when they appear, except for those that create social disturbances and classroom discipline problems.

Recent studies show that teachers are today more sensitive to maladjustment problems than was the case two or more decades ago. This perhaps stems from the greater emphasis being given to mental hygiene and related fields of study. Fenton has presented a valuable list of symptomatic expressions associated with the adjustive processes of aggression, compensation, and escape. These are presented for special study and consideration in Table 64.[15]

Aggression as symptomatic. According to the Yale frustration-aggression hypothesis, when the needs of a child are thwarted, one form of response may be that of an excessive amount of self-assertion which may take the form of belligerency. In this connection, two forms of aggression may be noted: (1) that growing out of self-confidence, and (2) behavior arising as a result of feelings of insecurity or the thwarting of some drive. Behavior arising as a result of thwartings may be observed in the temper tantrums of the small child or the bullying act of the overgrown boy on the playground.

It was pointed out in Chapter 7 that anger results from the restraint of actions or inhibitions imposed upon the individual. Thus, when a small child's toy is taken from him, he may resort to such forms of aggressive behavior as crying, biting, kicking, and the like. As the child learns through experience that such acts do not get

[15] Reprinted from *Mental Hygiene in School Practice*, 1943, p. 227, by Norman Fenton, with the permission of the author and of the publishers, Stanford University Press.

TABLE 64 The adjustive processes, associated feelings, and symptomatic expressions (after Fenton)

Forms of Mutually Overlapping and Interrelated Adjustive Processes	A Partial List of the Feelings Which May be Associated with Any of These Adjusted Processes	Some Examples of Symptomatic Expressions of the Three Adjustive Processes
1. Aggression (Attack, revolt against authority or social standards, destructiveness)	Anxiety Despair Fear Guilt Hatred Inferiority	Amnesia Antagonism Attention-getting behavior (boasting, showing off, bravado) Cheating Conceit Crankiness Criticalness Cruelty Destructiveness Discouragement Disobedience Dominance Evasiveness Fears (flight or concealment) Fighting (quarrelsomeness) Fretfulness
2. Compensation (Including rationalization, projection, "sour grapes")	Insecurity Jealousy Persecution Rejection Resentment	Headache Hypochondriasis Indecision Indifference Lying Negativism Nervousness Overdependence (overattachment) Overconscientiousness Phantasy (daydreaming) Prejudice Regression Revengefulness Sarcasm Self-abnegation
3. Escape (Evasion of reality or flight from it)	Revenge Self-pity (martyrdom) Shame Thwarting Uncertainty	Sexual problems (including crushes and perversions) Snobbery Stealing Submissiveness Timidity Vindictive gossip Wanderlust Withdrawal (seclusiveness) Worry

the desired results, these forms of behavior are given up in favor of conduct that is more effective.

Evasion of reality as symptomatic. One of the most common methods used by the child in meeting a frustrating situation is that of delving into phantasy or daydreaming. This may be observed in the classroom. The teacher calls on Jane, but Jane is staring into space and doesn't understand what the teacher has said, although she may have heard faintly that her name was called. Jane's attention was on things other than those with which the class is concerned. She might be said to be living in a world of phantasy, where she is able to find a happy retreat from the reality of inadequacy and insecurity. Perhaps all people may be said to live in such a world at times, since it provides opportunities to find satisfaction through the construction of a world that satisfies needs not satisfied in the world of reality.

A common form of phantasy among growing boys and girls is that of *identification.* Through this process the child identifies himself with some hero of his choice and escapes from the reality of insecurity, or lack of affection or attention. The boy of meager athletic ability becomes a superior athlete when he identifies himself with Joe Di Maggio. He may be able to throw off his fear nature when he identifies himself with the achievements of Buffalo Bill. These are tension-reducing devices that are symptomatic of unfulfilled needs in the life of the growing individual.

Children will resort to many different procedures in an effort to escape from unpleasant experiences resulting from thwartings of basic needs. Withdrawal behavior, shyness, and undue timidity which persists beyond childhood should be looked upon as symptomatic of emotional or social maladjustments. The prevalence of shyness and timidity will vary considerably with different home backgrounds and community patterns. Most studies agree, however, that such forms of behavior are quite widespread among children, and when these persist into adolescence and adulthood they should be looked upon as probably symptomatic of maladjustments either at this particular stage of life or emanating from early childhood experiences. The unwanted child, the child who feels insecure, and the child who lacks a feeling of personal worth or status are alike potential withdrawal cases.

Restlessness and irritability as symptomatic. When children suffer from malnutrition or fatigue, restlessness and irritability are likely to result. Also, frustrations and tensions may lead to irritability as well as to other nervous states. Cummins found from a study of the emotional symptoms among school children that restlessness, anxiety, and lack of concentration usually accompany a higher incidence of such symptoms.[16] Specific fears were found in over one-fifth of the children.

The obese child. From a physiological point of view, the problem of obesity is very simple. It is the direct result of a greater intake than output of energy, and, excluding certain rare cases of abnormal glandular functioning, treatment would consist of prescribing a diet that will reduce the energy intake below that of the output. This technique appears simple, but published data bearing on its success show that in most cases it fails to get the desired results.[17] The question naturally arises: Why should this simple method be so difficult? The answer to this has been presented by Freed as well as other investigators; they have pointed out that obesity is in most cases symptomatic of emotional maladjustments on the part of the child.[18]

A basic postulate set forth earlier in this chapter is that human behavior is explainable in terms of the satisfaction of certain basic needs. When this postulate is applied to the obese child, it becomes obvious that he must be taking in more food than is needed to satisfy his metabolic requirements in an effort to satisfy needs not otherwise satisfied. Thus, obesity becomes symptomatic in that it indicates that certain needs of the child are not being satisfied through normal channels. The importance of food as a means of reducing tension resulting from unsatisfied needs has been well described by Bayles and Ebaugh. They state:

The need may be for success, security, love, food, or whatever we have observed but cannot entirely explain the fact that food will temporarily relieve tension from sources other than metabolic ones and so, not infrequently, we find food being used to reduce the tension of emotional deprivation. Food can thus have the meaning of a medicine, perhaps a narcotic, to deaden the pangs of a frustrated life.[19]

[16] J. D. Cummins, The incidence of emotional symptoms in school children, *British Journal of Educational Psychology,* 1944, Vol. 14, pp. 151-161.

[17] See M. Trulson, E. D. Walsh, and E. K. Caso, A study of obese patients in a nutrition clinic, *Journal of the American Dietetic Association,* 1947, Vol. 23, p. 941.

[18] S. C. Freed, Psychic factors in the development and treatment of obesity, *Journal of the American Medical Association,* 1947, Vol. 133, p. 369.

[19] Spencer Bayles and Franklin G. Ebaugh, Emotional factors in eating and obesity, *Journal of the American Dietetic Association,* 1950, Vol. 26, pp. 430-434.

Laziness and inertia as symptoms. Laziness is a very general term applied to behavior that results from an apparent voluntary unwillingness to exert energy in the performance of a task. This is commonly listed as a major cause of poor schoolwork among children. Its apparent symptoms are such that parents, teachers, and others are likely to meet it with scorn, accusations, and punishments. There is considerable evidence, based upon case studies. that laziness is usually a result, rather than a cause. Thus, the appearance of laziness in a child should be looked upon as a symptom of maladjustment that should be given further study. One of the major causes of laziness is an undernourished state. The child who is undernourished will not have a long attention span. Furthermore, he will tend to show signs of nervousness and restlessness. Closely akin to an undernourished condition is a physical condition characterized by lack of energy resulting from diseased tonsils, anemia, diabetic conditions, and the like. When children are given annual physical examinations, these conditions are noted, and may be cared for. Many children, however, have been accused of being lazy when the real trouble resulted from some diseased condition that tended to deplete the child's physical energy.

Another factor oftentimes confused with laziness is *lack of interest*. This may result from overprotection in the home, or too much indulgence on the part of the parents.[20] It also appears in the authoritarian home and school. Where the child has no part in the planning of the various activities, he is not likely to be overly enthusiastic about the performance of such activities. Studies cited in Chapter 14 indicate that a democratic atmosphere in the home, at school, or in connection with club activities tends to promote an increased interest in the performance of the tasks with which the group is concerned. Sometimes, lack of success, closely related to a feeling of inadequacy, may lead to behavior classified as laziness. The case of W. H., a senior-high-school boy of average intelligence, described by White and Hussey, illustrates this.

This boy was not a conduct problem but was characterized by the teachers as "good, but very lazy and indifferent." They felt that he lacked drive and had poor work habits. ... Among other aids a personality questionnaire was given to him. This particular questionnaire

20 See David M. Levy, *Maternal Overprotection* (New York: Columbia University Press, 1941). Levy presents an outstanding study of maternal overprotection based upon many case studies. The types of overprotection encountered, and the special problems of the overprotected child, reveal some interesting facts related to maladjustments.

showed a profile for this boy running almost identically with that for the normally adjusted boy with the exception of one point, where the profile shot up into a high peak. This point was that of inferiority feelings. He felt that he was stupid, that there was no use trying, that he was different, even that his clothes didn't feel right on him. He was afraid that what he said would be wrong and he was discouraged. Feeling all these things, he had "sat down on the job." To allow this boy to express this in interviews, to talk out his discouragement, and from there to begin to build success-feelings by showing him his capacity in relation to other boys was a fundamental start. To find a spot where success and interest were fairly easy and to carry him along from there to other successes produced a better student and, we believe, a more adequate later adult.[21]

Children's behavior problems. The symptoms of maladjustment presented on the previous pages characterize the behavior of so-called "problem" children. Ackerson made an extensive study of the behavior problems of 5,000 children referred to the psychological clinic of the Illinois Institute for Juvenile Research.[22] The behavior items manifested by 25 per cent or more of these children are here presented in order of frequency.

1. Nervousness, restlessness
2. Disobedience, stubbornness
3. Retardation in school
4. Feeble-mindedness
5. Temper display, tantrums
6. Listless, dull, lack of ambition
7. Stealing
8. Childish, immature
9. Fighting, quarrelsome
10. Enuresis

Using a short time-sample observation procedure for each of forty-six nursery-school children, indexes were obtained of each child's tendency to indulge in each of eleven classes of "nervous habits" or mannerisms.[23] Scores for each class of "nervous habit" are based on behavior noted during 400 half-minute observation periods. The mean scores for the boys and girls are shown in Table 65.

[21] Helen M. White and Elmer H. Hussey, Self-description of personality and adjustment, reprinted from *Understanding the Child,* 1940, Vol. 9, p. 24. Published by the National Committee for Mental Hygiene, New York.

[22] Luton Ackerson, *Children's Behavior Problems* (Chicago: University of Chicago Press, 1931), pp. 102-103.

[23] H. L. Koch, An analysis of certain forms of so-called "nervous habits" in young children, *Journal of Genetic Psychology,* 1935, Vol. 46, pp. 139-170.

TABLE 65 Sex differences in mean number of mannerisms for an individual (after Koch)

Mannerism	Boys	Girls
Genital	2.31	.78
Pedal	2.98	3.02
Ocular	4.07	3.42
Hirsutal-caputal	1.79	8.62
Corporal-mass	114.90	113.90
Oral	104.65	101.50
Nasal	8.02	9.86
Aural	1.60	3.42
Digital	57.25	65.10
Corporal-limited	29.00	27.88
Respiratory	1.83	1.15

Significant sex differences appear in the masturbation tendencies and proneness to finger the scalp or hair. More mannerisms appeared in situations where there was considerable restraint and where there was least gross physical activity. The gross physical activity and free situations would appear to provide a release for body tension and thus decrease the tendency toward the display of nervous habits in the form of mannerisms. No pronounced age differences were observed, except for the tendency of older children to stand on the sides of their feet more often than the younger children did.

The problem child. There is considerable evidence, based on observations of children, that all normal children display behavior at some time that is commonly referred to as "problem behavior." [24] The average number of forms of problem behavior will vary with the age level of the children. Likewise, the general nature of the problem behavior varies with age. Younger children are given to less self-control; this is shown in their temper tantrums, fighting, and the like. It was suggested in an earlier chapter that the degree of emotional control manifested by a child is a good measure of his emotional maturity. According to Macfarlane, the average number of forms of problem behavior is from four to six per child. [25]

In the study reported by Martens and Russ, 109 problem children

[24] Elsie H. Martens and Helen Russ, *Adjustment of Behavior Problems of School Children*. A description and evaluation of the clinical program in Berkeley, California. U. S. Office of Education, Bulletin No. 18, 1932.

[25] J. W. Macfarlane, Study of personality development, in R. G. Barker, J. S. Connin, and H. F. Wright, eds., *Child Behavior and Development* (New York: McGraw-Hill Book Co., 1943), Chap. XVIII.

brought before the behavior clinic of Berkeley, California, were matched with 109 children who exhibited no problem behavior that warranted clinical attention. These children were equated by age, sex, intelligence, and grade in school. They were rated for a large number of general behavior traits. A comparison of the frequency of behavior problems reported by the problem and nonproblem children is shown in Table 66. The major difference between the two groups appears in the behavior activities frequently reported. It is the recurrent nature of certain forms of behavior regarded as undesirable that differentiates the problem from the nonproblem child. The persistent display of such activities as fighting, temper tantrums, showing off, lying, and the like labels the child as a problem child.

Emotional disturbances: A descriptive analysis

Some characteristics of the disturbed child. It was pointed out in Chapter 14 that personality development was affected by all the social and cultural forces with which the child comes into contact. Due to constitutional factors as well as these environmental forces and conditions, differences in personality become rather pronounced fairly early in life. Furthermore, symptoms of emotional disturbances appear early. Some of these symptoms have been studied by Herbert Archibald, and are presented in order to give the student of child growth and development a better understanding of the emotionally disturbed child.

1. The disturbed child has a short frustration tolerance. He is a poor loser. . . .

2. It is difficult for him to form a positive relationship, especially with children his own age. . . .

3. He is not well aware of his own feelings. He may be mad, but does not focus on the person responsible for his frustration and displaces his hostility onto other people and things. . . .

4. The disturbed child may be very impulsive and directly hostile.

5. The disturbed child may exhibit many or few so-called neuropathic traits. . . .

6. He may have difficulty telling the difference between fantasy and reality.

7. The disturbed child is always accompanied by a disturbed mother, who exhibits similar characteristics.[26]

[26] Herbert C. Archibald, Disturbed child—disturbed family, *Archives of Pediatrics,* 1950, Vol. 67, pp. 128-132.

TABLE 66 Comparison of the frequency of the behavior problems reported for 109 problem with those reported for 109 non-problem children (after Martens and Russ)

| Behavior Problem | Number of Children for Whom Problem Was Reported | | | |
| | PROBLEM | | NONPROBLEM | |
	Frequently	Total	Frequently	Total
Inattention	77	106	14	78
Carelessness, slovenliness in work	62	96	10	48
Restlessness, talking, etc.	61	90	9	48
Bad posture, slumping in seat	51	90	14	61
Laziness	44	74	9	45
Forgetting notes or books	32	74	1	42
Doing work other than assigned	50	74	10	45
Daydreaming	35	69	20	57
Teasing	25	66	1	35
Dirty hands, face, etc.	32	65	3	34
Fighting	26	63	1	24
Exuberance (laughing, giggling)	36	62	6	35
Showing off	31	62	3	18
Lying	33	61	1	6
Tardiness	19	60	2	31
Temper outbreaks	20	59	0	25
Sulkiness	21	59	2	26
Eating candy, fruit, chewing gum	18	56	7	42
Dirty belongings, books	23	47	2	15
Excessive reticence (easily embarrassed)	21	46	20	57
Impertinence	17	44	2	14
Dirty clothes	20	41	3	13
Cheating in schoolwork	13	40	0	13
Deliberate refusal to obey	22	39	0	6
Cheating in play	14	38	0	7
Stealing	14	37	0	4
Injury to others (not smaller)	21	33	0	8
Bullying	19	33	0	4
Damage to school property	9	32	0	3
Resistance to punishment	13	32	1	5
Profanity	12	32	0	4
Weeping (cries easily)	10	31	2	21
Damage to personal property	9	26	0	6
Hurting small children	15	26	0	1
Vulgar speech	9	24	0	1
Writing notes	7	24	2	14
Truancy	8	23	1	3
Damage to neighborhood property	6	18	0	0
Masturbation (suspected)	2	15	0	2
Sexual pictures or stories	4	14	0	1
Hurting animals	4	8	0	1
Heterosexual activity	2	5	0	0
Masturbation (known)	2	4	0	0
Vermin	1	2	0	2

The description of the disturbed child presented by Archibald applies primarily to the preschool child; however, many of these characteristics would also apply to preadolescents, adolescents, and adults. The inability to withstand frustrations would characterize also the emotionally disturbed adolescent. Likewise, the disturbed adolescent is unable to develop a satisfactory relationship with his peers. He is therefore likely to seek the company of someone younger or of an inferior social status. Exhibitionism characterizes the behavior of many emotionally disturbed preadolescents and adolescents, although a withdrawal tendency may be found in a number of boys and girls at this age. A study of the factors and forces underlying many disturbed adolescents will reveal the presence of too much "momism" in many, while others will seem to be lacking in favorable positive character traits. Just as habits become more stable with maturity, so do behavior activities that are an outgrowth of frustrations and tensions. The preadolescent has developed techniques for meeting frustrations that have proved fairly satisfactory to him, and these are used more consistently as he matures into adolescence and youth. Thus, the preadolescent years are preparatory years for adolescence, while early childhood years are preparatory years for preadolescence.

Resistance in early childhood. Many children pass through a period during which they are more or less resistive to adult direction and display an attitude of stubbornness, contrariness, and spitefulness.[27] This usually occurs during the preschool period. This period has at times been referred to as the "age of resistance." The reaction has been regarded as the "weaning period" and thus somewhat normal at this stage of life. Alfred Binet observed this among three-year-olds and attributed it to the timidity or bad mood of children at this age. Arnold Gesell has found this type of behavior among children observed in the Yale laboratory. From observations of 983 infants during testing periods, Levy and Tulchin found resistance to be pronounced at eighteen to twenty-three months in girls and thirty to thirty-five months in boys.[28]

Various explanations have been offered for resistive behavior, with many students of child development suggesting that this is a

[27] See Erich Benjamin, The period of resistance in early childhood, *American Journal of Diseases of Children,* 1942, Vol. 63, pp. 1019-1079. Some of the materials presented in the subsequent discussion of resistance during early childhood are adapted from this source.

[28] D. M. Levy and S. H. Tulchin, The resistance of infants and children during mental tests, *Journal of Experimental Psychology,* 1923, Vol. 6, p. 304.

normal feature of child development. The studies conducted by Erich Benjamin, based upon 167 problem children between the ages of one and five years, have yielded valuable information about the nature, causes, significance, and treatment of children exhibiting resistive behavior. The nature of such exaggerated behavior is illustrated by Benjamin in the case of Herbert:

Herbert was a boy 4 years and 2 months old. He had one sister, 6 years old. His development as an infant was excellent, and there were difficulties only after an attack of dysentery when he was 18 months old. Since that time he suffered frequently from diarrhea and gained hardly any weight. Speech developed relatively late, and was defective at the time of his admission to the Children's Home. About the middle of his third year Herbert became difficult to manage. He did not obey and usually did just the opposite of what he was supposed to do. He was excitable and suffered from convulsions, which had been considered as breath-holding spells. He was inclined to dominate his mother, was jealous when she did not pay him enough attention and wanted her always to put him on the chamber pot. When she refused to do so, he in turn refused to move his bowels. He was jealous also toward his sister; the fearfulness of the child was striking. There were good reasons for speaking of a kind of "nervous anxiety." He was afraid of animals and of Santa Claus; moreover, the anxiety was present during his dreams. The boy was restless. One year previous to admission a peculiar kind of shaking was observed, especially of the arms. It appeared when he was in a joyful excitement or when he was going to have a temper tantrum. There was also some salivation.

Herbert did not have confidence in himself, and he was a coward. He was still very dependent. In kindergarten he did not take part in the play of other children; he played by himself, mostly the same game in a monotonous manner. He masturbated and vomited occasionally. Enuresis had stopped one year previously.[29]

The most common symptom displayed by the resistive child relates to *feeding difficulties*. Some children may suffer from a lack of appetite; however, the majority of feeding difficulties stem from some other source. The major cause of resistive behavior is usually found in the attitudes of parents toward the child. Some of these were discussed in Chapter 14. Another symptom, closely related to feeding difficulty, is *vomiting habits*. During the period of resistance and oftentimes extending beyond early childhood, some children are able to vomit at will. Perhaps *constipation* gives the child more power over his environment than any other mode of resistive be-

[29] *Op. cit.*, pp. 1026-1027.

havior. Parents very often help the child in the use of this method by their anxieties and the ways in which they dramatize his eliminations. A fourth symptom relates to the *sleep habits* of children. Their unwillingness to go to bed, their requirements after being put to bed, and the ways used to get attention after going to bed are procedures useful to the child in his efforts to assert himself and gain attention. *Speech difficulties* and *breath-holding spells* are further means of resistance used by the preschool child. The breath-holding spell usually accompanies a severe test and is a rather violent form of resistant behavior. It is rarely observed after the fifth year. *Enuresis* has been listed as symptomatic of resistant behavior. One child was observed who continuously wet his clothes at kindergarten. This appeared from further study to be a resistive form of reaction to going to kindergarten. He wished to remain at home and play with his baby sister who was twenty months younger. Sometimes, undesirable habits, such as bumping the head, sucking the lip or thumb, scratching, grinding the teeth, and the like are forms of resistive behavior.

Anxiety and resistive behavior. A study of the case of Herbert reveals a case of anxiety about his status in the home. His desire to dominate his mother and the jealousy manifested toward his sister indicate a sort of feeling of insecurity. Benjamin has pointed out that "Behind the mask of spite reactions there is always anxiety or inner insecurity." This anxiety is more obvious, however, in some cases than in others. Resistive children are commonly found in homes of high-school and college graduates. Those children in need of special help usually come from families above average in their standard of living. However, many of them come from homes where there is much tension, and oftentimes the child is involved in some ways in this tension. Sometimes there is open tension between the parents over child-rearing practices and privileges given the child.

The development of resistive behavior. It is impossible to separate the influence of heredity and environment in the development of resistive behavior. There is considerable evidence that hereditary factors operate to predispose some children toward certain general forms of behavior, while other children are predisposed toward other forms. The constitutionally weak child should not be expected to have the same appetite as the constitutionally healthy child. And, although studies show that nervous conditions tend to run in families, one cannot solve statistically the problem of the relative importance of environment and heredity. It has been emphasized throughout this study of child development that heredity and environment are inextricably related from the date of the fertilization of the ovum. Furthermore, the assumption that hereditary factors are influential does not mean that nothing can be done to affect the course of the child's development. The influence of early home conditions has been observed in all studies of early child development. Several types of parental behavior have been listed as influential in the development of resistive behavior. These have been set forth by Benjamin as:

(1) Child rearing governed by autocratic methods
(2) Child rearing governed by submission to the wishes and demands of the child
(3) Child rearing based on fear of social disapproval
(4) Child rearing based upon blind obedience to dogmatic rules and principles
(5) The effects of parental ambitions for the child-parental anxiety
(6) Parental inconsistency in dealing with child behavior

In an attempt to cope with these, the child develops anxieties and meets with frustrations. Thus, frustration and added frustration fill the period of much of early childhood and preadolescence. Concerning this, Benjamin has stated:

It is understandable that the child tries to revolt against the manifold rules imposed on him. He cannot comprehend what it is all about. The most primitive way of rebellion is the temper tantrum, and therefore this reaction is the outstanding feature of the period of resistance. Some children, however, follow other roads. Some turn away from the common mode of establishing social relationship. They prefer to be alone, play exclusively with toys instead of with people and seek pleasure and satisfaction in the narrow sphere of the home and even more constrictedly, of the self. Another stops his development, turns back to infancy and presents signs of failure to "grow up" and develop independence. There is a tendency to retain privileges accorded to small children.[30]

Enuresis. Enuresis is generally defined as incontinence, or the inability to keep urine in the bladder for a reasonable period of time. Retention or evacuation of the contents of the urinary bladder depends upon the correct timing and action of the muscles involved. The achievement of co-ordination and control of such muscles is gradual in nature. It is accomplished earlier with the large muscles than with the smaller muscles. It was pointed out in Chapter 6 that

[30] *Op. cit.*, p. 1066.

the child develops skill in the use of the muscles of the arms earlier than in the use of the finger muscles. Since the muscles involved in the control of the bladder are of the small-muscle type, the child will not develop control over them and thus over the urination process as early as he can sit up or even stand erect.

Bladder and bowel control are usually established by the age of three years in most children. A child who still wets the bed at three years of age may be doing so for one of several reasons, which may be listed as follows:

1. His training may have been poorly handled from the start, so that he has never developed good bladder control habits.

2. A control poorer than that found in other children may result from his emotional make-up. Emotional situations, such as nursery-school experiences, may affect him to a greater degree than they affect other children.

3. Usually, bed wetting does not mean that there is something wrong with the child physically. However, when no other explanation can be found, the child should be given a physical examination.

4. A feeling of insecurity in the home is perhaps the most important factor that contributes to bed wetting on the part of a large percentage of children.

The notion that enuresis occurs as a result of unfavorable child-parent relationships is supported from many sources. Furthermore, there is considerable evidence that feelings of insecurity may produce such a condition. Observations of children in England evacuated from their home and neighborhood environment during World War II showed that bed wetting became one of the outstanding problems of many of these children.[31]

There are differences of opinion as to when the training in bladder control should begin. There are some who would advocate the beginning of such training during the third month, while others would delay the beginning of such training. It appears that the attitudes of the parents toward bladder control are more important than the question of the actual time when such training should begin. Undue alarm shown by parents of the enuretic child aggravates the problem rather than helps it. Bed wetting and diurnal enuresis (daytime enuresis) are often accompanied by other problems. The enuretic child is likely to be restless, excitable, and given to temper tantrums or nail biting. Parents should strive to develop a defense against

---

[31] See Cyril Burth, The incidence of neurotic symptoms among evacuated school children, *British Journal of Educational Psychology*, 1940, Vol. 10, pp. 8-15.

these rather than attempt to effect changes in behavior by a direct attack upon the acts. Children who feel secure in their home environment, who have developed self-reliance, and who feel wanted and loved are not likely to develop such habits. But, if the child is made to feel guilty, rejected, or insecure in his home and peer relations, his whole life, including bladder control, will be adversely affected.

Thumb or finger sucking. There is considerable evidence that thumb or finger sucking is an outgrowth of faulty feeding habits or insufficient feeding during the period of infancy. On the basis of studies of the feeding histories of numerous babies, Levy concluded that the primary cause of finger sucking was an insufficient amount of food from the breast or bottle.[32] This conclusion has been supported by findings from other studies. The study by Roberts indicated further that the amount of time spent by the baby in sucking was very important in connection with the sucking of the finger or thumb.[33] It appears, therefore, that thumb and finger sucking are closely related to the following feeding practices: (1) a rigid schedule not in harmony with the rhythm of the child's hunger development; (2) too short a feeding period on the part of the mother or nurse; and (3) insufficient food from the mother's breast or bottle to satisfy the child's hunger state.

Materials bearing on the effects of thumb sucking on the formation of the teeth were presented in Chapter 5. Massler and Wood have recently pointed out that among young infants with no teeth, thumb sucking produces no ill-effects.[34] The dentist and parent should not be concerned at this age, although the cause of the thumb sucking should be determined by the pediatrician. They suggest further that mechanical restraints serve to magnify the emotional causes and should be avoided. Enlightened feeding and closer parental relationship appear here, as in the case of other emotional disturbances, to be the most likely remedy.

Stuttering.[35] There are two ages when stuttering appears with a

[32] D. M. Levy, Thumb or finger sucking from the psychiatric angle, *Child Development*, 1937, Vol. 8, pp. 99-101.

[33] Ena Roberts, Thumb and finger sucking in relation to feeding in early infancy, *American Journal of Diseases of Children*, 1944, Vol. 68, pp. 7-8.

[34] Maury Massler and Arthur W. S. Wood, Thumb-sucking, *Journal of Dentistry for Children*, 1949, Vol. 16, pp. 1-9.

[35] See Isaac W. Karlin, Stuttering—the problem today, *Journal of the American Medical Association*, 1950, Vol. 143, pp. 732-736. Karlin gives a good abbreviated presentation of the following theories of stuttering: (1) As a psychoneuroses or a personality disorder; (2) As a habit or form of behavior that is learned; and (3) As an organic disorder related to language expression.

high degree of frequency. The peak of the stuttering curve appears when the child is about two or two and one-half years old, and is just beginning to talk freely. The other period when stuttering is conspicuous occurs when the child enters school for the first time. The first period is closely associated with the use of language in connection with social situations. At this age, the child has not developed a vocabulary sufficient to enable him to express himself freely and completely. Furthermore, his language habits have not formed to the degree that they have become automatic and stable. Perhaps it is safe to say that most children stutter to some extent at this age level when they are faced with social situations requiring language usage.

The other peak of stuttering is associated with the tension of the child when he reaches school age and is faced with new adjustments and situations for which he is not fully prepared. This nervous tension may result in nail biting, facial grimaces, enuresis, or stuttering. Although individual differences appear among children to withstand emotional conditions, it seems likely that any condition which produces nervous tension is likely to set off the beginning of stuttering. Julietta Arthur reports a case which illustrates this.

At thirty months, David, hitherto a bright, normal child. alarmed his parents by suddenly beginning to stutter violently. After some probing, the psychologist found the "attacks" had begun after David's six-year-old cousin and his parents had come for a prolonged visit. In order to spare the feelings of their relatives, David's parents scolded him, not his cousin, when the inevitable disagreements arose. But David, trying to ape his older companion, found the situation too complicated for him, and his parents' apparent withdrawal and disapproval of him too bewildering.[36]

A number of years ago there was a tendency to ascribe a considerable proportion of stuttering to a change of handedness when the child reaches school. The preponderance of ambidextrous children found among stutterers led Bryngelson and others to suggest that it is unwise to shift the left-handed child to right handedness in the case of the writing act.[37] Some suggestions set forth earlier relative to enuresis may also be applied to the prevention of stuttering. It is unlikely that a child would develop the habit of stuttering

[36] Julietta K. Arthur, Help for stutterers, *Parents Magazine,* April, 1946, pp. 153-156.

[37] B. Bryngelson, Sideness as an etiological factor in stuttering, *Pedagogical Seminar and Journal of Genetic Psychology,* 1935, Vol. 47, pp. 204-217.

upon entering school if his home environment were completely satisfactory and if his school adjustments did not put too much strain on his emotional constitution. The increased amount of stuttering found among school entrants tends to diminish as the necessary adjustments are made. Teachers should concern themselves with the factors associated with increased stuttering at this stage of the child's life and modify their activities and educational program so as to reduce to a minimum the frequency of the onset of stuttering among children upon entering school. Teachers need to understand the language problem of children, and need a better understanding of the principles of child development. The close relation between stuttering and emotional tension illustrates again the principle of the interrelatedness of growth. Children who are forced to recite under conditions calling forth emotional tension are likely to stutter. Children who are dealt with in a friendly manner, and who are not made to feel uneasy in connection with situations in their school environment, are not likely to develop habits related to nervous tension.

Summary and generalization

It has been pointed out throughout this chapter that the child is faced with many adjustment problems at home during the preschool period and with further adjustment problems when he enrolls in kindergarten or the first grade at school. These adjustment problems result from thwartings, frustrations, and anxieties relating to certain basic needs. Since these needs appear during infancy, adjustment problems appear at this stage. These needs, however, change with age so that the adjustment problems of the four-year-old will not be identical with those of the two-year-old. As the child develops, aggressive behavior and negativistic types of behavior appear under varying conditions. The form of aggressive behavior appearing will depend in a large measure upon the nature of controls with which the child is confronted at home and at school. The negative behavior manifested by a large percentage of preschool children is a means of expressing independence and is used by the child when conditions are such that he is unable to express his independence in a more natural and positive manner.

It has already been pointed out that maladjustments have been explained in relation to frustrations. The effects of such a condition will depend upon (1) the dynamic nature of the need, (2) the extent to which it is blocked, (3) the provisions made for a substitute goal, and (4) the extent to which the child's needs have been satisfied.

The symptoms of maladjustment have been presented and discussed in relation to the following adjustive processes: (1) aggression, (2) compensation, and (3) escape. There is a close relationship between disorder in school and maladjustments. Discipline problems in school are characterized by poor work habits, excessive nail biting, nervousness, social immaturity, aggressive antisocial behavior, temper tantrums, and the constant use of attention-getting devices. In general, however, problem children are most different from non-problem children in the frequency of the occurrence of certain forms of undesirable behavior rather than in the performance of different types of behavior.

The description of the disturbed child presented on page 434 should be useful to parents and teachers. Nail biting, stuttering, resistive behavior, sex disorders, and the like are outgrowths of conditions appearing earlier in the child's life. Some of these habits may be more or less natural to early childhood, while others are symptomatic of difficulties. The crying of the infant may signify hunger or pain. In such a case, there is little likelihood of its persisting into adulthood. The sex interests of the two- and three-year-old child have no particular relationship to sexual habits practiced during adolescence. The importance of distinguishing between activities that appear as part of the developmental process in our culture and activities that result from the frustration of some need should be emphasized in connection with the materials presented in this chapter.

Questions and Exercises

1. Study the four possible goals toward which disturbed behavior is directed, according to the idea presented by Rudolf Dreikurs. Give some type of behavior which would illustrate each of these.
2. Show how behavior problems change as a result of age. How would you account for the changes from two to four years of age?
3. Look up other classifications of needs. Upon the basis of your studies, what are the major needs of the child?
4. Show how child dynamics is related to adjustments. What factors determine the seriousness of a frustrated or blocked need? What would be the effect upon the child's development if no needs were ever blocked?
5. What are some of the major adjustment problems of the child when he reaches school? What factors determine how well the child will meet these situations or conditions?
6. What difference will it make if the teacher conceives of certain

behavior activities as symptomatic rather than as acts to be dealt with?
7. Consider some problem child of your acquaintance. What symptoms of maladjustment are manifested by this child? What do these suggest relative to possible causes of his maladjustment?
8. Study the different types of resistive behavior described in this chapter. What are some factors that will determine the type of resistive behavior used by a child?

Selected Readings

Ackerson, L. *Children's Behavior Problems*. Chicago: University of Chicago Press, 1931.

Anderson, John E. Personality organization in children, *Readings in Child Psychology*, Wayne Dennis, ed. New York: Prentice-Hall, 1951. Pp. 476-490.

Burton, Arthur, and Harris, Robert E. *Case Studies in Clinical and Abnormal Psychology*. New York: Harper & Brothers, 1947.

Cameron, Norman. *The Psychology of Behavior Disorders*. Boston: Houghton Mifflin Company, 1947.

Garrison, Karl C. *The Psychology of Exceptional Children*. Rev. ed.; New York: The Ronald Press Co., 1950. Chap. XIX.

Jersild, Arthur D. *Child Psychology*. 3rd ed.; New York: Prentice-Hall, 1947. Chap. XVI.

Kanner, Leo. *Child Psychiatry*. Springfield, Ill.; Charles C. Thomas, 1947.

Levy, David M. *Maternal Overprotection*. New York: Columbia University Press, 1943.

Louttit, C. M. *Clinical Psychology*, Rev. ed.; New York: Harper & Brothers, 1947.

Reynolds, Martha M. Negativism in preschool children, *Readings in Child Psychology*, Wayne Dennis, ed. New York: Prentice-Hall, 1951. Pp. 428-438.

Richards, T. W. *Modern Clinical Psychology*. New York: The Macmillan Company, 1946.

Thorpe, Louis P. *Child Psychology and Development*. New York: The Ronald Press Co., 1946. Chap. XV.

Tryon, Caroline, and Henry, William E. How children learn personal and social adjustment, *Learning and Instruction, Forty-ninth Yearbook of the National Society for the Study of Education*, Part 1, 1950. Chap. VI.

Wasten, Isabel Young. Behavior problems of elementary school children: a description and comparative study, *Genetic Psychology Monographs*, 1938. Vol. 20, pp. 123-181.

16

Mental Hygiene
of Childhood

Introduction: Mental hygiene today

Advanced knowledge of child growth and development has resulted in a better understanding of the forces and conditions that contribute to the development of personal and social maladjustments. Today, the term *hygiene* as used by the doctor, teacher, juvenile court judge, nurse, and social worker has an enlarged meaning over what it had several decades ago. The terms *hygiene* and *mental hygiene* are often used interchangeably. Their close relationship is recognized by the physician, teacher, and minister. It is the purpose of this chapter to present certain fundamental facts and principles of mental hygiene applicable to the preschool child as well as the school child. Many problems of adults have their inception during early childhood. Thus, the developmental concept of growth is well illustrated in studies of the development of personal and social maladjustments.

The purpose and goal of mental hygiene. The nature and purpose of mental hygiene have been presented by Isabel Parker as follows:

Mental hygiene offers a philosophy or objective in terms of optimum personality development. We may think of this objective from the standpoint of the individual in his striving to get along happily and effectively in his work or with his family and associates; or it may be considered from the standpoint of the study and prevention of the various forms of mental maladjustment. The aim in either case—mental health—involves the adjustment of individuals to themselves and to the world at large with the maximum of effectiveness, satisfaction, and cheerful-

446

ness. It implies socially considerate behavior and the ability to face and accept reality.[1]

A general recognition of the importance of sound mental health is one of the important developments of the twentieth century. The results and aftermaths of two world wars have helped to develop a more inclusive concept of mental health than that generally adhered to a few decades ago. There is ample evidence from different areas of learning that there is a close relationship between physical and mental well-being. Also, in harmony with developments in connection with the effects of various diseases, it is realized that prevention offers a greater reward than does cure. Pediatricians, psychiatrists, and others concerned with the mental well-being of growing boys and girls are constantly giving more attention to the preventive aspect of mental health. This, then, means that much of the work to be done in the development of healthy, well-adjusted individuals must be done during the early childhood period. The development of well-adjusted personalities should be the goal of mental hygiene. Platitudes on the part of parents and teachers will not suffice. Conditions, methods, and principles for the development of balanced and well-adjusted personalities during childhood and adolescence will be presented in this chapter.

Importance of emotional security

Bases of security. The needs of the child were given special consideration in the previous chapter. A careful study of these needs shows that they appear early in the child's life and are closely related to his security. This need for security dates back into infancy, and, of all forms of life, appears to the greatest degree in the human infant. The newborn child would not survive long if he were not cared for and nurtured by his parents or others. The necessity for this care continues longer in the human infant than among other mammals. In fact, technological developments have created conditions in which teen-age boys and girls must be provided for by their elders, thus prolonging the period of family security. Symonds has pointed out that "Security in its broad sense depends on a stable and secure environment which includes not only the home but the whole of society."[2] Security for the preschool child centers about

[1] Isabel Parker, Personality problems and reading disability, *Nineteenth Yearbook of the National Elementary Principals*, 1940, Vol. 19, p. 603.

[2] Percival M. Symonds, *The Dynamics of Parent-Child Relationships* (Teachers College, Columbia University, Bureau of Publications, 1949), p. 1.

the home, while security for the adolescent embraces the home, his peers, the school, and other social institutions.

Security involves more than providing for the child's physical needs. However, the child cannot be regarded as secure when the parents are unemployed, sick, or otherwise unable to provide for their physical needs. A comfortable home with an adequate diet will not in itself provide for the child's security. Variables reported in the study by Marian Radke which appear to be similar in their effect upon the child's feelings of security are: rejective attitudes by the parents, inharmonious family relations, and restrictive authority and discipline.[3] The child behavior found from this and other studies related to these home conditions seems to fall into the following constellations:

	Inharmonious homes	Rejective homes	Restrictive homes
Child behavior	aggressive	submissive	unpopular with
	hyperactive	aggressive	children
	neurotic	adjustment	
	lying	difficulties	nonrivalrous
	jealous	sadistic	passive, colorless
	delinquent	nervous	

Some parent-child relationships which contribute to the child's emotional security will be presented in the subsequent discussions.

Children's concepts of good parents. The child's concept of a desirable father or mother is different from that of the adult's; however, this does not indicate that either concept should be completely ignored. The concept that the child has of his father and mother is important in connection with the development of favorable attitudes and behavior patterns. Furthermore, there is good evidence that these concepts formed during childhood have an important bearing on the development of personality and favorable adjustments during adulthood. This problem was studied by Martin by means of interviews with children. From these interviews, he arrived at the following positive parental factors associated with good parents:

1. Parents are permissive or "giving."
2. Parents' first attitude toward a good school report is positive and acceptive, not coercive and exhorting. A poor report is taken as an indication of need for help, not punishment.

[3] Marian J. Radke, *The Relation of Parental Authority to Children's Behavior and Attitudes* (Minneapolis: University of Minnesota Press, 1946), p. 103.

3. Parents give time, thought, and effort, not material things.

4. Parents listen to and accept the child's early ideas and ambitions and do not foist theirs upon him.

5. Parents present the group as a place to go to play, to do things with others, and to make friends.

6. Parents and siblings are helpful.

7. Parents and siblings do things with him as well as for him.

8. Parents assign physical jobs with bulky objects involving lifting and carrying. This makes the child feel healthy and strong.

9. Playful companionship with parent.

10. Storytelling by parent.

11. Parents laugh and joke with the child.

12. The seniority of older brothers and sisters is recognized and respected by parent.

13. Father and mother live in the home and do things together.[4]

The rejected child. Rejection during childhood is closely related to a feeling of insecurity. The unwanted child feels his rejection very early in life. The selfish parent who didn't want the new baby, since he limits his or her freedom, will reveal this feeling in various ways. The earlier the rejection appears in the life of the child, the more serious will be the consequences. Concerning this, Florence Clothier has stated:

The future of the rejected child depends largely on his constitutional endowment and on the richness and meaningfulness of his early emotional experiences. The child deprived of love in the earliest years may never develop the capacity to give love and may even lose the capacity to accept love. Those are the children whose needs can theoretically be met by substituting mothering but who so often are unable to relate themselves to any foster mother provided for such a person.[5]

In a study of the parental attitudes of accepted and rejected children, Symonds was able to determine home attitudes related to rejection.[6] Home conditions of rejected children were especially characterized by (a) limited educational opportunities, (b) excessive punishment, (c) irritable mother, (d) the use of fear as a means of control, and (e) meager home environment. The experiences of the rejected child carry over into his relations with his playmates. Such

[4] A. B. Martin, A study of parental attitudes and their influence upon personality development, Education, 1943, Vol. 63, pp. 596-608.

[5] Florence Clothier, The treatment of the rejected child, *The Nervous Child,* 1944, Vol. 3, p. 106.

[6] Percival M. Symonds, *The Psychology of Parent-Child Relationships* (New York: Appleton-Century-Crofts, 1939), pp. 98-103.

children are in need of affection and moral support. Enough is known about the reactions of rejected children to present a positive mental-hygiene program based upon love and understanding. These children need more than food and clothing, if they are to develop as well-adjusted and useful boys and girls. Churches, schools, and clubs will be able to meet their needs to the extent that those agencies follow good mental-hygiene principles and are able to reach the emotional and spiritual side of the child's life. Many examples could be given to illustrate the fact that the rejected child will respond favorably to kindly treatment and fair play.

The effects of parental adjustments. The child's home life represents a crucial point in his adjustments. Perhaps the most important single factor in the home situation is that of well-adjusted parents. Maladjustments among the parents result in inconsistent and ambivalent practices in dealing with the reactions of the children. Good parental practices will be characterized by honesty, sincerity, and consistency in dealing with their children. Such parents have the ability to identify themselves with their children—to understand the basis for their action and to sense their feelings. Parents are not infallible, and the honest parent will admit his mistakes to his child without fear of losing status.

Among preschool children, whose environment is limited largely to the home situation, marital discord and personal maladjustments in either parent are more significant than is the case for older children. Children from homes where one or both parents are psychotic were found by Bender to show more behavior problems than was the case for children from homes where the parents are better adjusted.[7]

Essentials of good parent-child relationships

It is difficult to describe the ideal parent. It seems likely that there is no one pattern for the ideal parent or even for ideal parent-child relations. If one could set forth certain fundamental rules for good parent-child relations, the task of child-guidance clinics and schools would be much easier. Furthermore, desirable parent-child relations cannot be attained by adding together so many separable factors considered to be especially important. This relationship partakes of a pattern or unitary nature. The relationship that would best operate in a home with a kind and jovial father would not be

[7] L. Bender, Behavior problems in the children of psychotic and criminal parents, *Journal of Genetic Psychology,* 1937, Vol. 19, pp. 229-239.

the same as that which would operate in a home where the father was industrious, sympathetic, and stern. Also, the father-mother relationship must always be considered, since this has an important bearing on the parent-child relation. The goals, values, financial conditions, educational level, and other factors connected with the home will influence the nature of the parent-child relations. Some of the fundamental qualities of a more general nature will, however, be discussed in the following presentation.

Infant-mother relationships. A discussion of the mental hygiene of the child is too likely to give too much consideration to a method of changing the behavior of children and not enough emphasis to the parent. Many child behavior difficulties could have been avoided if the mother had had a better understanding of the child and herself during the period of infancy. The modern pediatrician appreciates the importance of favorable mother-infant relationships. He realizes that the intellectual and emotional aspects of child care are just as important and require as much attention as the physical aspects. Some questions with which they may be concerned are: Is the mother one who can adapt her schedule to the needs of the child? Is the mother so efficient and exact in her planning that she demands a rigid schedule and expects the child to behave like an automaton? Will the mother be sensitive to the child's needs, or is her life so artificial that she lacks this sensitiveness to the meaning of the child's behavior manifestations? Has the mother's emotion of love been so repressed or oriented that she is unable to express her true biological self in dealing with her baby? Martha MacDonald says: "A mother who has a neurotic attitude toward her baby needs all the help she can get in the way of reassurance and simplification of her duties during the first days and weeks of the child's life." [8]

A common complaint of infants brought to the attention of the pediatrician is anorexia (refusal to eat). This is usually a result of faulty training. The psychological aspect of infant feeding is as important as the nutritional. There are many degrees of complexity in this problem, most of them stemming from the interrelationships set up between mother and child during the period following birth. The importance of this in relation to personality development has been stated by Philip Jeans as follows:

. . . The infant-mother relationship is the simplest example of a social situation. Attitudes are communicated to the infant from the earliest

[8] Martha W. MacDonald, Mental hygiene in the child-health conference, *The Child,* 1944, Vol. 9, pp. 27-30.

moments and affect his behavior. The perception of impatience or hostility by the infant heightens the anxiety in him and produces physiologic changes which are not conducive to satisfactory feeding and digestion.[9]

Weaning is an important experience in the emotional adjustment of the child. This is the first important frustration that all children ultimately meet. The manner in which the child is helped in meeting this situation may affect the ways in which he meets future frustrations. Care should be taken that other frustrations do not enter into the child's life during the weaning period. Furthermore, the transition from the breast or bottle should be a gradual one. It is at this time that the mother should exercise patience and not be disturbed by some "doodling" with the spoon on the part of the infant or his spilling food on himself or the floor.

Another type of frustration appearing early in the child's life results from coercive toilet training. The period and manner in which this is undertaken may be very important for the child's future emotional adjustment. Despert found from a study of seventy-four children in which enuresis was a problem that thumb sucking, nail biting, and other nervous habits frequently appeared.[10] Enuresis during the early life stages may be closely related to biological maturation. Parents should not attempt to supersede maturation through a toilet-training program. Neither should they expect all children to develop at the same pace. When enuresis tends to persist, one should look to emotional factors for a more complete explanation. The behavior should again be regarded as symptomatic. The high incidence of enuresis found among children evacuated from London and other points during World War II is generally regarded by pediatricians and psychiatrists as a bodily reaction to loss of love and particularly to a separation from the home and mother. Referring further to Despert's study, it is pointed out that "training should be directed not at the relief of symptoms alone, but at the redirection of the motivating forces seeking expression. This involves the re-education of the total personality."

Temper tantrums and negativistic reactions of children are sources of anxiety to mothers and bring many of them to the guidance clinic or pediatrician. At all stages of the child's life, the mother should realize that what one says to a child is of less significance than how

[9] Philip C. Jeans, Feeding of healthy infants and children, *Journal of the American Medical Association*, 1950, Vol. 142, Pt. 2, p. 810.

[10] J. L. Despert, Urinary control and enuresis, *Psychosomatic Medicine*, 1944, Vol. 6, pp. 294-307.

it is said. Often the mother is advised what to do in meeting particular situations. She finds that the method she is using doesn't work. Perhaps the basic reason for this stems from how she behaved in her relations with the child. There is no substitute for motherly love. Furthermore, knowledge of child training unaccompanied by favorable attitudes and adjustments on the part of the mother will have little value in the development of well-adjusted personalities during early childhood.

Favorable home relationships. The influence of the home during early childhood has been emphasized throughout previous chapters. There is a need, however, to give attention to specific factors in the home environment that tend to promote good mental hygiene among the children. Meyer Nimkoff has described a good home as one in which the child has two parents who love each other, love him, understand his interests, capacities, and aspirations, and who provide opportunities to help him realize them and thus achieve adequate selfhood.[11] A home of this type will enable the child to satisfy his dynamic needs and will stimulate happy, well-adjusted personalities.

A few practical aspects of the ideal parent-child relationships deserve mention. These have been set forth by Nimkoff as: (1) carrying on activities together, (2) having mutual interests, (2) stimulating the child to put forth effort, and (4) encouraging self-reliance.[12] In the favorable home, parents share experiences with their children. It can thus be stated that the security that the child feels, the extent to which he becomes self-reliant, and the skill with which he assumes personal and social responsibilities depend in a large measure upon good home relationships. A study of the home life of 158 well-adjusted children was conducted by Stout and Langdon.[13] The children were chosen so as to represent a wide range of choice and a wide representation of family patterns. On the basis of a study of the factual information gathered and interviews with parents the following conclusions were reached: "In these attitudes toward the child and in the basic family unity growing out of them seem to lie the only common denominator to be found in the accounts of the family life of the 158 well-adjusted children of this study."

There is considerable evidence that behavior problems of later childhood can usually be traced to tensions growing out of early

[11] Meyer F. Nimkoff, *The Child* (Philadelphia: J. B. Lippincott Co., 1934), p. 165.

[12] *Ibid.*, pp. 167-171.

[13] Irving W. Stout and Grace Langdon, A study of the home life of well-adjusted children, *Journal of Educational Sociology*, 1950, Vol. 23, pp. 442-460.

childhood experiences. Child-guidance workers have found a direct relationship between school phobias in the young child and unfavorable parent-child relationships. Klein found that traumatic experiences in early childhood, especially among more primitive parents, coupled with increased tension at school, were responsible for the development of school phobias.[14] Anxieties developed through some sudden experience, such as fright from an attack by a dog, oftentimes prove difficult to eliminate. Concerning the treatment of such anxieties Paul Bergman has pointed out that according to psychoanalytical theory these disturbances will gradually disappear if the following conditions are fulfilled: "(1) the environment, particularly the mother, must not show exaggerated anxiety (because otherwise 'contagion' would add itself to fright); (2) the fright experience must not in its content or form be fit to appear as confirmation of some of the child's basic conflict anxieties; (3) there must not be a secondary gain from the maintenance of the anxiety, such as, for example, a greatly increased display of tenderness by the mother; for this would constitute a premium to the ego for holding on to its anxiety." [15]

Discipline and control. Charles Burlingame has pointed out that discipline in some homes is like a seesaw, with one parent holding down the "Spare the rod and spoil the child" end, while the other parent with equal determination keeps a seat on the end marked "Don't touch that child." [16] As a result, the youngster, who might be pictured as clutching at the center, must keep a sharp eye to see which end is up and which is down.

In order that the child may have the opportunity to learn what is right and what is wrong, he should be rewarded when his behavior meets the acceptable standard and punished when his behavior fails to meet this standard. That is the way society metes out its justice and accepts or rejects the individual. The child is being prepared to take his place in society. If he is allowed to violate the rules and regulations set forth by the group, he will ultimately pay the price in some institution designed for delinquents.[17] It has been suggested that every child needs from infancy a wise and continuous

[14] Emanuel Klein, The reluctance to go to school, *The Psychoanalytic Study of the Child* (New York: International University Press, 1945), Vol. 1, pp. 263-279.

[15] Paul Bergman, Neurotic anxieties in children and their prevention, *The Nervous Child,* 1946, Vol. 5, pp. 37-55.

[16] Charles Burlingame, Guideposts to mental health, *National Parent Magazine,* 1948, Vol. 37, pp. 4-5.

[17] William E. Brickman, Juvenile delinquency, *School and Society,* 1948, Vol. 6, p. 68.

discipline tempered with love. Every child has to be made to do some things or prevented from doing other things against his wishes. Compulsion has its place in curbing the unrestrained expression of impulses. The child actually needs some routines and rules to bolster his sense of security in an orderly world. A home in which Junior can do no wrong and feels no compulsions to do right, which, in short, exercises too little authority, gives him an inflated sense of his own importance and blinds him to the rights and needs of others. It thus develops delinquents from pampered children, some of whom eventually reach the juvenile courts.

Just as a child can be given too much discipline and control, so can he be given too much protection and direction. Overprotection, which is usually domination masquerading as love, can smother a child's initiative and tie him permanently to his mother's apron strings as a dependent and shy individual. Behind one mask or another, this absorption of the child's life appears to be a common fault among many mothers. Sincere affection for the child and his welfare, rather than the self, will provide for him the dynamics needed for wholesome development, provided such love and affection are tempered with justice and understanding. Only in this way can the child develop that inner discipline which is the surest shield against delinquency as well as the best safeguard of independence and self-control. Often the treatment of the emotionally disturbed child must begin with the treatment of the parent, if it is to be effective. A case described by Laderman illustrates this.

. . . A 4-year-old girl was brought in because of fearfulness, over-attachment to her mother and failure to talk to anyone but her family. In three months the nursery school experience had made her more self-reliant and a laughing, cheerful, talking little girl. But the mother is disturbed. She is more dependent upon the child than the child on her and she feels this relationship is in danger. Study of the mother revealed that the child was one of premature twins, the other died at birth. At that time the mother resolved that if the second lived, she would never let her out of her sight. That is just what happened. The mother began to worship the child abnormally, molded her to complete dependence, and reflecting her own fears, caused the child to develop hypochondriacal trends with an unnatural preoccupation with illness. The mother's childhood and adolescence were similarly full of fears and dependence. It is almost as if the mother is going to recreate her own life in the child.[18]

[18] Peter Laderman, Treatment of emotionally disturbed preschool children, *Archives of Pediatrics*, 1948, Vol. 65, pp. 36-37.

Feeding problems. Concerning feeding problems among preschool children, Stuart has stated: "Feeding problems tend to be (1) the outgrowth of special food needs, (2) relatively high food requirements, or (3) mismanagement of a child in consideration of his physiologic and psychologic needs determined by his maturity." [19] The years between one and five are important ones in the child's development of a sense of awareness of the meaning and significance of his environment. This thought is emphasized in Chapter 10. He is growing in independence and registers this by resisting parental direction in various ways. One of these ways relates to eating foods set before him by his parents. Improper training, insistence upon the child's eating certain foods, premature attempts to feed babies solid foods are among the most common causes of the poor appetite of the child. Also, poor appetite may follow an illness. Parents should recognize that it may take weeks for the normal appetite to return. There are a number of important principles which, if followed, will tend to insure desirable eating habits among children. [20]

1. A recognition on the part of the parents that the child gains weight slowly during the preschool years. Consequently, he does not need a large amount of food.

2. The child's eating habits and idiosyncrasies should not be discussed in the child's presence.

3. Parents should be urged to give less attention to calories, vitamins, and minerals and rely more on the child's appetite.

4. Parents should not continuously insist upon certain foods. Cereals could very well be omitted from the child's diet, if ample foods are provided in other forms.

5. Raw vegetables are often preferred by preschool children. In many cases these are more beneficial to them than the cooked foods. Furthermore, they provide good experiences needed for chewing foods.

6. Excessive insistence on milk should be avoided. A quart is a maximum amount needed, and a pint may be adequate when the needs are supplied through an assortment of other foods.

7. The child should be given the opportunity to feed himself without too much interference from adults insisting upon his eating according to some set pattern. His table manners should be taught by example rather than by percept.

8. The child should be permitted to sit at the table for a reasonable

[19] Harold C. Stuart, Children's nutritional needs during growth and development, *Journal of the American Dietetic Association,* 1949, Vol. 25, pp. 934-936.

[20] Some of the items here given are adapted from materials by Harry Bakwin, Poor appetite in young children, *Journal of Pediatrics,* 1947, Vol. 31, p. 584.

time and the food removed without a show of emotions because he hasn't eaten as much as the adult felt he should have eaten.

9. Meals should be served at regular hours. The child should be called to the meal a few minutes before the mealtime, in order that he will have ample time to put aside certain play materials with which he might be very much concerned.

10. The use of unusual devices bordering on sports, games, and trickery in order to get the child to eat should not be adhered to.

11. Placing the exact amount of food the child is to eat on his plate makes eating a chore for many children. The old family style has much to offer in this connection.

12. Children should be permitted to eat with the family as early as possible, and the mealtime should be a pleasant social function.

13. Tonics to increase the appetite and vitamins to supplement the nutrition needs at mealtime should be avoided. The tonics perhaps have no place in the nutritional program of the child.

The child's sleep habits. Twenty or more years ago there was a decided tendency not only to regulate the child's eating habits but also his sleep habits. Now we are inclined to be more lenient about sleep schedules. This does not mean that it is no longer believed that children need more sleep than adults, but rather that there is a movement toward a more flexible schedule in terms of the needs of the individual child. This presents a problem for parents, since they are required to pass judgment as to the exact nature of a schedule to be followed. Among both lower-middle-class and upper-middle-class groups, chronic resistance on the part of the children toward sleep is oftentimes quite pronounced. This is usually aggravated by parental anxiety, and this resistance tends to create even greater anxieties.

The policy of letting the baby "cry it out" is suggested by some, while others would have the mother soothe the baby. This first policy may be recommended for the infant who has developed a chronic resistance to sleep. The baby who unexpectedly wakes up and begins crying is another matter. Likewise, the child who suddenly becomes panicky around bedtime will need a different sort of treatment and consideration. It is safer for inexperienced parents to go on the assumption that it is generally right to comfort the child when he appears unhappy. The child may have a tendency to have colic after his meal just before bedtime. He is, therefore, in need of comfort and assistance. The parent should be on the alert for pins, tight clothing, and other conditions that might lead to pain and crying.

The school and mental hygiene

The school is assuming an increasingly important role in the guidance and development of boys and girls. The growing interest in kindergartens and nursery schools will increase the importance of the school as an agency for the development of well-adjusted personalities. The teacher is the crucial point in the school program. Teacher-pupil relationships become exceedingly important in the objectives of the modern school.

New objectives. One of the most difficult problems in education is the determination of objectives—just what teachers should try to do. The concept of behavior and adjustment presented throughout the previous chapters introduces new and enlarged roles for the school. The recognition that the whole child goes to school, that the whole child is involved in the learning and growth process, demands that emphasis should be given to the emotional and social development of the child as well as to his intellectual and physical development. Furthermore, the concept that all growth is interrelated requires a new type of emphasis in the guidance of the intellectual development of children.

Again, skills and subject matter, often dealt with in a purely quantitative manner, should be conceived of as learnings that have their qualitative aspects. Ideals and attitudes develop as part of any growth in skills. A child cannot learn to skate and swim without such learnings affecting other phases of his growth and development. The learnings involved in acquiring reading skill will affect the emotional development of the child and his attitudes toward reading materials and reading situations. Teachers should add to their objectives in teaching new objectives that embrace the personal and social adjustments of the child in his home, school, and community living. Teachers should realize that the formation of desirable attitudes and worth-while ideals are important objectives in the school program.

Importance of mental hygiene in the school program. It has already been pointed out that the school is a focal point in the child's personal and social development. New problems are faced; different routines are established; enlarged social relationships are presented; and many developmental tasks are encountered. During the early school period it is most important that the child's security and stability are insured against the influences that make for maladjustments. The whole child comes to school and the school must be responsible for the adjustments and development of the child as a whole while he is in school. The school must not think of the academic child only, but must regard the child as an individual who must learn to live as a social being in a social environment.

An important development related to child growth and mental health is the recognition of the close relationship between mental health and physical health. Evidence was presented in Chapters 7 and 8 showing how emotional development affected all phases of the child's growth and development, including the functioning of his intelligence. The organism functions as a whole, and anything that adversely affects the child's mental life will have a deleterious effect upon his physical well-being. In a study of the dynamics of nine-year-old elementary-school boys, Beatrice Lantz found that experience with success resulted in better performance and in better personal-social adjustments, while failure caused poorer performances, increased tension, and inferior personal-social adjustments.[21]

Mental health has at times been studied from the point of view of adjustment and integration. A person is well-adjusted if he meets the various day-by-day situations adequately and successfully. The unadjusted person, according to this point of view, is one whose habits and skills are inadequate to meet the situations or solve the problems confronted in everyday living. Integration is essential, then, if the individual is to meet a problem situation satisfactorily, since the child must focus the total self upon the problems at hand. Mental health is, therefore, regarded as satisfactory when the individual has integrated himself toward a problem situation so as to reach certain fairly well-defined goals. The school can function effectively in helping the child to set up goals and in stimulating the child to exert the total self in his efforts to reach these goals.

A large number of studies of the adjustments of elementary-school children deal with certain aspects of the child's adjustments, as if these aspects have no relationship to the child as a whole. The elementary-school child reacts to the classroom situation in terms of all that he has brought to school with him. This means that his health, his home relationships, and his relationship with the other pupils affect his reactions to classroom situations and conditions. Clifford Adams questioned forty-two teachers from different schools about wholesome and unwholesome practices in their schools.[22] A

[21] Beatrice Lantz, Some dynamic aspects of success and failure, *Psychological Monographs,* 1945, Vol. 59, pp. 1-40.

[22] Clifford R. Adams, Classroom practices and the personality adjustments of children, *Understanding the Child,* 1944, Vol. 13, pp. 10-12.

study of the responses of these teachers revealed that many school practices were designed to deal with immediate situations, with little regard for basic factors responsible for specific behavior activities. Many practices were such as to lead to feelings of insecurity and inferiority on the part of the children concerned.

Adjustments in school. The experience of entering school for the first time presents an adjustment problem for many children. If the home has failed to develop self-reliance, the first days at school may be characterized by emotional stress that will constitute a barrier to adequate personal adjustment. The child not only brings his home and neighborhood problems with him to school; he also encounters new problems at school. Here he must adjust to children from different homes and neighborhoods, must meet certain behavior requirements of the teachers and his peers, and must acquire the skills presented in the school program. Some progress toward adjustment is made when teachers and parents become aware of individual differences among children. When they realize that each child is a unique personality, they will be ready to give direction to each child in harmony with his needs and abilities. Lack of co-operation between parents and teachers results in confusion and conflicts on the part of the children concerned.

An important task of the teacher is to help the child make the transition from satisfactions that are brought about by dependence upon others to satisfactions that are based upon achievement. The teachers should strive, therefore, to guide the pupils so that they will grow increasingly self-reliant, intellectually and emotionally. It becomes the task of the teacher to aid the child in making satisfactory transition from dependence on the family, especially the mother, to self-reliance at school. To make this transition satisfactory, she must guide the child in his growth toward independence and at the same time furnish him with the needed security during this transition stage.

Problems related to school failure. The importance of emotional security on the part of the child applies to his school relations as well as to home conditions. The child who feels secure with his teacher and peers in his classroom and playground relations will be able to find release from many problems he may encounter, both at home and at school. This does not mean that the teacher should assume responsibility for his welfare in all phases of his school and out-of-school life. It is possible for the teacher to give the child too much attention and thus cause the individual to grow dependent rather than independent. The child must learn that he will have to solve most of his problems himself, and this should become increasingly true as he progresses through the school program. At the same time, the individual should be given guidance in the solution of his problems. The amount of help the child will need will depend upon a number of factors, among which are the following: (1) his mental and emotional development; (2) the extent to which he has developed habits of initiative and responsibility; (3) the seriousness and difficulty of the problem with which he is faced; and (4) the extent to which his needs are being met in his family, peers, and school relations.

At school, the child should learn to face reality in a larger sense than he has ordinarily come to learn at home. He must learn that he cannot receive all of the teacher's love and attention. He must learn to share experiences with others. He must learn that there are many tasks that he will not be able to do as well as others, and must at the same time learn that there are others who cannot successfully perform certain tasks. The teacher has a definite responsibility and many opportunities to help the child in these learnings. Individual morale is largely contingent on the possession of healthy techniques of adjusting to failure, and the successful teacher is one who can help the child develop such techniques.

Failure in school may be a major catastrophe to the school child. An important part of the healthy sense of emotional security making for zestful living is being able to handle one's routine assignments successfully. This problem is closely related to grades and report cards. Some constructive efforts have been made to develop a system of reporting grades and special information about the child's development in harmony with modern concepts of mental hygiene and the needs of children. During 1948, the Los Angeles County Research and Guidance Discussion Group studied this problem and worked out some valuable suggestions. The following principles were suggested, if the reports are to be carried home by the pupils:

1. The report card should serve as the child's and the teacher's interpretation of his progress to parents.

2. A good reporting plan furthers the child's growth in insight and self-direction.

3. The child should participate individually as a member of his group in evaluating his own growth toward clearly understood objectives.

4. Growth should be evaluated in relation to the individual's abilities

rather than in comparison to that of others or to the average of his group.

5. Those needs which can be met or those characteristics which the pupil can correct or improve should be reported rather than those that are the result of immediate inherent qualities.

6. Evaluations should describe the direction of growth in relation to the child's previous attainment rather than variation from the average of his group.

7. Reports should protect the child's self-respect and self-confidence since these are powerful incentives toward further effort and growth.

8. The relative effect of positive comment as compared with negative comment and reproof should be considered.

9. Descriptions of specific behaviors which the pupil can understand rather than abstract generalizations should be used." [23]

Guiding principles for mental hygiene

Positive habits. Good habits and desirable attitudes are started during the early years of life. Studies of child development indicate that many of our fundamental habits of adjustment have their origin in infancy. The first five years of life have been considered by many teachers, social workers, psychologists, and others as the most crucial ones for the development of fundamental character traits and patterns of behavior. This has been suggested by Symonds in his studies of the dynamic personality trends of parents in relation to child development. This is implied in the following statement: "Probably the first and most important factor making for a good parent is that the individual should have had a secure childhood and have grown up to be an emotionally secure person.... So one can look to good parents and a happy childhood as the prime ingredients in the making of a good parent in the next generation." [24] Parents who are secure will not be burdened with anxieties and feelings of guilt. They will not, therefore, attempt to satisfy their own unfulfilled ambitions through the development of their children. Freedom from anxiety and guilt enables the parents to deal more objectively and realistically with their children. This enables the child to develop positive habits rather than to suffer from rejection or overprotection at the hands of parents burdened with excessive anxieties or feelings of guilt.

[23] Los Angeles county studies its report cards, *California Journal of Elementary Education,* 1949, Vol. 18, pp. 41-42.

[24] Percival M. Symonds, *op. cit.,* pp. 128-129.

Children learn good habits by growing up in an environment where good habits are practiced. Since the child learns many things by imitating adults, it is important that good standards or models be available for the child to copy. The small boy will try to do the things he sees his father do. The little girl will play house and take care of her dolls in much the same manner in which she sees her mother carry on her household duties. A child tends to copy others at school, especially those whom he admires, and the teacher's ways serve more or less as models that children adopt as standards for their own behavior. Adults should remember at all times that what they do has more influence with children than what they say. The modes of expression do not develop miraculously but result from experiences in situations where these particular behavior activities are to be found.

Good physical health. An important foundation for good mental health is good physical health. The concept of the wholeness of the individual has increased the interest in good health habits as a partial basis for the development of desirable attitudes, adjustments, and outlooks on life. When a child shows symptoms of maladjustments, one of the first things to consider is his health status. The child who is undernourished, who does not get enough of active play, or who may have poor eyesight is certain to find difficulty in making proper adjustments in his daily activities. Good food and adequate recreation and rest help tremendously in favorable personal and social adjustments. This attention to physical well-being may not cure personality difficulties, but it furnishes an important element basic to satisfactory adjustments. A sound physical condition and abundant health are basic foundations for a well-adjusted and completely integrated life.

There is a common practice in nursery schools of serving a midmorning snack, usually fruit juice and crackers. Such a midmorning feeding is considered nutritionally valuable and also furnishes the children an opportunity to eat together in a group. That a midmorning feeding may be helpful in relieving fatigue and decreasing nervous tension is suggested from a recent experiment conducted in the University of Chicago Nursery School.[25] There were 133 different subjects in this study, which was carried on over four quarters. In each

[25] Mary E. Keister, Relation of midmorning feeding to behavior of nursery school children, *Journal of the American Dietetic Association*, 1950, Vol. 26, pp. 25-29. This study was presented as a *Ph.D. thesis,* Department of Education, University of Chicago, 1949. A rather complete review of previous studies bearing on this problem is presented in the original study.

quarter, two of the four groups served as experimental groups and the other two were control groups. The experimental groups were given pineapple juice at midmorning, while the control groups were given water at this time. During the period of the study each group served twice as experimental subjects and twice as control subjects.

The records of all the subjects in the expressions of negative behavior were secured. The negative behavior score was obtained by computing the percentage of negative behavior manifested in proportion to all the observations available on each of the subjects during a given experimental or control period. The results presented in Table 67 show rather clearly that negative behavior can be markedly lessened by a midmorning glass of pineapple juice. The differences shown are consistently in favor of the experimental group. A comparison of the effects on the various age groups showed further that the younger group of subjects were helped more than the older subjects, although this does not mean that the older children may not benefit from the midmorning snack. The results of this study are especially important in view of the fact that there is such a widespread criticism of eating between meals. The practice of serving a midmorning snack in school, if the snack is properly selected and administered, appears to be sound.

TABLE 67   Negative behavior in experimental and control periods over an entire year (after Keister)

Category of Behavior	Mean Percentage of Negative Behavior			
	CONTROL PERIODS		EXPERIMENTAL PERIODS	
Nervous habits	10.6	10.2	8.5	6.5
Hyperactivity	2.1	2.9	1.3	1.4
Withdrawing	1.3	1.6	1.1	1.4
Hostile behavior	2.0	2.9	1.5	1.5
All negative behavior except nervous habits	5.4	5.0	3.3	2.6
All negative behavior	5.2	11.5	11.4	7.5

Dealing with neurotic symptoms. It seems likely that the modern parent has a greater sense of responsibility and is more anxious to subordinate her own welfare to the development of the child as a well-adjusted personality than at any time in our history. Yet, in spite of these good intentions and the information available about child nature and growth, the children of today are faced with greater anxiety and are more likely to grow into maladjusted adults than was the case several generations ago, when parents did not consider child rearing, following the traumatic experience of birth, such a serious problem. The results of the efforts of many parents are out of proportion to their knowledge and good intentions relative to child training. No child is completely free of anxieties, conflicts, and minor neurotic symptoms. Parents and teachers should recognize this. The average parent, relying upon intuition, gives much help to the child. The father's playing "cowboy and Indian" with his four-year-old boy often fulfills this task quite adequately. Certainly, the intuitive methods of good parents should not be set aside for a strictly scientific approach. Scientific knowledge about child nature and growth may be used to explain these intuitive methods used by successful parents, it may suggest to unsuccessful parents methods that might be helpful, but it cannot in itself provide for the child's needs. Melitta Schmideberg has stated:

The parent may adopt various possible attitudes towards the child's difficulties. He may overlook them, suppress them or attempt to help the child get over them. In prescientific times the general attitude was that of neglecting them, interspersed with chance attempts both at giving help and suppressing them. In the early period of scientific education and pediatric advice, the tendency to suppress them pre dominated. The child should be forced to eat what he did not like, should control his fits of temper, should face up to situations he was frightened of.[26]

In many cases, parents expect their children to conceal their emotions, eat a well-balanced diet including spinach, and otherwise exercise self-control more than they as adults do. The children are punished when they fail to abide by the parents' dictates relative to self-control. The child, thus, conceals his terrors, fears, nightmares, and other difficulties. The parents, then, take pride in the fact that their children have never suffered from fear, nightmares, and other conflicts and difficulties. Concealment is mistaken for the absence of these forms of behavior. The issue arising here is whether the child is most likely to overcome these difficulties by concealment as far as possible or by expressing them under sympathetic guidance. It appears that when the difficulties are concealed, the parents may not even be aware of them until they appear in some major form

[26] Melitta Schmideberg, Environmental therapy based on psychoanalysis, *Journal of Child Psychiatry,* 1948, Vol. I, Section 3, p. 365.

at a later date. Then, parents are usually unable to understand their origin, nature, and source.

Helping the child to overcome fears. Pronounced fears and abnormal fears are devastating to the child's personality development. Certain fundamental principles essential for the development of emotional control were presented in Chapter 7. The importance of understanding and accepting the child's feelings was stressed. Also, suggestions were given for helping the child to meet frustrations. It was further emphasized that the child should be taught to respect certain dangerous situations and guided in the development of methods of dealing with such situations. It was pointed out that the beginning of emotional control lay in prevention, which receives a considerable amount of emphasis in mental hygiene today.

Those concerned with guiding the activities of children have observed that much fear behavior is not justified by reality. It is not sufficient simply to tell a child that he should not fear the particular situation. Neither is it especially helpful to explain that the situation is not one to be afraid of. The attack should be centered in helping the child in the attainment of the courage and confidence needed in dealing with the fear situation. It should be kept in mind in this connection that the fear emotion is not a causal agent, but rather that the fear is a response to a situation. This response is a learned response, just as other responses are learned. It is extremely problematic as to whether the response can be eliminated. The child can, however, be guided in the development of a substitute response to the fear situation.

One method useful in the development of a different way of meeting a particular fear situation is that of developing strength through achievement. It has been suggested that the development of leadership on the part of Disraeli resulted from his timidity or fear of social situations. The development of his abilities gave him the needed courage and confidence for leadership among his peers. At all times, the child's aspirations and wishes should be in harmony with his potentialities for development. The potentialities of most children are considerably greater than what is actually realized. The child may be guided in the development of potentialities that give him a feeling of success and the confidence needed for overcoming certain fears.

Sometimes, tension and friction in the home or at school is the source of the fear anxiety. An overly ambitious mother may be so demanding of her daughter that hysteria in the form of chronic headaches appears under trying conditions. When goals are set forth by both the child and the parent, and these goals are within the realm of possible fulfillment, there is little likelihood of such a condition developing. Sometimes the tension may result from the failure of the child to understand the goal or problem. Under such a condition the child should be aided in meeting the problem by suggestions and help from those concerned with his guidance. When goals are set forth by the parents and the child displays little or no interest in attaining the goals, fear anxieties are likely to be the ultimate result. The failure of parents and teachers to recognize the aspirations and limitations of the child may have serious consequences to his mental well-being.

A child may be helped in meeting a fear situation through careful guidance in a direct attack. A study of the elimination of the fear of fourteen nursery-school children who were afraid of a dark room was conducted by Frances Holmes.[27] The children were taught ways of orienting themselves to the room by learning to move successfully through the dark room, and to turn on a light at the back of the room. This method was successful in overcoming the fears of thirteen of the fourteen children. Such a procedure should be followed cautiously, since it is very important for the child's efforts to succeed—failure may aggravate the fear response. A child afraid to recite in class may be asked to participate in something in which he is greatly interested and in which he can succeed. He may be asked sometime when not in class if he would like to do this. A direct attack is successful only when the child is called upon to do something that he is capable of doing, and when he is in a state of readiness for the performance. Success breeds confidence. Since he is lacking in confidence, it is most important for him to develop the feeling of worth that comes from successful performance. Children who refuse to be led, or refuse to participate, are not necessarily stubborn. Such acts of behavior are motivated by the emotional patterns of the child, built up as responses to certain situations, and can be understood only when the child's nature and background are known. Healthy emotional growth seems to be best stimulated by the following procedures:

1. Providing an opportunity for every child to feel success which is in some measure commensurate with his ability.

[27] Frances B. Holmes, An experimental investigation of a method of overcoming children's fears, *Child Development*, 1936, Vol. 7, pp. 1-30.

2. Having standards fit the group and be adjustable to the individual child.

3. Providing the kind of competition wherein every child has a chance for success.

4. Having individual records so that the child can make comparisons which will show signs of betterment of his own record.

5. Providing constructive discipline of the child.

6. Giving sympathy and support to each child, developing in him a sense of security, making him into a social individual, with a genuine sense of responsibility to himself, his small group, his nation, and humanity.

7. Guiding the group so that fair play within the group, sympathy and respect for each other, and a practice of mutual help will characterize the actions of the members.

8. Presenting good emotional patterns by those in authority. Teacher serenity and emotional stability are affected by teacher load and security. Children suffer if the teacher is fatigued from too many outside interests.

9. Endeavoring to gain the child's friendship and confidence. A child may not progress unless he likes his teacher.[28]

Summary and implications

The last several decades have witnessed important developments in the field of mental hygiene. Its function today is concerned with optimum personality development of all children. Advanced knowledge of child growth and development, along with a better understanding of child dynamics, has provided the basis for formulating principles of mental hygiene. Since personal habit patterns are being formed during the early years of life, some have come to regard childhood as the important period for the application of good mental-hygiene principles in child guidance. Failures in the application of sound principles of mental hygiene will be reflected in nonsocial children, overly aggressive children, and delinquents.

Mental hygiene during the preschool period should begin with the child's security. Security for the preschool child will center around the home; with growth into the school year, it is shifted in a large measure to peer relations and activities at school. The school should provide for the child's security during the transition period when

[28] Cecil V. Millard (ed.), Child growth in an era of conflict, *Fifteenth Yearbook of the Department of Elementary School Principals,* Michigan Education Association, 1944, p. 107.

he is growing in self-reliance and independence. By providing opportunities for each child to achieve, the school is furnishing the means for the development of self-reliance. The real beginning of mental hygiene for preschool children should perhaps be with mothers and oftentimes with fathers. Favorable mother-infant relationship is generally recognized as the first step in the mental hygiene of the preschool child. Frustrations often appear during the first year, developing out of feeding habits, toilet training, and other matters relating to the schedule of activities of the child.

The enlarged concept of the objectives of the school has brought with it an increased consideration for the social and personal adjustments of children. There is an increased realization today that the pupils are preparing for adult living in a democratic society through harmonious social relations in the school. A school program based on a sound philosophy and planned to give the pupils experiences that will help them adjust to life situations about them will go a long way toward providing for the present and future needs of children and youth. The growing complexity of society has added new problems and put additional strains upon our institutions. This is having its effects upon the home, the school, the church, and various agencies concerned with child growth and development. The mental hygiene of parents, teachers, church leaders, Scout leaders, and others responsible for the guidance of boys and girls becomes very important. It is not enough that these people be keenly aware of good mental-hygiene principles; they should be well-adjusted individuals as well. Boys and girls look to these leaders for cues to behavior. It was pointed out in Chapter 13 that in many cases these leaders become the individuals that children tend to identify themselves with. It is the task of these leaders to teach boys and girls both by precept and example. They will need to provide many of these boys and girls with security and a feeling of personal worth—needs too often denied them in the home and neighborhood. The environment of the child, both in reality and in respect to his emotions and attitudes, should ideally, according to Richard L. Frank, provide for the following:

(a) A good degree of stability and security.

(b) The meeting of the child's essential needs and desires with appropriate outlets and satisfactions.

(c) Facilities and freedom for the development, training and use of the child's potential strengths and for the overcoming or minimizing of remedial difficulties.

(d) The relating of the demands made on the child to the resources available to the child.[29]

Questions and Exercises

1. Show how mental-hygiene problems follow the developmental concept presented throughout this text. What is the significance of this in terms of education?
2. Just what is meant by the statement, "What you say to a child is not nearly so important as how you say it"? Illustrate the operation of this idea.
3. Give an illustration from your observations of a parent dealing with neurotic symptoms by forcing the child to conceal his emotions. What are some likely results from such an approach?
4. Just what is your interpretation of the phrase, "The clinical point of view"? Why is it desirable for teachers to have this point of view?
5. In what ways have the problems of parents become accentuated by technological developments? Point out some changes that have occurred in parent-child relationships as a result of this.
6. What is the relationship between mental hygiene and physical hygiene? Cite illustrations to clarify your explanation.
7. What is meant by the "emotional climate"? Why is the emotional climate of the home, the kindergarten, and the school so important for a child's healthy growth and development?
8. Evaluate the factors listed on page 448 associated with good parents. What other factors would you add to the list presented? Which of these would you tend to question?
9. What are the major causes of childhood insecurity? What are the probable results of feelings of insecurity during childhood?

Selected Readings

American Educational Research Association. *Mental and Physical Health, Review of Educational Research,* 1949, Vol. 19, No. 5. This issue presents a review of the literature on mental and physical health published during the three-year period between December, 1946, and December, 1949.

Association for Supervision and Curriculum Development. *Fostering Mental Health in Our Schools.* 1950 Yearbook of the Association, National Education Association, 1950.

[29] Richard L. Frank, Problems of the parents, *The Emotional Climate of the Exceptional Child. Proceedings of the Spring Conference on Education and the Exceptional Child of the Child Research Clinic of the Woods Schools,* May, 1949, pp. 33-34.

Carroll, H. A. *Mental Hygiene*. New York: Prentice-Hall, 1947.

Crow, L. D., and Crow, Alice. *Mental Hygiene in School and Home Life*. New York: McGraw-Hill Book Co., 1942.

Fenton, Norman. *Mental Hygiene in School Practice*. Stanford University, Calif.: Stanford University Press, 1943.

Garrison, Karl C. *The Psychology of Exceptional Children*. Rev. ed.; New York: The Ronald Press Co., 1950. Chap. XXII.

Millard, Cecil V. *Child Growth and Development in the Elementary School Years*. Boston: D. C. Heath and Company, 1951. Chap. XV.

Myers, C. R. *Toward Mental Health in School*. Toronto: University of Toronto Press, 1939.

Rennie, Thomas, and Woodward, Luther. *Mental Health in Modern Society*. New York: The Commonwealth Fund, 1948.

Rivlin, H. N. *Educating for Adjustment*. New York: Appleton-Century-Crofts, 1936.

Thorpe, Louis P. *Child Psychology and Development*. New York: The Ronald Press Co., 1946. Chap. XV.

Thorpe, Louis P. *The Psychology of Mental Health*. New York: The Ronald Press Co., 1950.

Witty, Paul A., and Skinner, C. E., (eds.). *Mental Health in Modern Education*. New York: Farrar and Rinehart, 1939.

17

From Childhood
to Adolescence

Childhood growth

Graduating from infancy. By the time the child is fifteen months of age, he has graduated from "infancy," has reached a period of self-assertion, and begins to resist attempts to thwart his needs or too much adult interference with his activities. Some of the various forms of resistance used were discussed in the previous chapter. Having graduated from "infancy," however, the child does not stabilize himself, but rather continues to grow toward maturity. He exercises his newly formed abilities. Psychological needs become more prominent, and the child appears to be more demanding. This presents problems for parents who fail to realize that their infant child is reaching out and meeting a larger world; that he is being challenged and stimulated by new forces and conditions; and that his growing abilities introduce additional needs that provide a new pattern of dynamics for his growth and development.

By the time he reaches the two-year level, he has become adjusted to the environmental conditions about him. Any change in his pattern of living will require adjustments on his part, and may be crucial to his growth and development. He has developed an affection for his mother, provided normal home relations have been present. He is in need of affection at this stage, and the lack of such affection will present problems that the schools and other institutions will find it difficult to cope with at a later period. At the age of two years, he recognizes his sex group largely by the difference in the manner of dress and differences in the care of the hair.

Getting ready for school. Interest in self and curiosity about the things about him characterize the growing preschool child. It was pointed out in Chapter 9 that the word "I" becomes very prominent in his conversation at this time. The growing child has a past and at this stage is interested in his own past. He is interested in knowing what he was like and what he did as a baby. The import of growing out of babyhood is shown also in his attitude toward babies. By the age of four years, he becomes interested in the family constellation. For the boy, his smaller sister wears dresses, and plays with dolls. He looks to his father as the big brave man, and may be seen imitating him. The four-year-old girl likes to put on a long dress, the mother's high-heeled shoes, and her mother's hat. She can then be seen strutting around the room or over in the neighbor's yard.

The four-year-old is proud of his growth. He is conscious of his size and likes to be measured and weighed. Questions are likely to appear at this age about the birth of babies. He displays an increased interest in elimination, and demands greater privacy in the use of the bathroom. As he grows toward six years of age, he develops a better appreciation of the way things are done. He wants to become a part of the family and community culture. He enjoys playhouse, store, and other activities closely related to the adult world.

Growing into preadolescence. The desire for greater independence becomes especially noticeable at seven. The seven-year-old child is reaching out beyond the world of child activity into an enlarged world. He is now more sensitive to the presence, feelings, and attitudes of others. The tendency to daydream may show itself in an elementary manner at this age. He wants to grow up and become an integral part of the larger world which he now envisions. Since he cannot do this in actuality, he finds much satisfaction through daydreaming and make-believe.

The growing independence of the seven-year-old is manifested in his greater willingness to stand up for his rights, and oftentimes for the rights of others. A certain amount of aggressiveness is observed, which leads to an increased amount of rough play and fighting. In our American culture the spirit of competition develops and becomes stronger as the individual grows from seven to ten or eleven years of age. He likes to win the race, make the best grade, or paint the best picture. There is a keen desire to be first in line, to sit next to the teacher, or to be given special responsibilities at school or at home. At seven, boys and girls still play together, and little consideration is given to sex in competitive activities; however, best friends are usually chosen from the same sex.

Membership in the group and acceptance by one's age group are very important for nine-year-olds. In general, they may be regarded as conformists, and one who fails to conform is likely to be left out of the group. Thus, individual differences, largely ignored during the earlier years, are observed and become effective in the child's life at this age level. The child who is slow, the boy who can't run fast, or the girl who is large or bossy will be left out of the planning and activities of the nine-year-old group. Nine-year-olds can be very cruel to their peers, since they are brutally frank in their accusations and opinions.

Development into the preadolescent years brings with it further demands upon the members of the group to conform to the standards and practices of the group. This tends to bring the child into conflict with parents and teachers. By recognizing this need for approval from their age level, parents and teachers are better able to help the child who is being left out of the group, and to direct the activities of the group so as to achieve worth-while outcomes. The gang tendency is strong among preadolescents. This tendency may, through proper direction and stimulation, become a potent force for the development and maintenance of worthy standards of conduct and manners.

Reaching sexual maturity

Growth is characterized by changed attitudes toward members of the opposite sex. There has been much material written about the growth of sex consciousness, and the sexual nature of boys and girls at different age levels. Only a few objective studies have been made which provide an accurate basis for describing social-sex patterns of children at different age levels. The social development of the child was discussed in Chapter 12. It was pointed out at that time that the social development of the child was closely related to certain sexual changes and changed attitudes toward members of the opposite sex. The materials presented in the subsequent discussions are drawn from careful observations and studies of changes in the social-sex patterns of children as they grow from early childhood into adolescence.

The development of psychosexuality. It was once believed that the child was nonsexual, and that the sexual urge remained more or less dormant until the time of the glandular changes signifying the appearance of adolescence. The thinking of Freud and other psycho-analysts affected a change in the attitude toward the "sexuality" of the child. It is now generally recognized that sex feelings as well as sex attitudes have their beginning early in life. This idea has pro-duced changed attitudes toward the sex life and activities of chil-dren. No longer are the elementary sexual curiosities of children looked upon as works of evil spirits or the activities of children with evil minds and hearts. There is a need to help the child grow in understanding sex differences and sex feelings, rather assuming an attitude of censorship toward all ideas and feelings bearing on sex.

Most children begin showing signs of modesty during the later pre-school years, although modesty is learned and must be taught to children. This does not mean that the child must be taught to be ashamed of his body, or that he should come to look with disgust upon pictures and situations suggestive of nudity. Such an attitude ingrained in the child may be the beginning of sexual perversion. Most children encounter some minor sex episodes between the age of five and the beginning of adolescence. Such episodes should be looked upon as an opportunity to help the child develop a better understanding of sex and a more favorable attitude toward sexuality, rather than as a condition that requires punishment and shame for the child. Children must, of course, learn that these minor forms of sex activities should not be followed. A positive and reassuring ap-proach rather than one of blind repression should be followed. Parents and teachers tend to weigh the seriousness of the child's use of sex words, drawing of sex pictures, and other activities involving sex as extremely grave. They have in some cases heard of the dire effects that result from masturbation. There is no evidence that these experiences, if not participated in frequently, will have any serious ill-effects upon the child. There is evidence from case studies that the attitude parents take toward the child's sex life and activities may become paramount in relation to later sexual adjustments.

The preadolescent period. It has already been pointed out that sexual development follows a gradual and orderly process. However, the habits and attitudes to be observed among a group of boys and girls will be seriously affected by the cultural forces about them. In an effort to arrive at a more correct notion about the social-sex patterns of boys and girls at different periods of their development, and particularly during the preadolescent stage, Elsie Campbell con-ducted a careful study of the social-sex attitudes and behavior of boys and girls in the Merrill-Palmer recreational clubs.[1] The observations of the observers were recorded on a social-sex scale. The general development of boys during the period from nine to fourteen years, based on these observations, is described as follows:

At this stage the boy is found playing pursuit games with girls, such as informal tag games indoors. So much attention he will pay to girls, but in general he shows no interest in what they are doing and even in games not involving physical skill he prefers boys on his "side." When allowed to choose, he always sits next to boys rather than girls. He will not join in a game in which he is the only boy, but must have other boys with him when he plays with girls. Toward the end of the period he becomes sufficiently conscious of sex so that he does not wish to touch girls or show them any attention except under socially approved conditions, such as in games or dancing. If he finds himself in a group of girls, he leaves quickly. Still later in this period he begins a teasing, derogatory kind of talk about his friends who have girls, with the intention of "fussing" the boy in question. He is extremely self-conscious and modest about the physical aspects of sex and would not for the world undress or go to the toilet before girls or even women, except where the relationship is parental.

The general social-sex development of girls during the period from eight and one-half to thirteen years is described as follows:

In this period the girl shows no interest in what boys are doing merely because they are boys. She will not stay long in a group of boys if she is the only girl. In choosing sides she is likely to choose girls unless it is a game involving physical skill, when she may choose a boy in the interest of victory. She prefers men to boys. She sits next to girls if given a choice. She will not participate in an activity unless other girls are included. She will invite men to sit next to her, but never boys. She begins to be sufficiently conscious of sex so that she will not deliberately touch boys except under conventional circumstances, as in games or dancing. She classifies games according to sex—boys play this, girls play that.

Later she enters the "whispering period" with the girl contemporaries. She is shyer with a group of boys than with a single boy. If she dances, she prefers to dance with other girls. She would not admit that a certain boy is attractive to her, though she begins to take a covert interest. By this time she is modest about exposing her body or underclothing before boys—probably more so than she will ever be again. She is sufficiently

[1] Elsie H. Campbell, The social and sex development of children, *Genetic Psychology Monographs,* 1939, Vol. 21, pp. 461-552.

conscious of the sex attraction of clothes to admire the clothing of women and her girl friends. She begins frankly to enjoy dancing.

The ways in which the preadolescent deals with sex situations will depend primarily upon the situations established during the earlier years. One may conveniently list three attitudes to be found among preadolescents. In the first place, parents and teachers may have taken the attitude that sex as a topic should not be discussed. They feel that the best treatment is to try to keep it completely out of the lives of growing boys and girls by treating it as a subject not open for question or discussion in any form. A second method of dealing with the problem is that of facing the topic and related problems as one of the things one meets during the period of growing up. Farm boys often meet the problems of sex and birth through experiences with farm animals. They are constantly exposed to animals and have opportunities to learn, through caring for these animals, many things related to fundamentals of life and sex. A third attitude that may be found is one in which the child has been given a sordid picture of sex and the sex drive. He is made extremely ashamed of any sex thoughts he might have had, sex words or words of a sexual import he might have spoken, or any acts related to sex that he might have committed. Preadolescents oftentimes become very secretive and this characteristic may carry over into their sex attitudes. The experiences of the child during preadolescence will determine in a large measure how the child meets sex problems during adolescence, when the sex drive becomes much more potent and when his social outlooks and activities become more mature.

Glandular changes with age. Normal growth and development are largely conditioned by the reciprocal and proper timing of the action of the pituitary and gonadol hormones. Studies dealing with gonadotrophic hormone secretions in children indicate that the excretion of gonadotrophic hormones in early childhood in both sexes is too low to be detected by the methods used. These studies reveal that measurable amounts first appear in the urine during early adolescence. Data have been reported by Greulich and others, based upon the results of 120 urinary gonadotrophic assays performed on sixty-four boys. Concerning the importance of gonadotrophic excretion during adolescence, they conclude:

The results show that with advancing age and with advancing developmental status there is a general tendency for gonadotrophin to increase in amount from the undetectable levels of early childhood to levels more characteristic of the adult. There is as yet no direct evidence as to the biological nature of this gonadotrophin; on the other hand, it does not seem likely that it differs from the hormone found in the urine of the adult male. The properties of hormones of this type have been described earlier, and it seems reasonable to suppose that the primary changes of puberty, namely an increase in size of the testes and the initiation of spermatogenesis are related to the action of this gonadotrophin upon the seminiferous tubules. Secondary sex changes related to the secretion of the steroid sex hormones may be ascribed to the action of the hormone upon the interstitial gland of the testes.[2]

Somewhat similar results have been reported by Nathanson and others.[3] The average curves of secretion for boys and girls are

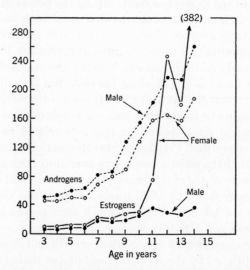

FIG. 43   Age changes in excretion of sex hormones. The female sex hormone, produced by the ovary, is the chief extrogenic hormone.

(After Nathanson and others)

shown in Figure 43. The amount of androgens secreted into the urine during the early years is only slightly less for girls than for boys. The difference, however, becomes more pronounced after age eleven. Prior to ages ten or eleven, both boys and girls excrete

[2] W. W. Greulich *et al.*, Somatic and endocrine studies of puberal and adolescent boys, *Monographs of the Society for Research in Child Development*, 1942, Vol. 7, No. 3, p. 62.

[3] I. T. Nathanson, L. E. Towne, and J. C. Aub, Normal excretion of sex hormones in childhood, *Endocrinology*, 1941, Vol. 28, pp. 851-865.

measurable amounts of male and female hormones. Although the differences are slight, the boys tended to secrete more of the male hormones, while the girls tended to secrete more of the female hormones. Beginning around the age of eleven, girls excrete a significantly increased amount of female sex hormones, while the boys excrete a markedly greater amount of the male sex hormones, but usually at a later date.

Physical symptoms of pubescence. Studies of the physical growth of boys and girls show that there is an increased rate of growth in height just prior to the onset of pubescence. This thought was presented in Chapter 5, and materials bearing on growth throughout childhood and adolescence were given. Since pubescence occurs earlier in girls than in boys, the accelerated rate of growth in height occurs earlier among girls. This is quite noticeable when one observes a group of girls and boys in the seventh or eighth grade of our schools. The girls at the ages twelve, thirteen, and fourteen will on the average be as tall or taller than the boys of these age levels.

There is also a pronounced increase in the rate of growth in weight just prior to the onset of pubescence. Some adolescents gain from twenty to thirty pounds during a single year. The girls again exceed the boys of their age level for weight during a two- or three-year period. Accompanying this increased growth, one finds important changes in body proportions. There is at first a rapid growth of the arms and legs, to be followed later by a more rapid growth of the trunk of the body. The hands, feet, and nose seem to undergo increased growth during this stage of life. By the time the boy is thirteen or fourteen years of age, his hands and feet have reached a large percentage of their total development at maturity.

In the study by Ellis, 208 boys, aged eleven to sixteen years, from the residential schools (British), were graded into three maturing groups: prepubescent, pubescent, and adolescent. Grading was based on the presence of pubic hair and/or pubescent genital development. Comparisons were made of the heights and weights of boys from the same school who fell into different maturity levels. These comparisons are presented in Table 68. These data show that the more mature groups are taller at all age levels than the less mature groups. Ellis concludes:

It was found that not only were boys of the higher maturity-group heavier and taller than their contemporaries in the lower maturity-group, but that differences between the growth curves could be demonstrated as far back as the sixth year (in the case of boys from School A, where records were reliable to this time.) [4]

The data presented about the relationship of the onset of pubescence and certain physical measurements indicate that wide differences exist with respect to the age of sexual maturity within a particular group of the same age level. Ellis has presented data showing the distribution range for a group of British boys. His data, given in Table 69, are based upon examinations of 561 boys aged

TABLE 68 Comparison of height and weight of different maturity groups (after Ellis)

Age group *	School	Height (cm)		Weight (K. g.)	
		Means	S.D. **	Mean	S.D.
12 to 13 years					
Prepubescent	A	142.10	5.26	33.32	3.06
Pubescent	A	148.01	6.09	37.74	6.66
13 to 14 years					
Prepubescent	A	146.30	7.23	36.30	5.73
Pubescent	A	151.53	6.93	41.49	5.63
13 to 14 years					
Prepubescent	B	146.53	5.59	38.33	3.31
Pubescent	B	158.88	6.20	47.73	5.64
14 to 15 years					
Pubescent	B	155.91	3.76	46.00	3.55
Adolescent	B	163.83	6.00	52.18	6.07
15 to 16 years					
Pubescent	B	154.53	6.76	45.30	5.96
Adolescent	B	164.31	10.29	53.59	8.00

* In the age groups here, adolescent refers to those who have passed through the period of pubescence—the postadolescent.

** S.D. is an abbreviation for standard deviation. This is a measure of variability based on the frequency distribution. A large S.D. in comparison with the mean indicates a wide distribution, while a small S.D. is an indication of greater homogeneity.

nine to seventeen in two residential schools of England, and examinations of 101 working boys aged fourteen to eighteen from the residential homes in Edinburgh.[5]

The study by Ramsey provides a rather complex analysis of sexual changes appearing among boys.[6] In his study, personal interviews

[4] Richard W. B. Ellis, Height and weight in relation to onset of puberty in boys, *Archives of Disease in Childhood*, 1946, Vol. 21, pp. 181-189.

[5] Richard W. B. Ellis, Puberty growth for boys, *Archives of Disease in Childhood*, 1948, Vol. 23, pp. 17-26.

[6] G. V. Ramsey, The sexual development of boys, American Journal of *Psychology*, 1943, Vol. 56, pp. 217-233.

TABLE 69 Analysis of 662 examinations of boys on the basis of maturity and age (after Ellis)

Age group (years)	No.	Nonpubescent (per cent)	Pubescent (per cent)	Adolescent * (per cent)
9-10	52	100	0	0
10-11	40	95	5	0
11-12	74	86.5	13.5	0
12-13	95	64.2	35.8	0
13-14	135	47.4	43.7	8.9
14-15	120	12.5	39.2	48.3
15-16	78	1.3	29.5	69.2
16-17	33	6.1	18.2	75.7
17-18	35	0	11.4	88.6

* In this study, adolescent is interpreted as those showing the physical symptoms of sexual maturity. These have been referred to elsewhere as postadolescents.

were conducted among 291 boys ranging in age from ten to twenty years. These boys were from middle-class and upper socioeconomic homes of a Midwestern city. The various aspects of sexual development studied are presented in Table 70. These data indicate that the appearance of the different sex characteristics follows a distribution range, and varies with the different characteristics studied. The thirteen-year level appears from this study to be the modal age for the appearance of each of these characteristics.

TABLE 70 Percentage of each age group, showing different aspects of sexual development (after Ramsey)

Age group	Ejaculation per cent	Voice change per cent	Nocturnal emission per cent	Pubic hair per cent
10	1.8	0.3	0.3	0.3
11	6.9	5.6	3.7	8.4
12	14.1	20.5	5.3	27.1
13	33.6	40.0	17.4	36.1
14	30.9	26.0	12.9	23.8
15	7.8	5.5	13.9	3.3
16	4.9	2.0	16.0	1.0

A study conducted by Katherine Simmons, using as subjects 200 girls from homes whose parents were above average in both education and economic status, and who were of Northern European stock, shows that pubescence among a fairly homogeneous group of girls falls in a rather wide distribution; however, more than two-thirds of the girls reached pubescence between 11.5 years and 13.62 years.[7] The average chronological age for the appearance of pubescence among these girls was reported as 12.56 years. This is significantly higher than the averages reported for the two groups presented in Table 71. These differences may be partially accounted for by the differences in the social and economic background of the groups studied. All studies seem to agree that pubescence is earlier among girls than among boys. Furthermore, the various studies furnish good evidence that such factors as climate, nutrition, living conditions, and the like affect the time of the onset of pubescence.

TABLE 71 Mean age and standard deviation of menarche for two groups of girls *

	No. of Girls	Mean Years	Standard Deviation
Adolescent study	92	13.16	13.3
Hebrew Orphan study	250	13.53	10.9

* The Adolescent Growth Study is a longitudinal study conducted at the University of California under the general direction of R. H. Jones.
The Hebrew Orphan Study was conducted by Leona M. Bayer. See her study, "Weight and menses in adolescent girls with special reference to build," *Journal of Pediatrics*, 1940, Vol. 17, pp. 345-354.

Pubescence and changed attitudes. One of the clearest indications of the beginning of adolescence may be observed in the changed attitude of boys and girls toward things about them and toward members of the opposite sex. No longer is the girl looked upon as an individual who merely gets in the way of the activities of boys. On the contrary, boys and girls begin showing an interest in the opposite sex and may resort to various devices to get their attention and admiration. This is brought out in a study by Jones and Bayley in which comparisons were made between two groups of boys equal in chronological age but approximately two years apart in skeletal development.[8] The results from a comparison of these two groups for "attention-seeking" behavior are presented in Figure 44. These results indicate that the late-maturing boys tended to vary around the

[7] Katherine Simmons, The Brush Foundation Study of Child Growth and Development. II. Physical growth and development, *Monographs of the Society for Research in Child Development*, 1944, Vol. 9, No. 1.
[8] Mary Cover Jones and Nancy Bayley, Physical maturity among boys as related to behavior, *Journal of Educational Psychology*, 1950, Vol. 41, p. 137.

average in the trait "matter-of-factness." Their lowest score is at age sixteen, where they fall on the "show-off" side of the scale. The early-maturing boys maintain at all age levels a score above the average in this trait. On the lower half of the figure, the mean score of the late-maturing boys tends to remain around the average at all

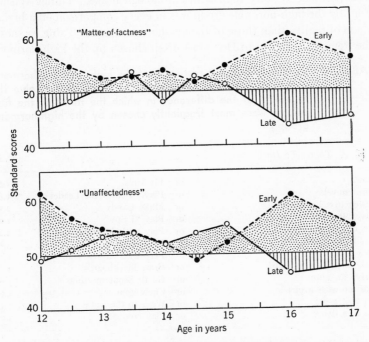

FIG. 44 Mean standard scores of early- and late-maturing groups, in attention-seeking behavior

age levels, while the mean scores for the early-maturing boys show less affection at all age levels. The average early-maturing boy thus appears to be relatively nonattention-seeking and unaffected.

A comparison of the ratings given early- and late-maturing adolescent boys shows the early-maturing boys to be less uninhibited and relatively less relaxed (more tense than the late-maturing boys. On a series of traits involving personal appearance, the early-maturing boys were consistently rated ahead of the late-maturing ones. As would be expected, the early-maturing boys displayed a greater interest in personal grooming.

Differences in the attitudes of early- and late-maturing boys are further shown in a study by Sollenberger.[9] Complete twenty-four-hour urine samples were obtained from twenty-three boys at a boys' reform school. The age range of the group was from twelve years, nine months to sixteen years, ten months. The degree of maturity of the expressed interests and attitudes of the boys correlated higher with hormone activity than with chronological age. "Things Wished For" by the high-hormone group was in every comparison on a higher plane of reality than those of the low-hormone group. Table 72 shows the items on "Things to Do" most often chosen by the high-hormone

TABLE 72 Comparison of the responses of the high- and low-hormone group on the items, "Things to Do." (The C.R.'s. give the reliability of the difference in which the items of the first column were most frequently chosen by the high-hormone group.)

Things To Do			C.R.
Bowl	or	Fly kites	1.0
Read novels	or	Play, "Follow the Leader"	1.6
Listen to a band playing	or	Make Candy	2.5
Play "Parchesi"	or	Play "I Spy"	1.2
Go out with a girl	or	Play with Meccano	1.2
Read sport news	or	Play checkers	3.8
Play soccer	or	Play with electric trains	1.1
Take a walk with a girl	or	Erase blackboards	1.3
Drive an auto	or	Go to Scout meetings	1.8
Go out with a girl	or	Chew gum	1.6
Go visit a girl	or	Wade in the water	1.3
Go to a dance	or	Play croquet	2.0

group. A study of these results reveals the change of interests toward girls with increased hormone activity. It is at this time, through a sort of subculture operating among adolescents, that existing sexual patterns are modified. According to the studies by Kinsey and others, individuals rarely adopt new patterns of sexual behavior after their middle teens.[10] Thus, changes made are those departures by pre-adolescents from the patterns of their parents and other adults. These early years are most important in the formation of individual and group patterns of sexual behavior. The influence of peers, ways of living, recreational activities, the church, the school, the home,

[9] R. T. Sollenberger, Some relationships between the urinary excretion of male hormones by maturing boys and their expressed interests and attitudes, *Journal of Psychology*, 1940, Vol. 9, pp. 179-189.

[10] Alfred C. Kinsey, Wardell P. Pomeray, and Clyde E. Martin, *Sexual Behavior in the Human Male* (Philadelphia: W. B. Saunders Co., 1948).

the movies, the press, and other institutions and forces within a culture will determine in a large measure the direction of these changes.

Development tasks of adolescents

Adolescence in America comprises a number of years in the lives of most boys and girls. These are important years, since they provide opportunities for development from childhood into adulthood. No longer does the boy leave school with development into adolescence and enter into the serious business of making a living and providing for a wife and children. And, although the needs and tasks of adolescents are to a certain degree an individual matter, there are developmental tasks which "they must achieve in order to lead a satisfactory life and to advance through the various stages of normal growth." [11]

Developing emotional independence from the parents. Throughout several of the previous chapters it has been emphasized that many mental-hygiene problems and personality difficulties are closely related to the attitudes of the child's parents. The unwillingness of parents to relinquish control may become a major source of difficulty to the child's successful adjustment as he grows into adolescence.

If the child has been given a reasonable amount of responsibility during the past years, and if he has been given the opportunity to exercise his own thinking without too much hindrance from adults, he is better prepared to face the task of growing up when he reaches adolescence. This has been referred to as *psychological weaning,* and is an essential task that must be learned as the individual passes out of childhood and into adolescence. This enables the individual to transfer his emotional attachment from his immediate family to that of his peers, and in so doing prepares him for the establishment of a family of his own, which will be discussed further in Chapter 18.

Understanding and accepting one's self. The problem of understanding and accepting one's self is closely related to that of facing reality. The adolescent should come to understand himself and accept himself and his role with her peers. He should recognize his limitations and potentialities. This implies a willingness to evaluate one's self without prejudice, bias, or favorable or unfavorable attitudes. This objective attitude is characterized by an impartial, dispassion-

[11] Robert J. Havighurst, What adolescence is like, *National Parent Teacher,* 1950, Vol. 45, pp. 26-28. Some of the materials in the following discussions of the developmental tasks of adolescents are adapted from this source.

ate regard for accurate, unbiased judgments and appraisal and thus assumes a scientific attitude toward the self. Perhaps this is expecting too much of the adolescent; however, with sound and sane guidance, the growing individual can come to weigh facts as they are rather than as he would like for them to be. In the end, this means being honest with the self. As Shakespeare says in *Macbeth:* "To thine own self be true and it must follow as the night the day, thou canst not then be false to any man."

The child does not have this objective attitude by natural endowment; neither does it appear as a result of physiological changes associated with pubescence. Such an attitude is an outgrowth of experiences involving honesty in thinking about matters relating to the self. It is extremely important that the child be guided into a fair and unprejudiced evaluation of his own worth. One of the first steps, perhaps, in training the child to think objectively about himself is for him to develop many wholesome interests outside the self. If he becomes less concerned about the self and more concerned about the things around him, he will be faced with fewer frustrations and conflicts. When he has developed the ability to accept the true self, he will have achieved an important step toward maturity and good personal adjustment.

Understanding one's sex role. The sex life of the child begins at birth. Parents have the responsibility of giving the child instruction suited to his age and needs, as well as giving him training in proper habits. The needed information should be given gradually, in proportion to the child's curiosity and capacity for understanding it. The information given a child of five or six will be different from that given a child of twelve, both in form and in certain features of content, but the one should be in harmony with the other. The child should feel perfectly free to ask his parents for information and he should feel confident that they will tell him the truth. His inquiries should be treated with candor because they are a result of natural curiosity, not of emotional tones. In this way the child will build up the right attitude toward sex and be prepared for puberty.

Boys and girls must learn social skills that tend to complement each other. They learn to work together, each playing the role of his or her sex. The boy is expected to develop a rather high degree of independence, and the capacity for looking after himself. The girl, on the other hand, is not faced with the problem of becoming independent. She is, however, faced with the task of gradually transferring the dependence and submission that characterized her earlier life from her parents to that of some growing man. This transference is much easier when the boy is several years older, and this factor is important in accounting for the interest that adolescent girls often have in older boys and men.

These sex differences are not as clear-cut, however, as they were a century or more ago. Boys and girls have developed a companionate relationship with each other, and they are often observed doing many things together. Even here, however, the boys and girls are likely to play different roles. Notice a group of boys and girls riding around in an old jalopy. The boys will be driving the car and making most of the noise, while the girls are giving attention to the boys and perhaps waving at some people as they pass by. An important developmental task that must be learned by adolescents, if they are to function satisfactorily with their group, is that of learning not only the role that their own sex must play in various activities but learning also about the role of the opposite sex and the ways these roles complement each other.

Attaining a satisfactory role. The attainment of a satisfactory role among one's peers is a developmental task which takes on added importance as the individual develops out of the early elementary-school stage. The nine- and ten-year-old child feels the need for attaining a satisfactory role, and will endure many things from his age group in order to attain such a role. The efforts at this age, however, are directed toward the attainment of a satisfactory role with his sex and age group. Gang life and gang activities are closely identified with this desire for attaining a satisfactory role. The insecure child and the rejected child find social development during this period a difficult and unpleasant undertaking. The failure to attain a satisfactory role during the preadolescent period makes it difficult for the individual to attain a satisfactory role during adolescence.

Growth into adolescence brings additional problems relative to the attainment of a satisfactory role. The boy who has failed to attain a satisfactory role with other boys of his age will not find it easy to attain a satisfactory role with girls of his age. The earliest dating activities of the adolescent are likely to be of an informal nature in groups. This is both wholesome and desirable; but the boy or girl who is unpopular with his own sex group probably will not find such activities pleasant experiences. Successful preparation for the attainment of a satisfactory role during adolescence should begin with the security of early childhood and continue with the attainment of a satisfactory role during the preadolescent years. Studies have revealed several important findings relative to the attainment of a satisfactory role during adolescence. The following generalizations are based on these findings:

1. The adolescent, like the preadolescent, desires the approval of his peers.

2. Good peer relations during preadolescence is perhaps the best assurance available for good peer relations during adolescence and post-adolescence.

3. With the onset of adolescence there appears the task of attaining a satisfactory sex role as well as satisfactory peer relations.

4. The attainment of a satisfactory sex role is inextricably related to the attainment of satisfactory peer relations.

5. Failure in the attainment of a satisfactory role may result in serious maladjustments and mental-hygiene problems.

6. Early adolescence is accompanied by the formation of cliques. These cliques play an important part in satisfying certain felt needs of adolescents.

7. There is a close relationship between favorable home conditions (see Chapter 14) and the attainment of a satisfactory role.

Developing social consciousness. The child is born neither social nor antisocial. He is born into a society where certain cultural patterns are found in the home, at church, at school, on the streets, and elsewhere. At first he is more or less oblivious to most of the culture that surrounds him, although he reacts within his limits to certain aspects of it from the very beginning of life. His behavior is largely concerned with providing for his physical needs—eating, sleeping, exercising, etc. Social consciousness is almost wholly lacking at this early period of life. The real beginnings of social consciousness are to be found in the activities of groups of children at play during the early school years. As they grow, they come to realize what the group expects of them, and how they must behave with respect to the various members of the group.

Adolescence has often been described as a period of heightened social consciousness. This fact was brought out in the discussions of adolescent peer relations in Chapter 12. Preadolescence is a period when this is being manifested in the formation of groups, gangs, and clubs. There is an extension and intensification of this during the adolescent period. If the adolescent is to secure and maintain a well-adjusted personality, he must develop out of his early egocentric nature into a social being who recognizes and appreciates the personality of others, and who is eager to become a part of his peer group.

The adolescent and his peers

Importance of peer relations. We have a tendency to explain a child's attitudes and behavior on the basis of his family, neighborhood, and the organized institutions with which he is identified. The importance of peer relations in day-by-day activities at play and school is either overlooked or minimized. Studies in social psychology and sociology show that a sort of subculture operates among growing boys and girls. The operation of this subculture is most obvious in towns and cities where family ties are likely to be less binding. This is observed in the activities of gangs, and appears as part of the child's growing independence and ability to share activities and experiences with others of his age level. The importance of peer relations during adolescence, when many personal and social problems appear, has been emphasized by Caroline Tryon, when she states:

If we were to examine the major developmental tasks which confront boys and girls in late childhood, during pubescence, and in later adolescence, it would become apparent that many of these can only reach a satisfactory solution by boys and girls through the medium of their peer groups. It is in this group that *by doing* they learn about the social processes of our culture. They clarify their sex roles by acting and being responded to, they learn competition, cooperation, social skills, values, and purposes by sharing the common life.[12]

It has already been suggested that growth into adolescence involves a number of developmental tasks among which are the development of satisfactory roles with one's peers. There is also, somewhat related to this, the problem of achieving independence. Parents and teachers often impose barriers to the attainment of these developmental tasks. The subculture operating in the adolescent groups enable boys and girls to achieve certain desired ends which they are not able to achieve satisfactorily within the adult culture. Furthermore, they receive sympathy and understanding from their peers that it would be impossible to get from most adult groups, since their peers are likely to be faced with problems similar to what they as adolescents are facing.

[12] Caroline M. Tryon, The adolescent peer culture, *Adolescence, Forty-third Yearbook of the National Society for the Study of Education*, Part 1, 1944, Chapter XII.

The culture operating in these adolescent groups may be conceived of as a mixture of that found among younger children, youths, and more mature adults. These groups, therefore, tend to have their own standards growing out of this mixture. They have their own values and purposes, and devise methods for protecting themselves from adult interference. They use the methods found among adult groups for securing conformity. Adults are frequently excluded from these groups by such indirect means as "Oh, this is just for us kids." Also, the expression "Other boys are able to do this" is used. The group remains somewhat constant for a number of years during the growing life of the adolescent, although it is never completely constant, since new members are being admitted and older ones drop out for one reason or another.

Desire for popularity. There is perhaps no period in the individual's life when he does not have the desire to be popular among his peers. However, this desire appears to be keener during the preadolescent and adolescent years than at any other time of life. This was indicated in the results of a survey by the Purdue University Opinion Poll, taken of more than ten thousand high-school students across the nation. Girls were found to be somewhat more concerned than boys with being popular. This difference is no doubt closely related to the greater restrictions placed on girls in making friends. Further data bearing on this will be presented in Chapter 18. The results from the survey for boys and girls were as follows:

Almost 50 per cent of the boys and 60 per cent of the girls checked the item *I want people to like me more.*

The item *I wish I were more popular* was checked by 30 per cent of the boys and 47 per cent of the girls.

The desire to make new friends was checked by 45 per cent of the boys and 56 per cent of the girls.[13]

Many of the young people felt the need for help in making better social adjustments. High-school students, writing to the panel, requested help in how to overcome shyness, how to carry on a pleasant conversation, how to keep from being embarrassed, and other questions concerned with good social relations. On the basis of the results obtained from the survey, girls apparently felt more secure than boys in conversational ability. They were, however, more concerned about gaining self-confidence than were the boys. Sixteen per cent wanted

[13] These results of the Purdue University Opinion Poll are adapted from the *Atlanta Journal* for July 4, 1949.

help in introducing people properly. Nineteen per cent felt that they should learn to be more tactful. Twenty per cent wanted help about how to act on formal occasions. Only 8 per cent felt that they should be less aggressive in their social behavior. In this connection, there is considerable evidence that popularity results from positive qualities of action. The boy or girl who does not initiate action and always awaits the actions of others may be accepted, but is not likely to be among the most popular. Certain outstanding negative qualities may lead to one's being unpopular; however, most individuals soon learn to control these qualities and thus achieve the need for peer approval.

The dominant desire for popularity during the teen years is further revealed in the variety of wishes and aspirations of boys and girls at this time. This was brought out in Chapter 13 in connection with the wishes of boys and girls at different age levels. An important characteristic of growing out of the period of early childhood is the desire for things concerned with relations with others rather than the desire for some particular thing or object.

First ventures in dating. Parents are beset with the problem of when their daughter or son should start having dates. The answer likely to be received is, "It all depends." Depends upon what? Perhaps it depends upon the rate of growth toward maturity, the habits of responsibility developed, the amount of good judgment possessed, and the customs and practices of the particular community. It has already been suggested that some youngsters mature considerably earlier than others. Furthermore, it has been pointed out that physiological maturity brings with it an increased interest in members of the opposite sex. Since girls usually mature earlier than boys, they are likely to display an interest in dating earlier than boys. Often, girls of fifteen are invited out by boys of seventeen, while the boys of fifteen are still in the stage where they prefer to mingle together in groups where both boys and girls are present.

Usually, the best sequence in the process of dating is that of starting with small groups of youngsters attending parties without any special pairing off. In the South, many youngsters begin dating in a very elementary way through attendance at Sunday-school parties or some of the church organizations designed especially for young people. "Teen-Age Centers" provide opportunities for youngsters to come together in groups under favorable conditions. Pleasurable social and recreational activities in groups over a period of one or two years give the teenage boys and girls the experiences and skills needed for later courtship. Ideally, the boys and girls will tend to find particular individual members of the gang more attractive to them, so that pairing off takes place gradually. They do not ordinarily "go steady" for another year or so, but have several boy or

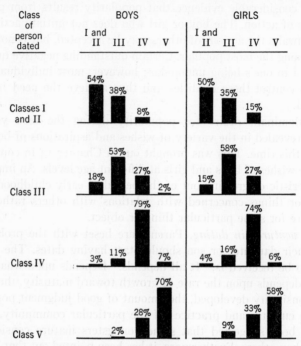

FIG. 45 Intra- and interclass dating patterns of boys and girls of Elmtown

(Reprinted by permission from *Elmtown's Youth* by A. B. Hollingshead, published by John Wiley and Sons, Inc., 1949, pp. 231-232.)

girl friends. There are, of course, exceptions to this general role. Many of these exceptions work out in a very satisfactory manner. The success of these exceptions will depend upon the attitudes of the parents concerned and the characteristics and values of the youngsters themselves.

The study of Elmtown's youth revealed some interesting facts regarding dating practices in relation to class structure (see Fig. 45). The families represented by these boys and girls were classified into five social-economic class groups. No dates were observed among these youth between members of class II and members of class V. On the other hand, 61 per cent of the dates belong to the same class; 35 per cent to an adjacent class; and 4 per cent to a class separated by one intervening class. This association of class with class in dating practices is shown in Figure 45. This chart shows that the boy is more willing than the girl to date someone in a lower class structure; conversely, the girl tends to date boys in a higher class structure. This means, then, that the girl in class V is less likely to have dates than any other groups of boys or girls classified on the basis of class structure.

Problems of adolescents [14]

Most of the problems of adolescents involve the fear element. Most of these fears are out of proportion to the seriousness of the problem. Most of these arise during childhood, and become modified in some manner as the child develops into adolescence. This may be observed from a study of the four fears, listed by Oliver Yoder Lewis, as characteristics of the average adolescent.[15] These are: (1) opinion of parents; (2) opinion of teachers; (3) opinion of peers; and (4) fear of the unknown. In order to determine the problems of adolescents enrolled in the Franklin Junior High School, Vallejo, California, each student was requested to list any personal problems he might have at the time. Blanks were received from 339 boys and 362 girls. These were then classified into seven general groups—school, home life, social, future, money, religion, and health and development. A comparison of the number of problems in each of these groups reported by boys and girls is presented in Figure 46. This figure shows that home life and social problems were reported by more than twice as many girls as boys. Health and development and the future presented problems for many more boys than girls.

Achieving independence. Among the problems faced by adolescents, that of achieving independence from home and family ties are of first magnitude. This problem is made more difficult by the failure of many parents to realize that the boys and girls are advancing toward maturity. Concerning this, George Gardner has stated:

The first problem of great concern during adolescent years is the drive for independence, and ... a successful solution of it is dependent upon, and in large part influenced by, solutions that have previously

[14] Some of the materials of this topic have been adapted from the writer's *Psychology of Adolescence* (4th ed.; New York: Prentice-Hall, 1951), chap. II.
[15] Olive Yoder Lewis, Problems of the adolescent, *California Journal of Secondary Education,* 1949, Vol. 24, pp. 215-221.

been made in earlier life to the aforementioned problems of security or insecurity, aggression, passivity, and the emergence of infantile sexual components. In other words, if the earlier adjustments to these have been inadequate, the problem of adolescence and freedom from parental con-

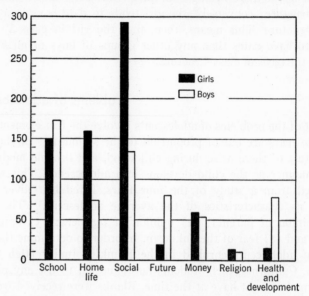

FIG. 46 Comparison of number of problems reported by boys and girls

(After Lewis)

trol, the overcoming of dependence and the gaining of a state of self-sufficiency, will be much more difficult. However, the internal pressures within the child, and the pressure from his colleagues, from his own parents, and from society as a whole *insist* that he find a solution to these problems in adolescence.[16]

Although adolescents may appear to repudiate their parents in certain respects, since they no longer consider them as their ideal in every way, the results of the *SRA Inventory* survey show that among teen-agers strong feelings against their parents are voiced by only a minority of the students. The three types of home problems most frequently checked were: (1) those indicating a lack of understanding between parents and adolescents, (2) those involving a limitation of their freedom, and (3) problems involving money or finances. In

[16] George E. Gardner, The mental health of normal adolescents, *Mental Hygiene*, 1947, Vol. 31, pp. 531-532.

harmony with results from other studies, problems connected with finances seemed more serious for the boys, although girls usually display less insight in the handling of money.

Problems relating to physical development. The pubescent spurt of growth does not occur simultaneously for the different parts of the body. The most rapid period of leg growth tends to precede the spurt of growth in sitting height. Bayley has reported some interesting features of the changes in build occurring at this stage.[17] Sex differences are noted first in growth, since girls reach pubescence earlier than boys. The degree of asynchrony of development as between leg length and body length, or hip width and shoulder width, becomes more pronounced at this stage and is itself in many cases a source of disturbances. Also, there is a lag in the increase in muscular strength in relation to the increase in the size of the muscles. This presents a significant problem to many boys.

Differences in build among early- and late-maturing boys is greater than that among early- and late-maturing girls. Early-maturing boys tend to be broad-hipped, while late-maturing boys tend to be slender-hipped and long-legged. The importance of variations in body build and variations in the onset of pubescence become sources of disturbances to many adolescents. Boys in particular are disturbed over conditions that may cause them not to look masculine. They are also disturbed over lack of strength, factors indicative of poor health, and muscular abilities required in the performance of motor skills.

The "sex appropriate physique" applies quite differently to girls from the way it applies to boys. Perhaps the phrase "sex appropriate face and figure" is more applicable to the girl. For the girl, too much strength may be regarded as undesirable. It was pointed out in Chapter 6 that girls upon reaching adolescence tend to discontinue the performance of motor skills, and there is an actual decline in the average motor ability of girls after the age of thirteen or fourteen years. Any condition that may cause the girl to be looked upon as less feminine becomes a problem to her. In connection with frustrations existing with regard to the appropriate sex physique, the girl is more likely to do something about it than is the boy. However, boys are often motivated to exert great effort and endure continued exercise in order to develop a so-called masculine physique. It seems likely, then, that even temporary deviations from the "sex appro-

[17] N. Bayley, Size and body build of adolescents in relation to rate of skeletal maturing, *Child Development*, 1943, Vol. 14, pp. 51-90.

priate physique" may produce significant adjustment problems for boys and girls.

Problems related to physiological growth. Many of the problems connected with physiological development are closely related to those discussed in connection with physical development. The physiological changes associated with adolescence present conditions and problems that the individual has not met up to this time and in many cases is ill-prepared to meet when they appear. The period of the first menarche may be a real problem for the girl, if she has not been properly prepared for it. There has been a tendency among some parents with the best of intention to give too much concern to this, and thus create undue anxiety in the girl over the appearance of the menstrual period. This is further reflected in the attitude and behavior of the girl toward physical activities during this period.

Problems of skin blemishes and acne disturb many boys and girls at this age. Also, closely akin to this are body odors. Some adolescents and postadolescents tend to go to an extreme in the use of perfumes, lotions, and other toilet articles in an effort to meet special problems of body odors at this stage. The appearance of axillary hair is in some cases a source of disturbance for girls, while the lack of the appearance of hair on the arms, legs, and chest has been regarded by many boys as a weakness in the development of a masculine type. The appearance of hair on the chin and upper lip at this stage presents one more problem for the adolescent boy, which he must learn to meet by shaving. Needless to say, problems related to physiological changes have been aggravated by cultural forces. These problems are inextricably related to the sex roles to be played by adolescent boys and girls. Any condition that interferes with the development and assertion of the masculine role on the part of boys is likely to be a source of difficulty; conversely, any condition that interferes with the development and assertion of the feminine role on the part of the girl is likely to be a source of difficulty.

Social demands upon adolescents. The development into adolescence brings forth impulses relating to the sex drive, and more sensitized social reactions. The changed physiological self causes the individual to take a different attitude toward members of the opposite sex. At this stage, the individual must learn to adapt to a society in which his role is complementary to that of the opposite sex. New demands are made upon him. A few years ago, he was excused for many acts because he was immature. Now, he is expected to assume the role of an adult on many occasions, even though he is inexperienced in living and participating as an adult in an adult society.

It is a common observation that the adolescent is a source of perplexity and anxiety to adults—particularly his parents and teachers. He feels, and perhaps rightly so, that he is misunderstood. Among his peers he is able to find the security and understanding that he is so often unable to secure from adults. Thus, peer relations become most important at this age. Pressed both internally and externally to conform to specified modes of behavior, he develops one technique for adjusting to adult demands and another one for adjusting to the demands of his peers. There is perhaps no period of life when individuals are so frequently misunderstood as they are in the adolescent period—the transition stage of life.[18]

Problems involving dating. Problems relating to dating appear with the onset of the sex drive and changed attitudes toward the opposite sex. This has been observed from various studies of adolescent problems. The question asked by a fourteen-year-old boy on a check list given by the writer illustrates the nature of this problem as encountered by many adolescent boys.

Girls are a problem of mine. I like a girl and I don't know whether she likes me or another boy, a friend of mine.

I would like to have a date with this girl but my mother won't let me.

At a later stage, problems related to "going steady," "wondering if I'll ever get married," and "not enough dates" are very prevalent. Among college girls, the writer found "wondering if I'll ever get married" checked more than any other problem of the Mooney problem check list.[19] The *SRA Inventory* survey revealed some of the problems and confusions that beset teen-agers in the areas of dating and personal-social relations. Some of the dating problems listed by these young people are as follows:

Boys

48% seldom have dates.

41% don't have a girl friend.

34% are bashful about asking girls for dates.

26% don't know how to ask for a date.

[18] See L. K. Frank, Introduction: adolescence as a period of transition, *Forty-third Yearbook of the National Society for the Study of Education,* Part i, 1944, Chap. 1.

[19] Unpublished data on file in the College of Education, University of Georgia, 1950.

25% don't know how to keep girls interested in them.

23% wonder whether anything is wrong with going places "stag."

GIRLS

39% seldom have dates.

30% don't have a boy friend.

23% feel they are not popular with boys.

33% don't know how to keep boys interested in them

36% would like to know how to refuse a date politely.

29% wonder whether it is all right to accept "blind dates."

22% don't know how to break up an affair without causing bad feelings.

20% wonder whether they should kiss their dates the first time they go out together.[20]

School problems of adolescents. Adjustments to different aspects of the school environment present problems at all age levels. It was pointed out in Chapter 15 that a pronounced increase in stuttering appears among a group of children upon entrance to school. Adjustment problems appear when the child transfers from one school to another. Furthermore, adjustment problems appear as the child moves out of the elementary-school program into a high-school program where he will meet a number of different teachers. The preadolescent and adolescent are required to adjust to a number of different teacher personalities. They may be called upon to listen and be attentive in one classroom, while the teacher lectures and expounds, but they may be expected to be responsive in another classroom. Again, they may be expected to obey and follow the dictates of an authoritarian teacher at one time, and then later to participate in the classroom planning under a teacher with more democratic methods and concepts.

Many situations in the traditional school involve competition. The adolescent must learn to adjust to failure and successes in his competitive school activities. Fear of failure, fear of disapproval of his teachers, fear of disapproval of his peers, and many other fears may loom large at this stage. Materials from the California adolescent

[20] Taken from the *Examiner's Manual for the SRA Youth Inventory,* Form A, 1949, p. 4, Chicago: Science Research Associates.

growth studies show that a large percentage of preadolescents, adolescents, and postadolescents dislike elements in the school situation that indicate unfair practices on the part of the teachers and snobbish as well as overly aggressive and dominating attitudes and practices on the part of their classmates. Some features of the curriculum and program disliked by a large percentage of boys and girls in the California study are listed in Table 73.[21]

TABLE 73 Aspects of the school curriculum and program disliked by adolescents

Aspect	H5L6		H8L9		H11L12	
	BOYS	GIRLS	BOYS	GIRLS	BOYS	GIRLS
There is too much homework	18	4	45	29	45	36
Assignments are too long	32	18	51	32	42	39
Many of the subjects are dull and un-interesting	55	32	63	56	63	53
No chance to pick out the subjects that one likes	48	25	44	25	20	6
Having to take subjects that one dislikes	63	31	61	57	48	42
School work is too monotonous	28	10	46	28	28	21
Having to take subjects which will be of no use to one when grown up	52	28	68	60	55	53

Many personal problems of adolescents involve school relations and conditions. Some of the personal problems most frequently checked by teen-agers in the *SRA Inventory* survey are:

35% say they worry about "little things."
35% can't help daydreaming.
29% must always be "on the go."
27% report that they are nervous.
26% have guilt feelings about things they have done.
25% are ill at ease at social affairs.
24% of the students report "I want to discuss my personal problems with someone."[22]

[21] Caroline McCann Tryon, *U. C. Inventory I: Social and Emotional Adjustment*. Revised form for presentation of cumulative record of individual and group norms for a seven-year period. Berkeley: University of California, 1939.
[22] The materials here quoted from the *SRA Inventory* survey are taken from the *Examiner Manual for the SRA Youth Inventory*, Form A, 1949, p. 3.

Summary and generalization

Graduation from infancy represents a stage in the child's development where he is able to explore the world about him by bringing himself in contact with many different things and conditions. This stage of life presents problems for parents, since the child is continuously examining, exploring, and trying out new ways of behaving. By the time he is two years of age, he displays affection toward those with whom he comes into daily contact. He is at this time differentiating personalities and may begin to sense that some children dress as boys while others dress as girls, although there is no understanding of sex differences as such at this time. The four-year-old child is quite conscious of size and likes to be measured. Four-year-olds like to copy adults, and may be seen doing this in their play and various activities in general. There is a need during this stage for the child to have a variety of experiences with other children, and experiences with things about him. This furnishes him with a background of readiness for school activities.

The seven- and eight-year-old child begins displaying considerable independence, although he is eager to co-operate in undertakings where he becomes a part of the total situation. He is beginning to show some interest in peer approval and membership in group activities, although this does not reach its peak until a few years later— the preadolescent stage. There is a demand at this age for the youngsters to conform to the ideals and activities of the gang. Secrecy is often manifested at this age, and methods are introduced for excluding adults from the group.

Growth into adolescence is especially characterized by changed attitudes toward members of the opposite sex. Boys and girls who were indifferent to the opposite sex just a few years ago are now anxious to secure approval from members of that sex. This affects changes in their ways of behaving and presents new problems to teachers and parents. Most children begin showing signs of modesty and oftentimes timidity in the presence of the opposite sex during late childhood. Most children encounter some minor sex episodes at this stage. These are usually not nearly as serious as many parents would seem to indicate or believe. The ways in which the preadolescent will deal with sex problems will depend largely upon the attitudes toward sex established prior to this period. Furthermore, the ways in which adolescents regard sex will depend upon the manner in which these problems were dealt with during childhood and preadolescence. There are a number of physiological symptoms that indicate the beginning of adolescence. There is an increased rate of growth just prior to adolescence, which heralds the beginning of adolescence. Accompanying this increased rate of growth are changes in body proportions, strength, and certain secondary sexual characteristics.

Havighurst has listed certain developmental tasks which adolescents face. Those discussed in this chapter are: (1) understanding and accepting one's self; (2) understanding one's sex role; (3) attaining a satisfactory role; (4) developing emotional independence from the parents; and (5) developing social consciousness. Peer relations become most important at this stage. It has been suggested that many of the developmental tasks of adolescents can only reach a satisfactory solution through good peer relations. In this connection, the desire for popularity becomes very important. Anything that interferes with the adolescent's good peer relations becomes a problem that is real and significant to him. This dominant desire for popularity is shown in the wishes, aspirations, and behavior activities of boys and girls at this age.

Many problems appear at this age. Some people have misunderstood the appearance of these problems and referred to the adolescent period as a problem age or problem group. It is more correct to say that individuals at this age are faced with many problems. Perhaps the problem of first importance is that of achieving independence from the family. This has sometimes been referred to as *emancipation* or *psychological weaning*. Studies of problems appearing during this age show that they tend to fall into the following general groups: (1) those relating to home life; (2) those relating to school activities; (3) social problems; (4) problems connected with the future; (5) problems involving money and finances; (6) problems connected with health and physical development; and (7) problems concerned with religion. A careful study of these problems will show that an individual fortified with affection, security, and a feeling of personal worth during childhood will be better prepared as an adolescent to meet and solve these problems.

Questions and Exercises

1. What essential adolescent needs should be satisfied in the emotional climate of the home? What are some of the dangers resulting from a failure to satisfy these needs?

2. Study the *developmental tasks* of adolescents listed in this chapter. Suggest several problems encountered by adolescents in connection with each of these.
3. Elaborate upon the statement: "Adolescents are not problem individuals, but rather individuals faced with problems."
4. Are adolescents of today different from those of a generation ago? In what ways are the problems adolescents face today different from those of a generation ago? In what ways are these problems the same?
5. What are some *social attitudes* that differentiate the preadolescent from the average child of eight or nine years of age?
6. Tom is now approaching eleven years of age. His father says he has never asked him any questions about sex. What are some reasons that might account for this?

Selected Readings

Beverly, Bert I. *A Psychology of Growth.* New York: McGraw-Hill Book Co., 1947. Chaps. X and XI.

Breckenridge, Marian E., and Vincent, E. Lee. *Child Development.* 2nd ed.; Philadelphia: W. B. Saunders Co., 1949. Chap. XIV. This chapter presents a good abbreviated account of moral judgments and psychosexual development during the preadolescent and adolescent years.

Cole, Luella. *Psychology of Adolescence.* 3rd ed.; New York: Rinehart and Co., 1948.

Douglass, Harl R. (ed.). *Education for Life Adjustment.* New York: The Ronald Press Co., 1950.

Frank, Lawrence K. *This is The Adolescent.* New York: National Committee for Mental Hygiene, 1946.

Garrison, Karl C. *Psychology of Adolescence.* 4th ed.; New York: Prentice-Hall, 1951.

Hurlock, Elizabeth B. *Adolescent Development.* 2nd ed.; New York: McGraw-Hill Book Co., 1949.

Merry, Frieda Kiefer, and Merry, Ralph Vickers. The First Two Decades of Life: A Revision and Evaluation of *From Infancy to Adolescence.* New York: Harper & Brothers, 1950.

Norvell, George W. *The Reading Interests of Young People.* Boston: D. C. Heath and Company, 1950.

Rothney, John W. M., and Roems, Bert A. *Guidance of American Youth.* Cambridge, Mass.: Harvard University Press, 1950.

Zachry, Caroline. *Emotion and Conduct in Adolescence.* New York: Appleton-Century-Crofts, 1940. Chaps. IV-VI.

18

From Adolescence
to Maturity

Introduction: The significance of maturity

During the period of growth and development, new needs are continuously appearing in the individual's life, while certain childhood needs relating to care and protection disappear or lose their potency. The development into adolescence introduces a different self and different concepts of the self. This though was presented in the previous chapter. Old goals are reorganized and new goals are introduced. Growth toward maturity brings with it increased abilities and independence, but with these come problems related to vocational choice, adjustment to a job, financial security, sex and marital adjustments, as well as other problems involved in assuming the role of an adult.

Manifestations of maturity. The essence of maturity lies not alone in the development of the bones, muscles, and reproductive organs. The nature of one's attitudes, outlooks, feelings, aspirations, and interests also determine one's maturity. The adult who persists in giving vent to his feelings by temper tantrums or some other child-like device is definitely manifesting immature characteristics. Perhaps no one is completely mature. Maturity, then, becomes a relative term. There are, however, certain behavior manifestations that are regarded as mature ways of behaving. The typical adolescent tends to manifest these characteristics to a greater and greater degree as he passes into the postadolescent stage. Conversely, immature ways of behaving are gradually discarded in favor of these more mature forms of behavior.

Although maturity is manifested in many ways and is revealed in different ways by various individuals, there are some characteristics which may be regarded as indicative of maturity. Some of these have been listed by Ruth Strang as follows:

1. Ability to feel with others, to see things from their point of view, and to be creative and happy rather than antagonistic or indifferent in one's relations with others.

2. Objectivity toward one's self, "ability to recognize and accept one's own emotions as natural," to project hypotheses about one's behavior, submit them to test, and, according to the results, further develop or discard them.

3. Ability to select suitable, worth-while, long-term goals and to organize one's thinking and acting around these goals.

4. Ability to make adjustments to situations; a certain amount of "role flexibility" is necessary to bring one's concepts into line with reality.

5. Ability "to meet unexpected stresses and disappointments without experiencing emotional or physical collapse, and without abandoning established lines of interest and activity."

6. Ability to give as well as receive affection.

7. Ability "to form opinions based on sound reasoning and to stand up for them, without abandoning willingness to accept such compromises as do not violate fundamental convictions." [1]

The mature person. It has already been suggested that maturity is a relative term. However, some individuals never reach an advanced stage of maturity, but remain infantile in much of their behavior. Some examples of infantilism, or childish behavior, may illustrate how this operates.

1. Louise became very angry and "lost her temper" when her younger brother slipped and read a letter of hers from her boy friend.

2. John became very angry at school when he failed to be elected to an office in his class, and refused to co-operate in future class activities.

3. Jack spent the evening printing pictures from negatives he had on hand, but didn't bother to clean up the dark room or put things back in their place after he was through.

Growth toward maturity is characterized by the individual *assuming personal responsibility*. This means that the individual has passed

---

[1] Ruth Strang, Manifestations of maturity in adolescents, *Mental Hygiene*, 1949, Vol. 33, pp. 563-569. Some of the materials for this study are taken from a paper read by Dr. John A. P. Millet at the annual conference of the New Jersey Welfare Council in New York, December, 1948.

through many stages in the development of responsibility. Human infancy was described in Chapter 3 as a period of helplessness. The previous chapters have described the growth process throughout the period of childhood. The radius of the individual's activities gradually increases. Likewise, if growth toward maturity has been complete, one's ability and readiness to assume increased responsibilities has gradually and continuously broadened. With maturity, the individual is able to make his own decisions and assume the responsibility for the consequences resulting from the decision made.

Growth toward maturity means *growth in independence.* An outstanding characteristic of most adolescents is their desire for independence, and one of the major developmental tasks they face is that of achieving a reasonable amount of independence. Oftentimes, the adolescent boy or girl has a keen desire for independence and the liberty that goes along with it, but does not care to assume the responsibility that independence and liberty bring with them. Liberty for the boy or girl reaching toward maturity without responsibility spells chaos, while responsibility without liberty is an empty dream in the lives of people.

Growing up means that *the individual must become a fundamental part of the larger society* of which he is a part. The world of the adolescent expands as he begins to look beyond his home, his school, and his immediate neighborhood. Friendships become wider, interests expand, and problems related to society become more meaningful and significant to him.

Just as early childhood is characterized by egocentric interests, growth toward maturity is characterized by *an expansion of interest beyond the self.* The young person or adult whose interests and conversation centers around himself may be mature physically, but has failed to grow up socially and emotionally. The mature person has a proper regard for the self; but he also has a wide range of interests outside and beyond the self, and reacts to situations in terms of values outside his own special interests and needs. If he is to take his place as an effective member of society, it is essential for him to weigh issues, consider events and happenings, and pass judgment on people in terms of the information and circumstances involved rather than in terms of their effect upon his personality.

The setting forth of goals and long-term purposes. One of the outstanding differences between the child and the mature individual is the way they react to remote or long-term goals. The immature individual is best motivated by goals that are within his reach over a short period of time. Any planning based on long-term purposes loses its force early and is thus short-lived. The following account of the vocational planning of a mentally superior seventeen-year-old boy is a manifestation of maturity:

My father died when I was ten years old, and left me a sufficient amount of money to provide for my college education. My mother has encouraged me during the course of the past several years to study pharmacy when I enter the state university.

This year I am graduating from high school and must soon decide what I will take when I enter college. Last week I had a long talk with our vocational counselor. At that time I told him of my mother's wishes about my professional future. He asked me some questions about my interests and what I would like to be doing ten or fifteen years from now. Thus, I have been doing lots of thinking about what I would like to be doing at that time. There are some things that I know that I don't want to be doing, so I am trying to decide between business, pharmacy, and teaching.

I have some literature dealing with a number of different fields of work, and have been reading some of it. Maybe after I have read more about the requirements of these different occupations, I will be able to make up my mind. Anyway, I am planning on going to the university this fall and will enroll in the liberal arts school. My counselor told me that the first year's work was basic anyway, and that I could make up my mind further after this first year. I don't want to put this off too long, though, for I think a fellow should decide soon after he goes to college just what field of work he is going to prepare to enter.

Changes of needs and goals with age. New needs or a change in existing needs may arise as a result of a variety of circumstances and conditions. In the previous chapter it was pointed out how development into adolescence brought with it new developmental tasks and modified existing needs and goals. As the individual grows from adolescence toward adulthood, new needs appear, existing needs are modified, and a changed outlook upon many problems gradually emerges. The individual begins to give more careful consideration to matters relating to financial independence, his life's work, and the establishment of a home. Problems relating to these appear, and decisions must be made.

Parents and teachers should be aware at all ages that the needs and goals of the growing individual are not static, but move from immediate situations toward more remote situations. Each period of life may be said to present a different individual with different needs, although life itself is a continuum and the individual life span is a continuous process of development and change. Concerning these conditions Kurt Lewin has stated:

Generally speaking, needs may be changed by changes in any part of the psychological environment, by changes of the inner-personal regions, by changes on the reality level as well as on the irreality level (for instance, by a change in hope), and by changes in the cognitive structure of the psychological future and of the psychological past. This is well in line with the fact that the total life space of a person has to be considered as one connected field.[2]

Developmental tasks of youth

The developmental tasks of adolescents were presented in Chapter 17. It was pointed out that adolescents are faced with the problems of accepting the self, attaining a satisfactory role, sexual adjustments, achieving independence from parental domination, and developing a social consciousness. Adolescence is for many American boys and girls a long period of frustrating experiences. Because of home influences, problems related to education, economic dependency, and lack of understanding and guidance from adults, the individual meets many difficulties as he attempts to acquire the developmental skills essential for satisfactory adjustment with his peers. The adolescent period has been aptly described as the in-between period or the transition stage. This is the period of life between childhood and adulthood. Just as many developmental tasks face the child as he moves from childhood into adolescence, many developmental tasks exist as the adolescent moves beyond the adolescent years into adulthood. The individual must satisfactorily complete these major developmental tasks if he is to be reasonably happy and well-adjusted as an adult. Some of the major developmental tasks that must be completed in our American culture will be summarized in the subsequent discussions.

The development of stable friendships. During the preadolescent years, friendships are often based upon factors related to a particular time or place, and are unstable in nature. The room in school and the neighborhood are the factors most important in determining friendships during this period. Growth into adolescence provides

---

[2] Reprinted by permission from Kurt Lewin, Behavior and development as a function of the total situation, in *Manual of Child Psychology,* L. Carmichael, ed., published by John Wiley & Sons, Inc., 1946, p. 284.

opportunities for a wider range of social contacts and a wider range for the choice of friends. Availability of social contacts and mutual satisfaction of needs were found by Reader and English to be the most important variables in adolescent friendships.[3] Girls with similar interests and tastes would thus appear more likely to be able to satisfy these mutual needs.

Comparative studies of friendship fluctuations of rural and urban adolescents and postadolescents have been made by Thompson and Horrocks.[4] In one study, 421 boys and 484 girls living in rural areas were studied over a two-week period. An increase in friendships from age ten to age seventeen was observed. In a later study, the friendship fluctuations of rural and urban adolescent girls were compared.

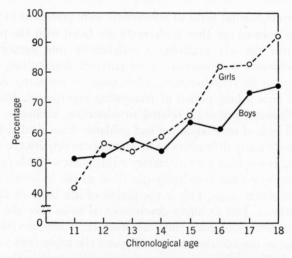

FIG. 47 The relationship between chronological age and percentage of boys and girls choosing the same person as their best friend on two occasions separated by a two-week interval
(After Horrocks and Thompson)

The 969 subjects used in this study were obtained from two cities in New York State and from one city in Pennsylvania. Girls were studied from families of approximately average socioeconomic

[3] Natalie Reader and H. B. English, Personality factors in adolescent friendships, *Journal of Consulting Psychology,* 1947, Vol. 11, pp. 212-220.

[4] J. E. Horrocks and G. G. Thompson, A study of the friendship fluctuations of urban boys and girls, *Journal of Genetic Psychology,* 1947, Vol. 70, pp. 53-63. Also, G. G. Thompson and J. E. Horrocks, A study of the friendship fluctuations of rural boys and girls, *Journal of Genetic Psychology,* 1946, Vol. 69, pp. 189-198.

status; a similar condition prevailed in the earlier study of rural adolescents. A comparison of the rural and urban boys in their fluctuations indicates a slightly greater stability in friendships among urban than among rural adolescents, although the differences found were not statistically reliable. The relationship between age and percentage of boys and girls choosing the same person as their best friend is shown in Figure 47. For both boys and girls there is a decided tendency toward an increased stability of friendship, with the girls showing the greater increase.

Development of the ideal self. The concept of an ideal self has been found useful by psychologists in their studies of personality development. By means of reports in which boys and girls were asked to write a brief essay on the subject "The Person I Would Like To Be Like," additional information was obtained concerning the development of the ideal self during childhood and adolescence.[5] Essays were secured from various groups, representing different cultures and different age levels. The results from two groups of boys and

TABLE 74   Comparison of ten-, eleven-, and twelve-year-olds (A) Ideals of self with those of sixteen- and seventeen-year-olds (B)—Percentage distribution (after Havighurst, Robinson and Durr)

	Boys		Girls	
Category	Group A N 60	Group B N 48	Group A N 100	Group B N 86
I P	7	6	6	3
II S	0	11	2	1
III G	12	6	16	1
IV H	3	2	2	4
V A	53	25	36	28
VI C	25	48	33	61
VII M	0	2	3	2
VIII NC	0	0	0	0

I P   Parents and other relatives of the parental or grandparental generation.
II S   Parent-surrogates: teachers, neighbors of parent generation.
III G   Glamorous adults: movie stars, military figures, etc.
IV H   Heroes: famous people, usually tested by time.
V A   Attractive and successful young adults within the individual range of observation.
VI C   Composite or imaginary character: may be a composite of several people within the individual's acquaintance.
VII M   Age-mates or youths only two or three years older.
VIII N C   Miscellaneous responses.

[5] Robert J. Havighurst, Myra Z. Robinson, and Mildred Dorr, The development of the ideal self in childhood and adolescence, *Journal of Educational Research*, 1946, Vol. 40, pp. 241-257.

girls from a typical small midwestern community are presented in Table 74. These results indicate that parents and members of the parental generation play a declining influence as the individual develops. Likewise, the glamorous person does not influence the sixteen- and seventeen-year-old groups to the extent that he does the early adolescent groups. Those of the older age groups who hold to the glamorous person as the ideal self are probably displaying immaturity of behavior.

A further analysis of the results presented in Table 74 shows that only 9 per cent of the older girls gave ideals of self that would fall in the first four categories (immature categories); while 25 per cent of the boys listed ideals of self in these categories. This is in harmony with the earlier maturity of girls. Also, a larger percentage of girls listed composite or imaginary characters as ideals of self. This, too, is related to the greater tendency of girls to daydream and engage in reading and similar types of activities.

Achieving a consistent and unified philosophy of life. As the adolescent grows into adulthood, he becomes more concerned about problems of living and the purposes of life. During the teen years, he is faced with many problems related to making choices, assuming an increased amount of responsibility, and securing the approval of his peers. During his adolescent years, he develops certain convictions, formulates ideals, and in many ways comes to function in a more stable manner. If he has received the proper guidance, his attitudes have become more consistent, and he has developed attitudes and outlooks that will enable him to grow more harmoniously toward maturity. During adolescence, he finds his role and comes to play it in relation to his peers as well as to others.

Growth from adolescence to adulthood is not an abrupt process; neither should these periods be looked upon as distinct from each other. It has been suggested that the best preparation for adulthood is that of a healthy and wholesome growth during childhood wherein the individual assumes a constantly increased amount of responsibility and is given the opportunity for increased initiative. The best preparation for adulthood is likewise a harmonious adolescence whereby the individual grows satisfactorily in the attainment of the developmental tasks set forth in Chapter 17. In such a case the individual gradually emerges into adulthood with a balanced set of values and worth-while ideals. His values and ideals furnish him with some standard by means of which he is able to arrive at clearer understandings and make sounder decisions. They provide a basis for passing judgments and making evaluations. Values give stability to one's actions and ideas, and provide for increased consistency in one's behavior. These values and concepts that make up one's philosophy of life are learned through individual and social experience.

As one enters into the responsibilities of adulthood, many choices must be made and responsibilities accepted. A guide in the form of unified concepts and values will contribute to the stabilization of behavior during adulthood. Spiritual values in this connection seem to give greater unity and meaning to life, and provide for a life of greater serviceableness and usefulness. This is part of the development of a unified philosophy of life, so essential for stability and growth of adolescent boys and girls into healthy, well-adjusted adults.

Education and maturity

Importance of the plasticity of youth. During the past decade, committees from the Higher Education Section of the National Education Association have called to our attention the great waste of human resources in the United States as a result of our failure to develop more fully the potential mental ability of the 60 per cent of our children from the lower socioeconomic groups. Allison Davis has described this waste as follows:

Half the ability of this country goes down the drain, owing to (a) the failure of intelligence tests to measure the real mental ability of children from the lower socio-economic groups, and (b) the failure of the schools to recognize and train this ability.[6]

At the present time, approximately three-fourths of the youth of this country between the ages of fourteen and seventeen years are enrolled in school. Most of these are in our secondary schools. The typical American high school is a comprehensive school. It provides a wide range of activities and experiences for boys and girls of varying abilities and interests. Members of all groups in our population are to be found in our high schools, although some groups are represented by a larger percentage than is the case for other groups. Concerning the influence of the educational forces, Harold Punke has stated the following:

[6] Allison Davis, Education for the conservation of human resources, *Progressive Education*, 1950, Vol. 27, p. 221.

Few thoughtful Americans are unaware of the great possibilities for improvement which exist in the nation's high schools and colleges of today—in content, methods, personnel, support, and other respects. On the other hand, few Americans fail to recognize the marked extent to which our educational institutions acquaint youth with the growing knowledge of the modern world, the techniques for adding and evaluating new information, and the methods for detecting the backgrounds out of which various types of domestic and international issues arise. Gaining acquaintance with such issues and attempting to analyze and resolve them, which furnishes the background of information and attitude that prevails in much of our secondary-school and college instruction, does a great deal to keep the mind and personality plastic and adaptable. From the standpoint of preventing early fossilization of mind and of lifting one's social and intellectual life above the level of trivial routine and habit, the situation regarding youth with the educational background suggested is substantially different from the situation regarding youth who at an early age settle into meticulous vocational routines or whose intellectual horizons become fenced in by a narrow range of family or social contacts and interests.[7]

Why adolescents and youth leave school. The American theory of education maintains that the public school system, extending through the high school, is designed to serve all; yet at least half of those who reach the fifth grade drop out before completing high school. These drop-outs are too often looked upon as statistics rather than as potential homemakers and citizens of tomorrow. Withdrawal from school is a complex process and any attempt to explain it is difficult because of the many intangible as well as tangible forces that determine whether or not a particular individual will remain in school. In order to determine the major reasons why young people leave school, the United States Department of Labor, in the spring of 1947, interviewed a sample of young people in Louisville, Kentucky—524 boys and girls, 440 of whom had not yet completed high school.[8] This survey showed that dissatisfaction with school was given as the major factor by 47.7 per cent of the young people, while economic need and lure of a job ranked second and third in importance. An analysis of the outstanding elements leading to dissatisfaction with schools is presented in Table 75. Failure in school, dissatisfaction with courses, and dislike of the social situations at

[7] Harold H. Punke, Neglected social values of prolonged human infancy, *School and Society,* 1950, Vol. 71, p. 371.

[8] Elizabeth S. Johnson and Caroline Legg, *Why Young People Leave School.* National Association of Secondary School Principals, 1948.

school were the most commonly mentioned elements leading to dissatisfaction with the school.

TABLE 75 Outstanding element in reasons for leaving school as given by nongraduates

Nature of dissatisfaction *	Young people who gave dissatisfaction with school as—		
	Principal Reason for Leaving	Contributory Reason for Leaving †	Either Principal or Contributory †
TOTAL	209	84	293
Failing grades—discouraged	38	22	60
Dissatisfied with courses	29	25	54
Disliked teachers or teaching methods	25	40	65
Disliked social relations, or the non-coed system	13	23	36
Unable to adjust after transfer	8	2	10
Thought discipline too severe	5	4	9
Other miscellaneous reasons	17	16	33
Disliked school generally—no specific reason given	74	33	107

* Excludes dissatisfaction specifically due to lack of personal funds, which is included with economic reasons.

† In this column one individual may appear one or several times, according to the number of ways in which dissatisfied; hence the figures add to more than the total here shown.

These results are in harmony with those obtained from a study of drop-outs in Syracuse, New York.[9] A sampling of drop-outs was obtained, representing seven semesters of the postwar period. Of these, 194 drop-outs—99 boys and 94 girls—were interviewed. The drop-outs represented all of the major occupational groups in the city, with the major proportion coming from families of craftsmen, foremen, factory operatives, and kindred workers. The reasons given by these drop-outs for leaving school are summarized in Table 76. Many graduates expressed dissatisfaction with the courses offered and the school services. They expressed a desire for more information about job opportunities and about how to get a job. They also expressed a need for further vocational training and advice on social living. The results of a survey of 5,500 high-school students in the state of Washington support these findings.[10] The percentage of boys

[9] *Syracuse Youth Who Did Not Graduate,* Research Division, Board of Education, Syracuse, New York, 1950.

[10] L. J. Elias, *High School Youth Look at Their Problems* (Pullman, Washington: The State College of Washington, 1949).

TABLE 76 Reasons given by Syracuse adolescents and youth for leaving school

	Frequency of Occurrence	Percentage
School situations		
Dissatisfaction with school	91	
Relation between school subjects and future work	51	
Inability to learn	48	
Teacher-pupil relationship	46	
Suitable subjects not offered	35	
Too old for grade	33	
Completion of course	22	
Principal—vice-principal—pupil relations	13	
Other	11	
Total	350	62
Personal or financial		
Family need or family situation	67	
Lack of personal funds	60	
Lure of job	59	
Illness	19	
Too poor in comparison with others	9	
Total	214	38

and girls (mainly seniors) checking the different things they thought the high school could have done to make them better prepared is listed in Table 77. The need for more courses, vocational courses, more friendly relationship with their teachers, vocational information and guidance, and the like were frequently checked by these students.

These studies reveal two outstanding needs, if the high schools are to function adequately for all of American youth. First, these schools must consider the needs of youth and organize a program designed to fit these needs, rather than continue a program based upon the needs of a small group which might be preparing for college or white-collar jobs. Secondly, our society must face the problem that equality of educational opportunity remains a myth when many boys and girls are forced annually to leave school because of financial conditions. The reticence on the part of youth to state poverty as the major cause for leaving school may have caused the number giving lack of money as the major cause to be understated in comparison to the number giving dissatisfaction with school. Due in a large measure to our emphasis upon individual responsibility, economic hardships are often taken for granted as a necessary element in connection with the school-leaving situation as well as elsewhere. There are many who would rationalize the situation with such a statement as: "If a boy has it in him, he will be able to rise above such hardships and difficulties." The importance of financial circumstances in connection with one's educational opportunities may be observed in many cases, such as the ones here illustrated in the cases of Harold and Tracy.

TABLE 77 Things high-school youth think the school could do to make them better prepared (after Elias)

	Boys	Girls	Total
Offer more courses	50.2%	46.8%	48.3%
Give more vocational courses	45.6	52.4	43.8
Teachers could be more friendly	16.8	18.6	17.8
Provide more guidance and counseling	29.2	29.9	29.6
Show interest in what they do after graduation	13.3	7.1	9.9
Tell them what vocation to follow	5.2	3.7	4.4
Give them practical vocational experience	28.8	26.9	27.8
More help with personal problems	11.2	9.9	10.5
Give them understanding of world problems	11.6	12.8	12.2
School and teachers are too strict	4.6	6.3	5.3

Harold, a better-than-average student, was in the tenth grade at the age of fifteen, when his father deserted the family. Harold's mother was working but did not earn enough to support herself and the boy. So Harold left school and obtained a full-time job in a chain grocery at $20 a week. Clinging to his ambition to become a lawyer, he enrolled in the academic course at night school. This double load was a serious tax on his strength, and when interviewed in the early spring, it seemed doubtful whether his health would hold.

When Tracy's father became ill and was unable to work, the family rented rooms to pay for the rent of their house, and Tracy's mother did washing and ironing to earn money but could not earn enough to pay for their food. So fifteen-year-old Tracy left school at the end of the eighth grade and got a job helping a vegetable peddler. He turned his earnings over to his mother, who supplied him with money for cigarettes and picture shows.[11]

Education and class status. Evidence has already been presented showing a close relationship between dropping out of school and socioeconomic level of the home. Studies conducted at New Haven, Connecticut, making use of the 1940 census data, revealed that a

[11] Elizabeth S. Johnson and Caroline Legg, *op. cit.*

significant correlation existed between dropping out of school and
(1) living in low-rental areas, and (2) the educational attainment
of the adults of a community.[12] Other factors associated with drop-
outs were (1) lack of central heating unit in home, (2) a high incidence of unemployment in the neighborhood, and (3) lack of
refrigeration equipment in the home. This study points again to the
influence of economic forces in determining who will remain in high
school. Closely related to this is an important problem, too often not
recognized by the teachers and others concerned with the school program, of reconciling the middle-class point of view of the schools
with the lower-class culture of so many of its pupils. This failure
on the part of the schools creates conditions that drive the lower-
class student from high school.

TABLE 78 School enrollment of Elmtown youth according to class
status (after Hollingshead)

Class	In School		Out of School	
	NUMBER	PER CENT	NUMBER	PER CENT
I	4	100.0	0	00.0
II	31	100.0	0	00.0
III	146	92.4	12	7.6
IV	183	58.7	120	41.3
V	26	11.3	204	88.7

A study of school retention among Elmtown's youth shows that
the dream of equality of educational opportunity is to a large degree a myth. An analysis of the per cent of adolescents (sixteen-year-
olds) from each of the five social-economic classes found in Elmtown
enrolled in school is presented in Table 78.[13] The great preponderance of school leavers appear among the underprivileged groups in
our rural areas, towns, and cities. The Elmtown study shows that
despite compulsory school laws requiring boys and girls to remain
in school until they are sixteen years of age, 74 per cent of the 345
young people out of school in the spring of 1942 had dropped out
before they had reached their sixteenth birthday. Neither the Elm-
towners nor the school authorities were aware of the large number

[12] William L. Gragg, Utilization of census data in statistical analysis of school
drop-out problems, *Journal of Experimental Education*, 1949, Vol. 18, pp. 147-151.

[13] Table 78 is reprinted by permission from *Elmtown's Youth* by A. B. Hollingshead, published by John Wiley & Sons, Inc., 1949. Elmtown is a fictitious name
given to a midwestern town of around 10,000 population.

of people that had dropped out of school. Such a condition is perhaps not by any means confined to Elmtown, but may become even more exaggerated in a larger urban area.

Youth and marriage

Falling in love. Falling in love is another milestone in the lives of boys and girls, and is a preliminary to a major decision relative to a mate and family life. It is not always easy for young people actually to know when they are in love. Being in love is very intangible, and may not affect all individuals in the same manner. The element of physical attraction is much stronger in some than in others. Infatuation alone, however, leaves very little to feed and grow upon and should be reckoned with in a cautious manner. Love in modern American courtship represents respect and comradeship to a higher degree than perhaps at any other period. The part of love involving partnership grows and develops through the enjoyment of common experiences. Similar tastes, ideals, aspirations, and outlooks are most important in the development of wholesome comradeship.

When the sexual attraction is combined with comradeship, which makes for growth in love and understanding, engagement and plans for the future are likely to follow. Love and marriage loom large in the lives of postadolescents. There is some evidence that the sex drive reaches its maximum during this period; however, the effects of technology and the demands for increased schooling have tended to prolong the period of adolescence and youth so that the individual is unable to assume the responsibilities of family life during the postadolescent period. This has no doubt affected the sexual lives and practices of the present generation so that many activities that were seriously frowned upon a generation or more ago are quite widely accepted today. It appears that a democratic society is faced with one of two choices in this connection. Either we must recognize the fact that the sex drive is powerful during this period and that guidance rather than repression of adolescents in their social activities must be followed, and that increased sexual activities will be found where such a program is not instituted, or we must provide in some way for earlier marriages. Although the latter may appear to many to be the ideal, it does not seem likely that this will be the alternative followed.[14]

[14] Karl C. Garrison, *Psychology of Adolescence* (New York: Prentice-Hall, 1950), chap. XIX.

Becoming engaged. Becoming engaged provides a couple with the final opportunity to make their choice relative to marriage. At this time the mature person is likely to weigh carefully just what he is hoping to get out of marriage. The less mature person is all too likely to be affected by some single factor. In one survey, young men and women were asked to list the things they wanted most from marriage. The results are presented in Table 79.[15] Romantic love and security were listed first by 60 per cent of the girls; companionship and tension reduction were listed by 70 per cent of the single men.

TABLE 79   Comparison of the replies of single men and single girls to the question: What do each of you want from marriage? (after Adams)

Single men		Single girls	
Companionship	40 per cent	Love	33 per cent
Tension Reduction	30 per cent	Security	27 per cent
Love	15 per cent	Companionship	20 per cent
Children	10 per cent	Children	11 per cent
Home	5 per cent	Tension Reduction	9 per cent

Tension reduction was, however, rated low among the girls. Perhaps much of what the girls are considering in relation to love may be called tension reduction, or perhaps tension reduction among the men may be regarded as closely related to love. Tension reduction refers to sexual attraction, the capacity to love and be loved. The girl, being more reserved in this connection, perhaps as a result of both biological make-up and cultural conditioning, does not sense the need for tension reduction to the extent that the man does. The importance of the desire for security is easily understood. The high rating given by the men to companionship is quite significant. Men appear to suffer more from loneliness and are more helpless in connection with activities involving daily living than are women. This is observable when one notes and compares the activities of single men and women who have passed their thirty-fifth birthday.

A somewhat similar study was conducted among college students by Vail and Staudt.[16] These students consisted of 118 males, eighteen to twenty-eight years of age, and 118 females, eighteen to twenty-

[15] Quoted from Clifford R. Adams, *Looking Ahead to Marriage,* Life Adjustment Booklet (Chicago: Science Research Associates, 1949), p. 30.

[16] James P. Vail and Virginia M. Staudt, Attitudes of college students toward marriage and related problems: I. dating and mate selection, *Journal of Psychology,* 1950, Vol. 30, pp. 171-182.

two years of age. These students were asked to check from a list of six characteristics the characteristic most essential and the one least essential in the selection of a marriage mate. The percentages of male and female subjects checking the different characteristics as most or least essential are presented in Table 80. It is significant that over 50 per cent of both men and women checked *moral character* as the most essential quality from the list presented. *Congenial in-laws* was considered least important by the men, while *good looks, beauty* was checked by the least number of females. Although education was not listed as one of the characteristics to be checked, a further study of their marriage choices revealed that most of them felt that it was highly desirable for college graduates to choose as a marriage partner someone with college training. In Chapter 17 it was pointed out that sixteen-year-olds tended to date from the same social and economic class. There is evidence available that marriages usually involve individuals of somewhat similar educational levels.

TABLE 80   Percentage distribution of most essential and least essential characteristics in a potential mate (after Vail and Staudt)

Characteristic	Most essential		Least essential	
	MALE	FEMALE	MALE	FEMALE
Beauty, good looks	1.78	0.00	25.00	66.10
Education	0.00	0.00	1.78	.85
Moral character	55.36	59.32	0.00	0.00
Similarity of interests	26.79	24.58	0.00	.85
Congenial In-laws	0.00	0.00	67.87	27.81
Intelligence	12.50	11.02	1.78	0.00
No report	0.00	2.54	0.00	2.54

Factors influencing dating and marriage. The small congenial community of yesterday furnished many opportunities for young people to meet each other and learn something of each other's interests and characteristics. Many young people today are employed in offices and factories in urban areas and find it very difficult to make acquaintances with a number of people of their age levels of the opposite sex. Girls employed in offices often find that the only men they meet are those around the office who are already married. Many men find employment in activities where few women are present. This displaced condition presents a problem which tends to reduce marriage or provides a condition in which young people are very limited in their choices. A study by Opal Wolford of the dating practices conducted during World War II in Highland Park High School, Michigan, showed that a relatively large number of young people, by their senior year in high school, were having few social contacts with the other sex.[17] This study showed the need for providing activities that would bring young people together so that they could better learn each other in particular and characteristics of the opposite sex in general. The first essential for young people in the case of marriage, according to customs existing in the United States, is for them to have opportunities to meet members of the opposite sex. In areas where such opportunities are limited, the number of people who never marry is relatively high.

It has already been suggested that individuals tend to marry within similar socioeconomic groups, and to marry people with somewhat similar interests and outlooks. Certain religious practices also cause individuals to restrict their choice of a mate to someone of their special religion. In addition, racial barriers may be set up which restrict marriages still further. Young people need information about the factors that tend to make for successful marriages and also about those that tend to make for unsuccessful marriages. Standards of social conduct, attitudes toward marriage, factors to be considered in choosing a marriage partner, ways of rearing children, and responsibilities involved in family life should be studied during the postadolescent years as a basis for preparing young people for marriage and successful family life.

Youth and the family. As boys and girls advance toward maturity, their outlook extends beyond the self and their mate toward having children of their own. This observation is borne out by data on marriages and children, especially during critical times. The high birth rate among the recently married during World War II is further evidence for such an observation. In the survey made by *Fortune* magazine, young people aged eighteen to twenty-five were asked to answer pertinent questions about themselves and the world in which they live.[18] These young people grew up in the depression years, experienced the war years as adolescents or youths, and were at the time of the survey experiencing the postwar inflation years with their uncertainties relative to depression or war. Despite these experiences, the results do not indicate that they have become cynical or

[17] Opal Powell Wolford, How early background affects dating behavior, *Journal of Home Economics,* November, 1948, pp. 505-506.

[18] Young people of the U. S. answer some pertinent questions about themselves, *Fortune,* December, 1948, pp. 40, 43-44.

defeatist. In answer to the question: How many children do you think makes the nicest-sized family? these young people showed again their desire for children to complete the family circle. The replies to this question are given for the different groups based on schooling in Table 81.

TABLE 81   Replies of youth to the question: How many children do you think makes the nicest-sized family?

	Total	Grade school	High school	College attending	College attended
None	1%	1%	1%	1%	1%
One	1	3	1	2	1
Two	32	32	35	26	31
Three	31	22	30	33	38
Four	23	22	22	27	22
Five	4	4	3	4	5
Six or more	2	4	2	1	1
Express no opinion	6	12	6	6	1

There were no pronounced differences in the replies of the different educational groups to the questions presented. There is, however, considerable evidence that the size of the family tends to decrease as we move up the sociocultural scale. The largest families are likely to be found in the rural areas among those with inferior incomes. This is unfortunate, since these families are least able to provide for the physical needs of their children. The hope of our social order here, as elsewhere, appears to lie in the production of some changed values among the maturing boys and girls. The crisis that the world has faced within recent years will no doubt cause youth even more than the older adults to question the importance attached by most people to material things as the source of all pleasure, and financial security as the sole basis of security. If youth can be made more proud of the new baby than of a new car, the problem will be partially solved. If youth can be brought to realize that family and friends provide a source of security never to be found in stocks and dollars, they will have learned a vital lesson not learned by most adults of the first half of the twentieth century. There is considerable evidence that youth are better prepared biologically for bearing children, and psychologically for rearing children, than are members of an older adult group. The marriage of youth is too often postponed, or, if not postponed, the bearing of children is postponed until the parents can get ahead financially.

The social and economic conditions that are responsible for this, therefore, tend to militate against childbearing and training during the most desirable years.

Prediction of family stability. The instability of the American family derives from many factors and conditions. A number of studies have been undertaken during the past two or more decades for the purpose of securing information relative to the factors that contribute to successful marriage. Students of marriage and the family agree that the concern with the high divorce rate and marital discord should be with causes rather than with effects, as is the case of lawmakers and others today. There is considerable evidence that the factors that make for unsuccessful and unhappy marriages are unwise mate selection and lack of preparation for marriage, rather than the type of marriage and divorce laws in existence. The early studies by Terman [19] and by Burgess and Cottrell [20] furnished evidence that there is a positive relationship between prediction test scores and marital happiness. Although a higher proportion of the couples were at the high-school and college level than is true of the general population, other studies conducted with low economic and low educational groups showed that the same chief background factors operated to make for marriage failure as those found by Terman and by Burgess and Cottrell.

It should be pointed out, however, that marriage prediction tests have their limitations as well as values. Perhaps the greatest value of such tests lies in the uses that can be made of the responses in counseling the parties concerned. Those couples having low predictive scores should be counseled with concerning possible conflicts and sources that are likely to appear in a marriage such as theirs and that contribute to marital discord. They should be made aware of the danger points and should thus be able to enter or refrain from entering the marriage relation with their eyes open and aware of sources of difficulty. Young people need opportunities to meet a large number of individuals of the opposite sex. They need to share wholesome experiences together, so that they may come to know and understand each other better. They also need information about the qualities that make for successful marriages. There is a need for more complete information and more accurate information about

[19] Lewis M. Terman, *Psychological Factors in Marital Happiness* (New York: McGraw-Hill Book Co., 1938).

[20] Ernest W. Burgess and Leonard S. Cottrell, *Predicting Success or Failure in Marriage* (New York: Prentice-Hall, 1939).

the responsibilities of marriage, and particularly the responsibility of the person concerned to his mate and to the establishment of a home. An increasing number of high schools and colleges are providing courses where such information is given. The home, the school, the church, and other institutions should be willing to face the problem of mate selection and the problem of preparation for marriage realistically. The trial-and-error process so commonly found today is perhaps less likely to produce a large percentage of happy and harmonious families than the method used earlier in which the parents played a very important role in the selection of the mate. Couples need to be taught in a forceful manner that happy marriages do not just happen, and that they need not be left entirely to chance. Sound principles of mate selection, along with sane instruction as a preparation for marriage and homemaking, would contribute a great deal to the reduction of marital discord and unfortunate marriages.[21]

Youth and the world of work

Changes in vocational interests. Adolescent boys and girls enter high school without too much concern about their future vocational plans. This should not be looked upon as unfortunate. The failure of the high school to help them become vocationally adjusted as they enter the world of work should be regarded as a catastrophe in the lives of many boys and girls. Since one's occupation and his attitudes toward it are extremely important in every phase of his life, the schools should give special consideration to the vocational needs and plans of adolescent boy and girls. A study by Roeher and Garfield dealt with the differences in vocational preferences of students in grades nine to twelve.[22] Data from questionnaires concerning occupational interests were secured from 912 boys and 1083 girls from twenty-two different schools. The results of this study indicate that students become more realistic in their vocational choices as they pass from the ninth to the twelfth grade, in that choices are made to a larger degree in harmony with vocational possibilities.

The vocational choice of the student and the task of the counselor relative to an individual's vocational choice on a higher occupa-

---

[21] For a splendid recent presentation of this and related problems see Toward Family Stability, *Annals of the American Academy of Political and Social Science,* November, 1950.

[22] E. Roeher and L. Garfield, A study of the occupational interests of high school students in terms of grade placement, *Journal of Educational Psychology,* 1943, Vol. 34, pp. 355-362.

tional level than that occupied by his father should be carefully studied. To many counselors and most secondary-school teachers, social mobility is a virtue that should be given encouragement. The American dream that if a child works hard he will be able to climb from an underprivileged place on our cultural ladder to a privileged place has infiltrated their thinking. Yet the counselor should be aware of the fact that only a few can actually move up the socioeconomic scale beyond the position occupied by their fathers.[23] Many boys and girls with the ability to move up and with aspirations to move up the socioeconomic ladder become frustrated because they are caught in their efforts and blocked by circumstances beyond their control.

The counselor and teachers face the problem of whether or not to encourage James in his aspirations to go to college and fulfill his ambitions to study law and become a lawyer, when the financial circumstances are such that James himself will have to find all the means for financing his education and the postcollege period of getting started in the practice of law. James will have to decide whether or not he will make the try, and whether he will sever to a large degree the ties of home and friends and take the right courses in school leading toward the aspired goal. The task of the counselor, when viewed in this context, has been described by Havighurst as follows:

(1) To help pupils decide whether they should make a try for upward social mobility.

(2) To help a minority of pupils achieve upward social mobility.

(3) To help the majority of pupils enjoy social stability. This means helping them to work out a school program that will make them skillful and happy workers at the occupational level of their fathers, and also helping them to develop extracurricular interests, such as music, dramatics, athletics, which will carry over into adult life and help them to enjoy their leisure time.

(4) To interpret cultural differences to other teachers. . . .[24]

The transition from school to work. Each year, about a million boys and girls enter into full-time work. For most of them, this is a rather abrupt change from school and home ties to employment in the factory, office, store, or on the assembly line. One day, they are

---

[23] See Robert J. Havighurst, Implications of cultural differences for guidance in the secondary schools, *Studies in Higher Education LXIX*, Purdue University, Division of Educational Research, 1949.

[24] *Ibid.,* p. 30.

in the sheltered environment of their peers at school and their parents at home. The next day, they find themselves on a job operating some machine, waiting on a customer at the counter, or filing materials away in the business office. They are now on their own and must assume responsibilities whether they desire to do so or not. Their task is to fit into this vast business and industrial machinery that we label today as technology.

The first job is a milestone in the life of the individual. It provides an opportunity for the extension of one's independence. A wrong start—getting fired, finding the job too difficult, clash with the foreman or management, or finding the work boring or unpleasant—is a frustrative experience for the young worker and may adversely condition him toward a working life. Thus, there is a definite need to prepare young people to make satisfactory vocational adjustments. A program related to youth employment is a matter of public concern. The vocational needs of youth must be recognized and dealt with in a realistic manner if the transition from school to work is to be a satisfactory one.

The fundamental difference between the problems of livelihood that confronted the adolescent and postadolescent several generations ago and those confronting the youth of today are: (1) specialized activities on the job may require a period of special training for the job today, although many jobs can be learned with a short period of training; (2) the great differentiation of work brought about by specialization gives a diversity of advantages to different types of work and to different abilities; (3) many new fields of endeavor have been opened to women, which has brought them into competition with men in an economic sense; (4) mass production has brought with it large organizations with large groups of workers engaged in a single enterprise. An outgrowth of this is the impersonal relationship often found between management and the workers. The problem of securing a job and of choosing the type of work to be done has undergone considerable change. The story of Jean Black indicates that graduation from high school does not necessarily assure one of a job or even of a satisfactory vocational orientation.

Jean was an attractive girl of 18 with intelligence, poise, and considerable musical ability. She not only completed high school but spent 6 months in college. She had 2 months' experience in sales work before going to college, and her parents gave their approval and financial support to her education.

Yet Jean was "in a quandary as to where to turn." She did not like her brief experience in selling. But she was also dissatisfied with the music course she took in college, because she considered it would not lead to practical employment. Jean had no interest in returning to school for a business course, however. She was marking time with a Saturday job in a downtown department store, and would have welcomed counseling from any source that could have helped her get a sense of direction.[25]

Youth and employment. A careful study of employment trends will show that youth plays an important role in such trends. This was clearly shown during the thirties, when there was widespread unemployment. A large percentage of the unemployed at that time were boys and girls between the ages of sixteen and twenty-four. A youth study conducted in Maryland at that time revealed that of the employable youth interviewed, all of whom had been out of school more than a year, 40 per cent had not obtained any sort of full-time employment. Government programs were set up primarily to help youth find some sort of employment. A few years later, however, World War II brought a great demand for the labor of youth. The draft was lowered to eighteen years, modifications were made in child labor laws, and school programs were adapted to the changed economic conditions. The few years after the close of World War II (the middle forties) brought back some of the conditions of the thirties; however, the clouds of a third world war soon appeared to change the picture again. A survey of work opportunities and activities of youth in Louisville, Kentucky, showed that a surprising number of boys and girls were unemployed.[26] Of those in the labor market, 46 per cent of the fourteen- and fifteen-year-old children, 36 per cent of the sixteen- and seventeen-year-olds, and 21 per cent of the eighteen- and nineteen-year-olds were unemployed. The younger the individual, the greater the likelihood of his being unemployed. "Inability to find jobs or to keep a job they found was a keenly felt difficulty with many of the Louisville young people."

The jobs these young people had been able to secure were in a large percentage of the cases undesirable from the standpoint of hours and working conditions. This was especially true for those sixteen years of age or under. When young people drop out of school, they are anxious to get a job and earn money. Many of them have felt the need for certain material things which they have been unable to buy because of their financial plight. In an effort to account for

[25] Hunting a career: a study of out-of-school youth in Louisville, Kentucky, *United States Department of Labor Bulletin No. 115,* 1949, p. 90.

[26] Elizabeth S. Johnson, Teen-agers at work, *The Child,* October, 1948.

their difficulties in getting a job, they reported such factors as: Someone always gets there first. You have to have a pull to get a job. They won't hire you when they find out your age. I can't get the kind of job I want without more education. In order to get on the other side of the issue, employers were interviewed. Many of them agreed that young people under eighteen years of age were too immature, or not dependable. The employers expressed an interest in employing youth who had completed high school rather than those who dropped out of school at an early age.

Vocational needs of youth. The fundamental differences between the problems of livelihood faced by the youth of a generation or more ago and those faced by today's youth were presented earlier in this chapter. These changed conditions have brought with them changed vocational needs. To a marked degree, the vocational pace of the modern worker is governed by the machine. The worker must be able and ready to perform the task at the accelerated rate that the machine has introduced. He is likely to be called upon to do some repetitive task. This will demand increased stability and willingness to subordinate the self to a single part of the process rather than the performance of all aspects of the task. The vocational needs of the new worker cannot be thought of in terms of specific skills alone. The new worker brings with him to the job attitudes, habits, outlooks, moral codes, health, and civic qualities that have important bearings on his success on the job. Industry, dependability, ability to follow directions, and willingness to co-operate in a common task are attributes that youth should acquire while in school, if they are to succeed on the job.

A community occupational survey, conducted in Kern County, California, revealed that local employers were especially concerned with desirable personal characteristics among their employees.[27] Excerpts from the interviews with managers and personnel directors gave emphasis to various personal qualities. An employer in the merchandising field gave the following characteristics as required: "pleasing appearance, honesty and dependability, ability to get along with other people, and an aptitude to learn merchandising."

The characteristics liked most by the employers included in this survey are listed in Table 82. Those concerned with the educational program for youth should note that proficiency is listed fifth on the list. Honesty, neatness, dependability, and ability to meet people are

[27] Ralph Prator, The employer survey and general education, *California Journal of Secondary Education,* 1950, Vol. 25, pp. 438-440.

more frequently listed by each of the employer groups than skill or training for the job.

TABLE 82 Personal and physical characteristics liked most by employers tabulated by major industry division survey area—1949

Personal or Physical Characteristics Named by Employers	Number of Times Named	Agricul- ture	Industrial Production and Utilities	Wholesale and Retail Trade	Insurance Real Estate and Government	Service
Honesty	476	27	43	201	37	168
Neatness	454	13	25	191	57	168
Dependability	378	19	59	110	50	140
Meeting Public	310	9	17	135	34	115
Proficiency	261	14	43	58	45	101
Ambition	247	15	25	100	29	78
Industry	215	20	28	83	17	67
Common Sense	202	16	19	54	27	86
Friendliness	189	7	20	66	18	78
Cooperativeness	175	10	19	59	25	62
Loyalty	171	10	23	51	24	63
Morality	105	12	21	34	9	29
Initiative	99	8	21	31	16	23
Versatility	37	—	4	11	6	16
Health	22	2	4	7	1	8
Married	8	—	1	2	—	5

Read Table as follows: Honesty was mentioned 476 times by all employees receiving questionnaires, 27 times by employees in agriculture.

A study of the factors associated with tenure of employment was conducted with 898 youth (469 boys and 429 girls) who had graduated from high school during the previous four-year period as subjects.[28] The median age of the boys was twenty-one years and one month and of the girls twenty years and seven months. These youth had been out of school for periods of time ranging from eighteen to sixty-six months. Basic data for the study were collected from two sources: the youth's school history and record, and a personal interview. No relationship was found between different aspects of academic success and tenure on the job, while a negative relationship was found between teachers' estimates and job tenure. The factors in school experiences positively associated with tenure on the job were as follows:

1. Boys who contributed to their own support during their last two years at school were employed to a considerably greater degree than

[28] C. Darl Long, School-leaving youth and employment, Teachers College, Columbia University, *Contributions to Education,* No. 845, 1941.

those who did not contribute to their own support. The same tendency was observed for the girls, although the differences were not as great as among the boys.

2. Both boys and girls who had work experience during their last two years at school were more regularly employed than those who had not had such experiences. The differences for the boys and girls were statistically reliable.

3. Boys who took their first job after leaving school because of their interest in that type of work exceeded all others in the percentage of time they had been employed. In the case of the girls, the differences were insignificant.

4. Intelligent behavior toward occupational situations, as found from interviews with the boys and girls, revealed a close relationship with tenure of employment.

These data, supported by other studies and observations, indicate that there is a wide gulf between the program of the school and the vocational demands of life. It appears that the secondary-school program contributes more realistically and more effectively to the needs of those going into the professions and certain skilled activities than it does to the larger group that will find employment on the assembly line, at routine clerical pursuits, and as helpers, repairmen, and in the transportation industry. This stems from the tradition of the high school designed to meet the needs of the select group that planned to continue some sort of an educational program after leaving high school. The vocational needs of most youth upon leaving high school may be summarized as follows: (1) a better understanding of their own aptitudes, limitations, and interests; (2) occupational information as a basis for choosing the type of work that will best satisfy their needs and interests; (3) work experiences supplemented by occupational information that will furnish them more accurate information about job requirements and possibilities; (4) opportunities for vocational training; and (5) the opportunity to use their abilities once developed, i.e., the right to a job.

Youth and citizenship

Youth and the socioeconomic outlook. Public-opinion polls show that interesting changes have taken place in the socioeconomic outlooks of the public during the past several decades. These changed attitudes have been reflected in our policies toward public-works projects, social-security legislation, labor-management relationships, public-health programs, international affairs, trade agreements, monetary standards, and employment. The increased educational opportunities for children in the lower economic groups and the large enrollments in our high schools and colleges have furnished a better-informed citizenry than at any time in our history. Even so, many of the problems of today have become too complex for the average citizen to understand their meaning and significance. The radio, the press, and advancements in television have also played an important role in keeping the public informed about domestic and international problems. All this means that important changes are being brought about in the aspirations, wants, outlooks, and values of the great mass of American citizens. Youth have been the quickest to accept these changes, since they were not bound so closely by traditional ties and concepts.

Comparative studies of the reactions of youth and older adults to present-day problems show that youth tend to show more idealism and at the same time perhaps more actual realism than do adults. These reactions stem from the fact that youth are not so closely bound with past prejudices. Less than 10 per cent of the youth studied in the 1948 *Fortune* survey believed that the United States should avoid war regardless of what happens in the rest of the world. They appear keenly aware of the danger of the expansion of communism under the domination of the Soviet Union. They show a more tolerant attitude toward the Negro than do the middle-aged group, and over three-fourths of them expressed the belief that Negroes should have the same chance to get good jobs as do white people, if they have the same qualifications. Their responses to the question: What two qualities, from a list presented, do you think really get a young person ahead the fastest today? are presented in Table 83.[29] The great majority of youth appear to realize that hard work, a pleasing personality, and brains are of utmost importance in getting ahead today; however, a rather large group seemed to believe that knowing the right person plays an important role. The responses of youth to this question were quite similar to those of the forty to fifty-five age group.

The idealism of youth. Contrary to what many adults think of youth, they are not always the lightheaded juveniles, hot-rod drivers, or unstable and unreliable youngsters that they are often pictured. Anyone who has counseled with high-school young people and college freshmen about their problems should be able to provide a

[29] *Op. cit.,* p. 43.

TABLE 83   The responses of youth to the question: What two qualities on this list do you think really get a young person ahead the fastest today?

	Total	Grade school	High school	College attending	College attended	Total 40-55 age group
Hard work	51%	45%	51%	50%	57%	46%
Having a pleasant personality	50	33	51	49	64	47
Brains	44	38	37	51	32	50
Know the right people	37	35	37	37	37	31
Good luck	9	20	10	5	2	1
Being a good politician	6	12	5	4	7	7
Express no opinion	1	7	—	1	1	2

different view of these youngsters. Adolescents and youth are beset with many problems. They are sensitive to moral and spiritual values, and are ready and eager to assume greater responsibilities in these areas, when they are approached in the right manner. The idealism of youth represents the greatest resource at the command of our society. The task of the home, school, and church, as well as other agencies, is to channel these idealistic impulses into worth-while channels. It is, furthermore, the task of those in control of these agencies to organize and direct their resources in such a way that these youngsters will not lose the faith that is so fervent during these early years of life. The question of how religion can be made to function in the home, the school, and community enterprises is one that is challenging the thoughts of many leaders today.

It has been emphasized throughout this study of child growth that the early years are of utmost importance in the building and establishing of the values and faiths that will endure throughout life. Many youth come from homes where such conditions were not in existence. The faith and beliefs of youth of today will determine their course of action tomorrow. Wise parents will not try to force the child into their particular religious mold. But, if these parents have been sincere in their religious ideals, have practised honesty and worth-while habits in their daily living, and have sound ideals and values as basic guides, the adolescent boys and girls will have a firm foundation of faiths and ideals. The writer recently asked an intelligent college freshman the reasons for his belief in God.

Among the answers received was, "My father and mother have much faith and believe in God." This is not a shallow answer, for it is well known that ideals and faiths are established during the early years of life. Where these are built upon quicksand they have not a firm foundation.

TABLE 84 The responses of youth to the question: Do you think steps should be taken right away to form a world government in which we'd become a member state, or do you think this should be done at all?

	Total	Grade school	High school	College attending	College attended	Total 40-55 age-group
Right away	34%	26%	33%	39%	39%	31%
More slowly	34	21	33	36	50	32
Not at all	17	11	19	18	9	.18
Express no opinion	15	42	15	7	2	19

Another problem with which the *Fortune* survey was concerned was the attitude of youth toward a world government. The fast-moving events that have taken place since this study was made would no doubt alter the results, if such a survey were made today. However, the over-all outlook on the part of youth would no doubt show the same general pattern. The idealism of youth is clearly revealed in their endorsement of a world government in which we would become a member state. This is shown in Table 84. The results of this study have been confirmed by more recent studies. Furthermore, there is evidence from these more recent studies that when youth are better informed they respond more favorably to the idea of a world court, world police powers, and other matters provided on a world co-operative basis. These ideals shown by the better-educated youth provide a hopeful sign. The church and the school must supplement any efforts being made in the home to influence youth in the development of sane and sound attitudes toward world problems. Farsighted educational and religious leaders recognize the dynamic force of the idealism of youth. Ideals that are far-reaching in their effects and based upon the needs of society will prove to be a stabilizing as well as a dynamic force in their lives. Such ideals have often been referred to as embodying spiritual values. Where the church takes into consideration the needs and characteristics of youth, it affects the lives of these boys and girls so as to produce citizens with a sense of spiritual as well as material security. The role of the school has come to be recognized as one extending beyond textbooks and academic pursuits. Many educators realize that the school must function in the spiritual and moral training of youth, if the advancements in science are to function for the benefit rather than the destruction of man.

Youth and the freedoms. Much is being written and said today about our freedom. Just a few years ago, the then President of the United States, Franklin D. Roosevelt, startled the world by proclaiming his famous Four Freedoms. Any consideration of these freedoms must take into account the social and economic forces that are operating in our society today. This problem, too, is closely related to the spiritual needs and values of youth. Concerning this, Kenneth Nye has stated: "In the most security-minded generation in history, sheer physical security has become more and more of a mirage." [30]

TABLE 85   Response of youth to the question: If you had to give up one of these things which one would you be most willing to give up?

	Men	Women
The right to earn more than $5,000 a year if you can	46%	48%
The right to change jobs if you want	15	15
Freedom of religion	8	5
Trial by jury	7	6
The right to vote	5	6
Freedom of speech	1	2
Express no opinion	18	18

The results of the 1948 *Fortune* survey of the opinions of American high-school youth are most encouraging to those who believe in the principles of our democratic government.[31] They reveal that youth have an ardent devotion to liberty and justice as provided for in our constitution. According to the results of the survey, presented in Table 85, the youth were most reluctant to give up such freedoms as: freedom of speech, the right to vote, trial by jury, and freedom of religion. These were also the freedoms cherished by the youth in the *Fortune* survey of 1942.[32] Closely related to this is the study conducted by Remmers and Weltman. They gave the Purdue Opinion

[30] Kenneth E. Nye, Faith for a lifetime, *National Parent Teacher,* 1950, Vol. 45, pp. 8-10.
[31] *Op. cit.,* p. 43.
[32] See the Fortune survey, *Fortune,* November, 1942, p. 8.

Poll for Young People to high-school students, their parents, and their teachers.[33] A strong positive relationship was found between the attitudes of members of the same family. The older adolescents were less like their parents in attitude patterns than were the younger adolescents, which indicates a gradual increase in independence in behavior patterns with growth toward maturity.

Responsibilities of youth. Self-reliance is one of the best measures available for evaluating the maturity of youth. The adolescent and postadolescent are capable of taking their place in the social group to the extent that they have developed habits of self-reliance. These habits are manifested in connection with the individual's social life, his educational and vocational choices, and in his civic responsibilities. The need for preparing youth for accepting the responsibilities of citizenship has already been suggested. Such a preparation involves more than academic courses in history and citizenship. This is a community responsibility. There has been a tendency among adults to regard youth as lacking in the ability to accept responsibility in home and community affairs. There is plenty of evidence from case studies of adolescents that when these boys and girls are prepared for responsibility, they are able to take their rightful place as capable and responsible citizens. This is perhaps the most important task facing the American community.

American boys and girls must be trained to detect the fallacies that led us into imperialism in one decade and into isolation a generation later. They need to be trained for a better understanding of the forces that make for peace and war. They need to develop a sense of values by means of which they are able to weigh the activities and attitudes of national leaders. In short, they will need to understand that material security alone for a group of people will not suffice. They must come to realize that security cannot be bought with dollars, but that it must begin in the minds and hearts of man. The American method of experimentation must enter the political and economic field, if our problems are to be satisfactorily solved. If the youth are trained in self-reliance, they will be more alert to the needs of our society. Such a training should bring youth to study the forces that affect the welfare of their own society as well as other societies. Young people need guidance in their life activities, but they also need opportunities for the practice of habits of responsibility. They need to have ideals brought to their attention, but they also need to view these ideals in terms of their relations to the world order of today. They need to be taught those things that have survived the trials of centuries, but they also need to study these as they have affected the lives and activities of the groups confronted with them. Character is a way of living, based upon values and ideals that have become a fundamental part of the self. Character cannot be imposed from without; neither can it be administered as a gift from within. The character that youth will need in meeting the world problems of tomorrow must be based upon a set of values in which the welfare of man and his relation to the cosmos is given first consideration. Such a set of values must be reinforced with self-reliance if they are to function in producing effective citizens in a troubled world.

Summary and generalization

As boys and girls pass through adolescence, they manifest more and more of the characteristics of adults. They have not, however, developed the stability found among adults, since life is still a period of transition for most of them. Maturity brings them closer to some of the decisions they will be called upon to make and some of the problems they will have to resolve in a satisfactory manner. These problems relate to (1) educational choices, (2) vocational planning, (3) attaining a more unified philosophy of life, (4) securing employment, and (5) maintaining satisfactory heterosexual relations, which means to most youth finding a mate.

Problems connected with educational choices and vocational planning become closely related during the latter part of the high-school program. The adjustment of youth to out-of-school work should be one of the major concerns of the secondary school. In general, the secondary schools have been seriously hampered in the discharge of this responsibility by the fact that they have little accurate information about the factors in the educational program that are associated with successful occupational adjustment. Some of the educational needs of adolescents and postadolescents that lead to successful vocational adjustment have been presented in this chapter. Character stands at the head of the list of qualities desired by a group of employers interviewed.

The importance of dating and choice of a mate appears at this period of life. There are a number of social and cultural factors operating at the present time to modify earlier restrictions upon sexual behavior. There is evidence, however, that the youth of today are faced with many of the same problems that youth have been faced with during the past several generations. Some of the forces operating to affect these changes have been listed by Claude Bowman as follows:

Women have more freedom; urban life, mobility, and the decline of religious control are conducive to the loosening of traditional restrictions; the dissemination of contraceptive knowledge reduces the risk of pregnancy; the motion pictures and popular literature provide erotic stimulation; and the automobile affords new opportunities for privacy.[34]

The high divorce rate and the large number of unhappy families, desertions, and other forms of marital discord indicate that there is a real need on the part of youth for counseling on problems relating to choice of a mate and marriage. The notion of leaving this to romantic impulse and chance is disastrous to the lives of a very large percentage of youth.

The youth of today are more interested in a job that will bring them security and the opportunities for enjoying good family relations than at any time in the history of the United States. Also, the youth of today cherish the freedoms, and reveal their idealism and zeal for democracy when the country is faced with a crisis. They are better informed than a large percentage of their parents on domestic and international issues. They are called upon to protect their country at the age of eighteen, and respond in a most favorable manner. All of this provides a good reason why they should have some voice in policy-making prior to the age of twenty-one years, which is the usual age when they are allowed to vote. Experiments in student government, youth organizations, religious activities, and the like furnish proof that youth are able to accept responsibilities, when these are so organized that youth are able to participate as adults in planning and implementing special programs and activities.

Questions and Exercises

1. When does the ability to make a wider variety of friendships begin? How can this be aided by the attitudes of parents? What special problems are sometimes encountered?
2. Why is good training in the handling of money so valuable for youth? When should this be begun? What are some special habits that adolescents should have acquired if they are to be successful as adults in handling money?

[34] Claude C. Bowman, Social factors opposed to the extension of heterosexuality, *American Journal of Psychiatry,* 1949, Vol. 106, p. 441.

3. Analyze one or two current motion pictures in terms of their treatment of love and marriage. What concepts do these give young people about love and marriage? Do these concepts appear to you to be realistic ones? Explain.
4. What bearing do a child's early years have on later happiness and marriage success? Be specific in your answers to this.
5. How would you define maturity? What are some of the evidences of maturity among a group of boys? Among a group of girls?
6. What do you understand the term "world citizenship" to mean? Why is it important to think in terms of world citizenship today as well as in terms of nationalism?
7. What are some of the freedoms cherished most by youth of today? Are these different from those cherished by youth a century ago? If these are different, how would you account for such differences?
8. What do you consider the major problems of youth today? Are these problems different from those of a generation or more ago?

Selected Readings

American Youth Commission. General Report, *Youth and the Future*. Washington: American Council on Education, 1942.

Chambers, M. M., and Exton, Elaine. *Youth—Key to American Future: An Annotated Bibliography*. Washington: American Council on Education, 1949.

Edwards, Newton. The adolescent in technological society, *Forty-third Yearbook of the National Society for the Study of Education*, Part I. Chicago: Department of Education, University of Chicago, 1944.

Fields, Mary R., Goldberg, Jacob A., and Kilander, Holger F. *Youth Grows Into Adulthood*. New York: Chartwell House, 1950.

Garrison, Karl C. *Psychology of Adolescence*. 4th ed.; New York: Prentice-Hall, 1951. Chap. XXI.

Jennings, Helen Hall. *Leadership and Isolation*. New York: Longmans, Green & Company, 1950.

Lawton, George. *How to be Happy though Young: Real Problems of Real Young People*. New York: Vanguard Press, 1949.

Pierce, Wellington G. *Youth Comes of Age*. New York: McGraw-Hill Book Co., 1948.

Rasey, Marie I. *Toward Maturity: The Psychology of Child Development*. New York: Hayden and Eldridge, 1947.

Ross, Murray G. *Religious Beliefs of Youth*. New York: Association Press, 1950.

Strang, Ruth, Manifestations of maturity in adolescents, *Mental Hygiene*, October, 1949, p. 563-569.

Appendix: A Selected List of Motion Pictures To Accompany Each Chapter

The following list of visual aids can be used to supplement some of the materials in the various chapters. The running time (min.) and whether the aid is silent or sound are listed with each title. All those not listed as color (C) are black and white. All motion pictures are 16 mm. The addresses of the distributors or producers are given at the end of the list. Although each film is listed only once, many of the films listed may be used advantageously in connection with other chapters.

Chapter 1—Studying Child Growth and Development

Life Begins (EBF, 60 min., sound). This furnishes a condensation of the individual Child Development films and gives an over-all view of the studies of Dr. Gesell at the Yale Clinic of Child Development. Individual growth patterns for different children are demonstrated.

Life History of Mary from Birth to Seven Years (NYU, 4 reels, silent). Mary is a healthy active child with superior ability. As the years pass, the story reveals the influence of experience and training in the shaping of her personality.

Conflict Situations in Childhood (CFC, 15 min., silent). The experimental and clinical techniques used by Kurt Levin in the study of child behavior is brought out in this film.

Chapter 2—Biological Inheritance and Prenatal Development

Heredity and Prenatal Development (M-H, 21 min., sound). The influence of the chromosomes and genes in determining sex and in transmuting traits to the offspring are presented. The fertilization of the ovum by the sperm is described and the development of the fetus until birth is shown.

In the Beginning (Cas. 17 min., sound). The development of the different stages of the human embryo in relation to the evolution of man is shown in this picture.

Chapter 3—The Period of Infancy

Growth of Infant Behavior: Early Stages (EBF, 10 min., sound). This film traces the rapid growth of early behavior patterns. Typical infant reactions at various ages are contrasted by means of the cinematic technique.

Growth of Infant Behavior: Later Stages (EBF, 10 min., sound). The increased ability of the infant to use his hands in manipulating objects is shown. Animated drawings showing the growth of the prenatal hand are included.

Reflex Behavior of Newborn Infant (Warden and Gilbert, 7 min., silent). The Moro reflex is illustrated along with the infant's movements in suspension grasping, crawling, stepping, and swimming.

Chapter 4—Some Fundamental Principles of Growth

Principles of Development (M-H, 17 min., sound). The fundamentals of growth and change are outlined and six basic principles of development presented. The variables that account for individual differences in development are also presented.

Life with Baby (EBF, 18 min., sound). Specific standards of development from infancy to age six are set forth.

Growth: A Study of Johnny and Jimmy (Warden and Gilbert, 41 min., silent). Comparative behavior is shown during the first two years, when the twins were the subjects of a special investigation. Further comparisons of motor development are made during the next six years. The interdependence of practice and maturation is illustrated in this production.

Chapter 5—Physical Growth and Health

Fundamentals of Diet (EBF, 1 reel, sound). This is especially helpful to elementary-school teachers, nurses, and parent groups. A good introductory study of diet is given.

Now I am Two (Dept. of Labor, 30 min., silent). This is a story of a two-year-old's activities involving his meals, sleep, and play.

Stages of Child Growth (EBF, 20 min., sound). Dr. Charlotte Bühler of Vienna demonstrates procedures which may be used in studying the growth of infants and children of preschool age.

Chapter 6—The Development of Motor Skills

From Creeping to Walking (EBF, 10 min., sound). This is a continuation of an earlier film entitled *Posture and Locomotion*. The correlation of abilities is illustrated in this film.

Behavior Patterns at One Year (EBF, 10 min., sound). A series of test situations showing normal behavior patterns for the infant at fifty-two weeks is presented. The reactions of the infants in manipulating objects are interpreted.

A Study in Human Development (PSC, 18 min., silent). This film supplements three previous productions. It continues a boy's growth to show physical and behavioral characteristics at ages three, four, and five years. The development of motor co-ordinations is well illustrated in the film.

Chapter 7—Emotional Growth and Control

Children's Emotions (M-H, 22 min., sound). The major emotions are illustrated, and the principal characteristics of children's emotions are discussed. The nature and causes of anger, fear, jealousy, and joy are illustrated.

Preface to Life (WFC, 29 min., sound). This film shows how the parents can influence child behavior and later character development by their consideration of the child's emotional needs. This film has been produced for the National Institute of Mental Health, Federal Security Agency, Public Health Service, Bethesda, Md., and arrangements to see the film may be made through the institute.

Chapter 8—Intelligence: Growth and Manifestation

Testing the IQ (Warden and Gilbert, 13 min., silent). The administration of Form L of the *Stanford Revision of the Binet Tests* (Revised) to a five-year-old child is shown. Methods of scoring the test and computing the IQ are also presented.

Normal Child Development (Rutgers, 15 min., silent, color). The responses of the preschool child to various test items is illustrated.

Chapter 9—Language Growth and Development

Learning and Growth (EBF, 10 min., sound). Several learning problems are presented showing the relationship between learning and growth. Some fundamental principles affecting learning in older children are brought out in the problems.

Preschool Adventures (Iowa, 42 min., silent). Through a wide variety of activities the child develops during the preschool period. These activities are in harmony with the major objectives set forth for child development at this stage.

Chapter 10—Growth in Knowledge and Understanding

Children Learning by Experience (UWF, 44 min., sound). As children grow they are absorbed in their own affairs and things about them. Through participation, striving, and doing they grow in understanding the world of which they are a part.

Chapter 11—Growth in Creative Expression

Finger Painting (NYU, 20 min., sound). Demonstrates the uses that may be made of finger-painting activities among young children. The differences observed in the paintings are shown in relation to personality patterns.

Chapter 12—The Development of Social Behavior and Attitudes

Children Growing Up With Others (UWF, 33 min., sound). Deals with the problems involved in achieving a balance between the individual self and the co-operative self.

Social Development (M-H, 16 min., sound). The reasons underlying the changes in the child's social behavior at different age levels are presented. The nature of the social changes are depicted, and the organization of social behavior at different ages shown.

Sharing Work at Home (CIF, 11 min., sound). Shows the importance of everyone's participating in the work of a well-managed home.

Chapter 13—Change of Interests with Age

Problem Children (OSU, 20 min., sound). This is a study of the development of the personalities of two children. The effects of their home and school contacts in producing changes in interests and activities are brought out.

Chapter 14—Personality Development: Its Nature and Evaluation

As The Twig is Bent (NYU 10 min., sound). The effects of a favorable and unfavorable environment on the child are shown; practical suggestions are given to help parents in meeting child and adolescent problems.

Learning to Understand Children, Part I (M-H, 21 min., sound). A case study of Ader Adams, an emotionally and socially maladjusted girl of fifteen, is presented for special study.

Learning to Understand Children, Part II (M-H, 23 min., sound). This is a continuation of the case study of Ader. Remedial action by the teacher proves effective.

Chapter 15—Personality Development: Conflicts and Adjustment

Feeling of Rejection (NFBC, 22 min., sound). A case history of an emotionally maladjusted woman is given. The influence of early childhood conditions, which contributed to her maladjustments, are clearly presented.

Overdependency (NFBC, 32 min., sound). This film shows how an oversolicitous mother and sister and an insensitive father produced an overdependent boy, who grew to maturity unable to face responsibilities.

A Criminal Is Born (TFC, 21 min., sound). The case history of three boys who develop criminal tendencies is shown. The influences of an inadequate home life are revealed in this study.

Chapter 16—Mental Hygiene of Childhood

Balloons: Aggressive and Destructive Games (NYU, 20 min., sound). Special techniques useful in the diagnosis of personality difficulties are demonstrated. A normal aggressive, destructive boy is compared with a suppressed normal boy.

Shy Guy (CIF, 12 min., sound). The shy adolescent is helped in his adjustment through the treatment of his fellow students and parents.

Body Care and Grooming (M-H, 17 min., sound). The social advantages of a clean, healthy physical appearance are emphasized. A daily program for the improvement of personal hygiene is presented.

Chapter 17—From Childhood to Adolescence

Youth in Crisis (MT, 22 min., sound). Many youth problems are solved when supervised playgrounds, recreational facilities for teen-agers, and improved school facilities are provided.

You and Your Parents (CIF, 15 min., sound). Some problems of parent-adolescent relationships are shown in this film.

A Family Affair (NYU, 2-reel, sound). Some of the social problems of adolescents are here presented in relation to his family and its attitudes and position in the community.

Chapter 18—From Adolescence to Maturity

Choosing for Happiness (M-H, 14 min., sound). This is a story of a college girl who attempts to mold the personalities of her male friends to suit her own desires, believing this to be for their good. She is helped by a girl friend in taking a different attitude toward her friends as well as a better understanding of herself.

It Takes All Kinds (M-H, 20 min., sound). A dramatic presentation of how the emotional factors hamper an objective evaluation of a potential marriage partner's personality. A number of illustrations are presented of the behavior of young people in identical emotional situations. The importance of young people's taking an objective view in judging the personality characteristics of the potential marriage partner is emphasized.

Sources of the Films Listed in the Appendix

Cas—Castle Films, 445 Park Ave., New York 22, N. Y.

CFC—College Film Center, 84 E. Randolph St., Chicago, Ill.

CIF—Coronet Instruction Films, 65 East South Water Street, Chicago 1, Ill.

Department of Labor, Children's Bureau, Washington, D. C.

EBF—Encyclopedia Britannica Films, 20 N. Wacker Dr., Chicago, Ill.

Iowa—Bureau of Visual Instruction, University of Iowa, Iowa City, Iowa.

M-H—McGraw-Hill Book Co., 330 West 42nd Street, New York 18, N. Y.

MT—March of Time, 369 Lexington Ave., New York 17, N. Y.

NFBC—National Film Board of Canada, 1270 Avenue of the Americas, New York, N. Y.

NYU—New York University, Film Library, Washington Square, New York 3, N. Y.

OSU—Ohio State University, Columbus, Ohio

PSC—Pennsylvania State College, Psychological Cinema Register, State College, Penna.

Rutgers Films, Rutgers University, Box 78, New Brunswick, N. J.

TFC—Teaching Film Custodians, 25 W. 45th Street, New York 18, N. Y.

UWF—United World Films, Inc., 105 East 106th Street, New York, N. Y.

Warden and Gilbert, Psychological Laboratory, Columbia University, New York, N. Y.

WFC—World Films Inc. (Castle Films), 1445 Park Avenue, New York, N. Y.

Author Index

Subject Index